Handbook of Automated Essay Evaluation

This comprehensive, interdisciplinary handbook reviews the latest methods and technologies used in automated essay evaluation (AEE). Highlights include the latest in the evaluation of performance-based writing assessments and recent advances in the teaching of writing, language testing, cognitive psychology, and computational linguistics. This greatly expanded follow-up to *Automated Essay Scoring* reflects the numerous advances that have taken place in the field since 2003 including automated essay scoring and diagnostic feedback. Each chapter features a common structure including an introduction and a conclusion. Ideas for diagnostic and evaluative feedback are sprinkled throughout the book.

Highlights of the book's coverage include:

- the latest research on automated essay evaluation;
- descriptions of the major scoring engines including the e-rater®, the Intelligent Essay Assessor, the IntelliMetric™ Engine, c-rater™, and LightSIDE;
- applications of the uses of the technology including a large-scale system used in West Virginia;
- a systematic framework for evaluating research and technological results;
- descriptions of AEE methods that can be replicated for languages other than English as seen in an example from China;
- chapters from key researchers in the field.

Ideal for educators, professionals, curriculum specialists, and administrators responsible for developing writing programs or distance learning curricula, those who teach using AEE technologies, policy makers, and researchers in education, writing, psychometrics, cognitive psychology, and computational linguistics, this book also serves as a reference for graduate courses on automated essay evaluation taught in education, computer science, language, linguistics, and cognitive psychology.

Mark D. Shermis, Ph.D. is a professor at the University of Akron and the principal investigator of the Hewlett Foundation-funded Automated Scoring Assessment Prize (ASAP) program.

Jill Burstein, Ph.D. is a managing principal research scientist in Educational Testing Service's Research and Development Division.

Handbook of Automated Essay Evaluation

Current Applications and New Directions

Edited by

Mark D. Shermis
The University of Akron

Jill Burstein
Educational Testing Service

NEW YORK AND LONDON

First published 2013
by Routledge
711 Third Avenue, New York, NY 10017

Simultaneously published in the UK
by Routledge
2 Park Square, Milton Park, Abingdon, Oxon OX14 4RN

Routledge is an imprint of the Taylor & Francis Group, an informa business

Library of Congress Cataloging in Publication Data
Handbook on automated essay evaluation : current applications and new directions / edited by
Mark D. Shermis, the University of Akron, Jill Burstein, Educational Testing Service. p. cm.
    1. Grading and marking (Students)—Data processing. 2. Educational tests and measurements—Data
processing. 3. Report writing—Study and teaching—Evaluation. I. Shermis, Mark D., 1953–
II. Burstein, Jill.
LB3060.37.H36 2013
371.27'2—dc23
2012042796

ISBN: 978–1–84872–995–7 (hbk)
ISBN: 978–0–415–81096–8 (pbk)
ISBN: 978–0–203–12276–1 (ebk)

Typeset in Sabon
by Swales & Willis Ltd, Exeter, Devon

SFI Certified Sourcing
www.sfiprogram.org
SFI-00453

Printed and bound in the United States of America
by Edwards Brothers, Inc.

Contents

Foreword

Carl Whithaus
University of California, Davis

When I was invited to write this foreword, I was both delighted and terrified. I was delighted because two of the leading researchers of Automated Essay Evaluation (AEE) software were asking a writing teacher and researcher to weigh in on a collection of essays about "the state of the art" in their field. I was terrified because the drumbeat of criticism about AEE, or "robo-grading" as its critics like to call it, had jumped from relatively obscure academic forums such as the Writing Program Administrators list-serv (WPA-L) to *The New York Times* and National Public Radio. While I had spent the last 11 years trying to chart a middle course between English teachers' rejection of robo-grading and computational linguists' impulse to ask only technical questions about how to build the systems rather than whether the systems should be build at all, I was worried because writing this foreword would very publically place me in the camp of being a proponent of AEE. No matter how guarded and nuanced my position in favor of AEE was, it was certain to be criticized by a wide range of my colleagues and friends in writing studies. I did wonder whether I should write this foreword or not.

Reading over the essays in this book, however, convinced me that Mark Shermis and Jill Burstein had not only put together the definitive collection of essays about AEE in 2012, but they had also worked to include perspectives from out in the field as well as within the developers' labs. This collection is not only a tour-de-force of the latest work in AEE from a testing and measurement or computational linguistics perspective, it is also an attempt to think about AEE in relationship with students in schools and colleges. The *Handbook of Automated Essay Evaluation* is written from within the lab, from within the AEE software developers' workrooms, but it is also written *in situ*—parts of it come from out here in the field where writing teachers, program administrators, and AEE researchers such as Norbert Elliot, Sara Cushing-Weigle, Paul Deane, and Changhua Rich are trying to work out the details of how particular AEE systems can, and how they cannot, be used to assess students' writing performances and effectively place students into college writing courses. In addition, Kenji Hakuta's "The Policy Turn in Current Education Reform" outlines the implications of the Common Core State Standards Initiative (CCSSI) for students and for natural language processing (NLP) software development. The *Handbook of Automated Essay Evaluation* attempts to address how AEE is situated in relationship to educational policy, psychometrics, NLP, and the teaching of writing. Even if the balance of its essays is tipped in favor of computational linguists instead of writing researchers, this collection strikes me as a vital move forward in the conversation.

Instead of joining the popular, and all too-easy-to-tell, narrative condemning robo-graders, writing teachers, researchers, and program administrators should engage with this research about AEE. In fact, this collection's title signals an important shift—Shermis and Burstein's last collection was *Automated Essay Scoring: A Cross-Disciplinary Approach* (Lawrence Erlbaum Associates, Inc., 2003). The software they were analyzing was AES, *scoring* software; this collection is about AEE, automated essay *evaluation* software. I realize that AES and AEE are most often used interchangeably. And I also realize that the current collection is focused on the latest iterations of the same three pieces of software that were key in the 2003 volume. However, the semantic shift from thinking about (1) Educational Testing Service's (ETS's) E-rater® and Criterion®, (2) Pearson's Intelligent Essay Assessor™ (IEA), and (3) Vantage's IntelliMetric® as essay *scoring* software to essay *evaluation* software is important. The shift indicates that feedback, interaction, and an altogether wider range of possibilities for software is being envisioned in 2012 than was seen in 2003. Hakuta notes that "For a linguist, what stands out about the Common Core is its privileging of the uses of language." He goes on to argue for the development of an epistemological linguistics, where knowledge construction is understood in relationship to language usage and to subject specific domains. Such an interdisciplinary form of linguistics could ask questions about AEE software development, NLP, and educational practices in a situated fashion.

Working *in situ*, in the field with students and the software tools that they use to write—and that are used to help evaluate their writing—rather than in the lab on the software development makes me acutely aware of the limitations and dangers of AEE software. Running one of the top Writing in the Disciplines (WID) programs in the country makes me aware of all that software—whether called AES or AEE—cannot do. However, as a writing teacher and writing program administrator, I believe that I need to know about the differences among the AEE software systems. The validity and reliability of these systems is not monolithic, they work differently, and writing specialists increasingly need to understand these differences. Writing specialists need to know the limits of AEE systems, but we also need to know about their potential. The Common Core State Standards will be reshaping educational practice in the United States for the next ten years; their emphasis on language usage might present a moment where a shift from No Child Left Behind's legacy of standardized, multiple choice testing could occur.

Does AEE have a place in the future of education, in the future of writing instruction and writing evaluation? The answer is an emphatic "Yes." And it is an emphatic yes whether or not English teachers immediately embrace software as one of the tools available for generating evaluative feedback. Software will, already is, in fact, reading and responding to students' writing. Students are using software as an evaluative, responsive tool when they type in Google Docs, on Tumblr, or on their status updates in Facebook. In these social media applications, software is evaluating and providing feedback on the intimate level of words and sentences for writers. For many teachers and students in the next ten years, AEE may become a far more common tool for providing feedback on the paragraph or even essay level. If so, writing teachers and educational administrators need to better understand AEE software.

To shift through the possibilities and limitations of AEE systems requires a sense of the field's history. The chapters in the *Handbook of Automated Essay Evaluation* go a long way toward providing a comprehensive overview of AEE developments. In the "Introduction to Automated Essay Evaluation," Shermis and Burstein trace the 40-year history of the field back to Ellis Page's Project Essay Grade (PEG) of the 1960s. Chapters 4, 5, and 6 each describe one of the major commercial AEE systems in use today. In Chapter 4, Jill Burstein, Joel Tetreault, and Nitin Madnani discuss ETS's e-rater and Criterion. Peter Foltz and colleagues describe how Pearson's Intelligent Essay Assessor (IEA) functions in Chapter 5. And in Chapter 6, Matthew Schultz provides an overview of Vantage's IntelliMetric. Schultz's contribution is particularly important, because while descriptions of the computational linguistics behind ETS's E-rater and Criterion and the early work on IEA have been shared in journal articles and whitepapers, researchers have had less access to information about how IntelliMetric functions. These three overviews of AEE systems are essential primers for writing researchers and applied linguists. I would argue that these chapters are also immensely valuable texts for mid- and upper-level administrators in colleges and school districts considering using AEE systems. If colleges and schools districts are going to use AEE for placement or as a tool to supplement teacher feedback on student writing, the administrators making these decisions should understand the logic that informed the development behind the AEE system they are selecting. These chapters provide that overview as well as references to the broader research literature on AEE.

Perhaps the biggest question about AEE facing writing teachers and researchers, applied and computational linguists, and psychometricians is where does the field go from here. The past has been marked by an argument rather than a dialogue. On one side there has been the computational linguists and psychometricians whose work is represented in Shermis and Burstein's *Automated Essay Scoring: A Cross-Disciplinary Approach* (Lawrence Erlbaum Associates, Inc., 2003). On the other side has been the critique of AEE from writing teachers and researchers; this rejection of AEE has been most forcefully articulated in Patricia Ericsson and Richard Haswell's collection *Machine Scoring of Student Essays: Truth and Consequences* (Utah State University Press, 2006). Extending the critiques in Ericsson and Haswell's collection, Les Perelman has tried to show that AEE systems can be gamed. He has argued that students can break these software tools at the outer edges and gain high scores from essays that are not only inaccurate but may in fact be nonsensical. But this argumentative past has neither halted the development of AEE nor produced AEE systems that fully address the many and varied needs of learners in primary, secondary, or postsecondary contexts.

The essays in the later chapters of the *Handbook of Automated Essay Evaluation* pick up these issues around the various needs of student learners and the possibilities for the future AEE developments. While writing teachers may not love large-scale writing assessment, it is important for the future of AEE that developers engage with the issues encountered in educational assessment. David Williamson examines how AEE relates to the psychometric concept of performance assessment. Yigal Attali and Brent Bridgeman each address critical issues around reliability and validity within AEE. Attali's chapter continues his valuable work on AEE, and Bridgeman's chapter examines variance among human raters compared with AEE. Another aspect of the future of AEE is thinking through how these systems relate to NLP.

Pretending that software systems, and particularly software agents that provide feedback, are not parts of students' writing processes, not parts of a broader ecology of available writing tools in the second decade of the 21st century, is simply naïve. The *Handbook of Automated Essay Evaluation* provides a variety of perspectives through which linguists, educational administrators, policymakers, psychometricians, writing teachers, researchers, and program administrators can approach the field of AEE development. It is not the final word. There will be more conversations about how AEE software can and cannot be used. But this collection is a running start—it's a key book for understanding the newly emerging dynamics among writing, software, and educational systems.

Preface

This volume arrives about ten years after the publication of the book, *Automated Essay Scoring: A Cross-Disciplinary Approach* (Lawrence Erlbaum Associates, Inc., 2003). The earlier volume documented a relatively new technology—automated essay scoring. These earlier automated essay scoring systems produced a "score" to rate the quality of an essay. We now have richer automated essay evaluation systems that generate descriptive feedback about linguistic properties of essays that are related to writing quality (see the introductory chapter). Recent developments in machine scoring of essays, and recognition of the need for explicit feedback, represent an awareness that more complex aspects of essay writing need to be analyzed. Advancements in methods of natural language processing (NLP) allow these more complex analyses of language in the context of machine scoring of essays.

The field has grown to the point where an updated, second volume, entitled the *Handbook of Automated Essay Evaluation* now makes sense. Compared with the small number of commercial vendors of AES ten years ago, there are now more than eight; that number is growing at a rapid rate as testing companies align their activities with the specifications of the Common Core Standards, requiring more complex writing tasks than we have seen on current assessments. As the breadth of writing tasks increases, and more innovative genres of writing, beyond the essay, make their way into the classroom, and onto assessments, and perhaps incorporate digital environments such as blog posts, NLP methods will continue to advance to capture and evaluate relevant aspects of the writing construct.

The field has recently expanded outside of the commercial arena. As is discussed in a chapter in this volume, there is an open source system, LightSIDE. Very recently, an open competition was sponsored by the William and Flora Hewlett Foundation in which the general public had access to essay data, and could build and evaluate a system. Over 150 teams participated. The motivation for this competition was to pool the larger intellectual community to see if new approaches might be developed. This public competition, and an earlier private competition among commercial vendors, is also discussed in detail in the Shermis and Hamner chapter.

As discussed in the earlier volume, the field of machine scoring and evaluation of essay writing has always been multi-disciplinary, and has included research from cognitive psychology, computer science, educational measurement, linguistics, and writing research. The interest in essay responses on standardized tests has been a large motivation for continued research in this field. With the Common Core, the need to align the technology appropriately with a large array of writing task types is essential. However, the field does not have to be "stuck", evaluating only a the small set of writing tasks types typically found on assessments, and conforming to current Common Core specifications which are likely to evolve. There are writing genres beyond the essay which have yet to be explored. Task types outside of the standard modes that we find in assessment are discussed by Carl Whithaus in the Foreword, as well as in the Introductory chapter, and

Chapter 2 (*Automated Essay Evaluation and the Teaching of Writing*). NLP methods can certainly handle a broader range of writing tasks that we might be more likely to see in instructional settings, where students have more time to write, interact and collaborate with peers, and where instructors might have more time to grade assignments. As well, NLP researchers are always excited about new challenges that can support growth in the discipline, and potential contributions to the communities that use the technology. The chapters in this book aim to cover perspectives from the major contributing disciplines. We hope that this volume can foster productive cross-disciplinary discussions to inform this technology as it continues to develop.

The book is organized into a number of sections. In the two chapters that follow the Introduction, authors who represent the writing research perspective discuss issues in writing research, and automated essay evaluation. In the next section, the volume highlights the capabilities of several automated essay evaluation engines, including one that focuses on short answer constructed responses. This, the system section, ends with a description of open-source machine scoring engines. In the following section, chapters address a number of the psychometric challenges and issues surrounding machine scoring and provide a framework for evaluating automated essay evaluation. Because machine scoring procedures for score prediction do not mirror the way humans rate essays, particular attention is given to providing a context for looking at the validity of machine-generated scores. The last section of the *Handbook* looks at cutting-edge advances in automated essay evaluation that may be achieved through research in NLP. We conclude the *Handbook* with a chapter that speculates on the short-term future of the field in the context of current education policy.

This volume is dedicated to Bo's memory and the advances that his work spawned in the field of automated essay evaluation. None of the work in this volume would have been possible without the enlightened vision of Dr. Ellis Batten "Bo" Page who envisioned the machine scoring technology in 1966, and implemented the first viable automated essay scoring engine 40 years ago in 1973. We honor him not only for his creativity, insight, and seminal contributions, but for his perseverance under sometimes harsh criticism. He had to endure the questioning of his motives and methods, and faced the naysayers with admirable composure, and elegance. As a true academic researcher, he incorporated the critics' questions and concerns in subsequent iterations of his innovative research agenda, and gladly involved others to participate in broadening the knowledge base of the field.

We also want to thank others who have supported this volume. Our colleagues in cognitive psychology, computational linguistics, educational measurement, and writing research have done a marvelous job in sharing their research and methods to help advance our knowledge. The first co-editor also wants to recognize several individuals who have made this research possible including Francis DiVesta, Sharon Apel Bursky, and Susan Hughes. He also would like to thank colleagues Jaison Morgan, Tom Vander Ark, Lynn Van Deventer, and Ben Hamner for their support and insights in helping shape his most recent research. He would also like to say "thank you" to both Ryan and Becky (especially wife Becky) in supporting all the craziness surrounding the book production process. Finally, a special tribute to his co-editor Jill who not only articulated the cutting edge of computational linguistics, ensured a balanced approach, but performed a marvelous job in communicating with colleagues. Thanks to you all.

Jill would like to, first of all, thank Mark for doing the legwork to get this second volume underway. As a computational linguist, and developer of automated essay scoring technology, she is also grateful for his long-term advocacy, and research ideas supporting the continued development of automated essay scoring and evaluation technology. The private and public competitions which he organized were critical to promoting greater cross-disciplinary dialogue which she hopes will continue. Mark and Jill would like to thank Jill's colleagues at Educational Testing Service (ETS) for their support in the internal technical review process (for all chapters on which ETSers are authors): Beata Beigman-Klebanov, Jim Carlson, Kim Fryer, Derrick Higgins, Ruth Greenwood, and Joel Tetreault. There were also many peer reviewers at ETS to whom we are very grateful. Jill would very much like to thank Norbert Elliot who has helped her gain a richer understanding of the writing research perspective about the development and application automated essay evaluation technology in instructional and assessment settings. As always, her family, Danny, Abby, and Marc, have been very supportive as her work day regularly continues at home.

We would like to thank all of the authors who contributed to this volume, and all of the readers who we hope will be inspired to make future contributions to this growing field. And finally we would like to thank the reviewers of the original book plan for their invaluable input: Gregory J. Cizek, University of North Carolina at Chapel Hill, Lawrence M. Rudner, Graduate Management Admission Council, Su Baldwin, the National Board of Medical Examiners, and one anonymous reviewer.

About the Editors

Mark D. Shermis, Ph.D. is a professor at the University of Akron and the principal investigator of the Hewlett Foundation-funded Automated Scoring Assessment Prize (ASAP) program. He has published extensively on machine scoring and recently co-authored the textbook *Classroom Assessment in Action* with Francis DiVesta. Shermis is a fellow of the American Psychological Association (Division 5) and the American Educational Research Association.

Jill Burstein, Ph.D. is a managing principal research scientist in Educational Testing Service's Research and Development Division. Her background and expertise is in computational linguistics with a focus on education technology for writing, reading, and teacher professional development. Dr. Burstein's inventions include e-rater®, an automated essay scoring system. In more recent work, Dr. Burstein has employed natural language processing to develop capabilities to support English learners, such as Language Muse[SM] which offers teacher professional development, and supports reading for English learners. Dr. Burstein holds 13 patents for her inventions. Dr. Burstein received her B.A. in linguistics and Spanish from New York University and her M.A. and Ph.D. in linguistics from the Graduate Center, City University of New York.

List of Contributors

Slava Andreyev is a senior software developer at Educational Testing Service. He earned a B.S. in computer science at the Polytechnic Institute in Ulyanovsk, Russia. After graduation, he worked in the Research Institute of Atomic Reactors in Dimitrovgrad, Russia. He has been with Educational Testing Service for more than ten years. His current focus of work is software systems that employ natural language processing algorithms implemented in Java, Perl, and Python. One of the products that he works on extensively is e-rater®, an automated essay scoring and evaluation system developed at Educational Testing Service.

Sharon Apel Bursky is a Ph.D. student in the Department of Counseling at the University of Akron. Her research studies include family interactions, interpersonal relationships, and forgiveness. She is currently being clinically trained as a marriage and family therapist and works with clients in the community as well as clients in an inpatient hospital setting. She previously received her M.A. in communication theory and methodology at Cleveland State University and her B.A. in psychology from Cleveland State University.

Yigal Attali is a principal research scientist in the Research and Development Division at Educational Testing Service in Princeton, New Jersey. He received his Ph.D. in cognitive psychology at the Hebrew University of Jerusalem in 2001, and joined ETS in 2002. Yigal is interested in the development and evaluation of innovative assessments and is co-inventor of the automated essay scoring system e-rater® V.2.

Beata Beigman-Klebanov is a research scientist in the Research and Development division at Educational Testing Service (ETS) in Princeton, New Jersey. Before joining ETS, she was a postdoctoral fellow at the Northwestern Institute for Complex Systems and Kellogg School of Management at Northwestern University, Evanston, Illinois, where she developed computational approaches to analyze political rhetoric. She holds a Ph.D. in computer science from the Hebrew University of Jerusalem, Israel. She received her M.S. degree (with distinction) in cognitive science from the University of Edinburgh in 2001. Her interests include automated semantic and pragmatic analysis of text. At ETS, her focus is on automatically scoring content and organization in student writing.

Daniel Blanchard is an associate research engineer in the Natural Language Processing and Speech Group at Educational Testing Service in Princeton, New Jersey. He is currently a Ph.D. candidate in computer science at the University of Delaware, where he received his M.A. in linguistics and his M.S. in computer science. His dissertation work focuses on the problem of how to identify word boundaries in unsegmented text. His research interests are language acquisition, machine learning, and native language identification.

Chris Brew is a senior research scientist at the Educational Testing Service (ETS), specializing in natural language processing (NLP). He previously held positions at the University of Edinburgh, University of Sussex, and Sharp Laboratories of Europe and most recently as an associate professor in computer science and engineering at Ohio State University. He holds a B.Sc. in chemistry from the University of Bristol, and an M.Sc. and D.Phil. from the Department of Experimental Psychology at the University of Sussex. His research interests include semantic role labeling, speech processing, information extraction, and psycholinguistics. At ETS, Chris leads the c-rater project as well as co-directing the content scoring vision for the NLP group. With Markus Dickinson and Detmar Meurers, he wrote *Language and Computers*, a textbook intended for general interest undergraduate courses in Natural Language Processing and Computational Linguistics.

Brent Bridgeman received his Ph.D. in educational psychology from the University of Wisconsin, Madison. He joined Educational Testing Service in 1974 after several years of college teaching; his current title is Distinguished Presidential Appointee in the Foundational and Validity Research area. His recent work focuses on validity and fairness issues, especially with respect to scoring methods, test format, timing, and automated essay assessments.

Martin Chodorow received a Ph.D. in cognitive psychology from MIT and completed a postdoctoral fellowship in computational linguistics at IBM Research before joining the faculty of Hunter College and the Graduate Center of the City University of New York, where he is a professor of psychology and linguistics. He also serves as a consultant for Educational Testing Service. His natural language processing (NLP) research interests include the measurement of text similarity and cohesion, and the detection of grammatical errors in non-native writing. His psycholinguistic research examines the processes that are used by readers when they proofread text.

Juan M. D'Brot is the executive director of assessment and accountability for the West Virginia Department of Education. He is responsible for the administration, development, and implementation of all aspects of the statewide summative assessments and all other assessments required by West Virginia code. He is also responsible for the co-oversight of the federal and statewide accountability system in West Virginia. Prior to this position, he worked in the Office of Research for WVDE providing research and evaluation services. He obtained his B.A. in communication data analysis and his M.A. in communication theory and research from West Virginia University. He is currently working toward his Ph.D. in industrial-organizational psychology with an emphasis in strategic planning and leadership consulting. He has training and certification in item response theory, hierarchical linear modeling, value-added modeling, experimental design, logic modeling, program development, strategic planning, and project management. He also serves as the state's lead for the Smarter Balanced Assessment Consortium and is a member of the Superintendent's Cabinet. D'Brot currently lives in Charleston, West Virginia, with his three-year-old son, Manny.

Paul Deane, a principal research scientist in research and development, earned a Ph.D. in linguistics at the University of Chicago in 1987. He is author of *Grammar in Mind and Brain* (Mouton de Gruyter, 1994), a study of the interaction of cognitive structures in syntax and semantics, and taught linguistics at the University of Central Florida from 1986 to 1994. From 1994 to 2001, he worked in industrial natural language processing, where he focused on lexicon development, parser design, and semantic information retrieval. He joined Educational Testing Service (ETS) in 2001. His current research interests include automated essay scoring, vocabulary assessment, and cognitive models of writing skill. During his career at ETS he has worked on a variety of natural language processing and assessment projects, including automated item generation, tools to support verbal test development, scoring of collocation errors, reading and vocabulary assessment, and automated essay scoring. His work currently focuses on the development and scoring of writing assessments for the ETS research initiative, Cognitively-Based Assessments Of, For and As Learning.

Norbert Elliot is professor of English at New Jersey Institute of Technology. With Les Perelman, he is, most recently, editor of *Writing Assessment in the 21ˢᵗ Century: Essays in Honor of Edward M. White* (Hampton Press, 2012).

Adam Faulkner is a doctoral candidate in linguistics at the Graduate Center, the City University of New York. His principal research interests lie in the fields of computational linguistics and formal semantics. His work involves the automated summarization of contrasting opinion in standardized essay responses and the sentence-level classification of stance. He is also employed as a computational linguist at an internet advertising company where he works on named entity clustering and sentiment analysis.

Peter W. Foltz is a founder of Knowledge Analysis Technologies. Peter serves as vice president of research and development for Pearson's Knowledge Technologies group and co-director of the Pearson Research Center for Next Generation Assessment. He also holds an appointment as senior research associate at the University of Colorado's Institute for Cognitive Science. Dr. Foltz holds a Ph.D. in cognitive psychology from the University of Colorado, Boulder. He previously worked as a research associate at the Learning Research and Development Center at the University of Pittsburgh and as a professor of psychology at New Mexico State University. He formerly was a member of technical staff at Bell Communications Research's Cognitive Science Research Group. He has authored over 80 journal articles, book chapters, conference papers, and other publications in the areas of cognitive modeling, natural language processing, discourse processing, and educational measurement, and holds a patent for automated scoring technology using Latent Semantic Analysis.

Michael Gamon came to the U.S. from his native country Germany in 1990 on a Fulbright scholarship to study linguistics at the University of Washington. He received his M.A. in 1992 and his Ph.D. in 1996. In the same year he joined the NLP group in Microsoft Research first as an intern, then as a German grammarian, working on the German grammar for the Microsoft Word grammar checker. Since then, Michael has worked and published on natural language generation, sentiment detection, social media, grammatical error correction, and, most recently, on problems around entity-centric search.

Kenji Hakuta is the Lee L. Jacks Professor of Education at Stanford University. His specialty is in psycholinguistics, bilingualism, and second language acquisition, and much of his work is directed toward practical and policy applications. He has a Ph.D. in experimental psychology from Harvard University, and has previously held faculty positions at Yale University (Department of Psychology), University of California, Santa Cruz (Education) and the University of California, Merced (Founding Dean of Social Sciences, Humanities and Arts).

Ben Hamner is responsible for data analysis, machine learning, and competitions at Kaggle. He has worked with machine learning problems in a variety of different domains, including natural language processing, computer vision, web classification, and neuroscience. Prior to joining Kaggle, he applied machine learning to improve brain–computer interfaces as a Whitaker Fellow at the École Polytechnique Fédérale de Lausanne in Lausanne, Switzerland. He graduated with a BSE in biomedical engineering, electrical engineering, and math from Duke University.

Andrew Klobucar, assistant professor of English at New Jersey Institute of Technology (NJIT), is a literary theorist and teacher specializing in internet research, electronic writing, semantic technologies, and Web 3.0. His research on experimental literary forms and genres continue to analyze the increasingly important role technology plays in contemporary cultural practices in both print and screen formats. More recently, looking at semantic technologies for the Web, he has worked on developing software for writing instruction and written on the use of programmable media in classroom instruction. Other projects include collaborative research between NJIT and the Educational Testing Service on placement and classroom use of automated assessment software. Recent publications include "The ABC's of Viewing: Material Poetics and the Literary Screen" in *From Text to Txting: New Media in the Classroom* (Indiana University Press, 2012).

Kristin L. K. Koskey is an assistant professor in the Department of Educational Foundations and Leadership in the College of Education at the University of Akron. She earned her Ph.D. in educational research and measurement at the University of Toledo in 2009. Dr. Koskey teaches courses in assessment, research design, evaluation, and statistics. In addition to teaching, she is a partner at MetriKs Amérique where she consults in psychometric analyses, development of measures, and facilitates item-writing workshops for different organizations. Additional professional experience includes serving as a fellow at the Consortium of Leadership in Evaluation, Assessment, and Research (CLEAR) at the University of Akron and co-editor of the *Mid-Western Educational Researcher*. Her research interests include psychometrics, applications of the Rasch model to constructing measures typically of constructs in the field of motivation, and mixed-method research.

Thomas K. Landauer has had a long career in pure and applied research on learning. His Ph.D. from Harvard was followed by teaching and research at Dartmouth, Stanford, and Princeton Universities. He spent 25 years at Bell Laboratories Research, 8 at the University of Colorado, and was the founder in 1998 of the company that in 2004 became Pearson Knowledge Technologies, where he is now Chief Scientist. Dr. Landauer has published more than 110 articles and authored or edited four books.

Claudia Leacock is a research scientist at CTB/McGraw-Hill who has been working on automated scoring and grammatical error detection for more than 15 years. Prior to joining CTB/McGraw-Hill in 2012, she was a consultant, for five years, at Microsoft Research, working with the team that developed *ESL Assistant*, a prototype tool for detecting and correcting grammatical errors of English language learners. As a research scientist at Pearson Knowledge Technologies, and previously at Educational Testing Service, she developed tools for both automated assessment of short answer content-based questions and grammatical error detection and correction. As a member of the WordNet group at Princeton University's Cognitive Science Lab, her research focused on word sense identification. Dr. Leacock received a B.A. in English from New York University, a Ph.D. in linguistics from the City University of New York, Graduate Center and was a postdoctoral fellow at IBM, T.J. Watson Research Center.

Karen E. Lochbaum is vice president of technology services for Pearson's Knowledge Technologies group. She holds a Ph.D. in computer science from Harvard University. At Pearson, she is responsible for the delivery of technology services to all of Knowledge Technologies' clients, having previously been responsible for development of the Intelligent Essay Assessor™. While earning her doctorate, Karen held a fellowship from Bellcore, where she worked as a technical staff member on projects involving development and applications of Latent Semantic Analysis. For five years, she was a member of technical staff at US West Advanced Technologies, where she performed exploratory software research and development, including work on two projects for Latent Semantic Analysis applications that led to patents. Karen has published numerous technical articles in areas related to the Intelligent Essay Assessor and computational linguistics.

Susan M. Lottridge is a respected professional in the field of psychometrics, and her research is regularly published and presented at national conferences. As the technical director for machine scoring for Pacific Metrics, Dr. Lottridge conceptualizes and leads research on Pacific Metrics' automated scoring engine, CRASE™, and is responsible for directing the development of new scoring modules and adjustments to the engine. Her academic experience included research positions at the Center for Assessment and Research Studies at James Madison University, and the Learning Through Evaluation, Adaptation and Dissemination Center. Dr. Lottridge holds a Ph.D. in Assessment and Measurement from James Madison University, an M.S. in computer science and mathematics from University of Wisconsin, Madison, and a B.A. in mathematics from the University of St. Thomas, graduating Summa Cum Laude.

Nitin Madnani is a research scientist with the Text, Language and Computation research group at the Educational Testing Service. He received his Ph.D. in computer science from University of Maryland College Park in 2010. His interests include paraphrase modeling, statistical machine translation, sentiment analysis, and grammatical error correction.

Elijah Mayfield is a Ph.D. student in the Language Technologies Institute at Carnegie Mellon University. His research studies the ways people signal authoritativeness and expertise when writing or speaking, with a special emphasis on conversation and interpersonal style. This work draws on influences from machine learning, natural language processing, and sociolinguistics. He is the primary developer of LightSIDE, a general-purpose tool for machine learning, designed for use by both experts and non-experts to analyze textual data. He previously received an M.S. in language technology from Carnegie Mellon University and a B.A. in computer science from the University of Minnesota, Morris, and was awarded the Class of 2011 Siebel Scholarship, which is awarded annually to 80 students from the world's leading graduate schools.

Howard C. Mitzel is the co-founder and president of Pacific Metrics and the chief architect of Pacific Metrics' psychometric software for equating and technical form construction. Formerly a senior research scientist with CTB/McGraw-Hill, Dr. Mitzel also serves on several state technical advisory committees and has worked with the National Assessment Governing Board (NAGB) to design and conduct a standard-setting procedure for the National Assessment of Educational Progress (NAEP) mathematics assessment. Dr. Mitzel is a co-developer of the Bookmark Standard Setting Procedure, the most widely used procedure in large-scale assessment for setting defensible standards in K–12 programs. Dr. Mitzel holds a Ph.D. in research methodology and quantitative psychology from the University of Chicago. Dr. Mitzel's contributions to the field of assessment also include over a dozen published papers, and numerous presentations at national conferences.

Changhua S. Rich is CTB's research director, Asia. She works closely with researchers and educators to develop assessment solutions for diverse learners and institutions from the U.S., China, India, and the Middle East. She also worked as a research scientist on the large-scale online writing assessment program for West Virginia, the McGraw-Hill EOS (English Online System) in China and testing programs for the state of Qatar. Recently, Dr. Rich collaborated with scholars and teachers from Beijing Foreign Studies University on the Ministry of Education funded research program of automated writing evaluation in the Chinese English as a foreign language (EFL) classrooms. Her work has been published in *English Teaching Reform in Digital Age – the Application of Educational Assessment Technology in English Writing Instruction, Chinese Journal of Applied Linguistics, Handbook of Experimental Economics Results*, and *American Economic Review*. Before joining CTB, Dr. Rich served as an assistant professor of economics at St. Lawrence University. She received the Ph.D. degree in international economics from the University of California, Santa Cruz.

Carolyn Penstein Rosé is an associate professor of language technologies and human–computer interaction in the School of Computer Science at Carnegie Mellon University. Her research program is focused on better understanding the social and pragmatic nature of conversation, and using this understanding to build computational systems that can improve the efficacy of conversation between people, and between people and computers. In order to pursue these goals, she invokes approaches from computational discourse analysis and text mining, conversational agents, and computer supported collaborative learning. She serves on the executive committee of the Pittsburgh Science of Learning Center and is the co-leader of its Social and Communicative Factors of Learning research thrust. She also serves as the secretary/treasurer of the International Society of the Learning Sciences and associate editor of the *International Journal of Computer Supported Collaborative Learning*.

M. Christina Schneider is a research scientist at CTB/McGraw-Hill. She is a psychometrician for custom state assessment programs, leads the psychometric work for automated essay evaluation within CTB/McGraw-Hill, and conducts standard settings across the United States. She has also authored two professional development curriculums in formative classroom assessment. Prior to joining CTB/McGraw-Hill Dr. Schneider managed the psychometric and data analysis unit within the Office of Assessment at the South Carolina Department of Education. Dr. Schneider began her career in education as a middle school band director. Her research has been published in *Applied Measurement in Education, Peabody Journal of Education, Journal of Psychoeducational Assessment*, and *Journal of Multidisciplinary Evaluation*. Her areas of expertise include formative classroom assessment, automated essay scoring, standard setting, identification of aberrant anchor items, and assessment in the arts. Dr. Schneider received her degrees from the University of South Carolina.

Matthew T. Schultz, Ph.D., director of psychometric services for Vantage Learning, is involved in all research design, data collection and analysis activities. Dr. Schultz has over 20 years of varied research experience in the areas of educational research, personnel selection, and market research. His work has focused on the application of analytic methodologies and statistical approaches for practical solutions to business and research questions. Prior to joining Vantage/McCann Associates, Dr. Schultz worked as a test and measurements specialist for the City of New York, a research scientist for the Law School Admissions Council, and a statistician/analyst at GlaxoSmithKline. He has taught statistics, research methods, tests and measures, and industrial psychology courses at Moravian College. Dr. Schultz earned his B.A. from Rutgers University and his M.A. and Ph.D. from Fordham University's Psychometrics program.

E. Matthew Schulz brings over 20 years of experience in the assessment industry, with a wide range of research accomplishments in the area of large-scale assessment, and has been published widely in the area of educational measurement. As the director of research for Pacific Metrics, he manages the psychometric components of online testing programs. Formerly the principal research statistician at ACT, Inc., Dr. Schulz earned national recognition as a leader in domain score theory and led the development of the bookmark-based standard setting method, Mapmark. He also previously served as the director of testing at the National Council of State Boards of Nursing. Dr. Schulz has a Ph.D. in measurement, evaluation, and statistical analysis from the University of Chicago, an M.S. in psychology from Washington State University and a B.S. in psychology from Iowa State University. He regularly serves as a consultant to state boards of education, licensure and certification boards, and local education agencies on the topics of equating, vertical scaling, job analysis, and computerized testing.

Lynn A. Streeter is the president of Pearson Knowledge Technologies, which provides automated scoring of speech and text for the education, corporate, and government markets with scoring as reliable as skilled human graders. Its products include: (1) the Intelligent Essay Assessor™ used in formative and summative assessment, and is the engine behind Pearson's literacy product, WriteToLearn® and (2) the Versant family of products, which assess speakers' ability to speak a particular language. Dr. Streeter has managed research and development organizations at Pearson, US WEST, Bellcore, and Bell Laboratories. Dr. Streeter holds a Ph.D. from Columbia University, and a bachelor's degree with honors from the University of Michigan. She attended the Stanford Executive Program and has advanced computer science training and experience. She shares a patent with Mr. Landauer and Ms. Lochbaum for Latent Semantic Analysis.

Joel Tetreault is a managing research scientist specializing in computational linguistics in the Research and Development Division at Educational Testing Service in Princeton, New Jersey. His research focus is natural language processing with specific interests in anaphora, dialogue and discourse processing, machine learning, and applying these techniques to the analysis of English language learning and automated essay scoring. Currently he is working on automated methods for detecting grammatical errors by non-native speakers. Previously, he was a postdoctoral research scientist at the University of Pittsburgh's Learning Research and Development Center. There he worked on developing spoken dialogue tutoring systems. Tetreault received his B.A. in computer science from Harvard University and his M.S. and Ph.D. in computer science from the University of Rochester.

Sara C. Weigle is professor of applied linguistics at Georgia State University. She received her Ph.D. in applied linguistics from UCLA. She has published research in the areas of assessment, second language writing, and teacher education, and is the author of *Assessing Writing* (Cambridge University Press, 2002. She has been invited to speak and conduct workshops on second language writing assessment throughout the world, most recently in Egypt, the United Kingdom, South Korea, and Austria. Her current research focuses on assessing integrated skills and the use of automated scoring for second language writing.

David M. Williamson is the senior research director for the Assessment Innovations Center in the Research and Development Division of Educational Testing Service (ETS). In this capacity he oversees fundamental and applied research at the intersection of cognitive modeling, technology and multivariate scoring models, with an emphasis on the development, evaluation, and implementation of automated scoring systems for text and spoken responses. The work of his center is an integration of several branches of research: cognitive science; psychometrics; and natural language processing (NLP) and speech processing. He earned his Ph.D. in psychometrics from Fordham University in 2000. He joined the Chauncey Group, a subsidiary of ETS, in 1996 and moved to ETS Research in 2001. From the outset his research has targeted advancing the field of measurement through innovation, with his dissertation targeting model criticism indices for Bayesian networks constructed from cognitive theory using Evidence Centered Design, work which won the 2001 NCME Brenda H. Lloyd Outstanding Dissertation Award. He has published multiple journal articles on simulation-based assessment, automated scoring, and related topics and an edited volume: *Automated Scoring of Complex Tasks in Computer-Based Testing* (Lawrence Erlbaum Associates, Inc., 2006). He directs the ETS research agenda for Innovations in Task Design and Scoring, which funds the development, evaluation, and implementation of automated scoring systems for essays, short answer content free-text entry responses, mathematics items, and spontaneous speech as well as design of innovative tasks. The results of this research have led to operational deployment of these capabilities for the Graduate Record Examination (GRE), Test of English as a Foreign Language (TOEFL), and multiple client programs as well as for practice and learning systems.

1 Introduction to Automated Essay Evaluation

Mark D. Shermis, Jill Burstein, and Sharon Apel Bursky

INTRODUCTION

Writing in the *New York Times*, educator Randall Stross (2012) recently noted that his long dream of the creation of a software program to help students learn to write may be close to reality. In dreams begin responsibilities, and so this present edited collection is offered to define and explicate the promises and complexities that occur when technologies advance to the point where they appear to be able to do what humans do.

A simple definition of automated essay evaluation (AEE) is "the process of evaluating and scoring written prose via computer programs" (Shermis and Burstein, 2003).[1] The *evaluation* label intentionally recognizes that the capabilities of the technology can go beyond the task of *scoring*, or assigning a number to an essay. For example, essay evaluation systems may incorporate natural language processing (NLP) capabilities that allow the analysis of the discourse structure of an essay to provide the writer with qualitative feedback specific to the structure of the writer's essay (e.g., "*Your essay appears to introduce three main ideas.*"). Most of the initial AEE applications have been in English; however, the technology has been applied to Japanese (Kawate-Mierzejewska, 2003), Hebrew (Vantage Learning, 2001), and Bahasa Malay (Vantage Learning, 2002).

AEE is a multi-disciplinary field that incorporates research from cognitive psychology, computer science, educational measurement, linguistics, and writing research. These are listed in alphabetical order, and not in order of importance in terms of relevant voices and contributions. Using computational linguistic methods, we are attempting to identify linguistic elements that measure writing constructs that cognitive psychologists and/or the writing community might identify as being key to successful writing. Research presented in this volume demonstrates that AEE has strong correlations with human rater behavior (Shermis and Hamner, 2012); possesses a high degree of construct validity (Keith, 2003); and, is related to external measures of writing (Page, 2003). For further discussions about how AEE systems represent aspects of the constructs related to writing quality, readers should see the following chapters, *Automated Essay Evaluation and the Teaching of Writing* (Chapter 2); *The E-rater® Automated Essay Scoring System* (Chapter 4); *Probably Cause: Developing Warrants for Automated Scoring of Essays* (Chapter 10); and, *Covering the Construct: An Approach to Automated Essay Scoring Motivated by a Socio-Cognitive Framework for Defining Literacy Skills* (Chapter 18).

AEE models (systems) have been developed for evaluating a single *genre* (Miller, 1984) of writing—*the essay*—which remains a primary discourse form in the context of instructional and assessment settings. *Modes* (Connors, 1981) of essay writing discussed in this volume include expository and persuasive writing, as well as summary writing. The field of research in AEE models is relatively new, and still has much room to grow. That said, a few chapters in this volume address new research that is likely to influence the evolution of essay evaluation systems, such that they might be applied more effectively and perhaps on a broader range of writing genres beyond the essay. This expansion is likely to include digital writing environments discussed in the book's Foreword and in Chapter 2 (*Automated Essay Evaluation and the Teaching of Writing*). The feasibility of producing engines with even greater utility will depend not only on the development of the technology, but also on a deeper understanding of specific writing environments and processes. This can be accomplished only through collaboration across the participating research communities

CONCERNS ABOUT AEE

There are a number of persistent questions about the use of AEE to evaluate student writing. For instance, the following questions about AEE are not uncommonly heard at the end of a conference talk. *Can systems be gamed? Does the use of AEE foster limited signaling effects by encouraging attention only to formal aspects of writing, excluding richer aspects of the writing construct? Does AEE subvert the writing act fundamentally by depriving the student of a true "audience"?* While each of these questions raises a slightly different issue, they all point to the issue of the writer not *truly* engaging in a specific writing task at hand, but attempting to follow some anticipated algorithm that is likely to result in a "good grade." All assessment carries a *signaling effect* (Bowen, Chingos, and McPherson, 2009)—specifically, the notion that tests carry implicit messages when they are widely used. In the case of automated essay scoring, we do not want to send a message that students and test-takers need to write only for purposes of machine scoring. It is important to note, however, that these questions may also be said to apply to certain modes of writing independent of the technological aspects of composing in digital environments. As pointed out in Connors (1984), the expository and persuasive modes typically found on writing assessments have been criticized as focusing on product, and not the process of writing. It may be said that these modes of writing are easily coached (and gamed), and they do not encourage the full complexity of engagement with a writing task, and a negative signaling effect that the process of writing can easily be boiled down to efficient writing tasks.

One consistent concern, more specific to the computer, is that it cannot possibly use the same processes as humans in making discerning judgments about writing competence (Neal, 2011). Yet another common issue voiced is that the aspects of a text being measured or evaluated by automated writing evaluation tools do not appropriately assess true qualities of writing, as specified in scoring guides used by human raters who use complex cognitive processes for reading. In many ways these assertions are correct. Who can disagree with the fact that scoring engines, as they exist now, do not use the same cognitive processes as humans to "read" written prose? Consider the following statement: "*I forgot what a boomerang was, but then it came back to me.*" While NLP methods can be used to provide linguistic analyses of texts, a system would not "get" the pun here, but a human reader would. NLP methods are currently limited to the more literal linguistic analyses. For instance, co-reference resolution tools can be used to determine if "me" in the sentence above refers back to the "I", and if "it" refers to the "boomerang." A syntactic parser could be used to identify the sentence as a "compound sentence" with two independent clauses. Statistical semantic similarity methods could be used to evaluate the topical similarity between the sentence and the essay topic. In order to analyze the pun, an NLP system would need to understand the relationships between "fought," the movement of the boomerang, and the idiomatic meaning of "came back to me." Chapter 4 (*The E-rater® Automated Essay Scoring System*) offers a summary of various NLP methods, as well as those used in AEE. Other chapters in this volume discuss how specific NLP methods are used to detect grammatical errors (Chapter 15), discourse coherence analysis (Chapter 16), and sentiment analysis (Chapter 17). Chapter 9 discusses short answer scoring, and addresses methods of automatic paraphrase detection.

Designers of AEE systems have always been aware of the limits of the models and have tried to introduce innovation in the service of improvement. Page and Petersen (1995), for instance, attempted to simulate human rater behavior. They used the terms *proxes* and *trins* as proxy variables that impact "good" writing. *Trins* represent the characteristic dimension of composing text such as fluency or grammar. *Proxes* (taken from ap*prox*imations) are the observed variables about which the computer gathers data. These are the variables that computer-based methods can capture, such as the length of a word, or a word's part of speech.

A clear explanation of how a contemporary AEE engine works is provided in Williamson (2009) and describes the elements that are used to develop the prediction models for e-rater®, the AEE system developed by the Educational Testing Service. The paper first discusses the intrinsic aspects of writing that e-rater is attempting to score and then specifies the observed variables that are used as approximations in making score predictions.

Part of the challenge in AEE reflects the challenges implicit in education itself: there is no "gold standard" consensus as to what constitutes good writing at a particular developmental level and for specific writing modes. We expect that, as in all scientific endeavors, variables and processes appropriate to the requirements of society will gradually emerge as an outcome established, in tandem, by evidence-based research (AEE empirical models) and conceptual research (rhetoric and composition/writing theory). More recently, there is a new influence in the educational landscape in the United States: the Common Core State Standards initiative. This initiative is coordinated by the National Governors Association Center for Best Practices and the Council of Chief State School Officers. The initiative has now been adopted by 46 states for use in Kindergarten through 12th grade (K–12) classrooms. This initiative is likely to have a strong influence on teaching standards in K–12 education. The Common Core standards describe what K–12 students should be learning with regard to Reading, Writing, Speaking, Listening, Language, and Media and Technology. With regard to writing, in particular, there is a strong focus in the Common Core for K–12 students to become college-ready writers. Further, there is a prominent focus on students' ability to write in different genres, and, consistent with this, there is an emphasis on the development of students' skills to develop argumentation in writing. In the context of these new standards, statewide writing assessments are being developed. AEE could be an excellent resource for scoring such large volumes of essays collected from statewide administrations of writing assessments. The strong emphasis on the importance of high-quality argumentation in writing motivates the need for research to advance automated text analysis capabilities to capture complex aspects of argumentation (see Chapter 16, *Automated Evaluation of Discourse Coherence Quality in Essay Writing*, and Chapter 17, *Automated Sentiment Analysis for Essay Evaluation*).

Despite the fact that machines do not read and evaluate essays using the same cognitive abilities as humans, the concerns about AEE might be in part allayed by the fact that different systems have been shown to achieve similar score prediction outcomes (Shermis and Hamner, 2012). As well, in addition to prediction, the development and application of AEE in appropriate settings is essential. Concerns about AEE are discussed further in *Automated Essay Evaluation and the Teaching of Writing* (Chapter 2), *English as a Second Language Writing and Automated Essay Evaluation* (Chapter 3), and *Validity and Reliability of Automated Essay Scoring* (Chapter 11).

Further, researchers reading this volume who are involved in the development of AEE systems should consider the following issues illustrated in Table 1.1, prior to developing systems (1) *What is the ecological setting* (e.g., individual classroom, or state-level assessment)? (2) *What is the task* (e.g., timed content-area essay task, or composing in digital environments)? (3) *Who is the audience* (e.g., classroom teacher or fictional test rater)? and, (4) *What are the relevant measureable writing skills* (e.g., use evocative imagery or demonstrate knowledge about a content area)?

A number of chapters in this volume offer descriptions of different systems that might be understood in the context of the system development issues identified in Table 1.1. Several other chapters discuss specific text evaluation capabilities that contribute to features that can be leveraged in AEE systems.

In sum, it might be suggested that, depending on setting, task, audience, and skill measured, it is not essential that machine scoring technology use exactly the same

Table 1.1 Considerations for Development of AEE Systems

Ecological Settings	*Tasks*	*Audience*	*Measureable Writing Skills*
Classroom			
• **writing assessment**	Timed, social studies essay requiring student to write a letter to the President of the U.S., defending some aspect of immigration policy	Barack Obama Classroom teacher	• Present a well-organized and coherent argument • Use appropriate letter-writing format and language appropriate for the President
• **in-class writing**	Practice writing for state assessment	Classroom teacher "imaginary" test rater	• Demonstrate appropriate use of standard English conventions • Present a well-organized and coherent argument
• **homework assignment**	Untimed, nature journal assignment for a high school English class Write in the style of "some author" (e.g., Emerson) who describes nature	Classroom teacher	• Use of evocative imagery to paint a picture for the reader about the nature settings • Use metaphor • Use appropriate English conventions
• **digital homework assignment**	Write to the teacher's Current Events blog, commenting on the "article of the day"	Classroom teacher Peers	• Content of blog posting appropriate for the digital genre
Assessment			
• **state-level**	Timed, biology test with essay task	Unknown test rater	• Demonstrate knowledge about biology topic • Present information in an organized manner
• **admissions**	Timed, expository writing task	Unknown test rater	• Demonstrate appropriate use of standard English conventions • Present a well-organized and coherent argument

processes as humans do for evaluation and score prediction of essay writing tasks. Indeed, even these human scoring processes remain to be accurately defined (Vaughn, 1991; Weigle, 1994; Wiseman, 2012). As in any scientific endeavor the identifications of such processes can evolve over time. And, as we show in this chapter, new developments don't just emerge randomly, but rather are fostered by the developments that preceded them in established programs of research.

A MULTI-DISCIPLINARY APPROACH

The development of AEE technology is a community enterprise. It continues to involve, the input of teams composed of writing teachers, test developers, cognitive psychologists, psychometricians, and computer scientists. Writing teachers are critical to the development of the technology because they inform us as to how AEEs can reflect research-based pedagogical practice and thus be most beneficial to students. As discussed in Chapter 18, research in cognitive psychology continues to help us to model systems in ways that reflect the thought processes of students who will use the systems. As is discussed in a number of chapters in this volume, psychometric evaluations give us essential information about the validity and reliability of these systems. So, psychometric studies help us to answer questions about how the evaluative information from the systems can be compared to similar human evaluations, and whether the systems are measuring what we want them to. Several chapters in this volume address AEE and measurement issues. Computer science plays an important role in the implementation of AEE systems, specifically with regard to linguistically-based feature development with NLP methods and machine learning in the context of feature modeling.

EARLY HISTORY

In 1966, Ellis Page wrote on "The imminence of grading essays by computer" in a landmark *Phi Delta Kappan* article (Page, 1966). The article, greeted with considerable skepticism, predicted the coming of automated essay grading—the capacity of the computer to score extended written responses. As a former high school English teacher, Page saw the technology as a tool for instructors who were burdened with hours of grading writing assignments. In particular, he recognized the grading burden as a significant impediment to the improvement of overall writing capacity in the United States. It led teachers of high-school writing classes to assign only two to three essays per semester, thereby limiting much needed experience in order to reach writing goals. His typical admonition was, "If you want to be a better writer, you simply have to write more." This point has also been made by Elbow (1973). The burden imposed by grading, he argued, was the biggest impediment to more writing.

His critics had considerable fodder for their skepticism. At the time, the necessary access to computers was rare. Moreover, the necessity of entering text into the computer was a huge obstacle. The primary medium for data entry in the 1960s was the IBM 80-column punch card. Though a remarkable invention, it was clumsy, costly, and not well-suited for the average student—much less for widespread use. Of greater importance, there was no existing software that purported to do even part of what Page was proposing, since basic word processing packages were not to become available until the beginning of the *next* decade.

In addition to the lack of availability of the necessary hardware for essay grading machines, there were objections to the whole idea of displacing human raters; a society that was becoming increasingly depersonalized in so many other ways did not require further depersonalization by computerizing educational practices. There were concerns from the writing community about homogenizing writing instruction; failure of the machine to capture the writing construct and thus having a detrimental impact on writing instruction; disenfranchising writing faculty; and focusing on the summative rather than the formative aspects of writing. Some of these concerns are also discussed in Chapter 3. Nevertheless, Page wrote the article as a way to launch his ideas for the development of Project Essay Grade (PEG).

Page and his colleagues at the University of Connecticut reported on a continuation of their work: a stable working version of PEG (Ajay, Tillett, & Page, 1973). Given the context and the type of data to which his team had access (e.g., short college-level essays), PEG performed remarkably well. The 1973 study predated the entrance of high-stakes state-administered accountability assessments at United States public schools, a period in which exact agreement rates for human raters were in the low .70s. Prior to that time, it was common to see trained raters achieving agreement rates in the low to mid .60s (Page, 2003). Even so, PEG was able to perform as well as and sometimes better than the inter-rater performance of two trained human raters. As impressive as the technology performance was at the time, it was not long-lasting due to the limitations, including a lack of computer access and a time-consuming method for data entry.

Enter William Wresch, who retrospectively concluded the following from reading Pages' reports,

> The fact that 25 years have now passed since the original studies were published and no high schools or colleges use computer essay grading sums up the reaction to these studies. Statistics or no, there is little interest in using computers in this way.
>
> (Wresch, 1993)

Wresch's conclusion, however, did not consider other ongoing forces at work that were to facilitate the future of AEE, including (a) the creation and widespread adoption of the Internet, (b) word processing software, and (c) the use of NLP in the evaluation of writing.

TECHNOLOGY INFLUENCES ON AEE

AEE notably has employed computer-based technology innovation as it has advanced from one stage to the next. Web-based interfaces have supported the sharing of ideas to foster collaboration and interaction among writers. Specific developments, including word processing and the Internet, have facilitated the use of AEE. Word processing facilitates the creation of electronic texts, which are required for automated text scoring. The Internet is "leveling the playing field" regarding information that that might be used for composition content. And, of course, feedback on one's writing can take place instantaneously and often in the context of web-based essay evaluation systems.

Word Processing

Word processing is the application of technology to produce printed text, which includes composition, formatting, editing, and printing. It was not until the 1980s that this technology was accessible. During the 1980s and 1990s, more than 60 commercial word processing programs became available, and each one proved to be more time-saving and user-friendly than the previous (Kunde, 1996). Additions such as outlining and formatting capabilities transformed basic word processing into desktop publishing. The systems added features that either corrected or identified potential writing errors, including spell-checking, grammar parsing, and stylistic features.

The notable features of word processing must be considered in forecasting the advent of AEE systems. It was now possible for young writers to deal with not only putting words on paper, but with all the formatting, punctuation, and correction devices previously unavailable or, perhaps, even unknown to the writers. Word processing made it possible to create electronic texts that appear to have a positive impact on successful writing instruction (Graham & Perin, 2007) and are essential input to AEE systems.

The Internet

When Page created the first version of PEG in 1973, there was no Internet. At the time, the Department of Defense had assembled a basic communications network known as ARPANET, a project of the Advanced Research Project Agency Network. The project was initiated by connecting four computers located at UCLA, Stanford Research Institute, UCSB, and the University of Utah. In 1986 the National Science Foundation funded NSFNet as a cross-country backbone to the Internet, and maintained sponsorship, with rules for non-commercial government and research usage, for almost a decade. Commercial applications of the Internet were prohibited unless they had a related goal for educational or research purposes. In 1992, Delphi, the first national commercial Internet online service, offered subscribers email connection and full Internet service. In May 1995 the limitations placed on the commercial use of the Internet disappeared; the National Science Foundation ended sponsorship of the Internet backbone. All traffic now relied on commercial networks; AOL, Prodigy, and Compuserve came "online."

The creation and expansion of the Internet was an important development for AEE because it ultimately provided a platform upon which AEE could be administered. Instead of requiring essays to be written, stored, and transported, the platform could incorporate all of these steps with a simple Internet connection (Gleik, 2011).

NLP

NLP is a computer-based approach for analyzing language in text. NLP may be defined as "*a range of computational techniques for analyzing and representing naturally occurring texts at one or more levels of linguistic analysis for the purpose of achieving human-like language processing for a range of task applications*" (Liddy 2001). This somewhat labored definition can be analyzed in this way: The *range of computational techniques* refers to the multiple methods and techniques chosen to accomplish a particular type of language analysis. "*Naturally occurring texts*" refers to the ability to use any language, mode, genre, etc. that one might encounter in written or spoken mode. The main requirement is that it is in a language used by humans to communicate with one another. Analyses related to text-based NLP are likely to include morphology (word structure), syntax (sentence structure), and semantics (meaning). Chapter 4 contains descriptions of several commonly used NLP applications, such as machine translation and Internet search engines.

Research in NLP dates back to the 1940s. The first computer-based application of NLP, related to natural language, was Machine Translation (MT) introduced by Weaver and Booth for the purpose of breaking enemy military codes during World War II.

The *Automatic Language Processing Advisory Committee of the National Academy of Sciences, National Research Council* (ALPAC) created a report in 1966 that discussed the inadequacies of the systems and concluded that MT was not achievable, and recommended that it should not be funded (ALPAC, 1966). During the years after the ALPAC report, research and development in language-based computing included theoretical work in the 1960s and 1970s which focused on how to represent meaning and develop computationally-tractable solutions. Chomsky (1965) introduced the transformational model of linguistic competence. This was followed by the work of other transformational generativists, including case grammar of Fillmore (1967), semantic networks of Quillan (Collins and Quillan, 1971), and conceptual dependency theory of Schank (Schank and Tesler, 1969) in order to explain syntactic anomalies and provide semantic representations. In the early 1980s, NLP began to facilitate the development of new writing tools as well: Writer's Workbench was designed to help students edit their writing. This software provided automated feedback mostly related to writing mechanics and grammar (MacDonald, Frase, Gingrich, & Keenan, 1982).

The NLP field began growing rapidly in the 1990s, in part due to the increased availability of electronic text, the availability of computers with high speed and high memory capabilities, and the Internet.

NLP now contributes to a number of technologies in our everyday lives, including automated grammatical error detection in word processing software, Internet search engines, and machine translation, which is now freely available on most Internet sites. NLP has become a main driver in the development of AEE technologies. Readers should refer to Chapter 4 for a discussion of "everyday NLP," and for illustrations of how specific methods are utilized in the context of AEE.

EVOLUTION OF COMMERCIAL AEE

In this section, we offer a description of the evolution of the first commercial AEE systems. For detailed discussions of each of these systems, readers should refer to the system chapters in this volume.

By the early 1990s the advances of the Internet and word processing had sufficiently unfolded, and electronic processing and evaluation of student written papers became a real possibility. Page and his colleagues began to update the Fortran-coded PEG and convert it to the C-programming language. The program still processed the text in batch mode.

The original version of PEG used shallow NLP as part of its repertoire. The text was parsed and classified into language elements such as part of speech, word length, and word functions PEG would count key words and make its predictions based on the patterns of language that human raters valued or devalued in making their score assignments. Page classified these counts into three categories: simple, deceptively simple, and sophisticated. An example of a simple count would be the number of adjectives in an essay. Empirically, writers tend to be rewarded by human raters for using more adjectives. Breland, Bonner, and Kubota (1995) also noted that essay word count was correlated with human score, consistent with a PEG feature, specifically the fourth root of the number of words in an essay.

A deceptively simple count might be the number of words in an essay. Longer essays tend to be assigned higher scores by human raters. However, Page found that the relationship between the number of words used and the score assignment was not linear, but rather logarithmic. That is, essay length is factored in by human raters up to some threshold, and then becomes less important as they focus on other aspects of the writing.

A sophisticated count would be attending to words that are proxies for something that might have greater meaning. For example, a count of the word "because" may not be important in and of itself, but as a discourse connector it serves as a proxy for sentence complexity. Human raters tend to reward more complex sentences.

Page and Petersen (1995) summarized their approach in their *Phi Delta Kappan* article, "The computer moves into essay grading: Updating the ancient test," at which point they introduced the terminology of *proxes* and *trins*. As discussed earlier in this chapter, *trins* represent the characteristic dimension of interest such as fluency or grammar whereas *proxes* (taken from approximations) are the observed variables with which the computer works. These are the features that a computer might extract from a text, as described above. In social science research, a similar distinction might be made between the use of latent and observed variables. Observed variables are what one operationally measures (i.e., the score from an intelligence test) while the latent variable represents the underlying construct that one is attempting to measure (i.e., intelligence).

PEG's empirical approach has been characterized in a pejorative way as "brute-empirical" by some (Ben-Simon & Bennett, 2007) since it employed only the surface features of language in formulating its models. Moreover, PEG models were typically comprised of approximately 30–40 individual predictors that were selected on a prompt specific basis. Although the models formed from one prompt and population performed reasonably well when applied to other prompts and groups (Keith, 2003), the models failed to emulate human rater behavior and provided little rationale for creating norms that might be applied across a variety of prompts. The predictors seemed to take on an idiosyncratic arrangement and weighting. The third level, "explain," in the hierarchy of scientific purpose (i.e., describe, predict, explain) was difficult to achieve since the PEG models did not seem to conform to any particular theory of writing or communication. PEG also did little with the evaluation of content. Page had programmed PEG to evaluate the presence of key words and synonyms, but his early work suggested that content was either masked by other predictor variables or did not account for very much variance in human rater scores when modeling with PEG. He did, however, employ the content capabilities of PEG to create a "topicness index" which determined how "on-topic" a particular essay was. This was critical in identifying what he termed as "bad faith" essays—well-written essays that seemed to be off-topic.

In 1998, a web interface was added to PEG that permitted students to enter their essays remotely (Shermis, Mzumara, Olson, & Harrington, 1998, 2001). This new capability had few word processing features other than the basic editing of text, but it meant that student writers could enter their responses from anywhere in the world. After clicking a "submit" button, the essay would be processed by a PEG server and would return a score assigned by PEG. It would also store the results in a database that could later be retrieved for analysis.

At about the same time Vantage Learning released its first version of their IntelliMetric scoring engine (Elliot, 1999). The IntelliMetric scoring engine used empirical relationships to derive its predictive models, but also incorporated elements, computational linguistics, and classification (Elliot, 2003). The IntelliMetric scoring engine analyzes more than 300 semantic, syntactic, and discourse level features that fall into five major categories: focus and utility, development and elaboration, organization and structure, sentence structure, and mechanics and conventions. It was the first scoring engine to be marketed with an electronic portfolio, MyAccess!, where students could store past work. The portfolio system also provided writing aids, sophisticated word processing capabilities, and analytics for teachers to monitor student writing progress.

The original PEG and IntelliMetric scoring engines could provide assessments of content, but only in an indirect way. That is, using a list of key words and synonyms, one could determine the frequency with which a candidate essay employed the same terminology as that drawn from an expert list or from a normative model. Intelligent Essay Assessor's primary evaluation is based on the essay's content using a technique known as *Latent Semantic Analysis* (LSA) (Landauer, Foltz, & Laham, 1998; Landauer, Laham, & Foltz, 2003). LSA is a corpus-based statistical modeling approach that uses large corpora to model word usage. LSA generates information about statistical word usage in a document without regard to word ordering. This information for a single document is compared to other documents to determine the similarity between that source document and a large set of reference documents in terms of vocabulary use. Reference documents used for comparison purposes can be textbook material in a particular domain or a corpus of essays. LSA modeling requires a very large corpus of reference documents (several thousand) to reliably model a given domain. The underlying claim is that if LSA determines that two documents are similar with regard to word usage, then they are likely to be semantically similar (i.e., have the same meaning). In the context of essay scoring, LSA is trained on reference documents in a particular domain, such as textbook passages and/or human-scored essay responses to an essay topic. This training creates a semantic representation of topical knowledge. This method focuses on essay content and can be used to score essays that respond to opinion- or fact-based topics.

E-rater represents the first hybrid approach that leveraged NLP-derived linguistic properties in texts that were aligned with human scoring rubric criteria, and empirical relationships between human ratings (Attali & Burstein, 2006; Burstein, Kukich, Wolff, Lu, Chodorow, Braden-Harder, & Harris, 1998). E-rater features aligned with human scoring criteria included features related to writing conventions, sentence variety, topical vocabulary usage, sophistication of vocabulary, and organization and development. The system can also identify anomalous essays, for example, essays that appear to be off-topic. E-rater was the first system to be used in a large-scale, high-stakes assessment setting with the Graduate Management Admissions Test. In addition to assessment settings, e-rater features were also used in one of the first instructional settings, Criterion® to provide individualized feedback for student writers, directing students' attention to areas of success or improvement (Burstein, Chodorow, & Leacock, 2004).

CONCLUSION

Automated essay evaluation technology continues to evolve. This invites all of the communities who are stakeholders in AEE to become involved and to shape future developments. The technology still remains open to criticism about its current features and insufficient coverage of the writing construct. We expect that there will be greater interest in automated essay evaluation when its use shifts from that of summative evaluation to a more formative role, i.e., the research will contribute to 'evaluation of writing in learning contexts in contrast to only the evaluation of writing in assessment contexts.' For example, Shermis (2003) proposed that one mechanism for incorporating AEE into electronic portfolios is the possibility of having students "pre-submit" their essays before submitting the final product. The writing products would then be reviewed by the AEE system for elements covered by their model, so that students would be comfortable with their ability to demonstrate proficiency related to, for example, patterns of organization and knowledge of writing conventions. With their instructors, students could then review writing aspects not covered by the AEE model such as rhetorical strategies and audience.

By incorporating such requirements as part of a writing assignment, AEE systems would be viewed as helpful, rather than competitive tool. Chapters 2, 3, and 20 provide discussion about formative assessment and AEE. Chapter 2 offers a more detailed discussion of electronic portfolio assessment. National norms developed for writing models would permit educational institutions to track the developmental progress of their students using a measure independent of standardized multiple-choice tests. A school would have the opportunity to document the value-added component of their instruction or experience.

Research into the development and understanding of AEE programs can provide thoughtful and creative insights into the components of good writing. As the foregoing general discussion indicates, it might be appropriate to think of the technology as being where microcomputers were during the early 1980s, when writers still had a choice between the new technology and the typewriter, at which time computers represented a technology with promise for the general population but which had yet to undergo development. (Today, there is no longer an American manufacturer of typewriters.)

Until recently, one major hindrance to advancing research in the field centered on the lack of publicly-available AEE engines. Almost all AEE research and development has been conducted by commercial or not-for-profit companies that have protected their investments by restricting access to the technology. This has had the overall effect of limiting investigations to the areas of primary interest to technology owners. The first scoring engine to be made available publicly was Larry Rudner's BETSY (Rudner and Gagne, 2001). It was designed for, and worked well as a demonstration tool using a Bayesian approach to scoring essays. More recently, Mayfield and Rosé (2010) of the Teledia Lab at Carnegie Mellon University released LightSIDE, an easy-to-use automated evaluation engine with both compiled and source code publicly available. This scoring engine does not implement NLP features, but does support multiple scoring algorithms. Moreover, anyone with a penchant for basic Java programming could supplement the LightSIDE code with customized programming that incorporates NLP AI feature sets, and use the modified version for research or development.

Along similar lines, the Automated Student Assessment Prize,[2] with funding from the William and Flora Hewlett Foundation (Stross, 2012), recently concluded a study that involved eight commercial vendors and the LightSIDE scoring engine in a demonstration of AEE's capacity to score high-stakes essay assessments. Chapter 19 details the promising results (Shermis and Hamner, 2012). In addition, there was a public competition to complement the private vendor demonstration. The results from the public competitors showed that given sufficient time and motivation (the first prize was US$60,000), data scientists from around the world could develop automated essay scoring engines that, from a system performance perspective, could compete with the commercial vendors (at least on the data sets provided). In formulating the prize, the hope was that the public competitors would develop new analytic techniques or approaches that would either supplement or replace existing algorithms. A number of the public competitors committed to sharing their scoring engines with those who would want to extend field research.

AEE was first introduced in the 1960s (Page, 1966), and has since evolved into its own field of study. As discussed earlier in this chapter, the field of AEE involves research from several communities, including cognitive psychology, computer science, educational measurement, linguistics, and writing research. When large-scale use of automated essay scoring systems was first introduced for high-stakes testing in the late 1990s, the communities were not necessarily of one mind. On the one hand, there was excitement about the advantages of this new technology which created savings in terms of time and costs associated with human rater scoring. In addition, system reliability is 100%. Specifically, systems will predict the same score for a single paper each time that paper is input to the system. This is not necessarily true of human raters (Mitchell, 1994) as discussed in Haswell (2008), and in Chapter 2 (*Automated Essay Evaluation and the Teaching of Writing*).

At present, the writing community remains concerned about how machine scoring might send an inappropriate signal that fails to embrace the essentially rhetorical nature of writing instruction and assessment over the longer term. There are concerns that students and test-takers would learn to write to a machine, and there might be a longer-term degradation of writing instruction offered to students in classroom and assessment settings. As all shareholders recognize, writing *only* in a standardized, formulaic style, is an undesirable outcome *not only* in the context of technology but in instructional contexts in general. Additionally, there are similar concerns for conventional paper-and-pencil test prep coaching, where test-takers are coached about how they should respond to writing tasks on standardized assessments, and instructed to write to an audience of human essay raters. Coaching to a specific mode of writing, whether for machine- or human-rater scoring, is certainly a valid concern. Undermining evidence-based instruction is always a serious concern in the consequence of any assessment.

In this volume, we have tried to be sensitive to the AEE community at large and all of its stakeholders, inviting authors to write chapters from the communities shaping the design and impact of these technological systems. The book foreword and early chapters were written by researchers from the writing community, and present this perspective for native and non-native English speaking populations, while discussing an array of writing tasks and settings. Among the remainder of the book chapters, several are written from the perspective of the educational measurement, cognitive psychology, and education policy communities. As might be expected from the book title, several chapters offer descriptions of the current state of the art in AEE systems. Authors of these chapters were asked to offer descriptions that discussed the underlying motivations behind the system design, and provided readers with a clear understanding of the underlying algorithms.

As a result of the publication of this new volume, we hope that its breadth of multi-disciplinary discussion will support an ongoing and meaningful dialogue among the communities working in this area. We anticipate that such a discussion will inform the technology so that it can offer substantive support to educators and students, respectively, in instructional and assessment settings.

ACKNOWLEDGMENTS

We would like to thank Doug Baldwin, Brent Bridgeman, Frank DiVesta, Norbert Elliot, and Derrick Higgins for thorough and substantive reviews of earlier versions of this chapter. We would like to offer a special thank you to Norbert Elliot for adding elegant refinements and substance to our prose.

NOTES

1 Note that the terms automated essay scoring (AES) and automated essay evaluation (AEE) are used interchangeably in this volume. Historically, the term automated essay grading (AEG) has also been applied to research and development in this area.
2 http://www.scoreright.org/asap.aspx

REFERENCES

Ajay, H. B., Tillett, P. I., & Page, E. B. (1973). Analysis of essays by computer (AEC-II) (p. 231). Washington, DC: U.S. Department of Health, Education, and Welfare, Office of Education, National Center for Educational Research and Development.

ALPAC (1966). Languages and machines: computers in translation and linguistics. A report by the Automatic Language Processing Advisory Committee, Division of Behavioral Sciences, National Academy of Sciences, National Research Council. Washington, DC: National Academy of Sciences, National Research Council, 1966. (Publication 1416.) 124pp.

Attali, Y., & Burstein, J. (2006). Automated essay scoring with e-rater 2.0. Retrieved August 4, 2012, from http://www.jtla.org

Ben-Simon, A., & Bennett, R. E. (2007). Toward more substantively meaningful automated essay scoring. *Journal of Technology, Learning, and Assessment,* 6(1). Retrieved August 4, 2012, from http://www.jtla.org

Bowen, W. G., Chingos, M. M., & McPherson, M. S. (2009). *Crossing the finish line: Completing college at America's public universities.* Princeton, NJ: Princeton University Press.

Breland, H. M., Bonner, M. W., & Kubota, M. Y. (1995). Factors in performance in brief, impromptu essay examinations (College Board Rep. No. 95–04). New York: College Entrance Examination Board.

Burstein, J., Kukich, J., Wolff, S.,. Lu, C., Chodorow, M., Braden-Harder, L., & Harris, M. D. (1998). Automated scoring using a hybrid feature identification technique. *Proceedings of the 36th Annual Meeting of the Association for Computational Linguistics and 17th International Conference on Computational Linguistics,* 1, 206–210.

Burstein, J., Chodorow, M., & Leacock C. (2004) Automated essay evaluation: The Criterion online writing service. *AI Magazine, 25*(3), 27–36.

Chomsky, N. (1965). *Aspects of the theory of syntax.* Boston, MA: The MIT Press.

Collins, A. M., & Quillan, M. R. (1971). *Categories and subcategories in semantic memory.* Paper presented at the Psychonomic Society Convention, St. Louis, MO.

Connors, R. J. (1981). The rise and fall of modes of discourse. *College Composition and Communication, 32*(4), 444–455.

Elbow, P. (1973). *Writing without teachers.* New York: Oxford University Press.

Elliot, S. M. (1999). *Construct validity of IntelliMetric™ with international assessment.* Yardley, PA: Vantage Technologies.

Elliot, S. M. (2003). *IntelliMetric:* From here to validity. In M. D. Shermis & J. Burstein (Eds.), *Automated essay scoring: A cross-disciplinary perspective* (pp. 71–86). Mahwah, NJ: Lawrence Erlbaum Associates, Inc.

Fillmore, C. J. (1967). *The case for case.* Paper presented at the Texas Symposium on Linguistic Universals, Austin, TX.

Gleik, J. (2011) *The information. A history. A theory. A flood.* New York: Pantheon Books.

Graham, S., and Perin, D. (2007). A meta-analysis of writing instruction for adolescent students. *Journal of Educational Psychology, 99*(3), 445–476.

Haswell, R. (2008). Teaching of writing in higher education. In Charles Braverman (Ed.), *Handbook of research on writing: History, society, school, individual, text.* New York: Lawrence Erlbaum Associates.

Kawate-Mierzejewska, M. (2003). *E-rater software.* Paper presented at the Japanese Association for Language Teaching, Tokyo, Japan, March 23.

Keith, T. Z. (2003). Validity and automated essay scoring systems. In M. D. Shermis & J. Burstein (Eds.), *Automated essay scoring: A cross-disciplinary perspective* (pp. 147–168). Mahwah, NJ: Lawrence Erlbaum Associates, Inc.

Kunde, B. (1996). A brief history of word processing (through 1986). Retrieved March 1, 2012, from http://www.stanford.edu/~bkunde/fb-press/articles/wdprhist.html

Landauer, T. K., Foltz, P. W., & Laham, D. (1998). Introduction to latent semantic analysis. *Discourse Processes, 25*(2–3), 259–284.

Landauer, T. K., Laham, D., & Foltz, P. W. (2003). Automated scoring and annotation of essays with the Intelligent Essay Assessor. In M. D. Shermis & J. Burstein (Eds.), *Automated essay scoring: A cross-disciplinary perspective* (pp. 87–112). Mahwah, NJ: Lawrence Erlbaum Associates, Inc.

Liddy, E. D. (2001). Natural language processing. In *Encyclopedia of library and information science* (2 ed.). New York: Marcel Decker, Inc.

MacDonald, N. H., Frase, L. T., Gingrich, P. S., & Keenan, S. A. (1982). The writer's workbench: Computer aids for text analysis. *IEEE Transactions on Communications, 30*(1), 105–110.

Mayfield, E., & Rosé, C. (2010). *An interactive tool for supporting error analysis for text mining.* Paper presented at the Demonstration Session at the International Conference of the North American Association for Computational Linguistics, Los Angeles, CA.

Miller, Carolyn. (1984). Genre as social acton. *Quarterly Journal of Speech, 70*, 151–167.

Mitchell, F. (1994). Is there a text in this grade? The implicit messages of comments on student writing. *Issues in Writing, 6*(2), 187–195.

Neal, M. R. (2011). *Writing assessment and the revolution in digital technologies.* New York: Teachers College Press.

Page, E. B. (1966). The imminence of grading essays by computer. *Phi Delta Kappan, 48*, 238–243.

Page, E. B. (2003). Project Essay Grade: PEG. In M. D. Shermis & J. Burstein (Eds.), *Automated essay scoring: A cross-disciplinary perspective* (pp. 43–54). Mahwah, NJ: Lawrence Erlbaum Associates, Inc.

Page, E. B., & Petersen, N. S. (1995). The computer moves into essay grading: Updating the ancient test. *Phi Delta Kappan, 76*(7), 561–565.

Rudner, L., & Gagne, P. E. D. N. (2001). An overview of three approaches to scoring written essays by computer. *Pareonline, 7*(26). Retrieved July 22, 2012, from http://pareonline.net/htm/v7n26.htm

Schank, R. C., & Tesler, L. (1969). *A conceptual dependency parser for natural language.* Paper presented at the 1969 Conference on Computational Linguistics, Stroudsburg, PA.

Shermis, M. D. (2003). Facing off on automated scoring. *Assessment Update, 15*(2), 4–5.

Shermis, M. D., & Burstein, J. (2003). Introduction. In M. D. Shermis & J. Burstein (Eds.), *Automated essay scoring: A cross-disciplinary perspective* (pp. xiii–xvi). Mahwah, NJ: Lawrence Erlbaum Associates.

Shermis, M. D., & Hamner, B. (2012). *Contrasting state-of-the-art automated scoring of essays: Analysis.* Paper presented at the National Council of Measurement in Education, Vancouver, BC, Canada.

Shermis, M. D., Mzumara, H. R., Kiger, B. S., & Marsiglio, C. (1998). The testing center annual report 1998. Indianapolis, IN: IUPUI Testing Center.

Shermis, M. D., Mzumara, H. R., Olson, J., & Harrington, S. (2001). On-line grading of student essays: PEG goes on the web at IUPUI. *Assessment and Evaluation in Higher Education, 26*(3), 247–259.

Stross, Randall. (2012). The algorithm didn't like my essay. *New York Times*, June.

Vantage Learning. (2001). *A preliminary study of the efficacy of IntelliMetric™ for use in scoring Hebrew assessments.* Newtown, PA: Vantage Learning.

Vantage Learning. (2002). *A study of IntelliMetric™ for responses in scoring Bahasa Malay.* Newtown, PA: Vantage Learning.

Vaughan, C. (1991). Holistic assessment: What goes on in the raters' minds? In L. Hamp-Lyons (Ed.), assessing second language writing in academic contexts (pp. 111–126). Norwood, NJ: Ablex.

Weigle, S. (1994). Effects of training on raters of ESL compositions. *Language Testing, 11*(2), 197–223.

Williamson, D. M. (2009). *A framework for implementing automated scoring.* Paper presented at the American Educational Research Association, San Diego, CA.

Wiseman, C. (2012). Rater effects: Ego engagement in rater decision-making. *Assessing Writing. 17,* 150–173.

Wresch, W. (1993). The imminence of grading essays by computer—25 years later. *Computers and Composition, 10*(2), 45–58.

2 Automated Essay Evaluation and the Teaching of Writing

Norbert Elliot and Andrew Klobucar

INTRODUCTION

The relationship between instruction and assessment has always been problematic. Framed as a struggle between the force of systems and integrity of individualism, *writing assessment* stands as a term symbolizing contested space. Research in writing assessment operates on a continuum between nomothetic span and idiographic representation (Borsboom, 2005; Embretson, 1983). In one tradition, the field seeks information about the performance of entire populations (National Center for Education Statistics, 2012); in another, investigation of individual student ability is the proper assessment aim (Sternglass, 1997).

Nowhere is this tension more apparent than in the contrasting ways to stump automated writing assessment systems. For Powers, Burstein, Chodorow, Fowles, and Kukich (2001), the test was to see if e-rater®, the automated essay evaluation (AEE) platform developed by the Educational Testing Service (ETS), could be tricked into awarding scores that were judged by human readers to be too low in their value. Winner Jason Eisner, then a computer science graduate student at the University of Pennsylvania, wrote and repeated paragraphs 37 times. For Herrington and Moran (2012), the trick was to write one essay, submit it to the Criterion® Online Writing Evaluation Service—the platform hosting e-rater that provides formative review along with a total score—and identify the ways that the machine gaffed by incorrect identification of errors that were not actually in the essay. In their conclusions, the Powers research team calls for software improvement—a view supported in the Introduction to this volume; Herrington and Moran offer a more extreme view, arguing that the software should be banished from our classrooms—a view congruent with the position taken by Cheville (2004). Responsible for large-scale assessment, testing organizations benefit by improvements in the software that yield accuracy; responsible for the individual student at her desk, the teacher benefits by curricular improvements that reinforce learning.

Such value dualisms are inherent in the history of writing assessment (White, 2001) and, if we believe Derrida (1976), in the history of western thought itself. Binary opposition—nomothetic versus idiographic, sampling plans versus students, science versus the humanities, organizations versus individuals, researchers versus teachers—results in an epistemological juxtaposition that is, at once, both artificial and harmful. As Hirschmann (1992) has observed in the case of obligation theory, these discourse patterns prevent us from seeing critical relationships and interconnections that are beneficial to all.

In this chapter, our position is one of mediation. In this volume, readers will find descriptions of the AEE systems and their scoring capability, generalizations that may be made from that capability, extrapolations of score interpretations, and implications of AEE use. The multi-disciplinary orientation of this volume suggests that understanding AEE is a complex endeavor that can best be understood in the context of research traditions: Applied Linguistics; Business Administration and Management; Cognitive Psychology and Psycholinguistics; Computer and Information Sciences; Educational Assessment, Testing, and Measurement; Psychometrics and Quantitative Psychology; and Rhetoric and Composition/Writing Studies. This chapter will provide a context for these taxonomic programs of research by focusing on writing instruction, its assessment, and the unique role of AEE in this relationship. The chapter begins with an overview of contemporary research on teaching and assessing writing. Following an examination of writing construct models, we then turn to our experiences with an AEE over a three-year period at a public science and technology research university. Based on the present state of AEE research and our own experiences, we conclude with directions for the future of writing assessment in digital environments. Our explorations at this point do not yet warrant a position of authority in this rapidly evolving field; rather, we take our contingent position as teachers–researchers in the field of Rhetoric and Composition/Writing Studies working to understand and use the technology of AEE for the benefit of our students and the institution that provides their education.

TEACHING AND ASSESSING WRITING IN THE 21ST CENTURY

Meta-analysis indicataes that the best practice in writing instruction may be described as environmental, a term used by Hillocks (1986) in his meta-analysis and re-categorized as process writing by Graham and Perin (2007) in theirs. Empirical research has now demonstrated that an effective curriculum is characterized by clear and specific objectives, with tasks selected to engage students cognitively in small settings. In a language arts model where writing, reading, speaking, and collaborating are viewed as interrelated communicative activities, students have been shown to make substantial gains in their writing performance. Graham and Perin provide ten recommendations regarding curricular emphasis on strategy instruction, summarization, peer assistance, product goals, word processing, sentence combining, professional development, inquiry, prewriting, and model analysis. Attendant to these recommendations are the following: explicit and systematic instruction, creation of collaborative environments where students help each other with their writing, and use of word processing.

Similarly, the writing community has found that assessments are most meaningful when they are site based, locally controlled, context sensitive, rhetorically informed, accountable, meaningful, and fair (Huot, 1996; Lynne, 2004). The more that can be understood about the situated ecology of writing, Wardle and Roozen (2012) have proposed, the better an institution can identify the multiple sites where writing takes place, strengthen the possibility for student learning at these sites, and respond to multiple shareholders involved in assuring that graduates have the knowledge and skills needed to be productive citizens and professionals.

The contemporary ecological model for teaching and assessing writing is congruent with the description given by Yancey (2012) of the present state of writing assessment. Yancey sees the history of writing assessment as a series of phases, often overlapping: the period from 1950 to 1970 highlighted multiple-choice tests (Palmer, 1961); from 1970 to 1986, attention was focused on the holistic essay (White, 1985); and from 1986 to the present, portfolio assessment was viewed as the optimal evaluation method (Hamp-Lyons & Condon, 2000). Today, calls for greater knowledge about local exigency—greater emphasis on how writers respond to contingency—mark contemporary writing assessment practices. In this fourth wave, Yancey and her colleagues (Cambridge, Cambridge, & Yancey, 2009) are especially attentive to composing in digital environments. Interaction with digital artifacts, the significance of reflective analysis, the desire for comparison without standardization, and knowledge generation—all are new areas targeted for study as students shift from print-based to web-based communication environments.

From the reliable certainties of instruction and assessment in a print environment to the wonky contingencies involved in digital communication, this history has been accompanied by position statements from the Conference on College Composition and Communication (CCCC), the college section of the National Council of Teachers of English (NCTE). The professional voice of Rhetoric and Composition/Writing Studies since 1949, CCCC position statements are influential in their ability to frame significant issues for members and the postsecondary institutions they serve. Two statements are of special interest to the reception of AEE by those who teach and assess writing in postsecondary institutions. The 2004 "Position statement on teaching, learning, and assessing writing in digital environments" begins with the observation that the focus of writing instruction is expanding to include a literacy of print and a literacy of the screen. Since work in one medium may enhance learning in the other, the position statement recommends reflective engagement with the epistemic characteristics of information technology that yield opportunities to use digital technologies to solve important social problems. Both teachers and administrators are called upon to institute best practices to support student learning, curricular development, and infrastructure support. The 2009 revision of "Writing assessment: A position statement" attends to the relationship between teaching and assessing writing. The statement identifies guiding principles that focus on assessment as a means to improving instruction and learning, the social nature of writing and the need for contextualized writing, the need for multiple measures, the significance of anticipating the consequences of assessment, and the need for research-based practice.

These two position statements are unified in their opposition to electronic rating. "Because all writing is social," the 2004 statement claims, "all writing should have human readers, regardless of the purpose of the writing." Objections are twofold: writing-to-a-machine sends a message that human communication is not valued, a message that reduces the validity of the assessment; as well, we cannot know the criteria by which the computer scores the writing and so we cannot understand the kinds of bias that may have been built into the scoring. The 2009 position statement references the opposition to the use of machine-scored writing:

> Automated assessment programs do not respond as human readers. While they may promise consistency, they distort the very nature of writing as a complex and context-rich interaction between people. They simplify writing in ways that can mislead writers to focus more on structure and grammar than on what they are saying by using a given structure and style.

Taking their stand with idiographic representation, the authors of these documents oppose AEE. Aligned with arguments taking their origin in philosophy of technology, these two documents—along with Ericsson and Haswell's *Machine Scoring of Student Essays: Truth and Consequences* (2006)—object to the design and determinism of AEE. In its design, technology is not neutral. It is a product of dominant social forces and, as such, tacitly articulates their assumptions. In the tradition of Mumford (1934) and Ellul (1964), the leaders drafting these position statements call attention to the fact that artifacts embody politics (Winner, 1980). Lack of disclosure, or blackboxing, is evidence of technological determinism. "When a machine runs smoothly," Latour notes in his definition of blackboxing, "when a matter of fact is settled, one need focus only on its inputs and outputs and not on its internal complexity. Thus, paradoxically, the more science and technology succeed, the more opaque and obscure they become" (Latour, 1999, p. 204). With Winner (1980), many in the writing community believe that artifacts have politics, and these individuals want to know all they can about the gears of the machine.

Those who assess writing as part of the educational measurement community involved in the commercialization of AEE see the technology quite differently. With Carr (2003), they realize that information technology involved in AEE is proprietary. Because AEE can be owned, it can be the foundation of strategic marketplace advantages that can allow both higher profits and greater good. In the tradition of focus on nomothetic span, these researchers realize that AEE is a disruptive technology, that particular artifact described by Christensen (1997) as an innovation that holds the potential to displace established competitors—those weary-eyed readers, paid by testing companies (Farley, 2009). If a machine can do what a human can do with a timed, impromptu essay, then why not let the machine do the work at a fraction of the time and cost?

Affirmative answers have been swift. On the postsecondary level, AEE has been used in the Graduate Record Examination (GRE), the Test of English as a Foreign Language (TOEFL), and the Graduate Management Admissions Test (GMAT). In the elementary and secondary schools, the Race to the Top assessment consortia—fuelled by US$330 million provided by the U.S. Department of Education (2012)—will almost certainly use some form of AEE to evaluate literacy as it is manifested in the essay or in short text response. The design of the Common Core State Standards, a curricular model led by the National Governors Association Center for Best Practices and the Council of Chief State School Officers, ensures that an evidence-based assessment model will emerge during the competition, with AEE integral to that model. It is not a bridge too far to imagine the use of the Cognitively-Based Assessments of, for, and as Learning (CBAL) (Forgione, 2012; Sabatini, Bennett, & Deane, 2011), an ETS research-based initiative described by Paul Deane in this volume, for both the Common Core State Standards and the National Assessment of Educational Progress.

As is the case with many disruptive technologies that displace markets right before our eyes, AEE is based on a counterintuitive premise: the machine does not read the essay at all. In the case of the e-rater, the machine predicts a human-like score. The machine is not a better interpreter of the essay; it merely extrapolates data we already have more efficiently and therefore more productively than a typical human scorer. At present, there are at least nine AEE systems capable of essay scoring, and this volume contains chapters describing several of them: AutoScore, LightSIDE, Bookette, e-rater, Lexile Writing Analyzer, Project Essay Grade, Intelligent Essay Assessor, CRASE, and IntelliMetric. In their analysis of 22,029 essays from grades 7, 8, and 10, Shermis and Hamner (2012) found that AEE was capable of producing scores that are similar to human scores. As they find in this volume, two human scores (as measured by quadratic weighted kappas) ranged in rates of agreement from 0.61 to 0.85; machine scores ranged from 0.60 to 0.84 in their agreement with the human scores. Shermis and Hamner provide additional discussion of the limitations and potential for AEE in this volume.

So, if these known and commonly used AEE systems so well reflect the scores given by human raters, why not build upon the success GRE, GMAT, and TOEFL? Why not expand AEE use in the SAT Writing section, allowing the cost savings for a second human reader to fund evaluation of a second writing sample on a different discourse mode? Why not implement AEE in the National Assessment of Educational Progress?

The answer is deceptively simple: Because writing is a complex socio-cognitive construct, the issues involved in its measurement are often as complex as the construct itself. Because AEE does not read the essay but is trained to behave as a human rater would, the validity of the human score itself is called into question. (Again, as Latour correctly points out, both the concepts and the empirical tools for representing such measurements will seem more and more difficult to understand.) We know a great deal about the reliability of AEE regression analysis scoring procedures, but the factors that impact human scoring decisions are multiple and varied (Bejar, 2012; Wiseman, 2012). If the human readers do not follow the scoring rubrics, the machine will follow a path leading to inaccurate scores because the machine is trained (that is, modelled) based on sets of human-scored essays. Machine modelling methods are described by Brent Bridgeman in this volume.

The complexities associated with the digital format of these systems are breathtaking: if the platform hosting the test is not usable for students, construct irrelevant variance is introduced; if the reporting system is poor, scores will not be usable for decision making. As well, if proprietary issues stand in the way of any disclosure whatsoever, it will become simply impossible to recommend AEE adoption. As Bennett and Bejar (1998) wryly observed in the early days of automated assessment, it's not only the scoring. In order to find a thread through the maze of barriers that arise as constructs are mediated in digital environments, Bennett (2011) offers sound recommendations: to reduce construct irrelevant variance, we should design platforms according to usability analysis; to increase transparency, we should base the AEE on articulated constructs validated by experts; to ensure accurate AEE modelling to human readers, we should strengthen operational human scoring; to enhance AEE scoring systems, we should conduct empirical studies on the bases upon which humans assign scores; to lessen undesired impacts associated with proprietary development of technology, we should ensure that vendor contracts disclose AEE scoring designs; to ensure increased construct representation, we should require a broad base of validity evidence to evaluate score meaning. If all fails, there should be a failsafe: unless the base of validity evidence is compelling, we should include supervised human raters in the assessment system. In similar fashion, Williamson, Xi, and Breyer (2012) have offered a baseline approach for the assessment of AEE that emphasizes the consequences of test use. Their framework emphasizes the following: fit between the scoring capability and the assessment purpose; agreement between human and automated scores; associations with independent measures; generalizability of automated scores across different tasks and test forms; and the impact and consequences for the population and subgroups.

If we seek an intersection among the research-based curricular recommendations of Graham and Perin (2007), the desire for local validation of Huot (1996) and Lynne (2004), the policy recommendations of Conference on College Composition and Communication (2004, 2009), and the recommendations for AEE development and use of Bennett (2011), we would do well to pursue validity evidence through construct modelling (Kane, 2006).

MODELS OF THE WRITING CONSTRUCT

Resonating with calls for precise conceptual definitions of the writing construct (Slomp, 2012), the three major associations in the writing community have offered the *Framework for Success in Postsecondary Writing*. In 2011 the Council of Writing Program Administrators (CWPA), NCTE, and the National Writing Project (NWP) published a writing model for instructors, parents, policymakers, employers, and the general public. Licensed under the Creative Commons in order to facilitate non-proprietary sharing and creative use, the *Framework for Success* focuses on the critical juncture between high school and college. Emphasizing habits of mind and experiences with writing, reading, and critical analysis, the *Framework for Success* is intended to serve as a foundation for college-level, credit-bearing courses. The intent of the model is straightforward: "Students who come to college writing with these habits of mind and these experiences will be well positioned to meet the writing challenges in the full spectrum of academic courses and later in their careers" (p. 2). As such, the *Framework for Success* defines of the specific competencies for first-year writing classes.

Defined as "ways of approaching learning that are both intellectual and practical" (p. 2), the habits of mind include the following: curiosity (the desire to know more about the world); openness (the willingness to consider new ways of being and thinking); engagement (a sense of investment and involvement in learning); creativity (the ability to use novel approaches for generating, investigating, and representing ideas); persistence (the ability to sustain interest in and attention to short- and long-term projects); responsibility (the ability to take ownership of one's actions and understand the consequences of those actions for oneself and others); flexibility (the ability to adapt to situations, expectations, or demands); and metacognition (the ability to reflect on one's own thinking as well as on the individual and cultural processes and systems used to structure knowledge). Acknowledging that "particular writing, reading, and critical analysis experiences contribute to habits of mind that are crucial to success in college" (p. 6), the experiences include the following: rhetorical knowledge (the ability to analyze and act on understandings of audiences, purposes, and contexts in creating and comprehending texts); critical thinking (the ability to analyze a situation or text and make thoughtful decisions based on that analysis); writing processes (the multiple strategies writers use to approach and undertake writing and research); knowledge of conventions (the formal rules and informal guidelines that define what is considered to be correct [or appropriate] and incorrect [or inappropriate] in a piece of writing); and composing in multiple environments (the ability to create writing using everything from traditional pen and paper to electronic technologies). While the habits of mind are new to the *Framework for Success*, the writing, reading, and critical analysis experiences are not. The CWPA Outcomes Statement for First-Year Composition identified a common set of objectives for first-year writing over a decade ago, and it use has been documented (Behm, Glau, Holdstein, Roen, & White, 2012; Harrington, Rhodes, Fischer, & Malenczyk, 2005).

A constructive literate act, Flower (1994; see also Hayes, 2012) proposed involves social, cognitive, and rhetorical processes. Flower's social cognitive theory of writing defines literacy as an action involving discourse processes dependent on knowledge of social conventions. Influenced by this view of writing, the *Framework for Success* is also indebted to knowledge gleaned from theories of personality and cognition. The habits of mind are part of this tradition, commonly known as the Big Five model of personality: extraversion, agreeableness, conscientiousness, emotional stability, and experiential openness (De Raad, 2000; O'Connor & Paunonen, 2007). As well, the writing, reading, and critical analysis experiences are associated with cognitive psychology and knowledge acquisition (Dillon & Sternberg, 1986; Wells, Christiansen, Race, Acheson, & MacDonald, 2009). Figure 2.1 provides a visual rendering of the *Framework for Success*.

Understood contextually, the Outcomes Statement and the *Framework for Success* provide a good context for understanding AEE. If we define the construct domain as a set of interrelated variables that can be used as a unified model for validation of test use (Kane, 2006; Messick, 1989), we can better understand the role of AEE within that

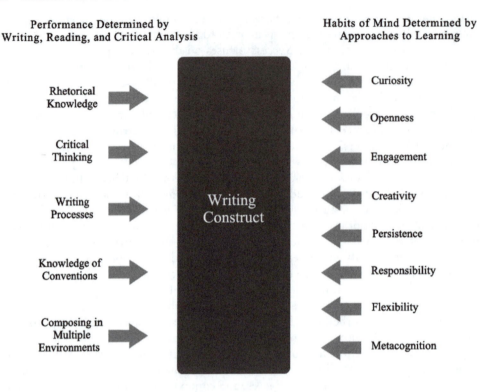

Figure 2.1 Framework for success in postsecondary writing: the writing construct.

framework. We turn now to our experiences with the AEE system *Criterion* to provide examples of the value of construct modelling.

CASE STUDIES AT A SCIENCE AND TECHNOLOGY UNIVERSITY

At our institution, a study of the use of AEE for placement purposes resulted in an appetite to learn more about its potential (Elliot, Deess, Rudniy, & Johsi, 2012). Because the Criterion construct model is transparent, it allows an ideal investigation of the relationship between the traits it measures and those of the *Framework for Success*.

At the present, e-rater—the AEE platform that serves the assessment function in Criterion—is currently able to identify the following features; grammatical and word usage errors (based on native and non-native speaker writing data); mechanics errors (e.g. spelling); the presence of essay-based discourse elements (e.g., a thesis statement); the development of essay-based discourse elements; and style weaknesses (e.g., overly repetitious words). As well, content vector analysis—a statistical technique that compares the frequency of word use in a given AEE scored essay to the set of related essays scored by humans—allows comparison of an essay to the set of training essays that received a score of 6 (the highest score), average word length, and word frequency (how often a word occurs given a document). Based on this information, an overall score is computed for an essay and given to students and their teachers within the Criterion system, along with an annotation of the student essay suggesting areas for possible revision (Burstein, 2012). As Burstein, Tetreault, and Madnani show in their chapter in this volume, these features—organization, development, grammar, usage, mechanics, style, lexical complexity, and topic-specific vocabulary use—are commonly associated with rubrics for instruction and assessment. As does the *Framework for Success*, Criterion offers a defined construct model.

When students write to carefully structured persuasive topics, they produce constructed responses—ideally, well structured writing samples that demonstrate their ability to achieve proficiency in the specified domain (Bennett, 1993). Because our institution has a long history of using portfolios as a form of outcomes assessment (Elliot, Briller, & Joshi, 2007)—and conceptualizing these portfolios as showcases of student constructed responses to a defined set of course tasks and program objectives (Camp, 1993)—the relationship between ETS's Criterion and our curriculum provided an ideal experimental that focused on placement of admitted students and embedded assessment of those students.

During the fall of 2009, information was gathered on admitted student writing performance at our science and technology research university. Under timed conditions, first-year students (n = 862) wrote on two 12th grade level ETS persuasive prompts in Criterion at the beginning of the semester. Prompt-specific models were then built and evaluated for four prompts, and models meeting designated performance criteria were further evaluated against the SAT Writing section and holistic portfolio scores. As Ramineni (2013) has demonstrated, the Criterion scores correlated at statistically significantly levels with all significant measures, including the holistic portfolio score ($r = .41, p < .05$). These correlations supported an analysis of the ability to Criterion to place students in patterns similar to the SAT Writing section, the admissions test that had been validated by our university as a placement tool. At the present, Criterion is used as a placement system for students who do not have SAT Writing scores or who wish to challenge their placement with the submission of two essays scored by e-rater. Both administrators and faculty see this use of Criterion as a clear advantage. In place of the combined multiple-choice and essay format of the SAT Writing section, students produce two essays written to constructed-response tasks.

Concurrent with this study, we substantially decreased the remediation rate by revising the placement system. We were able to reduce remediation rates, often as high as 39%, while maintaining record low failure grades. Essentially our new model demonstrated that establishing empirically-warranted placement scores on the SAT Writing would place approximately 10% of our admitted students in honors courses, 80% of our students in traditional, credit bearing courses, and 10% of our students in basic writing classes (Elliot et al., 2012). Because admissions criteria, based on high school grades and SAT Critical Reading and Mathematics, are consistently at or above the national mean score for all populations (men, women, White, Asian, Black, and Hispanic students), it was clear that we had been over-remediating our admitted students before 2008. Calls at our institution for increased retention and graduation rates were part of a national trend severely questioning the premises of remediation (Scott-Clayton, 2012) and its effects (Complete College America, 2012), a trend that is expected to gain support from students, parents, administrators, and legislators.

Nevertheless, the construct represented in the SAT Writing—the purchased admissions test that we had validated for placement purposes with its combined essay and multiple-choice sections was only a part of the writing assessment environment shown in Table 2.1 with respect to the *Framework for Success* as its curricular and assessment implementation.

Because we did not want to put students who may have been misplaced at risk, we decided to use Criterion as a rapid assessment system (Klobucar, Elliot, Deess, Rudniy, & Joshi, 2013). During the first two weeks of school, students in traditional, credit bearing courses responded to two college-level argumentative prompts supplied by ETS in a 90-minute time period. Both the posted rubric associated with two scores of 4 and

Table 2.1 A Writing Assessment Ecology

System and Sponsor	Purpose	Content Coverage	Scoring and Time Allowed	Sequence
SAT Writing, College Board	Placement: individual student placement into first-year writing	Essay: develop and support point of view; follow conventions of standard written English Multiple choice: improving sentences; identifying sentence errors; improving paragraphs	Essay: two human readers Multiple choice: automated Time: 60 minutes	Before admission
Criterion, Educational Testing Service	Formative: individual student rapid assessment; individual student end of semester assessment	Essay: grammar, usage, mechanics, style, vocabulary, organization, and development	e-rater scoring engine Time: 45 minutes for each essay	Third through fifth week of semester; 11th through 14th week of semester
Traditional Portfolios, New Jersey Institute of Technology	Summative: writing program assessment	Portfolio: rhetorical knowledge, critical thinking, writing process, conventions, holistic score	Two human readers, neither the student's instructor Time: 15 weeks	End of semester, after final grades posted
EPortfolios, New Jersey Institute of Technology	Summative: writing program assessment	EPortfolio: rhetorical knowledge, critical thinking, writing process, conventions, composing in electronic environments, holistic score	Two human readers, neither the student's instructor Time: 15 weeks	End of semester, after final grades posted
Course Grades, New Jersey Institute of Technology	Summative: individual student end of semester assessment	Final grade: rhetorical knowledge, critical thinking, writing process, conventions, composing in electronic environments, information literacy	One human reader, the student's instructor Time: 15 weeks	End of semester

our own placement system allowed us to determine that a student scoring below 8 would be identified by Criterion as in need of additional help. Our traffic light system identified in red scores of 7 or below on an Excel spreadsheet given to instructors in the days immediately following the rapid assessment. Scores of 8 through 12 were highlighted in yellow, a signal that the just qualified student—the student who would find the course neither too challenging nor too difficult—was in need of attention. Upon receipt of the spreadsheet in e-mail, the instructor was to review the Criterion print out, complete with overall score and feedback based on the AEE writing assessment model, with the student and determine the best course of action. With expert readers familiar with the course and its content now actively engaged in the interface between the AEE and the student (Smith, 1992), a supportive plan of action—extra office time, writing center visits, additional work in the AEE platform—could be made that was targeted toward areas identified by Criterion as in need of attention. Resonance between the construct models in the *Framework for Success* and Criterion could be identified and emphasized.

Such a comparison offers significant insight into relationships within our institutional assessment. Table 2.2 presents the inter-correlations in the writing assessment environment shown in Table 2.1.

Table 2.2 Summary of Inter-correlations, Writing Performance Measures for First-Year Writing, Fall 2010

	1	2	3	4	5	6	7	8	*n*	*M*	*SD*
				Fall 2010							
1. SAT Writing	—	.22**	.22ns	.18ns	.14ns	.09ns	.18ns	.21**	572	530.82	61.59
2. Combined Criterion Scores		—	.14ns	.12ns	.23**	.05ns	.25**	.25**	582	6.99	2.92
3. Portfolio: Rhetorical Knowledge			—	.76**	.54**	.74**	.61**	.23*	79	7.94	1.89
4. Portfolio: Critical Thinking				—	.66**	.76**	.75**	.32**	79	8.29	1.67
5. Portfolio: Writing Processes					—	.58**	.65**	.29**	79	7.2	2.17
6. Portfolio: Conventions						—	.69**	.22*	79	8.16	1.73
7. Portfolio: Holistic Score							—	.4**	79	8.1	1.85
8. Course Grade								—	572	2.93	1.09

*p < 0.05, ** p < 0.01

In early course measures, the SAT Writing correlated with the Combined Criterion Scores. In relationship to the end of course measures, the SAT Writing correlated with the course grade but not with the portfolio scores. The Combined Criterion Scores correlated with Writing Processes, the Holistic Score, and course grades. And, as it always has, the Holistic Score correlated with the course grade at a moderate level. The correlations between portfolio scores range from .54 to .76, a moderate to strong association that is the highest in Table 2.2.

In a study of high-stakes placement exams and their relationship to college success, Scott-Clayton (2012) has observed that "there is no obvious or absolute standard for how large a correlation coefficient should be to be considered sufficiently predictive" (p. 6). Local practice, however, does provide a sense of longitudinal trends among traditional measures, such as portfolio scores and course grades, which allow a better understanding of new measures. In fall 2009, for instance, the predictive relationship between the Holistic Score and the course grade was approximately as it has been since we began the portfolio assessment program at our institution in 2003: $R = .39$, $R^2 = .16$, $F = 14.02$, $p < .01$. That is, about 16% of the variance in the model is explained by the relationship between the variables. The Combined Criterion Scores predict the Holistic Score at 6%, a lower coefficient of determination ($R = .25$, $R^2 = .06$, $F = 4.99$, $p < .05$). The Combined Criterion Scores predict the course grade at similar levels ($R = .25$, $R^2 = .06$, $F = 37.96$, $p < .01$). This model is slightly higher that that using the SAT Writing as the predictor variable of the course grade ($R = .21$, $R^2 = .04$, $F = 24.39$, $p < .01$). As it did in 2010, the SAT Writing failed to predict the Holistic Score at statistically significant levels ($R = .18$, $R^2 = .03$, $F = 2.65$, $p = .11$). Table 2.2 therefore reveals relationships that are consistent with previously observed trends at our institution: correlations within portfolio scores are strong, yet the Holistic Score is moderately correlated and weakly predictive of the course grade. Interestingly, the relationship between the Holistic Score and the course grade is similar to the relationship of the SAT Writing to first-year grade point average noted in a study of 726 institutions (Kobrin, Patterson, Shaw, Mattern, & Barbuti, 2008). As Willingham, Pollack, and Lewis (2002) have observed, there are multiple sources of discrepancy between recorded grades and test scores.

In light of this truth, the moderate to low correlations in Table 2.2 may not be an isolated case of laboratory results at one intuition; rather, Table 2.2 may be representative of such data patterns. It should therefore come as no surprise that the statistically significant relationships between the AEE scores (two 90-minute writing samples) and the course grade are approximately half of what they are between the Holistic Score (the most robust representation of writing performance presently available) and the course grade. In light of the complexities involved in aligning performance measures with course grades, moderate to low correlations may be as good as it gets.

In an analysis of the predictive ability of Criterion for our diverse student population, we found that Criterion predicted the course grades for all groups with sufficient sample size except Hispanic students in 2009. In 2010, Criterion predicted course grades for all groups with sufficient sample size. We also found that the Combined Criterion Scores predicted the course grade at statistically significant levels for men, women, White, Asian, and Hispanic, students. Criterion did not, however, predict the course grades of Black students in the sample (Klobucar et al., 2013). Attention to construct modelling, relation to other variables, and impact suggested that Criterion might be used, with qualification, as a system of rapid assessment.

In the fall of 2010, 26% of participating students, a number much greater than we had anticipated, were identified as potentially at risk, and appropriate supportive action was recommended. At the end of the semester, of 116 students, only 13 students (11%) received grades of D or F in the course. Overall, these at-risk students proved quite capable: 19 students received grades of C, 21 students received grades of C+, 24 students received grades of B, 14 students received grades of B+, and 25 students received grades of A. Significantly, for those students whose Combined Criterion Scores were 8 or above (n = 321)—and therefore identified as just qualified students at 73% of the total population—only 9% (n = 29) received grades of D or F. Rapid assessment and early warning had reduced the course failure rate of 13% in the previous year to 11%, while simultaneously countering arguments that students who performed poorly early in the course in the rapid assessment could not succeed (Klobucar et al., 2011).

In the fall of 2011, similar patterns emerged as we again used Criterion as a rapid assessment system. Of the students participating in the study (n = 168), 32% fell below the Combined Criterion Score of 7. Of these, only 4 students (8%) received a grade of D or F. Of the 115 students identified as just qualified for the course and appropriately placed with scores of 8 or above, only 7 students (6%) failed the course.

Clearly, Criterion identified students placed in our credit-bearing first-year course who might be at risk. We had achieved construct modelling at our institution using both the *Framework for Success* and Criterion, and we had identified specific targets of the construct domain of each, along with meaningful levels of student performance to con-structed-response tasks. In pursuing an evidence-centered assessment design (Mislevy, 2007), we were able to offer the validation argument shown in Figure 2.2. Our arguments to shareholders are framed in categories that are conceptual (with attention to relationships), scholarly (with attention to current research), empirical (with attention to quantitative and qualitative evidence), and operational (with attention to impact). Because we wish to support our claim that AEE is a valuable addition to our first-year writing program, arguments are framed according to the Toulmin (1958) model. As Figure 2.2 shows, the argument is situation-dependent (Toulmin, 2001) to our specific

We have identified **evidence** to support the use of AEE in first-year writing

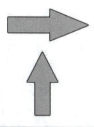

We **claim** that AEE is a valuable addition to first year writing

Conceptual: Congruent relationships exist among institutional mission, writing program goals, and the AEE construct.

Scholarly: Existing and emerging theoretical and empirical studies constitute a body of knowledge about AEE.

Empirical: Quantitative and qualitative studies suggest the appropriateness of AEE use at our specific institution.

Operational: Unwarranted remediation of admitted students impedes timely course engagement, first-year retention, and time to graduation.

We wish to **warrant** the reasons our evidence supports our claim.

Concurrently, we wish to present **qualifications** to our claim.

Conceptual: AEE serves a valuable role in both the institution and its writing program regarding defined models of learning and assessment and the use of technology to improve the lives of students.

Scholarly: Multidisciplinary literature reviews reveal convergent and divergent validation arguments of the usefulness of AEE.

Empirical: Commitment of the writing program to quantitative and qualitative investigation will document the usefulness of AEE in the program's ecological environment for teaching and assessing writing.

Operational: Experiments with admittance of just qualified students into credit-bearing courses will send a signaling effect that a commitment exists between instruction and assessment.

Conceptual: Because the institution and its writing program both value defined models of learning, assessment, and technological use, the AEE model is only a part of a robust conceptual model of writing.

Scholarly: Unless a multidisciplinary view of writing and its assessment is fostered, it will become increasingly difficult to understand the role of writing and its assessment in digital environments.

Empirical: Unless the institution and its writing program are uniformly committed to quantitative and qualitative investigation of AEE in the writing program's ecology, the relationship between instruction and assessment will deteriorate and technological determinism may result.

Operational: While experiments with admittance into credit-bearing courses may document AEE usefulness, special care must be taken for student populations who may be subject to disparate impact.

Figure 2.2 A validity argument for automated essay evaluation use.

institutional site. In this volume, David M. Williamson also examines the Toulmin model as the basis for a validity argument.

Experimentation with AEE is congruent with our institutional mission, and an ever-expanding program of research suggests that a body of knowledge is now present that allows informed decision making. The use of AEE with students admitted to credit-bearing courses obviated unwarranted remediation rates while allowing students who may truly remain at risk to receive additional support.

In fact, the rhetorical argument in Figure 2.2 can also be used to demonstrate the congruency between AEE and our approach for instruction and assessment.

Conceptually, just as AEE relies on a multi-disciplinary approach, so too does the study of writing. As Bazerman observes in his *Handbook of Research on Writing* (2008), methods from many fields are needed "to understand the human capacity for writing," a capacity that leads to a greater appreciation of the cultural significance of writing (p. 3). From deployment of computer technologies in the classroom to the use of educational measurement in analysis, our approach is always and everywhere multi-disciplinary. Analytically, a broad literature review is required to understand recent advances in all forms of writing assessment. As the present volume demonstrates, the value dualisms that interrupted collaborative research are being dismantled so that frameworks can be developed for evidential and consequential research. Empirically, both AEE and our approach to assessment rely on standard statistical techniques tailored to the assessment at hand. At the heart of each are regression analyses used for construct modeling and correlations used to estimate the relationship between scores and independent measures. Operationally, the disheartening descriptions commonly given to the measurement of writing ability (Farley, 2009) simply do not match the research described in this volume. The AEE system, we conclude, may be used for low-stakes rapid assessment to help admitted students succeed in credit-bearing classes without undue remediation; portfolio scores are then used to gauge student performance in the writing program. In both instances, it is information about performance that is most important—to help an individual student and to improve our program. We have not used assessment to determine student advancement. That is a role that can only be played by teachers who have observed their students over an entire semester.

Nevertheless, we remain vigilant in reminding all shareholders that AEE is but part of the writing assessment program at our institution. Within this ecology, we work to maintain a multi-disciplinary view of writing informed by research within and beyond the field of Rhetoric and Composition/Writing Studies. This view of writing, in addition, must continue to be research based lest the efficiency of the AEE will appear to be more desirable and the construct model associated with the *Framework for Success* and portfolio assessment will deteriorate. Perhaps our greatest qualification remains with our diverse student population and the potential for disparate impact that arises when the performance of a minority group is lower than that of the majority group—a condition that impacts test use (Sireci & Parker, 2006). Because it is test use not individual tests that are validated, the impact of any assessment on a diverse student population remains the subject of constant research. In this volume, Lottridge, Schulz, and Mitzel offer methods for evaluating the fairness of AEE.

Qualifications continue. Troubling is the drift downward in those students actively using Criterion for rapid assessment. From 2010 to 2011, mean scores ($M = 8.25$, $SD = 1.6$; $M = 7.82$, $SD = 1.74$) declined by statistically significant levels ($t(597) = 2.85$, $p < .01$). Indeed, an experiment in 2011 to use Criterion at both the beginning ($M = 8.4$, $SD = 1.32$) and end of the semesters ($M = 8.15$, $SD = 1.56$) showed that paired samples of students (n = 92) actually declined in performance ($t(94) = 61.83$, $p < .01$). Yet the empirical evidence to justify the use of Criterion is not alone in declining in its meaningfulness. Instructor use of EPortfolios as part of the assessment ecology shown in Table 2.1 is also experiencing implementation barriers. Too often used as merely a digital filing cabinet instead of a rhetorically-based showcase for posting evidence of proficiency and reflection, EPortfolio scores (a mere 47 portfolios were submitted for 2011) correlated at lower levels ($r = .198$, $p < .05$) with course grades than had the traditional portfolio holistic scores shown in Table 2.2.

At the present, a substantial effort is underway at our institution to identify the reasons for the decline in use of technologies associated with digital assessment. As Chomsky (1987) reminds us, despite the continuous demands of modernization upon almost every facet of social existence, few aggregates of authority—no matter how progressive they claim their values and aims to be—ever willingly compromise established influence and attendant power in the name of further technological development. As a tool for rapid assessment, Criterion has enormous capability to dispel unwarranted beliefs that additional testing and subsequent remediation of admitted students is necessary; as an instructional tool allowing both in-class and at-home writing practice, the advantages of Criterion—indeed, of writing in digital environments in general—are not yet universally apparent at our institution.

CONCLUSION

Higher education is currently in the midst of what is likely its most significant transition since the university transformed itself to reflect processes of industrialization between 1870 and 1944 (Cohen & Kisker, 2010). In the years following the Civil War, when education became complementary to a technically skilled, literate, and rapidly industrializing society, learning environments developed accordingly. Specific practices and applications, notable for their uniformity, comprehensiveness, and, most importantly, capacity to be examined, were introduced in a format that allowed a single educator, equipped with the right tools, to impart skills to a mass audience. No longer tethered to neo-Aristotelian thought and the Socratic Method, modern education capably replaced western culture's long-standing relationship between learning and moral improvement with more production-oriented, professionally-directed objectives. Here was a system ideally suited to those who attend college under the Servicemen's Readjustment Act of 1944. That system held until the early 21st century when a series of political, economic, and technological changes destabilized markets associated with metaphors of stability. Just as the industrialization of the classroom challenged precepts about knowledge and its social value and function that extended to origins in the classical world, the shift into a post-industrial learning environment does not arrive without significant politico-ethical ramifications.

What is distinctly interesting about this latest period of cultural intransigency is how many of the same arguments originally used to critique the shift into factory-based learning models find themselves being referenced yet again to preserve the very same conditions they opposed over a century ago. Irony abounds. Thus we find typical in response to the introduction of technologies developed specifically for digital writing practices a negative stance that tends to re-situate the industrial classroom as an ethically superior, culturally valuable approach to higher education. Writing to a machine, we are told, is not writing at all. It was the legion of dedicated instructors who were the only ones worthy to read, in flawless fashion, the never-ending conveyor belt of student papers. Derrida, it seems, was right after all. Binary opposition is a cultural constant. (Once again, Latour's critique of epistemology is relevant: as both the practice and evaluation of writing become more complex, a truly accurate measurement seems increasingly impossible to accomplish.)

It remains a tempting—and, at times, amusing—parlor game: alignment of education and its social value with the more instrumental and functional significance generally associated with technological progress. As DeMillo (2012) notes, technological advances ensure that incumbent methods along with any cultural attitudes they support tender no respect of tradition. The Socratic is displaced by the industrial; the industrial is displaced by the digital. It is a fun game but not especially productive. As in all games, someone must lose. In this case, that someone is likely to be our students.

To work with students in digital writing is to teach them to build multimodal worlds, to understand learning as participating in an information-based environment. From trying out sentence patterns in an AEE to posting reflective statements in an EPortfolio, experiment is the order of the day. Just as importantly, students must realize that the material and technical qualities of these environments ensure that their epistemological and social value is hardly fixed, but forever evolving, fluctuating. Encouraging digital experimentation, Whithaus (2006) argues that a variety of software packages such as Microsoft Word are reading and responding to student writing without our approval. As such, the "discourse of rejection" is not viable (p. 167).

Assessment itself must accordingly target functional objectives, noting that accomplished essay writing practices describe at a very fundamental level the discursive organization and formulation of observed phenomena in digital environments. Hence, emphasis on the capacity of technology to mediate instruction and assessment suggests a subsequent need to adopt a unique kind of inquiry toward early developments in next generation assessments. This emphasis on the capacity of technology to mediate instruction and assessment suggests a subsequent need to adopt a unique kind of inquiry toward early developments in next generation assessments.

If we accept that there are many roads to literacy, then AEE can and arguably should be viewed as but one tool to help students and their instructors along the way (Warschauer & Grimes, 2008). Helpful here is the work of Christensen and his colleagues (Christensen & Raynor, 2003; Christensen, Horn, Caldera, & Soares, 2011; Christensen, Horn, & Johnson, 2008) in disruptive innovation:

> the process by which a sector that has previously served only a limited few because its products and services were complicated, expensive, and inaccessible, is transformed into one whose products and services are simple, affordable, and convenient and serves many no matter their wealth or expertise.
>
> (2011, p. 2)

As a form of disruptive innovation, AEE has the potential to move relentlessly across markets to displace the established competition of human scoring. Forgione (2012) has documented cost reduction in the case of the Common Core State Standards. If tests in English Language Arts and mathematics are scored by humans, the cost will be US$11.01 per test. If the tests are scores 50% by humans and 50% by machines, the cost drops to US$9.54 (p. 19). As Christensen (1997) observed when he first identified the dilemma of innovation, products that may not appear to be useful today may squarely address the needs of tomorrow; with cost savings apparent and validity claims emerging, strategies will be needed to understand and manage the new population of consumers. Informed by our experiences with AEE, we close this chapter with the following three strategies. These strategies are intended to ensure that validation processes are in place that will result in wise AEE use.

First, successful management of AEE should focus not on the technology but on innovation. This is a point made consistently by Christensen, and our experience demonstrates its truth. The decline in technology-based instruction and assessment we have experienced at our institution may be related to our incorrect emphasis on Criterion and EPortfolios as artifacts of instructional technology. Viewing our colleagues as managers of digital environments rather than researchers in innovation is a mistake not to be replicated by others. Appropriate here is the role of the teacher–researcher (Cochran-Smith & Lytle, 1993), one adopted by the NWP and an essential conceptual orientation for the management of AEE. With the potential to generate knowledge about instruction and assessment, our colleagues would probably have made the investment in topics of inquiry and exerted control over research strategies that would have been their own; as a result, instructional and assessment technologies would have increased due to engagement (Chandler-Olcott, 2002). Had we adopted the teacher–researcher orientation with our colleagues, we would have encouraged them, for example, to create instructional modules for experiments in both Criterion (such as sentence combining and cohesion exercises) and EPortfolios (such a use of blogs for reflection on course content). Observation and reporting on the impact of such modules would, perhaps, have allowed both digital innovations to be more broadly used.

Second, barriers to innovation should be identified. Here, the emphasis again is not on identification to barriers to the technology of AEE—a "thing," in Christensen's terms—but to the innovation. In this case, the recommendations of Bennett (2011) are essential to follow, as are those by Williamson, Xi, and Breyer (2012). Especially important here is emphasis on a broad base of validity evidence. Needed to justify wise use will be studies of the following elements of assessments involving AEE—or, for that matter, EPortfolios and other forms of assessment associated with digital environments: evidence based on content, response processes, internal structure, relationship to other variables, and consequence (American Educational Research Association, American Psychological Association, & National Council on Measurement in Education, 1999). While investigating the sources for validity evidence offered on the *Standards for Educational and Psychological Testing* is a good start, it is equally necessary to remain alert to shifting concepts of validation processes (Lissitz, 2009) so that the focus will remain on innovation and not on the things that accompany it. Chapters in this volume by David M. Williamson and Yigal Attali offer further guidance.

Third, because our focus must be on innovation, reasonable estimates of capability should drive decision making. Conversely, sole focus on meeting today's needs with the disruptive technology of AEE will ensure failure. Current investigations into writing processes and construct representation are two areas of AEE that appear to be clearly in reach. Deane and Quinlan (2010) have offered new lines of research that are taking advantage of computer administration protocols to collect keystroke logs—detailed records of student writing processes which may help us learn more about the significance of pauses first established by Perl (1979). Features derived from such logs may reflect different aspects of writing skill related to writing processes. The second trend, involving sentiment analysis (Shanahan, Qu, & Wiebe, 2006; Taboada, Brooke, Tofiloski, Voll, & Stede, 2011), allows automated opinion detection. Incorporated into AEE, the evaluation of attitude and affect would allow assessment of the writing construct shown in Figure 2.1 to extend beyond its present limitations. Non-cognitive construct attributes of personality, difficult as they are to measure, have long been of interest to researchers (Kahenman, 2011; Messick, 1979). As Burstein, Beigman-Klebanov, Madnani, and Faulkner show in this volume, an automated opinion detection feature allows the potential to learn more about the ways that student expression of sentiment contributes to writing quality.

A promising future for AEE—the kind described by Kenji Hakuta in the last chapter in this volume—will be determined by a deep understanding of the forces at play that swirl around and through this disruptive innovation. Through innovative practice, barrier identification, and realistic estimates of capability, a path for success can be charted.

REFERENCES

American Educational Research Association, American Psychological Association, & National Council on Measurement in Education. (1999). *Standards for educational and psychological testing*. Washington, DC: American Educational Research Association.

Bazerman, C. (2008). Introduction. In C. Bazerman (Ed.), *Handbook on research on writing: History, society, school, individual, text* (pp. 1–4). New York, NY: Lawrence Erlbaum.

Behm, N., Glau, G. R., Holdstein, D. H., Roen, D., & White, E. M. (2012). *The WPA outcomes statement: A decade later*. Anderson, SC: Parlor Press.

Bejar, I. (2012). Rater cognition: Implications for validity. *Educational Measurement: Issues and Practice, 31*, 2–9.

Bennett, R. E. (1993). On the meanings of constructed response. In R. E. Bennett & W. C. Ward (Eds.), *Construction versus choice in cognitive measurement: Issues in constructed response, performance testing, and portfolio assessment* (pp. 1–27). Hillsdale, NJ: Lawrence Erlbaum.

Bennett, R.E. (2011). *Automated scoring of constructed-response literacy and mathematics items*. Washington, DC: Arabella Philanthropic Investment Advisors.

Bennett, R. E., & Bejar, I. I. (1998). Validity and automated scoring: It's not only the scoring. *Educational Measurement: Issues and Practice, 17*(4), 9–17.

Borsboom, D. (2005). *Measuring the mind: Conceptual issues in contemporary psychometrics*. Cambridge, UK: Cambridge University Press.

Burstein, J. (2012). Fostering best practice in writing assessment and instruction with e-rater®. In N. Elliot & L. Perelman (Eds.), *Writing assessment in the 21st century: Essays in honor of Edward M. White* (pp. 187–217). New York, NY: Hampton Press.

Cambridge, D., Cambridge, B., & Yancey, K. B. (2009). *Electronic portfolios 2.0: Emergent research on implementation and impact*. Sterling, VA: Stylus Publishing.

Camp, R. (1993). The place of portfolios in our changing views of writing assessment. In R. E. Bennett & W. C. Ward (Eds.), *Construction versus choice in cognitive measurement: Issues in constructed response, performance testing, and portfolio assessment* (pp. 183–212). Hillsdale, NJ: Lawrence Erlbaum.

Carr, N. G. (2003). IT doesn't matter. *Harvard Business Review, 81*, 41–49.

Chandler-Olcott, K. (2002). Teacher research as a self-extending system for practitioners. *Teacher Education Quarterly, 29*, 23–38.

Cheville, J. (2004). Automated scoring technologies and the rising influence of error. *English Journal, 93*, 47–52.

Chomsky, N. (1987). *On power and ideology: The Managua lectures*. Boston, MA: South End Press.

Christensen, C. (1997). *The innovator's dilemma: When new technologies cause great firms to fail*. Boston, MA: Harvard Business School Press.

Christensen, C., Horn, M. B., Caldera, L., & Soares, L. (2011). *Disrupting college: How disruptive innovation can deliver quality and affordability to postsecondary education*. Washington, DC: Center for American Progress.

Christensen, C., Horn, M. B., & Johnson, C. W. (2008). *Disrupting class: How disruptive innovation will change the way the world learns*. New York, NY: McGraw Hill.

Christensen, C., & Raynor, M. E. (2003). *The innovator's solution: Creating and sustaining successful growth*. Boston, MA: Harvard Business School Press.

Cochran-Smith, M., & Lytle, S. (1993). *Inside/outside: Teacher research and knowledge*. New York, NY: Teachers College Press.

Cohen, A. M., & Kisker, C. B. (2010). *The shaping of American higher education: Emergence and growth of the contemporary system*. San Francisco, CA: Jossey Bass.

Complete College America. (2012). *Remediation: Higher education's bridge to nowhere*. Washington, DC: Complete College America.

Conference on College Composition and Communication (2004). Position statement on teaching, learning, and assessing writing in digital environments. Retrieved from http://www.ncte.org/cccc/resources/positions/digitalenvironments

Conference on College Composition and Communication (2009). Writing assessment: A position statement. Retrieved from http://www.ncte.org/cccc/resources/positions/writingassessment

De Raad, B. (2000). *The big five personality factors: The psycholexical approach to personality*. Gottingen: Hogrefe & Huber.

Deane, P., & Quinlan, T. (2010). What automated analyses of corpora can tell us about students' writing skills. *Journal of Writing Research, 2*(2), 152–177.

DeMillo, R. A. (2012). So you've got technology. So what? *Chronicle of Higher Education.* Retrieved from http://chronicle.com/article/So-Youve-Got-Technology-So/131663/

Derrida, J. (Ed.). (1976). *Of grammatology* (G. C. Spivak, Trans.). Baltimore, MD: Johns Hopkins University Press.

Dillon, R. F., & Sternberg, R. J. (Eds.). (1986). *Cognition and instruction.* San Diego, CA: Academic Press.

Elliot, N., Briller, V., & Joshi, K. (2007). Portfolio assessment: Quantification and community. *Journal of Writing Assessment, 3*, 5–30.

Elliot, N., Deess, P., Rudniy, A., & Johsi, K. (2012). Placement of students into first-year writing courses. *Research in the Teaching of English, 46*, 285–313.

Ellul, J. (1964). *The technological society* (J. Wilkinson, Trans.). New York, NY: Knopf.

Embretson, S. (1983). Construct validity: Construct representation versus nomothetic span. *Psychological Bulletin, 93*, 179–197.

Ericsson, P. F., & Haswell, R. (Eds.) (2006). *Machine scoring of student essays: Truth and consequences.* Logan, UT: Utah State University Press.

Farley, T. (2009). *Making the grade: My misadventures in the standardized testing industry.* Sausalito, CA: PoliPoint Press.

Flower, L. (1994). *The construction of negotiated meaning: A social cognitive theory of writing.* Carbondale and Edwardsville, IL: Southern Illinois University Press.

Forgione, P. D. (2012). Coming together to raise achievement: New assessments for the Common Core State Standards. Retrieved from http://www.k12center.org/rsc/pdf/Assessments_for_the_Common_Core_Standards.pdf

Graham, S., & Perin, S. (2007). A meta-analysis of writing instruction for adolescent students. *Journal of Educational Psychology, 99*, 445–476.

Hamp-Lyons, L., & Condon, W. (2000). *Assessing the portfolio: Principles for practice, theory and research.* Creskill, NJ: Hampton Press

Harrington, S., Rhodes, K., Fischer, R. O., & Malenczyk, R. (Eds.). (2005). *The outcomes book: Debate and consensus after the WPA outcomes statement.* Logan, UT: Utah State University Press.

Hayes, J. R. (2012). Modeling and remodeling writing. *Written Communication, 29*, 369–388.

Herrington, A., & Moran, C. (2012). Writing to a machine is not writing at all. In N. Elliot & L. Perelman (Eds.), *Writing assessment in the 21st century: Essays in honor of Edward M. White* (pp. 219–232). New York, NY: Hampton Press

Hillocks, G. (1986). *Research on written composition: New directions for teaching.* Urbana, IL: National Council of Teachers of English.

Hirschmann, N. J. (1992). *Rethinking obligation: A feminist method for political theory.* Ithaca, NY: Cornell University Press.

Huot, B. (1996). Towards a new theory of writing assessment. *College Composition and Communication, 47*, 549–566.

Kahenman, D. (2011). *Thinking, fast and slow.* New York, NY: Farrar, Straus and Giroux.

Kane, M. T. (2006). Validation. In R. L. Brennan (Ed.), *Educational measurement (4th ed).* (pp. 17–64). Westport, CT: American Council on Education/Praeger.

Klobucar, A., Elliot, N., Deess, P., Rudniy, O., & Joshi, K. (2013). Automated scoring in context: Rapid assessment for placed students. *Assessing Writing, 18*, 62–84.

Kobrin, J. L., Patterson, B. F., Shaw, E. J., Mattern, K. D., & Barbuti, S. M. (2008). Validity of the SAT® for predicting first-year college grade point average (College Board Report 2008–5). Retrieved from http://professionals.collegeboard.com

Latour, B. (1999). *Pandora's hope: Essays on the reality of science studies.* Cambridge, MA: Harvard University Press.

Lissitz, R. W. (Ed.) (2009). *The concept of validity: Revisions, new directions, and applications.* Charlotte, NC: Information Age Publishing.

Lynne, P. (2004). *Coming to terms: A theory of writing assessment*. Logan, UT: Utah State University Press.

Messick, S. (1979). Potential uses of noncognitive measurement in education. *Journal of Educational Psychology, 71*, 281–292.

Messick, S. (1989). Validity. In R. L. Linn (Ed.), *Educational measurement* (pp. 134–103). New York, NY: American Council on Education and Macmillan.

Mislevy, R. J. (2007). Validity by design. *Educational Researcher, 36*, 463–469.

Mumford, L. (1934). *Technics and civilization*. New York, NY: Harcourt, Brace.

National Center for Education Statistics (2012). *The nation's report card: Writing 2011* (NCES 2012–470). Washington, DC: Institute of Education Sciences, U.S. Department of Education. Retrieved from http://nces.ed.gov/nationsreportcard/pdf/main2011/2012470.pdf

O'Connor, M., & Paunonen, S. (2007). Big five personality predictors of post-secondary academic performance. *Personality and Individual Differences, 43*, 971–990.

Palmer, O. (1961). Sense or nonsense? The objective testing of English composition. *English Journal, 50*, 314–320.

Perl, S. (1979). The composing process of unskilled college writers. *Research in the Teaching of English, 13*, 317–336.

Powers, D. E., Burstein, J., Chodorow, M., Fowles, M.E., & Kukich, K. (2001). *Stumping e-rater: Challenging the validity of automated essay scoring*. Princeton, NJ: Educational Testing Service.

Ramineni, C. (2013). Validating automated essay scoring for online writing placement: A case study. *Assessing Writing, 18*, 40–61.

Sabatini, J. P., Bennett, R. E., & Deane, P. (2011). *Four years of cognitively based assessment of, for, and as learning (CBAL): Learning about through-course assessment (TCA)*. Princeton, NJ: Educational Testing Service.

Scott-Clayton, J. (2012). Do high-stakes placement exams predict college success? (CCRC Working Paper 41). New York, NY: Community College Research.

Shanahan, J. G., Qu, Y., & Wiebe, J. (Eds.). (2006). *Computing attitude and affect in text: Theory and applications*. Berlin, Germany: Springer.

Shermis, M. D., & Hamner, B. (2012). *Contrasting state-of-the-art automated scoring of essays: Analysis*. Paper presented at the annual meeting of the National Council of Measurement in Education, Vancouver, BC, Canada. Retrieved from http://www.scoreright.org/NCME_2012_Paper3_29_12.pdf

Sireci, S. G., & Parker, P. (2006). Validity on trial: Psychometric and legal conceptualizations of validity. *Educational Measurement: Issues and Practices, 25*, 27–34.

Slomp, D. H. (2012). Challenges in assessing the development of writing ability: Theories, constructs and methods. *Assessing Writing, 17*, 81–91.

Smith, W. L. (1992). The importance of teacher knowledge in composition placement testing. In R. J. Hayes (Ed.), *Reading empirical research studies: The rhetoric of research* (pp. 289–316). Hillsdale, NJ: Erlbaum.

Sternglass, M. (1997). *Time to know them: A longitudinal study of writing and learning at the college level*. Mahwah, NJ: Lawrence Erlbaum.

Taboada, M., Brooke, J., Tofiloski, M., Voll, K., & Stede, M. (2011). Lexicon-based method for sentiment analysis. *Computational Linguistics, 37*(2), 267–307.

Toulmin, S. E. (1958). *The uses of argument*. Cambridge, UK: Cambridge University Press.

Toulmin, S. E. (2001). *Return to reason*. Cambridge, MA: Harvard University Press.

U. S. Department of Education. (2012). Race to the Top Assessment Program. May 25. Retrieved from http://www2.ed.gov/programs/racetothetop-assessment/index.html

Wardle, E., & Roozen, K. (2012). Addressing the complexity of writing development: Toward an ecological model of assessment. *Assessing Writing, 17*, 106–119.

Warschauer, M., & Grimes, D. (2008). Automated writing in the classroom. *Pedagogies: An International Journal, 3*, 22–26.

Wells, J. B., Christiansen, M. H, Race, D. S., Acheson, D. J., & MacDonald, M. (2009). Experience and sentence processing: Statistical learning and relative clause comprehension. *Cognitive Psychology, 58*, 250–271.

White, E. M. (1985). *Teaching and assessing writing: Recent advances in understanding, evaluating, and improving student performance*. San Francisco, CA: Jossey Bass.

White, E. M. (2001). The opening of the modern era of writing assessment: A narrative. *College English, 63*, 306–320.

Whithaus, C. (2006). Always already: Automated essay scoring and grammar checkers in college writing courses. In P. E. Ericsson & R. Haswell (Eds.), *Machine scoring of student essays: Truth and consequences* (pp. 166–176). Logan, UT: Utah State University Press.

Williamson, D. M., Xi, X., & Breyer, F. J. (2012). A framework for evaluation and use of automated scoring. *Educational Measurement: Issues and Practices, 31*, 2–13.

Willingham, W. W., Pollack, J. M., & Lewis, C. (2002). Grades and test scores: Accounting for observed differences. *Journal of Educational Measurement, 39*, 1–97.

Winner, L. (1980). Do artifacts have politics? *Daedalus, 109*, 121–136.

Wiseman, C. S. (2012). Rater effects: Ego engagement in rater decision-making. *Assessing Writing, 17*, 150–173.

Yancey, K. B. (2012). The rhetorical situation of writing assessment: Exigence, location, and the making of knowledge In N. Elliot & L. Perelman (Eds.), *Writing assessment in the 21st century: Essays in honor of Edward M. White* (pp. 475–492). New York, NY: Hampton Press.

3 English as a Second Language Writing and Automated Essay Evaluation

Sara C. Weigle

INTRODUCTION

Much of the published work on automated scoring of writing has focused on writing instruction and assessment in K–16 education in the United States, with the implicit assumption that the writers being assessed have native or native-like command of English. In this context, English language learners (ELLs) appear to be of somewhat peripheral concern. However, readers may be surprised to find out that there are more people learning and communicating in English in the world than there are native speakers (Kachru, 1997; McKay, 2002); some are immigrants or children of immigrants in the United States (U.S.) or other English-speaking countries; some intend to work or study in an English-speaking country; and some use English for professional reasons in their home countries. Given the importance of written communication for global education and business and thus the need to teach and assess writing throughout the world, the interest in reliable and efficient automated scoring systems for assessing the writing of ELLs is increasing, and the applicability of automated essay scoring (AES) systems to non-native speakers (NNSs)[1] of English is an ever-more important concern. One might even argue that the largest market for automated scoring of English writing is not in assessing the writing ability of native speakers, but rather that of NNSs of English.

The goal of this chapter is to lay out some groundwork for understanding the potential place for AES systems for ELLs, whether they are in school with their native speaker peers in the U.S. or learning English as a foreign language (EFL) in a country where English is rarely encountered outside the classroom. I will discuss both AES, defined as "the provision of automated scores derived from mathematical models built on organizational, syntactic, and mechanical aspects of writing" and automated feedback, or "computer tools for writing assistance rather than for writing assessment" (Ware, 2011, p. 769), since these two applications of AES have different considerations for use.

The chapter is organized as follows. First, I discuss the main contexts for assessing writing among ELLs, both in English as a second language (ESL) and EFL settings. Then, I discuss the construct of writing for different populations of ELLs, specifically with regard to the relative importance of second language proficiency and writing ability in different contexts, and current trends in teaching writing to ELLs. Next, I describe briefly the two main functions of computer-assisted writing evaluation: scoring and feedback, and how these functions are implemented in existing systems. Finally, I discuss considerations for implementing automated scoring and automated feedback in different contexts.

CONTEXTS FOR TEACHING AND ASSESSING ELL WRITING

Second language writing instruction and assessment varies widely depending on the context and population of concern. The first major distinction is between ESL and EFL contexts. In the U.S. and other English-speaking countries, there are two main populations of ELLs for whom writing assessment is important. Many NNSs in schools and universities in the U.S. and other English-speaking countries are in writing classes with native speakers, and thus are assessed in the same way, e.g., for placement into composition courses or achievement in class. Even if these students frequently do not have complete control over English vocabulary and grammar, their language proficiency is presumed to be strong enough so that the focus of assessment can be writing *per se*, not language proficiency as demonstrated through writing. The main question for these students is whether assessments designed for native speakers, whether scored by human raters or computers, are valid and fair for NNSs.

The other main writing assessment purpose for ELLs in English-speaking countries is to evaluate English language proficiency through writing. In these settings, there is a greater focus on control over syntax and vocabulary, along with rhetorical concerns such as development and organization. In K–12 and university settings, NNSs are often tested to determine whether they need additional English language services before or concurrent with their regular program of study. In the U.S., the No Child Left Behind law (NCLB) requires ELLs to be tested annually in listening, speaking, reading and writing (No Child Left Behind Act, 2001). For this population, the focus of the assessment tends to be language proficiency as demonstrated through writing, rather than strictly writing skills *per se*, especially at lower levels of proficiency. The question here is whether one or more writing samples can provide sufficient information about a student's language proficiency to make useful decisions about whether he or she needs additional language support to access academic content and perform successfully.

In EFL contexts, there are three main purposes for assessing English writing ability. A large testing industry has grown around the need to assess English language proficiency for students coming to the U.S. or to other English-speaking countries. In the U.S. the main test for this purpose is the Test of English as a Foreign Language (TOEFL); in the U.K. and Australia the most familiar test is the International English Language Testing System (IELTS). More than 27 million people have taken the TOEFL to date (ETS 2012), and 1.7 million take the IELTS (IELTS.org). Secondly, English is a requirement for university students in many countries. For example, in China, approximately 13 million students took the College English Test (CET) in 2006 (Zheng & Cheng, 2008), and South Korea is currently developing its own English language test; both of these major examination systems including writing tests.

Third, there is a great deal of international interest in developing English language tests for workplace certification, particularly tests aligned with the Common European Frame of Reference (CEFR) standards (Europe, 2001) that have been promulgated over the past ten years. Among the most well known of these tests are the Cambridge suite of exams, including the First Certificate in English (FCE) and the Certificate in Advanced English (CAE) (http://www.cambridgeesol.org/index.html).

English examinations have fairly high stakes for students, as their future may depend on their test scores. Thus, test preparation is a large industry in many places, including general English courses or courses specifically tailored towards preparation for a specific exam. To the extent that writing is a central component of the examination, writing will be part of the curriculum. In all of these situations, the primary purpose of these assessments is to evaluate language ability in a specific context—academic or vocational, for example—through writing.

Second Language Writing Ability

The discussion of contexts above highlights the fact that ELLs differ greatly in terms of a number of variables (e.g., age, educational level, ESL vs. EFL, proficiency level) that influence how the construct of writing is defined for a given purpose. Crucially, these variables are related to the degree to which the focus of instruction and assessment is on linguistic or rhetorical concerns; that is, concerns about mastering sentence structure, morphology, and vocabulary vs. concerns about higher-level issues such as audience, voice, and genre. This focus, in turn, has major implications for the use of AES and to its acceptance by stakeholders, including students, teachers, administrators, and users of test scores.

There is a general consensus in the field that second language writing ability is dependent upon both writing ability and second language ability (e.g., Cumming, 1989; Weigle, 2002; Williams, 2005), though the exact contribution of each, and indeed, the degree to which they can be neatly separated, are a matter of dispute. Native English speakers learning to write essays in school generally have automatic control over basic text production processes and extensive experience with English texts; thus, although their academic vocabulary and control over advanced structures such as relative clauses and non-finite subordination strategies may still be growing, they do not need to devote cognitive effort to subtler aspects of English grammar such as article and preposition use or the formation of verb tenses. NNSs of English, on the other hand, vary tremendously in their control over English syntax, morphology, and vocabulary, their familiarity with English written genres, and their experience in writing, either in English or in their home language. Those who are strong writers in their first language can often transfer writing skills to their second language given a certain level of proficiency. However, limited English proficiency can hamper student writing because of the need to focus attention on language rather than content (Weigle, 2005). At lower levels of language proficiency, then, the focus of assessment is generally on linguistic issues; that is, the degree to which writers have control over basic vocabulary, syntax, and paragraph structure. As writers gain more control over these skills, the focus can shift to higher order concerns such as development, strength of argument, and precision in language use. Finally, at the highest levels of proficiency, second language writers may still retain an "accent" in writing but otherwise do not need to be distinguished from first language writers in terms of assessment.

From this discussion it is clear that what is meant by writing in assessment can be very different in different contexts, and that therefore when we talk about automated scoring of writing we need to be clear about what kind of writing is meant. While automated scoring of writing has been quite controversial in the composition community (e.g., Conference on College Composition and Communication, 2004; Crusan, 2010), it may be less controversial when the focus of the assessment is on English language proficiency rather than composition ability (Weigle 2010, 2011). Deane (in press) argues that

> when the use case emphasizes the identification of students who need to improve the fluency, control, and sophistication of their text production processes, or affords such students the opportunity to practice and increase their fluency while also learning strategies that will decrease their cognitive load, the case for AES is relatively strong; but if the focus of assessment is to use quality of argumentation, sensitivity to audience, and other such elements to differentiate among students who have already achieved fundamental control of text production processes, the case for AES is relatively weak.

The former is precisely the case for many ELLs both in ESL and EFL settings, and thus a relatively strong argument can be made for automated scoring and feedback systems if they can be implemented wisely.

Writing Instruction for L2 Learners

Before discussing the use of AES for scoring or feedback on writing, it is important to examine practices in writing instruction for ELLs. As discussed above, writing instruction for L2 learners varies by age, proficiency level, and context. However, some pedagogical principles apply across instructional settings. A good place to start is Silva's (1993) conclusion from an extensive literature review that composing in a second language is generally "more constrained, more difficult, and less effective" than writing in a first language. Depending on how proficient they are, therefore, students learning to write in their second language need more of everything: they need more examples of written texts to learn from, more practice writing, more opportunities to develop effective writing strategies, more familiarity with genres, more practice with vocabulary and grammar, and more feedback. Writing teachers, especially in second language academic contexts such as first-year composition courses, need to find ways to balance the need to provide opportunities to learn and practice new language structures with opportunities to improve written fluency without getting bogged down in grammatical concerns.

It is well known that language proficiency, as it relates to writing, develops slowly over a number of years and depends on extensive exposure to different texts in different genres. Certain elements of grammar, for example, appear to be resistant to explicit instruction and acquired late, such as the use of relative clauses and the English article system (Ellis, 2005). However, other aspects of writing seem to be amenable to instruction regardless of English proficiency level. For example, Roca de Larios, Murphy and Marin (2002) suggest that writing strategies such as problem-solving strategies, goal setting and organization, and having a sense of audience can be effectively taught within the course of a single semester.

The major paradigm in writing instruction in the U.S. for teaching students who are at a stage of language development where they are able to compose texts of a paragraph or longer is the so-called "process approach," also dominant in L1 writing instruction (e.g., Emig, 1971; Flower & Hayes, 1981). That is, the process of idea generation, drafting, giving and receiving feedback, and revising, which is used by expert writers, is modeled and supported by the teacher. In such an approach, students submit multiple drafts of essays and only the second or third draft of the essay is graded. The process approach is contrasted with a "product approach" (e.g., Kroll, 2001) in which students are graded on the basis of a single draft, with no opportunity to revise.

In other countries, of course, writing instruction varies across educational settings. In many places writing is viewed as a support skill for reinforcing and practicing the grammar and vocabulary learned in class, rather than as a skill to be developed in its own right for communication. As many EFL teachers are NNSs themselves, they often do not feel equipped to write or comment on student writing in English, and much of the writing that is done in class is in preparation for examinations. As a result there are many settings where a process approach is not implemented; rather, the focus may be explicitly on practicing strategies for writing timed essays of the kind that are typical on large-scale assessments (see, for example, You, 2004).

The Role of Error Correction in Second Language Writing Instruction

One of the features of AES systems emphasized by proponents is the ability to provide instantaneous feedback on writing, and particularly on sentence-level errors in grammar and usage. Thus, it is important to explore the role of error correction in L2 writing instruction. After all, if error correction is not useful and does not lead to improvements in writing, as claimed by Truscott (1996, 1999, 2007) and others, there is little point in automating it.

In the U.S., the process movement for some time de-emphasized the language aspect of writing instruction for L2 learners. However, the pendulum has swung back the other direction with the understanding that second language writers need and want to improve their knowledge of academic English grammar and vocabulary. One implication of this is that students want feedback on their writing, particularly about the errors that they make. The issue of error correction is one that has caused a great deal of controversy and anxiety for second language writing teachers, particularly in light of some scholarship that suggests that error correction is unhelpful or even harmful (e.g. Truscott, 1996, 1999, 2007). It is clear from the research that L2 writers want comprehensive error correction; it is also clear that teachers frequently do not always know how to provide useful feedback on errors or feel that the time spent in providing comprehensive error feedback reaps useful benefits.

Ferris (2011) provides a thorough review of the research on corrective feedback in L2 writing. This research suggests that students welcome feedback on errors, and that focused feedback which can be used in revising has both short-term and longer-term effects on their control over specific structures targeted in feedback. In particular, Ferris notes that students feel that "teacher feedback on grammar and errors is extremely important to their progress as writers" (p. 46); they prefer comprehensive marking of errors and strategies for correcting them rather than direct correction; on the other hand, they often find teachers' marking systems confusing.

The degree to which L2 teachers actually provide accurate and comprehensive feedback is unclear. Although an often-cited paper by Zamel (1985) reports that teachers are inconsistent, arbitrary, and contradictory in their comments, there are no statistics in the paper to substantiate this assertion, and it is quite likely that 25 years of improved teacher education has improved the situation substantially. In a study designed to gather data on the nature and effect of teacher feedback, Ferris (2006) collected writing samples from six sections of an ESL composition course containing teacher feedback on 15 error types (e.g., word choice, verb tense, word form, articles) using a coding system that the instructors had agreed on. Ferris found that teachers correctly marked 89% of errors identified by independent researchers in one sample, and 83% in another sample. While these results cannot be generalized to other settings, they at least provide a baseline on which to judge automated scoring systems: if 80–90% agreement is a reasonable outcome for experienced teachers working within the same program, one could argue that this would be a reasonable ultimate goal for automated scoring engines to achieve.

To summarize, in some contexts writing instruction for ELLs is very much focused on language acquisition, while in others such instruction is focused on writing strategies. In reality, most ELLs need both types of instruction; one complication is that teachers dealing with ELLs are often trained either in second language acquisition or in composition pedagogy, but frequently not both. For example, in many MA TESOL programs, a course in teaching writing is not required; on the other hand, graduate students from English departments in U.S. universities teaching first-year composition frequently have second language writers in their courses but do not necessarily have specific ESL training. In order to understand an appropriate role for AES in L2 writing assessment, it is important to take what we know from both perspectives.

Specifically, for automated scoring, it is important that scoring systems be able to identify the features of language that characterize learners at different proficiency levels (and not just errors), and, at the same time, allow learners who are still developing in their language to demonstrate their writing competence (overall content development, quality of ideas, organization, etc.) without being penalized for errors that do not interfere with comprehension or that are late acquired and not amenable to instruction. This is particularly important when ELLs are assessed along with their native speaker peers.

In terms of automated feedback, ELLs want and need specific feedback on language, but such feedback must be digestible and written in a way that is useful for learning. ELLs also want and need feedback on content and organization, but features associated with these aspects of writing are more challenging from a computational perspective to provide automatically. As Chapelle and Chung (2010) have suggested, the ideal hybrid may be one in which sentence-level feedback is provided by an automated mechanism, leaving the teacher free to comment on higher order concerns. Nevertheless, research in natural language processing is focusing on these higher-order concerns, as discussed in later chapters: Automated Short-Answer Scoring (at Educational Testing Service); Automated Evaluation of Discourse Coherence Quality; and, Automated Sentiment Analysis for Essay Evaluation.

AUTOMATED ESSAY EVALUATION: SCORING AND FEEDBACK

The difference between automated scoring and automated feedback is important when considering their use for ELLs. Automated scoring is primarily intended for large-scale tests (that is, beyond the level of the classroom) and automated feedback is primarily intended for instructional use, although these two functions are sometimes blurred. For instance, it is possible, and may be very welcome, to provide diagnostic feedback on essays in large-scale tests. It is also possible, though perhaps less desirable, to incorporate automated scoring along with automatic feedback in a classroom setting. For the moment, however, we will make a distinction between scoring—that is, using automated tools to produce a score that is intended to be equivalent to a human score on the same essay for the purpose of some decision, such as admission or placement—and feedback: the use of automated tools to provide information that will help students improve their writing. As noted above, automated scoring for high-stakes decisions is a highly controversial issue within mainstream composition studies. Automated feedback, on the other hand, is viewed somewhat more positively as a supplement to teacher feedback in classroom use (Ware, 2011; Warschauer & Grimes, 2008).

Large-scale tests are often produced by private companies employing testing and measurement experts and are used to make relatively high-stakes decisions, such as admission to higher education, graduation, and placement. Examples of such assessments include the TOEFL, the CET required of all Chinese students graduating from any college in China (Zheng & Cheng, 2008), and the Entry Level Writing Requirement required of all incoming first-year students in the University of California system (California, 2012). Some tests, such as the Graduate Record Examination, are taken by L1 and L2 students without distinction; others are designed specifically as English proficiency tests for L2 speakers; and yet others, such as the University of California test, incorporate mechanisms for determining whether students who need writing courses would benefit from classes specifically designed for L2 speakers. Some of these assessments currently use

AES systems; for example, e-rater® has been used along with human raters on both the TOEFL® and the GRE® (Educational Testing Service, 2012). In other cases, AES is not currently used but may be under consideration or development for the future.

The most obvious potential advantage of AES for large-scale assessment is the savings in terms of time and cost, given the labor-intensive nature of human scoring of writing, as well as the reliability of AES in producing the same score for a given essay. Most large-scale tests require essays to be double-rated for reliability, with a third rater used if the first two raters disagree. At a single university with a test for only a few hundred students, scoring essays can require several raters working over multiple days, and many tests are much larger. An automated scoring system that can accomplish this scoring in a matter of minutes represents a major savings of time, if not necessarily money.

On the other hand, the major objection to automated scoring for high-stakes exams is the argument that a computer cannot "read" an essay and that the most important features that contribute to essay quality are not quantifiable. Furthermore, the decisions made on the basis of test scores are too important to be made by machines. Other objections have to do with the lack of transparency about the algorithms used to score essays, the de-professionalization of teachers, the narrowing of the construct, and the potential consequences of using computers to score writing (Cheville, 2004; Condon, 2006; Crusan, 2010; Herrington & Moran, 2001). One of the goals of this volume was to address the issue of system transparency. Several systems are described in the chapters that follow.

In contrast to large-scale testing, much writing assessment is done at the classroom level by a teacher who knows the students, is in control of the curriculum, and understands the context for the assessment. Within classroom assessment we can distinguish summative and formative assessment. Summative assessment is used to evaluate how much students have learned in a course and whether specific aims have been met. Formative assessment, on the other hand, is used to help teachers and students diagnose and address specific writing problems during a course, before a final grade is recorded.

Considerations for the use of automated scoring and feedback differ for these different situations. A better argument can be made for AES—both scoring and feedback, but particularly feedback—for formative assessment rather than for summative assessment. In the context of formative assessment, systems that allow students to submit an essay for instant scoring, receive useful feedback, and revise an essay with the goal of getting a better score can be motivating for students (Grimes & Warschauer, 2010). However, in terms of summative assessment, the final determination of what a student has achieved in terms of meeting the instructional goals for a course is surely better left to the judgment of the teacher rather than to an automated system.

In summary, it is possible to make a plausible case for AES in high-stakes large-scale assessment, provided that there are sufficient checks within the system to ensure ongoing accuracy and reliability of scoring and evidence in addition to computer-generated scores on which to base important decisions about a student's writing proficiency such as placement or university admission. It is also possible to make a plausible case for AES in very low-stakes assessment, that is, automated feedback for formative assessment within the classroom. Here, the important checks to be made are the degree to which feedback can be understood and used by students and how well teachers are trained in system use so that they can make use of its advantages appropriately. On the other hand, the case for AES is weakest as a tool for summative assessment in the classroom, where the classroom teacher is the most appropriate person to make the ultimate evaluation as to how much students have learned or achieved. Teachers are rightly concerned about the dangers of handing over critical decision making to a computer that may be focusing on the wrong skill, and de-professionalizing teaching by using automating grading to make critical decisions about students' education.

Features of AES Systems

Given the potential for using AES systems with ELLs, I now turn to a discussion of what AES systems can and cannot do. Commercially available AES systems, such as e-rater, created by Educational Testing Service (ETS), and IntelliMetric, from Vantage Learning, can produce ratings on a holistic scale that agree with one human rater as often as two human raters agree with each other, and can do so much faster than human beings (Attali & Burstein, 2006; Burstein, 2002; Burstein & Chodorow, 1999; Elliot, 2003; Landauer, Laham, & Foltz, 2003; Page, 2003). Automated scoring systems may use natural language processing or Latent Semantic Analysis techniques that provide measures of quantifiable aspects of essays, which can be combined mathematically to predict human scores with a high degree of accuracy. Readers should refer to the e-rater chapter for a brief discussion of natural language processing methods.

It is important to recognize that the features identified and counted by AES systems are not necessarily the things that human raters pay attention to in rating essays; however, the argument can be made that the quantifiable features stand in as proxies for the features that raters value (see, for example, Connor-Linton, 1993; Cumming, 1990; Huot, 1993; Lumley, 2002; Milanovic, Saville, & Shen, 1996; Vaughan, 1991 for discussions of rater behavior and decision-making processes). For example, e-rater evaluates organization and development by automatically identifying the presence or absence of relevant discourse units (e.g., introduction, thesis statements, main ideas, supporting details, and conclusion). In addition to identifying discourse element types to represent organization, the system also takes into account the length of each element identified to represent development. (See the chapter about the Automated Evaluation of Discourse Coherence Quality for a discussion of natural language processing research in this area.) By comparison, raters pay attention to the organization and flow of an essay, in terms of an introduction, body paragraphs with supporting statements, and a concluding paragraph. The human rater will consider whether the organization is easy to follow, whether it makes logical sense, and whether the conclusion wraps up the essay in a satisfactory way. These things may not be quantifiable, as they rely on the fact that the reader brings background knowledge and expectations to the reading and intuitively compares the essay to others that he or she has read in the past, and often to knowledge about the writers. However, even if neither the human rater nor e-rater explicitly considers essay length as a central indicator of writing quality, the length of discourse units (in the case of e-rater) frequently corresponds with human judgments of development, as it is difficult to develop an essay well without expanding on main points and supporting them with relevant details, all of which have the effect of increasing the length of such units.

Similarly, text analysis research has suggested several features of essays that tend to correlate well with essay scores, ranging from final free modifiers (Nold & Freedman, 1977) to the number of words before the main verb (McNamara, Crossley, & McCarthy, 2010), or error-free T-units (Homburg, 1984). Again, even though raters may not specifically focus on such features, the relationship between these features, which can be counted automatically, and rater scores reflects the fact that writers who are able to express complex ideas generally have mastered the syntactic means to do so in a sophisticated way. Thus, while some of the features of automated scoring systems cannot replicate what human raters respond to, they may stand in as proxies for those constructs.

Another reason why automated scores are generally consistent with human scores has to do with the fact that the features that raters pay attention to in scoring tend to be highly correlated with each other. There are two possible explanations for this: first, the different sub-skills develop more or less in tandem, as the writer gains more experience reading and writing, and second, raters are not necessarily able to distinguish one from another, even when using an analytic scoring rubric (Marsh & Ireland, 1987). For example, the word choices that a writer uses, which is frequently captured in a scoring rubric under the category of language use, can influence the reader's understanding of content or organization.

There certainly are some cases in which an automated scoring system will not give the same score as a trained human rater. For one reason, AES systems cannot "read" a text in the same way that a person does. That is, while it is possible for AES systems to parse sentences and identify propositions, they cannot relate those propositions or texts to a body of world knowledge or judge the reasonableness of certain types of evidence in support of a thesis. Thus, AES systems are not currently well suited to evaluate features of writing such as authorial voice or strength of argument, which depend on shared background knowledge and assumptions between reader and writer. However, as is discussed in the Sentiment Analysis and Discourse Coherence Quality chapters later in this volume, there are current research efforts intended to address features related to both authorial voice, and argumentation.

By the same token, the computer cannot detect features of an essay that might be rewarded by a human rater, such as allusions to well known literature, people, or events that may be unusual but apt in the circumstances, or the use of humor or irony. One example of this can be seen in ETS's own materials. In a screen shot in the online Criterion demo, for example, the sentence "monkey see, monkey do" is marked as having subject/verb agreement errors. From a strictly grammatical perspective this is true, but from a pragmatic perspective the sentence is perfectly well formed, evoking the reader's (stereotyped) world knowledge about monkey behavior and the appropriate use of proverbs in writing, among other things. We have not yet reached a point in automated scoring where the computer can recognize pragmatically skillful uses of 'incorrect' language like this.

Furthermore, the computer cannot easily judge the intended meaning of a writer when errors are made. ESL errors are notoriously difficult to categorize, and AES systems may not able to use context reliably to distinguish among possible interpretations of ill-formed sentences. Chodorow, Gamon and Tetreault (2010, p. 422) give the example "I fond car": does this involve a misspelling of 'found' and a missing article (I found the car) or a missing copula, preposition, and plural marking (I am fond of cars)? In the context of an actual essay a human rater would be able to deduce from the context what the most likely interpretation would be, but AESs are not yet at the point where they can reliably do so. Another aspect of concern is that there are degrees of seriousness of errors, in terms of what errors are stigmatizing and what create confusion. Because it is impossible to predict exactly what errors will lead to difficulties in comprehension, it is difficult for an AES system to predict and evaluate the seriousness of different error types.

Despite these differences, in the majority of cases, automated scoring systems correlate with human judgments about as well as humans do with each other. A few advantages of AES are that they are not affected by factors that make human raters unreliable, such as fatigue, inattention, or distraction. On the other hand, there are still several validity questions that need to be answered regarding automated scoring. Xi (2010) provides a list of questions that should be asked of automated scoring systems, corresponding to the different steps in a validity argument (Chapelle, Enright, & Jamieson, 2008; Kane, 1992, 2006). These questions are listed in Table 3.1.

Table 3.1 Validity Questions Related to Automated Scoring

Inference	Validity Questions
Domain representation: the performance represents the target domain	Does the use of assessment tasks constrained by automated scoring technologies lead to construct under- or misrepresentation?
Evaluation: the scores are accurate representations of the performance	Does automated scoring yield scores that are accurate indicators of the quality of a test performance sample? Would examinees' knowledge of the scoring algorithms of an automated scoring system impact the way they interact with the test tasks, thus negatively affecting the accuracy of the scores?
Generalization: the observed score is an appropriate estimate of other scores obtained from other, similar observations	Does automated scoring yield scores that are sufficiently consistent across measurement contexts (e.g., across test forms, across tasks in the same form)?
Explanation: the scores can be attributed to the construct	Do the automated scoring features under- or misrepresent the construct of interest? Is the way the scoring features are combined to generate automated scores consistent with theoretical expectations of the relationships between the scoring features and the construct of interest? Does the use of automated scoring change the meaning and interpretation of scores provided by trained raters?
Extrapolation: the scores are indicative of performance in the target domain	Does automated scoring yield scores that have expected relationships with other test or non-test indicators of the targeted language ability?
Utilization: the scores provide useful information for decisions and curriculum	Do automated scores lead to appropriate score-based decisions? Does the use of automated scoring have a positive impact on examinees' test preparation practices? Does the use of automated scoring have a positive impact on teaching and learning practices?

Source: Xi, 2010.

A complete treatment of these validity questions is beyond the scope of this chapter. However, the literature has paid more attention to some of these questions than to others, and it is to those that I turn my attention now. First is the issue of construct underrepresentation; that is, whether the use of automated scoring constrains the assessment tasks that can be used. Typically, the independent expository or argument/persuasive essay has been the most frequent candidate for automated scoring. However, the types of tasks used in L2 writing assessment are expanding to cover a more broadly conceived notion of writing ability. A recent trend in large-scale tests such as the TOEFL is the use of integrated tasks, in which students receive input through listening and/or reading and use this information in a written response. Such tasks are claimed to be more authentic than traditional independent tasks because academic writing nearly always involves reading as well (Carson, 2001; Feak & Dobson, 1996; Weigle, 2004). It is not clear how automated scoring systems would be used to evaluate integrated responses. One complication is how to deal with the presence of language from the source texts in the written responses, some of which may be appropriately or inappropriately used (see Weigle & Montee, in press, for a discussion of rater perceptions of source text borrowing in integrated tasks). The investment in automated scoring systems to evaluate a specific type of writing may make companies reluctant to experiment with other task types, which could have the effect of narrowing the construct.

A perhaps more serious challenge with regard to construct narrowing comes from scholars such as Condon (2009), who notes that the writing produced in a typical writing test is of very little interest beyond the assessment itself. Condon presents an alternative type of writing assessment task at the university level, which requires students to reflect on and write about what they have learned at the university. Condon claims that the content of the writing is not only more engaging and interesting to the readers, but serves an authentic communicative purpose that extended beyond the specific testing situation. Condon's argument is not necessarily specific to automated scoring; his focus is on rethinking the whole notion of timed essay tests as a way of evaluating writing. In his view, automated scoring serves to reify the essay exam as the main assessment tool, and scholars should be cautious in developing automated scoring systems without critically examining the basis of the assessment.

A related question is whether actual or perceived knowledge of the algorithms will change the way students prepare for an exam. In situations where test scores have very high stakes for students, the curriculum tends to focus on strategies for passing the test. You (2004), for example, describes the English curriculum at a Chinese university, noting that

> a typical college English curriculum in China works under the guidance of the College English Syllabus and is evaluated almost exclusively by the results of students' scores on the CET. In such a curriculum, students' individual needs for English are hardly acknowledged; many teachers are predominantly concerned about teaching language knowledge and test-taking skills, instead of language skills for communication purposes. English writing is still taught in the current-traditional approach, focusing on correct form rather than helping the students develop thoughts. Systematic language instruction is severely constrained by simulation tests and various test-preparation exercise manuals when the CET draws near.
>
> (p. 108)

Thus, the possibility of automated scoring algorithms affecting the way students learn to write is quite real. Both Grimes and Warschauer (2010) and Chen and Cheng (2008) report that teachers and students believed that the scoring algorithm favored the traditional five-paragraph essay and that the scoring algorithms discouraged creativity in writing, suggesting that students wanting to get higher scores may be less likely to take risks in their writing.

One important validity question is whether automated scores and human scores have the same relationship with other indicators of writing ability. This issue was taken up by Weigle (2010, 2011) in the context of the Internet-based (iBT) TOEFL. In the study, relationships between human and automated scores on TOEFL iBT essays, on the one hand, and a variety of indicators of writing ability, including self-assessment, instructor assessment, and ratings of non-test writing samples, on the other, were investigated. Correlations between essay scores (whether generated by human raters or computers) and these indicators were moderate, with higher correlations with more global language proficiency measures such as self-assessment than with more specific writing-related issues. Human and e-rater scores differed in their relationships to indicators of writing ability only in a few cases. Most strikingly, the scores of human raters on TOEFL iBT essays were more strongly correlated with judgments made by content area teachers about the seriousness of language problems faced by participants than were e-rater scores, suggesting that both the human raters and the instructors were more sensitive to some aspects of student writing than was e-rater. Weigle's data supports the use of e-rater with the

TOEFL, bearing in mind that the main use of the TOEFL is to assess the "ability to use and understand English at the university level" (Educational Testing Service, 2012), rather than writing *per se*.

Xi (2010) notes that the higher the stakes, the more validity evidence needs to be presented to justify any use of automated scores, particularly if automated scores are used alone. At present there are no plans to use e-rater on any large-scale assessment without a human rating as well, and the results from Weigle (2011) support the idea that automated scoring should be complemented by human judgments, even if the focus of the assessment is on linguistic rather than rhetorical issues such as argumentation and voice.

Automated Feedback

I now turn to consideration of automated feedback, which holds a promise of reducing teacher's burdens and helping students become more autonomous. AES systems can recognize certain types of errors and offer automated feedback on correcting these errors, in addition to providing global feedback on content and development. One benefit of automated feedback for many students is that it is anonymous and not personal, allowing students to save face in a way that submitting their writing to teachers does not allow. Another benefit is that students can receive instant feedback, repeatedly, on an essay. Teachers may not have time to give detailed feedback on numerous drafts of essays before giving a final grade; on the other hand, students can submit their essays to the computer for scoring as many times as they choose and can continue to improve until they feel ready to submit it to their teacher. Furthermore, many teachers would prefer to focus on higher-level concerns, such as argumentation and voice when responding to student writing, and automated feedback has the potential to remove some of the burden of giving feedback on grammar to give teachers more time for these higher-level concerns.

Xi (2010) provides the following list of questions that can serve as a guide for evaluating automated feedback systems (see Table 3.2). Note that several of these questions could be asked, and have been asked, of feedback in general, as discussed above. Recent

Table 3.2 Validity Questions Related to Automated Feedback

Inference	Validity Questions
Evaluation: the scores are accurate representations of the performance	Does the automated feedback system accurately identify learner performance characteristics or errors?
Generalization: the observed score is an appropriate estimate of other scores obtained from other, similar observations	Does the automated scoring feedback system consistently identify learner performance characteristics or errors across performance samples?
Explanation: the scores can be attributed to the construct	Is the automated feedback meaningful to students' learning?
Utilization: the scores provide useful information for decisions and curriculum	Does the automated feedback lead to improvements in learners' performances? Does the automated feedback lead to gains in targeted areas of language ability that are sustainable in the long term? Does the automated feedback have a positive impact on teaching and learning?

Source: Xi, 2010.

research on automated feedback has focused on two questions: the accuracy of automated feedback, and its usefulness to students. I will discuss each of these questions briefly.

Does the Automated Feedback System Accurately Identify Learner Performance Characteristics or Errors?

The most common type of automated feedback is feedback on sentence-level errors (e.g., grammatical and mechanical errors), as opposed to content and organization. If automated feedback on errors is to be useful, it should be able to correctly identify the kinds of errors that ESL students are likely to make, and recent advances in AES systems have improved this ability, particularly in the areas of articles and preposition usage. Equally importantly, an automated feedback engine should be able to identify errors that are important for students to address, given the multiplicity of things that students need to think about when revising their writing. The general consensus is that the most important errors to address are those that (a) interfere with comprehension of the message; (b) are frequent; (c) are important for the particular genre or in the context of a particular teaching situation; and (d) are ones that the student is developmentally ready to address (Bates, Lane, & Lange, 1993; D. Ferris, 2011; Frodeson & Holten, 2003; Williams, 2005). While a computer can be programmed to identify errors that are likely to cause comprehension problems (for example, wrong words and verb formation errors tend to be more serious than article errors) and errors that occur frequently, the other considerations require teacher input and interpretation and may not be as easy to automate.

As noted above, automated scoring systems, like people, cannot always categorize ESL errors reliably, particularly in cases of garbled syntax, where the overall sense is clear but trained humans may not agree on the appropriate correction. For example, "he lead a good life" can be interpreted as a subject–verb agreement error or a tense error, depending on the context. Another problem is that humans do not always agree on whether or not something is an error. Preposition errors fall into this category (Chodorow et al., 2010; Tetreault & Chodorow, 2008) because of the variety of factors that influence their use and variability in their usage among native speakers. Given these complications, creators of AES algorithms need to decide whether false positives (identifying something as an error is actually not) or false negatives (failing to identify an actual error) are the greater problem. Chodorow et al. (2010) report that the developers of Criterion decided to minimize false positives; as a result, Criterion is able to identify with 80% accuracy only 25% of preposition errors. With article errors, these figures are slightly better: identifying 40% of errors with 90% accuracy. Recall that Ferris (2006) found that teachers agreed with trained raters 80–90% of the time, but this count included all errors, not only preposition and article errors, which are somewhat more difficult to categorize than errors such as verb tense or word form.

Thus, if e-rater can be considered the most advanced AES system for non-native writing, it appears that automated scoring engines have a similar accuracy rate as human raters, but may not identify as many errors as human raters do. Grimes and Warschauer (2010), commenting on low rates of identifying errors in MyAccess!, argue that automated feedback, even if imperfect, serves a useful pointing function, in that it identifies structures that are likely to be errors, thus reducing cognitive load on the writer.

It should also be noted that imperfect targeted feedback may have different consequences for learners at different levels of ability. In a study of Microsoft Word's spelling and grammar checker, Galleta, Durcikova, Everard and Jones (2005) found an interaction between verbal ability and use of software. In cases where the software correctly identified errors, both high and low ability students performed equally well. In the case of false positives (errors falsely identified by the software) both groups of students were influenced by the incorrect error messages and wrongly corrected them. In the case of false negatives (errors not detected by the software) the high ability students' performance was particularly degraded; these students were much more likely to detect such errors when the software was turned off than when it was turned on. This result suggests that high ability students rely on the software too much and have an unrealistic expectation of how credible the software is. While this was only a single study, it serves as a reminder that teachers and students should not rely too heavily on automated feedback alone but must always interpret it.

Is the Automated Feedback Meaningful to Students' Learning?

Another critical question regarding automated feedback is whether it is effective in helping students improve their writing. Some recent research has begun to answer this question by investigating students' use of such feedback in their classrooms. Two studies in particular are relevant. Chen and Cheng (2008) studied the classroom use of My Access!, which provides both a score and specific feedback, in three university classrooms in Taiwan. The teachers received only one hour of training and were given free rein in determining how the software would be used. In the class where automated feedback was most well received by students according to a survey, the teacher used the software for formative assessment only, requiring that students achieve a certain computer score before turning their drafts in for teacher comments. In the second class, the teacher stopped using the software after six weeks of class, stating that the automated feedback was unhelpful and required more work on her part to help students interpret and use it, and also citing technical difficulties using the software. In the third class, the teacher used both the feedback and grading components of the software but did not provide much guidance to students on how to make use of the feedback features. Students in all classes had negative reactions towards the scoring features, and only some students found the feedback features useful. Students found in some cases that the feedback helped them attend to specific language problems such as sentence variety and the use of the passive voice, but they also felt the feedback was "vague," "abstract," and "repetitive" and did not help them revise their essays, particularly in development and coherence. Moreover, they felt that the automated system discouraged creativity in writing and overemphasized the use of transition words. They also thought that automated feedback would be more appropriate for students at lower levels of language proficiency who were still learning basic writing skills.

Grimes and Warschauer (2010) studied the implementation of MyAccess! in eight middle schools in Southern California. They found that the use of the software simplified classroom management and increased student motivation to write. However, some of their findings regarding automated feedback support the notion that teacher support is essential for effective implementation of automated feedback. They found that MyAccess! provided too much low-level feedback for students to absorb, and that they needed to supplement the feedback with handouts or checklists to help students prioritize and use the feedback. They also reported that some of the feedback (e.g., "adverb placement") was difficult for students to interpret, particularly ELLs.

Although the research in this area is limited, it does suggest several strategies for implementing automated feedback successfully. First of all, teacher training and support is crucial. Grimes and Warschauer (2010) report that lack of administrative support was one reason that automated scoring was discontinued in one district; similarly, the one hour of training received by teachers in Chen and Cheng's (2008) study was not sufficient to make teachers feel confident in their use of the software. Teachers need to be trained in the technical aspects of using the system and sufficient support must be available to deal with inevitable technological breakdowns. Teachers also need to know how to make best use of the features in the software for their specific classroom situation. For example, the strategy of requiring students to achieve a certain score from the automated system before turning a paper in to the teacher appeared to be a useful motivating strategy.

Second, it is incumbent upon teachers to help their students interpret and prioritize feedback. Both studies found that the amount of low-level feedback was overwhelming, and some teachers reported that their workload increased because of the need to help students interpret the feedback.

Third, students are likely to take on the attitudes towards AES systems that their teachers adopt (Chen & Cheng, 2008), so teachers should be careful about how they present the tools to their students. Finally, teachers should remember that the most common AES systems are a commercial product (Chapelle & Chung, 2010) and their claims of success deserve critical scrutiny from scholars and teachers.

Just as teachers need to decide on their own strategies for error correction and feedback in writing, they need to be careful in how they present and use automated feedback in their own classrooms. Perhaps automated feedback is most useful as a "third voice" (Myers, 2003) in student–teacher conferences, where it provides some objective information about the essay and an evaluation based on that information with which the student and teacher can agree or disagree. As Grimes and Warschauer (2010, p. 34) state,

> Mindful use of [Automated Writing Evaluation] AWE can help motivate students to write and revise, increase writing practice, and allow teachers to focus on higher level concerns instead of writing mechanics. However, those benefits require sensible teachers who integrate AWE into a broader writing program emphasizing authentic communication, and who can help students recognize and compensate for the limitations of software that appears more intelligent at first than on deeper inspection.

While Grimes and Warschauer were addressing teachers of native speakers, their advice is equally valid for those who teach ELLs.

CONCLUSION

Despite calls by some to eliminate or reduce the use of AES systems in teaching and evaluating writing, it would be naïve to suggest that AES systems will not be used for scoring and feedback in the future. AES is here to stay, and the focus should be on continuing to improve both the human and technological sides of the equation. On the technological side, recent insights into differences between native and non-native writing and between lower- and higher-level proficiency writers that go beyond error counts may help improve automated scoring engines used for ELL writing. For example, Crossley and McNamara (2011) found significant differences between native and non-native college-level writers on four word-based indices (hypernymy, polysemy, lexical diversity, and stem overlap), suggesting that these indices may be useful indicators of native vs. ESL writing. Similarly, Friginal and Weigle (2012) found that co-occurrence of specific language features such as agentless passives, attributive adjectives, and lack of other features such as second person pronouns, mental verbs, and that-complement clauses were associated with higher essay scores, suggesting that as students gain proficiency, their academic writing becomes more informational and less descriptive.

As for the human side of the equation, it has been shown that failures in the implementation of educational technology are often due to teacher resistance rather than problems with technology (Curan, 2003, 2005, cited in Grimes & Warschauer, 2010). Administrative and peer support, training, and willingness of teachers to experiment can be important in reducing such resistance. One possible path is to expose teachers to non-commercially produced automated tools that can be used to explore dimensions of their own students' writing. For example, Cotos (2012) reports improvement in writing among students using the Intelligent Academic Discourse Evaluator (IADE), a web-based, automated writing evaluation program that analyzes the discourse elements in the introduction section of research articles. Other corpus tools may be used by researchers or teachers wishing to do specific analyses on their own students' data. For example, the Gramulator (McCarthy, Watanabe, & Lamkin, 2012), can be used to identify the linguistic differences between two data sets—expert and novice papers, for example—and the LexTutor website (http://www.lextutor.ca/) includes numerous tools for analyzing vocabulary use automatically. Teachers who are familiar with such tools and can see their advantages and disadvantages may be more comfortable with commercially produced automated evaluation tools.

To quote Stewart Brand, editor of the *Whole Earth* journal: "Once a new technology rolls over you, if you're not part of the steamroller, you're part of the road" (http:// famousquoteshomepage.com/2012/02/01/stewart-brand/). (Teachers of ELLs would do well to make sure they are part of the steamroller when it comes to automated essay evaluation.)

NOTE

1 ELL and NNS are used interchangeably in this chapter. Other terms frequently encountered in the literature are English as a second language (ESL) or Limited English Proficiency (LEP) students. For a useful overview of terminology, see Wolf and Farnsworth (in press).

REFERENCES

Attali, Y., & Burstein, J. (2006). Automated essay scoring With e-rater V.2. *Journal of Technology, Learning, and Assessment, 4*(3), Available from http://www.jtla.org.

Bates, L., Lane, J., & Lange, E. (1993). *Writing clearly: Responding to ESL compositions.* Boston, MA: Heinle.

Burstein, J. (2002). The e-rater scoring engine: Automated essay scoring with natural language processing. In M. Shermis & J. Burstein (Eds.), *Automated essay scoring: A cross-disciplinary perspective* (pp. 113–121). Mahwah, NJ: Lawrence Erlbaum Associates.

Burstein, J., & Chodorow, M. (1999). Automated essay scoring for nonnative English speakers. *Proceedings of the ACL99 Workshop on Computer-Mediated Language Assessment and Evaluation of Natural Language Processing.*

California, Regents of the University of. (2012). University of California Office of the President Student Affairs: Entry Level Writing Requirement, from http://www.ucop.edu/elwr/index.html

Carson, J. (2001). A task analysis of reading and writing in academic contexts. In D. Belcher & A. Hirvela (Eds.), *Linking literacies: Perspectives on L2 reading-writing connections* (pp. 246–270). Ann Arbor, MI: University of Michigan Press.

Chapelle, C., Enright, M. K., & Jamieson, J. (Eds.). (2008). *Building a validity argument for the Test of English as a Foreign Language.* New York: Taylor & Francis.

Chapelle, C. A., & Chung, Y. (2010). The promise of NLP and speech processing technologies in language assessment. *Language Testing, 27*(3), 301–315.

Chen, C.-F., & Cheng, W.-Y. (2008). Beyond the design of automated writing evaluation: Pedagogical practices and perceived learning effectiveness in EFL writing classes. *Language Learning & Technology, 12*(2), 94–112.

Cheville, J. (2004). Automated scoring technologies and the rising influence of error. *English Journal, 93*, 47–52.

Chodorow, M., Gamon, M., & Tetreault, J. (2010). The utility of article and preposition error correction systems for English language learners: Feedback and assessment. *Language Testing, 27*(3), 419–436.

Condon, W. (2006). Why less is not more: What we lose by letting the computer score writing samples. In P. F. Ericsson, & R. H. Haswell (Eds.), *Machine scoring of student essays: Truth and consequences* (pp. 211–220). Logan, UT: Utah State University Press.

Condon, W. (2009). Looking beyond judging and ranking: Writing assessment as a generative practice. *Assessing Writing, 14*(3), 141–156.

Conference on College Composition and Communication. (2004). *CCCC position statement on teaching, learning, and assessing writing in digital environments*, February 25. Retrieved from http://www.ncte.org/cccc/resources/positions/digitalenvironments

Connor-Linton, J. (1993). Looking behind the curtain: What do L2 composition ratings really mean? *TESOL Quarterly, 29*(4), 762–765.

Cotos, E. (2012). Potential of automated writing evaluation feedback. *CALICO Journal, 28*(2), 420–459.

Crossley, S. A., & McNamara, D. S. (2011). Understanding expert ratings of essay quality: Coh-Metrix analyses of first and second language writing. *International Journal of Continuing Engineering Education and Life-Long Learning, 21*(3), 170–191.

Crusan, D. (2010). *Assessment in the second language writing classroom*. Ann Arbor, MI: University of Michigan Press.

Cumming, A. (1989). Writing expertise and second-language proficiency. *Language Learning 39*(1), 81–141.

Cumming, A. (1990). Expertise in evaluating second language compositions. *Language Testing 7*, 31–51.

Deane, P. (in press). On the relation between automated essay scoring and modern views of the writing construct. *Assessing Writing*.

Elliot, S. (2003). IntelliMetric: From here to validity. In M. Shermis & J. Burstein (Eds.), *Automated essay scoring: A cross-disciplinary perspective* (pp. 71–86). Mahwah, NJ: Erlbaum Associates.

Ellis, R. (2005). Principles of instructed language learning. *System 33*(2), 209–224.

Emig, J. (1971). *The composing processes of twelfth graders*. Urbana, IL: National Council of Teachers of English.

Educational Testing Service. (2012). About the TOEFL iBT Test. Retrieved December 14, 2012, from http://www.ets.org/toefl/ibt/about/

Europe, Council of. (2001). *Common European framework for reference for languages: Learning, teaching assessment*. Cambridge: Cambridge University Press.

Feak, C., & Dobson, B. (1996). Building on the impromptu: A source-based writing assessment. *College ESL, 6*(1), 73–84.

Ferris, D. (2006). Does error feedback help student writers? New evidence on the short- and long-term effects of written error correction. In K. Hyland & F. Hyland (Eds.), *Feedback in second language writing: Contexts and issues* (pp. 81–104). Cambridge, UK: Cambridge University Press.

Ferris, D. (2011). *Treatment of error in second language student writing*. Ann Arbor, MI: University of Michigan Press.

Flower, L., & Hayes, J. R. (1981). A cognitive process theory of writing. *College Composition and Communication, 22*, 365–387.

Friginal, E., & Weigle, S. C. (2012). *Exploring multiple profiles of academic writing using corpus-*

based, multi-dimensional and cluster analysis. Paper presented at the Georgetown University Roundtable (GURT), Washington, DC.

Frodeson, J., & Holten, C. (2003). Grammar and the ESL writing class. In B. Kroll (Ed.), *Exploring the dynamics of second language writing* (pp. 141–161). Cambridge, UK: Cambridge University Press.

Galleta, D. F., Durcikova, A., Everard, A., & Jones, B. (2005). Does spell-checking software need a warning label? *Communications of the ACM, 48*(7), 82–85.

Grimes, D., & Warschauer, M. (2010). Utility in a fallible tool: A multi-site case study of automated writing evaluation. *Journal of Technology, Learning, and Assessment, 8*(6). Retrieved September 1, 2012, from http://www.jtla.org

Herrington, A., & Moran, C. (2001). What happens when machines read our students' writing? *College English, 63*(4), 480–499.

Homburg, T. J. (1984). Holistic evaluation of ESL composition: Can it be validated objectively? *TESOL Quarterly, 18*(1), 87–107.

Huot, B. (1993). The influence of holistic scoring preocedures on reading and rating student essays. In M. Williamson & Brian Huot (Eds.), *Validating holistic scoring for writing assessment* (pp. 206–236). Cresskill, NJ: Hampton Press.

Kachru, B. B. (1997). World Englishes and English-using communities. *Annual Review of Applied Linguistics, 17,* 66–87.

Kane, M. T. (1992). An argument-based approach to validation. *Psychological Bulletin, 112,* 527–535.

Kane, M. T. (2006). Validation. In R. L. Brennan (Ed.), *Educational measurement (4th ed).* (pp. 17–64). Westport, CT: American Council on Education/Praeger.

Kroll, B. (2001). Considerations for teaching an ESL/EFL writing course. In M. Celce-Murcia (Ed.), *Teaching English as a second or foreign language* (3rd ed.) (pp. 219–232). Boston, MA: Heinle.

Landauer, T. K., Laham, D., & Foltz, P. W. (2003). Automated scoring and annotation of essays with the Intelligent Essay Assessor. In M. D. Shermis & J. Burstein (Eds.), *Automated essay scoring: A cross-disciplinary perspective* (pp. 87–112). Mahwah, NJ: Lawrence Erlbaum Associates, Inc.

Lumley, T. (2002). Assessment criteria in a large-scale writing test: What do they really mean to the raters? *Language Testing, 19,* 246–276.

Marsh, H.W. & Ireland, R. (1987). The assessment of writing effectiveness: A multidimensional perspective. *Australian Journal of Psychology, 39,* 353–367.

McCarthy, P., Watanabe, S., & Lamkin, T. (2012). *The gramulator: A tool to identify differential linguistic features of correlative text types.* Hershey, PA: IGI Global.

McKay, S. L. (2002). *Teaching English as an international language.* Oxford, UK: Oxford University Press

McNamara, D. S., Crossley, S. A., & McCarthy, P. M. (2010). The linguistic features of quality writing. *Written Communication, 27*(1), 57–86.

Milanovic, M., Saville, N., & Shen, S. (1996). *A study of the decision-making behaviour of composition markers* Paper presented at the 15th Language Testing Research Colloquium, Cambridge and Arnhem.

Myers, M. (2003). What can computers contribute to a k-12 writing program? In M. D. Shermis & J. Burstein (Eds.), *Automated essay scoring: A cross-disciplinary perspective* (pp. 3–20). Mahwah, NJ: Lawrence Erlbaum Associates.

No Child Left Behind Act, 115 Stat. 1425 (2001).

Nold, E. W., & Freedman, S. W. (1977). An analysis of readers' responses to essays. *Research in the Teaching of English, 11,* 164–174.

Page, E. B. (2003). Project Essay Grade: PEG. In M. D. Shermis & J. Burstein (Eds.), *Automated essay scoring: A cross-disciplinary perspective* (pp. 43–54). Mahwah, NJ: Lawrence Erlbaum Associates, Inc.

Roca de Larios, J. R., Murphy, L., & Marín, J. (2002). A critical examination of L2 writing process research. *Studies in Writing, 11,* 11–47.

Silva, T. (1993). Toward an understanding of the distinct nature of L2 writing: The ESL research and its implications. *TESOL Quarterly, 27*(4), 657–677.

Tetreault, J., & Chodorow, M. (2008). *The ups and downs of preposition error detection.* Paper presented at the COLING, Manchester, UK.

Truscott, J. (1996). The case against grammar correction in L2 writing classes. *Language Learning, 46,* 327–369.

Truscott, J. (1999). The case for grammar correction in L2 writing classes: A response to Ferris. *Journal of Second Language Writing, 8,* 111–122.

Truscott, J. (2007). The effect of error correction on learners' ability to write accurately. *Journal of Second Language Writing, 16,* 4, 255–272.

Vaughan, C. (1991). Holistic assessment: What goes on in the rater's mind? In L. Hamp-Lyons (Ed.), *Assessing second language writing in academic contexts* (pp. 111–125). Norwood, NJ: Ablex.

Ware, P. (2011). Computer-generated feedback on student writing. *TESOL Quarterly, 45,* 769–774.

Warschauer, M., & Grimes, D. (2008). Automated writing in the classroom. *Pedagogies: An International Journal, 3,* 22–26.

Weigle, S. C. (2002). *Assessing writing.* New York: Cambridge University Press.

Weigle, S. C. (2004). Integrating reading and writing in a competency test for non-native speakers of English. *Assessing Writing, 9*(1), 27–55.

Weigle, S. C. (2005). Second language writing expertise. In K. Johnson (Ed.), *Expertise in language learning and teaching* (pp. 128–149). Hampshire, England: Palgrave Macmillan.

Weigle, S. C. (2010). Validation of automated scores of TOEFL iBT tasks against non-test indicators of writing ability. *Language Testing, 27*(3), 335–353.

Weigle, S. C. (2011). Validation of automated scores of TOEFL iBT tasks against non-test indicators of writing ability. TOEFL iBT Research Report TOEFL iBT-15. Princeton, NJ: Educational Testing Service.

Weigle, S. C. & Montee, M. (in press). Raters' perceptions of textual borrowing in integrated writing tasks. In M. Tillema, E. Van Steendam, G. Rijlaarsdam. & H. van den Bergh (Eds.) *Measuring writing: Recent insights into theory, methodology and practices.* Bingley, UK: Emerald Books.

Williams, J. (2005). *Teaching writing in second and foreign language classrooms.* Boston, MA: McGraw-Hill.

Wolf, M., & Farnsworth, T. (in press). The use of English proficiency assessments for exiting English learners from ESL services: Issues and validity considerations. In A. Kunnan (Ed.), *The companion to language assessment.* Hoboken, NJ: Wiley-Blackwell.

Xi, X. (2010). Automated scoring and feedback systems: Where are we and where are we heading? *Language Testing, 27*(3), 291–300.

You, X. (2004). The choice made from no choice: English writing instruction in a Chinese University. *Journal of Second Language Writing, 13,* 97–110.

Zamel, V. (1985). Responding to student writing. *TESOL Quarterly, 19,* 79–102.

Zheng, Y., & Cheng, L. (2008). College English Test (CET) in China. *Lanuage Testing, 25*(3), 408–417.

4 The E-rater® Automated Essay Scoring System

Jill Burstein, Joel Tetreault, and Nitin Madnani

INTRODUCTION

Automated essay scoring (AES) is a well-established technology in educational settings. The technology is now supported by a number of commercial vendors, and is used to evaluate millions of essay responses in instructional and assessment settings in Kindergarten through 12th grade (K–12), undergraduate, and graduate-level contexts. Earlier motivations for this technology stemmed from issues related to the time and costs associated with human scoring. Continued development on e-rater® (Attali & Burstein, 2006; Burstein et al., 1998) has deliberately focused on the development of a greater variety of features to more comprehensively address the writing construct (specifications for characteristics of writing being measured, or evaluated), using tangible markers in scoring rubric criteria.[1] The focus of this chapter is two-fold. It includes a description of the e-rater automated essay scoring system and its natural language processing (NLP)-centered approach, and a discussion of the system's applications and development efforts for current and future educational settings.

E-rater uses NLP methods to identify construct-relevant linguistic properties in text. Since we anticipate that many reading this book may not be familiar with NLP, a general discussion of NLP is provided as background. In the first volume of this book, a similar discussion was included. That discussion has been updated here, and offers a broader discussion, highlighting more recent applications. The chapter follows with a description of e-rater's features and their relevance to the writing construct, and the approaches used to identify those features derived from NLP methods. The reader should also refer to Chapter 15 (*Grammatical Error Detection in Automatic Essay Scoring and Feedback*) which includes a comprehensive description of grammatical error detection methods used in automated essay scoring, including e-rater scoring. Chapter 16 (*Automated Evaluation of Discourse Coherence Quality in Essay Writing*), and Chapter 17 (*Automated Sentiment Analysis for Essay Evaluation*) discuss novel features in development for use with e-rater. These features will address aspects of the writing construct related to argumentation in essays, specifically, *discourse coherence*, and *sentiment* as it pertains to claims and opinion in essay writing.

In the development of educational technology, in general, but specifically in the development of building automated essay scoring systems, researchers should consider how their system fits into the different educational problem spaces, including *curriculum and assessment development, curriculum delivery*, and *score reporting* (Burstein, Sabatini, & Shore, in press). The chapter discusses these different problem spaces, and, more specifically, how e-rater is used in the context of *curriculum and assessment development and delivery* (practice, instructional settings) such as Criterion®, Educational Testing Service's (ETS's) online essay scoring system, and for *score reporting* with large-scale writing assessments.

The chapter discusses the importance of continued e-rater development that is aligned with the writing construct in light of Common Core State Standard Initiative (CCSSI) specifications that stress the teaching and evaluation of argumentation in student writing. E-rater and automated essay scoring applications, in general, can support Common Core goals both for classroom settings and large-scale state assessments.

WHAT IS NLP?

Some Basics

NLP is the application of computational methods for the purpose of analyzing language-related characteristics of electronic files of text or speech. E-rater is a text-based application, and so this chapter discusses NLP-based applications related to the analysis of *text*.

Statistical and rule-based methods are the two approaches used to develop a variety of NLP-based tools designed to carry out various types of language analyses. Statistical methods rely on very large corpora to automatically cull out and model language patterns. These methods employ *supervised* and *unsupervised* modeling approaches which are discussed in Chapter 16 in the context of automated evaluation of discourse coherence. Briefly, *supervised* modeling approaches require human annotated data. In the context of e-rater, for instance, human-scored essays are an example of human-annotated data. Essays are assigned scores based on scoring guide criteria. These human scores (annotations) are used to build e-rater scoring models. Supervised e-rater model-building methods are described later in the chapter. *Unsupervised* modeling does not use annotated data. Language features are automatically generated that are often statistically-based, such as bigram frequencies (proportional number of occurrences of two-word sequences in a corpus). These features are used to build a model for predicting certain characteristics in language. For instance, an example of an unsupervised learning approach is *content vector analysis* (CVA) (Salton, 1989), a method originally developed for information retrieval. In a nutshell, CVA uses automatically-derived information about word frequency to evaluate the similarity between two documents. The unsupervised aspect here is that the lexical similarity between two essays is determined independent of human annotations. In *rule-based methods*, specific rules are designed, such as syntactic patterns, to guide the identification of language structures. Specific examples of *supervised, unsupervised*, and *rule-based* methods used for e-rater feature generation will be discussed below.

Everyday NLP

One of the earliest research efforts in NLP was for *machine translation*. This application involves using computational analyses to translate a text from one language to another. A well-known research effort in machine translation took place during the Cold War era, when the United States was trying to build programs to translate Russian into English. More recently, statistical machine translations systems have become quite advanced and have moved beyond translating word by word (Chiang, 2007; Koehn, Och, & Marcu, 2003; Marcu & Wong, 2002; Zollmann & Venugopal, 2006). Off-the-shelf machine translation software is readily available with internet search engines. For example, Google, Yahoo!, and Bing all offer machine translation.

Another NLP application that has been researched since the 1950s is automated summarization. *Summarization* systems, such as Columbia University's *Columbia*

NewsBlaster system[2] that produces news summaries from various news sources, are used to automatically extract the most relevant text from a document. A familiar application of automated summarization is the *Auto Summarize* feature in Microsoft Word.

Internet search engines, such as Google, Yahoo!, and Bing may also use NLP methods (Brin & Page, 1997; Broder, 2002). When we enter a search phrase, or query into a browser's search engine, automated analysis must be done to evaluate the content of the query. An analysis of the vocabulary in the original query is performed that enables the search engine to return the most relevant responses. NLP methods for *automated question answering* were used to develop *Watson*, IBM's system used to participate in *Jeopardy* (Moschitti, Chu-Carroll, Patwardhan, Fan, & Riccardi, 2011).

Sentiment analysis systems use NLP to identify if a text contains opinion statements, and further, to categorize these statements by polarity, specifically, determining if they contain positive or negative sentiment, or both. Industry applications of sentiment analysis systems can be used to analyze the expression of opinion in blogs (Godbole, Srinivasaiah, & Skiena, 2007), and also in customer service settings, where product reviews can be examined and analyzed (Ghose & Ipeirotis, 2007; Kim, Pantel, Chklovski, & Pennacchiotti, 2006; Zhang & Varadarajan, 2006).

E-RATER

Background

E-rater is a commercial automated essay evaluation and scoring system that was developed at ETS (Attali & Burstein, 2006; Burstein et al., 1998). The computational methodology underlying the system is NLP. E-rater first became operational in 1999 when it was deployed to provide one of two scores for essays on the writing section of the Graduate Management Admissions Test (GMAT)—a high-stakes assessment designed for graduate business school admissions. (The second score for each essay was provided by an expert, human rater.) Prior to e-rater deployment, each GMAT essay had been scored by two human raters. Since the first version of e-rater proved to be highly reliable, and the system was shown to agree with an expert rater as often as two expert raters agree with each other, it made sense from a cost perspective to use e-rater to generate one of the two scores. So, essentially, the motivation for the first use of e-rater was a highly practical one.

Research and development around e-rater has *always* incorporated e-rater features that reflected the *writing construct*—specifically, tangible markers in essay writing that can be used to measure (evaluate) writing quality, given a specific writing task. For instance, in expository writing tasks that are used on assessments, human raters are instructed to focus on features in writing that contribute to a high quality essay. Depending on the task, and the scoring rubric criteria, these might include the writer's *organization and development of ideas, the variety of syntactic constructions, the use of appropriate vocabulary,* and *the technical correctness of the writing in terms of its grammar, usage, and mechanics.* Scoring rubric criteria can be argued to be tangible aspects of the writing construct (also see Chapter 18).

Human raters then need to collectively evaluate these aspects of an essay in order to assign a score that reflects the overall, *holistic* quality of the essay. Using this approach, raters take into account all aspects of writing as specified in the scoring guide, often using a 6-point scale, where a score of "6" indicates the *highest* quality essay, and a score of "1" indicates an essay of the *lowest* quality.

E-rater has made a considerable number of advances since its first release to provide greater coverage of the writing construct. From this perspective, the most notable changes were enhancements to the set of linguistic features extracted for use in the e-rater model building and scoring procedures. E-rater features are described in the following section.

E-rater Features

In this section, a high-level description is provided of the set of features used for e-rater modeling building and scoring (also see Attali & Burstein, 2006). Space constraints in this chapter do not allow a full description of the different feature algorithms. The chapter offers high-level descriptions of the subset of e-rater features that are generated using statistical or rule-based NLP methods. Table 4.1 offers a list of suggested additional readings associated with writing construct feature. These readings offer

Table 4.1 Suggested Readings for E-rater Features by Construct Feature

E-rater Features	Selected Publications
Grammatical errors	• Leacock, C., & Chodorow, M. (2003) Automated grammatical error detection. In M. Shermis and J. Burstein (Eds.), *Automated Essay Scoring: A Cross-Disciplinary Perspective*, pp. 186–199, Hillsdale, NJ: Lawrence Erlbaum Publishers • Han, N. R., Chodorow, M., & Leacock, C. (2004). Detecting errors in English article usage with a maximum entropy classifier trained on a large, diverse corpus. In *Proceedings of the 4th International Conference on Language Resources and Evaluation.* • Han, N. R., Chodorow, M., & Leacock, C. (2006). Detecting errors in English article usage by nonnative speakers. *Natural Language Engineering, 12*(2), 115–129. • Tetreault, J., and Chodorow, M. (2008). *The Ups and Downs of Preposition Error Detection.* Manchester, UK: COLING. • Chodorow, M., Gamon, M., & Tetreault, J. (2010). The utility of article and preposition error correction systems for English language learners: feedback and assessment. *Language Testing, 27*(3), 419–436.
Discourse structure Organizational development	• Burstein, J., Marcu, D., & Knight, K. (2003). *IEEE Intelligent Systems: Special Issue on Advances in Natural Language Processing, 18*(1), 32–39.
Topic-relevant word usage	• Burstein, J., Kukich, K., Wolff, S., Lu, C., Chodorow, M., Braden-Harder, L., & Harris, M. D. (1998). Automated scoring using a hybrid feature identification technique. In *Proceedings of the 36th Annual Meeting of the Association for Computational Linguistics and 17th International Conference on Computational Linguistics*, Vol. 1, pp. 206–210. • Attali, Y., & Burstein, J. (2006). Automated essay scoring with e-rater v.2.0. *Journal of Technology, Learning, and Assessment, 4*(3), 3–30. • Attali, Y. (forthcoming). Modified Content Vector Analysis Features for E-rater. ETS Research Report.
Style-related word usage	Burstein, J., & Wolska, M. (2003). Toward evaluation of writing style: finding overly repetitive word use in student essays. In *Proceedings of the 10th Conference of the European chapter of the Association for Computational Linguistics, Budapest.*
Sophistication or register and relevance of word usage	Attali, Y., & Burstein, J. (2006). Automated essay scoring with e-rater v.2.0. *Journal of Technology, Learning, and Assessment, 4*(3), 3–30.

more detailed descriptions of the methods used to identify NLP-based features used in e-rater scoring.[3]

Using statistical and rule-based NLP methods, e-rater currently identifies and extracts the several *feature classes* for model building and essay scoring (Attali & Burstein, 2006; Burstein, Chodorow, & Leacock, 2004). Each feature class may represent an aggregate of multiple features. The feature classes include the following (1) grammatical errors (e.g., *subject–verb agreement errors*), (2) word usage errors (e.g., *their* versus *there*), (3) errors in writing mechanics (e.g., *spelling*), (4) presence of essay-based discourse elements (e.g., *thesis statement, main points, supporting details*, and *conclusions*), (5) development of essay-based discourse elements, (6) style weaknesses (e.g., *overly repetitious words*), (7) two CVA-based features to evaluate topical word usage, (8) an alternative, *differential word use* content measure, based on the relative frequency of a word in high-scoring versus low-scoring essays (Attali, 2011), (9) two features to assess the relative sophistication and register of essay words, and (10) a feature that considers *correct usage* of prepositions and collocations (e.g., *powerful computer* vs. **strong computer*) (Futagi, Deane, Chodorow, & Tetreault, 2008), and variety in terms of sentence structure formation. The set of ten features represent positive features, rather than errors in conventions. Prepositions and collocations represent two structures that are especially difficult for English learners. The addition of these features also represents a focus on common English learner challenges in writing.

More details about specific features aggregated within a feature class may be found in Attali and Burstein (2006).

E-RATER FEATURES USING NLP APPROACHES

In this section, descriptions are provided for e-rater features that use NLP methods.

Grammar Error Detection

E-rater identifies grammar, usage, and mechanics errors, including agreement errors, verb formation errors, incorrect word usage (e.g., determiner errors), and missing punctuation. Two approaches are used to detect violations of general English grammar. For *rule-based* methods, essay data are parsed using *syntactic parsers*. Parsers automatically analyze texts and assign syntactic structures to sentences and the syntactic units within a sentence (e.g., noun phrases, verb phrases, relative clause). Rules can then be developed to identify patterns of error. In e-rater, an example error type that is identified using rule-based methods is *sentence fragments*. Sentence fragments, for instance, can be identified if a "sentence" contains only a dependent clause, for example, "*Because they did not wear their school uniforms.*" Using a syntactic parse, a rule might look for both an independent and a dependent clause, but when finding only a subordinate clause, the "sentence" would be flagged as a fragment.

The other method is statistical, and can be explained as follows. The system is trained on very large corpora (billions of words), including well-edited text and noisy essay data, from which it extracts and counts sequences of adjacent word and part-of-speech pairs called *n-grams*. Statistical models are built that determine which n-grams (typically those that occur less frequently) are more likely to be evidence of grammar or usage errors (Burstein et al., 2004; Chodorow & Leacock, 2000). Example error types detected using statistical methods are determiner and preposition errors (Han, Chodorow, & Leacock, 2006; Tetreault & Chodorow, 2008; Tetreault, Foster, & Chodorow, 2010). It should also be noted that new research in automated error detection also takes into account errors more likely to appear in essays of non-native English speakers in order to handle the large volumes of essays from this population. The focus has been on error types such as determiner and preposition errors. There is an extensive body of work presenting statistical methods for error detection, especially for grammatical and usage error detection in the context of e-rater scoring and other applications (Leacock, Chodorow, Gamon, & Tetreault, 2010). The reader should also refer to Chapter 15 for a detailed description of research in grammatical error detection methods.

Essay-Based Discourse Analysis

The approach to discourse analysis in essays is based on a linear representation of the text. It assumes the essay can be segmented into sequences of discourse elements, which include introductory material (to provide the context or set the stage), a thesis statement (to state the writer's position in relation to the prompt), main ideas (to assert the writer's ideas related to the thesis), supporting ideas (to provide evidence and support the claims in the main ideas, thesis, or conclusion), and a conclusion (to summarize the essay's argumentation). In order to automatically identify the various discourse elements, language modeling and machine learning methods were applied to a corpus of over 1400 essays that had been manually annotated with the discourse segment types listed above. The language model and machine learning models were combined to build a large system that can accurately identify the presence of the set of essay-based discourse segments listed (Burstein, Marcu, & Knight, 2003). This segmentation supports the calculation of e-rater features that give us information about aspects of organization and development in essays. In terms of organization, we know if the essay contains a thesis statement, for instance. Presence of a thesis statement would indicate that the essay is off to a good start, while absence of a thesis statement might be an indicator of a less well-organized essay. With regard to essay development, the presence of three longer main ideas might be an indicator of a more well-developed essay, whereas the presence of only a single, very short main idea might indicate less development.

CVA

CVA was described earlier as an example of an unsupervised modeling approach. E-rater uses CVA to examine vocabulary of an essay by comparing its vocabulary to the vocabulary found in manually-graded training essays for a particular topic. Higher-quality essays better reflect the assigned topic. They also tend to use a more specialized and precise topic-specific vocabulary than do lower-quality essays. Therefore, we expect a higher-quality essay to resemble other higher-quality essays in its choice of words and, conversely, a lower-quality essay to resemble other lower-quality ones.

CVA is used to compare an essay to a range of essays at different score points to determine how the language in the essay compares to other essays on the same topic at different score points. To do this, the use of a word in a document (term frequency) is computed, and the frequency of that term in a collection of documents is computed that tells us the relative frequency of that term in general (e.g., *the* will have a higher frequency in a set of documents than a content word, such as *rule*). The frequency of the word in the document in relation to its frequency in the corpus is used to assign a weight to that word in a text. The document now is composed of a vector of weights. To figure out the similarity between two documents, a cosine correlation is performed between the vector of weights in one document and another.

Collocation Detection

E-rater includes a module designed to identify collocations in test-taker essays (Futagi et al., 2008). Details about how this collocation detection system works and complete evaluations can be found in Futagi et al. (2008). The module essentially identifies collocations in a text that occur in seven syntactic structures identified as the most common structures for collocations in English based on the *BBI Combinatory Dictionary of English* (Benson, Benson, & Ilson, 1997). For instance, the following examples are given in Futagi et al. (2008): noun *of* noun (e.g., *swarm of bees*), and adjective + noun (e.g., *strong tea*), and noun + noun (e.g., *house arrest*). It uses a reference database containing collocations that have been created from the Gigaword Corpus[4] which is 1 terabyte. However, the majority of the data turn out to be almost entirely non-word strings, which are unusable for collocation reference. Therefore, it has been filtered to keep only the usable strings, and the final size of the corpus is about one-third of the original (approximately 1 billion n-grams retained). The collocation module identifies bigram, trigrams, and 4-grams in text, and computes pointwise mutual information (PMI) values between these n-grams extracted from the text, and collocations in a reference database. PMI is a statistical measure of association. In this context, it yields a value that establishes the likelihood of association of n-grams. Higher PMI values between the n-grams in the text and collocations in the reference database indicate a greater likelihood that the collocation in the essay is correctly formed.

E-RATER MODEL BUILDING AND EVALUATION

E-rater modeling was motivated specifically to predict a *rating* based on the holistic rubrics designed for human reader scoring (discussed earlier). To build a scoring model, a randomly-selected sample of human-scored essays (at least 250 essays) is run through e-rater which extracts a variety of linguistic features, as described above. The linguistic features are each converted to a numerical value. Using a regression modeling approach (Attali & Burstein, 2006), the values from this training sample are used to determine an appropriate weight for each feature. To score a new, unseen essay that may appear in a real test administration, for example, e-rater extracts the set of linguistic features, converts the features to a vector (list) of values on a numerical scale. These values are then multiplied by the weights associated with each feature, and a sum of the weighted feature values is then computed to predict the final score. This final, single score represents the overall quality of an essay.[5] For a discussion about empirical scoring evaluations, see Attali, Bridgeman, and Trapani (2010).

Three kinds of e-rater models can be built. *Topic-specific models* are built using a set of human-scored essays on a given topic, and all features are typically used for these models. A topic-specific model can be built only when there is sufficient human-scored data for the topic. *Generic models* are built using a set of human-scored essay data written by students in a particular grade or test-taker population, across a number of essay topics. All features, except for the content-specific features created for CVA-related features are used to build these models, since CVA features are designed to tell us how well a writer addresses a particular topic. These models are applied to essay responses for any topic written by students without new training when new topics are introduced (Attali & Burstein, 2006). There is a third *hybrid model* type. The model is like the generic model in estimating its feature weights within a testing population, but across multiple topics. The difference is that the model's intercept parameters are estimated from prompt-specific samples. For details about the hybrid model approach, see Davey (2009).

Before any kind of e-rater model can be operationally deployed, the model is evaluated on large samples of essays that have been scored by expert raters. It is critical that evaluations are performed on large samples to yield meaningful outcomes. In terms of sample sizes, generic e-rater models intended for operational use are evaluated on thousands of essays, and topic-specific on hundreds. A new model is released if it meets pre-established measurement criteria which require both Pearson correlation and weighted kappa for agreement with human raters to be at least 0.70.

E-rater Advisories

E-rater provides advisories that point out if an essay is off topic; has problems with discourse structure; and, contains disproportionately large numbers of grammatical errors (Higgins, Burstein, & Attali, 2006). Typically, these essays are not assigned a score by e-rater. These *off-topic* essays may be classified in the following categories. *Keyboard-banging* essays typically contain gibberish text such as "alfjdla dfadjflk ddjdj8ujdn," with little or no substantive lexical content. The *copied-prompt* essay is one which consists entirely or primarily of text copied and pasted from the essay topic itself. The prompt may be reproduced in its entirety, or only selected sentences may be included. The *unexpected-topic* essay is a well-formed, possibly very well-written essay, but is written to a topic that does not respond to the expected test question. This can happen if a student or test-taker misunderstands the prompt or inadvertently responds to the wrong question. The latter is more likely to happen in an instructional setting, where, perhaps the student responds to a question from a different assignment. The *bad-faith* essay is one in which the examinee enters a chunk of text which may be of substantial length, and may even be fairly coherent, but which is entirely unrelated to the essay topic. These essays do not make an attempt to respond the essay topic or task. It is important to handle these kinds of essays for the sake of ensuring score validity; however, our experience suggests that such essays occur very rarely in operational contexts. Other advisories are used to detect essays with a disproportionate number of grammatical errors given the length of the essay, and essays with anomalous discourse structure (i.e., structures which are disproportionately long given essay length).

Keyboard-banging essays are handled by a capability that considers ill-formed part-of-speech sequences in an essay. *Unexpected topic* and *bad faith essays* are handled using two CVA methods. An additional method is applied to capture *bad faith* essays. All measures for flagging *unexpected topic* and *bad faith* essays are described below. Two measures are derived from a CVA program for determining vocabulary usage in an essay. For each essay, z-scores are calculated for two variables: (1) the relationship to words in a set of training essays written to a prompt (essay question), and (2) the relationship to words in the text of the prompt. The z-score value indicates a novel essay's relationship to the mean and standard deviation (SD) values of a particular variable based on a training corpus of human-scored data. As discussed earlier in the chapter, the score range for many ETS large-scale assessments is 1 through 6, where 1 indicates a poorly written essay, and 6 indicates a well-written essay. To calculate a z-score, the mean value and the corresponding SD for maximum cosine or prompt cosine are computed based on the human-scored training essays for a particular test question. The formula for calculating the z-score for an unseen essay is: $z\text{-}score = \dfrac{(value - mean)}{SD}$. The z-score indicates how many SDs from the mean our essay is on the selected dimension. For our task, z-scores are computed for: (1) the *maximum cosine*, which is the highest cosine value among all cosines between an unseen essay and all human-scored training essays, and (2) the *prompt cosine*, which is the cosine value between an essay and the text of the prompt (test question). The *maximum cosine* value is used to flag *bad faith* essays, and the prompt cosine to flag *unexpected topic* essays. A second non-CVA-based method used to flag *bad faith* essays is the following. It is based on calculating two rates for each word used in essays: (1) the proportion of word occurrences across many topics (generic, or prompt-independent, rate), and (2) the proportion of word occurrences within a topic (prompt-specific rate). The generic rate of occurrence for each word (G_i) across the large sample is calculated one time only from a large sample of essays across different prompts from within one program, or within similar grade levels. It is interpreted as the base-rate level of popularity of each word. The prompt-specific rate (S_i) is computed from a training sample of essays that were written to the specific prompt for which an individual essay is to be compared. These two rates are used to compute an overall index for each individual essay:

$$\frac{1}{N} \sum_{i=1}^{n} \sqrt{S_i(1 - G_i)}$$

Equivalently, in order to compute this index, we carry out the following steps:

1. identify S_i and G_i values for all words in an essay based on predetermined values from training sets;
2. for each word, compute $S_i(1-G_i)$ and take the square root. Now sum these square roots over all words; and,
3. multiply the sum of square roots by $1/N$, where N is the number of words in the essay, and the two rates are computed for all words in the essay.

The methods described above for detection of *unexpected topic* and *bad faith* essays require a set of essays responses to a particular topic. In *Criterion*, a teacher might want to introduce a new topic for a class, and so methods requiring a set of training essays could not be applied. New advisory detection methods needed to be developed for this scenario. Our topic-independent model for off-topic essay detection uses CVA to computed similarity scores between student essays and the text of the assigned prompt (essay topic). This method uses a set of reference essay prompts to which a new essay is compared. *Criterion* offers a number of topics for teachers to use for writing assignments. *Reference prompts* are taken from the set of existing prompts offered in *Criterion*. The similarity scores from all of the essay-prompt comparisons, including the similarity score that is generated by comparing the essay to the *assigned prompt*, are calculated and sorted. If the assigned prompt is ranked amongst the top few vis-à-vis its similarity score, then the essay is considered on topic. Otherwise, it is identified as off topic.

As mentioned earlier in this section, advisories exist to identify essays with disproportionately large number of grammatical errors, and, similarly, disproportionately large discourse structures. Essays with large numbers of errors related to technical issues are computed as follows. In e-rater there are different error classifications, specifically: grammar, usage, mechanics, and style. Advisories are computed by calculating the proportion of each error type, given the total number of words in the essay. For example, all errors found that are related to grammar are summed and divided by the number of words. The same procedure is used for the set of usage, mechanics, and style errors. An empirical threshold value is predetermined that triggers the flag. The advisory that flags essays with excessively large discourse structures is computed by counting the total number of discourse units detected in an essay, and dividing this number by the total number of words in an essay. An empirical threshold value is also predetermined for this advisory and used to invoke the related advisory.

Detection of Essay Similarity

In the case of the GRE exam, e-rater also employs an NLP system for detecting unusual amounts of similarity between two or more essays. Some test-takers may prepare and memorize stock passages or even whole paragraphs which could be used across several prompts. This practice poses a threat to the validity of the assessment since it is meant to measure original writing. Given that over a million GRE essays are processed each year, it is intractable for human raters to catch suspiciously similar essays. To address this, ETS uses a tool known as Essay Similarity Detection which compares all essays to each other using different NLP similarity techniques. If the system flags an essay as being unusually similar to material found in another essay or essays, the essay in question is then reviewed by test developers from ETS who have the option of forwarding the essay in question to the ETS Board of Review. The Board may choose to clear the essay in question or to cancel the test scores for the test-taker. In the event of a cancellation, all scores (including Verbal and Quantitative) will be canceled.

CONCLUSION

As discussed in the Introduction to this chapter, researchers should consider how their system fits into the different educational problem spaces. In addition, it is critical that developments in AES align with new ideas in the educational landscape. In this section, we discuss educational problem spaces and how e-rater technology applies in these spaces. We also discuss how e-rater enhancements are aligned with the Common Core State Standards.

AES and Educational Problem Spaces

Three educational problem spaces were introduced earlier in this chapter: (1) *curriculum and assessment development*; (2) *curriculum and assessment delivery*; and (3) *score reporting*. In this section, we offer a discussion about how e-rater applications fit into these different problem spaces.

In the *curriculum and assessment development space*, teachers interact directly with the essay evaluation applications to prepare classroom materials (including assessments), such as essay prompts (questions). Teachers can interact with instructional applications, such as *Criterion*, the online essay evaluation system developed by ETS (Burstein et al., 2004). Briefly, *Criterion* offers students a platform for essay writing, where writing is evaluated and relevant feedback is provided immediately. Feedback includes a score and specific feedback, for instance, about technical quality (e.g., grammar and spelling errors), and organization and development. In terms of *curriculum and assessment delivery*, students interact directly with the technology and receive immediate feedback. In *Criterion*, for instance, students will receive feedback that illustrates specifically where they may have made a grammatical error (e.g., subject–verb agreement error), or if they are missing a critical organizational segment (e.g., thesis statement). This feedback is tailored to multiple aspects of the writing construct, as typically specified in scoring guide (rubric) criteria, and students can use this feedback to write revised essays. Users of applications that *generate and report scores (outcomes)* for test-taker assessments might include teachers, school administrators in K–12 or higher education settings (e.g., colleges and universities), or state or national agencies that review aggregate outcomes (e.g., measuring student performance in a domain at state and national levels). In this context, AES is probably the most widely-used NLP application in education for low- and high-stakes large-scale assessments. The technology has been used to develop efficient and relevant methods to automatically score test-taker writing so that scores can be used for the intended purpose (such as university admissions, evaluation of performance on state or national levels) by users such as admissions committees, and state and national policy makers. With appropriate attention to validity concerns in order to ensure that scores remain meaningful, AES systems can provide cost-effective and efficient scoring for operational testing programs.

AES and the CCSSI

The practical need for language-analysis capabilities, in general, has been driven by increased requirements for state and national assessments, and a growing population of foreign and second language learners. As is discussed in this chapter, and in other AES chapters in this volume, commercial systems do exist that handle automated scoring of free text and speech in the context of assessment as well as systems that address linguistic complexity in text—commonly referred to as readability measures (Nelson, Perfetti, Liben, & Liben, 2012). More recently, the need for applications for language analysis is emphasized by a new influence in the educational landscape in the United States, specifically, the CCSSI that is coordinated by the National Governors Association Center for Best Practices and the Council of Chief State School Officers (http://www.corestandards. org/; Loveless, 2012). The initiative has been adopted by most states for use in K–12 classrooms. This initiative is likely to be a trend-setter and influence teaching standards in K–12 education.

The CCSSI standards describe what K–12 students should be learning with regard to reading, writing, speaking, listening, language, and media and technology. In addition, the CCSSI describes the array of linguistic elements that learners need to grasp as they progress to the higher grades.[6] In the case of writing which is relevant to AES systems, the evaluation of students' writing includes criteria that are closely tied to linguistic elements and structures, for instance, the quality of argumentation (e.g., well-organized claims and supporting reasons, use of relevant transition terms, identification of text aspects indicating writer's perspective); use of precise, domain-specific vocabulary (e.g., vocabulary choice); and, use of formal English conventions (e.g., grammatical correctness). CCSSI thereby introduces language requirements that have clear alignments with NLP research and applications. The goals of CCSSI with regard to a student's ability to produce essays with sophisticated argumentation motivate advanced research in AES—specifically, to develop linguistic analysis capabilities that can evaluate linguistic features that contribute to an AES system's ability to evaluate aspects of argumentation in essay writing. Capabilities that might be used to evaluate the quality of argumentation in essays include the analysis of discourse coherence quality (see Chapter 16), and the automated detection of sentiment (opinion or claims) (see Chapter 17).

AES that can capture the structure of argumentation in student writing is critical, especially as constructed-response tasks appear in large-scale statewide assessments. It is essential that we continue to develop capabilities that capture as many as possible of the features of writing that are explicitly valued in contemporary writing assessments.

NOTES

1 For a more in-depth discussion about the notion of the writing construct, the reader should refer to Chapter 2 (*Automated Essay Evaluation and the Teaching of Writing*), and Chapter 18 (*Covering the Construct: An Approach to Automated Essay Scoring Motivated by a Socio-Cognitive Framework for Defining Literacy Skills*).
2 See http://newsblaster.cs.columbia.edu/
3 For a full list of publications about e-rater see http://www.ets.org/research/topics/as_nlp/ bibliography/.
4 http://www.ldc.upenn.edu/Catalog/CatalogEntry.jsp?catalogId=LDC2006T13
5 Readers should be aware that in operational scenarios, the e-rater score can be used in different ways. For high-stakes scoring, at the time that this chapter was written, the e-rater score is typically considered in combination with a human score to determine the final essay score. How the e-rater score is used depends on the client. In lower-stakes, instructional settings, such as Criterion, the e-rater score may be the sole score.
6 Refer to: http://www.corestandards.org/assets/Publishers_Criteria_for_3-12.pdf,and http://www.corestandards.org/assets/Appendix_A.pdf (both retrieved February 25, 2012).

REFERENCES

Attali, Y. (2011). *A differential word use measure for content analysis in automated essay scoring (ETS RR-11–36)*. Princeton, NJ: Educational Testing Service.

Attali, Y., Bridgeman, B., & Trapani, C. S. (2010). Performance of a generic approach in automated essay scoring. *Journal of Technology, Learning, and Assessment, 10*(3), 4–16.

Attali, Y., & Burstein, J. (2006). Automated essay scoring with e-rater V.2. *Journal of Technology, Learning, and Assessment, 4*(3), available from http://www.jtla.org.

Benson, M., Benson, E., & Ilson, R. (Eds.). (1997). *The BBI combinatory dictionary of English: A guide to word combinations.* Amsterdam, The Netherlands: John Benjamins.

Brin, S., & Page, L. (1997). The anatomy of a large-scale hypertextual web search engine. *Computer Networks and ISDN Systems, 30*(1–7), 107–117.

Broder, A. (2002). A taxonomy of web search. *SIGIR Forum 36*(2), 3–10, September.

Burstein, F., Chodorow, M., & Leacock, C. (2004). Automated essay evaluation: The Criterion Online Writing Service. *AI Magazine, 25*(3), 27–36.

Burstein, J., Kukich, K., Wolff, S., Lu, C., Chodorow, M., Braden-Harder, L., & Harris, M.D. (1998). *Automated scoring using a hybrid feature identification technique.* Paper presented at the Proceedings of the 36th Annual Meeting of the Association for Computational Linguistics and 17th International Conference on Computational Linguistics.

Burstein, J., Marcu, D., & Knight, K. (2003). Finding the WRITE stuff: Automatic identification of discourse structure in student essays. In S. Harabagiu and F. Ciravegna (Eds.), *Special issue on advances in natural language processing, IEEE Intelligent Systems* (pp. 32–39).

Burstein, J., Sabatini, J., & Shore, J. (in press) Developing NLP applications for educational problem spaces. In R. Mitkov (Ed.), *Oxford handbook of computational linguistics.*

Chiang, D. (2007). Hierarchical phrase-based translation. *Computational Linguistics, 33*(2), 201–228.

Chodorow, M., & Leacock, C. (2000). *An unsupervised method for detecting grammatical errors.* Paper presented at the 1st Annual Meeting of the North American Chapter of the Association for Computational Linguistics, Seattle, WA, April/May.

Davey, T. (2009). *Principles for building and evaluating e-rater models.* Paper presented at the annual meeting of the National Council on Measurement in Education.

Futagi, Y., Deane, P., Chodorow, M., & Tetreault, J. (2008). A computational approach to detecting collocation errors in the writing of non-native speakers of English. *Computer Assisted Language Learning, 21*, 353–367.

Ghose, A., & Ipeirotis, A. (2007). *Designing novel review ranking systems: Predicting usefulness and impact of reviews.* Paper presented at the International Conference on Electronic Commerce (ICEC).

Godbole, N., Srinivasaiah, M., & Skiena, S. (2007). *Large scale sentiment analysis for news and blogs.* Paper presented at the ICWSM.

Han, N. R., Chodorow, M., & Leacock, C. (2006). Detecting errors in English article usage in nonnative speakers. *Natural Language Engineering, 12*(2), 115–129.

Higgins, D., Burstein, J., & Attali, Y. (2006). Identifying off-topic student essays without topic-specific training data. *Natural Language Engineering, 12*(2), 145–159.

Kim, S., Pantel, P., Chklovski, T., & Pennacchiotti, M. (2006). *Automatically assessing review helpfulness.* Paper presented at the Conference on Empirical Methods in Natural Language Processing (EMNLP), Sydney, Australia.

Koehn, P., Och, F., & Marcu, D. (2003). *Statistical phrase-based translation.* Paper presented at the Human Language Technology and North American Association for Computational Linguistics Conference (HLT/NAACL), Edmonton, Canada, May 27–June 1.

Leacock, C., Chodorow, M., Gamon, M., & Tetreault, J. (2010). *Automated grammatical error detection for language learners.* Paper presented at the Synthesis Lectures on Human Language Technologies.

Loveless, T. (2012). *How well are American students learning?* (Vol. 3; pp. 3–32). The 2012 Brown Center Report on Education. Washington, DC: The Brookings Institution.

Marcu, D. and Wong, W. (2002). *A phrase-based, joint probability model for statistical machine translation.* Paper presented at the Conference on Empirical Methods in Natural Language Processing (EMNLP-2002), Philadelphia, PA, July 6–7.

Moschitti, A., Chu-Carroll, J., Patwardhan, S., Fan, J., & Riccardi, G. (2011). *Using syntactic and semantic structural kernels for classifying definition questions in Jeopardy!* Paper presented at the Conference on Empirical Methods for Natural Language Processing.

Nelson, J., Perfetti, C., Liben, D., & Liben, M. (2012). Measures of text difficulty: Testing their predictive value for grade levels and student performance, from http://www.ccsso.org/Documents/2012/Measures%20ofText%20Difficulty_final.2012.pdf

Salton, G. (1989). *Automatic text processing: The transformation, analysis, and retrieval of information by computer.* Reading, MA: Addison-Wesley.

Tetreault, J., & Chodorow, M. (2008). *The ups and downs of preposition error detection.* Paper presented at the COLING, Manchester, UK.

Tetreault, J., Foster, J., & Chodorow, M. (2010). *Using parse features for preposition selection and error detection.* Paper presented at the ACL '10, Uppsala, Sweden.

Zhang, Z., & Varadarajan, B. (2006). *Utility scoring of product reviews.* Paper presented at the ACM SIGIR Conference on Information and Knowledge Management (CIKM).

Zollmann, A., & Venugopal, A. (2006). *Syntax augmented machine translation via chart parsing.* Paper presented at the NAACL 2006 – Workshop on statistical machine translation, New York, June 4–9.

5 Implementation and Applications of the Intelligent Essay Assessor

Peter W. Foltz, Lynn A. Streeter,
Karen E. Lochbaum, and Thomas K Landauer

INTRODUCTION

In 1998 Pearson Knowledge Technologies (formerly Knowledge Analysis Technologies) entered the business of automatically scoring text, such as essays. Prior to that, founders Landauer and Foltz had experimented with using automated essay grading in their large psychology lecture courses beginning in 1994. A typical prompt from that era was: "Describe the differences between classical and operant conditioning."

The innovation that Pearson Knowledge Technologies (PKT) brought to bear on scoring text was incorporating an automated, mathematical way of representing and assessing the content of text that corresponded to judgments that people make about the similarity in meaning between passages of text and individual words. This scoring technology is based on Latent Semantic Analysis (LSA), a machine-learning method that acquires and represents knowledge about the meaning of words and documents by analyzing large bodies of natural text. LSA is all of the following:

- A theory of how people learn the meanings of words.
- A mathematical system for computational modeling of thinking processes.
- A text analysis tool.

Thus, in addition to measures that traditionally are used to characterize text, incorporating natural language processing (NLP), readability measures, grammar and spelling errors, LSA measures gave a way to assess the semantics or content of what was written, not just its form.

LSA's ability to gauge the quality of a text's meaning at the level of human raters has produced over the last 25 years a cottage industry of new applications where content coverage and quality are the core metrics (e.g., there are about 20,000 references to LSA according to Google Scholar). Early demonstrations of this by PKT showed that LSA discriminated between high school students, undergraduates, and medical students in assessing the same essay prompt, "Describe the functioning of the human heart." Foltz and Landauer used LSA scoring in their undergraduate psychology courses for several years, with Foltz giving students the option of having him grade their psychology essay if they were dissatisfied with the machine score. Oddly enough, no one ever took him up on his offer.

Because the word "essay" connotes English Language Arts to most people, the initial market was scoring language arts essays. While LSA-based content scoring accounted for roughly 80% of the prediction variance, the English Language Arts community required stylistic and grammatical judgments, and feedback. Over the years the scoring algorithms evolved to support measurement and feedback on aspects of style and mechanics such as grammar, punctuation, and spelling. Today approximately 60 variables have the potential to contribute to an overall essay score, as well as trait scores such as organization or conventions.

The Common Core State Standards (CCSS) change the landscape of how writing will be evaluated and what writing assignments will be. The CCSS reify the role of content in students' writing as an indication of mastery and higher order thinking skills. So, we have come full circle—PKT's shibboleth that substance matters more than form is now front and center of American curriculum reform.

In this chapter, first, far-reaching applications of PKT's Intelligent Essay Assessor (IEA) are described. Next, how the technology works for various types of scoring is described, and, finally, how well the technology works as compared to humans is described.

APPLICATIONS OF IEA

Automated Essay Scoring

The first major market for automated essay scoring was for English Language Arts (ELA). Educators, test publishers, and the public were reluctant to use automated scoring alone for summative assessment, but there was an appetite for giving students more practice writing essays in preparation for state writing exams. Teachers could grade on average three to four essay assignments a year; whereas, with computer-delivered automated scoring with instant feedback, much more writing practice could be given. For example, one teacher of PKT's WriteToLearn product has 120 students annually who produce 25,000 revisions to essays and summaries in the school year. Recognizing that writing is a contact sport that can be better played with technology, leads to students who markedly improve their writing skills.

Typical ELA curriculum includes writing in response to particular prompt types, such as narrative, expository, descriptive, and persuasive. Feedback in formative settings models the rubrics used to score state writing exams; usually a holistic score on a 4- or 6-point scale and trait scores, such as: ideas, organization, conventions, word choice, and sentence fluency. In addition, grammar and spelling errors are flagged. Figure 5.1 shows the system's scoring of a 12th grade persuasive prompt, "Should students upon graduating from high school be required to give a year of compulsory community service?"

WritetoLearn is implemented as a formative tool to continuously assess and improve skills rather than provide just an annual snapshot measure. For example, in South Dakota, it is incorporated as a formative writing assessment to replace the year-end summative state writing assessment for grades 5, 7, and 10. On average, students would revise an assignment four times: more revision practice than could or would occur in a conventional classroom with teacher grading. The results of using the system showed that student writing improved an average of one point on a six-point scale over those revisions (Foltz, Lochbaum, & Rosenstein, 2011).

Automated Scoring and Feedback of Paragraphs

Pearson's Writing Coach product is a grammar and writing curriculum program that includes automated evaluation of paragraphs as well as essays. With Writing Coach, students can write and receive feedback on each individual paragraph as they build toward a complete essay. Students receive paragraph feedback on the following features:

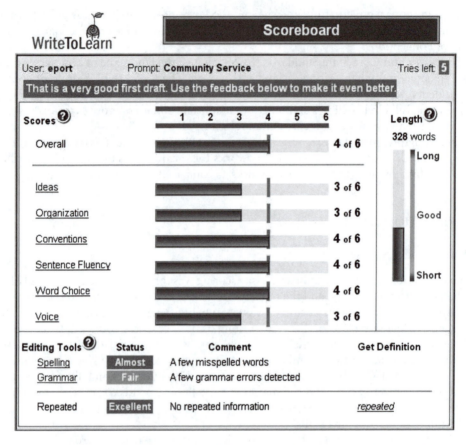

Figure 5.1 Essay feedback scoreboard. WriteToLearn provides students with an overall score as well as scores on six popular traits of writing. Passing scores are shown by the bars. Analysis of spelling, grammar, and redundancy (Repeated) is available by clicking on the links provided. Clicking on individual traits, such as Ideas or Organization provides more detailed explanations of how to improve those particular aspects of writing.

- Topic Focus: How well the sentences in the paragraph support the topic, as well a listing of those sentences that don't appear to support it.
- Topic Development: How well developed the ideas in the paragraph are.
- Variety of sentence length, sentence beginnings, and sentence structure.
- Transitions, vague adjectives, repeated words, pronouns, spelling, grammar, and redundancy (see Figure 5.2).

Summary Writing to Improve and Measure Reading Comprehension

Pearson's WriteToLearn tool expands the role of writing across the curriculum by automatically evaluating written summaries of informational texts in disciplines other than language arts. WriteToLearn's summary component evaluates writing across academic subjects, such as science, social studies, and history. Student feedback on a summary includes an assessment of how well the student covered the content in each major section of the reading, hints for how to improve content coverage in a particular section, and feedback on length, unimportant content, redundant content, and direct copying from

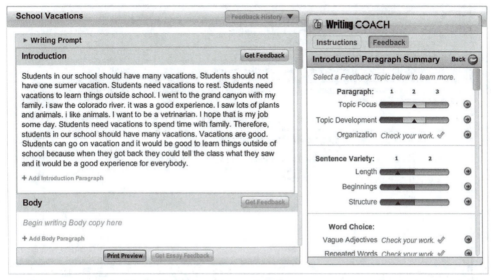

Figure 5.2 Writing Coach feedback for paragraphs. Writing Coach provides students with feedback on individual paragraphs including ratings for topic focus, topic development, and sentence variety, as well as feedback on word choice and spelling, grammar, and redundancy.

the original text. Scoring is accomplished by analyzing both the passage sections and summary for their holistic meanings, not by looking for particular key words.

Figures 5.3a through 5.3c show the summarization flow. First, a student reads a passage about penguins. Next, the student writes a summary of the passages that was just read. After submitting the passages for scoring, feedback is provided in the *scoreboard* which shows how well the student covered the content of each major section in the

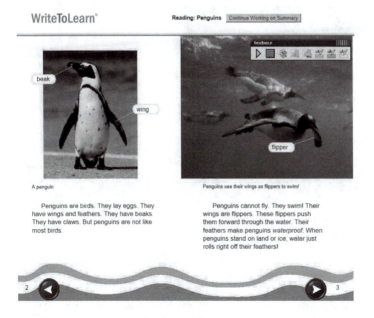

Figure 5.3a Text for student to read.

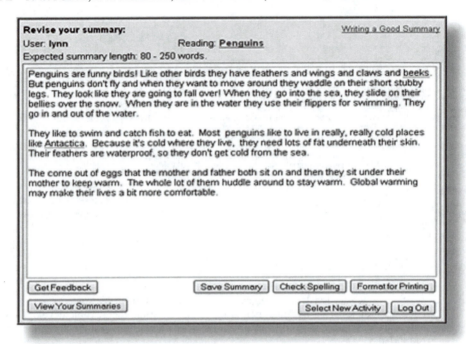

Figure 5.3b Student summary writing.

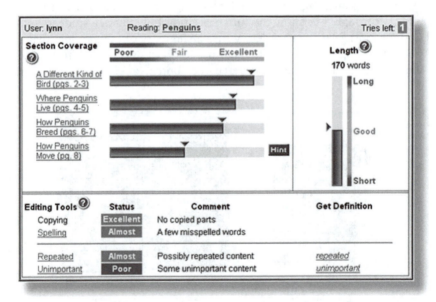

Figure 5.3c Summary Street feedback screen. This scoreboard is presented immediately after the student clicks "Get Feedback."

reading. The triangles above the content coverage bars show performance achieved on a previous submission. Students are encouraged to re-read the sections on which they are not doing well and revise their summary to push the score bars for each section over the passing threshold shown between Fair and Excellent.

Summary Writing to Improve Reading and Writing Skills

Summary Street was the result of joint development between researchers at the University of Colorado and scientists and software developers at Knowledge Technologies.[1] Several controlled studies were performed on the effects of Summary Street in the classroom. In one study 60 students in two sixth-grade classes each wrote two texts, one class using Summary Street and the other using a standard text editor. Results from this small study (see Figure 5.4) indicated that the students who used Summary Street:

- received higher grades on their summaries as assessed by teachers blind to the condition to which the student was assigned
- spent more time on the writing task
- retained the skills they learned even after they stopped using the tool.

In another study (Franzke, Kintsch, Caccamise, Johnson, & Dooley, 2005), 121 students used Summary Street for four weeks or were in a control group who received the same training but did their summary writing on word processors, which did not give the automated summary feedback. Students with Summary Street improved their content summary scores by an overall effect size of $d = 0.9$ compared to the control students. The results indicate that for a class of mixed-ability students, students scoring at the 50th percentile improved their writing performance with more difficult materials to the 82nd percentile. When the performance of low- and medium-ability students (the lower 75% of the distribution) was considered, the effect size increased to $d = 1.5$ for the most difficult materials. (An effect size of 1.0 corresponds to approximately a one-grade difference, e.g. from fifth to sixth grade.)

In a third study, University of Colorado researchers conducted a large two-year evaluation of 2,851 students in grades 5–9 in nine Colorado schools districts (Caccamise et al., forthcoming). Classes of students were assigned to either use Summary Street or

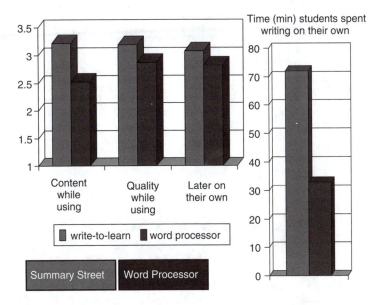

Figure 5.4 Summary Street produces better essays as judged by teachers in a two-week trial of sixth-grade students.

to receive traditional teacher-provided summarization instruction. Of the students who used Summary Street, most of them used it for an average of five to six different texts throughout the year. Students were given a summarization pretest at the beginning of the school year and at the end of the school year, as well as a standard short reading comprehension test (Test of Reading Comprehension, or TORC) at the beginning and end of the year. The experimental group was superior to the control group in summary writing for both years. Improvement in summarization was highly related to the number of texts a student studied during the year, as well as the amount of time students spent using the tool. Comprehension improvements on the TORC test were highly related (p < .002) to the amount of Summary Street use (see Figure 5.5).

Automated Essay Scoring in Postsecondary Environments

Use of automated essay scoring has been less prevalent in the postsecondary arena. The greatest impediment to adoption is that in college settings each professor creates his or her own assignment for a class of 10 to 500 students. When subject-area content needs to be evaluated, scoring models for unique (new) prompts typically need to be created. Thus, automated essay grading requires economies of scale in order to be cost-effective. Florida Gulf Coast University offers an example of IEA use where scale preconditions were met. "*Understanding the Visual and Performing Arts*" was a required freshman course with 800 students taught across 30 sections by adjunct professors. For the essay writing requirement, students analyzed a work of art—such as a painting, a sculpture, a piece of architecture, or a performing arts piece such as music, dance or theater. The essay prompts asked students to provide an objective analysis of particular elements of the art work, as well as to explain the meaning created by the particular work. While grading a "creative" essay might seem to be a particular challenge for automated assess-

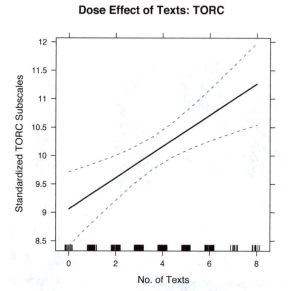

Figure 5.5 Performance on a standard reading comprehension test as a function of the number of texts studied with Summary Street during the school year with the 95% confidence interval shown as a solid line. The pretest scores for the same test were used as a covariate to control for student ability.

ment, professors were very pleased with the results. An analysis of IEA's reliability in grading showed it was more consistent than human scoring, matching human graders' scores 81% of the time vs. 64% when scored by two independent graders.

About 40% of students enrolling in community college need remediation in literacy, math or both. This is an ideal situation for automated essay grading. The size of this population is large, heterogeneous, and growing. To make progress in literacy skills such as writing requires dedicated hours of practice. And there are so many students in need that dedicated tutors are not an option. Pearson uses IEA in MyWritingLab, a web-based practice and assessment environment for the developmental writing market. As of the writing of this chapter, additional writing programs in the areas of science, history, social science, and business programs are implementing IEA to assess content knowledge in several MyLab learning environments for mainstream college students.

Performance Task Scoring

The ability to automatically evaluate content enables scoring of complex tasks, such as responding to scenarios, which require application and synthesis of complex knowledge either already possessed by the learner or gained experientially by taking a vocational or academic course. The first example of performance-based scoring comes from the Collegiate Learning Assessment, an assessment that is scored operationally by Pearson's automated scoring services. One task type involves presenting students with a scenario and a variety of information sources and asking the student to synthesize the information in a written response. An example of such an item is shown in Figure 5.6. Automated scoring performance on these types of items has an average Pearson correlation of 0.88 with the human consensus score, whereas the human–human correlation was 0.79.

Automated Assessment of Diagnostic Skills—National Board of Medical Examiners

A final example of automated assessment of performance tasks comes from a study done with the National Board of Medical Examiners where IEA was used to rate a physi-

---

You advise Pat Williams, the president of DynaTech, a company that makes precision electronic instruments and navigation equipment. Sally Evans, a member of DynaTech's sale force, recommends that DynaTech buy a small private plane (a SwiftAir 235) that she and other member of the sales force could use to visit customers. Pat was about to approve the purchase when there was an accident involving a SwiftAir 235.

Resources: Document Library
Newspaper article about the accident
Federal Accident Report on in-flight breakups in single engine planes
Internal Correspondence (Pat's email to you and Sally's e-mail to Pat)
Charts relating to SwiftAir's performance characteristics
Excerpt from magazine article comparing SwiftAir 235 to similar planes
Pictures and descriptions of Swiftair Models 180 and 235

Using the resources provided, the student writes a memorandum to the president presenting a reasoned decision of whether or not to purchase the Swiftair jet.

Figure 5.6 Sample performance task.

cian evaluation in simulations in which doctors examine and diagnose actors posing as patients feigning diseases. The patient notes produced by the doctors in this evaluation are illustrated in Figure 5.7. The notes are divided into text sections by patient's history, the findings of the doctor's physical examination of the patient, the potential diagnoses, and the additional diagnostic tests to be performed. IEA correlated more highly with the rating of the patient notes than did the expert physician ratings (Swygert et al., 2003).

The Collegiate Learning Assessment and medical example are just two examples in which IEA has been used in assessment other than standard language arts essays. Pearson has also done work with the military studying automated assessment of *Think Like a Commander* scenarios in which officers are presented with a scenario and asked to write a response detailing their approach to the scenario and the steps they would take. Automated scoring performance on such scenarios was shown to match that of the expert military evaluators (Lochbaum, Psotka, & Streeter, 2002).

Knowledge Technologies has used IEA to assess learning and performance in online collaborative work environments (see Foltz & Martin, 2008; Streeter, Lochbaum, LaVoie, & Psotka, 2007) to automatically monitor online discussion groups to alert the instructor to discussion drift; to assess relative contributions of participants; and to enhance the value of the discussion by automatically placing expert commentary into the discussion based on assessing the quality of the student discussion (LaVoie et al., 2010). IEA has also been used in psychiatric settings as a means of assessing clinical disorders to predict depression and schizophrenia from retelling familiar stories or from LSA analysis of transcribed psychiatric interviews in which the patient describes routine daily tasks (Elvevåg, Foltz, Weinberger, & Goldberg, 2007).

Short-Answer Scoring for Science

Pearson and the Maryland State Department of Education have worked together since 2007 on evaluating automated scoring for the Maryland Science Assessment (MSA). Since 2010, Pearson's automated scoring system has been used as a second scorer for short-answer science items that are best suited to automated scoring techniques. Short-

History	L-upper arm dull pain upon exertion (walking x2 weeks, each episode lasting <5 minutes, one episode at rest last night. 2. No associated chest pain, shortness of breath, numbness, parasthesia, weakness/paralysis, dizziness, syncopal episodes. 3. Past medical history of hypertension. 4. Post-menopausal, no hormone replacement therapy. Occupational history, social history, social history negative for activities that may contribute to arm strain.
Physical Examination	1. No focal tenderness, erythema, warmth. 2. L-upper extremity exam with normal pulse, capillary refill, motor/sensory function, reflexes.
Differential Diagnosis	Tendonitis Bursitis Angina Pectoris
Diagnostic Workup	EKG CBC Plain film X-ray L-upper extremity

Figure 5.7 Sample text from patient diagnostic notes.

> *Use the technical passage 'Green Ocean Machine' to answer the following.*
>
> *The passage states that "the new green partner [alga] seems to provide Hatena with most of its energy needs."*
>
> *Describe the process that enables organisms to use energy from light to make food. In your description, be sure to include:*
> *the specialized features needed to produce food*
> *the substances needed to produce food*
> *the substances produced during this process*

Figure 5.8 Sample Maryland science short answer item.

answer science questions on the Maryland assessment, which average about 50 words, are scored automatically on a 4-point holistic scale. For some types of prompts, students read a passage on a scientific question and write a response after reading the relevant text. For others, they simply respond to a given scientific question. One example item scored successfully using automated scoring is as follows.

HOW IEA SCORES

The IEA uses machine-learning techniques to learn how to score based on the collective wisdom of trained human scorers. Training IEA involves first collecting a representative sample of essays that have been scored by human raters. IEA extracts features from the essays that measure aspects of student performance such as the student's expression of knowledge and command of vocabulary and linguistic resources. Then, using machine-learning methods, IEA examines the relationships between both the scores provided by the human scorers and the extracted features in order to learn how the human scorers weigh and combine the different features to produce a score. The resulting representation is referred to as a "scoring model." This section provides details of the scoring features used in IEA, how the features are combined to score different traits of writing, and considerations for building and evaluating the performance of scoring models.

IEA Scoring Features

The quality of a student's essay can be characterized by a range of features that measure the student's expression and organization of words and sentences, the student's knowledge of the content of the domain, the quality of the student's reasoning, and the student's skills in language use, grammar and the mechanics of writing. In developing analyses of such features, the computational measures extract aspects of student performance that are relevant to the constructs for the competencies of interest (e.g., Hearst, 2000; Williamson et al., 2010). For example, a measure of the type and quality of words used by a student provides an effective and valid measure of a student's lexical sophistication. However, a measure that counts the number of words in an essay, although it will likely be highly correlated with human scores for essays, does not provide a valid measure of sophistication of writing. Because a student's performance on an essay typically requires showing combined skills across language expression and knowledge, it is critical that the scoring features used in the analysis cover the construct of writing that is being scored. Thus, multiple language features are typically measured and combined to provide a score. IEA uses a combination of features that measure aspects of the content, lexical sophistication, grammar, mechanics, style, organization, and development within essays. Figure 5.9 illustrates some of the features used in IEA and how they relate to specific constructs of student writing performance.

Content-Based Features in IEA

One of the hallmarks of IEA has been its ability to score essays in content domains. IEA uses LSA, a statistical semantic model (Deerwester et al., 1990; Landauer & Dumais, 1997) as the basis for scoring content features. LSA derives semantic models of English (or any other language) from an analysis of large volumes of text. For essay scoring applications, we typically use a collection of texts that is equivalent to the reading a student is likely to have done over their academic career (about 12 million words). LSA builds a co-occurrence matrix of words and their usage in paragraphs and then reduces the matrix by Singular Value Decomposition (SVD), a technique similar to factor analysis. The output of this analysis is a several hundred dimensional semantic space in which every word, paragraph, essay, or document is represented by a vector of real numbers to represent its meaning. The semantic similarity between words, paragraphs, and essays can be determined by computing the cosine between the vectors of two units of text. For example, the sentence "Surgery is often performed by a team of doctors" has a high semantic similarity to "On many occasions, several physicians are involved in an opera-

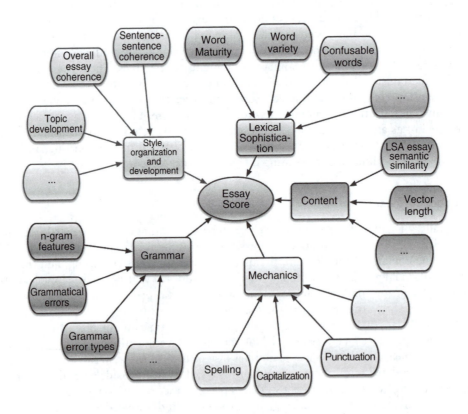

Figure 5.9 Features used in the IEA.

tion" even though they share no words in common. Although the technique is based on the statistics of how words are used in ordinary language, its analysis is much deeper and more powerful than the simple frequency, co-occurrence, or keyword counting and matching techniques that have sometimes been used in traditional NLP techniques. For an overview of NLP methods, see Chapter 4.

LSA is now in wide use around the world in many applications in many languages, including Internet search, psychological diagnosis, signals intelligence, educational and occupational assessment, intelligent tutoring systems, and in basic studies of collaborative communication and problem solving. The accuracy of the LSA meaning representation has been empirically tested in many ways. For example, LSA improves recall in information retrieval, usually achieving 10–30% better performance *cetera paribus* by standard metrics (Dumais, 1994; Landauer & Dumais, 1997) by matching documents with similar meanings, but utilizing different words. After training on domain corpora from which humans learned or might have learned, LSA-based simulations have passed multiple choice vocabulary tests and textbook-based final exams at student levels (Landauer, Foltz, & Laham, 1998). In rating the similarity of meaning between pairs of paragraphs and the similarity of meaning between pairs of words, LSA measures the similarity of meaning 90% as well as two human raters do when agreeing with each other about word and paragraph meanings (Landauer et al., 1998). LSA has been found to measure coherence of text in such a way as to predict human comprehension as well as sophisticated psycholinguistic analysis, while measures of surface word overlap fail badly (Foltz, 2007; Foltz, Kintsch, & Landauer, 1998).

Within IEA, LSA is used to derive measures of content, organization, and development-based features of writing. For example, the "LSA essay semantic similarity" measure compares the semantic similarity of a student essay against a set of training essays of known quality. A content score is assigned to the essay based on the scores of the most similar essays, weighted by their semantic similarity. This correlates highly with human scores of essays (see Landauer, Laham, & Foltz, 2001, 2003; Rehder et al., 1998). LSA-based measures are also used to compare the content of individual sentences to each other to compute measures of coherence (see Foltz et al., 1998) as well as to computing semantic similarity of the content of sentences or paragraphs against gold standard samples (see Foltz, 1996; Foltz, Gilliam, & Kendall, 2000). Finally, measures based on the LSA-based vector length of an essay in the semantic space are used. The vector length in an LSA-based semantic space provides an index of the preciseness of content within an essay (Rehder et al., 1998).

Other Language Features in IEA

Along with content-based measures, a range of other automatically computed measures are also used to score the lexical sophistication, grammatical, mechanical, stylistic, and organizational aspects of essays. Measures of lexical sophistication include measuring the developmental maturity of the words used (see Landauer, Kireyev, & Panaccione, 2011) as well as the variety of types of words used. Grammar and mechanics measures use NLP-based approaches to analyze the specific linguistic features of the writing. For grammar, such measures detect run-on sentences, subject–verb agreement, and sentence fragments use of possessives, among others. For assessing mechanics, measures are used that examine appropriate spelling, punctuation, and capitalization.

The assessment of stylistic and organizational aspects of essays are evaluated using a combination of LSA-based measures to analyze coherence in the essay, as well as

NLP-based measures that assess aspects of the organization, flow, and development across the essays. In addition, for specific essay types, additional features are incorporated which assess aspects of topic development, such as the strength of an introduction, use of supporting arguments, and the quality of the conclusion. Unless explicitly called for by a test design and documented for users, measures based on raw counts of words, sentences, or paragraphs are not included (e.g., counting words, adjectives, number of occurrences of "therefore"). While these measures can be predictive, students can be too easily coached to exploit such count-based measures.

Building a Scoring Model

IEA is trained to associate the extracted features in each essay to scores that are assigned by human scorers. A machine learning-based approach is used to determine the optimal set of features and the weights for each of the features to best model the scores for each essay. From these comparisons, a prompt and trait-specific scoring model is derived to predict the scores that the same scorers would assign to any new responses. Based on this scoring model, new essays can be immediately scored by analysis of the features weighted according to the scoring model.

Training on Human-Scored Data

The sample of student responses used for training and evaluating the scoring engine should represent the full range of student responses and scores. Typically the set of essays should represent a normal distribution, while ensuring that there are sufficient (e.g., at least a minimum of 10–20) examples at each score point. During training of the system, the responses should be 100% double-scored by human scorers and also receive resolution scores for non-adjacent agreement. By having scores from multiple human scorers, IEA can be trained on something closer to the true score (e.g., the average of multiple human raters) rather than the scores of an individual rater. The goal is to have as much and as accurate information as possible about the range of possible responses and how those responses should be evaluated. Generally, essay sets that are not as accurately scored by human raters will result in less accurate automated scoring models (e.g., Foltz, Lochbaum, Rosenstein, & Davis, 2012).

The number of responses typically required to train the scoring engine varies depending on the type of prompt and expected use of the response. For general formative and content-based scoring, 200–300 essays are required to train the scoring engine. For an essay prompt in a high-stakes assessment, a sample of about 500 student responses is preferred, while for a short-answer prompt 1000 responses are recommended for best performance (see Foltz et al., 2012) These numbers allow for using part of the data to train the scoring engine while holding out the other part for testing and validation. If such numbers of responses do not exist, a smaller testing and validation set can be used, or, alternatively, techniques such as jack-knife methods can also be used for evaluating expected performance based on the training set results alone.

Types of Scorable Traits

Human scorers are able to score essays for different traits within essays by focusing on different features of the essays in their evaluation. For example, to score an essay on conventions, a human scorer would focus on a student's grammar, spelling, and punctuation. Similarly, IEA can generalize to scoring different traits by choosing and weighting different combinations of features. A subset of the features can be used in the training, for example just choosing features related to conventions if scoring a convention trait. By then training IEA on human scores, it learns to associate the features within the IEA set that best model judgment on a specific trait. IEA has been used to accurately score a range of traits including:

- overall quality
- content
- development
- response to the prompt
- effective sentences
- focus and organization
- grammar, usage, and mechanics
- word choice
- development and details
- conventions
- focus
- coherence
- reading comprehension
- progression of ideas
- style point of view
- critical thinking
- appropriate examples, reasons and other evidence to support a position.
- sentence structure
- skilled use of language and accurate
- apt vocabulary.

Evaluating Responses for Scorability

Before scoring a student response, IEA analyzes the response to determine the confidence with which it can score it accurately. IEA uses a variety of statistical and probabilistic checks to make this determination based on characteristics of the response on which it was trained and experience with a variety of both good- and bad-faith responses. Responses that appear to be off topic, not English, or highly unusual or creative will be directed to a human for scoring.

Variants on IEA for Scoring Different Types of Student Responses

Short-answer scoring

Short-answer responses (e.g., responses on the order of 5 to 50 words) pose somewhat different scoring problems than longer essays. A sample student response is shown in Figure 5.10 that illustrates some of these problems.

A first problem is that responses of a sentence or two can be challenging because they contain very little information with which to evaluate a student's knowledge and ability. Second, spelling has a critical effect on short responses. If the majority of the words in a response are misspelled, it is very difficult to evaluate anything but the student's spelling ability. Third, short-answer items can often be very open-ended and so the range of

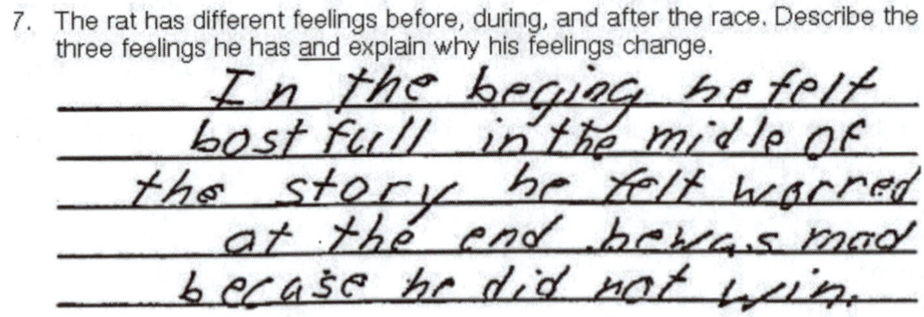

7. The rat has different feelings before, during, and after the race. Describe the three feelings he has <u>and</u> explain why his feelings change.

In the beging he felt bost full in the midle of the story he felt worred at the end he was mad becase he did not win.

Figure 5.10 Short answer student response.

acceptable possible responses very broad. In contrast with essays, the quality of short-constructed responses is also characterized more by word choice and the usage of specific terminology. To address these differences, a variant of IEA is used for scoring short-answers. In addition to the features from IEA, the short-answer variant uses statistical classifiers and assessment-specific heuristics for treating ordering of events in a process or explanation to model each short answer. In addition, compared to essay scoring, the development of short-answer-response scoring requires more student data to reach the accuracy required for high-stakes use. Based on research with the State of Maryland over five years, we have found that about one half to two-thirds of the short-answer science items can be scored automatically with similar accuracies to human scorers (see Thurlow, Hermann, & Foltz, 2010; Thurlow, Hermann, & Lochbaum, 2011). In these cases, the automated scoring system operates as a second scorer on those questions. For the remaining items, double human scoring is used exclusively.

Summary scoring

Summary writing allows students to practice both reading comprehension and writing across content areas. Automatic evaluation of summaries enables students to participate in a read, write, and revise cycle that encourages them to re-read, rethink and re-express those parts of the text that they have not yet fully understood. Our automatic summary evaluation process measures how well a student's summary covers the content of each major section of a reading by calculating the semantic similarity between the summary and each section of the text. Studies of its use in classrooms have shown that it produces improved reading comprehension and improved content writing when compared to students who did not receive automated feedback (Franzke et al., 2005).

Prompt-independent scoring models

In the examples of scoring models described above, IEA is trained specifically on each prompt for scoring traits associated with the particular assessment. When educators are mainly interested in gauging the stylistic and mechanical aspects of writing, a variant of IEA has been developed that provides a generalized grading (prompt-independent) scoring method. The prompt-independent method was calibrated on thousands of essays across multiple topics and prompts. Prompt-independent scoring is somewhat less reliable (self-consistent) than prompt specific scoring (generally about 10% lower reliability).

However, for formative instructional use, prompt-independent scoring enables teachers to author essay prompts that are tied to their own lesson plans and curriculum.

EVALUATION OF SCORING ENGINE PERFORMANCE

Evaluation of the performance of a scoring engine is critical throughout the test development process. In the pilot testing phase of item development, evaluation is performed to determine how amenable items are for automated scoring. Before deployment, finalized scoring models are evaluated on held-out tests sets to determine generalizability and robustness of scoring. During deployment, evaluation of the scoring engine is often performed to ensure that the scoring remains consistent with the goals of the testing. In the case of IEA being used as the sole scorer, random samples of essays can be chosen for backreads by human scorers as a check on the automated scoring. When IEA is being used as a second scorer, agreement rates with the other human scorer as well as with resolution scorers can be constantly monitored for performance. In addition, when used as a second scorer, evaluation of the agreement with human scorers can be used to detect drift in the human scorers and scorer consistency.

The performance of a scoring model can be evaluated both in how well the scores match human scoring, but also how well the scores align with the constructs of interest (see also Williamson, Chapter 10). The most common benchmark is to compute the reliability of the scoring engine by examining the agreement of IEA's predicted scores to human scorers, as compared to the agreement between human scorers. Metrics for computing the reliability include correlation, kappa, weighted kappa, and exact and adjacent agreement. Using "true scores" (e.g., the average of multiple scorers or the consensus score) for the comparison can provide more accurate measures of IEA's accuracy. However, human agreement is seldom sufficient as a means to evaluate performance. IEA performance can be compared against external variables that provide a measure of the validity of the scoring, including comparison of IEA scores with scores from concurrent administrations of tests with a similar construct, agreement with scores from subsequent tests, predicting student age or grade level, agreement to scorers with different levels of skill, and tests of scoring across different population subgroups. It should be noted though that when used in a formative context, evaluation should also be considered within a framework of measuring learning gains. As students receive formative feedback, revise their essays and resubmit, automated scoring can be evaluated in how well it improves students' content knowledge, reading skills (e.g., Franzke et al., 2005) and writing abilities (e.g., Foltz et al., 2011).

IEA has been evaluated across a range of different types of essays at different levels of student ability. Table 5.1 presents correlation coefficients between automated scores and consensus human scores for a sample of written constructed responses. For example, the third row shows score accuracy indicators for a set of five information-integration items, the Collegiate Learning Assessment items described above. For each item, students were asked to write memos that synthesized information from multiple sources, including letters, memos, summaries of research reports, newspaper articles, maps, photographs, diagrams, tables, charts, and interview notes or transcripts. The resulting set of 1239 written responses was then scored by machine and by independent scorers. One can compare the average Pearson correlation between pairs of human scorers, shown as the human–human correlation of 0.79, with machine–human correlation of 0.88. Thus, for this example, automatic scores are closer to a stable consensus human score than one expert score is to another.

Table 5.1 Indicators of Scoring Quality for Four Operational Item Sets. N is the average the number of test-takers per test or item used in the calculations. Machine–human correlations are between one fully automatic score and a consensus human score (rating the same material). For comparison, the human–human column shows correlations between scores from two human scorers for the same materials.

Assessment Prompt Material	N	Machine–Human Pearson Correlation	Human–Human Pearson Correlation	Source
81 published essay prompts (grades 6–12)	200	0.89	0.86	Prentice Hall
18 research-leveled essay prompts (grades 4–12)	635	0.91	0.91	MetaMetrics
5 performance tasks using multiple sources	1239	0.88	0.79	Council for Aid to Education
10 essay prompts used for placement	4858	0.90	0.90	ACCUPLACER

Note that the correlations shown in Table 5.1 are item-level correlations. Assessments typically include many different types of items designed to get as accurate a measure as possible of a student's knowledge, ability, and skill level. At the assessment level, taking all items into account, correlations between human scorers and between human and automated scorers are typically higher, approaching 0.95 or above.

Trait Scoring

While Table 5.1 shows scores for the overall quality of the essays, IEA can provide scores for individual traits of writing as well. The performance for scoring six writing traits based on six prompts is shown in Table 5.2. For each of the prompts, students were directed to read a particular text and respond in the context of the text. The prompts asked students to compare and contrast components of the reading, identify and synthesize particular aspects of the reading, and use important and specific details from the reading to support their response.

Table 5.2 Performance on Essay Prompts. Correlation and exact agreement between automated and human scores for the six traits based on six different prompts.

Traits	Machine–Human Pearson Correlation	Machine–Human Exact Agreement Mean (%)	Range (%)
Ideas	0.93	73	58–87
Organization	0.93	69	60–74
Word Choice	0.93	68	63–74
Sentence Fluency	0.90	64	58–70
Conventions	0.85	60	52–66
Voice	0.92	65	62–68

IEA Applied to Content Scoring

Because IEA can score content-based essays, it has been applied to a range of content areas including history and social science topics for students ranging from grade school to college level. Because the automated scoring system is trained on the semantics of the domain (subject area), it is able to provide reliable scores of the content knowledge of students. For example, tests were performed on high school and entry-level undergraduate writing prompts on the history of the Great Depression, the history of the Panama Canal, ancient American civilizations, alternative energy sources, business and marketing problems, psychology of attachment in children, aphasia, and Pavlovian and operant conditioning (Foltz, Laham, & Landauer, 1999; Landauer et al., 2001). The average inter-rater correlation of two human scorers was 0.75 and the average correlation of the automated scoring to each single rater was 0.73—which was not significantly different from each other. The results further showed that the greater the expertise of the human rater, the greater the correlation to the automated scorer, thereby providing a measure of the validity of the scoring. In addition to providing scores on content, the methods are able to provide feedback about different aspects of the content where students have stronger or weaker knowledge. Feedback from this automated scoring has shown to significantly improve student content learning (see Foltz et al., 2000).

Short-Answer Scoring

As described above, short-answer scoring uses a modified version of IEA to account for different language and content features found in short responses. This version of IEA is being used operationally for scoring the State of Maryland's science assessment. Maryland's approach to item development is to create items independently of automated scoring considerations. The items are then evaluated for how well they can be scored automatically. Those responses that can be scored reliably by automated scoring techniques are scored by one human scorer and the automated system. Those responses that cannot be scored automatically continue to be scored by two human scorers. Since 2010, Pearson's automated scoring system has participated in operational scoring, acting as the second scorer for roughly two-thirds of the items on the Maryland assessment (see Thurlow et al., 2010, 2011). Table 5.3 summarizes scoring performance for ten

Table 5.3 Short Answer Scoring Performance

	Human–Human				IEA–Human			
Prompt	N	R	Exact	Adj	N	R	Exact	Adj
1	1507	0.71	79	100	1471	0.76	75	100
2	695	0.52	70	100	674	0.66	71	100
3	675	0.76	75	99	642	0.85	75	99
4	661	0.68	77	100	638	0.79	78	100
5	680	0.64	71	100	669	0.73	73	100
6	885	0.70	81	100	843	0.75	82	100
7	702	0.80	76	99	672	0.85	76	100
8	1674	0.57	70	99	1624	0.68	71	99
9	1666	0.81	78	100	1610	0.89	83	100
10	500	0.87	81	100	500	0.86	78	100

operational prompts showing the correlation, exact, and adjacent levels of agreement for human–human and IEA–human scoring. Overall, IEA–human performance is at an equivalent level as human–human performance.

CONCLUSION

Every year millions of elementary, secondary, and college and career essays and summaries are evaluated by IEA. It is used as a backend scoring system for summative tests, publishers' textbooks, for test preparation, as well as for products like WriteToLearn and Writing Coach. IEA provides a means to incorporate accurate scoring for a wide range of written responses including language arts, content, reading comprehension summaries, and short-answer essays, as well as responses in performance items, situation judgment tasks and clinical assessments.

As a formative tool, IEA provides more revision practice than could occur in a conventional classroom with teacher grading. As such, it helps support the trend to replace annual summative assessments with formative tools to improve skills rather than use an annual snapshot measure. This permits more personalized learning for the student and allows the teacher to focus on students that need help by monitoring the learning of individual students and the class as a whole. Because there is a great deal of commonality among state rubrics for evaluating essays, the secondary market for automated scoring is very large and the tools are widely applicable. Across America there is tremendous appetite to improve students' writing and reading skills as the situation is dire and is rightfully labeled a crisis by the educational establishment, employers, parents, and students. Tools that make practice simple and enjoyable and provide meaningful feedback can be keys to remediating literacy.

NOTE

1. WriteToLearn's Summary Street component is based on ten years of research and evaluation, as part of an Interagency Educational Research Initiative (IERI) research and effectiveness trial project, combined with seven years of professional educational software development and both software and educational effectiveness testing at Knowledge Analysis Technologies (since 2004, Pearson's Knowledge Technologies group). At University of Colorado, the research was performed under the direction of Professors Walter Kintsch and Tom Landauer, and at New Mexico State University under Professor Peter Foltz. Landauer and Foltz currently direct research at Pearson's Knowledge Technologies group. Professor Louis Gomez at UCLA Policy and Dr. Jack Stenner of MetaMetrics, Inc have also collaborated in the WriteToLearn research.

REFERENCES

Caccamise, D., Snyder, L., Allen, C., DeHart, M., Kintsch, E., Kintsch, W., & Oliver, W. (forthcoming). *Summary street: Scale-up and evaluation*.

Deerwester, S., Dumais, S., Furnas, G. W., Landauer, T. K, & Harshman, R. (1990). Indexing by Latent Semantic Analysis. *Journal of the American Society for Information Science, 41*(6), 391–407.

Dumais, S. T. (1994). Latent Semantic Indexing (LSI) and TREC-2. In D. Harman (Ed.), *The Second Text REtrieval Conference (TREC2)* (pp. 105–116). National Institute of Standards and Technology Special Publication 500–215.

Elvevåg, B., Foltz, P. W., Weinberger, D. R., & Goldberg, T. E. (2007). Quantifying incoherence in speech: An automated methodology and novel application to schizophrenia. *Schizophrenia Research*. doi: doi:10.1016/j.schres.2007.03.001.

Foltz, P. W. (1996). Latent Semantic Analysis for text-based research. *Behavior Research Methods, Instruments and Computers, 28*(2), 197–202.

Foltz, P. W. (2007). Discourse coherence and LSA. In W. Kintsch, T. K. Landauer, D. McNamara, & S. Dennis (Eds.), *LSA: A road to meaning.* Mahwah, NJ: Lawrence Erlbaum Publishing.

Foltz, P. W., Gilliam, S., & Kendall, S. (2000). Supporting content-based feedback in online writing evaluation with LSA. *Interactive Learning Environments, 8*(2), 111–129.

Foltz, P. W., Kintsch, W., & Landauer, T. K (1998). The measurement of textual coherence with Latent Semantic Analysis. *Organizational Process, 25*(2–3), 285–307.

Foltz, P. W., Laham, D., & Landauer, T. K. (1999). The intelligence essay assessor: Applications to educational technology. *Interactive Multimedia Electronic Journal of Computer-Enhanced Learning, 1*(2). Available at http://imej.wfu.edu/articles/1999/2/04/

Foltz, P. W., Lochbaum, K. E., & Rosenstein, M. B. (2011). *Analysis of student ELA writing performance for a large scale implementation of formative assessment.* Paper presented at the the Annual Meeting of the National Council for Measurement in Education (NCME).

Foltz, P. W., Lochbaum, K. E., Rosenstein, M. B., & Davis, L. E. (2012). *Increasing reliability throughout the automated scoring development process.* Paper presented at the Annual Meeting of the National Council for Measurement in Education, Vancouver, CA.

Foltz, P. W., & Martin, M. J. (2008). Automated communication analysis of teams. In G. F. Goodwin, E. Salas, & S. Burke (Eds.), *Team effectiveness in complex organizations and systems: Cross-disciplinary perspectives and approaches.* New York: Routledge.

Franzke, M., Kintsch, E., Caccamise, D., Johnson, N., & Dooley, S. (2005). Summary street: Computer support for comprehension and writing. *Journal of Educational Computing Research, 33,* 53–80.

Hearst, M. A. (2000). The debate on automated essay grading. *IEEE Intelligent Systems & Their Applications, 15*(5), 22–27.

Landauer, T. K, & Dumais, S. T. (1997). A solution to Plato's problem: The Latent Semantic Analysis theory of acquisition, induction, and representation of knowledge. *Psychological Review, 104,* 211–240.

Landauer, T. K, Foltz, P. W., & Laham, D. (1998). Introduction to Latent Semantic Analysis. *Discourse Processes, 25*(2–3), 259–284.

Landauer, T. K, Kireyev, K., & Panaccione, C. (2011). Word maturity: A new metric for word knowledge. *Scientific Studies of Reading, 15*(1), 92–108.

Landauer, T. K, Laham, D., & Foltz, P. W. (2001). Automated essay scoring. *IEEE Intelligent Systems,* September/October, 27–31.

Landauer, T. K, Laham, D., & Foltz, P.W. (2003). Automated scoring and annotation of essays with the Intelligent Essay Assessor. In M. D. Shermis & J. Burstein (Eds.), *Automated essay scoring: A cross-disciplinary perspective* (pp. 87–112). Mahwah, NJ: Lawrence Erlbaum Associates, Inc.

LaVoie, N., Streeter, L., Lochbaum, K., Wroblewski, D., Boyce, L.A., Krupnick, C., & Psotka, J. (2010). Automating expertise in collaborative learning environments. *Journal of Asynchronous Learning Networks, 14*(4), 97–119.

Lochbaum, K., Psotka, J., & Streeter, L. (2002). *Harnessing the power of peers.* Paper presented at the Interservice/Industry, Simulation and Education Conference (I/ITSEC), Orlando, FL, December.

Rehder, B., Schreiner, M. E., Wolfe, M. B, Laham, D., Landauer, T. K, & Kintsch, W. (1998). Using Latent Semantic Analysis to assess knowledge: Some technical considerations. *Discourse Processes, 25,* 337–354.

Streeter, L., Lochbaum, K., LaVoie, N., & Psotka, J. (2007). Automated tools for collaborative learning environments. In D. McNamara, T. Landauer, S. Dennis, & W. Kintsch (Eds.), *Latent Semantic Analysis: A road to meaning.* Mahwah, NJ: Lawrence Erlbaum.

Swygert, K., Margolis, M., King, A., Siftar, T., Clyman, S., Hawkins, R., and Clauser, B. (2003). Evaluation of an automated procedure for scoring patient notes as part of a clinical skills examination. *Academic Medicine, 78,* 10, S75–S77.

Thurlow, M. M., Hermann, A., & Foltz, P. W. (2010). *Preparing MSA science items for artificial intelligence scoring.* Paper presented at the Maryland Assessment Group Conference, Ocean City, MD, November.

Thurlow, M. M., Hermann, A., & Lochbaum, K. E. (2011). *Preparing MSA science items for artificial intelligence scoring.* Paper presented at the Assessment Group Conference, Ocean City, MD, November.

Williamson, D. M., Bennett, R., Lazer, S., Bernstein, J., Foltz, P. W., Landauer, T. K., Sweeney, K. (2010). Automated scoring for the assessment of Common Core Standards. doi: http://www. ets.org/s/commonassessments/pdf/AutomatedScoringAssessCommonCoreStandards.pdf

6 The IntelliMetric™ Automated Essay Scoring Engine – A Review and an Application to Chinese Essay Scoring

Matthew T. Schultz

INTRODUCTION

IntelliMetric™ was designed as a tool for scoring essay-type, constructed response questions across a number of environments and content areas, including K–12, higher education, and professional training. This paper describes IntelliMetric and reviews an application of IntelliMetric for scoring foreign language content.

OVERVIEW OF INTELLIMETRIC

IntelliMetric is an intelligent scoring system that emulates many of the processes carried out by human scorers in writing assessment. IntelliMetric is theoretically grounded in a cognitive model often referred to as a "brain-based" or "mind-based" model of information processing and understanding. To this end, IntelliMetric seeks to identify features of scored essays that are associated with high rater assigned scores, developing models that emulate the results of the scoring process used by human raters.

Minsky (1986) captured the perspective embodied by IntelliMetric in his view of the brain presented in *The Society of Mind*, where understanding is conceptualized as the result of billions of interacting subprograms, each doing simple computations. Most recently Baum's (2004) work has extended this search and produced an integrated view of meaning.

The IntelliMetric system must be "trained" with a set of previously scored responses drawn from expert raters or scorers. These papers are used as a basis for the system to "learn" the rubric and infer the pooled judgments of the human scorers. The IntelliMetric system internalizes the characteristics or features of the responses associated with each score point and applies this intelligence to score essays with unknown scores.

Because writing scores and feedback from IntelliMetric are virtually instantaneous, students can submit their work on a more frequent basis as a means to improve their writing. In the context of writing instruction, IntelliMetric can aid the teacher by providing immediate feedback in a number of diverse areas including grammar, syntax, organization, and development (Attali, 2004; Lipnevich & Smith, 2008).

IntelliMetric utilizes the same holistic scoring approach commonly employed by human raters to evaluate large-scale writing assessments. See Chapter 4 for a description of holistic scoring. At a high level, the holistic score of a response represents the overall impression that it makes on a reader. The score provided by this reader (rater) is typically based on a formal scoring rubric, which focuses on the discourse elements, content, organization, word use, and grammar/mechanics of the response as a whole. To become proficient and reliable in scoring responses to a given prompt, expert raters are provided anchor papers specific to the prompt, are given scores to those papers, and are taught why each paper should receive a certain score. The human raters are given additional scored papers for training and are ultimately asked to score some papers on their own. If the human scoring is acceptable with regards to a set standard of agreement with other raters, the human rater is then allowed to score new essays for that particular prompt.

Much like human scorers who are generally trained to score a specific prompt, IntelliMetric creates a unique solution for each prompt. This process leads to higher levels of agreement between the scores assigned by IntelliMetric and those assigned by human scorers. A summary of representative agreement rates by grade level is presented in Table 6.1. IntelliMetric can be used for standardized assessments where a single essay submission is required as well as for various instructional applications where a student can provide multiple submissions of an essay response and receive frequent feedback. IntelliMetric provides feedback on overall performance in the form of a holistic score, and further can provide diagnostic feedback on the following dimensions as shown in Table 6.2.

TEXT FEATURES EXAMINED

IntelliMetric analyzes more than 400 semantic-, syntactic-, and discourse-level features to form a composite sense of meaning as illustrated in Figure 6.1 (Elliott, 2003).

These features fall into two major categories: content and structure. Examples of the types of features IntelliMetric looks at in each of these categories is provided below.

Table 6.1 Representative Agreement Rates by Grade Level

Prompt Level	Exact	Adjacent	Discrepant	Pearson Correlation
Elementary	76%	24%	0%	0.93
Middle School	73%	26%	1%	0.92
High School	70%	29%	1%	0.91
Higher Ed	66%	34%	0%	0.83

Source: Vantage Learning, 2012.

Table 6.2 Domain Scoring Rubric for IntelliMetric

Focus and Meaning	Content and Development	Organization	Language Use, Voice, and Style	Mechanics and Conventions
The extent to which the response establishes and maintains a controlling idea (or central idea), an understanding of purpose and audience, and completion of the task.	The extent to which the response develops ideas fully and artfully using extensive, specific, accurate, and relevant details *(facts, examples, anecdotes, details, opinions, statistics, reasons, and/or explanations).*	The extent to which the response demonstrates a unified structure, direction, and unity, paragraphing, and transitional devices.	The extent to which response demonstrates an awareness of audience and purpose through effective sentence structure, sentence variety, and word choice that create tone and voice.	The extent the response demonstrates control of conventions, including paragraphing, grammar, punctuation, and spelling.

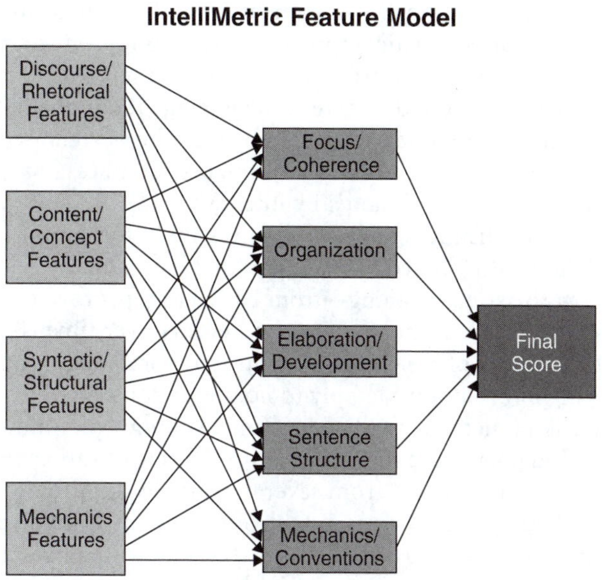

IntelliMetric Feature Model

Figure 6.1 A conceptual diagram about how IntelliMetric works.

Content

Features of text evaluate the topic covered, the breadth of content, and the support for concepts advanced (e.g., vocabulary, concepts, support, elaboration, word choice). Similarly, features suggesting cohesiveness and consistency in purpose and main idea (e.g., unity, single point of view, cohesiveness), and features targeted at the logic of discourse including transitional fluidity and relationships among parts of the response (e.g., introduction and conclusion, coordination and subordination, logical structure, logical transitions, sequence of ideas) are evaluated.

Structure

Features examining standard writing conventions of edited American English include grammar, spelling, capitalization, sentence completeness, and punctuation. Features targeted at sentence complexity and variety include syntactic variety, sentence complexity, usage, readability, and subject–verb agreement.

Based on these features, IntelliMetric identifies the underlying semantic structure for a given piece of writing. Fundamentally, IntelliMetric synthesizes broader meanings from many more molecular features.

How does IntelliMetric use this information to score essays?

KEY PRINCIPLES

In developing IntelliMetric, Vantage sought to integrate current thinking about the human brain and how the brain processes text to develop meaning. IntelliMetric is based on this brain-based model of understanding reflecting several central principles. There are four primary principles that guide IntelliMetric. They include:

1. IntelliMetric is modeled on the human brain and its ability to synthesize discrete information. A neurosynthetic approach is used to reproduce the mental processes used by human experts to score and evaluate written text. The specific aspect of intelligence we are interested in here is the intelligence applied by human experts to score and evaluate written text provided by examinees when writing essay question responses. The information contained in the text of an essay is processed, and then organized into a meaningful model by IntelliMetric.

2. IntelliMetric is a learning engine. It acquires the information it needs by learning how to evaluate writing based on examples that have already been scored by experts. Humans learn to assign meaning—from basic concepts to social patterns of behavior—through exposure to phenomena and events over time (Baum, 2004; Schank, 1999). In the context of developing IntelliMetric, learning is a process of acquiring and organizing information to apply to new situations.

3. IntelliMetric is inductive. IntelliMetric makes judgments inductively rather than deductively. Judgments are made based on inferences rather than rules. Inductive reasoning derives a principle from several example situations (specific to general). IntelliMetric largely employs an inductive process as it involves inferences rather than following a rule-governed protocol. It makes inferences about how an essay should be evaluated based on its acquired knowledge from specific examples, previously evaluated by experts. IntelliMetric models the human scoring process by using information gained from "reading" the text to make an inference about the score to be assigned. IntelliMetric makes an inference based on several pieces of information in the form of the features of text in the major feature categories described above.

4. IntelliMetric uses multiple judgments based on multiple mathematical models. It is based on several different types of judgments using many types of information organized using mathematical tools.

    *   Most attempts at automated essay scoring rely primarily on a single mathematical methodology. IntelliMetric uses a hybrid of techniques, including linear analysis, Bayesian, and Latent Semantic Analysis.
    *   The independent judges are treated like a "panel of experts." In the human essay scoring arena, it is better to have several judgments of the score rather than a single judgment. This is no less true in automated essay scoring. IntelliMetric calculates likely solutions (potential scores) from the different mathematical models and sources of information (by bootstrapping from various combinations of cases from the training set). It then combines this information using proprietary algorithms to obtain the optimal solution, or more simply the solution that is most likely to produce an accurate score. This approach produces the most stable and accurate score possible. Since any single judge is less reliable than several judges, relying on a broader array of information and looking to the optimal solution improves the accuracy and stability of IntelliMetric scoring decisions.

INTELLIMETRIC PROCESS

To this point we have examined the theoretical and conceptual basis for IntelliMetric modeling. This section describes the specific process IntelliMetric uses to score essays.

Overview of the Process

IntelliMetric uses a multi-stage process to evaluate responses. First, *the scoring engine* is exposed to a subset of responses with known scores from which it derives knowledge of the scoring scale and the characteristics associated with each score point. Second, the model reflecting the knowledge derived is tested against a smaller set of responses with known scores to cross-validate the model. Third, after making sure that the model is scoring as expected, the model is applied to score novel responses with unknown scores. Using Legitimatch™ technology, responses that appear off topic, are too short to score reliably, do not conform to the expectations for edited American English, or are otherwise "unusual" are identified as part of the process.

To provide a better understanding of how IntelliMetric works, this process is broken into steps presented in Figure 6.2, accompanied by a description of the individual steps.

Step 1: Create Essay Files

IntelliMetric requires that essays be provided in electronic form (ASCII text). Essay responses can either be transcribed versions of handwritten essays or more commonly essays entered electronically. The software can accept information as an individual response or as a "batch" of many responses. Increasingly, information is submitted using the Internet as part of a broader educational application, such as MY Access!™.

Step 2: Preprocessing

After the information has been received in electronic form, IntelliMetric prepares the information for further analysis. This preprocessing stage ensures than all materials are

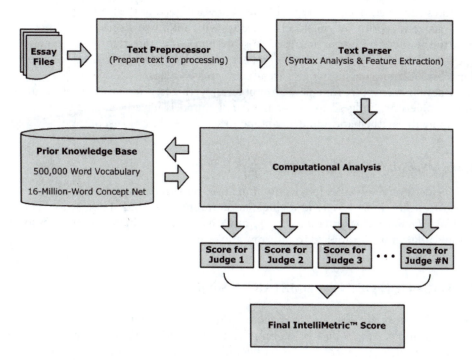

Figure 6.2 IntelliMetric architecture.

in a form that is readable and understandable. The preprocessor removes extraneous characters and corrects formatting.

Step 3: Analyze Text

Once converted to a usable form, the text is then parsed to understand the syntactic and grammatical structure of the language in which the essay is written. Each sentence is identified with regard to parts of speech, vocabulary, sentence structure, and concept expression. Several patented techniques are used to make sense of the text including morphological analysis, spelling recognition, collocation grammar, and word boundary detection. A 500,000 unique word vocabulary and 16 million word concept net are consulted to form an understanding of the text.

Step 4: Calculate Information

After all the information has been extracted from the text, it is translated into numerical form to support computation of the mathematical models. This process relies on a variety of statistical techniques and computational linguistics to create the more than 400 features described earlier.

Step 5: Evaluate Text Based on Virtual Judges (Mathematical Models)

The information obtained as a result of Step 4 is used as a basis to calculate models linking features to assigned scores.

While the number of judges used by IntelliMetric varies depending on several factors, they all share certain things in common. At the highest level, each judge seeks to associate the features extracted from the text with the scores assigned in the training set in order to make accurate scoring judgments about essays with unknown scores. They differ with respect to the specific information used to score and more importantly the underlying mathematical model used to make judgments. Several statistical, artificial intelligence and machine learning methodologies are used to create judges.

In the development stage for a new prompt or topic, this step actually creates the mathematical models or "judges" to be used. After the models have been created, this step would apply the mathematical understanding to score novel essay responses.

Step 6: Resolve Multiple Judges' Scores

Step 5 yields several possible judgments. IntelliMetric then integrates the information obtained from the judges to yield a single accurate, reliable, and stable score. This is much like human scoring situations where multiple scorers evaluate an essay response and some model must be applied to integrate those diverse opinions.

AN APPLICATION OF INTELLIMETRIC IN SCORING CHINESE

While IntelliMetric has demonstrated success in scoring text written in English, there have been a number of studies evaluating the effectiveness of the software applied to text written in other languages. The remainder of the paper will discuss and evaluate the performance of IntelliMetric in scoring essays written in Chinese.

Data Collection

Responses from approximately 600 essays were gathered for use in this study. Essays were written to the same prompt, which focused on Environmental Protection, hand written in Chinese by native speakers who were residents of mainland China, then transcribed into electronic files (in Chinese) for processing. Figure 6.3 presents a sample essay.

Each essay was subsequently scored holistically by two human native speaking raters, on a six-point scale (scores ranging from 1–6). An IntelliMetric model was created from the essays submitted as a training set. In addition to the training set, a separate set of 120 essays with human scores were randomly withheld for model validation purposes. A total of 613 essays were used in the evaluation: 493 for model building, and 120 for testing.

Table 6.3 provides the score distributions for the training and validation sets.

Evaluation

To determine the accuracy of the model on Chinese essay data, three different measures were compared.

在国家经济发达的时候，人们不断地制造千千万万的垃圾，堆成像一座高山。这将会对人们的健康带来有害，如果人们一直地制造垃圾。这将让政府无可奈何把垃圾都丢入海里，造成环境一片黑暗。

为了不让此事再发生，政府应该举办一项生活营活动，主题为加强青少年对环保的意识和知识。这项活动能够让青少年自由发挥他们对环保的知识以及重要性，如在会画，辩论，游戏以及其它能让青少年发挥的活动。政府也应该鼓励青少年们参加和出席对环保的意识，如收旧可以再用的物品，例如报纸，衣服等的东西。

除此之外，政府也要灌输青少年对环保意识的知识，也教导青少年如何保护环境，如何环保可以再用的东西。政府也可以通过电视上，电台上和报纸上把环保意识灌输和鼓励青少年。这将让青少年能够更快的知道对环保的知识，也能够让青少年容易看到或者听到对环保的知识。

对于学校也应该举办环保讲座会，让学生们能够知道更多的环保知识。老师也需要鼓励学生们参加环保比赛，如，打扫课室和环保考试比赛等，让学生们能够从中学习知识，和能够培养学生们的兴趣。

要加强青少年的环保意识，家长也不能够错过。家长应该从小教导和灌输环保的意识给孩子们。让孩子们能够在小时候培养对环保的习惯，使孩子们长大的时候能够把环保成为良好的习惯。

加强青少年的环保意识是人人有责的事情。青少年应该对一些细听对环保的意识以便让将多的环境良好，给于刚离的儿子和孩子能够在一个美好的环境里生活。

Figure 6.3 Sample Chinese Essay.

Table 6.3 Counts and Percentages for Training and Validation Sets

Human Scores	1	2	3	4	5	6	Total
Training Counts	39	67	65	112	142	68	493
Training Percent	7.9%	13.6%	13.2%	22.7%	28.8%	13.8%	
Validation Counts	20	6	8	14	40	32	120
Validation Percent	16.7%	5%	6.7%	11.7%	33.3%	26.7%	

Overall Mean Scores

The overall means of the human scores and IntelliMetric scores were contrasted. A general rule of thumb suggests that an accurate model will yield scores in which the overall mean calculated by IntelliMetric is not significantly different from the overall mean of the human scores.

Agreement Rates

Agreement rates between the human and IntelliMetric scores were also calculated. Scores are designated as "exact" if the IntelliMetric model and human rater agree with each other. Scores are designated as "adjacent" if IntelliMetric has exact + adjacent agreement with the human score. Finally, scores are designated as discrepant if the human and machine scores differ by two or more (non-adjacent) points.

Pearson Correlations

The Pearson Correlation between the IntelliMetric scores and human scores were also calculated. The correlation indicates the degree to which the two sets of scores covary. A high Pearson correlation indicates a very strong relationship between the scores. For the purposes of automated essay evaluation, correlations of 0.70 are considered minimally acceptable, 0.80 very good and 0.85 excellent.

Results

To calculate the agreement rate between the human rater scores and the machine scores on the Chinese data, the human rater score was averaged. If this resulted in a decimal-level score, the score was rounded to the nearest whole number. None of the differences in mean scores between the individual and rounded human scores were statistically significant.

Training Set

The agreement rates and Pearson correlations between the human–human comparisons and the average human rater score and the IntelliMetric model are shown in Table 6.4.

Additional Validation Set

The agreement rate and Pearson correlation between the average human rater score and the IntelliMetric model score on the Chinese data are shown in Table 6.5.

Table 6.4 Agreement Rates and Pearson Correlation Between Two Human Raters and Human Versus IntelliMetric on Chinese, N = 493

Comparison	Exact (%)	Adjacent (%)	Discrepant (%)	Pearson Correlation
Human–Human Agreement	43	100	0	0.95
Human–Machine Agreement	49	96	4	0.86

Table 6.5 Agreement Rates and Pearson Correlation Between Two Human Raters and Human Versus IntelliMetric on Chinese, N = 120

Comparison	Exact (%)	Adjacent (%)	Discrepant (%)	Pearson Correlation
Human–Human Agreement	56	100	0	0.96
Human–Machine Agreement	61	99	1	0.93

CONCLUSION

Overall, the results indicate that IntelliMetric is accurate in scoring the Chinese essays. In all score comparisons, all calculated scores were either exact or adjacent at 99% for the validation set. Indeed, there was only one discrepant essay in the validation set. The Pearson correlations between human and IntelliMetric scores were also very high, ranging between 0.86 (for the training set) and 0.93 (for the additional 120 essay validation set), indicating that the linear relationship between the human and IntelliMetric scores was very strong. However, the Pearson correlations between the two human raters for both the training set and additional validation set exceeded the Pearson correlations attained by comparing IntelliMetric with the average human rater score. Although overall agreement between IntelliMetric and the human raters was nearly equivalent to the agreement amongst the two raters, the small amount of discrepant scores resulted in a reduced Pearson correlation. It is possible that the atypical finding of a higher correlation for the validation set than the training set is most likely due to the distributions of 5s and 6s in validation set being higher (33% 5s and 27% 6s for validation, contrasted to 29% 5s and 14% 6s for training). Similarly, the exact agreement for human raters on the 120 validation essays was higher than for the training sets (56% versus 43%). These results suggest that in the end the training and validation samples were fundamentally different.

For both the training set essays and the validation set essays, the exact agreement between the IntelliMetric model and the human raters exceeded the agreement between the two human raters.

The quality of the training set is of the utmost importance in the IntelliMetric modeling process. It is vital that all of the following criteria are addressed to optimize the models created:

- *Include at least 300 training papers.* Although accurate models have been constructed with as few as 50 training papers, an ideal training set consists of 300 or more papers.
- *Provide sufficient coverage across each score point including the tails.* For example, on a 1–6 scale it is important to include at least 25 papers defining the "1" point and the "6" point. For a 4-point scale, it is recommended to have at least 50 papers at the score points of 1 and 4. The reason for this is the inductive nature of the modeling; without examples of a particular score point, the rubric may become truncated or IntelliMetric may not be as precise at the tails.
- *Include multiple raters if possible.* Two or more scorers typically yield better results than one scorer. Any one scorer is subject to inconsistencies that will raise confusion during the model creation process.
- *Ensure the human markers are well calibrated.* While IntelliMetric is very good at eliminating "noise" in the data, ultimately the engine depends on receiving accurate training information. If the training set is scored inconsistently, the software will not be able to accurately model the human scoring process.

For this example, the first three of these criteria were clearly met. There were approximately 500 essays used to train IntelliMetric, with a sufficient number of essays at each of the tails. Also, two raters reviewed each essay, and scored it using the same 6-point rating scale.

There are two potential areas where we believe that, if slight changes are made, the resulting IntelliMetric model would be even more robust in scoring foreign language essays. First, when an essay is determined by a human rater to be non-scorable for any reason (illegible, repetitive, or too short, for example) the essay receives a score of "0." Since this essay is not representative of an appropriate response to the writing prompt, this essay should not be included in the training set, despite one rater assigning a score. IntelliMetric is able to filter out this information to an extent, but it ultimately depends on receiving the highest quality, and most representative, set of essays with scoring information, as possible. The training set used for this study contained eight responses that received scores of "0" by one of the raters (the other rater gave them a score of 1). Had these responses not been part of the training set, the accuracy of the model may have improved slightly. In the future, only the essays which are the most representative of anticipated responses to the prompt should be included in the training set.

Second, in order for the resulting IntelliMetric model to be as accurate as possible, it must receive accurate scoring data. If the agreement between the two human raters is low, the agreement with the model is likely to be low. The agreement for the training set is of particular importance, since this data is ultimately used to create the model (the validation essays were not used to create the model). As displayed in Tables 6.4 and 6.5, the exact agreement rate between the two human raters is just 43% for the training set and 56% for the additional 120 essay validation set. This agreement rate is lower than is typically acceptable. While the agreement rate between IntelliMetric and the average human rater score exceeded the rate of agreement between the two human raters, with improvement in human scoring, it is likely that future models will be even more accurate. Typical requirements for agreement include a minimal threshold of 70% exact agreement between two human raters, with few, if any, discrepancies. If that rate is not met, additional rater training and essay re-scoring occur, ensuring that the information that IntelliMetric receives is the most accurate possible.

Despite these potential concerns, IntelliMetric was able to produce a functional model. If the concerns noted above are properly addressed, it is anticipated that new models would provide even more accurate scoring, more directly comparable to typical results seen with essays written in English.

REFERENCES

Attali, Y. (2004). *Exploring the feedback and revision features of Criterion.* Paper presented at the National Council on Measurement in Education, San Diego, CA, April.
Baum, E. B. (2004). *What is thought?* Cambridge, MA: Bradford Books/MIT Press.
Elliott, S. (2003). IntelliMetric: From here to validity. In M. D. Shermis & J. Burstein (Eds.), *Automated essay scoring: A cross-disciplinary perspective* (pp. 82–106). Mahwah: NJ Erlbaum.
Lipnevich, A. A., & Smith, J. K. (2008). *Adding praise to other forms of feedback: Does it matter?* Paper presented at the American Educational Research Association Conference, New York.
Minsky, M. (1986). *The society of mind.* New York: Simon and Schuster.
Schank, R. (1999). *Dynamic memory revisited.* New York: Cambridge University Press.
Vantage Learning. (2012). *Representative agreement rates by grade level (RB 2012–01).* Yardley, PA: Vantage Learning.

7 Applications of Automated Essay Evaluation in West Virginia

Changhua S. Rich, M. Christina Schneider, and Juan M. D'Brot

INTRODUCTION

The National Commission on Writing (2003) summarized the importance of writing in American schools: "Writing is not a frill for the few, but an essential skill for the many" (p. 11). West Virginia policymakers have focused on the importance of writing in students' education. For over 25 years West Virginia has been a leader in writing instruction and assessment. The state began a statewide, stand-alone assessment of writing in 1984. In 2005, West Virginia was among the first states to adopt automated essay evaluation (AEE) in both formative and summative assessments. In 2008, the West Virginia Department of Education (WVDE) joined the Partnership for 21st Century Skills (P21), a national organization advocating the instruction of critical thinking, problem solving, communication, collaboration, creativity, and innovation. West Virginia policymakers consider effective writing to be one of the most powerful methods of communication. As such, stakeholders prioritized writing instruction by placing it into the state's curriculum standards, the West Virginia 21st Century Content Standards and Objectives. Beginning in 2009, the WVDE made writing a sizeable part of the reading/language arts (RLA) portion of West Virginia Education Standards Test 2 (WESTEST 2), the state's assessment for accountability under the *No Child Left Behind* statute. The WVDE intended to emphasize writing through a performance task on WESTEST 2 to collect evidence of the 21st century skills of critical thinking, problem solving, creativity, and communication.

West Virginia dedicated considerable resources toward measuring student writing ability by incorporating real-life, relevant writing prompts into the state's summative assessment and by providing AEE software to help teachers measure student writing skills so they can spend more time individualizing classroom instruction. The early decision to adopt AEE technology was made based on the state's vision of 21st century skills and performance assessment, the practical need to reduce costs and improve the reliability of essay grading at the classroom level, and the desire to provide instructional feedback to teachers and students.

The West Virginia application of AEE has three unique aspects: AEE-based scoring for the large-scale state summative assessment, AEE-based scoring that connects formative assessment to summative assessment, and ongoing teacher professional development in AEE technology applications as well as teacher validation of engine scores. This chapter describes West Virginia's application of AEE technology in summative and formative assessment contexts. We begin by describing the unique challenges associated with large-scale AEE implementation in West Virginia and provide descriptions of the following:

- West Virginia's summative writing assessment, the Online Writing Assessment (OWA) program;

- the state's formative writing assessment, *West Virginia Writes™*, a customized version of CTB's off-the-shelf solution, *Writing Roadmap 2.0™*;
- the engine that powers the OWA and *West Virginia Writes™*, CTB's Bookette AEE engine; and
- results from three studies of the effect of AEE formative assessments on the summative assessments.

We close the chapter by offering discussion centered on teacher professional development, future AEE applications in West Virginia, and concluding remarks.

CHALLENGES OF AEE IMPLEMENTATION IN WEST VIRGINIA

The implementation of new approaches—especially those reliant on technology—are not without their challenges. The following section presents challenges of large-scale summative and formative AEE implementation.

Summative Assessments

In the spring of 2005, the first summative West Virginia online writing assessment was administered to 44,000 students in grades 7 and 10 over a four-week testing window. The state faced many initial implementation challenges including security of online administration, bandwidth and connectivity, lack of computer labs and technology personnel in schools, lack of teacher training in the use of AEE and technology in instruction, students' lack of keyboard skills, a shortage of writing prompts, and questions about AEE scoring accuracy. West Virginia policymakers worked to address each concern systematically, but they struggled with many issues along the way. The three major challenges were technology access; the availability of AEE technology support staff at the state, county, and school levels; and the interaction between the AEE summative and formative applications.

In 2008, the state transitioned to a more rigorous assessment, WESTEST 2, which currently annually tests more than 182,000 students in grades 3–11 using AEE. Challenges to the implementation of the AEE tools came from an access perspective (i.e., primarily technology concerns) and the degree to which sites exhibited standardized implementation. West Virginia addressed the issue by requiring mandatory online administration for WESTEST 2, which ameliorated much of the concern about technological problems in the first year's administration. However, even after seven years of AEE adoption, there is still a need to continuously reassess the capacity of the online educational system. The state provides ongoing support for increased needs for bandwidth and hardware replacement cycles that are appropriate for changing technology.

Formative Assessments

While many states are currently working to implement balanced assessment systems that link formative and summative assessments, West Virginia has provided and supported such a system since the implementation of WESTEST 2 in 2009. Since the 2009 WESTEST 2 operational application of AEE, greater attention has been paid to teachers' effective use of AEE in the classroom to support the link between instruction and assessment. To that end, ongoing professional training and day-to-day availability of the technical support staff became necessary. One crucial issue was to have sufficient personnel at the state and district levels. Because educators often ignore the availability of vendor customer support systems in lieu of speaking directly to someone in the state department, the WVDE employs a small team to (a) support the effective use, administration, and interpretation of formative tools, such as *West Virginia Writes™*, and (b) provide comprehensive and responsive support with an escalation plan to provide timely responses and solutions to any AEE user issues.

During classroom writing practice sessions, teachers need foundational information and support to effectively use the AEE score for instruction. For example, the teacher must have a clear understanding of the rubrics on which the AEE score is based. Additionally, there must be a concerted plan for how results from the tool will be used. Without an effective approach to interpreting the information, a teacher may inadvertently remove himself or herself from the instructor role and allow the student to interact with the AEE program without appropriate guidance. Conversely, a teacher may have doubts about the AEE score and be reluctant to use the AEE system. In West Virginia, it would seem that reluctance to use the AEE program stems primarily from lack of experience and/or awareness of its capabilities.

Recent research studies on the classroom use of AEE provide some insights into the formative use of AEE. Grimes and Warschauer's (2010) multisite case study in Southern California identified that teachers and students found automated scoring unreliable at times. Some teachers resisted using the automated scoring software and preferred using conventional writing instruction methods. In West Virginia, AEE is provided to all schools for formative use. However, Rich, Harrington, Kim, and West (2008) found that approximately 40–50% of students did not use AEE in the classroom. Tang and Rich's (2011) study of AEE use in Chinese English as a Foreign Language (EFL) classrooms found that AEE as a formative assessment tool, when used appropriately, can assist teachers in student-centered instruction and student independent learning. Both Rich et al. (2008) and Tang and Rich (2011) found AEE can provide a motivational function to stimulate students' writing. This finding has important policy implications because low-performing students who were disengaged or uninterested were motivated to practice writing using AEE in the classroom and in assessment settings. Teacher training, experience sharing, and professional development efforts in AEE application are necessary to assist teachers in understanding the limitations of AEE and the appropriate uses of the tool for formative assessment.

DESCRIPTIONS OF THE SUMMATIVE ASSESSMENT, FORMATIVE ASSESSMENT, AND AEE ENGINE

The following section provides a description of the summative and formative applications of AEE in large-scale settings, and presents an overview of the engine on which both applications are based. One unique aspect of the West Virginia application is the high-stakes use of AEE scores in the RLA portion of WESTEST 2, the state's assessment for accountability under the *No Child Left Behind* statute.

Summative Assessment Program: WESTEST 2 OWA

The OWA requires students to write an essay on a specific topic referred to as a prompt. The prompts were field tested in 2008 using West Virginia students in grades 3–11. Each prompt is general in nature, which eliminates the need for students to have specific content or technical knowledge in order to address the topic. The prompts were written to elicit descriptive, informative, narrative, and persuasive texts from students. For the administration of the West Virginia OWA, one prompt from these four genres is randomly given when a student logs onto the testing website.

Because the writing process includes completing a rough draft, students have the option of prewriting and revising before submitting their final draft. The assessment is not timed so that every student is given the time needed to complete the assessment within the testing session. There is an approximately nine-week testing window to accommodate school scheduling and the use of computer labs across the three levels: elementary, middle, and high school. In order to provide learning feedback and support the instructional application of WESTEST 2 data, student writing trait scores are reported along with scores on the RLA multiple-choice items in the WESTEST 2 Individual Right Response Report. Table 7.1 presents demographic information for students who used the AEE system during the 2009 administration of the WESTEST 2 RLA.

The OWA is scored using the West Virginia Writing Rubric (see Table 7.2 for the rubric for grade 8). West Virginia English/language arts professionals developed and modified grade-level appropriate criteria that best exemplify the elements of the writing process. The rubric requires that a score of 1 to 6 be assigned to each of the five analytic traits: (a) Organization, (b) Development, (c) Sentence structure, (d) Word Choice/Grammar Usage; and (e) Mechanics. The scoring rubric underpins the AEE engine training and validation process. Additionally, this same rubric is used for *West Virginia Writes*™.

Formative Assessment Program: *West Virginia Writes*™

West Virginia Writes™, a customized version of CTB's *Writing Roadmap*™, was first introduced in 2010. It is a web-based, online essay scoring tool that provides students with the opportunity for unlimited essay writing practice sessions on a variety of prompts. The WVDE made this tool available to teachers and students to reduce the time teachers spend scoring essays and to provide students with valuable practice to build writing skills and confidence. It also stimulates and encourages student interest through technology-based applications in the classroom. It has novel features including a colorful, user-friendly interface; a West Virginia scoring engine trained using sample student papers from the 2008 WESTEST 2 Online Writing Field Test; scoring based on the West Virginia Writing Rubrics; and immediate feedback.

The WVDE made a conscious decision to provide this tool to all districts in the state in an effort to concretize the link between the state's more rigorous 21st Century Content Standards and Objectives and the more rigorous WESTEST 2 assessment. Through training and use of the AEE tool, educators and administrators would have a better sense of how increased focus on writing translated to increased student expectations in demonstrated knowledge, skills, and abilities. In addition, the state hoped to exhibit the need for and benefit of a formative instructional toolset linked with the state summa-

Table 7.1 Student Demographic Information for 2009 WESTEST 2 RLA

Grade	N	Male	Female	White	Black	Hispanic	Asian	Native American	Low socio-economic status	Special Education
4	19,874	10,052	9,822	18,356	1,147	209	142	18	11,046	3,298
8	20,550	10,507	10,043	19.047	1,153	190	139	21	10,387	2,869
11	17,546	8,832	8,714	16,391	859	140	137	19	6,941	2,232

Table 7.2 West Virginia Writing Rubric, Grade 8. Copyright © 2011 by the West Virginia Department of Education

	Organization	Development	Sentence structure	Word choice/grammar usage	Mechanics
6	**Exemplary Organization** • Clear and logical progression of ideas • Strong introductory paragraph, supporting paragraphs and concluding paragraph • Sophisticated transition conveys relationships among ideas and paragraphs	**Exemplary Development** • Clear focus maintained for intended audience • Strong development of the topic for narrative and descriptive writing • Strong thesis statement for development of informative and persuasive writing • Strong use of examples, evidence or relevant details • Strong use of analogies, illustrations or anecdotes	**Exemplary Sentence Structure** • Sophisticated sentence structure; complete and correct sentences • Sentence variation ➤ Simple ➤ Compound ➤ Complex	**Exemplary Word Choice/ Grammar Usage** • Vivid, specific, economical, connotative • Consistent grammar usage ➤ Subject/verb agreement ➤ Singular/plural nouns ➤ Verb (tense and usage) ➤ Pronoun usage ➤ Adjective/Adverb	**Exemplary Mechanics** • May have minor errors ➤ Punctuation ➤ Capitalization ➤ Spelling • Needs little or no editing
5	**Effective Organization** • Logical progression of ideas • Introductory paragraph, supporting paragraphs and concluding paragraph • Purposeful transition conveys relationships among ideas and paragraphs	**Effective Development** • Effective focus maintained for intended audience • Appropriate development of the topic for narrative and descriptive writing • Appropriate thesis statement for development of informative and persuasive writing • Clear use of examples, evidence or relevant details • Use of analogies, illustrations or anecdotes	**Effective Sentence Structure** • Complete and correct sentences • Sentence variation ➤ Simple ➤ Compound ➤ Complex	**Effective Word Choice/ Grammar Usage** • Economical, specific, clear meaning, connotative • Mostly consistent grammar usage ➤ Subject/verb agreement ➤ Singular/plural nouns ➤ Verb (tense and usage) ➤ Pronoun usage ➤ Adjective/Adverb	**Effective Mechanics** • Few errors ➤ Punctuation ➤ Capitalization ➤ Spelling • Needs some editing
4	**Adequate Organization** • Some evidence of a logical progress of ideas • Introductory paragraph, supporting paragraphs and concluding paragraph	**Adequate Development** • Adequate focus maintained for intended audience • Adequate development of the topic for narrative and descriptive writing	**Adequate Sentence Structure** • Minor errors in sentence structure • Some sentence variation ➤ Simple	**Adequate Word Choice/ Grammar Usage** • Appropriate, specific, somewhat simplistic • Somewhat consistent grammar usage	**Adequate Mechanics** • Some errors ➤ Punctuation ➤ Capitalization ➤ Spelling

Table 7.2 Continued

	Organization	Development	Sentence structure	Word choice/grammar usage	Mechanics
	• Appropriate use of transition; transition between paragraphs	• Adequate thesis statement for development of informative and persuasive writing • Sufficient use of examples, evidence or relevant details • Use of analogies, illustrations or anecdotes	➤ Compound ➤ Complex (errors in more complex sentences do not detract)	➤ Subject/verb agreement ➤ Singular/plural nouns ➤ Verb (tense and usage) ➤ Pronoun usage ➤ Adjective/Adverb	• Needs editing but doesn't impede readability
3	**Limited Organization** • Limited evidence of a logical progression of ideas • Introductory paragraph and concluding paragraph with limited supporting paragraphs • Repetitive use of transition	**Limited Development** • Some evidence of focus for intended audience • Limited development of the topic for narrative and descriptive writing • Limited thesis statement for development of informative and persuasive writing • Some use of examples, evidence or supporting details • Some use of analogies, illustrations or anecdotes	**Limited Sentence Structure** • Some errors in sentence structure • Limited sentence variation ➤ Simple ➤ Compound ➤ Complex (errors in more complex sentences begin to detract)	**Limited Word Choice/Grammar Usage** • Vague, redundant, simplistic • Several inconsistencies in grammar usage ➤ Subject/verb agreement ➤ Singular/plural nouns ➤ Verb (tense and usage) ➤ Pronoun usage ➤ Adjective/Adverb	**Limited Mechanics** • Frequent errors ➤ Punctuation ➤ Capitalization ➤ Spelling • Begins to impede readability
2	**Minimal Organization/Minimal Response** • Lacks evidence of a logical progression of ideas • Lacks introductory paragraph, supporting paragraphs and/or concluding paragraph • Ineffective or overused transition	**Minimal Development/Minimal Response** • Lacks focus on intended audience • Lacks development of the topic for narrative and descriptive writing • Lacks thesis statement for development of informative and persuasive writing • Lacks sufficient examples, evidence or other supporting details • Lacks sufficient analogies, illustrations or anecdotes	**Minimal Sentence Structure/Minimal Response** • Contains fragments and/or run-ons • Minimal sentence variation ➤ Simple ➤ Compound ➤ Complex (errors in more complex sentences detract)	**Minimal Word Choice/Grammar Usage/Minimal Response** • Inadequate, imprecise, repetitive • Frequent inconsistencies in grammar usage ➤ Subject/verb agreement ➤ Singular/plural nouns ➤ Verb (tense and usage) ➤ Pronoun usage ➤ Adjective/Adverb	**Minimal Mechanics/Minimal Response** • Consistent errors ➤ Punctuation ➤ Capitalization ➤ Spelling • Impedes readability

1

Inadequate Organization	Inadequate Development	Inadequate Sentence Structure	Inadequate Word Choice/ Grammar Usage	Inadequate Mechanics
• Little or no progression of ideas; difficult to follow • Inadequate paragraphing • Little or no transition	• Unclear or no focus • Little or no development of narrative or descriptive writing • Little or no development of informative or persuasive writing • Few or no examples, evidence or other supporting details • Few or no analogies, illustrations or anecdotes	• Contains numerous fragments and/or run-ons • Inadequate sentence variation ➤ Simple ➤ Compound ➤ Complex (errors in sentence structure detract)	• Rambling, inappropriate, incorrect • Distracting inconsistencies in grammar usage ➤ Subject/verb agreement ➤ Singular/plural nouns ➤ Verb (tense and usage) ➤ Pronoun usage ➤ Adjective/Adverb	• Serious and consistent errors ➤ Punctuation ➤ Capitalization ➤ Spelling • Impedes understanding/ communication

tive assessment, to highlight how ongoing student evidence spoke to his/her summative, grade-level expectations.

Overview of the CTB Bookette Engine

CTB's Bookette "scoring engine" is an automated essay evaluation system designed to score student essays submitted online into its interface. The scoring engine provides scores for student essays by statistically modeling what trait-level and/or holistic-level scores humans would give to the essays. The CTB Bookette scoring engine scores student essays with a similar degree of reliability as one would obtain with an expert human rater. Expert human raters are senior hand-scoring personnel that monitor and read behind trained human raters in the rater pool during operational scoring. The engines use a natural language processing (NLP) system with a neural network to model expert human rater scores. The engines are trained using essays that have been scored by expert raters and validated against a separate set of papers also scored by expert raters during the model building phase. The engines are then monitored by using human-to-engine comparisons during the implementation phase for uses in which students are scored "live" for accountability purposes.

CTB has been using AEE in large-scale accountability testing contexts since 2009 and in classroom settings since 2005. CTB has expertise in building prompt-specific and generic engines. Prompt-specific engines have demonstrated high fidelity to human scoring on a prompt-by-prompt basis, but they may only be reliably used with the particular prompt for which they have been trained. Generic engines, on the other hand, are not quite as reliable as prompt-specific engines, but they generalize better to a variety of prompts, thereby allowing them to be more flexibly used in the classroom. When applied in the classroom for formative purposes, our technology provides students feedback on their writing performance. This feedback is both holistic and at the trait level by applying the scoring rubrics and providing feedback on grammar, spelling, and writing conventions at the sentence level.

Scoring Model

CTB's Bookette engines operate on approximately 90 features of student-produced text. These features may be classified as structural, syntactic, semantic, and mechanics-based. Most commonly, the features are used to model trait-level scores, which may be reported separately and/or combined to produce a total writing score. The analytic scoring guide that underpins the CTB system produces integer scores (ranging from 1 to 6 points) based upon well-recognized traits of effective writing (see Table 7.2 on p. 103):

- Organization.
- Development.
- Sentence structure.
- Word Choice/Grammar Usage.
- Mechanics.

CTB's Research

When used in a state accountability testing context, CTB's Bookette engine-to-human comparison studies typically become publically available in the program's technical report (CTB/McGraw-Hill, 2010). CTB's AEE system and supporting practices attend to validity and reliability considerations, and extensive comparisons between the scores produced by sets of expert raters and those produced by the CTB Bookette engines are analyzed. An array of statistical characteristics is examined to evaluate the quality of the scoring engine for each prompt (for a discussion, see Williamson, Xi, & Breyer, 2012). This use of multiple measures provides a more complete and global view of engine scoring validity, reliability, and quality.

CTB AEE Grammar Error Detection

The CTB Bookette system has an embedded NLP-based grammar and style error detection tool. The system detects the following eight major types of common writing errors:

1. Agreement errors (e.g., The school for boys *were* established.).
2. Missing words (e.g., Beijing is *(the)* capital of China.).
3. Extra words (e.g., You should *be* try this.).
4. Wrong words (e.g., Listen to *she*!).
5. Confusion of similar words (e.g., then versus than).
6. Wrong word order (e.g., How you *are*?).
7. Punctuation errors and white space errors (i.e., additional space between words and sentences).
8. Spelling errors.

AEE LARGE-SCALE IMPLEMENTATION HYPOTHESIS AND RESEARCH METHODS

The large-scale application of AEE in West Virginia is one of the earliest statewide implementations of AEE in high-stakes testing. In advance of implementation, we hypothesized that AEE technology would produce AEE scores that were valid and reliable for high-stakes, large-scale assessment accountability reporting. This section describes the processes and procedures used to support the validity and reliability of the AEE scores for WESTEST 2.

Validity and Reliability

The terms validation and validity have two related, yet distinct, meanings in the measurement of student learning (Kane, 2006). Validation is the accumulation of evidence to support a test score's proposed interpretation and use, and validity is a user's judgment that the validation evidence is sufficient to warrant the proposed interpretation and use. For traditional paper-and-pencil writing assessments, evidence is collected and documented in the technical report. The same is true when AEE is used to measure student writing ability.

The WESTEST 2 validation evidence (CTB/McGraw-Hill, 2010) includes:

- content-related validity supported by item maps, alignment studies, and text discussing item development procedures;
- content and instructional validity supported by content and bias reviews;
- measurement accuracy supported by measures of test reliability, measurement error, and standard-level validity;

- construct-related validity supported by dimensionality investigations and analysis of content standards;
- discriminant validity correlations between student test scores on different content area tests;
- fairness supported by examination of effect size differences of ethnic/racial group means, differential item functioning (DIF) studies, and documentation of allowable accommodations;
- procedural validity supported by descriptions of the methodology and standardized processes we use; and
- quality control procedures we undertake to eliminate construct irrelevant variability.

Beyond the traditional evidence collection, there are additional pieces of validation evidence that CTB collects when AEE is used to measure student writing ability. Kolen (2011) pointed out that the content of an assessment, the conditions of measurement, and the examinee population are the three broad characteristics of an assessment. These characteristics define the construct represented by the test scores. When AEE is used to score student essays, it is one facet of the measurement conditions. Simultaneously, AEE is also one facet of test content. Though the essay prompt remains the same regardless of whether AEE or human scoring is used, the content assessed depends on the features that the AEE engines use to model human scores. The accuracy of the modeling process also affects the content assessed by AEE. The central validity question when using AEE is whether the scores reflect what a student knows and can do in writing or whether the scores measure some other characteristics (Keith, 2003).

The reliability and validity of the AEE system essentially rests on how well expert human scores are modeled. Two main sources of rater errors are rater inconsistency and sampling bias in direct writing assessments (Breland, 1983). In the case of West Virginia's application, as well as others using CTB's AEE program, two rater scenarios are evaluated: (a) the human-to-human rater reliability upon which an engine is modeled and (b) the AEE engine-to-human rater score consistency. The AEE scoring process is uniform across all essays based on the algorithm determined during the AEE engine training. Scoring engines do not have issues such as the halo effect, fatigue, or rater drift as found in the traditional human hand scoring process (Cizek & Page, 2003), which is one of the many reasons West Virginia felt this was an amenable approach to high-stakes and instructional application of AEE. Keith (2003) wrote that correlations of AEE scores and human scores provide evidence that these scores measure the writing construct, as well as provide reliability and criterion-related validity evidence. Similarly correlations of AEE scores with scores from reading, mathematics, science, and social studies provide discriminant validity evidence. To ensure that the OWA AEE application is valid, a robust model building process provides construct validity evidence using best practices. The following section provides an overview of the model building process used for the West Virginia OWA, followed by a section on cross-validation. Using the unified concept of validity discussed previously, we provide evidence for the intended usage of the AEE scores in the WESTEST 2 high-stakes assessment. CTB's AEE engine training and validation process has been conducted under the above-mentioned principles from the literature.

AEE Model Building for the WESTEST 2 OWA

Expert human rater scores are used to train and build the AEE model. The quality of the AEE training process therefore begins with obtaining high-quality human scores that underpin the modeling process. In the 2008 field test, about 10% of the essays were double-scored by expert human raters. These human double-read scores served as the human-to-human benchmark to which AEE scores were compared in the 2009 AEE-to-expert comparison studies. In addition to providing a human-to-human benchmark, the 2008 field test scored papers were used in the modeling building process.

CTB has found it optimal to have senior hand-scoring experts create the AEE training paper set and the blind validation paper set with support provided by research scientists with expertise in AEE. Training papers at each score point should (a) have exact agreement among human raters, (b) be a unique response, and (c) represent the population that will receive AEE scores.

Although the number of papers at each score point may vary, the general expectation is to have a minimum of 60 essays for each score point. A challenge in training engines in West Virginia, and noted by Elliott (2003), is having sufficient numbers of papers to score the "1" point and the "6" point for each trait. Historically, West Virginia has less than 1% of students score a "6" on each trait of the writing rubric. Due to the large number of field test prompts administered in 2008, there were insufficient numbers of papers to train the engines to score the "6" point. To solve the problem, student essay responses from the 2009 WESTEST 2 operational test were scored by expert human raters to create additional training papers at the "6" point. These training essays were added to the training sets during the model building process to train and validate the engine before the AEE implementation of WESTEST 2 operational scoring.

Cross-Validation

Once training has been completed for a given prompt, the AEE system is ready to score the validation set. CTB typically uses about 250 responses to examine the quality of the 6-point trait AEE engine. Several inter-rater reliability statistics are used to evaluate the quality of the AEE scores. If AEE agreement rates are comparable to the human-to-human benchmarks and the engines closely model the human means and standard deviations, then the claim is made that the scoring algorithm functions at a level similar to that of two humans.

Table 7.3 presents the 2009 AEE-to-human agreement for the validation set for three grades on the West Virginia OWA. These statistical values represent a more uniform distribution and tend to be lower than those that would be found if papers were used to represent the score distribution of the census population. CTB uses a more uniform score distribution of papers in the validation work during the model building phases to assess how well the engine performs at the tails of the score distribution. Were a census population approach to be used at this stage, too few "6"-point papers would be available in the population to determine whether or not the engine was sufficiently modeling this score point. Table 7.3 shows the AEE-to-human score agreement for the exact and adjacent agreement rates. Exact agreement ranges from .39 to .74 while adjacent agreement ranges from .83 to 1.00. The quadratic weighted kappa for each trait score on each of the writing prompts ranges from .76 to .93.

Quality Assurance and Control

Quality assurance and control are essential to establishing the validity of an AEE system. Bejar (2010) described a framework researchers can use to scrutinize the AEE system for quality control. For example, Powers, Burstein, Chodrow, Fowles, and Kukich (2001) found that students can "game" some AEE systems into giving high scores by

Table 7.3 AEE-to-Human Validation Agreement for 2009 WESTEST 2 OWA

Grade	Genre	Trait	N	Weighted Kappa	% Perfect Agreement	% Perfect and Adjacent	Engine M (SD)	Expert M (SD)	r
4	Descriptive	Organization	220	0.83	58	97	3.38 (1.20)	3.36 (1.25)	0.83
		Development	220	0.85	61	97	3.40 (1.26)	3.34 (1.26)	0.85
		Sentence structure	220	0.82	58	97	3.36 (1.11)	3.47 (1.28)	0.83
		Word choice	220	0.80	57	95	3.48 (1.15)	3.53 (1.35)	0.81
		Mechanics	220	0.78	48	90	3.48 (1.25)	3.66 (1.48)	0.80
	Informative	Organization	219	0.81	61	97	3.17 (1.04)	3.33 (1.24)	0.83
		Development	219	0.86	72	96	3.19 (1.08)	3.34 (1.25)	0.88
		Sentence structure	219	0.83	63	97	3.14 (1.06)	3.33 (1.26)	0.85
		Word choice	219	0.82	60	97	3.19 (1.05)	3.37 (1.28)	0.85
		Mechanics	219	0.78	47	91	3.48 (1.23)	3.59 (1.50)	0.80
	Narrative	Organization	266	0.83	53	96	3.42 (1.40)	3.24 (1.35)	0.84
		Development	266	0.84	57	94	3.39 (1.44)	3.12 (1.47)	0.86
		Sentence structure	266	0.83	50	93	3.59 (1.54)	3.24 (1.42)	0.86
		Word choice	266	0.81	50	92	3.62 (1.40)	3.39 (1.45)	0.82
		Mechanics	266	0.84	50	93	3.68 (1.55)	3.56 (1.64)	0.84
	Persuasive	Organization	331	0.80	50	97	3.27 (1.15)	3.34 (1.29)	0.81
		Development	331	0.80	56	95	3.30 (1.33)	3.25 (1.27)	0.80
		Sentence structure	331	0.82	56	98	3.17 (1.11)	3.23 (1.27)	0.83
		Word choice	331	0.79	53	98	3.26 (1.01)	3.38 (1.21)	0.81
		Mechanics	330	0.79	48	92	3.42 (1.27)	3.61 (1.47)	0.80
8	Descriptive	Organization	167	0.85	51	99	3.51 (1.10)	3.49 (1.44)	0.88
		Development	168	0.86	52	100	3.47 (1.19)	3.52 (1.46)	0.88
		Sentence structure	168	0.84	50	98	3.70 (1.17)	3.57 (1.48)	0.87
		Word choice	168	0.80	51	96	3.51 (1.06)	3.51 (1.44)	0.83
		Mechanics	170	0.87	54	94	3.94 (1.49)	3.78 (1.68)	0.88
	Informative	Organization	135	0.87	67	96	3.33 (1.22)	3.30 (1.34)	0.87
		Development	142	0.83	61	96	3.47 (1.20)	3.37 (1.32)	0.84
		Sentence structure	137	0.88	58	99	3.64 (1.38)	3.46 (1.42)	0.89
		Word choice	142	0.86	56	99	3.55 (1.19)	3.49 (1.40)	0.87
		Mechanics	150	0.82	43	83	4.33 (1.69)	3.99 (1.80)	0.83
	Narrative	Organization	155	0.92	69	99	3.51 (1.41)	3.37 (1.46)	0.92
		Development	154	0.89	57	97	3.55 (1.50)	3.46 (1.54)	0.89
		Sentence structure	154	0.91	64	97	3.75 (1.52)	3.47 (1.58)	0.92

Grade	Genre	Trait	N	α	N	M (SD)	M (SD)	α
		Word choice	157	0.90	60	3.69 (1.39)	3.50 (1.55)	0.91
		Mechanics	156	0.89	54	3.88 (1.64)	3.57 (1.64)	0.90
	Persuasive	Organization	151	0.84	55	3.60 (1.47)	3.40 (1.43)	0.85
		Development	153	0.88	67	3.61 (1.42)	3.49 (1.49)	0.88
		Sentence structure	154	0.83	50	3.84 (1.51)	3.47 (1.46)	0.86
		Word choice	151	0.83	56	3.70 (1.32)	3.40 (1.40)	0.85
		Mechanics	162	0.83	39	4.05 (1.39)	3.86 (1.74)	0.86
11	Descriptive	Organization	199	0.86	51	3.85 (1.35)	3.85 (1.67)	0.88
		Development	203	0.88	56	3.66 (1.40)	3.88 (1.71)	0.91
		Sentence structure	191	0.89	61	3.70 (1.39)	3.84 (1.66)	0.91
		Word choice	195	0.88	59	3.75 (1.40)	3.87 (1.66)	0.90
		Mechanics	192	0.87	57	3.78 (1.54)	3.91 (1.69)	0.88
	Informative	Organization	149	0.86	59	3.34 (1.43)	3.27 (1.48)	0.86
		Development	146	0.82	61	3.26 (1.40)	3.25 (1.49)	0.83
		Sentence structure	159	0.88	62	3.40 (1.40)	3.44 (1.57)	0.89
		Word choice	155	0.84	62	3.44 (1.38)	3.39 (1.54)	0.85
		Mechanics	182	0.79	51	3.58 (1.37)	3.78 (1.70)	0.82
	Narrative	Organization	145	0.93	74	3.37 (1.48)	3.41 (1.50)	0.93
		Development	145	0.90	65	3.50 (1.57)	3.41 (1.51)	0.90
		Sentence structure	143	0.90	66	3.36 (1.54)	3.36 (1.49)	0.90
		Word choice	144	0.91	70	3.40 (1.54)	3.39 (1.50)	0.91
		Mechanics	144	0.91	69	3.33 (1.56)	3.38 (1.49)	0.91
	Persuasive	Organization	139	0.87	59	3.21 (1.25)	3.19 (1.48)	0.88
		Development	136	0.87	57	3.24 (1.34)	3.14 (1.45)	0.87
		Sentence structure	159	0.80	54	3.30 (1.27)	3.40 (1.49)	0.82
		Word choice	155	0.83	54	3.26 (1.19)	3.34 (1.49)	0.85
		Mechanics	166	0.76	49	3.40 (1.23)	3.62 (1.68)	0.80

repeating paragraphs. As a quality assurance procedure, during the validation process CTB checks the AEE scoring of condition-coded papers. These are papers that are off topic, repeat the prompt, have repetitious text, or have other non-scorable issues. In addition, content experts conduct reviews of papers with maximally discrepant scores to determine if any scoring anomaly exists that has gone undetected during the statistical reviews of the engine quality. Finally, the AEE system is reviewed during the operational test scoring implementation phase through a 5% human read behind of AEE scores. That is, 5% of the essays are randomly selected and independently scored by human raters to calculate the overall agreement rate and to determine the presence of rater drift, if it exists.

Validation After Implementation

Trapani, Bridgeman, and Breyer (2011) wrote that in order to obtain comparable AEE engine-to-human agreement results from the model building phase to multiple operational implementations for the same AEE engine, three assumptions must be met: (a) the general ability levels of examinees must be constant, (b) the features of submissions must be constant, and (c) the human rating standards must be constant. Given that the long-term goal of any assessment system is to improve student achievement, it is likely that engines may not generalize over sustained periods of time as student proficiency grows or as the distributions of the features shift over time. For these reasons, as a component of our standard quality assurance, CTB enacts an implementation study each year the AEE system is used.

Table 7.4 presents the AEE-to-human agreement for the 2009 operational implementation for three grades of the West Virginia OWA. These values are based upon a 5% second read of the census population. Because the score distribution is relatively normal, these values could be compared to the human-to-human benchmarks established for these same prompts in 2008. As indicated in the weighted kappa column, all values obtained with the engines were higher than that of two human raters except in two cases: (a) for the grade 8 informative prompt, trait of mechanics, the weighted kappa value was the same as that of human raters, and (b) for the grade 8 persuasive prompt, trait of mechanics, the value was lower than that of human raters. For grades 4, 8, and 11, AEE-to-human score agreement for exact agreement ranges from 33% to 83% and for perfect and adjacent agreement ranges from 85% to 100%. The quadratic weighted kappa for each trait score on each of the writing prompts ranges from .58 to .93. Fifty-one of the 60 traits met or exceeded 0.75.

WESTEST 2 RLA Scaling and Reporting

To report RLA scores, first, the student's total writing raw score is calculated as the sum of the five trait scores, with a maximum possible score of 30 points. These points are added to the student's raw score from the multiple-choice items. For example, the grade 8 RLA test consists of 46 items and 75 total raw points. Thirty-three multiple-choice points measure reading, 12 multiple-choice points measure writing, and 30 performance task points measure writing. Raw score-to-scale score conversation tables are used to obtain each student's scale score.

The RLA scale score is an ability estimate based on Item Response Theory (IRT). To produce raw score-to-scale score conversation tables by grade, the multiple-choice items and the writing prompt are scaled together. This is not an uncommon approach with writing items, and psychometric support exists in the literature. De Ayala, Dodd,

Table 7.4 AEE-to-Human Implementation Agreement for 2009 WESTEST 2 OWA

Grade	Genre	Trait	N	Weighted Kappa	% Perfect Agreement	% Perfect and Adjacent	Engine M (SD)	Expert M (SD)	r
4	Descriptive	Development	244	0.88*	74	99	3.11 (1.15)	3.06 (1.08)	0.88
		Mechanics	244	0.85*	69	98	3.12 (1.17)	3.03 (1.06)	0.86
		Organization	244	0.85*	72	99	3.11 (1.11)	3.01 (1.04)	0.86
		Sentence structure	244	0.85*	75	98	3.12 (1.04)	3.00 (0.99)	0.86
		Word choice	244	0.86*	73	99	3.16 (1.03)	3.04 (0.98)	0.86
	Informative	Development	241	0.90*	83	99	3.22 (1.00)	3.22 (0.98)	0.90
		Mechanics	241	0.83*	71	97	3.45 (1.15)	3.28 (1.06)	0.84
		Organization	241	0.88*	79	100	3.18 (0.95)	3.19 (0.97)	0.88
		Sentence structure	241	0.85*	76	99	3.16 (0.97)	3.10 (0.96)	0.85
		Word choice	241	0.88*	80	100	3.24 (0.93)	3.16 (0.96)	0.88
	Narrative	Development	240	0.87*	68	98	3.39 (1.23)	3.34 (1.17)	0.87
		Mechanics	240	0.82*	65	97	3.53 (1.13)	3.36 (1.10)	0.83
		Organization	240	0.81*	68	95	3.45 (1.18)	3.33 (1.10)	0.82
		Sentence structure	240	0.80*	60	96	3.51 (1.23)	3.31 (1.12)	0.81
		Word choice	240	0.82*	68	96	3.57 (1.16)	3.35 (1.08)	0.83
	Persuasive	Development	233	0.83*	69	95	3.07 (1.36)	3.10 (1.16)	0.84
		Mechanics	233	0.82*	62	96	3.27 (1.28)	3.09 (1.13)	0.84
		Organization	233	0.85*	76	97	3.19 (1.12)	3.09 (1.05)	0.85
		Sentence structure	233	0.84*	73	97	3.11 (1.08)	3.00 (1.06)	0.85
		Word choice	233	0.87*	74	100	3.12 (1.01)	3.08 (1.04)	0.87
8	Descriptive	Development	255	0.72*	69	98	3.31 (0.81)	3.31 (0.95)	0.73
		Mechanics	255	0.73*	64	96	3.41 (1.01)	3.29 (0.95)	0.74
		Organization	255	0.73*	64	98	3.34 (0.86)	3.28 (0.91)	0.73
		Sentence structure	255	0.74*	64	98	3.39 (0.89)	3.28 (0.91)	0.74
		Word choice	255	0.72*	67	98	3.31 (0.78)	3.29 (0.92)	0.73
	Informative	Development	255	0.80*	69	98	3.20 (1.00)	3.11 (0.95)	0.80
		Mechanics	255	0.65^	52	85	3.57 (1.36)	3.16 (0.92)	0.75
		Organization	255	0.77*	63	98	3.30 (0.98)	3.07 (0.90)	0.79
		Sentence structure	255	0.79*	61	100	3.35 (1.01)	3.13 (0.93)	0.81
		Word choice	255	0.77*	66	99	3.29 (0.92)	3.13 (0.91)	0.78
	Narrative	Development	259	0.77*	54	97	3.45 (1.09)	3.81 (1.09)	0.81
		Mechanics	259	0.77*	54	96	3.83 (1.28)	3.76 (1.10)	0.79
		Organization	259	0.77*	60	97	3.59 (1.11)	3.76 (1.06)	0.78
		Sentence structure	259	0.78*	57	97	3.73 (1.25)	3.75 (1.08)	0.79
		Word choice	259	0.79*	61	98	3.59 (1.16)	3.76 (1.06)	0.80

Table 7.4 Continued

Grade	Genre	Trait	N	Weighted Kappa	% Perfect Agreement	% Perfect and Adjacent	Engine M (SD)	Expert M (SD)	r
	Persuasive	Development	254	0.76*	63	100	3.44 (0.94)	3.25 (0.80)	0.79
		Mechanics	254	0.58	33	91	3.91 (1.12)	3.28 (0.82)	0.73
		Organization	254	0.75*	67	98	3.37 (0.94)	3.22 (0.78)	0.77
		Sentence structure	254	0.69*	54	96	3.63 (1.07)	3.24 (0.77)	0.79
		Word choice	254	0.71*	60	98	3.48 (0.97)	3.26 (0.80)	0.74
11	Descriptive	Development	220	0.87*	78	99	3.75 (0.98)	3.84 (1.07)	0.88
		Mechanics	220	0.90*	82	99	3.69 (1.05)	3.66 (0.99)	0.90
		Organization	220	0.86*	75	99	3.86 (1.00)	3.83 (1.05)	0.86
		Sentence structure	220	0.91*	82	100	3.72 (1.01)	3.70 (0.98)	0.91
		Word choice	220	0.89*	81	100	3.75 (0.98)	3.70 (1.00)	0.90
	Informative	Development	221	0.87*	80	100	3.37 (0.94)	3.44 (0.99)	0.88
		Mechanics	221	0.83*	72	98	3.46 (1.03)	3.44 (0.99)	0.83
		Organization	221	0.84*	72	99	3.46 (0.98)	3.48 (0.99)	0.84
		Sentence structure	221	0.85*	72	99	3.40 (1.05)	3.43 (1.02)	0.85
		Word choice	221	0.83*	70	99	3.43 (1.04)	3.41 (1.00)	0.83
	Narrative	Development	215	0.92*	75	99	3.67 (1.41)	3.61 (1.28)	0.93
		Mechanics	215	0.91*	76	99	3.60 (1.32)	3.58 (1.24)	0.92
		Organization	215	0.93*	79	100	3.53 (1.25)	3.57 (1.21)	0.93
		Sentence structure	215	0.91*	75	99	3.62 (1.32)	3.56 (1.19)	0.91
		Word choice	215	0.89*	77	97	3.60 (1.26)	3.51 (1.20)	0.90
	Persuasive	Development	224	0.88*	74	100	3.39 (1.05)	3.45 (1.03)	0.88
		Mechanics	224	0.85*	73	98	3.40 (1.12)	3.38 (1.03)	0.86
		Organization	224	0.89*	79	100	3.34 (1.06)	3.40 (1.01)	0.90
		Sentence structure	224	0.88*	80	98	3.38 (1.09)	3.38 (1.03)	0.88
		Word choice	224	0.89*	78	100	3.34 (1.01)	3.38 (1.00)	0.89

* Weighted kappa is higher than that obtained from two humans for the same prompt.
^ Weighted kappa is the same as that obtained from two humans for the same prompt.

and Koch (1991) scaled writing essays using the Master's Partial Credit Model. Breland (1996) discussed measurement of writing skills and argued that "combining assessment item types, essays and multiple choice, is a way to improve reliability." Sykes and Yen (2000) explained the advantages of scaling mixed item types using the three-parameter logistic model and the two-parameter Partial Credit Model (3PL/2PPC).

To scale the writing prompt using the 2PPC IRT model, the trait score points were averaged and rounded to the nearest integer to obtain a holistic writing score of 0–6. Sykes and Yen (2000) found that item discrimination for performance tasks scaled with the 3PL/2PPC IRT model generally decreases as the number of score points increase. The WVDE and CTB felt that scaling the writing prompt as a 6-point item rather than a 30-point item provided a good balance between item discrimination and information. Figure 7.1 shows the item category characteristic curves of the grade 8 narrative prompt by score level. Table 7.5 presents the number of students at each score point for each of the four grade 8 prompts on the 2009 WESTEST 2 OWA. As shown in Table 7.5, the narrative prompt was slightly easier than the other prompts; the *p*-values of the four

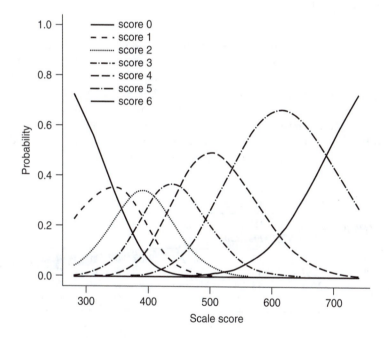

Figure 7.1 Item category characteristic curves for the 2009 Operational WESTEST 2 RLA Grade 8 narrative prompt.

Table 7.5 Raw Score Statistics for Grade 8 Writing Prompts From 2009 WESTEST 2 OWA

Writing Prompt	Item difficulty	Total N	Score level 0	Score level 1	Score level 2	Score level 3	Score level 4	Score level 5	Score level 6
Descriptive	0.54	5002	53	21	1009	1843	1747	295	34
Informative	0.53	5023	74	321	833	1322	2390	79	4
Narrative	0.58	5001	55	205	649	1388	1928	752	24
Persuasive	0.55	4990	51	132	872	1717	1729	359	130

administered prompts were 0.54, 0.53, 0.58, and 0.55, respectively. The prompts were scaled together with the multiple-choice items to obtain IRT parameters for the prompts and to provide estimates of RLA ability.

IRT model fit was evaluated using a generalization of Yen's (Yen, 1981) Q_1 statistic (Fitzpatrick et al., 1996). The fit statistics for the four grade 8 prompts are presented in Table 7.6. CTB conventionally uses both fit statistics and the graphic trace line comparison to evaluate IRT model fit for a scaled item. To adjust for differences in degrees of freedom among items, Q_1 was transformed to Z_{Q_1} where

$$Z_{Q_1} = (Q_1 - df) / (2\ df)^{1/2}.$$

The value of Z still will increase with sample size. To use this standardized statistic to flag items for potential misfit, it has been CTB's practice to vary the critical value for Z as a function of sample size. For the operational tests, which have large calibration sample sizes, the criterion $Z_{Q_1}Crit$ used to flag items was calculated using the expression

$$Z_{Q_1}Crit = \left(\frac{N}{1500}\right) * 4\ ,$$

where N is the calibration sample size. An item was considered to have poor fit if the value of the obtained Z_{Q_1} was greater than the value of $Z_{Q_1}Crit$. If the obtained Z_{Q_1} was less than $Z_{Q_1}Crit$, the item was rated as having acceptable fit. The misfit flagging criterion was 13.3 for grade 8, for example, and the AEE scored writing prompt Z-values ranged from 1.9 to 2.97 (informative and persuasive prompts, respectively) as shown in Table 7.6. None of the writing prompts selected for the West Virginia summative operational RLA test forms was flagged for misfit. In fact, we found that the AEE scored writing prompts in general had very good IRT model fit.

Table 7.6 IRT Scaling Fit Statistics for Grade 8 Writing Prompts From 2009 WESTEST 2 OWA

Writing Prompt	Model	Chi Square	Degree of Freedom	Total N	Z	Observed	Predicted	Observed-Predicted
Descriptive	2PPC	73.84	53	5002	2.02	0.5410	0.5384	0.0026
Informative	2PPC	72.51	53	5023	1.90	0.5286	0.5249	0.0038
Narrative	2PPC	82.91	53	5001	2.91	0.5760	0.5731	0.0029
Persuasive	2PPC	83.58	53	4990	2.97	0.5517	0.5494	0.0023

RESULTS OF AEE LARGE-SCALE IMPLEMENTATION STUDIES

This section examines three studies of the effect of AEE on student performance. The decision to use AEE in West Virginia was in large part driven by the ability to collect valid and reliable data on student writing ability for accountability and to report the data in an efficient, cost-effective manner to parents, students, and teachers. However, the WVDE also saw this as an opportunity to provide a different kind of support to teachers and students in the field. In this section, three research studies (Rich et al., 2008; White et al., 2010; White, Hixson, & Whisman, 2011) are described that investigated the use of AEE software for both summative and formative online writing assessment in West Virginia. The methods and results are described, showing the relationship between in-classroom writing practices using CTB's *Writing Roadmap™*, the precursor to *West Virginia Writes™*, for formative purposes and the relevant summative writing assessment.

Study 1

Rich et al. (2008) investigated the relationship between the year-end, stand-alone summative assessment administered in 2007 and the formative assessment use of *Writing Roadmap™* 2.0. The study used a quasi-experimental design. *Writing Roadmap™* users and non-users were matched based on the performance levels for the WESTEST RLA assessment. The study examined the differential performance based on community type of rural versus urban schools, gender, and ethnicity to provide insight into fairness issues in the use of AEE in West Virginia classrooms. Positive score gains on the state writing test were found for students who used *Writing Roadmap™* compared to students who did not. The largest gain was found for the lowest performing group with an effect size of 0.7. The results were statistically significant for rural, urban, female, male, and white subgroups of students (p < 0.001). One inference made from the study is that AEE technology could have an important impact on student writing in West Virginia. When AEE technology was successfully integrated into teaching and learning in the classroom, the regular practice of writing and real-time feedback raised students' writing performance. This study investigated frequency of use and did not investigate what strategies teachers implemented to make effective instructional use of the tool.

Study 2

In 2010, after five years of integrating AEE in classroom assessment and summative assessment, White et al. (2010) investigated the impact of *Writing Roadmap™* 2.0 on WESTEST 2 OWA scores. Students who had completed five or more *Writing Roadmap™* essay assignments during the 2008–2009 school year were randomly selected for the study. These students were matched to *Writing Roadmap™* non-users based on grade level, geographic location, and socioeconomic status. The final sample in the study included 8,430 randomly selected students in the treatment group and 8,430 students in the comparison group. The summative online writing test score means from the treatment groups and the comparison groups are shown in Figure 7.2. A positive association between using *Writing Roadmap™* 2.0 and student achievement as measured by the WESTEST 2 OWA was found. Effect sizes calculated using Cohen's d ranged from 0.17 for grade 9 to 0.59 for grade 4. The effect sizes tended to be larger among elementary school students compared to middle school and high school students. Based upon the findings, White et al. (2010) recommended continued use of *Writing Roadmap™* 2.0 as a formative assessment tool in West Virginia.

Study 3

White et al. (2011) analyzed the impact of AEE usage in classrooms by controlling the variance of students' prior year academic performance in RLA. A linear regression model was developed to predict 2010 online summative writing scores using five variables: number of writing assignments in *Writing Roadmap™*, male gender, low socioeconomic status, special education eligibility, and 2009 RLA scale score. These variables were chosen due to observed performance gaps in writing assessment among these subgroups

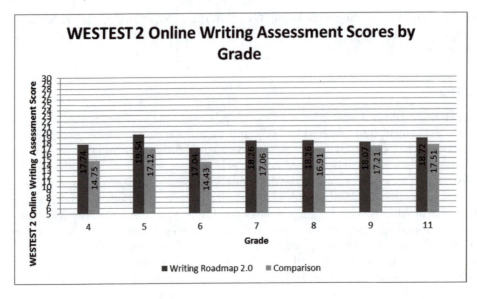

Figure 7.2 Impact of AEE classroom use on the end-of-year writing assessment. Reprinted by permission of the WVDE.

of students. Samples of 5% of the population were randomly selected from grades 4 through grade 11 based upon students who had taken the WESTEST 2.

Bivariate correlation and multiple regression analyses were performed on the sample data of 8,577 students from grade 4 through grade 11. All variables were significant predictors in the multiple regression equation and accounted for approximately 37% of variance in students' summative writing scores. White et al. (2011) concluded that even after controlling for students' prior academic achievement and gender in a representative sample, a modest but statistically significant positive relationship was found between *Writing Roadmap*™ 2.0 usage and students' subsequent online summative writing scores for grades 4 through 11, with the exception of grade 10.

DISCUSSION

This section provides discussion focused on teacher professional development, future directions, and concluding remarks.

Professional Development Supporting Implementation

When the WVDE began widespread implementation and use of AEE, there was a clear need to educate the educational community on the writing rubrics for instruction, the purpose of the assessments, the process of AEE, and the validity and reliability of the engines. One of the challenges for state adoption of AEE was to promote understanding of the limitations of and trust in AEE technology and the AEE scores. The WVDE was concerned that the statistical evidence of engine score validity would not be sufficiently convincing to teachers. Therefore, during the early years of AEE adoption, the WVDE conducted teacher believability workshops (Rich et al., 2008).

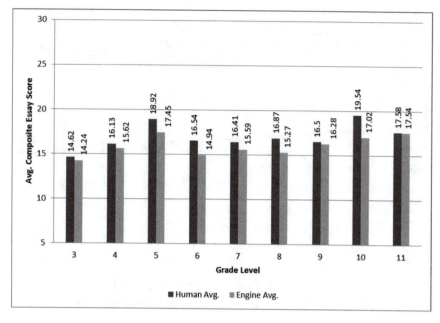

Figure 7.3 WVDE internal study of human-to-engine score means comparison. Reprinted by permission of the WVDE.

Since that time, the WVDE has conducted annual teacher workshops that support AEE-to-human score comparability studies using essays from the summative assessment (Rhudy, 2011). The purposes of these studies are to (a) provide professional development to selected West Virginia educators in the use of the West Virginia Writing Rubrics, (b) gain understanding of AEE scoring in relationship to human scoring, (c) compare West Virginia educator scores to each other's scores and to computer scores, (d) independently validate the AEE-to-human score agreement and build a research data base, and (e) make findings available to the public to assure the credibility of AEE technology.

During these workshops, teachers from the state writing committees score a set of representative essays, compare scores among themselves, and compare their scores with the engine scores. During the workshops, teacher training initially focuses on understanding engine scoring and the training process. Teachers discuss the reasons for differences and similarities in scores between teachers, and they compare those similarities and differences to scores from the engine. In addition, the WVDE uses these workshops to independently validate the WESTEST 2 AEE scores.

White, Hixson, and Rhudy (2010) reported results from the 2009 independent validation of AEE scores. As shown in Table 7.7, they randomly sampled 500 student essays per grade from grades 3–11 for a total of 4,500 student essays. Four to seven teachers scored each essay. The rounded average scores from the teachers were then compared to the AEE scores. The results shown in Figures 7.3 and 7.4 indicate that the teachers tend to agree with each other more than they do with the AEE engine and that they tend to give slightly higher scores to students on average. However, these results are not unexpected given that teachers tend to be more lenient than hand-scoring experts.

The WVDE validation exercises have provided teachers important professional development opportunities to better understand the expected quality of student writing. Through this process teachers see exemplars of student writing for each score point, and examples of good student performance are made explicit. Such opportunities are an

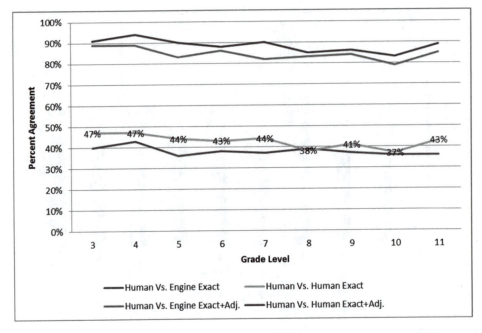

Figure 7.4 WVDE internal study of human-to-engine score agreement rates. Reprinted by permission of the WVDE.

Table 7.7 WVDE Internal Human-to-Engine Score Comparability Study: Number of Essays Selected and Number of Human Ratings per Prompt. Reprinted by permission of the WVDE.

Grade	Prompt	No. of essays selected	Total No. of human ratings by prompt*
3	Narrative	500	2642
4	Informative	500	2500
5	Persuasive	500	2527
6	Descriptive	500	2651
7	Informative	500	2562
8	Descriptive	500	2500
9	Descriptive	500	2485
10	Persuasive	500	2839
11	Narrative	500	2655
		TOTAL = 4500	

* This number varies based on the number of human scorers that scored essays within each prompt.

important step in helping each teacher reflect on the attributes of his or her own students' work and analyze how well his or her students meets the stipulated criteria, and hopefully will lead teachers to fostering better writers. These principals are consistent with the formative assessment practice of self-assessment (Andrade & Boulay, 2003).

Future Directions

It is expected that the WVDE will continue to draw upon its independent research database to conduct additional studies over time. In future teacher workshops, the WVDE may consider extending the teacher task to comparing teacher scores to scores of (a) their peers, (b) the AEE system, and (c) trained expert raters.

One important policy issue to address in future is the number of recommended uses of *West Virginia Writes™* during the school year and what pedagogical supports should be enacted to better support teachers in making instructional adaptations based on the assessment data. Tang and Rich (2011) found that pedagogical changes need to be made with AEE integration in the classroom. Currently, the WVDE finds that teachers with the lowest performing students exhibit the highest usage of *West Virginia Writes™*. There is a difference, however, between frequent and effective use of such a system.

There is little margin for error when AEE is used in the high-stakes settings. To ensure AEE score reliability and validity, quality assurance and controls are put in place to monitor engine quality to ensure high rates of agreement between AEE and human scores. AEE engines developed for classroom practice sessions do not typically have the same level of rigor as those used for high-stakes purposes. There are several reasons for this, and among these reasons are cost and capacity. For example, generic AEE engines are used for classroom assessment purposes because this allows AEE scores to be provided for teacher-created prompts. Formal evaluation of AEE score quality for every teacher-created prompt would be prohibitively expensive. Although there is often a perception that assessment data used for formative purposes can be less rigorous than those used for high-stakes purposes, this may be a necessary, albeit faulty, practice.

Teachers must make instructional decisions based upon formative assessment data. Inaccurate decisions lead to inaccurate instructional interventions and potentially lost opportunities for student learning. Thus, though high-stakes and low-stakes assessments have different purposes, the intended uses of scores are arguably equally important. However, there is a tension between the teacher-perceived need to have their prompts scored using AEE and the need for accurate information about student writing over time. This is an area that warrants future research.

Ironically, the low-stakes use of AEE may cause more public relation issues than the high-stakes use of AEE. A lack of score consistency for 5–10% of essays for each prompt administered in the classroom over time will inevitably cause teachers and students confusion and create distrust of AEE. These discrepant scores coupled with more lenient or stringent teacher scoring of student essays can make it appear to teachers that engines may provide more discrepant scores than they do in reality. For these reasons it would be optimal for the WVDE to develop professional development programs, similar to the teacher workshops described previously, which would be accessible to all teachers in the state at any time. Online training specific to diagnosing teacher-perceived discrepant scores would be optimal. Moreover, online or pre-recorded workshops designed to showcase exemplar papers and scoring standards could also be accessed by students.

Ideally, classroom teachers monitor AEE and teacher-derived scores across writing genres and across time, especially if an AEE score is unexpected or extreme. In addition, teachers need to review any essay the system flags for their review or as nonscorable. Teacher professional development and online forums for experience sharing on the topics of the interpretation of writing scores and appropriate uses of the student scores also serve to assist teachers in monitoring AEE score quality. In addition, small implementation studies are always warranted when possible.

For both the formative and summative applications of AEE, it is necessary to monitor the engine scoring accuracy as the student population increases its writing skill over time—the AEE engines trained on an earlier population may no longer generalize, thus the accuracy of the scores may degrade. It is likely in future years that the WVDE may consider small-scale studies to determine at what point both sets of scoring engines should be retrained on a student population with higher writing proficiency.

CONCLUSION

West Virginia continues to foster innovation in writing instruction and assessment. The state was quick to adopt performance-based measures of writing ability with the understanding that writing represents important 21st century skills: critical thinking, problem solving, creativity, and communication. As standards and assessments evolve, West Virginia continues to seek the best ways to assess 21st century skills. With the development and widespread adoption (45 states, the District of Columbia, and 2 territories at the time of publication) of the Common Core State Standards (CCSS), states are collectively thinking about how to push instruction through evidence-based frameworks that call for fewer, clearer, and more rigorous standards. This evolution has a direct effect on the way in which these skills will be measured in the future.

By using authentic evidence-based measures, educators may have richer evidence of students' current levels of understanding that permit them to make more precise instructional adaptations to the learning targets found in the CCSS. Such evidence will assist teachers, policymakers, parents, and students in determining whether or not students are acquiring the requisite knowledge, skills, and abilities to be competitive in the 21st century. To that end, West Virginia is considering how best to support the transition to the CCSS as well as manage and support the use of longitudinal data systems.

The five traits West Virginia uses in its scoring rubric support effective writing regardless of the content area or application. Writing has been clearly articulated as one of the main points of English/language arts (ELA) in the CCSS. The CCSS take that consideration one step further in the application of writing to non-ELA content. Specifically, the CCSS propose explicit literacy standards, which include writing, for history/social science, science, and technical subjects. To that end, West Virginia is considering whether it is feasible to use AEE outside of ELA. In practice, the vocational-technology classes could rely on AEE technology to score content-specific prompts for the foundational components of writing. This writing score could then supplement the content-specific score the technical instructor provides to the student. This application of AEE technology may have substantial merit in supporting the instructional needs of technical education students.

As AEE software and programs become more robust in their ability and reporting, the WVDE and local educational agencies will continue to collect evidence of student writing ability, potentially across content areas as described in the CCSS. West Virginia intends to continue using such data along the continuum of assessments—from formative to summative—to support both system-based and teacher-based evaluations for the improvement of schools and student learning.

REFERENCES

Andrade, H., & Boulay, B. (2003). The role of rubric-referenced self-assessment in learning to write. *Journal of Educational Research, 97*(1), 21–34.

Bejar, I. (2010). *Towards a quality control and assurance framework for automated scoring.* Paper presented at the annual meeting of the National Council of Measurement in Education, Denver, CO, May.

Breland, H. M. (1983). *The direct assessment of writing skill: A measurement review.* College Board Report, No. 83–6. New York: College Board Publications.

Breland, H. M. (1996). *Writing skill assessment: Problems and prospects.* Princeton, NJ: Educational Testing Service.

Cizek, G. J., & Page, B. A. (2003). The concept of reliability in the context of automated essay scoring. In M. D. Shermis & J. Burstein (Eds.), *Automated essay scoring: A cross-disciplinary perspective* (pp. 125–145). Mahwah, NJ: Lawrence Erlbaum Associates, Inc.

CTB/McGraw-Hill. (2010). WVDE WESTEST 2 technical report. Monterey, CA.

De Ayala, R. J., Dodd, B. G., & Koch, W. R. (1991). Partial credit analysis of writing ability. *Educational and Psychological Measurement, 51*, 103–104.

Elliott, S. (2003). IntelliMetric: From here to validity. In M. D. Shermis & J. Burstein (Eds.), *Automated essay scoring: A cross-disciplinary perspective* (pp. 82–106). Mahwah: NJ Erlbaum.

Fitzpatrick, A. R., Link, V., Yen, W. M., Burket, G. R., Ito, K., & Sykes, R. (1996). Scaling performance assessments: A comparison of one-parameter and two-parameter Partial Credit Models. *Journal of Educational Measurement, 33*, 291–314.

Grimes, D., & Warschauer, M. (2010). Utility in a fallible tool: A multi-site case study of automated writing evaluation. *Journal of Technology, Learning, and Assessment, 8*(6). Retrieved from http://www.jtla.org

Kane, M. T. (2006). Validation. In R. L. Brennan (Ed.), *Educational measurement* (4th ed., pp. 17–64). Westport, CT: Council on Education/Praeger.

Keith, T. Z. (2003). Validity and automated essay scoring systems. In M. D. Shermis & J. Burstein (Eds.), *Automated essay scoring: A cross-disciplinary perspective* (pp. 147–168). Mahwah, NJ: Lawrence Erlbaum Associates, Inc.

Kolen, M. J. (2011). *Comparability issues associated with assessments for the common core state standards.* Paper presented at the annual meeting of the National Council on Measurement in Education, New Orleans, LA.

Powers, D., Burstein, J. C., Chodrow, M., Fowles, M. E., & Kukich, K. (2001). *Stumping E-Rater: Challenging the validity of automated essay scoring GRE Board Professional (Rep. No. 98–08bP).* Princeton, NJ: Educational Testing Service.

Rhudy, V. G. (2011). Presentation on WESTEST 2 online writing comparability study. West Virginia Department of Education, Office of Assessment and Accountability.

Rich, C. S., Harrington, H., Kim, J., & West, B. (2008). *Automated essay scoring in state formative and summative assessment.* Paper presented at the American Educational Research Association, New York, NY, March.

Sykes, R. C., & Yen, W. M. (2000). The scaling of mixed-item-format tests with the one-parameter and two-parameter Partial Credit Models. *Journal of Educational Measurement, 37*(3), 221–244.

Tang, J., & Rich, C. (2011). *Online technology-enhanced English language writing assessment in the Chinese classroom.* Paper presented at the annual meeting of the American Educational Research Association, New Orleans, LA.

Trapani, C., Bridgeman, B., & Breyer, J. (2011). *Using automated scoring as a trend score: The implications of score separation over time.* Paper presented at the annual meeting of the National Council on Measurement in Education, New Orleans, LA.

White, L., Hixson, N., D'Brot, J., Perdue, J., Foster, S., & Rhudy, V. (2010). Impact of Writing Roadmap 2.0 on WESTEST 2 Online Writing Assessment Scores, Research Brief. Charleston, WV: West Virginia Department of Education.

White, L. J., Hixson, N., & Rhudy, V. (2010). WESTEST 2 Online Writing Scoring Comparability Study, Research Brief. Charleston, WV: West Virginia Department of Education.

White, L., Hixson, N. K., & Whisman, S. A. (2011). Writing Roadmap usage and additional predictors of WESTEST 2 Online Writing Scores. Charleston, WV: West Virginia Department of Education, Division of Curriculum and Instructional Services, Office of Research.

Williamson, D., Xi, X., & Breyer, J. (2012). A framework for evaluation and use of automated scoring. *Educational Measurement: Issues and Practice, 31*, 2–13.

Writing, National Commission on. (2003). The neglected "R": The need for a writing revolution. *College Entrance Examination Board*, from http://www.collegeboard.com/prod_downloads/writingcom/neglectedr.pdf

Yen, W. M. (1981). Using simulation results to choose a latent trait model. *Applied Psychological Measurement, 5*, 245–262.

8 LightSIDE

Open Source Machine Learning for Text

Elijah Mayfield and Carolyn Penstein Rosé

INTRODUCTION

Machine learning, as an approach for managing large scale challenges in text, has seen a strong uptick in interest in recent years. Tasks which were once unimaginable to automate computationally are now becoming commonplace. Few domains showcase this advancement so clearly as natural language understanding, and the application of machine learning to written text. In this work, we present LightSIDE, a software tool enabling new, non-expert users to access this technology for text assessment for the domains and tasks relevant to them.

Up to this point, access to the computational power of machine learning has largely been limited to experts in technical fields. Because of the complex statistical models required to perform machine learning, non-technical users have few ways to make use of the computational power available to them. Some tools, such as Weka (Hall et al., 2009), have made strides for general data mining. However, those tools still assume that your data is pre-formatted in a tabular format. Qualitative research software, such as MaxQDA (software for qualitative data analysis, 1989–2013, VERBI Software), allows researchers to understand data they've collected, but does not offer any way to extend that understanding to new data. In particular, this qualitative software does not reduce the labor cost of reproducing annotations and analysis on new data as it is collected (nor does it aim to), even in an identical format and domain.

One reason for this disconnect is that text data is challenging to process. Content, style, structure, and the voice of the author do not lend themselves to simplistic representation. Balancing the desire to fully represent this complexity and the practical limitations of machine learning requires an innovative approach. Researchers and industry professionals have been pushing the boundaries of this balance for years in fields such as sentiment analysis (Wiebe, Wilson, & Cardie, 2005), automated dialogue systems (DeVault, Sagae, & Traum, 2011), and facilitating collaborative learning (Mu, Stegmann, Mayfield, Penstein Rosé, & Fischer, 2012) and online groups (Mayfield, Adamson, & Penstein Rosé, 2012).

Our primary focus in this chapter will be on the particular task of automated essay evaluation. Automated scoring systems which are specialized to this task are numerous and effective (see Burstein et al., this volume). However, we wish to focus on the general techniques that can be used to solve this problem. This chapter explains our task-agnostic approach to automated evaluation of texts using machine learning. LightSIDE, the software package this chapter centers on, provides the user interface to follow that approach.

For the remainder of this chapter, we begin with an introduction to machine learning, with a focus on iterative, data-driven development of representations of text data. The models resulting from machine learning must be effective at reproducing human assessment, which requires weighing the complexity and thoroughness of a representation against the generality of that representation. We introduce the workflow used within LightSIDE, which moves from a set of scored texts to a trained model, and show how this workflow generalizes to a variety of tasks. We describe the ways that this workflow excels, particularly through detailed error analysis, in assisting non-expert users in achieving a balance of representation complexity and generality. We then present three case studies of ways that LightSIDE has been used. The first two focus on essay assessment, while the third applies machine learning to contributions in a collaborative learning environment. We conclude by discussing the advantages of a general framework for applying machine learning techniques to text.

SUPERVISED MACHINE LEARNING

Recent years have seen an explosion in interest in machine learning technologies (Mitchell, 1997). While artificial intelligence more generally captures the notion of computers understanding and interacting with their environments, machine learning is a particular subset of that research with an emphasis on two points. First, machine learning emphasizes well-defined, specific tasks with well-defined inputs and outputs, where some *classifier* performs the mapping between these two stages. Second, machine learning requires that the decisions made by the classifier are based on empirical evidence from examples it has seen before—*training data*. The function that takes this training data and optimizes the mapping used by a classifier based on those examples is called an *algorithm*.

In this work, we focus on machine learning algorithms as they can be applied to text input. This excludes entire fields of work on computer vision (Sebe, Cohen, Garg, & Huang, 2005), audio processing (Chiu, Raj, & Stern, 2009), and purely numeric data, as might be present in a database. What this allows us to do, though, is focus on the question of representation. The most challenging problem for improving performance of classifiers for text is this representation of data, so it will be the first focus in the remainder of this section.

INPUT

Machine learning algorithms can only work with objective data, such as numbers or labels. In reality, text does not naturally fit into a series of numeric values. The challenge for machine learning researchers, then, is to identify how to simplify an input into some representative set of these objective values. This set of *features* is a simplified representation of reality. Each individual feature attempts to answer one question about the input data, in a way that can be represented objectively. Before a text can be used at all by machine learning, it must be replaced with the features to be used to represent that text.

The simplest feature of text possible may be a count of the number of words the text contains. This feature functions as an objective measure of the text's length. In this case, the mapping between reality and representation is simple. However, what if we want objective values describing the *content* of a text? What single numeric value can represent that question effectively?

In short, the answer is that one number cannot capture content. Instead, a set of many features must be used to approximate that content. As an example, consider the "bag of words" representation (also known as "unigrams"). Each feature in a bag of words corresponds to a single word, and takes on a value of 1 if that word is present in the text, and 0 if the word is not present. This simple representation has proven to be surprisingly robust and is the basis of more complex, specialized methods such as latent semantic analysis (Foltz, 1996) and topic modeling (Blei, Ng, & Jordan, 2003).

While robust, the bag of words representation of a text is only a baseline for most tasks. An advantage of state-of-the-art machine learning algorithms is that they are not limited to a particular set of features. Instead, they allow any arbitrary representation of an input. This enables researchers to design task-specific features based on domain knowledge and experience. As examples of this type of feature specialization, researchers have designed targeted lists of vocabulary for specific tasks (Pennebaker, Booth, & Francis, 2007) or methods for domain-specific specialization of existing groups of features (Daumé III, 2007).

LightSIDE allows users flexibility in choosing what set of features are best suited to their task. Both the length feature and unigram bag of words features are available through the user interface, as are additional configurations for adjacent pairs of words (bigrams), which capture phrases; part-of-speech tags, which approximate sentence structure and grammaticality; and other more specific options such as stopword removal (non-contentful words such as "the" or "in") and stemming (removing verb tense, pluralization, and other grammar forms from words).

Beyond these basic features, LightSIDE is open source and designed for easy extension through plugins. With minimal programming, new features can be designed and added to a model without having to rewrite every other step of the machine learning process. LightSIDE is distributed with a small number of these plugins as examples for interested users with programming backgrounds; for instance, one plugin allows users to define search queries using regular expressions (the value of the resulting feature, for each query, matches whether that query was successful on a given input text). Another finds "stretchy patterns" (Gianfortoni, Adamson, & Rosé, 2011), a formal method for matching sequences of nearby words in a text without needing them to be exactly adjacent. In addition to examples, the LightSIDE users' manual offers guidance for creating these plugins.

Whatever the representation, the result is the same: an input text has been transformed in some way such that the original content has been replaced with the features extracted from that content. It is with this new representation that machine learning can map the input to a label. That process is described in the next section.

OUTPUT

After a text has been converted to a set of features, LightSIDE's workflow assumes that some label should be assigned to each text. In some tasks, this label is the numeric score that the text should receive, but in other tasks the label can be *nominal*, meaning that exactly one of a set of possible outputs is chosen. A nominal task might be Boolean, offering exactly two choices, or it may have multiple options.

The purpose of the features extracted from a text is to determine the label that is most appropriate for a document. In the case of a numeric output, features can only direct the model in one direction—either the feature is indicative of higher scores or lower scores. This is identical to the way variables are used in regressions and, in fact, one classifier available within LightSIDE is a linear regression (using all features of a text as variables). On the other hand, in a classification task, a feature might be present almost exclusively in one class, resulting in a high-confidence indicator that this label should be chosen by the classifier; or a feature might be equally common among all classes, meaning that the feature should not be highly valued by the classifier.

To make this example more concrete, we return to the example task of essay evaluation. If this task were to be treated as having a numeric label, the output would be a single number representing the quality of the text. Each feature of the text would have to be used by a classifier to indicate whether the essay was of higher or lower quality. On the other hand, in a nominal classification, each possible score would have to be enumerated (such as an A–F scale). A feature then might appear almost exclusively in examples which were assigned a grade of A; or appear commonly in essays with grades of C, D, or F, but very rarely in essays with a grade of A or B; or evenly distributed throughout. In a binary decision, on the other hand, a single choice would have to be made—is this essay of suitable quality, or does it fail to meet that standard? This representation is more well-suited to targeted evaluations and is discussed in greater detail in "Trait-Based Essay Assessment" later in this chapter.

We are now equipped with both our input (a set of features representing relevant facets of a text) and output (a single label corresponding to the task we are attempting to automate). The mapping between them can then be learned from training data. This is the most important element of the machine learning process. Rather than hand-crafting rules determining which features should be used and in what way, a set of examples allow this to be learned.

LightSIDE offers a number of algorithms to perform this learning, primarily using implementations of classifiers from Weka (Hall et al., 2009). Exhaustively describing that learning process is outside of the scope of this chapter, but to establish an intuition, we provide a summary of two example classifiers: the Naïve Bayes model and linear support vector machines.

In a Naïve Bayes classifier, two factors are considered. First, the model learns the probability of each possible label, without regard for the features of a text. Therefore, all else being equal, the model will tend to assign labels that were more frequent in training data it observed. Then, for each possible label, the model estimates the probability that the observed features of a text would have occurred. These probabilities, again, are derived from training data. After making this estimation for each possible label, the label with the highest probability is chosen.

Alternatively, consider the linear support vector machine classifier. In this case, for a given label, a model is trained comparing that label to all other possible labels. Remember, if this is an A–F nominal classification, then a model will be trained to discriminate grades of A from grades of B; a separate model will be trained to discriminate A from C; and so on for every possible pair. In each of these models, each feature will be assigned a weight (similar to a linear regression). This weight assigns relative value to the presence of that feature, in the direction of one choice or another. For instance, the A vs. C model might determine that a particular vocabulary item is much more indicative of A essays, and assign it a high weight in that direction. After summing the weights for all features present in a text, a final value is reached for each of these pairs, with weights for one option outweighing the other. In the Boolean classification task, of course, choosing a label then amounts to selecting the label with more weight. In multi-class nominal problems, the final label is chosen based on which label was selected in the largest number of pairings.

This is nowhere near a thorough representation of LightSIDE's algorithms; for further detail consult Hall et al. (2009). Instead, it is meant to give an intuition to possible ways that the mapping from features to label can be performed.

ERROR ANALYSIS AND COMPARING MODELS

One stumbling block for new users of machine learning software is the complexity of the models like those outlined in "Output," above. Because most classifiers use some elements of probability, there is a barrier to entry for non-technical users. In LightSIDE, as features are extracted, their ability to predict labels in the data is assessed and reported to the user, and as models are trained, their accuracy is laid out to the user, along with details about the types of errors that model makes.

Whenever possible, LightSIDE reports classifier and feature performance based on behavior, not the internal structure of a classifier. This allows for a unified interface across many different types of classifiers, and requires only minimal mathematical intuition. The foundation of this reporting is the confusion matrix, as shown in Figure 8.1. In this example, from an essay evaluation task with an A–D nominal grading system, the system reported that 183 of the 1,772 training documents were labeled with an A grade by the model and were given the same A grade by humans. In contrast, there were only two cases where the model predicted a grade of A, but human graders assigned a grade of D. Thus, our representation of error is fundamentally based on comparing a confusion matrix's columns (predictions from the trained model) and rows (actual distributions of labels).

The remainder of LightSIDE's error analysis interface is built on this analysis framework. One question that might be asked, for instance, is the difference between those examples that the model correctly assessed and those where it made an error. The distribution of individual features is also visible. As an example of how this might be useful, a feature appearing almost exclusively in a single column of the confusion matrix is likely to be key in the model's predictions for that particular label. By clicking on a given error cell in the confusion matrix, the interface ranks features based on their proneness to error.

We make a distinction between *horizontal* and *vertical* error-prone features. Understanding this distinction begins with the understanding that examples along the diagonal of the confusion matrix are ideal output, the cases where model output matched human assessment perfectly. For each row and column, then, we can compare the examples along the diagonal with any other given cell in the matrix table. A horizontal comparison, then, compares across rows—training input assigned the same human-assessed label but which appeared different to the model. Ranking features by horizontal comparison describes what makes those incorrectly labeled texts appear most different from the correctly classified texts. In contrast, a vertical comparison is concerned with cells within the same column, texts assigned the same label by the

Model Confusion Matrix:

Act \ P...	A	B	C	D
A	183	65	3	2
B	106	366	96	2
C	8	105	335	189
D	2	17	76	217

Figure 8.1 Model confusion matrix.

model even though they were labeled differently by humans. In this case, then, it is similarity that is most interesting. The goal of such a comparison is to identify those features appearing the same in examples in the entire column, despite occurring in texts assigned different labels by humans.

Understanding the relationship between features and predicted labels is key to improving performance of a model. Features with large discrepancies in horizontal comparison identify the attributes or places in a text where distinctions are being drawn incorrectly, while identifying similarities in vertical comparison gives intuition to what features are most common to examples where the model is making predictions corresponding to the targeted column's label. Notably, the intuition gained from these comparisons is agnostic to the classification algorithm used, meaning that comprehensive understanding of the underlying algorithms is not necessary for an initial intuition into the behavior of the resulting model. Improvement of the features representing a text can be based on this intuition.

EXAMPLE APPLICATIONS

LightSIDE has been developed with the explicit purpose of being easily applicable to new domains and to problems that are specific to a researcher. A question remains, though: in practice, how flexible is this workflow? Can it be applied quickly to a specific task? We now seek to answer that question through a series of studies.

In the first study, we evaluate LightSIDE in the context of holistic essay assessment, where a score assigned to an essay does not correspond to a particular trait or attribute but instead provides a rough overall judgment. The second study still focuses on student responses to prompts, but specializes the task. It questions whether individual constructs are present in a text, providing not just an overall assessment but a targeted evaluation of understanding. That study also tests the generality of these models, showing the extent to which models may generalize based on different examples or populations. Finally, we provide an example applying LightSIDE to a collaborative learning setting. Individual utterances from an online chat conversation were tagged for information sharing behavior; the resulting annotations provide a useful, automated representation of student interactional styles in small groups.

For each study, we will follow the same general pattern. We describe the context in which the study took place and outline the aims of the research. The features extracted and the models used by LightSIDE are specified. Then, we discuss the results, in terms of LightSIDE's accuracy, and implications that these results have on the use of automated assessment in general.

HOLISTIC ESSAY ASSESSMENT

In early 2012, LightSIDE was invited to act as a vendor in the Hewlett Foundation's study on automated assessment of student essays. This study was framed as a comparison of the state of the art in essay assessment, to inform decision making and policy by giving a robust comparison to human scorers. In addition to LightSIDE, eight commercial vendors were invited, collectively representing over 95% of the market in this field. The organizers of this competition collected a large number of essays from eight different long-form prompts; participants in the competition, which included multiple commercial vendors in addition to LightSIDE, were asked to build models to evaluate responses to this prompt, given the large number of available examples. Performance would be compared against agreement between humans. The full details of the study are reported in Shermis & Hamner, 2012.

The eight prompts provided in this study represented a wide range of scenarios. Some were source-based, requiring students between seventh and tenth grade to read from an excerpted text before writing, while others were more open-ended, fitting into common structures such as persuasive essays. In one case, essays were graded on two different rubrics, one in terms of writing style and the other measuring content quality; however, by and large the study involves holistic scoring only.

Each model was trained only on the data sets provided for each prompt, ranging from 918 to 1,805 example essays. Scoring ranges also varied between prompts, ranging from as small as a 4-point scale up to a 60-point scale. After experimentation, models trained by LightSIDE for this study used only unigram and part-of-speech (POS) bigram features (as described in "Input," above). Only the 500 most predictive features were used, as evaluated using a χ^2 statistical test. The classifier was trained using the Naïve Bayes model. Testing other algorithms demonstrated weaker performance; this was especially evident through LightSIDE's error analysis interface. With a linear support vector machine, for instance, frequent classes were overemphasized; if more scores in multiples of 5 were prevalent in the 60-point scale, for instance, the support vector machine (SVM) would overcompensate for this imbalance and group a larger number of responses into those categories. Naïve Bayes, on the other hand, had a more even distribution (while still taking prior label probabilities into account).

For the purposes of this chapter we report agreement using Pearson r correlation. The specific details of these examples are not vitally important; they serve only to provide context for the task. Human agreement on this task was reasonably high, from a low of 0.61 r on the 60-point data set to a high of 0.85 r on one of the source-based, 4-point data sets. LightSIDE's performance, when compared to the human consensus score, ranged from a low of 0.64 to a high of 0.81, with an average across all datasets of 0.75 r. On five prompts, LightSIDE's reliability exceeded inter-rater agreement between humans; in only one case was performance substantially below human agreement.

This study generalized across a great number of mitigating factors. Specific conclusions about the benefits and drawbacks of the model are therefore hard to draw. Instead, we can make a different and more general claim. In this study, various difficulties came into play regarding data sources, transcription processes, scoring patterns, and other logistic issues regarding the essays. Despite these difficulties, LightSIDE's performance was remarkably high, matching or exceeding human performance nearly universally. This suggests that the representations and models used by LightSIDE are very robust to the technical challenges of data collection.

TRAIT-BASED ESSAY ASSESSMENT

A drawback of the previous study is that it is overly broad. Models did not seek to identify particular aspects of the content of essays. However, in the next study (originally reported in Ha, Nehm, Urban-Lurain, & Merrill, 2011 and Nehm, Ha, & Mayfield, 2012), these more specific issues were brought to the forefront and studied in great detail. The end result showed that across a large number of variations in conditions, the classifiers trained by LightSIDE were robust and effective. Those conditions are detailed in this section.

For these studies we focus particularly on the domain of biology essay assessment. Students (all college undergraduates) were given a prompt requesting an explanation of trait gain and loss in species. Classifiers were built which assessed not a holistic score, but instead whether an essay contained an individual concept considered key to the curriculum. For instance, one classifier was trained to detect whether a student displayed satisfactory understanding of the heritability between generations of variation in traits.

The purpose of this study was not just to assess whether such models could be built reliably; it also tested the limits of the generality of these models. In the most straightforward case, a single population of students was given a prompt, and a model was trained; then a new set of students from that same population responded to the exact same prompt. Classification was performed using LightSIDE, using unigrams and line length as features, and a linear support vector machine as the classification algorithm. As hoped, performance was near perfect, with agreement above 0.9 kappa (which measures agreement beyond chance). The question, then, became one of generality.

One evaluation of robustness is based on the precise example given to a student. In this study, prompts were given examples from one of four different species: an elm, a penguin, a rose, and a snail. The constructs to be described by students were the same in each case. The second experiment involved training a model that was general across all four examples; performance remained high, above 0.8 kappa in most cases. Next, models were evaluated when tested on examples they had never seen before; for instance, a model might be trained on examples of snails, roses, and penguins, and tested entirely on essays responding to an example of elm trees. Because the training data contained varying examples, the classifier was still able to find generalizable features describing each construct. Performance remained high, with kappa agreement still above 0.8 in most cases. In the most challenging case, classifiers were trained on responses to a single example—for instance, a classifier might be trained exclusively on rose examples, but tested exclusively on snail examples. In this case, the robustness of the model became more dependent on the construct being identified. When predicting the construct "presence and variation of traits" classifier agreement remained above 0.8 kappa, while the construct "differential reproduction and survival of individuals" was more reliant on the particular example trained, resulting in cross-example performance nearer to 0.5 kappa.

After evaluating the generality of a model based on the exact prompt given to a student, the study went on to test more practical issues. For instance, LightSIDE was tested when assessing the same core concept, using the same example, but with human assessors trained on a different instrument. This captures whether these classifiers are being trained specific to a particular grading rubric or whether they are truly learning a general model for identifying a core construct. Again, results were studied at a fine-grained level based on the number of varying examples given to the classifier as training data. When all four species were included in the training data, the drop in performance when LightSIDE's classifiers were tested on a new instrument was around 0.1 kappa, dropping performance from above 0.9 to above 0.8, still resulting in highly predictive classifiers. When trained on individual examples, however, the LightSIDE models did not transfer well; performance dropped to merely moderate agreement above chance. What this suggests is that when presented with robust training data, LightSIDE was able to build classifiers which mapped more generally to key concepts; when presented with very narrow examples, LightSIDE tended to overfit to the rubrics used by human graders.

Classifier performance was also tested on varying answer lengths. Testing examples were divided into quintiles; it was found that performance became erratic only in the shortest 20% of responses, with very high performance (above 0.9 kappa) among the 80% of responses making up the top four quintiles.

LightSIDE was then tested in new student populations. In particular, two variations were studied: classifiers trained on responses from students within a biology major and tested on responses from non-majors (or vice versa), and responses collected on a different campus from the location where training data was collected. Across five of the six constructs tested, it was found that neither of these conditions affected classifier performance, with performance remaining high in all conditions.

The one case where performance varied strongly between different conditions is instructive for a different reason: a skewed distribution of labels. Only a very small number of students, less than 5% of the total number of collected responses, were labeled by human assessors as having demonstrated that construct. Thus, performance as measured by percent accuracy was very high, and agreement as measured by kappa was substantially lower than among other constructs. Thus, while student population did not affect model performance, the design of the constructs themselves was more sensitive.

Overall, this study proved the effectiveness of LightSIDE for the task of identifying key constructs in written responses. Across varying examples, assessment instruments, response lengths, and student populations, trained classifiers were able to replicate human assessment with very high agreement. Particular cases where the classifier performance was weakest were highlighted, especially models trained on only a single example prompt, and tested in unusual conditions such as across campuses or against humans assessing a concept with a different instrument. These examples are instructive for designing scenarios where machine learning may be used within a curriculum.

APPLICATION TO COLLABORATIVE LEARNING

The results described above have shown that when given a large amount of long-form, asynchronous essays, machine learning can reproduce the evaluations of humans reliably. They show that the use of machine learning is robust against different methods of data collection and against variations in the exact population that produced that data. However, they do not address the challenge of applying LightSIDE to a new domain entirely.

In Howley et al., 2012, we showcase the use of LightSIDE for automated analysis of collaborative learning discussions. To understand how this is comparable to essay assessment, and how the same framework can be applied in both contexts, we revisit the notion of inputs and outputs.

The setting for this study was an online chat room between students, facilitated by a computerized and scripted intelligent agent participating in the conversation. The participants, undergraduate college students, were instructed to discuss the construction of a power plant. The goal of the study was to characterize the effect of group composition on certain student behaviors and attributes, such as self-efficacy (Bandura, 1997). To facilitate this analysis, conversation transcripts were annotated and the behaviors of students were analyzed. This annotation scheme was based on the Negotiation framework from Systemic Functional Linguistics (Martin & Rose, 2003), a branch of discourse analysis that pays special attention to the social roles between speakers.

These annotations differ from the evaluations performed in the previous two sections. While those texts were well-formed responses written and edited by students with the intention of being assessed, conversational transcripts have an entirely different structure. Student writing is impromptu and is not polished or structured for evaluation from an instructor. Instead, a text may consist of a short phrase or even lack words entirely (such as a line of chat consisting of an emoticon). The features extracted from these texts are therefore much sparser; however, the same methods for extracting those features, such as a unigram model, can be applied with no adjustment. The labels being considered for output, similarly, are no longer the same domain. Rather than assign an evaluation or score to a text, the classifier's goal is merely to describe the line of dialogue in a single, coarse-grained label, such as "requesting information" (a label usually applied to questioning lines of chat).

The complexity of this domain makes it a useful test bed for error analysis capabilities of LightSIDE. For instance, a major difference between this domain and essay assessment is context. The output label of one line of a dialogue is related to the output of the previous line, a marked difference from the arbitrary ordering of a set of essay responses. In error analysis, it became apparent that this context was not being captured by a bag-of-words feature space or any default options available in LightSIDE. Singling out individual lines of dialogue indicated that short utterances like "Okay" could have entirely different labels based on whether they were answering a question, indicating attentiveness, or trying to grab attention when initiating a long claim. These multipurpose acknowledgments dominated certain cells when viewed as a horizontal comparison, and new features (taking context into account) had to be designed. The new model included features representing a comparison of the length between the current turn and the previous turn, a measure of vocabulary similarity from one line to the next, and the predicted label of the previous turn (using a simpler machine learning model), amid others. The full model, with that contextual information, approaches human reliability in annotating conversations in multiple domains (Mayfield & Rose, 2011; Mayfield et al., 2012).

These results assume that human-labeled examples already exist both to train the model and to compare effectiveness of different algorithms and features. If an annotation task such as this were being performed for the first time, LightSIDE would not be particularly effective. LightSIDE requires ample training data in order for classifiers to effectively reproduce human labels. However, in this study, we had an advantage. The annotations that we wished to reproduce had already been applied to data from a previous year's study in the same domain (Howley, Mayfield, & Penstein Rosé, 2011). This meant that training data existed and could be applied to new data instantaneously. Scenarios such as this serve as an effective use case for LightSIDE, in a task where the same styles of conversation, in similar domains, are occurring over time in different classrooms with new students.

CONCLUSION

In this chapter, we have attempted to describe the use and practice of supervised machine learning for text data in an educational context. By breaking down the machine learning "black box" into its component parts and shedding light on each step of that process, our goal is to demystify the state of the art and provide a stepping stone for interested researchers. This process is exemplified within the LightSIDE workflow, which mirrors this process of feature extraction and classifier training, along with tools for error analysis and understanding of the behavior of classifiers.

One of the most important attributes of the LightSIDE framework is that it is open source. Users can extract features, build models, and label new data entirely through the interface if they desire, but they are not limited to the basic representations available in that interface. Instead, LightSIDE actively encourages new feature extraction and machine learning technology. This allows the LightSIDE architecture to be rapidly adjusted to new problems and to be used for a wide variety of research interests.

We demonstrated this flexibility here with three example applications. First, we showed that for a holistic essay evaluation task, LightSIDE agreement with human graders is at approximately human levels of reliability. Next, we showed that individual traits could be detected effectively across a very wide variety of conditions. Finally, we showed that this architecture is not limited to long-form, edited essays, but can be applied to texts of many different lengths, down to individual lines of chat in a collaborative learning dialogue.

With this level of flexibility in hand, many communities can advance because of the tools LightSIDE makes available. Researchers in education can continue to explore the implications of automated assessment and its application to new, exciting domains such as collaborative learning. Experienced machine learning researchers can use LightSIDE as a test bed for new feature representations, free of the burden of constructing an end-to-end pipeline for machine learning and prediction. Real-world practitioners can make use of LightSIDE's current, high-accuracy evaluation to implement automated assessment in real-world applications. Even more excitingly, the use of a shared platform between these communities can bring forth new collaborations built on vocabulary and understanding of shared processes that can only come with a unified technology framework.

REFERENCES

Bandura, A. (1997). *Self-efficacy: The exercise of control*. New York: Freeman.

Blei, D. M., Ng, A. Y., & Jordan, M. I. (2003). Latent Dirichlet Allocation. *Journal of Machine Learning Research, 3*, 993–1022.

Chiu, Y., Raj, B., & Stern, R. (2009). *Towards fusion of feature extraction and acoustic model training: A top-down process for robust speech recognition*. Paper presented at the Interspeech.

Daumé III, H. (2007). *Frustratingly easy domain adaptation*. Paper presented at the Association for Computational Linguistics.

DeVault, D., Sagae, K., & Traum, D. (2011). Incremental interpretation and prediction of utterance meaning for interactive dialogue. *Dialogue and Discourse, 2*(1), 143–170.

Foltz, P. W. (1996). Latent semantic analysis for text-based research. *Behavior Research Methods, Instruments and Computers, 28*(2), 197–202.

Gianfortoni, P., Adamson, D., & Rosé, C. P. (2011). *Modeling of stylistic variation in social media with stretchy patterns*. Paper presented at the Workshop on Modeling of Dialects and Language Varieties at the Conference on Empirical Methods in Natural Language Processing.

Ha, M., Nehm, R., Urban-Lurain, M., & Merrill, J. (2011). Applying computerized scoring models of written biological explanations across courses and colleges: prospects and limitations. *CBE-Life Sciences Education, 10*(4), 379–393.

Hall, M., Franke, E., Holmes, G., Pfahringer, B., Reutemann, P., & Witten, I. (2009). The Weka Data Mining Software: an update. *ACM SIGKDD Explorations, 11*(1), 10–18.

Howley, I., Adamson, D., Dyke, G., Mayfield, E., Beuth, J., & Penstein Rosé, C. (2012). *Group composition and intelligent dialogue tutors for impacting students' academic self-efficacy*. Paper presented at the Intelligent Tutoring Systems.

Howley, I., Mayfield, E., & Penstein Rosé, C. (2011). *Missing something? Authority in collaborative learning*. Paper presented at the Computer Supported Collaborative Learning.

Martin, J., & Rose, D. (2003). *Working with discourse: Meaning beyond the clause*. London: Continuum.

Mayfield, E., Adamson, D., & Penstein Rosé, C. (2012). *Hierarchical conversation structure prediction in multi-party chat*. Paper presented at the SIGDIAL Meeting on Discourse and Dialogue.

Mayfield, E., & Rose, C. P. (2011). *Recognizing authority in dialogue with an integer linear programming constrained model*. Paper presented at the 49th Annual Meeting of the Association for Computational Linguistics: Human Language Technologies.

Mitchell, T. (1997). *Machine learning*. Boston, MA: McGraw-Hill.

Mu, J., Stegmann, K., Mayfield, E., Penstein Rosé, C., & Fischer, F. (2012). The ACODEA Framework: developing segmentation and classification schemes for fully automatic analysis of online discussions. *International Journal of Computer Supported Collaborative Learning,* *7*(2), 285–305.

Nehm, R., Ha, M., & Mayfield, E. (2012). Transforming biology assessment with machine learning: automated scoring of written evolutionary explanations. *Journal of Science Education and Technology, 21*(1), 183–196.

Pennebaker, J., Booth, R., & Francis, M. (2007). *Linguistic inquiry and word count: LIWC2007.* Austin, TX: University of Texas at Austin.

Sebe, N., Cohen, I., Garg, A., and Huang, T. (2005). *Machine learning in computer vision.* Berlin: Springer.

Shermis, M. D., & Hamner, B. (2012). *Contrasting state-of-the-art automated scoring of essays: analysis.* Paper presented at the National Council on Measurements in Education, 2012, Vancouver, BC.

Wiebe, J., Wilson, T., & Cardie, C. (2005). Annotating expressions of opinions and emotions in language. *Language Resources and Evaluation, 39*(2–3), 165–210.

9 Automated Short Answer Scoring
Principles and Prospects

Chris Brew and Claudia Leacock

INTRODUCTION

In educational assessment, there is an obvious role for the short answer item as a complement not only of longer essays but also of the traditional selected response item. It is now well established that automated scoring can contribute to the reliability, feasibility, and cost-effectiveness of large-scale essay grading. Can automated scoring do the same for the short answer? In our view, the answer to the question is a qualified "Yes." The purpose of the present chapter is to introduce the technology, explain some of the uses to which it can be put, and indicate why our generally positive conclusion still has to be qualified. We will refer primarily to Educational Testing Service's (ETS's) c-rater engine, because that is what we know best. The main points of this chapter are:

1. Short answer items are not the same as essays. Typical essay tasks emphasize grammar and mechanics, while typical short answer tasks emphasize content. Also, there is much more variation between short answer rubrics than there is between essay rubrics.
2. Along with the substantive differences between essays and short answers come corresponding differences in the technological approaches that are needed. One reason for the difference is the simple fact that short answers are short, and therefore usually contain a smaller amount of exploitable information than do longer responses.
3. Much of the work of an automated scoring engine for essays can be done at the levels of spelling, grammar, and vocabulary, whereas an engine for short answers must address meaning as a primary concern. From the perspective of computational linguistics, an essay scoring engine is primarily, but not exclusively, an application of *computational syntax and stylistics*, while a short answer scoring engine is primarily an application of *computational semantics*. The former fields have the more mature technology.
4. The automated components cannot work alone, but are dependent on prompt-specific analysis and knowledge engineering using human expertise. It is possible to get extremely good results when this preparatory work is done well, but not currently feasible to build a generic engine capable of scoring unseen items for which this work has not been done.
5. From an assessment perspective it is desirable that items be as rich as possible, with test-takers being given the maximum opportunity to show their knowledge and skills, but from the perspective of automated scoring it is desirable that the open-endedness of the items be restricted. Successful designs will strike a balance between these desiderata. One way to do this is to ensure that both the needs of assessment and the needs of automated scoring are represented in the design process. This suggests that

an effective strategy for achieving high quality in automated scoring of short answer items will be to foster long-term collaboration between content specialists and automated scoring experts.

SHORT ANSWER RESPONSES ARE NOT SHORT ESSAYS

It often surprises people when it is claimed that automated scoring of short answer questions poses more of a challenge than does automated essay scoring. But experience, both at ETS and its competitors, firmly validates this claim (Streeter, Bernstein, Foltz, & DeLand, 2011). Essays are by nature repetitive, short answers are shorter and less repetitive. This matters because scoring engines are fallible. If an essay-scoring engine fails to notice a piece of crucial evidence about the student's abilities and understanding, it may well get another chance later in the piece. But with short answer responses, there is rarely any repetition. Thus, when the scoring engine fails to notice a feature of the student response, it is unlikely that there will be another opportunity.

In addition, scoring short responses is a relatively young field: we do not yet have the luxury of a consistent stream of scored operational data against which to train and tune our systems:

> There is less operational experience with automated scoring systems of short texts than with essay scoring. Also, it is often the case that human raters score short content responses at considerably higher agreement rates than they do essay responses, which creates a higher standard for automated scoring methods to attain. Thus, there is still progress to be made in developing a clear understanding of which kinds of items will work best with automated scoring in a short-response format.
>
> (Williamson et al., 2010)

For practical purposes, short answer scoring and essay grading have very different scientific, commercial, and technical profiles. While both rely on generic natural language processing (NLP) technologies, they use these technologies in quite different ways.

BACKGROUND AT ETS

In 1999, in collaboration with New York University Virtual College, ETS started the c-rater short answer scoring project with constructed responses from a post-graduate database management course. The scoring engine went operational in 2003 to score the Indiana end-of-year assessment for 12th grade students (Leacock, 2006).

The c-rater engine identifies content in free-text responses that can range in length from a single word or phrase to four or five sentences. It has been tested in many domains including biology, reading comprehension, mathematics, information technology, literacy, business, psychology, and physics. C-rater can also support both summative assessments, where a score is assigned in a test, and formative assessments, where the engine gives feedback to guide instructional/learning activities. In order to capture as much content as possible, c-rater conducts a thorough and deep linguistic analysis of each student response.

There is general consensus that the primary purpose of short answers is to assess content. However, in discussing them, there sometimes seems to be an implicit assumption that all short answer questions are of the same type. This is *not* the case. Some questions elicit information that is given in a reading passage, others ask students to draw on knowledge that they already have, and yet others ask for a summary of a reading passage, to name just a few differences. The effectiveness of automated scoring will vary along with the task. Systems will do well when looking for specific information in a passage, but less when assessing the more open-ended task of a brief summary of the same passage. As a result, it is not possible to predict, in advance, which items will be amenable to automated scoring. We assume that this is what is behind Pearson's findings that "With short answers we typically find that about two-thirds of the items survive" (http://www.pearsonassessments.com/hai/images/automatedscoring/downloads/Automated_Workshop_faq.pdf).

In the next section, we give an extended description of c-rater's architecture. Then we discuss the evaluation of c-rater, focusing on measures that can guide future development. Next, we note some directions that we expect to be important in the future development of c-rater and its applications to automated scoring. Finally, we provide a brief summary of conclusions and recommendations.

C-RATER ARCHITECTURE

The task for c-rater is to determine whether a response either does or does not provide evidence of understanding (or misunderstanding) the target concept. Imagine a very simple item that would include a reading passage about Marie going to the movies and watching a comedy. A prompt could then ask the students to describe Marie's reaction to the movie. Possible correct answers might include, but certainly would not be limited to:

- Marie liked the film a lot.
- She just loved it.
- It was awesome.
- Amusement.
- She was floored.
- She had a greet time there.
- It cracked her up.
- Mari totally went for it.
- She fell over laughing.
- She thought that the movie were alot of fun.
- She laffed out loud.
- Hillarious.
- She had terific time.
- It was an absolute riot.
- Fantastic!!!!!!!!
- Marie thought it was one of the funniest movies she has ever seen in her whole life.

For the purposes of this hypothetical test item, all of these responses have essentially the same meaning. They all express, in one way and another, that she found the movie funny. But even this very simple concept can be expressed in an enormous variety of ways. It can be expressed in a single word or in a full sentence with a relative clause. Pronouns can be used instead of *Marie* and *movie*. The concept of enjoyment can be expressed with a noun, a verb, an adjective, or a variety of idiomatic expressions. In addition, the responses will contain ungrammatical sentences, sentence fragments, and run-on sentences. Finally, they will certainly include a variety of spelling errors. It is c-rater's job to recognize, in spite of all of this variation, that these are all correct responses.

Item Development

The c-rater engine is designed to score items for which the intended response is a free-text short answer, and for which points are assigned on the basis of demonstrated awareness and understanding of identifiable concepts. This need arises in tests of reading comprehension, science, and social studies.

There is, however, a limit to the kinds of questions that c-rater can score. The items need to elicit explicit concepts or facts. If an item is open-ended and asks, for example, for an opinion or information drawn from the student's experience, c-rater will *not* be able to score it, because there is no way to anticipate how the student will respond. Aside from this restriction, there is a wide array of question types that c-rater will be able to score. However, as with the Pearson team quoted in the Introduction, we also find that results for a number of items do not reach the threshold for practical use. In the item development phase, a test developer defines the concepts that a response must contain in order to receive credit and generates examples of anticipated correct responses. A typical short answer item, taken from the domain of writing instruction, presents the test-taker with a short poem, asking the student to identify and explain lines in which the writer is using imagery that achieves a particular effect. Such an item is shown in Figure 9.1.

Next, the test developer supplies one or more model sentences to represent each concept. These model sentences are written expressions of the ideas that the item writer expects to see expressed in student responses. These ideas may include expected misconceptions (wrong answers) as well as evidence of good understanding.

The item in Figure 9.1 first asks the test-taker to select an appropriate line. This first part of the item is a selected response, and does not pose a challenge to c-rater's NLP

Berkshires in April
by Clement Wood
1. It is not Spring – not yet –
    But at East Schaghticoke I saw an ivory birch
    Lifting a filmy red mantle of knotted buts
    Above the rain-washed whiteness of her arms.

5. It is not Spring – not yet –
    But at Hoosick Falls I saw a robin strutting,
    Thin, still, and fidgety,
    Not like the puffed, complacent ball of feathers
    That dawdles over the cidery Autumn loam.
    . . .

Prompt: The poet uses a variety of images to convey the notion that spring is coming. For example, the phrase "the willows are young and golden" shows that spring is coming because willows are "young and golden" only in the springtime. Select one other line from the highlighted stanzas and explain why it shows that spring is coming. How does this line suggest that spring is coming?

Figure 9.1 C-rater stimulus and prompt.

technology. Test-takers are then asked to explain why their selected line shows that spring is coming. Examples of model answers are in Figure 9.2. The responses to this part of the question are genuine free-text, and their assessment makes full use of both human judgment and NLP technology. For this item, the test designer provided just one model sentence for each concept. However, it is usually advantageous for a larger set of model sentences to be used.

The final step for the test developer is to create a set of scoring rules by identifying which concepts are required for a response to be given partial and full credit. A very simple set of scoring rules are shown in Figure 9.3

Once a test developer completes the prompt and provides required concepts and scoring rules, the item is pretested on a sample of students. The results of the pretest are passed to a team of human raters.

The human raters are asked to evaluate whether each response contains an expression of these concepts. This requires considerable judgment, both because it is not likely that test-takers will use the exact words of the model sentence, and because the rubric requires that considerable latitude be given on deficiencies in spelling and grammar. For items of this type, any clearly identifiable expression of the relevant concepts is deemed acceptable. This presents challenges both for the human raters and for the automated scoring engine. It is expected that both human raters and automated scoring engines will have non-trivial error rates in making their judgments about the presence and absence of this latter set of concepts.

The raters use a graphical user interface (Sukkarieh & Blackmore, 2009) to highlight that portion of the response that indicates understanding of one of the required concepts. Scores for the responses are calculated based on these annotations. That is, instead of reading the response and assigning a score, the human annotators highlight which part(s) of the response should receive credit and, when they are done, the interface calculates the score based on the annotations. Once the training, development, and blind cross-validation sets have been annotated, c-rater's processes are *fully automated*. There is no further human intervention unless the results are unsatisfactory and there is a need to redesign the item.

In the early versions of c-rater, the scoring engine was driven by hand-crafted rules and some of the modules, such as synonym identification, were fashioned manually. Although this system scored short answer responses with good accuracy, the process did not scale up—it was too costly and time-consuming to build models in assessments that required many short answer questions. In subsequent c-rater versions, the hand-

---

C4:   Trees only bud in the spring
C5:   Rain is often seen in the spring
C6:   Robins are only found in the spring

Figure 9.2 Constructed-response concepts for c-rater.

SR1:   If line number and C4 match, score is 1
SR2:   If line number and C5 match, score is 1
SR3:   If line number and C6 match, score is 1

Figure 9.3 Scoring rules for c-rater.

crafted modules have been replaced with machine-learned algorithms (Sukkarieh, 2010). In addition, the model-building process that was originally manual has been automated (Sukkarieh & Stoyanchev, 2009). A description of the original version can be found in Leacock and Chodorow (2003). In this chapter, the current (2012) version is described. More details are given in Sukkarieh (2010).

Building a Model

Once the student responses have been annotated the *automated model expander* builds a model using (1) the original model sentences provided by the test developer, (2) the set of annotated student responses, and (3) databases of synonyms/similar words. A set of heuristic methods selects additional model sentences from the annotated responses and assigns one or more *required words* for each of the expanded set of model sentences (Sukkarieh & Stoyanchev, 2009). For example, the required words for C6 in Figure 9.2 are "robin" and "spring." Each required word is associated with a set of similar words that could stand in for them. For example, if a similar word for "robin" were "redbreast" and a similar word for "spring" were "early," the response sentence "Redbreasts only come early in the year" might be assessed as having no missing required words when compared to "Robins only come out in spring." This is desirable, and increases the chance that a correct student response will be matched. This can be seen as a principled, data-driven way of increasing the flexibility and coverage of the automated scoring system.

The data presented later in the chapter will show that this process of automated model expansion is effective, and that it usually increases the coverage of the system without significantly impairing the precision with which responses are categorized. However, if mistakes are made in the choice of model sentences, in the selection of required words, or in the assignment of synonyms, the process can have a negative effect. The intent behind the heuristics is to identify model sentences that are not only present in the training set but also likely to occur in similar form in the test set and in subsequent student responses. To give a simple example, if the item designer did not consider the possibility that responses might contain the term "red breast" instead of "redbreast," this may be picked up by the automated expansion process and result in the addition of model sentences.

If this happens, the required words for the new sentences should include both "red" and "breast." Both words are needed, because we want to ensure that the new model sentences match all and only the responses that they should. If a mistake is made and "red" is selected as the only required word, there is a risk that the matching process will pick up all sentences that talk about anything red, and jump to the erroneous conclusion that all these sentences are talking about robins. Such errors may affect the final score that is assigned. Since the process of assigning required words is automated and reliant upon heuristics, it can sometimes give results that strike humans as blatantly wrong, with corresponding effects on the scores. Our data show that the process works well on average, but mistakes are inevitable, and do occur. Similarly, the process that assigns similar words can fail in interesting ways. For example, if we are working with an item about insects, and the target word which we want to match is "jump," it is probably a good idea to assign the words "leap' and "spring" as similar, because "the cricket leaps high" or "the cricket springs 10 inches in the air" is probably expressing the same concept as "the insect jumps high." However, in the context of an item about the season called "spring" it would be inappropriate to assign "jump" as a similar word, since that would run the risk of matching against sentences that have nothing to do with the intended concept. Incremental improvements in NLP technology will be able to improve the process that assigns similar words, but, once again, it is unlikely that errors will be entirely eliminated unless major advances occur.

Laying the Foundation for Deriving a Score: Preprocessing Responses

The desired final product is a score for each student response. As discussed in the previous section, the role of c-rater is to simulate the human raters' ability to detect concepts in the response. The basic process is that c-rater examines each sentence in the response and tries to match it against the model sentences that represent each concept. A concept matches if any of its model sentences match. Once concepts have been identified, scoring rules can be applied yielding a final score.

In preparation for deriving a score, the responses are preprocessed to normalize their variation as much as possible. There are five preprocessing steps that normalize across the kinds of variation typically found in student responses: misspellings, syntactic and morphological variation, use of words that are synonyms or similar in meaning, and the use of pronouns in the place of nouns.

- **Spelling:** Human raters are instructed to "see through" spelling errors and to identify the students' intention. People are very good at accomplishing this task; it is more difficult to get a computer to accomplish it. The spell correction algorithm operates in the same manner as other spell-checkers do, except that it is not interactive. When generating a score, c-rater cannot ask the student which, from a list of candidates, is the intended word. However, we do have a good idea of the *domain* of the item. For c-rater, the domain of the item is defined as the language contained in the reading passage, in the prompt, in the model answers, and a small set of words that are commonly found in responses (e.g., *because*). The spell-checker's suggestions are filtered through the words within the domain, and only suggestions that are in the domain are accepted. Thus, "*how com iicy hail fall*" is corrected to "*how come icy hail fall.*" This spelling correction algorithm is able to correct about 80% of the students' spelling errors. A second contextually-based spell-checking algorithm corrects confused homophones or near homophones such as *their, there,* and *they're.*
- **Pronoun Resolution:** The pronoun resolution module identifies whom or what is the referent of a pronoun (*he, she, it, them,* etc.). The module identifies all of the noun phrases in the response, as well as in the prompt, and selects the one that the pronoun is most likely to refer to (Morton, 2000). This module was especially important in a prompt that asked the students to compare and contrast three U.S. presidential inaugural speeches, where the pronoun *he* needed to be resolved in order to score the response accurately.
- **Morphological Normalization:** C-rater uses a morphological analyzer to normalize across word forms. It normalizes across inflectional morphology by identifying the base forms of inflected words. For example, *wrote, written,* and *writing* share the base form of *write.* The morphological analyzer also identifies derivational variants. For example, it recognizes the derivational relation between the verb *succeed* and the noun *success.*
- **Synonyms and Similar Words:** To fill in lexical gaps, a proprietary database developed for ETS by Dekang Lin (Lin, 1998) is searched for words that are synonyms of, or have similar meanings to, the words that were found in the student responses. For example, words that are similar in meaning to *choose* include *select, elect, decide, nominate, pick,* etc. The system also extracts synonyms and semantically related words from WordNet, a lexical database of English (Fellbaum, 1998).

- **Syntactic Analysis:** To get at syntactic variation, the c-rater engine looks for patterns in which words tend to appear in correct responses. As a first step, the responses are parsed to identify grammatical relations within each sentence. Features that identify grammatical and semantic roles are then automatically extracted from the parse trees. These are subsequently used in a classifier based on the artificial intelligence technology of machine learning that tries to recognize equivalent structures.

Generating a Score

The next step of the c-rater process consists of a Maximum Entropy module called the *sentence match module* that compares model sentences to student responses using the features that were extracted from the parse. When it finds a match, it records the fact that the concept associated with the relevant model sentence is active. A concept is deemed active if any of its model sentences match. After this stage, c-rater has found a set of concepts for which it thinks that there is sufficient evidence in the student response.

The sentence matching process relies on *features* that are extracted from pairs of parsed sentences. Each pair (M,R) consists of one model sentence (M) and one sentence (R) drawn from a response. The idea is that the features are measurable properties of the sentence pair, and that the presence or absence of each feature gives evidence for or against the possibility that R matches M. The role of the sentence matching module is to weigh the evidence provided by the features and arrive at an overall decision. Since not all the evidence will point in the same direction, the sentence matching module begins by learning a vector of weights that can be used to resolve conflicts. These weights are set by fitting a so-called *maximum entropy model* to the training set. Details of this process are in Sukkarieh, 2010.

The specific features used in the sentence matching module, summarized from Sukkarieh, 2010, are:

- A set of surface-based features that measure whether M's required words are present in R. These include:

  o (a) features representing the exact number of missing required words. These features include "nmw = 0," "nmw = 1" and so on.
  o (b) a coarser set of features representing roughly how many required words are missing. Possible values are "nmwlevel = none," "nmwlevel = some," "nmwlevel = all." "nmwlevel = none" is a redundant encoding of "nmw = 0," but "nmwlevel = some" is useful because it collapses across several different numbers of missing words, reducing data sparsity.

- A set of linguistically-informed features that measure detailed correspondences between the linguistic analyses of M and R. Comparisons rely on analyses in terms of parts of speech, in terms of parse trees, and in terms of verb–argument tuples. This is the level at which the system has a chance of accurately making the distinction between the season of spring (which will be marked as a noun) and the activity of springing, in which the relevant instance of the word "spring" would be marked as some kind of verb-form. In early versions of c-rater, similar linguistic comparisons were made, but they were fed directly to a rule-based program, rather than being, as now (Sukkarieh, 2010), transformed into features and used by the maximum entropy classifier.

A simple and effective way to make decisions about sentence pairs is to ask whether the number of missing words is zero. In experiments later in the chapter, we use this criterion as a baseline. One reason for its effectiveness is the presence in the training data of a much larger number of non-matching pairs than of matching pairs. Most of the matching pairs have "nmw = 0," and it is absent from most of the non-matching pairs. A system that uses "nmw = 0" as a decision criterion is not going to make many mistakes.

But it is desirable to make use of all the evidence that is available, weighing the evidence in accordance with the weights provided by the maximum entropy model. In practice, it turns out that the maximum entropy model gives very high weight to "nmw = 0," ensuring that the results often agree with those of the simple baseline, but this is not universally the case. When the linguistically informed features are present, they can sometimes ensure that the signal from "nmw = 0" is overridden. This is the point at which "The insects are eaten by the birds" would be successfully separated from "The insects eat the birds."

Scoring

In the final stage of processing, c-rater uses an analytic rubric that spells out, in full detail, the connection between the concepts that are active and the scores that will be assigned when particular combinations of concepts are present. The analytic rubric can be seen as a simple decision list, whose input is a collection of matched concepts and whose output is a final score. C-rater goes through the list, top to bottom, until a scoring rule is found for which all the relevant concepts are present. Misconceptions will be associated with rules that give lower scores, and correct understandings with ones that give higher scores.

We have found that this scoring rule format makes sense to content experts, and that they are able, after a little training and familiarization, to apply it effectively. Sometimes users forget that the list is processed in order, top to bottom, and place more specific rules after their less specific counterparts. A rule requiring concepts two, three, and five can never match if it is placed later in the list than a rule which specifies only concepts two and five. For safety, the next version of the scoring software will issue a warning when it detects this situation.

TOOLS FOR MEASURING AND ASSESSING THE EFFECTIVENESS OF AUTOMATED SCORING

There are multiple reasons for measuring the effectiveness of automated scoring systems. Potential clients have a direct interest in knowing whether an automated system can safely be used as a (perhaps partial) substitute for expensive human scoring or, more modestly, in understanding the applicability of automated scoring to new use cases for which human-level performance is not required. The speed, scalability, and objectivity of automated systems may allow uses for which human scoring is too costly. But even for these limited uses, it is appropriate to understand the tradeoffs that are involved, so measurements are necessary.

In educational assessment, the primary measure of an automated system's agreement with human scoring (or, indeed of inter-rater reliability for pairs of humans) is a quadratically weighted form of Cohen's kappa. Both clients and providers are familiar with this measure, and it is widely accepted as a broad measure of quality. Organizations typically link decisions about the deployment of items to thresholds on the kappa statistic, deeming that items for which kappa is too low are probably inappropriate for use in high-stakes tests. It is well established that a low kappa is a contraindication for deployment of an item. Typical thresholds fall in the range from 0.7 to 0.8, but this is a matter of policy and commercial judgment rather than a purely technical decision.

In addition, quadratic kappa, averaged over nine tasks, was used as the criterion for ranking essay grading systems in the public competition for Hewlett Foundation's Automated Student Assessment Prize. The organizers gave prizes to the top three teams, who all achieved averaged kappas in the range between 0.815 and 0.805 on the test set. Although figures for individual tasks were not reported, it is likely that the winning systems, and several others, all reached threshold on the majority of the tasks presented. So, while there may be differences in the quality of the systems, it is not clear that the differences correspond to real differences in operational potential.

Figure 9.4 shows a kernel density plot of quadratic weighted kappa (QWK) for four conditions, based on a sample of 65 diverse items for which the agreement with human scoring is known. Kernel density estimates are similar to histograms, but smoother, and allow, as here, several distributions to be presented simultaneously. Since we want kappa to be close to 1 for as many items as possible, we are hoping to see high values to the right of the graph and low values elsewhere.

We are engaged in exploratory data analysis, and our primary goal is insight into the system. Our ongoing research includes studies designed to provide formal statistical tests that correspond to the diagrams presented here. These studies extend the work of Tryon and Lewis (2008). One aspect which is not further addressed in the present chapter is the dependence of the results on the sizes of the samples of human-annotated responses. Because human annotation is costly, it is important to be sure that these samples are large enough to draw firm conclusions, but not so large as to be wasteful.

The samples are drawn from various pilot studies, from several grade levels and subject areas, including science, math, and reading comprehension, some for which the rubrics were designed in close collaboration with the c-rater team, others for which the rubrics were handed to us in nearly final form. Sample sizes range from small pilots with under

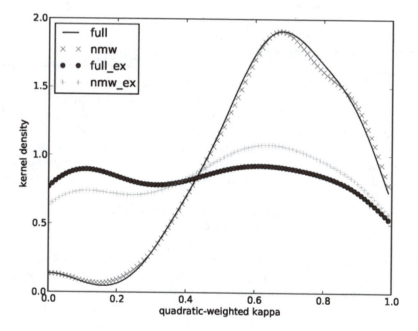

Figure 9.4 Kernel density estimates for QWK.

200 responses to more substantial studies with around 2000 responses. All graphs presented in this article are based on the cross-validation sets, which contain 20% of the total sample. In each case 60% of the data was used as a development set from which additional model sentences were collected, and 20% was reserved as a blind sample for use in final validation of the item.

In Figure 9.4, the solid line labeled "full" is the density for the operational system, using both the original exemplars and the evidence collected from the development sample. This version of the system uses the most complete linguistic matching that we have available. The line labeled "nmw" also uses both the original exemplars and the evidence from the development sample, but restricts linguistic processing to a simple check whether the number of missing words is zero. It can be seen that these two distributions are very similar indeed. Both have a mode around 0.65, which is lower than ideal, but reasonably encouraging.

Because the distributions of "full" and "nmw" are so similar, arguments in support of the fuller linguistic processing cannot be made on the basis of differences in performance on these items as measured by QWK. Just one of the many alternative arguments for thorough linguistic processing is the point that a system based solely on the presence of required words would potentially give good scores to extremely ungrammatical "word-salads" that no human rater would accept. A system with these properties would be very difficult to justify in the event that test-takers turned out to produce ungrammatical word-salads.

The third line, labeled "full_ex" shows the results of applying a version of the system that uses full linguistic processing but uses only the exemplars provided by the item designer. It does not make any use of student responses mined from the development set. This system is clearly inferior to the first two, with greater density towards the low end of the scale. The fourth system uses only the exemplars, and only the simplified linguistic processing. This is also clearly inferior to the first two, but little different from the third. On the basis of this data, we feel justified in continuing our practice of mining additional response sentences from the development set.

The majority of academic studies on automated assessment report quadratic kappa. Notice, however, that QWK is a measure of agreement, and that a system that consistently under-scores by some amount may have a kappa identical to one that consistently over-scores by the same amount. Yet, in c-rater, the remedies for underscoring and overscoring are quite different, and the same presumably holds for all other scoring systems with a similar architecture. If, as is likely, underscoring can be attributed to a failure to identify correctly expressed concepts, we will want to increase the chance that these concepts will be detected, either by adding new model sentences, by adjusting the threshold for matching a response sentence, or by some other means. Conversely, if underscoring is due to erroneous recognition of concepts associated with misconceptions, it will be desirable to reduce the chance that these concepts are matched. Similar arguments apply in the case that the system is overscoring. Since kappa does not distinguish between overscoring and underscoring, it is not, on its own, sufficient as a guide for system development. Therefore, Sukkarieh (2010) did not use kappa alone but also quoted the standard information-retrieval metrics of precision, recall, and f-measure. We are doing the same, on a larger sample of 65 items.

Figure 9.5 presents kernel density plots of the precision with which concepts are identified. Precision measures the probability that a concept to be present by the system actually is present in the gold standard. Hence, if TP is the number of true positives and FP is the number of false positives, precision = TP/(TP + FP). All four distributions have the same broad shape, indicating that the addition of extra model sentences has not affected the system's false positive rate.

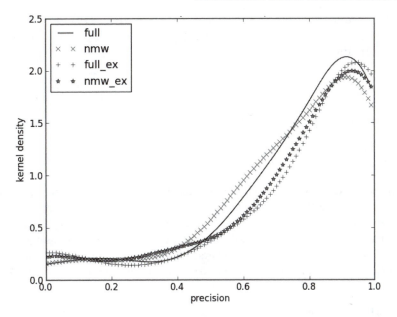

Figure 9.5 Kernel density estimates for precision.

Figure 9.6 presents the same plots for recall. Recall measures the probability that the system will correctly identify a concept when it is present in the gold standard. It is therefore defined as TP/(TP + FN) where FN is the number of false negatives. There are real differences between the systems here, indicating that the use of extra model sentences mined from the development set does improve recall for many items. This is reflected in the fact that the "full" and "nmw" distributions are more skewed towards the right than the "full_ex" and "nmw_ex" distributions, which use only the original exemplars.

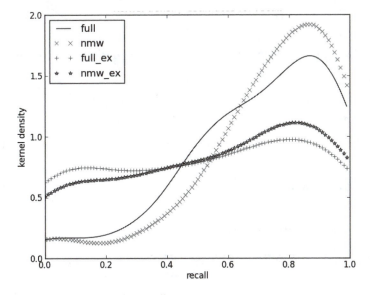

Figure 9.6 Kernel density estimates for recall.

For completeness, Figure 9.7 shows the distribution for F-measure, which is the harmonic mean of precision and recall. The harmonic mean F of two quantities P and R is defined by the equation:

$$\frac{2}{F} = \frac{1}{P} + \frac{1}{R}$$

Algebraic manipulation leads to the standard formula for F-measure:

$$F = \frac{2PR}{P + R}$$

F-measure is a standard choice because it strikes the balance between precision and recall, and offers a measure that avoids giving high scores to trivial systems. Since precision hardly changed across systems, but recall did, the graph for F-measure shows essentially the same patterning as that for recall, once again showing that the choice between full linguistic processing and the simplified version cannot be made on the basis of performance alone, but that the use of examples mined from the development set is effective.

RECOMMENDATIONS

Our exploratory data analysis has shown that the mining of model answers from the development set is effective, but that variations in the depth of linguistic processing cannot be motivated from performance considerations alone. There are certainly further exploratory analyses that can help give insight. For example, the distribution of the *difference* between recall using exemplars only and additional model sentences is shown in Figure 9.8.

In Figure 9.8, the difference is positive if the use of extra exemplars has improved recall. We see that for a significant number of items, there is no difference between the different versions of the system, that there are many items for which the extra exemplars

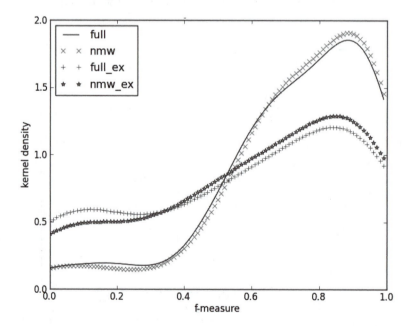

Figure 9.7 Kernel density estimates for f-measure.

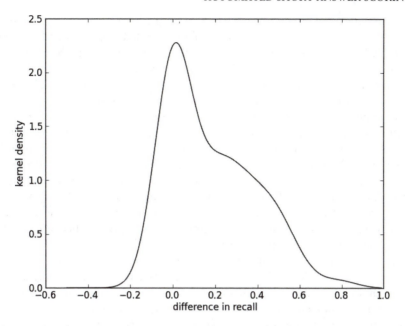

Figure 9.8 Kernel density estimate for difference in recall.

have improved concept recall, and some for which it has slightly reduced it. This presentation is useful because it tells us that the change in the system is generally beneficial, but also that there is variability in the effects.

At some point analysis must stop and we should step back and examine the big picture. The variability is no surprise, because the items we are working with were collected over a period of years, with changes in the details of the practices used. Some of the models pre-date the automated model expansion of Sukkarieh and Blackmore (2009). For these earlier items, more effort was put into manual selection of model sentences, there being no other option. Given this, there may be little remaining for the automated model expansion to do. Measurements on these items likely understate the potential of automated expansion.

More fundamentally, the variability is no surprise, because short answer items do vary, both in their difficulty, their suitability for use in automated scoring, and in the difficulties that they pose for any form of rigorous scoring. It is clear that large samples of scored responses for the items in question will allow more reliable scoring, and that careful expert analysis of the items may lead to very effective formulations of the scoring rubric in terms of concepts and scoring rules. But the pipeline from initial design idea to finalized scoring model is long, and there are several potential points of failure. Some items, especially those calling for creativity on the part of the test-taker, are simply not amenable to description in terms of a finite list of concepts. Others could in principle be described by finite lists, but the concepts are hard to pin down. The content focus of short answer items makes this especially problematic, because automated scoring researchers cannot be content area experts in all the relevant domains, and content area experts may struggle to understand what can and cannot be done with automated scoring.

For other items, the concepts are well-defined, but the language used in correct answers turns out to be too similar to the language used in incorrect answers. When this happens, even human raters are likely to struggle. Automated systems are less able than human raters to pick up on subtle linguistic cues, so they are even more likely to get into difficulties. In practice, the remedy is to try to rewrite the item so as to elicit responses that are easier to rate. It may be helpful to replace open-ended questions with more specific formulations. For example, in an item about electricity, it would be better to ask "why does the current flow through bulb A?" than to ask "what happens to the bulb?" Clearly, such changes must not violate the item designer's original intent, so it would be risky for automated scoring experts to make such changes without consultation.

It is also unpredictable how varied the student responses will be. This can be affected by the difficulty of the question, the details of its formulation, whether or not the test-takers have been prepared for the question by specific instruction, and many other factors. This is critical for short answer scoring, because every system that we are aware of relies on the assumption that data used in training and development will be sufficiently similar to the data on which the system will eventually be used. Even if this assumption is valid, a question that induces highly variable responses will call for more training and development data than one that produces stereotyped responses, because the data will need to cover a larger range of possibilities.

Finally, it is a truism (originally attributed to Helmuth von Moltke) that "no plan survives contact with reality." This is true for automated scoring of short answers. To date, the technology has been tested mainly in pilot studies and low-stakes environments. When it is deployed in a high-stakes situation, it will be subject to greater rigors. We do not know what strategies will be available to test-takers and their coaches once the strengths and weaknesses of the technology become generally known. This can only complicate the already challenging task of designing items and assessment systems that are effective and fair.

It is, of course, extremely common for potential users of automated scoring to ask potential providers for estimates of unknown future success rates, and for providers who are aware of the variability and its sources to be hesitant about providing definite answers. This is especially delicate if the items that will be used are already well-advanced in their design, or if the potential user has made plans on the assumption that automated scoring will be feasible. This is in part an issue of effective communication of expectations, and will reduce in seriousness as the capabilities of automated scoring engines become better understood by users. One way to achieve this understanding is to disseminate automated scoring into low-stakes application areas where users will encounter it and become more familiar with it.

A plausible path towards improved quality in automated scoring is for the automated scoring researchers to be involved in early stages of the item design process. As this process proceeds, it will be important to measure aspects of the items that are predictive of eventual success, and to guide the process towards items that are readily scoreable. A caveat is that scoreability should not dominate the process at the expense of rich content and pedagogical appropriateness. Nonetheless, it seems clear that the collaboration between content experts and automated scoring specialists is important.

Such collaboration will decrease the chance that the items that are designed will have fundamental flaws that preclude automated scoring, and increase the chance that automated scoring researchers will become aware of design features that are desired by item designers. One example of such a feature is the common rubric requirement that a set of sub-parts of the question be answered in particular order. This requirement is a potential boon for automated scoring, because it imposes constraint and structure on the task, and reduces variability. This feature can clearly be provided if necessary, but is not currently available in c-rater.

A more challenging requirement is that students provide answers "in their own words" (i.e., that they provide paraphrases rather than direct quotes of a reading passage provided with the question). It is straightforward to provide a filter that flags direct quotes from the reading passage. A more detailed conversation will be needed if the rubric is intended to be more subtle than this, and the item designers want, for example, to legislate against quotes that are not exact, but still too close to the passage.

A consequence of the content focus of most short answer items is that organizations that commit to the use of short answer items will need to plan for a long-term collaboration between content specialists and automated scoring experts. New items will be needed on a regular basis as old items are exposed to the test-taking population and their teachers, and reach the end of their practical lifetime. It will therefore be especially important to design an item production process that is sustainable and efficient in its use of scarce expertise.

GOALS FOR FUTURE RESEARCH

In the long term, short answer scoring engines need to become easier to train and use, easier to deploy, and to come with clear promises and expectations about when an item will, with high probability, meet the quality threshold for use in high-stakes tests. Progress in artificial intelligence and NLP will contribute to the fulfillment of these goals, but the human component cannot be neglected. If the goal is to optimize performance figures, it is, at least in the short term, clearly more promising to work on streamlining and supporting the process of item design than to hope for benefit from major advances in linguistic technology.

The content focus of short answer scoring offers additional possibilities. With minor modifications c-rater and similar systems output sets of identified concepts instead of or in addition to scores. This richer output can be useful in instructional and test preparation settings, where it can form the basis of individualized feedback. Work of this type is already under way, but it is clear that more can be done. See Dzikovska et al. (2011), Graesser et al. (2004), and Mislevy and Haertel (2006) for examples of the work that has already been done in this area.

A further, more technical, direction for research is to refine the training objective that c-rater uses. The maximum entropy model at the heart of c-rater optimizes success in sentence matching, which is an intermediate purpose rather than the final goal. As training proceeds, parameters will be adjusted so as to remove errors in sentence matching. But this may not result in a concomitant improvement in concept matching, although it will certainly tend to. It will not help to remove a false positive at the sentence level if another model sentence associated with the same concept continues to match. Similarly, the removal of an error in concept matching will only improve the score if the scoring rules map this into a change in score. It is known from Och (2003) and Zaidan (2009) that performance on NLP tasks can often be improved by directly tuning the system to optimize the measure on which the system will finally be evaluated, rather than on intermediate objectives. This approach needs to be investigated for automated short answer scoring.

CONCLUSION

Can automated scoring benefit the short answer? In our view, the answer to the question is a qualified "Yes." The potential benefits in terms of cost, objectivity, and scalability are similar to those of the essay. The largest caveat is that it is currently impossible to buy an off-the-shelf short answer scoring engine that will work for all items. It will take a very large increment in the quality of artificial intelligence and NLP systems to change this. Therefore, organizations wishing to provide short answer scoring must instead develop a process for maintaining a sustainable flow of content-rich items suitable for automated scoring. This fact makes the demands in terms of collaboration with content experts more severe, and the need for careful management and measurement of the item generation process more pressing. In addition, organizations that undertake the careful conceptual analysis of content that is needed for short answer scoring will be in a position to offer assessments that give more than a simple score, especially ones that give useful and informative feedback.

REFERENCES

Dzikovska, M. O., Isard, A., Bell, P., Moore, J. D., Steinhauser, N., & Campbell, G. (2011). Beetle II: An adaptable tutorial dialogue system. In *Proceedings of the 12th Annual SIGdial Meeting on Discourse and Dialogue*, Portland, Oregon (pp. 338–340).

Fellbaum, C. (1998). *WordNet: An electronic lexical database.* Cambridge, MA and London: The MIT Press.

Graesser, A. C., Lu, S., Jackson, G. T., Mitchell, H., Ventura, M., Olney, A., & Louwerse, M. M. (2004). AutoTutor: A tutor with dialogue in natural language. *Behavioral Research Methods, Instruments, and Computers, 36*, 180–193.

Leacock, C. (2006). Automated marking of content-based constructed responses. In M. Sainsbury, C. Harrison, and A. Watts (Eds.), *Assessing reading: From theories to classrooms.* Slough, UK: NFER Publishing Co.

Leacock, C., & Chodorow, M. (2003). C-rater: Automated scoring of short answer questions. *Computers and the Humanities, 37*(4), 389–405.

Lin, D. (1998). Automatic retrieval and clustering of similar words. In *Proceedings of the 38th Annual Meeting of the Association for Computational Linguistics.* Hong Kong.

Mislevy, R. J., & Haertel, G. D. (2006). Implications of evidence-centered design for educational testing. *Educational Measurement: Issues and Practice, 25*(4), 6–20.

Morton, T. S. (2000). Coreference for NLP applications. In *Proceedings of the 38th Annual Meeting on Association for Computational Linguistics* (ACL '00). Association for Computational Linguistics, Stroudsburg, PA, USA. pp. 173–180.

Och, F. (2003). Minimum error rate training in statistical machine translation. In *Proceedings of ACL*, Sapporo, Japan, pp. 160–167.

Streeter, L., Bernstein, J., Foltz, P., & DeLand, P. (2011). Pearson's automated scoring of writing, speaking, and mathematics. Retrieved from http://www.pearsonassessments.com/hai/images/tmrs/PearsonsAutomatedScoringofWritingSpeakingandMathematics.pdf

Sukkarieh, J. Z. (2010). Using a MaxEnt Classifier for the automatic content scoring of free-text responses. *Bayesian Inference and Maximum Entropy Methods in Science and Engineering: Proceedings of the 30th International Workshop on Bayesian Inference and Maximum Entropy Methods in Science and Engineering, AIP Conference* Proceedings, V 1035, pp. 41–48.

Sukkarieh, J. Z., & Blackmore, J. (2009). C-rater: Automatic content scoring for short constructed responses. In *Proceedings of the 22nd International FLAIRS Conference for the Florida Artificial Intelligence Research Society*, Sanibel Island, FL.

Sukkarieh, J. Z., & Stoyanchev, S. (2009). Automating model building in c-rater. in *Proceedings of TextInfer: The ACL/IJCNLP 2009 Workshop on Applied Textual Inference*, pp. 61–69.

Tryon, W. W., & Lewis, C. (2008). An inferential confidence interval method of establishing statistical equivalence that corrects Tryon's (2001) reduction factor. *Psychological Methods, 13*(3), 272–277.

Williamson, D. M., Bennett, R. E., Lazer, S., Bernstein, J., Foltz, P. W., Landauer, T. K., Rubin, D. P., Way, W. D., & Sweeney, K. (2010). Automated scoring for the assessments of Common Core Standards. Princeton, NJ: Educational Testing Service. Retrieved from https://www.ets.org/s/commonassessments/pdf/

Zaidan, O. (2009). Z-MERT: a fully configurable open source tool for minimum error rate training of machine translation systems. *The Prague Bulletin of Mathematical Linguistics, 91*, 79–88.

10 Probable Cause

Developing Warrants for Automated Scoring of Essays

David M. Williamson[1]

INTRODUCTION

When the idea of scoring an essay with a computer was first introduced (Page, 1968) it was a radical concept, but now such an application of technology almost seems mundane when contrasted with computer systems that can translate text across dozens of languages (http://translate.google.com/), best the top human competitors in the game show Jeopardy (Ferrucci et al., 2010), and perform personal assistant services from verbal commands (http://www.apple.com/iphone/features/siri.html). If computers can perform these kinds of tasks, then why shouldn't they be able to score a basic academic essay typical of those used in standardized testing programs? The potential benefits of using computers to score essays include improving the quality of scores by eliminating idiosyncratic behaviors of human raters (e.g., halo effects, fatigue, central tendency), reducing the time for score reporting, allowing for immediate performance feedback, and reducing the cost and coordination effort of recruiting and managing human raters. An automated essay scoring[2] (AES) system that provides performance feedback could also encourage broader use of essays in learning and assessment, which would facilitate greater alignment between the kinds of tasks that appear in assessments and the kinds of performances most valued in education. Of course, there are potential drawbacks to automated scoring as well, including the cost of development and validation and uncertainty regarding the extent to which these systems produce scores in the same *way* as human raters.

It is the pursuit of the benefits of automated scoring that brought the field of AES from its origins with Page (1968) to the current state, which now fields no less than nine commercial vendors of automated scoring systems for essays (Chapter 19, this volume). These are used in a variety of learning products, such as Criterion™, Write-ToLearn™, and MyAccess!™, for academic placement (Ramineni, 2013), and in college admissions tests, including the Graduate Management Admissions Test (GMAT®), the Test of English as a Foreign Language (TOEFL®) and the Pearson Test of English (PTE®). While the use of AES is growing, validation of automated scoring tends to emphasize the agreement between human and automated scores relative to the baseline agreement between two independent raters (Chapter 19, this volume). But is this alone sufficient justification for the use of AES systems? If not, what other evidence is critical and/or relevant to decisions about using AES to supplement or replace human raters in scoring essays?

In this chapter I provide a structure for considering the strength of a validity argument for AES by exploring the chain of reasoning that supports the assignment of scores to essays under traditional human scoring and how this argument may be different when automated scoring is used. It begins with a brief orientation to the structure of validity arguments and Toulmin's (1958) model for reasoning. This is followed by the construction of a Toulmin model for human scoring of essays, elaborating on the elements that make up the argument. This model serves as the basis for contrast with an analogous Toulmin model for AES. Implications of the similarities and differences in the models are discussed and the chapter closes with some implications for use of AES and current directions in advancing the state-of-the-art of AES systems.

THE STRUCTURE OF A VALIDITY ARGUMENT

As elaborated in Kane (2006), *validity* is the extent to which there is a convincing argument supporting an interpretation or use of test scores. There are two arguments involved: the *interpretive argument*, which provides the structure for the chain of reasoning that leads from observations of performance to the conclusions drawn on the basis of those observations, and the *validity argument*, which fleshes out the interpretive argument with direct evaluations of the assumptions, relationships, and exceptions that comprise the interpretive argument. In describing the interpretive argument, Kane discusses four major inferences that are commonly made when drawing conclusions from test scores, proceeding in the following sequence from task performances to decisions based on test scores:

1. *Scoring*, in which scoring rules are used to generate scores that are most appropriate for performances on each task in the test.
2. *Generalization* extends the interpretation from observed score across all tasks on a particular test to the domain score; the score expected if the examinee were administered the entire universe of potential tasks allowed by the testing procedure.
3. *Extrapolation* extends the interpretation to a level of examinee ability in the domain of interest, with implications for expected future performance on domain-relevant tasks that might be beyond the scope of tasks allowed by the testing procedure.
4. *Decision* uses estimates of examinee ability to make decisions about examinees, such as whether the examinee is competent to practice a profession, would be appropriate for a particular academic institution, or would benefit from a certain academic course.

When we consider use of AES in tests, our focus is on the first of these inferences, scoring, in which the key question of validity of AES is the extent to which there is a convincing argument supporting the inference from performances to task scores when AES is the mechanism for determining scores. So, how can we evaluate the validity argument for such a use of AES? Toulmin (1958) provides a framework and terminology for structuring and analyzing arguments that has found applications in measurement (Clauser, Kane, & Swanson, 2002; Kane, 2006; Mislevy, 1996; Mislevy, Steinberg, & Almond, 2003), and is applied here for the question of AES (it is also referred to for AES in Chapter 2, this volume). Specifically, I provide an orientation to the Toulmin terminology and structure and in subsequent sections provide an elaboration of these as the interpretive argument for the scoring of essays, both by human raters and with AES.

I use the example of someone checking in to a secure testing center as our "check-in" to the terminology and structure of Toulmin argumentation, which is provided as Figure 10.1. The fundamental part of the Toulmin argument is the connection between a *datum*, or observation that is made, and a *claim*, or conclusion whose support we are evaluating. For the purposes of our example of secure test check-in, the datum is that there is a woman presenting herself as Helen Derrell and holding a government ID with her picture on it and the claim we wish to evaluate is that the woman taking the test is in fact Helen Derrell. The *warrant* is a concise representation of the basis upon which the claim can be supported from the observed datum. In the case of our check-in example, the warrant is that if a person presents a government-issued identification with their picture on it they are probably the person named on the ID. In order to support this warrant there needs to be sufficient *backing*, or assurances that support the warrant, for the warrant to establish its authority. Continuing with our example, the backing for this warrant is that the government undertakes sufficient steps to establish the identity of the person before issuing the ID, takes their picture at a government location, and produces the ID at a government institution.

The final part of the Toulmin model is the potential for *rebuttal*, a counter-argument that would undermine the ability to support the claim from the datum and warrant provided. For example, a potential rebuttal to the claim that the person taking the test is Helen Derrell is that the government ID presented at check-in to the test could be a forgery. In order to represent this potential as a formal part of the argument structure there may be a need for a *qualifier* to the argument that makes explicit that there are potential exceptions to the veracity of the claim even with the datum and warrant as presented. With these components of the argument structure specified, the Toulmin structure from Figure 10.1 is represented as Table 10.1 for the case of identity verification of Helen Derrell for test check-in.

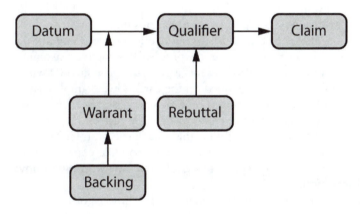

Figure 10.1 Toulmin model of argumentation.

Table 10.1 Interpretive Argument for Test Check-In

Datum: There is a woman at the entrance presenting a government ID and indicating that she is Helen Derrell.
Claim: The person taking the test is Helen Derrell.
Warrant: If a person presents a government-issued identification with their picture on it they are probably the person named on the card.
Backing: The government undertakes sufficient steps to establish the identity of the person before issuing the ID, takes their picture at a government location, and produces the ID at a government institution.
Rebuttal: The government ID provided could be a forgery.

Note: The qualifier is not explicitly called out, but is represented by the word "probably" in the warrant.

Even with a common structure there are different types of arguments. Some arguments are focused on the application of existing and accepted warrants to make a claim about a new datum. These "warrant-using" arguments represent cases of *deductive* reasoning, in which existing warrants are the mechanism by which claims are made about new data (Toulmin, 1958). In assessment this corresponds to warrants already established through the validation process and applied to make claims about examinees based on their performance on test items. Therefore, the warrant rests on the presence of existing backing.

Another class of arguments are "warrant-establishing." These are concerned with the *inductive* reasoning required for the creation of a novel warrant through a process of applying it in numerous cases in which both data and conclusion are independently verified (Toulmin, 1958). In assessment the provision of novel warrants is consistent with the concept of validating the use of a test. For an unproven assessment it is necessary to gather sufficient evidence of the veracity of the warrant(s) to establish their general applicability. Once established the warrant can be applied to draw appropriate conclusions (and appropriately consider rebuttals) about examinees. As such, the emphasis of inductive reasoning arguments is on the accumulation of sufficient backing that the warrants are compelling. Once accumulated, this backing constitutes the core of a validity argument for application in operational testing (deductive reasoning). I refer to this development of new warrants as establishing "probable cause"[3] for the warrant through the accumulation of sufficient backing to make the warrant a compelling case for supporting the claim on the basis of the datum. Or, in concrete terms for scoring with AES, to accumulate sufficient evidence to establish the relationship (warrant) between the performance of an examinee on an essay (datum) and the score that should be assigned to that essay (claim) when AES is part of that relationship.

As an illustration of this distinction between deductive reasoning and inductive reasoning for our check-in example, consider the process of inductive reasoning necessary to establish the warrant that if a person presents a government-issued ID with their picture on it they are probably the person named on the card. This example assumes a need to positively verify identity for the purposes of a high-stakes assessment. For such tests an examinee could want a high-ability person to take the test on their behalf in order to achieve a score higher than they would be able to achieve on their own. Therefore, the nature of the warrant must be sufficiently rigorous to have confidence in the identity of the examinee. There are two aspects to establishing this warrant: an investigation of process and observation.

The investigation of process targets understanding how rigorous the government is in establishing someone's identity before issuing an ID. Governmental processes such as comparing reported information on the ID application with existing government documents (e.g., birth certificates, social security numbers, immigration records, legal records), asking questions of the person to see if they have personal knowledge of personal information from other government documents, and taking a photo of the person on-site upon verifying identity all provide support for the proposed warrant. So too does knowledge that the government actively seeks to prevent, identify, and confiscate IDs that may be forgeries, such as through security elements of the ID itself (e.g., tamper-proof lamination, holograms, magnetic strips), laws encouraging confiscation of suspected fake IDs (such as at bars and liquor stores), and police efforts to track down and prosecute those who may manufacture fakes. A sufficiently rigorous process for issuing IDs and policing possession of fake IDs strengthens a proposed warrant.

The other part of establishing of a warrant is through observation and is largely an empirical approach. By selecting a person at random and checking their government-issued ID against other methods of verifying their identity (such as fingerprints, government records, etc.) it can be established whether the ID is accurate. With a sufficient number of people sampled and verified one can establish a percentage of IDs that are accurate. Understanding the probability that an ID is an accurate indicator of identity helps to establish the strength of a potential warrant. Of course, such empirical investigations do not have to be conducted directly by those who are admitting examinees to the test. They can instead rely on others who have conducted such efforts (such as law enforcement) to establish empirical support for the warrant. It is a matter of argument whether the number of such observations and the quality of those observations are sufficient to fully establish the warrant.

While presented as though it is focused on a single warrant, the inductive reasoning to establish a warrant simultaneously considers multiple competing variations on a warrant and eventually selects the one most appropriate for the test. For example, a test that requires less rigorous identity verification (practice test) might simultaneously consider several alternate warrants, such as "if a person presents the receipt from registration for the test they are probably the person named" or "if a person provides a name and address that matches the record of pre-registered examinees they are probably the person named." A test requiring more rigor might consider warrants based on biometric data, such as "if a person's fingerprints and retinal scan match those in the database for that name they are probably the person named." This warrant selection and modification process may undergo several iterations in proposing and evaluating potential warrants before a final warrant is selected for the claim.

This section has provided a brief orientation to validity theory and Toulmin reasoning as the basis for evaluating the strength of a validity argument for AES. It will serve as a roadmap for discussion of the argumentation structure and validity evidence for AES. However, I first present the Toulmin argument for the more commonly accepted model of scoring with human raters as a baseline against which to consider the implications of AES.

HUMAN SCORING OF ESSAYS

Human scoring is a commonly accepted model for evaluation of essays and is typically the standard against which the merits or deficiencies of AES are contrasted. In this section I provide an interpretive argument for the use of human raters for scoring essays, followed by a brief review of some of the elements of the corresponding validity argument to substantiate the interpretive argument. In this example I presume that the test in question has the potential for consequential impact to individual examinees, such as granting a license to practice a profession or admission to an institution of higher education. Therefore, each essay is scored by two independent raters as is common practice for such tests. I also presume that the essay score is combined with scores from other tasks and other sections of the test to produce a final score intended to be sufficient for the purposes of the test, so that the essay score is an item score and not the test score itself.

Interpretive Argument for Human Scoring

The interpretive argument begins with the datum observed and the claim that would be made on the basis of this datum. Continuing from the check-in example we now have the datum that Helen (having been admitted to the test) responded to writing prompt #23 with an essay, which has characteristics A, B, and C. In this characterization of the datum several notes are worthwhile. First, it is common for high stakes tests that use essays to have a pool of writing prompts that are treated interchangeably in the assessment, with an examinee receiving a prompt at random from the pool of available prompts. In this case, it is presumed that Helen received prompt #23 from such a pool. Second, the term "an essay" cites the particular response that Helen produced during the test and which has certain inherent characteristics indicated as A, B, and C. By necessity this description of the datum uses placeholders A, B, and C to indicate that there are multiple inherent characteristics of the essay that are indicative of the degree to which the essay is good vs. poor in quality. The number of potential characteristics of the essay relevant to determining quality are too numerous to list all of them explicitly in this example and are potentially far-ranging, including such characteristics as spelling, punctuation, use of language, word choice, accuracy of content, and sensitivity to audience, to name just a few. So in our representation this notation simply indicates that there are inherent observable qualities of the essay Helen produced.

The purpose of the interpretive argument is to establish the link from this datum to the claim, which for this example is that the essay is most consistent with a score of 5 on a scale of 1–6. The warrant that would establish this link between datum and claim is that essays with characteristics A, B, and C usually get a score of 5. Together these establish the chain of reasoning from the essay that Helen produced during testing to the claim that the essay is a 5 on a 6-point scale.

The extent to which the warrant connecting the response to the score is supportable will depend on the backing. Therefore, the backing may be the most elaborated portion of the interpretive argument and if fully elaborated could be quite extensive. For the human scoring of Helen's essay the interpretive argument is provided as Table 10.2, including an expanded backing consisting of four primary areas:

1. The rubric is appropriate
2. Raters have appropriate qualifications
3. Raters have appropriate training
4. Scoring is conducted in a way as to ensure appropriate application of the rubric

Each of these primary areas of backing has a number of secondary areas that further support the primary backing. These are discussed further below, organized by area of primary backing.

The Rubric Is Appropriate

The first part of the backing is that the scoring rubric applied to Helen's essay is appropriate. This is supported by three secondary areas (1a–1c) that further elaborate on this primary backing. The first of these, that the construct is well-represented in the rubric (1a), has several elements to it. First, that the rubric covers the full range of the construct of interest. If the rubric only covers a subset of the areas of interest in scoring then the paucity of the rubric could negatively impact the meaning of scores since important parts of the construct would remain unmeasured. By contrast, if the rubric is over-reaching and incorporating scoring elements that are beyond the targeted construct then scoring can incorporate construct irrelevant variance that detracts from the purpose of the assessment. The second element is that the rubric is appropriate for the targeted population such that the expectations of performance are neither too great, and therefore

Table 10.2 Interpretive Argument for Essay Scoring With Human Scores

---

Datum: Helen responded to prompt #23 with this essay, which has characteristics A, B, and C.
Claim: The essay is most consistent with the score of 5 on a scale from 1–6.
Warrant: Essays with characteristics A, B, and C usually get a score of 5.
Backing:

1. The rubric is appropriate

   a. The construct is well-represented in the rubric. It covers the range of the construct of interest, is appropriate for the abilities of the targeted population, and is explicitly represented for each scale point in the rubric.
   b. The rubric is clear. The rubric is clearly expressed, is appropriately specific, makes clear distinctions among neighboring points on the scale, and has illustrative examples from examinee submissions that distinguish meaning in scale points.
   c. The rubric was developed using an appropriate process. A committee of experts was convened, they had the right qualifications, were appropriately representative of various perspectives on writing, they followed an appropriate process for development (orientation, draft iteration, discussion, refinement, finalization), and the results were reviewed and refined by additional experts in the field.

2. Raters have appropriate qualifications

   a. Raters have appropriate education and experience to interpret the rubric.
   b. Raters have sufficient knowledge of the examinee population.
   c. Raters are unbiased.

3. Raters have appropriate training

   a. Raters completed an appropriate training session (orientation to task, to rubric, to performance variations in the population, to standard and exception cases for rubric application).
   b. Raters successfully scored exemplar papers as part of the training.
   c. The raters passed a certification trial to demonstrate their ability to implement the rubric.

4. The scoring process encourages appropriate application of the rubric

   a. Inappropriate scores were identified and corrected (quality control). Quality control is the mechanism by which *interventions* are imposed to prevent poor quality scores from being issued.

      i. Double human scoring – the second score serves to verify or call into question the first score
      ii. Adjudication of discrepant scores
      iii. Benchmark papers scored accurately (or else raters are retrained)

   b. Success of scoring process was empirically verified. Empirical verification is the process by which post-hoc analyses are conducted to provide evidence of the success of scoring.

Possible Rebuttals:
- Both of two human raters may have misapplied the rubric in a similar fashion for this essay.
- The essay might have some special characteristics not addressed in the rubric.

---

beyond the capabilities of the examinees (such as expecting sophisticated writing styles or concepts from 4th graders), nor too lax and representing an inappropriately low set of expectations of performance. This represents the overlay of a normative perspective on the production of a standard for a criterion-referenced process. The third element is that the expectations of the scoring rubric are explicitly represented for each scale point, rather than being general and ambiguous, in order to make clear how points in the scale are distinguished from one another.

The next area of secondary backing (1b) specifies that the rubric is clear. This refers to the language of the rubric so that the intent of the rubric will not be ambiguous to those who are applying it. The language is concise and appropriately specific in directions to the rater. This includes making clear distinctions among neighboring points in the scale and using examples from examinee submissions to illustrate distinctions between score points. The illustrative examples are critical to conveying the meaning of the rubric, as most essay scoring rubrics are vague and therefore only allow for meaningful distinctions among score points through examples from examinee submissions. For example, the rubric for the Graduate Record Examination® (GRE) Issue prompt articulates the characteristics of essays at each score point on a six-point scale. The description of a six-point essay and five-point essay is provided as Table 10.3 (ETS, 2010). The rubrics in Table 10.3 are different in their expression, but a rater would be unable to effectively implement the rubric without supporting examples from examinees that exemplify the intended differences between score points.

The third area of secondary backing, that the rubric was developed using an appropriate process (1c), is somewhat different from the first two in that it is process-oriented. It elaborates a process expected to produce appropriate rubrics. This process begins with selection of a committee of experts on the basis of their experience, qualifications, and representativeness of important perspectives on the topic (such as variations in training, experience, or demographic background). Other elements of an appropriate process include orientation to the goals, sensitization to characteristics of the examinee population that could bear on decisions, and iteratively developing draft rubrics and discussing and revising rubrics in the context of examinee examples. The resultant rubric may be subjected to additional independent review, discussion and refinement from a second panel of experts. Such processes are intended to ensure that the right expertise is brought to bear on rubric development and that multiple viewpoints are represented in developing the rubric.

Table 10.3 GRE Rubric for Scores of 5 and 6 for the Issue Prompt

---

Score 6
In addressing the specific task directions, a 6 paper presents a cogent, well-articulated analysis of the issue and conveys meaning skillfully.

A typical paper in this category
- articulates a clear and insightful position on the issue in accordance with the assigned task
- develops the position fully with compelling reasons and/or persuasive examples
- sustains a well-focused, well-organized analysis, connecting ideas logically
- conveys ideas fluently and precisely, using effective vocabulary and sentence variety
- demonstrates facility with the conventions of standard written English (i.e., grammar, usage, and mechanics) but may have minor errors.

Score 5
In addressing the specific task directions, a 5 paper presents a generally thoughtful, well-developed analysis of the issue and conveys meaning clearly.

A typical paper in this category
- presents a clear and well-considered position on the issue in accordance with the assigned task
- develops the position with logically sound reasons and/or well-chosen examples
- is focused and generally well organized, connecting ideas appropriately
- conveys ideas clearly and well, using appropriate vocabulary and sentence variety
- demonstrates facility with the conventions of standard written English but may have minor errors.

Raters Have Appropriate Qualifications

Having a quality scoring rubric is one part of scoring essays, but the quality of scores also depends on the characteristics of the human raters who implement the rubric during scoring. The second area of backing, that raters have appropriate qualifications, is necessary to implement the rubric. In the interpretive argument in Table 10.2 there are three areas of secondary backing that support the qualifications of raters. The first (2a) is that raters have appropriate education and experience to interpret the rubric. This represents that there are expectations of educational achievement and experiences that are necessary to understand and interpret the rubric and to recognize when an essay has characteristics that are consistent or inconsistent with the scale points of the rubric.

In addition to education, secondary backing 2b expresses the need for raters to have sufficient knowledge of the examinee population. Familiarity with the range of performances of the examinee population (both typical and lower/upper bounds) facilitates mapping characteristics of essays to elements of the rubric. Part of this mapping is having appropriate expectations of performance for the examinee population in order to map normative aspects of performance onto the criterion-referenced components of the rubric.

The secondary backing that raters are unbiased (2c) is intended to ensure the fairness of the scoring procedures. In this case bias refers to any tendencies the raters may have to deviate from the rubric in selected subsets of cases that share a common characteristic, such as a score, topic addressed, or demographic characteristic of the examinee population.

Raters Have Appropriate Training

Ensuring that raters have appropriate qualifications is a prerequisite, but raters also need training before they are ready to score. Thus, the third primary backing is that raters have appropriate training. One secondary backing for training of raters is the successful completion of an appropriate training session (3a). Such a training session typically includes several distinct sections, including orientation to the purpose of the assessment, the examinee population, and their roles as raters. It also typically includes familiarization with the rubric and the application of the rubric to example cases, with discussion of how the samples are more characteristic of one scale point over another. This often includes review of examinee submissions that are typical of score points in the rubric as well as those that are challenging to classify.

Secondary backing 3b, that raters successfully score exemplar papers, is also part of training. This backing is distinguished from the training process in that the raters must independently apply the rubric to examinee papers and produce appropriate scores. This allows for feedback and correction to raters after review of their scores.

The final secondary backing (3c) for training raters is that they pass a certification trial establishing their ability to score essays according to the rubric. This establishes confidence in rater ability to independently score essays. Of course, this requires a certification measure that includes a sufficient number and range of essays to evaluate ability to score a variety of performances. These may vary among multiple dimensions, including writing styles, assigned topics, levels of performance across multiple features, and the full range of scores.

The Scoring Process Encourages Appropriate Application of the Rubric

The final primary backing is that the scoring process encourages appropriate application of the rubric. This process-oriented backing is intended to facilitate operational scoring that is consistent with rater training. This has two areas of secondary backing, with the first being that any inappropriate scores were identified and corrected (4a). This is a quality control procedure applied during scoring. Double-human scoring for each essay allows for comparison of the two independently-produced scores. If there is a discrepancy between the scores an adjudication process allows for additional, often more experienced, human raters to review the essay and determine the appropriate score. Another method is the use of benchmark papers; examinee essays for which the correct score has been previously established and which are inserted at random into the sequence of essays for raters to score. If a rater has patterns of systematic discrepancy from the scores for benchmark papers then they may require retraining and their previous scores may need to be revisited to ensure that they are correct.

The other secondary backing is that the success of the scoring process was empirically verified (4b) and is an aggregate post hoc evaluation rather than a quality control procedure. Such post hoc analysis includes a variety of aggregate measures, such as inter-rater agreement rates (agreement between two independent raters) that meet or exceed an established expectation, distributions of scores that suggest raters making full use of the score scale, accuracy rates for benchmark papers, and related measures.

The final portion of the interpretive argument for human scoring of essays has to do with potential rebuttals to the claim of a score of 5 for Helen's essay. There are two potential rebuttals for this interpretive framework. The first is that both of the two human raters may have misapplied the rubric in a similar fashion for Helen's essay. For example, they may have both been inappropriately influenced by surface features such as essay length rather than a more thorough examination of the essay. Similarly, they may have both encountered some aspect of the essay that was remarkable (either positively or negatively) and which results in their lending more weight or influence to that aspect of the essay. Or further still, by resorting to a central tendency pattern in their scoring in which they favored scores toward the center of the score scale rather than making full use of the scale. While the potential ways two independent raters could inappropriately agree on a score are many, the fundamental effect for rebuttal purposes is fairly straightforward as stated.

A second potential rebuttal is that the essay may have some special characteristics not addressed in the rubric that make it difficult to assign a score. For example, perhaps the style of the essay is inconsistent with what was expected for the prompt, such as providing the response in the form of a fable rather than as a direct response. A failure of the rubric and training process to anticipate some more unusual variations in the response, either intentional or unintentional on the part of the examinee, could undermine the ability to provide an appropriate score.

It is noteworthy that there is interplay between the potential rebuttals and the backing provided for the warrant. For example, anticipation of a rebuttal that an individual human rater may not have been attending sufficiently to their task when scoring an essay could be a factor in deciding that double-human scoring should be routinely conducted rather than single human scores. This allows for quality control procedures that might detect such inattention (presuming the second rater was attending). As test designers anticipate the range of rebuttals they may provide for greater or lesser backing of warrants, as influenced by the circumstances and consequences of the test.

This concludes an overview of the interpretive argument for human scoring of essays for the example of Helen Derrell's essay. Of course, the representation of the interpretive argument for Helen's essay presumes that the characteristics cited (A, B, and C) are represented in the rubric as being most consistent with the score of 5, rather than one of the other values between 1 and 6. Otherwise, a different claim would be made relating those characteristics to a different score point. This highlights the fact that the deductive reasoning of operational scoring is somewhat different from the representation above. A specific claim, from among the six potential claims about score, is not made about a datum until the warrant has been exercised to determine the appropriate claim. However, the structure of the argument remains constant, even if the specifics of the claim may change based on the essay examined, with the datum, warrant, and claim being instance-specific while the backing and rebuttals are general to the process of scoring essays with human raters.

Validity Argument for Human Scoring

With the interpretive argument for scoring essays with human raters explicated we have one of the two components of validity as defined by Kane (2006). The other component, the validity argument, provides the empirical basis for validity through direct evaluation of the assumptions, relationships, and exceptions of the interpretive argument. This section provides examples of investigations that would support the validity argument for the interpretive argument provided above. Much like the interpretive argument above, the examples here are not exhaustive. They are offered to provide further grounding for the validity of human scoring as the baseline against which to contrast similar argument structures for AES.

Evaluations constituting the validity argument are focused on the backing supporting the warrant. Of course, there are many kinds of studies that could support the validity of human scores and they may be related to multiple aspects of the interpretive argument rather than isolated to a single area of backing. Some may also be relevant beyond the inference about scoring and be relevant to the other inferences of validity as well. In the following I present some illustrative studies and discuss how they provide backing for the scoring inference.

One of the most versatile methods for constructing the validity argument is through subject matter expert (SME) review. This method is useful wherever the evaluation of backing is dependent on human judgment and for which it may be difficult to secure empirical support independent of such judgment. These methods engage experts who have not been involved in test development in a formalized process of review and evaluation of the assessment design. The outcomes are typically documentation of endorsements and criticisms of the design, the latter of which may suggest areas of weakness (and therefore opportunities for strengthening validity). There may also be empirical aspects to SME review, such as computing measures of correspondence between an SME review committee and the design team on aspects of the design or sample scoring. In the case of scoring essays there are multiple areas of backing that could be evaluated through SME review, including:

- How well does the scoring rubric cover the construct of interest? Are there areas of the construct notably lacking in the rubric or areas included that should be omitted? (backing 1a)
- Is the rubric well positioned for the target population, without incorporating expectations that are too great or too lax for the examinees? (backing 1a)
- Are performance levels for aspects of the construct made sufficiently explicit for each score point in the rubric? (backing 1a)
- Is the language of the rubric clear and unambiguous? (backing 1b)
- Does the rubric make clear and concrete distinctions among score points, illustrated with examples from examinee essays? (backing 1b)
- Was the process used to develop the rubric sufficient to the purpose? (backing 1c)

- Are the qualifications of the experts who developed the rubric appropriate? (backing 1c)
- Are the expectations of education and experience of raters appropriate? (backing 2a)
- Is the criterion for raters having sufficient knowledge of the examinee population appropriate? (backing 2b)
- Are the processes and support materials for rater training appropriate? (backing 3a)
- Are the exemplar papers used for practice scoring by raters during training sufficiently diverse to illustrate the important variations in essays that must be scored? (backing 3b)
- Are the essays and procedures of the certification trial sufficient to assure that raters have the skills to score appropriately? (backing 3c)
- Is the quality control process sufficient to ensure that issued scores are consistent with the rubric? (backing 4a)

While SME studies may seem universally applicable they are not sufficient for a strong validity argument and direct empirical evidence is also necessary. Some examples of empirically-based evaluations include[4]:

- Score distributions. If the distribution of scores is notably skewed (either positive or negative) or notably higher/lower than a priori expectations it may suggest a problem with scoring. Of course such a discrepancy between expected and observed scores would require further investigation to determine whether this is attributable to a problem with the rubric or with the human scoring (or the sample of examinees). Similarly, if raters tend not to use the high and/or low end of the scale there may be a problem with the scoring as well, either as a result of raters not making full use of the scale or a rubric that is not sufficiently designed to recognize performances at the extremes of the distribution. (backing 1a, 2a, 2b, 3, 4b)
- Rater agreement. The rate at which two independent raters agree on the score to be assigned an essay is relevant to assessing quality of human scoring. A variety of measures may be applied, including kappa, weighted kappa (unit or quadratic), and correlations, among others. While percent agreement (exact agreement or agreement +/- one scale point) is commonly provided I recommend other measures due to the potential for agreement rate to be influenced by score scale. For example, chance agreement would tend to increase percent agreement on a four-point rating scale over that on a six-point scale. (backing 1a, 1b, 2a, 2b, 3)
- Adjudication rates. The rate at which two independent human raters are discrepant in their scores and require additional human raters (often more experienced raters) to adjudicate and determine the assigned score. (backing 1a, 1b, 2a, 2b, 3)
- Benchmark papers. The rate at which raters correctly score benchmark papers is another simple measure of rater ability to score essays according to the rubric. (backing 1b, 2, 3)
- Timing. If raters are scoring essays quickly it could be an indicator of inattentiveness to the essay or attending to more cursory features of the essay. (backing 4)
- Certification rates. The rate at which raters successfully certify and are ready for scoring after training may be relevant to some aspects of the quality of scoring. (backing 3c)
- Readability metrics. Indices of readability, such as Flesch–Kincaid, may help ensure that rubrics are clear and well-written. (backing 1b)
- Rater drift/trend. To evaluate the consistency of scoring over time it is common to

insert benchmark papers from a prior cohort into the current cohort scoring. By comparing scores on the trend sample across occasions to the overall score distributions between occasions it is easier to determine whether differences (or consistency) in scores can be attributed to changes in scoring behavior of raters or to ability levels of the examinee cohort. (backing 4)

- Sequencing. The sequence in which raters view essays could impact their judgment of essays in systematic ways (Attali, 2011). (backing 4)
- External variables. Examining the relationship between human scores and external variables of interest may be informative about the quality of the rubric and scoring. For example, if there is another portion of the test that is designed to measure a similar or identical construct to writing ability, comparing the association between this measure and the essay score to a measure of association between the essay score and an unrelated construct (such as mathematics) may be of interest. If the patterns of relationship are consistent with expectations this may encourage confidence in the scoring of essays, while if patterns are inconsistent with expectations it may be cause for further investigation. (backing 1, 2, 3, 4)

Many of these measures can be applied at the aggregate level, for an entire cohort of raters, as well as at the individual level so that individual raters could have empirical profiles related to agreement rates, score distributions, adjudication rates, benchmark paper performance, timing and other measures. Of course, it is beyond the scope of this chapter to fully elaborate on the many kinds of studies that could be conducted, how they might be executed, and how they might pertain to the interpretive argument for essay scoring. The intent is to illustrate how the backing of an interpretive argument is supported through the validity argument for human scoring of essays. A review of research conducted or planned can help identify which parts of the interpretive argument are more/less strongly supported. This can draw attention to the need for additional studies to strengthen weaker or more critical parts of the interpretive argument. So while the development of a validity argument is initially a two-stage process (interpretive argument followed by a validity argument), it is potentially an iterative process as the interpretive argument may suggest new studies for the validity argument, which in turn may reveal a need for further refinement of the interpretive argument. This discussion has been restricted to the interpretive argument and validity argument for the Scoring inference, and as such does not address other inferences of a more complete validity argument: Generalization, Extrapolation, and Decision, as these are beyond the scope of the chapter. The reader interested in a more general treatment of human scoring may refer to Johnson, Penny, & Gordon (2009).

AUTOMATED SCORING OF ESSAYS

Given this structure for validity of scoring essays with human raters, is the structure for validity of AES notably different than for human scoring? This section provides an interpretive argument for AES, followed by a validity argument that could accompany the interpretive argument.

Interpretive Argument for Automated Scoring

Use of AES to score essays instead of human scores implies a somewhat different interpretive argument and I again turn to the example of Helen Derrell to illustrate. The new interpretive argument for Helen's performance on the essay is provided as Table 10.4 and

Table 10.4 Interpretive Argument for Essay Scoring With Automated Scores

Datum: Helen responded to prompt #23 with this essay, which has characteristics A, B, and C.
Claim: The essay is most consistent with the score of 5 on a scale from 1–6.
Warrant: Essay's with characteristics A, B, and C usually get a score of 5
Backing:

    1.   AES covers the construct appropriately
        a.   The construct is well-represented in automated scoring. The features of automated scoring are accurate, construct-relevant, capable of representing the full range of performance, and leave no important aspect of the construct unmeasured.
        b.   The automated scoring system was developed using an appropriate process. Conceptualization and design of scoring features is appropriate, is empirically verified as accurate, and has been reviewed by experts regarding their construct representation.

    2.   Automated scoring models are appropriately derived
        a.   The mechanism by which scoring features are aggregated to produce a summary score (calibrated) for an essay is appropriate and the influence of individual features on the score is acceptable.
        b.   Automated scoring is unbiased.
        c.   Automated scoring models pass a certification trial and have been demonstrated to be issuing appropriate scores.

    3.   The scoring process encourages appropriate scores
        a.   Essays were sampled at random for human confirmation to ensure performance of automated scoring.
        b.   Success of scoring process was empirically verified.

Possible Rebuttals:

- The essay may have some special characteristics not reflected in the AES construct.
- The essay may be unusual relative to the sample of essays included in the calibration process.

has several differences from the interpretive argument for human scoring. The datum, claim, and warrant are identical to those in Table 10.2 but the backing is modified to reflect a shift from human scoring to AES, now consisting of three areas of primary backing:

1. AES covers the construct appropriately
2. Automated scoring models are appropriately derived
3. Scoring is conducted so as to ensure appropriate scores

Just as for human scoring, each of these primary areas of backing includes secondary areas which are discussed further below, organized by area of primary backing.

AES Covers the Construct Appropriately

The backing that AES covers the construct appropriately represents that AES measures the aspects of writing that, in the aggregate, embody the meaning of writing for the assessment. There are two areas of secondary backing supporting the primary backing of encompassing an appropriate construct: that the construct is well-represented in AES (1a) and the AES was developed using an appropriate process (1b).

    The first of these secondary backing statements, that the construct is well-represented in AES (1a), addresses several characteristics of AES and the relationship to the construct of writing. These include that the scoring features of AES are accurate, construct-relevant, capable of representing the full range of performance, and leave no important aspect of the construct unmeasured. As there are multiple aspects to this backing, some discussion of these characteristics and how they can support or undermine construct representation in AES is relevant.

Most AES systems consist of a potentially large number of scoring features (Attali & Burstein, 2006; Chapters 4, 5, and 6 of this volume) each of which is designed to address an aspect of the construct of writing. For example, some features may focus on the rates at which certain errors occur, such as spelling errors, punctuation errors, grammatical errors, or preposition errors. Other features may be designed to measure aspects of language use, such as the sophistication of vocabulary through measures of how unusual words are. Others may be concerned with the content of the essay, typically through measures of statistical association summarizing how the words used in an essay coincide with words in texts related to the essay topic and to previously scored essays in the calibration sample. Each of the potentially many scoring features in an AES system are designed to measure a relatively small part of the construct and may vary with respect to how well they address the aspect of the construct they are designed to measure. The result is that some features may be very accurate while other features may be relatively inaccurate in distinguishing higher quality aspects of the feature from lesser quality aspects of the feature. As an illustration, we might reasonably expect that a feature addressing spelling errors would be more accurate than a feature designed to evaluate whether a thesis statement is supported with facts. The inconsistent accuracy of AES features is not necessarily a flaw and may reflect the fact that some aspects of writing are relatively easy for experts to define, identify, and agree upon (more concrete) while other aspects of writing may be difficult to define and be subject to greater discrepancy in opinion among experts (DiPardo, Storms, & Selland, 2011). Regardless of whether the cause of lower accuracy is in the technology of natural language processing or ambiguity about the portion of the construct the feature is intended to target, an AES score is an amalgamation of many such features, each of which may vary in the accuracy with which they fulfill their purpose. This part of the backing states that each of the features of AES are sufficiently accurate for the purpose for which they are defined and the context in which they are used.

Accuracy is not the only way in which features of AES may vary. Features may also differ in the degree to which they are construct-relevant in their design, with some being direct measures of an aspect of the construct of interest and others being proxies that may be marginally (or not at all) related to valued aspects of writing. For example, a spelling-error detection feature that maps the words in an essay against a defined set of English language words and marks discrepancies is a direct measure of the spelling part of the writing construct. By contrast, the number of words in an essay has been used as a feature in some AES systems because it has a high correlation with human scores. Therefore, it is a powerful mechanism for increasing the correlation between AES scores and human scores. Despite the ability of number of words to predict human scores English writing experts do not highly value length as an important aspect of writing fluency; the ability to write extensively under timed conditions. The potential for inclusion of AES features that are statistically predictive of human scores but weakly related to the construct of writing underscores the need for backing that specifies the degree to which the features are construct-relevant.

Each of the features in AES systems must also be broad enough that it can represent a full range of examinee performance with respect to that feature. If a feature of AES is only capable of measuring a limited range of performance then it may be able, for example, to distinguish those at the low end of performance on that characteristic from those at the middle range but be unable to distinguish those at the high end of performance on that characteristic from those at the middle range. Therefore, one of the elements of secondary backing is that features are capable of representing the full range of performance in the portion of the construct each feature targets.

In the aggregate, the full set of features that make up an AES system represents the entirety of the construct of writing as evaluated by AES. So another aspect of secondary backing 1a is that the complete set of features in AES leaves no important aspect of the construct unmeasured. Omission, or incomplete coverage, of aspects of the writing construct threatens the construct representation of the AES scores.

The secondary backing for the construct of AES being appropriate also includes that the AES system was developed using an appropriate process (1b). The design process for scoring features begins with conceptualization of the feature, which should specify how the feature represents an important part of the writing construct. This representation needs to be carried over into the design and computation of the feature, whether the computation is rule-based or based on statistical methods such as machine learning. Once implemented, a rigorous design process includes empirical verification that the feature is functioning as intended and at a level of accuracy expected for assessment use. Together, these processes help to ensure that the feature represents a positive contribution to scores, both conceptually and statistically.

Automated Scoring Models Are Appropriately Derived

While the features of AES systems represent individual elements of the construct of writing, scoring models specify how these features are combined to produce a summary score. In practice, scoring features tend to be static parts of the AES system and perform the same operation regardless of the context in which they are applied (e.g., spelling error detection functions the same fundamental way for 4th grade state assessment as it does for college entrance exams). By contrast, scoring models are typically empirically calibrated for the population of interest for the assessment (therefore the relative contribution of spelling to the overall score may differ substantially between 4th grade state assessment and college entrance exams). The most straightforward approach to such calibration is to obtain a sample of essays from the target population, conduct human scoring for the essays, and then regress these human scores on AES features. The result is a statistically optimal set of feature weights for producing scores similar to those of human raters. There are a variety of different calibration techniques that might be employed for AES and a full representation is beyond the scope of this chapter, but each method has a fundamental similarity in that multiple features are statistically aggregated to produce the score. Just as the process of feature development is part of the backing so too is the process of developing the scoring models. Regardless of the method of calibration there is an expectation that automated scoring models are appropriately derived (backing 2). There are several secondary backing statements associated with this backing, including that the calibration process is appropriate (2a), automated scoring is unbiased (2b) and that the models for automated scoring have passed a certification trial (2c).

The calibration process cited in secondary backing 2a includes multiple aspects. These include the method by which features are aggregated to produce a score is appropriate, the statistical influence of features on the resultant score is consistent with the definition and quality of the feature, the statistical methods for calibration are appropriate, and the sample used for calibration is sufficiently large and consistent with the population of examinees whose essays will be scored by the model. It should be noted that empirical calibration can complicate the goal of having meaningful representation of the writing construct in AES scores. A feature of AES might be conceptually very important to the construct definition, but be poorly measured by AES.[5] Similarly, another feature may be less important to the construct but measured with great accuracy and have notable variance in the population.[6] An empirical calibration process may assign the more accurately measured features higher weight in computing scores than less accurately measured features. The resultant scoring model could have conceptually important features with little influence on the essay score and conceptually minor features with great influence on the score due to their higher statistical association with human scores in calibration. Such a model may pose an interesting dilemma in evaluating its merits.

Another secondary backing is that automated scoring is unbiased (2b). This may at first appear to be an unusual point to specify about automated scoring. After all, AES treats every essay in the same way and is not subject to any variability in scoring practices based on characteristics of the examinee. However, prior research (Bridgeman, Trapani, & Attali, 2012) suggests there can be differences between human scores and scores from AES for certain subgroups despite having been successfully calibrated for the examinee population as a whole. It is unclear whether this discrepancy in scores for certain subgroups stems from some characteristic of the AES system or some pattern of scoring practice of human raters, or both. It could also be related to real differences in patterns of writing by subgroups. The potential for these differences and ambiguity regarding root causes necessitates the representation of potential bias in the backing for AES scores.

The final secondary backing is that automated scoring has passed a certification trial (2c) to assure the user that AES issues appropriate scores for the use and population in question. The design and implementation of such certification trials may vary based on the intended use and the interests of the assessment program. However, it is common for such trials to include multiple kinds of evaluation of AES scores against human scores on the same response. It is somewhat less common, but still quite relevant, to contrast the association of human and AES scores with scores on alternate responses, external criteria, or on alternate occasions.

The Scoring Process Encourages Appropriate Scores

The backing that scoring is conducted so as to encourage appropriate scores (backing 3) is a variation on the human scoring backing that the scoring process encourages appropriate application of the rubric. The secondary backing 3a states that subsets of essays were sampled at random for human scoring to confirm performance of the AES system. This serves as the quality control mechanism to ensure that AES is performing as expected, with the nature and extent of the control based on the proportion of cases sampled for review. The other secondary backing, that success of the scoring process was empirically verified (3b), indicates that post hoc analyses are conducted to provide evidence that scoring is consistent with a priori expectations.

The backing is not the only difference in transitioning from human scoring to AES. The potential rebuttals are also impacted by this shift. The first of the possible rebuttals for AES is that the essay may have some special characteristics not reflected in the AES construct. To the extent that there are elements of the essay that are not addressed in the features of AES, but are relevant to the construct of interest for the assessment, the score could be inconsistent with the characteristics of the essay.

The second rebuttal, that the essay may be unusual relative to the sample of essays included in the calibration process, is an inevitable by-product of an empirical calibration. The scoring models for AES are trained on a sample of essays and the statistical aggregation of features to produce a score is based on patterns of association between features and human scores in these data. If an essay is notably atypical of the essays used for calibration, the statistical model for scoring may not be robust to the differences in this essay, allowing for an AES score that might be different than the score human raters would provide.

Validity Argument

The validity argument for AES serves the same purpose as it does for human scoring: to provide the empirical support for the interpretive argument. The differences in the interpretive arguments for human scoring and AES, however, suggest some corresponding difference in the nature of the empirical support for AES relative to human scores. This section provides some examples of empirical support for the AES interpretive argument. As with prior examples, this summary is not exhaustive and serves as an illustration of a validity argument that supports the interpretive argument.

Just as with human scoring, there are some areas of backing that can be supported through direct empirical evidence and others that are best supported through soliciting the judgment of experts. In the latter case SME evaluations are again useful and some examples include:

- Are the features of automated scoring designed and programmed in such a way that they represent a truly valued part of the construct, or are they instead statistical proxies of what is valued? (backing 1a)
- Are the processes and methodologies (statistical and argumentative) used to develop the AES features appropriate? (backing 1b)
- Does the collection of features that constitute the score from an AES system represent the full construct of interest for writing? Are there aspects of the construct that are not represented or are underrepresented in the AES? (backing 1a)
- Is the calibration process appropriate for the intended use? (backing 2a)
- Are there notable discrepancies between the statistical influence of certain AES features on the essay score and their importance from a construct perspective? (backing 1a)

These represent just a few of the areas in which SME review could substantiate or call into question the backing of the interpretive argument.

Evaluations based on SME judgments are typically only part of the validity argument and are often de-emphasized relative to empirical evidence, examples of which include the following:

- Evaluation of the performance of scoring features against test sets. For example, by determining the extent to which a feature of AES designed to identify preposition errors is successful relative to human annotations on a corpus of data (Burstein & Marcu, 2003; Leacock & Chodorow, 2003). (backing 1a)
- Experimentation with AES features to establish limits of performance. For example, if an AES were to have a feature for whether a thesis statement is supported by facts,[7] how much of the range of factual support does it measure? Does it only distinguish at the low end of the scale, such as those that are not supported from those that are modestly supported? Or can it also distinguish circumstances when there is compelling factual support for the thesis statement? Again, these kinds of questions might be explored through empirical comparisons of feature performance against human annotated data. (backing 1a)
- Evaluation of multiple approaches to calibration of AES to select a preferred approach. Comparing the performance of different calibration methods, such as regression-based procedures, empirical neural networks, and rule-based methods, may lead to a preference for one method on substantive grounds. (Clauser, Margolis, Clyman, & Ross, 1997). The implication being that selection of a more appropri-

ate calibration model from competing methods strengthens confidence in the use of those models operationally. Of course, the criterion for "preferred approach" deserves some attention since models with high association with human scores can have features that influence scores in ways inconsistent with how writing experts view the construct of writing. (backing 2a).

- Comparisons between human scoring and AES scores for key demographic subgroups. An example would be comparison of standardized mean score differences in distributions of scores between human and AES scores for subgroups of interest (Bridgeman et al., 2012). Observed differences for demographic groups of interest may suggest differences between how human raters and automated scoring evaluate responses from a subgroup, which may imply a need for addressing behaviors of one or both to ensure fairness of scoring. (backing 2b).

- Agreement with human scores. Do AES scores agree with human scores on the basis of measures of association such as correlations, kappa, weighted kappa? (backing 2c)

- Distributions of scores. Are the distributions of AES scores similar to those of human raters? Do they make similar use of the scale of measurement, with similar means and variances? This question would appear transparently true, since an empirical calibration of scores on existing human scores would be expected to produce distributions of AES similar to those of the human scores used for calibration. However, several aspects of model calibration and use may suggest otherwise. For example, calibrating using regression will tend to match the mean scores but reduce the variance of the distribution of scores. This begs the question of whether the reduced variance is desired (as regression to the mean is a real effect) or whether the AES models are better served by variances that make use of the scale in the way that human raters do. Further, calibration in the aggregate (pooling examinees and prompts) may produce an appropriate score distribution in the aggregate, but examination of the disaggregated data by examinee demographic or by prompt within the pool of prompts may reveal systematic differences in the distributions of AES and human scores.[8] (backing 2c)

- Contrasting human and AES scores with external criteria. Comparison of the relationships (e.g., correlations) between AES scores and external criteria to the relationship between human scores and external criteria can elicit assurances or questions about the relative relationships of human and AES scores and the construct of interest. If the relationships are similar it suggests a correspondence between scores produced by human raters and AES, but if they are different these differences may reveal important distinctions in the meaning of scores between human and AES scores. The nature of the interpretation would depend on the external variable to which they are being compared, with the expectation of stronger relationships with variables more closely related to the writing construct, such as grades in a writing course, scores on a portfolio assessment, or scores on an alternate essay. By contrast, there would be an expectation of weaker relationships with measures of constructs different from writing, such as scores on a multiple-choice mathematics test or grades in a physical education course. (backing 1b)

As in the section on human scoring, the intent is not to represent all research that is relevant to the validity argument but to provide examples of empirical evidence that is relevant. It also illustrates the relationship between the elements of backing for an interpretive argument and the validity argument that supports the use of scores, with implications for how the findings from each of these inform the other iteratively in the course of developing a new warrant.

CONTRASTING HUMAN AND AUTOMATED SCORING OF ESSAYS

It follows from the representations above that there are similarities and distinctions in both the interpretive argument and validity argument between human scoring and AES. In this section I briefly discuss a few of the more substantial contrasts and commonalities, focusing on construct, consistency, and the interrelatedness of human and AES scoring.

The human scoring backing 1, that the rubric is appropriate, and the AES backing 1, that AES covers the construct appropriately, serve the same fundamental purpose: to specify that the construct targeted by the assessment has the opportunity to be represented appropriately in the scoring. However, to interpret this purpose in the context of scoring, it is necessary to have a more complete understanding of what is meant by the "construct" of writing. There are three areas of focus regarding the construct of writing. The first is a naturalistic definition of the construct, the second is a definition of the construct of writing for assessment purposes, and the third is the construct of writing addressed in scoring. These may be viewed as a sequence of limiting factors on the construct of writing from a very generalized construct to the explicit (and more narrow) construct represented in a score.

In the naturalistic definition of the construct of writing the focus is on what aspects of writing are valued by a field of practice, regardless of whether those characteristics can be reasonably measured. Ideally this definition would be irrespective of field of practice, but since different fields of use value different characteristics of writing such a universal definition is impractical. For example, we might expect that those practicing in the area of English literature would have very different values in writing than those who practice in the field of scientific reporting, particularly around writing style. An example of a naturalistic definition of writing in basic education is the six-trait model (Culham, 2003), which has gained some currency among educators who teach writing. Another model is provided by Deane, Fowles, and Sabatini (2012) and focuses on the skills of the writer rather than features that define text quality.

In defining the construct of writing targeted by an assessment, the naturalistic definition may serve as a starting point, but typically requires certain modifications to constitute the construct for assessment. A common constraint is to consider the use of the assessment and focus the definition of writing construct for assessment to be consistent with test use. For example, if the test is a certification test targeting minimal competence it may eschew aspects of the naturalistic construct that are more advanced and focus solely on entry level aspects of writing. The construct may be further constrained by the circumstances of assessment, such as being conducted under timed conditions, requests for spontaneous essays rather than planned writing, providing writing prompts unanticipated by the examinee, and with more limited resources (such as references, source materials, or knowledgeable colleagues) than would occur under naturalistic conditions.

The third definition of the writing construct is the construct actually measured in assessment and serves as the point of comparison between human scoring and AES. Backing 1 in both AES and human scoring represents a measured construct as similar as possible to the construct of writing targeted by the assessment. In the case of human scoring the construct measured is embodied as the scoring rubric and therefore the rubric is the focus of backing 1. If the rubric fully embodies the construct targeted by the assessment and is expressed in a way that it can be readily implemented by human raters then we might expect a stronger relationship between the writing construct embodied in scores and the construct targeted by assessment. By contrast, deficiencies in the rubric would undermine the goals of alignment between constructs embodied in scores and targeted by assessment. Similarly, the parallel backing 1 for AES addresses the extent to which the scoring features in AES are capable of representing the construct of interest for the assessment. To the extent that they are a complete and accurate representation there is greater confidence that the AES scores represent a targeted construct of assessment.

The fundamental contrast in construct representation between human scoring and AES rests on the distinction between what *can* be measured and what *is* measured. In theory, human scoring is fully capable of representing the entire construct of interest for the assessment. That is, human raters have the capacity to recognize any and all relevant characteristics of a response and consider them in determining a score. However, in order for this to occur several aspects of the backing must work in harmony. The rubric must be appropriate and well specified through adequate examples, the human raters must have a fundamental ability to recognize elements of performance and classify them appropriately, they must be trained to use the rubric, and they must faithfully implement the rubric conscientiously throughout the scoring process. While this is theoretically possible, research suggests that it is difficult to achieve as there is a constant need to guard against common problems in human scoring that include inattentiveness, halo effects, sequence effects, central tendency effects, lenience, severity, bias, and other undesirable characteristics of human scoring (Rudner, 1992; Saal, Downey, & Lahey, 1980). As such, human raters have the capacity to recognize any and all elements of a response that are relevant to scoring, but may be challenged in consistent identification of these elements and in consistent aggregation of these features into summary scores, resulting in multiple approaches attempting to identify and quantify the effects of these tendencies on scoring (Leckie & Baird, 2011; Myford & Wolfe, 2003; Wolfe, 2004).

By contrast, AES is the inverse of human scoring in that the primary challenge of AES is in whether it can adequately identify all of the characteristics of a response that are relevant to the construct of the assessment, but it can be relied upon to consider those elements it can measure consistently and to always aggregate them to a summary score in the same way. In concrete terms, the scoring features targeting essay characteristics A, B, and C represented in the interpretive argument for both human scoring and AES may not be exactly the same A, B, and C in each instance. There may be some representations of A's, B's, and C's that share a common definition in human scoring and AES, but which are implemented differently. For example, the definition of spelling errors may be largely held in common, but an AES system is more capable of identifying spelling errors consistently and completely than human scoring. Other representations of A's, B's, and C's may have a common goal, but be defined somewhat differently. For example, for a scoring feature that a thesis statement is supported with facts a human rater may be able to directly determine the extent to which the thesis statement is factually supported. In contrast, an AES may not be capable of the kind of analysis required for directly assessing this feature and, if the feature is part of an AES system, it may be a statistical proxy developed to identify and evaluate the kind of text indicative of thesis and factual support rather than a direct measure. As such, even when features are held in common between human scoring and AES they may be operationally defined differently. Finally, there are some aspects of writing that human raters are able to identify that AES systems are currently not yet able to address and as such may be areas of the construct of interest for the assessment that are unmeasured by AES.

This potential construct challenge of AES is offset by strength in the consistency of identification and aggregation of features to a summary score. Some features of AES can measure elements of writing with greater precision and consistency than human raters. Further, there is complete consistency in how these precisely measured features are used to produce summary essay scores. The combination of a large number of precisely measured features and a statistically optimized model for aggregation to a summary score can be an effective method that can compensate for potential deficiencies in the construct representation (an example can be found in Ramineni, Trapani, Williamson, Davey, & Bridgeman, 2012b).

In summary, the most notable distinction between human and AES scoring is that with human scoring we have greater confidence in the *potential* for the construct to be well-represented but less confidence in the conscientiousness and consistency of scoring, while AES scoring may entail some inadequacies in construct representation but provide highly conscientious measures and complete consistency in the use of features to determine summary scores. In this way, a transition from human scoring to AES is an exchange of the random error of human scoring for systematic error of AES. Such an exchange may be advantageous if it can become a mechanism for better identification of sources of error in scoring and successful efforts to control those sources of error.

Despite the emphasis on contrast, there is more similarity between AES and human scoring than may be immediately apparent. Several aspects of human scoring are implicit parts of AES, one of which stems from the calibration process for AES. If the calibration process is conducted by optimizing statistical associations of features with a set of human scores then the human scores used in the calibration are an implicit introduction of the rubrics, the training, and the human scoring processes into AES scoring. If the human scores used for calibration are of poor quality then we might expect the AES scores to suffer as a result. It is an open question whether AES models are better served by calibrating on large samples of essays with human scores obtained under operational scoring conditions (potentially lower quality, but greater representation of essays) or small samples of essays scored by highly trained experts who are very conscientious in scoring, with more independent ratings per essay (higher quality but limited representation of essays).

It is not only calibration that implicitly folds human scoring into AES. Several of the methods used to demonstrate that AES is unbiased and passes a certification trial rely in some part on comparisons with human scores, including when referencing external validation criteria. To the extent that AES methods are endorsed, rejected, or modified on the basis of these comparisons constitute further influence of human scoring.

Thus far human scoring and AES have been treated as contrasting methods in which a replacement model is assumed that would transition from human scoring to AES, with implications for how the interpretive argument and a validity argument would change in this transition. However, it is not simply a question of the contrasts and similarities between human scoring and AES for replacement purposes as these methods can also be used in conjunction with each other, as described in the following section.

COMBINED HUMAN AND AUTOMATED SCORING OF ESSAYS

Whenever presented with methods with relative strengths and weaknesses, as is the case with the interpretive and validity arguments for human and automated scoring, there is the question of whether a combination of methods could combine the strengths of alternate approaches and minimize weaknesses. The use of human scoring and AES as complementary methods for scoring essays is consistent with this goal and simply replaces one of the two human raters from the human scoring approach with a score from AES. This is the most common approach to using AES in consequential assessments and has been used in tests such as TOEFL and GMAT. The interpretive argument for combined use of human and AES scores is simply a merger of the two interpretive arguments provided for human and AES scoring alone and is provided as Table 10.5. The backing reflects this by simply appending the interpretive argument for AES in Table 10.4 into the

Table 10.5 Interpretive Argument for Essay Scoring With Human and Automated Scores

Datum: Helen responded to prompt #23 with this essay, which has characteristics A, B and C.
Claim: The essay is most consistent with the score of 5 on a scale from 1–6.
Warrant: Essay's with characteristics A, B, and C usually get a score of 5.
Backing:
1. The rubric is appropriate

   a. The construct is well-represented in the rubric. It covers the range of the construct of interest, is appropriate for the abilities of the targeted population, and is explicitly represented for each scale point in the rubric.
   b. The rubric is clear. The rubric is clearly expressed, is appropriately specific, makes clear distinctions among neighboring points on the scale, and has illustrative examples from examinee submissions that distinguish meaning in scale points.
   c. The rubric was developed using an appropriate process. A committee of experts was convened, they had the right qualifications, were appropriately representative of various perspectives on writing, they followed an appropriate process for development (orientation, draft iteration, discussion, refinement, finalization), and the results were reviewed and refined by additional experts in the field.

2. AES covers the construct appropriately

   a. The construct is well-represented in automated scoring. The features of automated scoring are accurate, construct-relevant, capable of representing the full range of performance, and leave no important aspect of the construct unmeasured.
   b. The automated scoring system was developed using an appropriate process. Conceptualization and design of scoring features is appropriate, is empirically verified as accurate, and has been reviewed by experts regarding their construct representation.

3. Raters have appropriate qualifications

   a. Raters have appropriate education and experience to interpret the rubric.
   b. Raters have sufficient knowledge of the examinee population.
   c. Raters are unbiased.

4. Raters have appropriate training

   a. Raters completed an appropriate training session (orientation to task, to rubric, to performance variations in the population, to standard and exception cases for rubric application).
   b. Raters successfully scored exemplar papers as part of the training.
   c. The raters pass a certification trial to demonstrate their ability to implement the rubric.

5. Automated scoring models are appropriately derived

   a. The mechanism by which scoring features are aggregated to produce a summary score (calibrated) for an essay is appropriate and the influence of individual features on the score is acceptable.
   b. Automated scoring is unbiased.
   c. Automated scoring models pass a certification trial and have been demonstrated to be issuing appropriate scores.

6. The scoring process encourages appropriate scores

   a. Inappropriate scores were identified and corrected (quality control). Quality control is the mechanism by which *interventions* are imposed to prevent poor quality scores from being issued.

      i. Double scoring – the second score serves to verify or call into question the first score
      ii. Adjudication of discrepant scores
      iii. Benchmark papers scored accurately (or else raters are retrained)

   b. Success of scoring process was empirically verified. Empirical verification is the process by which post-hoc analyses are conducted to provide evidence of the success of scoring.

Potential Rebuttals:

- The human rater may have misapplied the rubric for this essay *and* the essay may have characteristics that cause the automated scoring system to issue a similarly inappropriate score.
- The essay might have some special characteristics not addressed in the human scoring rubric *and* may be unusual relative to the sample of essays included in the calibration process for AES.

interpretive argument for human scoring from Table 10.2. The rebuttals are not simply appended, but are changed somewhat with the merger so that for each potential rebuttal there is a requirement that both the human and AES share a certain commonality in the potential mis-scoring of an essay. The validity argument that would support the interpretive argument is likewise simply replicated as an appending of the previously presented discussions into a single set of potential empirical support.

DISCUSSION

The focus of this chapter has been in contrasting the interpretive arguments for scoring essays with human scoring and AES, with implications for the nature of evidence that would be required for the validity argument that complements the interpretive arguments. The examples have largely been from the perspective of deductive reasoning cases in which evidence has already been developed to support the backing for the warrants and are being applied to score essays. Of course, in the absence of such a pre-existing body of evidence there is the need to develop this evidence, or "probable cause," through the inductive reasoning process so that the warrant is sufficiently strong to support the intended use. While presented largely as a discussion of deductive reasoning, the argument structures and potential evidence discussed in this chapter are equally applicable in inductive reasoning, just that the emphasis shifts to refining the interpretive argument and accumulating validity evidence rather than using pre-established arguments. The question of just how strong the argument needs to be to support the warrant will depend in part on the use of scores, with lower-stakes uses requiring less rigorous justification than more consequential uses.

Uses that target practice and learning environments may require less rigor to support warrants, particularly since these often emphasize the feedback capabilities of AES to improve writing rather than the summary scores. Software designed to improve writing through use of AES are numerous, of which Criterion™ and MyAccess!™ are two examples. These systems rely on the individual features of AES as the basis for alerting writers to errors and aspects of writing that could be improved in subsequent drafts. Such learning and practice environments require less extensive backing due to the relatively modest consequences of inaccurate scores.

Uses of AES as part of course placement (Ramineni, 2013), require somewhat more support than practice environments, stemming from the potential consequences of inaccurate scoring. Inaccurate scores could contribute to incorrect placement, with negative impact including unnecessary expenditure on course credit and lost educational opportunity. This potential risk is offset somewhat by the expectation that other evidence beyond the essay score (such as prior courses and grades) would be used in the placement decision and there could be early semester opportunities to transfer to a more appropriate class if a misclassification occurs.

For more consequential assessments, such as admissions testing, employment testing, and licensure programs, there is a need for extensive support for the use of AES scores. The a priori consideration of what evidence is needed and how well the AES should perform against pre-established expectations is particularly important for these kinds of tests. The interested reader may see Williamson, Xi, and Breyer (2012) for a more applied perspective on an a priori validity framework for use of AES scoring along with some benchmark measures that have been used at Educational Testing Service for approving AES as one of two scores in consequential assessments that include GRE and TOEFL. A more general perspective on validity and automated scoring can be found in Yang, Buckendahl, Juszkiewicz, and Bhola (2002).

There is another potential use of AES that has not been as widely emphasized, and that is as a tool for trend scoring. Trend scoring is required when the consequence of test scores is substantial and the scores need to have a consistent meaning over time. Scores of human raters are subject to "rater drift" in which the scoring practices of raters change over time, either due to changes in the performance of the same raters or as a result of changes in the pool of raters who score the test. Trend scoring targets determining whether scores from a current scoring are consistent in meaning with the performances from a prior cohort by systematically inserting essays from the prior scoring into the series of essays that the current raters are scoring. If the scores of the current raters match the original scores on these trend essays then there is some confidence that the same scoring standards and practices are being applied. Therefore, any differences in aggregate scores for the cohort may be more readily attributed to differences in examinee performance. In trend scoring applications AES may play a role as a known consistent scoring methodology that could be applied to multiple cohorts of essays and used as the basis for determining differences in performance on essays across cohorts (Trapani, Bridgeman, & Breyer, 2011). A variation on this theme is to use AES for monitoring rater drift directly in an ongoing assessment to alert the assessment developers to changes that may be occurring in human scoring over time (Trapani et al., 2011; Chapter 14, this volume).

The consequences of score use are one aspect that will influence the nature and degree of evidence required to support a warrant, but so too is the philosophical position regarding the purpose of automated scoring. Several such purposes have been proposed, each of which has implications for the interpretive and validity arguments necessary to support the position. These potential positions on AES are:

1. Prediction. The automated score predicts the human score that would have been provided
2. Complement. Automated scores represent some aspect of the construct of writing better than human raters, and other aspects less well than human raters.
3. Replication. Automated scores do exactly what human raters do, replicating both the positive aspects and the negative elements of human scoring.
4. Improvement. Automated scores represent the construct of writing better than human raters, having incorporated all of the desirable characteristics and eliminated the undesirable characteristics of human raters.

The philosophy adopted in defining what AES scores are designed to do will impact how the scores are positioned in the interpretive argument, how they are informed by the validity argument, and ultimately how they are determined to be appropriate (or not) for certain uses in assessment. The interpretations above are roughly ordered in sequence of more modest to more ambitious perspectives on of AES (with the distinction between 2 and 3 admittedly debatable).

The prediction model is very primitive and simply presents AES as a predictor of human scores, thus making few demands on the interpretive argument for scoring, particularly around construct representation. For example, there are many essay prompts in common usage for which the correlation between the number of words in an essay and the score of a human rater is almost as high as the correlation of scores between two independent human raters. From a purely predictive perspective on AES, then, simply counting the number of words in an essay and adding a few other basic elements of the construct of writing, such as a spell-checker, might be sufficient to predict the score a human rater is likely to provide for an essay. Of course, this is a very weak argument for the use of AES as such an approach also makes such an AES system prone to the surrogation fallacy (Kane, 2006). Still, if the only evidence provided for the validity of AES is agreement with human scores then the validity argument is by default a prediction model.

The complementary model is one that is commonly cited to support use of AES as one of two scores in consequential assessment. When applied, it typically references the contributions of human raters to ensure full construct representation and the contributions of AES for specificity and consistency of scoring. Examples of the use of the complimentary model include application of AES to the GRE (Ramineni, Trapani, Williamson, Davey, & Bridgeman, 2012b) and TOEFL (Ramineni et al., 2012a), with the Integrated prompt of TOEFL offering an interesting example of the contrast between construct and consistency in scoring.

The replication model is seldom cited as a goal of AES. While it would represent a notable advance in the construct representation capability of AES, it bears with it the continuation of many aspects of human scoring that are undesired and that AES is well positioned to improve upon. As such, it is not elaborated here other than to note it has been previously referenced as a role for AES.

The improvement model is the fundamental driver for advancing the state of the art of AES and represents a goal to aspire to with ongoing research. It represents the ability of AES to provide all the desirable characteristics of human scoring without any of the undesirable characteristics. For most conceptualizations of the construct of writing the current state of the art of AES is not yet capable of analyzing text as richly as an expert human rater, particularly for higher-order aspects of writing such as sophisticated reasoning, extended argumentation structures that call for precise factual support, or use of irony. Of course, it is currently possible to take this position for AES if the construct of writing for assessment is defined very narrowly to be consistent with the capabilities of current AES systems for construct representation.

CONCLUSION

Interest in AES has been growing substantially, fueled in part by the desire of two consortia of states, SBAC (www.smarterbalanced.org) and PARCC (www.parcconline.org), to implement assessments of Common Core State Standards (National Governors Association Center for Best Practices & Council of Chief State School Officers, 2010) that include AES of essays. With this growth in interest has come increased efforts to advance the state of the art by encouraging contributions from researchers in fields outside the traditional areas of assessment and natural language processing to contribute to AES (Quillen, 2012). This interest has also led to a certain degree of democratization of the development of scoring features for AES through an open-source movement. Such an open-source environment for AES is a commitment of the SBAC consortium, and at least one system, LightSIDE (Chapter 8, this volume) has already been released as an open-source AES. Increasing access and interest in AES may well help advance the state of the art, but substantial progress is still needed and years of research lie ahead before AES will be able to approach an improvement model for the most sophisticated construct definitions for writing. As new features representing expansions of construct of writing are developed, whether open source or private, the design and performance of an integrated system for AES must still be sound and defensible, both at the level of the overall scores produced and for the features that comprise the AES system. Towards that goal, this chapter has provided a perspective on validity of AES based on the validity theory of Kane (2006) and the Toulmin framework for argumentation. It has elaborated interpretive arguments for human scoring and AES, as well as their combination, as a basis for demonstrating fundamental similarities and differences in the necessary support for a convincing validity argument. These serve as a basis for understanding the evidence needed to establish "probable cause" to support a warrant for appropriate use of AES in a variety of assessments.

NOTES

1 The author thanks Michael T. Kane, James E. Carlson and Brent Bridgeman for their helpful advice and comments on earlier versions of this chapter. Any remaining flaws are entirely attributable to the author.
2 Technically these are systems for automated scoring of essays since it is the scoring and not the essay that is automated, but the term AES has become common and so is used here.
3 Admittedly somewhat tongue-in-cheek.
4 While beyond the scope of this chapter, two points are worth noting. First, that some research spans multiple validity inferences, such as G-theory designs that can contribute to the Scoring inference, but also the Generalizability inference. Second, high-stakes assessments tend to have pools of essay prompts considered exchangeable and selected at random for administration. There is an open question regarding where the continuum from prompt #23 to other prompts in the test pool to the universe of all possible essay prompts crosses from the Scoring inference to the Generalizability inference. But as long as this issue is addressed, it does not matter whether it is under one heading or another.
5 An example might be "Voice" from the six-trait model of writing commonly used in instruction.
6 An example might be number of words in the essay, or spelling errors as a function of length.
7 To my knowledge, no AES system uses such a feature and this example is provided for illustrative purposes.
8 This again invokes the question raised in note 4 of where the inference of Scoring ends and the inference of Generalizability begins.

REFERENCES

Attali, Y. (2011). Sequential effects in essay ratings. *Educational and Psychological Measurement, 71,* 68–79.

Attali, Y., & Burstein, J. (2006). Automated essay scoring with e-rater V.2. *Journal of Technology, Learning, and Assessment, 4*(3). Available from http://www.jtla.org

Bridgeman, B., Trapani, C., & Attali, Y. (2012). Comparison of human and machine scoring of essays: Differences by gender, ethnicity, and country. *Applied Measurement in Education, 25,* 27–40.

Burstein, J., & Marcu, D. (2003). A machine learning approach for identification of thesis and conclusion statements in student essays. *Computers and the Humanities, 37*(4), 455–467.

Clauser, B. E., Kane, M. T., & Swanson, D. B. (2002). Validity issues for performance-based tests scored with computer-automated scoring systems. *Applied Measurement in Education, 15,* 413–432.

Clauser, B. E., Margolis, M. J., Clyman, S. G., & Ross, L. P. (1997). Development of automated scoring algorithms for complex performance assessments: A comparison of two approaches. *Journal of Educational Measurement, 34*(2), 141–161.

Culham, R. (2003). *Six + 1 traits of writing.* New York, NY: Scholastic Professional Books.

Deane, P., Fowles, M., & Sabatini, J. (2012). Rethinking K-12 writing assessment to support best practices. In C. Bazerman & S. Null (Eds.), *New directions in international writing research.* Anderson, SC: Parlor Press.

DiPardo, A., Storms, B. A., & Selland, M. (2011). Seeing voices: Assessing writerly stance in the NWP analytic writing continuum. *Assessing Writing, 16,* 170–188.

ETS. (2010), from http://www.ets.org/toefl/news/toefl_testtakers_exceed_25_mil_globally

Ferrucci, D., Brown, E., Chu-Carroll, J., Fan, J., Gondek, D., Kalyanpur, A. A., & Welty, C. (2010). Building Watson: An overview of the DeepQA Project. *Al Magazine, 31*, 59–79.

Johnson, R. L., Penny, J. A., & Gordon, B. (2009). *Assessing performance: Designing, scoring, and, validating performance tasks.* New York, NY: Guilford.

Kane, M. T. (2006). Validation. In R. L. Brennan (Ed.), *Educational measurement (4th ed)*. (pp. 17–64). Westport, CT: American Council on Education/Praeger.

Leacock, C., & Chodorow, M. (2003). Automated grammatical error detection. In M. D. Shermis & J. Burstein (Eds.), *Automated essay scoring: A cross-disciplinary perspective* (pp. 195–208). Mahwah, NJ: Lawrence Erlbaum Associates, Inc.

Leckie, G., & Baird, J. (2011). Rater effects on essay scoring: A multilevel analysis of severity drift, central tendency, and rater experience. *Journal of Educational Measurement, 48*, 399–418.

Mislevy, R. J. (1996). Test theory reconceived. *Journal of Educational Measurement, 33*, 379–416.

Mislevy, R. J., Steinberg, L. S., & Almond, R. G. (2003). On the structure of educational assessments. *Measurement: Interdisciplinary Research and Perspectives, 1*, 3–67.

Myford, C. M., & Wolfe, E. W. (2003). Detecting and measuring rater effects using many-facet Rasch measurement: Part I. *Journal of Applied Measurement, 4*, 386–422.

National Governors Association Center for Best Practices & Council of Chief State School Officers. (2010). Common core state standards. National Governors Association Center for Best Practices & Council of Chief State School Officers. Washington, DC. Available from http://www.corestandards.org/the-standards

Page, E. B. (1968). The use of the computer in analyzing student essays. *International Review of Education, 14*, 210–225.

Quillen, I. (2012). Hewlett Automated-Essay-Grader Winners Announced, May 9. Retrieved from http://blogs.edweek.org/edweek/DigitalEducation/2012/05/essay_grader_winners_announced.html

Ramineni, C. (2013). Validating automated essay scoring for online writing placement. *Assessing Writing, 18*, 40–61.

Ramineni, C., Trapani, C. S., Williamson, D. M., Davey, T., & Bridgeman, B. (2012a). *Evaluation of e-rater® for the GRE® issue and argument prompts (ETS RR-12-02).* Princeton, NJ: Educational Testing Service.

Ramineni, C., Trapani, C. S., Williamson, D. M., Davey, T., & Bridgeman, B. (2012b). *Evaluation of e-rater® for the TOEFL® independent and integrated prompts (ETS RR-12-06).* Princeton, NJ: Educational Testing Service.

Rudner, L. M. (1992). Reducing errors due to the use of judges. *Practical Assessment, Research & Evaluation, 3*(3).

Saal, F. E., Downey, R. G., & Lahey, M. A. (1980). Rating the ratings: Assessing the psychometric quality of rating data. *Psychological Bulletin, 88*, 413–428.

Shermis, M. D., & Hamner, B. (2013). *Contrasting state-of-the-art automated scoring of essays.* In Shermis & Burstein (Eds.), *Handbook of automated essay evaluation: Current applications and new directions* (pp. 313–346). New York, NY: Routledge.

Toulmin, S. E. (1958). *The uses of argument.* Cambridge, UK: Cambridge University Press.

Trapani, C., Bridgeman, B., & Breyer, J. (2011). *Using automated scoring as a trend score: The implications of score separation over time.* Paper presented at the annual meeting of the National Council on Measurement in Education, New Orleans, LA.

Williamson, D. M. Xi, X., & Breyer, J. (2012). A framework for evaluation and use of automated scoring. *Educational Measurement: Issues and Practice, 31*, 2–13.

Wolfe, E. W. (2004). Identifying rater effects using latent trait models. *Psychological Science, 46*, 35–51.

Yang, Y., Buckendahl, C., Juszkiewicz, P., & Bhola, D. (2002). A review of strategies for validating computer-automated scoring. *Applied Measurement in Education, 15*, 391–412.

11 Validity and Reliability of Automated Essay Scoring

Yigal Attali

INTRODUCTION

The purpose of this chapter is to develop a plan to support the use of automated essay scoring (AES) systems. Such a plan involves a clarification of the purpose of AES, how it could achieve this purpose, and what evidence exists that it is successful. This plan elaborates and expands upon previous proposals that were concerned with the validity of automated scoring in general (Bennett, 2006; Bennett & Bejar, 1998; Clauser, Kane, & Swanson, 2002; Yang, Buckendahl, Juszkiewicz, & Bhola, 2002) or specifically with automated essay scoring (Keith, 2003). That such a plan is needed is evidenced by the skepticism and criticism that have accompanied AES over the years. For example, in a *New York Times* column, Scott (1999) remarks cynically that ". . . it has come to this. The essay, the great literary art form that Montaigne conceived and Virginia Woolf carried on . . . has sunk to a state where someone thinks it is a bright idea to ask a computer if an essay is any good." Criticism of AES has been especially harsh within the community of writing professionals (Ericsson & Haswell, 2006). A major organization for writing professionals, the Conference on College Composition and Communication (CCCC), summarizes its position on AES (Communication, 2004), with the words: "We oppose the use of machine-scored writing in the assessment of writing." That this statement has not been revised in the last eight years, in spite of the widespread adoption of AES, suggests that AES developers have not been successful in explaining the intrinsic qualities of AES beyond the obvious logistical benefits of speed and cost.

Supporting the use of test scores is the purpose of test validation. The Standards for Educational and Psychological Testing (AERA, APA, and NCME, 1999) define validity as "the degree to which evidence and theory support the interpretation of test scores entailed by proposed uses" (p. 9). Developing support for a proposed interpretation of test scores involves the development of an argument for the interpretation (Cronbach, 1988; Kane, 2006). To validate an interpretation or use of measurements is to evaluate the plausibility of the intended interpretation. It includes the evidence for and against the proposed interpretation and alternative interpretations.

CAN AES BE VALID?

Therefore, our first goal is to clarify the purpose and uses of AES. On the face of it, the answer to this question is straightforward. By and large, AES has been conceived (Page, 1966) as a *replacement* for human scoring and the purpose of automated scores has been to *emulate* human scores (Shermis & Burstein, 2003). However, this conceptualization gives rise to two difficulties that considerably complicate the *validation* process of AES.

The first of these difficulties is that, if AES is to function as a replacement for human assessment, then it is necessary for AES validation to show that machine scores measure the same construct(s) as human ratings. One problem with this requirement is that we do not actually have a good understanding of what human raters do in their evaluation of student essays. In the context of large-scale, high-stakes writing assessments in particular, a primary goal is to ensure that human raters think similarly enough about what constitutes a high- or low-quality student response to achieve reasonable consistency of scores across ratings. Achieving this goal is a continuous challenge, as numerous studies of rater behavior have shown substantial differences in the way raters interpret scoring criteria (see, e.g., Bachman, Lynch, & Mason, 1995; Eckes, 2008; Engelhard, 1994; Engelhard & Myford, 2003; Lumley & McNamara, 1995; Weigle, 1998). Moreover, rater training has not been able to completely eliminate these differences (Barrett, 2001; Elder, Knoch, Barkhuizen, & von Randow, 2005; Lumley & McNamara, 1995; Weigle, 1998, 1999).

A second difficulty with machine scoring as replacement for human scoring is that it allows (even invites!) what can be considered the most fundamental objection to AES: if AES is supposed to replace a human reader, then it should be rejected out of hand since a machine cannot truly understand the essay, cannot read it as a human reader would, and cannot interpret its meaning. In other words, if machine scores are to be interpreted and used in the same way as human scores, they will never be able to meet this expectation because the machine is not able to understand the text and therefore cannot evaluate aspects of the quality of writing that depend on such understanding. This argument is at the heart of several chapters in Ericsson and Haswell's book (Anson, 2006; Condon, 2006; Ericsson, 2006).

Most validation efforts of AES have implicitly or explicitly tried to answer this objection by showing that machine *scores* are indistinguishable from human scores. In a description of the first AES system, Page (1966) showed that the patterns of agreement between machine and human scores were indistinguishable from patterns of agreement between scores from two human raters. Page and Petersen (1995) even suggest a version of the Turing test (where one has to determine if a rater is a human or a machine by passing essays under a door and getting back essay scores) to emphasize the importance of score imitation for the acceptability of AES. However, score similarity is not a sufficient answer to this objection because the argument concerns the meaning of machine scores, not their empirical correspondence with human scores.

Regardless of the difficulties in establishing what exactly human raters measure (and whether different raters measure the same constructs), we believe that a serious consideration of the construct argument against AES should lead one to accept its basic premise—because the machine is not able to read the essay, it will not be able to assess such aspects as the quality of argumentation or the development of characters in a narrative, as human readers do.

What should we do then? How can validation of AES proceed if its primary purpose cannot be achieved? We believe that AES should be based on an alternative definition of its intended use. Specifically, it should be construed primarily as a *complement* to (instead of replacement for) human scoring, *limited* in its ability to measure a subset of the writing construct. The advantages of this alternative definition are substantial. It implies that AES should not be judged exclusively against the criterion of human ratings. Bennett and Bejar (1998) suggested that using human scores as the sole criterion for judging the success of automated scoring is counter-productive because human raters are highly fallible. Here we stress two other reasons. First, the holistic nature of the human reading process provides little guidance for AES on how to emulate it. Second, the limited nature of machine processing makes it highly unlikely that it could imitate this process. The use of AES as a complement to human scoring also suggests that machine scores should be interpreted directly with respect to what they claim to measure instead of indirectly through what human scores could measure. This in turn could help researchers refocus validation efforts towards a clarification of the traits being measured by AES instead of demonstrations of similarities between human and machine scores. Last but not least, defining AES as a complement to human scoring acknowledges the limited nature of machine analysis and thus may remove an obstacle for a productive discussion with the writing community about the possible merits of AES.

With AES as a complement to human scoring, we can proceed to outline a plan for its validation. The plan should answer the following questions: if machine scores are not the same as human scores, what are the elements of the writing construct that AES measures and how well are they measured? As an alternative method of scoring essays, how similar are machine scores to human scores, are there fairness issues that emerge from the use of machine scores, and how to combine human and machine scores? To answer these questions, we start with the validity of features, the elements that are extracted from the text to serve as measures of essay quality, because they are the most important determiners of the meaning of machine scores. We turn next to the issue of combining features into essay scores, as it affords some flexibility in establishing the meaning of machine scores. Only then we turn our attention to scoring issues, mainly the relation with human scores and other measures, as sources of evidence about the quality of AES. We conclude with implementation issues—how to combine human and machine scores and how to measure the effects of using machine scores on student writing.

THE VALIDITY OF FEATURES

As a complement to human scoring, it is easy to see how AES could directly measure certain aspects of the writing construct, such as adherence to conventions of writing, and may even produce more precise evaluations of these writing aspects than human raters because of its mechanical nature. AES and the use of technology in administering assessments may even provide opportunities to measure aspects of the construct that human raters are not capable of evaluating. For example, tracking the complete keystroke record produced by the student can provide a rich source of information about writing fluency (Almond, Quinlan, & Attali, 2011).

This section will discuss ways to establish the meaning of individual features, of relating features to writing skills, and of establishing the quality of measurement of features.

Meaning of Features

A fundamental problem in developing and considering features for AES is one of interpretation. This is because features, based on extracting elements from the text, bear an indirect relation with the linguistic or writing quality they are supposed to represent. It should be noted that this problem of interpretation is shared by any assessment—the relation between any test item and what it claims to measure is indirect. This suggests a useful analogy between AES features and test items. Although items normally elicit student responses whereas features decompose a student response, the process of item development shares affinities with feature identification. Consequently, content validity activities, such as logical or empirical analyses of the adequacy with which the test content represents the content domain, could similarly be applied to enhance the validity of features.

An important aspect in establishing the meaning of a feature is the degree of its interpretability, or the logical argument that connects a feature with the linguistic or writing quality it is supposed to measure. The interpretation of some features is straightforward—a feature that identifies subject–verb agreement errors measures grammatical conventions, the number of words in an essay measures fluency, and the choice of words in terms of their norms of developmental acquisition measures vocabulary level. Obviously, each of these features is only one of many possible signals (each of them imperfect), but their relation is intuitive. On the other extreme, it is possible to develop features based on aggregating many (sometimes thousands) tiny signals through their statistical relation with human essay scores. These features are "black boxes" in the sense that it is not possible to interpret feature values beyond the fact that high values are predictive of high human scores.

In establishing the meaning of features, AES can also draw on linguistic and cognitive research that characterizes different types of non-essay texts. One line of research analyzed the linguistic characteristics (through normalized frequency counts) of different spoken and written genres through a wide range of linguistic features (Biber, 1988). These include such features as tense and aspect markers, place and time adverbials, pronouns, questions, nominalizations, passive forms, and subordination features. Another line of research on language (particularly second language) development also analyzed measures of fluency, lexical and syntactic complexity, and accuracy in writing (Wolf-Quintero, Inagaki, & Kim, 1998). The long tradition of research on readability and complexity of (well-written) texts (Flesch, 1974; Sheehan, Kostin, Futagi, & Flor, 2010) uses some of the same kinds of linguistic features. Lastly, the rules of writing provide many opportunities to directly identify deviations from these conventions.

By using these sources to identify and develop AES features, it is usually possible to develop (or borrow) a theory of the writing quality that is measured by the feature and the type of effect that variations in this feature will have on essay quality, independently of human essay scores. For example, text features that are more prevalent in academic writing should have a positive relation with human scores of essays that stress an academic writing style. Similarly, text features that are more prevalent later in language development or by native (as opposed to non-native) speakers should have a positive relation with human essay scores.

However, adopting features that have been validated in other contexts does not guarantee their usefulness for AES. An example of this case is a feature used by the Lexile Framework for Reading (Stenner, Horabin, Smith, & Smith, 1988), a reading complexity measure widely used to assess the readability of textbooks and other reading materials in American elementary and middle schools. The Lexile Framework considers two dimensions of text variation: syntactic complexity and semantic difficulty. Syntactic complexity is assessed via log average sentence length. However, computing this feature on student essays does not prove useful in predicting human essay scores. For example, in a large data set of essays written as part of a large-scale, high-stakes assessment, the correlation of this feature with the human essay score is .16 and the partial correlation of this feature after controlling for essay length (log number of words) is −.01, not significantly different from 0. This result is replicated in other essay assessments, including in assessments for middle and high school students. Should we use this measure in AES and accept it as a measure of syntactic complexity, even though in student essays it appears to be a weak proxy of essay length?

An even stranger example is the case of the type/token ratio, the ratio between number of unique words in a text (types) to all words in the text (tokens). A high ratio results from the use of many different lexical items in a text (less repetition). Therefore it presumably indicates lexical diversity and lexical complexity. In Biber's (1988) analysis, this feature was a strong marker of literary (versus oral) discourse. However, in student essays it usually correlates *negatively* with human scores (−.05 in the previous data set), contrary to expectation. Moreover, after controlling for essay length the sign of the correlation is reversed (.27). This reflects the finding that the number of types is very highly correlated with the number of tokens (.85). Should we use this feature in AES, even though in student essays it appears to measure production fluency?

Interpretation of Features as Measures of Writing Skills

These two examples suggest that in developing features, both the rationale for the feature and its empirical relation with human scores and other features should be considered. In particular, through factor analysis methods, the patterns of correlations between features could provide additional support for their interpretation as measures of particular dimensions of writing quality. For example, in an analysis of Test of English as a Foreign Language (TOEFL) essays written by English-as-second-language students, Attali (2007, 2011b) found support for a three-factor structure of the non-content e-rater features, with a factor of word-choice features, a factor of features that measure grammatical conventions within a sentence, and a factor of features that measure fluency and organization aspects. Attali and Powers (2008) replicated these results in an analysis of essays written by students in five grade levels (4th, 6th, 8th, 10th, and 12th). Deane, Quinlan, and Kostin (2011) replicated these results in a re-analysis of the data in Attali and Powers (2008) that was augmented with features used to develop text readability measures (Sheehan et al., 2010). Finally, Attali (2012a) replicated these results with both Graduate Record Examination (GRE) tests and TOEFL writing and showed that the e-rater content features measure a distinct fourth factor.

These results strengthen the validity argument of AES by further clarifying what individual features measure and how related features can be interpreted as measures of writing constructs. Factor analyses can also be useful in supporting (or refuting) the intuitive rationale for new candidate features. As the examples above show, there are often alternative interpretations of what in fact a feature measures. For example, content analysis in the context of AES has always been based on prompt-specific vocabulary analysis (Attali & Burstein, 2006; Landauer, Laham, & Foltz, 2003). Attali (2011a) proposed a task-level feature, on the assumption that specific tasks (such as the GRE issue or the GRE argument tasks) elicit distinct types of vocabularies that have commonalities across prompts. However, such a feature can also be interpreted as a general word-choice vocabulary feature. Nevertheless, factor analyses confirmed that the new feature clearly loads on the content factor and not on the word-choice factor.

Quality of Measurement

Beyond the question of what a feature measures, quality of measurement will also have an effect on feature validity, as it affects our ability to generalize from observed scores to universe scores (Kane, 2006). Empirical evidence needed to support generalization over replications of a measurement procedure is collected in various types of reliability studies (Haertel, 2006). Attali and Burstein (2006) report alternate-form e-rater feature reliabilities for 6th to 12th grade students who wrote two essays on similar topics. Reliabilities are mostly in the mid-40s (with a median of .45), with the exception of very low reliability for content features. Attali (2012a) reports alternate-task e-rater feature reliabilities for GRE and TOEFL examinees who wrote essays on the two assessment tasks (argument and issue for GRE, independent and integrated for TOEFL). Reliabilities are slightly higher for GRE (with a median of .47) but significantly lower for TOEFL (median of .35). However, as the two pairs of writing tasks are not identical (by design) it is not possible to separate the task effect from feature measurement error.

Test-retest and parallel-form reliability analyses are not feasible when students write only one essay. However, with AES it is possible to conduct *internal consistency* reliability analyses of many features (such as word-choice and conventions features) by dividing the essay text into parallel parts and computing the consistency of feature values across these parts. To demonstrate this method, data from Attali and Powers (2009) was reanalyzed. For 6,069 8th, 10th, and 12th grade students who wrote two persuasive essays as part of the study, alternate form reliability was estimated for the grammar (.45), usage (.38), mechanics (.65), vocabulary (.62), and word length (.40) e-rater features. The features were then recalculated for the odd and even sentences of each essay. The stepped-up[1] correlation between the two parts can serve as an estimate of the internal consistency reliability of an entire essay. These estimates for grammar, usage, mechanics, vocabulary, and word length were .66, .63, .83, .74, and .78, respectively. A comparison of the two types of reliability estimates shows a differential effect of prompt (e.g., word length is more affected than vocabulary).

VALIDITY OF FEATURE AGGREGATIONS INTO SCORES

Identification of features can be thought of as the first phase in automated scoring. In the second phase, the features should be aggregated into essay scores. Whereas the previous section discussed the meaning of individual features, this section discusses the implications of different aggregation approaches on the meaning of essay scores. As Bennett and Bejar (1998) note, an advantage of automated scoring is that it makes it possible to control (to some degree) what Embretson (1983) calls the construct representation (the meaning of scores based on internal evidence) and nomothetic span (the meaning of scores based on relationships with external variables) of automated scores. This section will focus on construct representation and the next section will review consequences on nomothetic span.

Feature Weighting

Aggregation can be performed in many ways, but the simplest is to compute a weighted average of the features (this weighted average can then be transformed to a desired scale). In this computation, the weights represent the relative importance of the different features (assuming they have the same scale, for example by standardizing the features). Different weighting schemes will result in scores that have different meanings depending on the traits that are emphasized. These different meanings will surely have an effect on the relation of these scores with other measures. Therefore, the choice of a weighting scheme and its rationale is of utmost importance for the validity of AES.

Nevertheless, weighting schemes for AES have been based almost exclusively on the concept of optimizing the relation of automated scores with human scores of the same essays. For example, by using multiple regression to predict human scores from the set of features calculated on the same essays, weights will be obtained that maximize the relation between the predicted scores and the human scores on this set of essays. Clearly, the rationale for human-prediction weighting is to imitate human scores as best as possible on the premise that machine scores should replace human scores. However, since the computer cannot really imitate human evaluation of essays, statistically optimal weights will not necessarily reflect the relative importance of *human* measured traits. For example, imagine we could somehow determine that a human rater values facility with conventions at 20%, effective vocabulary at 20%, and an insightful position on the issue at 60%. Because the computer is not very good at measuring insightful positions, and since effective vocabulary probably does not mean the same for the human rater and for the machine, it is anybody's guess what would actually be the human-prediction weighting scheme. One possibility is that, because insightful positions may entail generally longer essays, features that are more highly correlated with fluency and essay length will receive a higher weight through the regression analysis. As this example shows, human-prediction weights may be driven more by statistical artifacts than by what drives human scoring. Even more significantly, by adopting human-prediction weights we lose control over what is measured by machine scores. An extreme consequence of this lack of control is the occurrence of negative weights in specific cases, signifying that the effect of a feature on scores will be opposite to the intention of its developers. This of course does not contribute to the validity of machine scores.

Evidently, human-prediction weights are also meant to provide the best prediction of human scores. However, as we show next, this is not necessarily the case when the generalizability of scores is evaluated across different prompts or tests. There are several alternatives to the human-prediction approach. With judgment-based weighting, experts set weights according to judged importance of AES features or measured dimensions of writing. Ben-Simon and Bennett (2007) carried out this approach with two independent committees of writing experts. They found that judgment-based e-rater scores generalized well to new prompts, compared to the "brute-force" human-prediction-based e-rater scores. In the absence of expert judgments, an alternative approach that is similarly not based on empirical data is to assign equal weights to features or dimensions. The rationale of this approach is that the features are all measures of a single underlying construct, similarly to a fixed set of items or components of a test. Attali (2007) compared equal weights with human-prediction weights and found almost identical test-retest reliabilities and slightly lower correlations across tests (e.g., human scores on the first test with machine scores on the second test, with a different prompt) between equal weight scores and human scores (.56 versus .60). Interestingly, human-prediction scores had the highest cross test correlation with essay length (.61), followed by human scores (.53 for a single human score) and equal-weight scores (.47).

A related approach starts with equal weights, but takes into account the quality of measurement of features. In other words, although all features in principle measure the same underlying writing construct, features with higher reliability are more heavily weighted to optimize the measurement of this underlying trait. Indeed, psychometric theory suggests a weighting scheme[2] that maximizes the reliability of the composite score (Haertel, 2006). Another related approach is based on factor analysis. In particular, with a one-factor solution that again assumes all features measure the same underlying construct, the loadings of features represent the strength of relation between each feature and this underlying construct and can be used as the basis of a weighting scheme. Attali (2012a) compared these two weighting schemes to the human-prediction scheme and found again similar cross-task correlations with human scores, similar cross-task reliabilities, and much lower correlations with essay length.

An approach that combines expert judgment of the validity and construct representation of AES features with reliability evidence of features starts with judgments of the importance of dimensions for the construct measured by AES and updates these estimates with reliability of the different dimensions. It is important, however, that judges relate their judgments to the construct measured by the machine and not by human ratings. For example, although organization may be an important trait to measure, it is likely to be measured crudely by the machine and its importance appropriately reduced by judges.

Level of Score Definition

One of the most difficult psychometric issues in human scoring of constructed response assessments is the maintenance of scoring standards across tasks and forms. An advantage of AES is the possibility to assure constant scoring standards across prompts by using the same weights and scaling parameters (Attali, Bridgeman, & Trapani, 2010). This also contributes to the validity of AES as it fixes the meaning of scores across prompts and contributes to score generalizability. These advantages cannot be realized under a human imitation approach that seeks to optimize prediction of human scores for each prompt separately. In prompt-specific AES, both the weights of features could change from prompt to prompt (and hence the construct representation of scores) as well as the scoring standards (depending on changes in human scoring standards).

RELIABILITY

Reliability is concerned with consistency of test scores and is based on the idea that the observed score on a test is only one possible result that might have been obtained under different conditions—another occasion of the test, a different form of the test, or a different rater scoring the test. Reliability contributes to the validity argument because it provides evidence on the repeatability of scores across different measurement conditions. To the extent that scores reflect random errors of measurement, their potential for accurate prediction of other behaviors or for beneficial examinee diagnosis is limited.

In the context of a particular AES system, there is only one possible "rater," and therefore the generalizability of scores across raters is not applicable. As a consequence, it is important to realize that inter-rater agreement coefficients between human and machine scores do not provide information about the reliability of machine scores, because they do not estimate consistency of machine scores in different conditions (e.g., for different prompts). Rather, they provide information about the validity of machine scores as an alternative method for human scoring. This type of information will be discussed in the next section.

Consequently, reliability of AES is principally concerned with precision of scores across test forms (prompts). To estimate this type of reliability, a large group of students would write an essay on one prompt and after a suitable amount of time would write another essay on another prompt. The observed correlation between automated scores on those two prompts is an *alternate forms* estimate of reliability, also referred to as a coefficient of *stability and equivalence*. It reflects the uncertainty in scores arising from students' idiosyncratic reactions to different prompts (lack of equivalence between prompts), lack of stability across time, as well as any other random effects on scores. When the two prompts are administered on the same occasion, reliability estimates cannot indicate variability over time and are referred to as coefficients of equivalence. In any case, the observed correlation between scores on two prompts estimate the reliability of a single essay test. To estimate the reliability of a test comprised of two (or more) essays from the reliability of a single essay test, one can use the Spearman-Brown formula. Note that because the principal interest in this context is in generalizing over only one type of condition (or facet), namely prompts, the application of generalizability theory (Brennan,

2001) to the measurement of AES reliability will not provide any additional insights over the use of the Spearman-Brown formula. In other words, Spearman-Brown estimates will be the same as generalizability coefficients.

The reliability of e-rater was estimated in several studies. Attali and Burstein (2006) estimated a reliability coefficient of .59 for scores of 6th to 12th grade students who submitted two essays as part of an instruction and practice program within a time frame of a few weeks. Attali and Powers (2009) estimated reliability coefficients of .67 to .75 for scores of 4th to 12th grade students who participated in a research study and submitted four essays within a time frame of a few weeks. Attali (2009) estimated reliability coefficients for students who repeated the GRE and TOEFL tests within six months. Estimates of reliability were .73, .69, and .79 for the GRE argument, GRE issue, and TOEFL independent tasks, respectively. Finally, Attali (2012a) reports cross-task reliability coefficients for GRE and TOEFL, which can be thought of as lower bounds for same-task reliability estimates. The correlation between GRE argument and issue e-rater scores was .75 and the correlation between TOEFL independent and integrated e-rater scores was .70. All the above figures estimate the reliability of a single essay test. To estimate the reliability of a test comprised of two essays from the reliability of a single essay test, one can use the Spearman-Brown formula. For example, if the single essay reliability is .70, the reliability of two essays is estimated to be .82. It should be noted that the reported reliability of human scores is considerably lower. For example, the cross-task reliability coefficients for a single human rater in Attali (2012a) are .56 and .51 for GRE and TOEFL, respectively (about .20 lower than e-rater reliability).

RELATION WITH HUMAN SCORES

The relation of machine scores with human scores provide important information about the validity of AES because, on the one hand, it is reasonable to assume that machine scores do not measure the same construct as human scores, but, on the other hand, machine scores are used as an alternative *method* of scoring essays. Because machine scores cannot be claimed to be completely interchangeable with human scores, it is important to empirically estimate the degree of similarity between the two methods of scoring. As two methods for scoring essays, the relationship between human and machine scores provide convergent evidence on their validity.

Several types of statistics have been used to measure the degree of relation between machine and human scores. The percent of time a human rating agrees with the machine rating is easy to communicate but does not take into account the expected agreement due to base rates in the use of different categories, and therefore cannot be compared across applications. The kappa measure corrects this shortcoming, but it requires (as do percent agreement) that machine scores be rounded to conform to the same discrete categories used by human raters. An advantage of machine scores from a measurement perspective is that they are continuous by nature, and therefore the use of kappa measures artificially lowers the measurement quality of machine scores. Consequently, the correlation coefficient, as a general purpose measure of association between scores, should be preferred as a measure of the relation between machine and human scores.

The vast majority of evaluations have compared the score correlations between human and machine ratings to those between one human rating and another human rating, all on the same prompt task. In the earliest experiments with AES, Page (1966) found that human–machine correlations were as high as human–human correlations. These results were replicated many times (see different chapters in this volume) but a careful examination reveals interesting differences across tasks. For example, Ramineni, Trapani, Williamson, Davey, and Bridgeman (2012a) show that for the GRE issue task human–human correlations (.74) are lower than human–machine correlations (.80), but for the GRE argument task human–human correlations (.78) are at least as high as human–machine correlations (.78). Similarly, Ramineni, Trapani, Williamson, Davey, and Bridgeman (2012b) show that for the TOEFL independent task human–human correlations (.69) are lower than human–machine correlations (.75), but for the TOEFL integrated task human–human correlations (.82) are higher than human–machine correlations (.73). These differences can be explained by considering the writing requirements of the four tasks. The GRE issue and TOEFL independent tasks ask students to present their opinion on a general issue (e.g., "In our time, specialists of all kinds are highly overrated. We need more generalists—people who can provide broad perspectives"); the GRE argument and TOEFL integrated tasks are more focused on quality of argumentation by presenting a rich and specific context for the writing task. To the degree that human scoring takes into account the quality of arguments and since AES is limited in its ability to understand arguments, it is reasonable to expect a lower degree of relation between human and machine scores on the later two tasks.

A second type of evaluation of human–machine relations can be based on comparisons of score correlations *across* prompt tasks. In other words, the human–human and human–machine correlations are based on performance in different prompts. The advantage of different-prompt correlations is that they incorporate idiosyncrasies in the way different human raters evaluate different tasks, a significant possible source of inconsistencies in human scoring. Another advantage of cross-task evaluations is that they permit estimation of true-score correlations between human and machine scores. True-score correlations estimate what would be the degree of relation between scores if they were measured without error (or with perfect reliability) and are computed by dividing the raw correlation by the square root of the product of the reliabilities. Scores that measure the same construct would have the largest raw correlation that their respective degree of unreliability could permit. Computing true-score correlations for such scores would yield a value of 1.

Cross-task human–machine correlations and true-score human–machine correlations were computed in several studies that were mentioned previously. Attali and Burstein (2006) estimated true-score human–machine correlation of .97 for 6th to 12th grade student essays. Attali (2007) estimated true-score correlation of .97 for TOEFL independent essays. Attali (2009) estimated true-score correlations of .89, .97, and .94 for the GRE argument, GRE issue, and TOEFL independent tasks, respectively. These results show again that machine scores can be very highly correlated with human scores for tasks that elicit less constrained writing and where human evaluation is not primarily focused on quality of argumentation.

The previous approaches treated human and machine scoring as distinct alternative methods of scoring. However, when human ratings are available from a large number of raters, machine scores can be interpreted as a distinct "rater" among other raters. Similarities and differences in rating styles can then be studied by conducting factor analyses of all raters' scores. Page (1966) conducted a similar analysis but did not focus on individual differences (and conducted the factor analysis with pairs of human raters). In unpublished work, Attali (2012b) analyzed GRE argument and issue essays for which ratings from 16 different GRE raters were collected. Results of a principal component analysis (a form of factor analysis) on the 17 ratings (16 human and e-rater) showed that the first (most important) component accounted for a large proportion of total variance (81% for argument and 75% for issue), indicating that, overall, rater scores measure a strong single component. Figure 11.1 shows the loadings (or correlations) of raters with

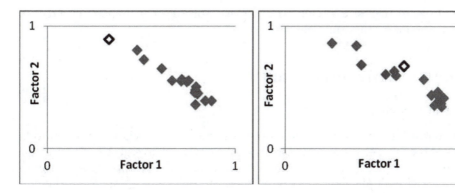

Figure 11.1 Two-component solution loadings for argument (left) and issue (e-rater empty symbol)

the two principal components (after a Varimax orthogonal rotation to better differentiate between components). The figure clearly shows that e-rater is a "typical" rater for issue (on both dimensions), whereas on argument it exemplifies most strongly the second component. Nevertheless, even for argument, some human raters are quite similar to e-rater—their scoring may be identified as "machine-style." Results like these provide a detailed illustration of the similarities and differences between machine and human scoring.

Another test of the degree of similarity between the two scoring methods can be based on developmental data. Specifically, differential sensitivity of human and machine scores to developmental trends in writing quality could provide hints about differences in the measurement of the construct. For example, if human raters were more sensitive to different aspects of mature writing, human scores of older students would increase more dramatically than machine scores. To test this possibility, Attali and Powers (2009) compared the human ratings of essays written by 6th, 8th, and 10th graders (human raters did not know the grade level of the writer) to e-rater scores that applied the same scoring standards to all essays and were not based on prediction of the human scores. Results indicated that human and machine scores were equally sensitive to student grade level.

Subgroup Differences

Because writing is a complex construct, groups of examinees with different linguistic and cultural backgrounds could develop distinct patterns of writing skills. Because machine scores measure the writing construct differently than human scores, these skills may be more or less influential in human or machine scores. Consequently, specific groups of examinees may have, on average, higher or lower machine scores than human scores. Bridgeman, Trapani, and Attali (2012) explored this possibility across gender, ethnic, and country of origin groups, for both the GRE and TOEFL. Human and machine scores were very similar across most subgroups, but there were some notable exceptions. Chinese speaking examinees, and in particular examinees from mainland China, earned relatively higher e-rater scores than human scores, and Arabic speaking examinees earned relatively lower e-rater scores. These results were in the same direction as found by Burstein and Chodorow (1999) with an earlier version of e-rater. Although these results could emerge from distinct writing styles of certain language groups, lack of differences for countries that share the same or similar languages (Korea, Japan, and even Chinese-speaking Taiwan) suggest that cultural differences, or even test preparation practices, could also account for these findings.

RELATION WITH OTHER MEASURES

Convergent Evidence

Comparison of human and machine scores in terms of their relationship with other measures of the same or a similar construct could serve as convergent evidence against the threat of construct under-representation. One particularly important measure in this context is a multiple-choice test of writing. Multiple-choice tests of writing indirectly measure writing skills through recognition tasks of the knowledge of writing conventions. Because AES emphasizes conventions and other lower level aspects of writing skills, it could be argued that machine essay scores would be more correlated with multiple-choice test scores than human essay scores. However, both Petersen (1997) and Attali (2007) found similar correlations for human and machine scores. Moreover, Attali (2007) found that the TOEFL multiple-choice writing scores had slightly higher true-score correlations with human essay score (.89) than with e-rater scores (.85).

Several studies examined the relations of automated and human essay scores with other sub-scores from the same general ability test (Attali, 2007, 2009; Petersen, 1997; Ramineni, et al., 2012a, 2012b). These measures are relevant for validation of essay scores especially when their purpose is to measure other aspects of language proficiency (like reading, speaking, and listening for TOEFL and verbal scores for GRE), because they can serve as additional convergent evidence on the validity of scores. The general finding in the above studies is that human and machine essay scores correlate roughly equally with other sub-scores. However, it is important to remember that with AES these correlations can be partly manipulated through feature weights. For example, Attali (2007) shows that true-score correlations between e-rater and TOEFL reading and listening scores are higher with an equal-weight scheme.

Powers, Burstein, Chodorow, Fowles, and Kukich (2002a) examined the relationship of GRE essay scores, both automated scores derived using (an older version of) e-rater and human scores, to several non-test indicators of examinees' writing skills. These included self-evaluations of writing ability and various self-reported accomplishments in writing. These measures provide important information on the validity of essay scores because they are related to "real-world" achievements in writing. Results showed somewhat weaker correlations for automated scores than for human scores with these indicators.

Divergent Evidence

The relationship with measures of other proficiencies, such as mathematical reasoning, can serve as further evidence that machine scores are not influenced by construct irrelevant factors. Ramineni et al. (2012a) found that GRE quantitative scores had slightly higher correlations with e-rater (.13 and .24 for argument and issue) than with human scores (.07 and .22).

The relationship between response length and response quality for constructed-response measures is a controversial issue (Powers, 2005). Essay length is very highly correlated with human essay scores—e.g., Attali (2007) computed true-score correlations of .85. Because essay length is highly predictive of human scores, correlations of machine scores with essay length can also serve as evidence of divergence—that machine scores are not overly dependent on this easily computable feature. Indeed, Attali (2007) found that e-rater scores based on human-prediction weights had significantly higher true-score correlations with essay length (.86), compared with equal weights (.66).

Because the machine does not understand the essay, it is possible that test-takers develop strategies to produce text that do not depend on writing ability and are blatantly incoherent, but nevertheless it allows them to receive high machine scores. Powers, Burstein, Chodorow, Fowles, and Kukich (2002b) investigated the importance of this source of construct irrelevance by asking writing experts to write essays that would trick e-rater into awarding scores that are higher (but also lower) than deserved. The experts were successful in producing essays that would earn a higher machine score in 26 of 30 cases, with an average discrepancy of 1.3 points, on a 6-point scale. The most successful of these essays repeated sentences many times and thus clearly qualify as a strategy that is easy to implement during a test. Other successful essays attempted to ramble, missed the point, used faulty logic, or were haphazard in their progression, but used relevant content words and complex sentence structure. The results of this study show the importance of developing techniques for automatically detecting unusual essays that should not be processed through the regular AES system. These techniques could be especially useful in detecting incoherent repetition or off-topic essays (Higgins, Burstein, & Attali, 2006).

CONSEQUENCES OF AES USE

In making decisions about whether and how to incorporate AES in the evaluation of essays, an assessment program has to take into account the range of evidence for the validity of machine scores. It has to weigh the possible benefits in cost savings and reliability against the possible risks of shifting the measured construct, changes in subgroup differences, and susceptibility to large errors in scoring.

One possibility for AES implementation is the contributory model, where the human machine ratings are averaged with some predetermined weights to determine the final score for the writing task. As a more conservative approach, in the "check score" or confirmatory score model the machine score is used only to confirm that the human and machine scores are within an allowable discrepancy threshold. If they are, the human rating would constitute the final score for the writing task. If their discrepancy exceeds the threshold, a second human rating is produced and the average of the two human ratings would constitute the final score for the task.

However, regardless of the model of implementation, an evaluation of the intended and unintended consequences of AES use should be part of the evidence for the validity of automated scores. A possible unintended consequence of AES use is that students change their writing strategies to accommodate automated scoring. Although evidence for this possibility can indirectly be drawn from monitoring of human and machine scores (as well as individual features), a useful way to approach this issue is to ask test-takers directly about their reactions to AES and whether they had approached test taking differently as a result of the use of automated scoring. Powers (2011) surveyed TOEFL test-takers and asked them what would be good strategies for writing essays that are scored automatically. The most frequently endorsed strategies were to pay more attention to spelling and grammar and to the form or structure of the essay, such as making certain to include sections like an introduction and a conclusion. Other popular strategies were to use more transition words and more diverse vocabulary. On the other hand, test-takers were far less likely to endorse such strategies as writing lengthy essays or using complex sentences and long words. In addition, most did not think it a good strategy to focus less on the content or logic of their essays.

The intended consequences of AES should also be investigated. Tests are administered to realize some benefit from their scores, such as better educational placement decisions or better selection decisions into academic institutions. Typically, criterion measures can be identified (e.g., success in the academic institution), and the degree to which test scores predict the criterion measure is evaluated to assess the predictive validity of test scores. In this context, the predictive validity of machine scores can be compared to that of human scores.

SUMMARY

AES has been defined as a *replacement* for human scoring and the purpose of automated scores has been to *emulate* human scores. This chapter proposes that AES would benefit if it was redefined primarily as a *complement* to human scoring. The main reason for this proposal is that machine processing of text cannot achieve an understanding of the essay, and is therefore limited to measuring a subset of the writing construct. The task of mimicking human raters is further complicated by the difficulty to deduce what factors drive human essay evaluations.

Therefore, it is proposed that AES validation should proceed by first clarifying the construct it can measure, independently of what humans measure, and only then evaluate the similarity in measured constructs. The following issues are important to address in this process:

- *Meaning of individual features.* What linguistic or writing quality attributes features are meant to be measured? What is the logical argument that supports this interpretation? Does empirical evidence support this interpretation through group comparisons (comparing feature values for high and low quality essays, younger and older students, native and non-native speakers), direct human evaluation (is this really a subject–verb agreement error), and factor analysis (do features that are supposed to measure word choice cluster together)?
- *Meaning of clusters of features.* What interpretation emerges from factor analysis of features about the writing qualities that clusters of features measure? What is the quality of measurement (or reliability) of features and feature dimensions?
- *Aggregating features into essay scores.* What criteria are used to determine the importance (weight) of features in scores? The choice of criteria—prediction of human scores, expert judgments, factor analysis, reliability information—have implications to construct representation. At what level are scores defined? Standardizing feature weighting and scaling across prompts of the same assessment provides important benefits in terms of the meaning of scores across tasks.
- *Reliability.* As a method for evaluating essay writing performance, what is the evidence about the expected consistency of scores across occasions and prompt tasks?
- *Relation with human scores.* As alternative methods for evaluating essay writing performance, what is the empirical evidence about the degree of convergence between human and machine evaluation? In the context of individual differences between human raters, how similar are machine scores to scores of different raters? What is the evidence of differential subgroup differences across the methods?

- *Evidence of convergence.* As an essay writing measure of writing skills, what is the evidence of convergence with other measures of writing skills (multiple-choice tests or self-evaluations of writing ability)? As a measure of a specific aspect of language proficiency, what is the evidence of convergence with measures of other language proficiencies (reading or listening)? How does this evidence compare with the method of human evaluation of essays?
- *Evidence of divergence.* What is the evidence of divergence with measures of other proficiencies (math ability)? Is the correlation with essay length similar for human and machine scores? How susceptible is machine scoring to incoherent writing?
- *Consequences of AES use.* Is there evidence for unintended consequences—for example, that examinees are changing their writing strategies as a result of AES implementation? What is the predictive validity of AES in situations where it is used for selection or placement purposes?

CONCLUSIONS

I believe that with AES one should remember Carl Sagan's famous quote that "extraordinary claims require extraordinary evidence." This chapter outlined the range of evidence required to support a validity argument for AES, with a particular emphasis on the methods for gathering evidence. I believe that a review of the published data does provide support for the less extraordinary claim that AES can measure *some* useful aspects of the writing construct. However, this support is not solid for the most important piece of the argument—what exactly are these aspects of the writing construct that are measured by an AES system?

I would like to conclude with a proposal to consider a broader view of the validity of writing assessments. For a long time the goal of an AES system was to produce scores that are as similar as possible to human scores. However, considering that AES is here to stay but that it is best understood as a complement to human scoring, I believe that a broader assessment perspective should lead us to favor greater separation of the evaluation roles that are assigned to humans and to the machine. A "division of labor" approach, where each method focuses on the aspects of writing quality it measures best, could lead to better and broader measurement of the construct. Although with AES it is possible to control construct representation to some degree, the limited nature of machine processing suggests that this goal could be achieved more easily by inducing human evaluation to focus more on higher-order writing skills. This change in human evaluation could, paradoxically, improve the validity of both methods of scoring.

NOTES

1 The correlation r between the two halves is an estimate of the reliability of half an essay. Using the Spearman-Brown formula, $2r/(1+r)$ is an estimate of the reliability of an entire essay.
2 Setting feature weights proportional to $\sqrt{r}/(1-r)$, where r is the reliability of the feature.

REFERENCES

AERA, APA, and NCME (1999). *Standards for educational and psychological testing.* Washington, DC: American Psychological Association.

Almond, R., Quinlan, T. H., & Attali, Y. (2011). *Using timing logs to diagnose problems in writing performance.* Paper presented at the annual meeting of the American Educational Research Association, New Orleans, LA.

Anson, C. M. (2006). Can't touch this: Reflections on the servitude of computers as readers. In P. F. Ericsson & R. H. Haswell (Eds.), *Machine scoring of student essays: Truth and consequences* (pp. 211–220). Logan, UT: Utah State University Press.

Attali, Y. (2007). *Construct validity of e-rater in scoring TOEFL essays (ETS RR-07–21).* Princeton, NJ: Educational Testing Service.

Attali, Y. (2009). *Evaluating automated scoring for operational use in consequential language assessment.* Paper presented at the National Council on Measurement in Education, San Diego, CA.

Attali, Y. (2011a). *A differential word use measure for content analysis in automated essay scoring (ETS RR-11–36).* Princeton, NJ: Educational Testing Service.

Attali, Y. (2011b). *Automated subscores for TOEFL iBT Independent essays (ETS RR-11–39).* Princeton, NJ: Educational Testing Service.

Attali, Y. (2012a). *Factor structure of the e-rater automated essay scoring system.* Paper presented at the National Council of Measurement in Education, Vancouver, CA.

Attali, Y. (2012b). *When raters score like a machine: Exploring rating styles among essay raters.* Manuscript in preparation.

Attali, Y., Bridgeman, B., & Trapani, C. S. (2010). Performance of a generic approach in automated essay scoring. *Journal of Technology, Learning, and Assessment, 10*(3). Available from http://wwwjtla.org

Attali, Y., & Burstein, J. (2006). Automated essay scoring with e-rater V.2. *Journal of Technology, Learning, and Assessment, 4*(3). Available from http://www.jtla.org

Attali, Y., & Powers, D. (2009). Validity of scores for a developmental writing scale based on automated scoring. *Educational and Psychological Measurement, 69*, 978–993.

Attali, Y., & Powers, D. E. (2008). *A developmental writing scale.* (ETS RR-08-19. Princeton, NJ: Educational Testing Service.

Bachman, L. F., Lynch, B. K. & Mason, M. (1995). Investigating variability in tasks and rater judgments in a performance test of foreign language speaking. *Language Testing, 12*, 238–257.

Barrett, S. (2001). The impact of training on rater variability. *International Education Journal, 2*, 49–58.

Ben-Simon, A., & Bennett, R. E. (2007). Toward more substantively meaningful automated essay scoring. *Journal of Technology, Learning, and Assessment, 6*(1). Available from http://www.jtla.org.

Bennett, R. E. (2006). Moving the field forward: Some thoughts on validity and automated scoring. In D. M. Williamson, R. J. Mislevy, & I. I. Bejar (Eds.), *Automated scoring of complex tasks in computer-based testing* (pp. 403–412). Mahwah, NJ: Erlbaum.

Bennett, R. E., & Bejar, I. I. (1998). Validity and automated scoring: It's not only the scoring. *Educational Measurement: Issues and Practice, 17*, 9–17.

Biber, D. (1988). *Variation across speech and writing.* Cambridge, England: Cambridge University Press.

Brennan, R. L. (2001). *Generalizability Theory.* New York, NY: Springer-Verlag.

Bridgeman, B., Trapani, C., & Attali, Y. (2012). Comparison of human and machine scoring of essays: Differences by gender, ethnicity, and country. *Applied Measurement in Education, 25*, 27–40.

Burstein, J., & Chodorow, M. (1999). Automated essay scoring for nonnative English speakers. *Proceedings of the ACL99 Workshop on Computer-Mediated Language Assessment and Evaluation of Natural Language Processing.*

Clauser, B. E., Kane, M. T., & Swanson, D. B. (2002). Validity issues for performance-based tests scored with computer-automated scoring systems. *Applied Measurement in Education, 15*, 413–432.

Communication, Conference on College Composition and. (2004). *Position statement on teaching, learning, and assessing writing in digital environments.* Paper presented at the Conference on College Composition and Communication, http://www.ncte.org/cccc/resources/positions

Condon, W. (2006). Why less is not more: What we lose by letting the computer score writing samples. In P. F. Ericsson & R. H. Haswell (Eds.), *Machine scoring of student essays: Truth and consequences* (pp. 211–220). Logan, UT: Utah State University Press.

Cronbach, L. J. (1988). Five perspectives on validity argument. In H. Wainer & H. Braun, (Eds.), *Test validity* (pp. 3–17). Hillsdale, NJ: Lawrence Erlbaum Associates, Inc.

Deane, P., Quinlan, T., & Kostin, I. (2011). *Automated scoring within a developmental, cognitive model of writing proficiency* (ETS RR-11-16). Princeton, NJ: Educational Testing Service.

Eckes, T. (2008). Rater types in writing performance assessments: A classification approach to rater variability. *Language Testing, 25,* 155–185.

Elder, C., Knoch, U., Barkhuizen, G., & von Randow, J. (2005). Individual feedback to enhance rater training: Does it work? *Language Assessment Quarterly, 2,* 175–196.

Embretson, S. (1983). Construct validity: Construct representation versus nomothetic span. *Psychological Bulletin, 93,* 179–197.

Engelhard, G., Jr. (1994). Examining rater errors in the assessment of written composition with a many-faceted Rasch model. *Journal of Educational Measurement, 31,* 93–112.

Engelhard, G., Jr., & Myford, C. M. (2003). Monitoring faculty consultant performance in the Advanced Placement English Literature and Composition Program with a many-faceted Rasch model. *College Board Research Report* (No. 2003–1). New York, NY: College Entrance Examination Board.

Ericsson, P. F. (2006). The meaning of meaning: Is a paragraph more than an equation? In P. F. Ericsson & R. H. Haswell (Eds.), *Machine scoring of student essays: Truth and consequences* (pp. 28–37). Logan, UT: Utah State University Press.

Ericsson, P. F., & Haswell, R. H. (Eds.). (2006). *Machine scoring of student essays: Truth and consequences.* Logan, UT: Utah State University Press.

Flesch, R. (1974). *The art of readable writing.* New York, NY: Harper & Row.

Haertel, E. H. (2006). Reliability. In R. L. Brennan (Ed.), *Educational measurement* (4th ed., pp. 65–110). Westport, CT: American Council on Education/Praeger.

Higgins, D., Burstein, J., & Attali, Y. (2006). Identifying off-topic student essays without topic-specific training data. *Natural Language Engineering, 12*(2), 145–159.

Kane, M. T. (2006). Validation. In R. L. Brennan (Ed.), *Educational measurement (4th ed.,* pp. 17–64). Westport, CT: American Council on Education/Praeger.

Keith, T. Z. (2003). Validity of automated essay scoring systems. In M. D. Shermis & J. Burstein (Eds.), *Automated essay scoring: A cross-disciplinary perspective* (pp. 147–168). Mahwah, NJ: Lawrence Erlbaum Associates, Inc.

Landauer, T. K., Laham, R. D., & Foltz, P. W. (2003). Automated scoring and annotation of essays with the Intelligent Essay Assessor. In M. Shermis & J. Bernstein (Eds.), *Automated essay scoring: A cross-disciplinary perspective* (pp. 87–112). Mahwah, NJ: Lawrence Erlbaum Associates, Inc.

Lumley, T., & McNamara, T. F. (1995). Rater characteristics and rater bias: Implications for training. *Language Testing, 12,* 54–71.

Page, E. B. (1966). The imminence of grading essays by computer. *Phi Delta Kappan, 48,* 238–243.

Page, E. B., & Petersen, N. S. (1995). The computer moves into essay grading: Updating the ancient test. *Phi Delta Kappan, 76,* 561–565.

Petersen, N. S. (1997). *Automated scoring of writing essays: Can such scores be valid?* Paper presented at the National Council of Measurement in Education, Chicago, IL.

Petersen, N. S., & Page, E. B. (1997). *New developments in Project Essay Grade: Second ETS blind test with GRE essays.* Paper presented at the American Educational Research Association, Chicago, IL.

Powers, D. E. (2005). *"Wordiness": A selective review of its influence, and suggestions for investigating its relevance in tests requiring extended written responses (ETS RM-04–08).* Princeton, NJ: Educational Testing Service.

Powers, D. E. (2011). *Scoring the TOEFL independent essay automatically: Reactions of test takers and test score users (ETS RM-11–34).* Princeton, NJ: Educational Testing Service.

Powers, D. E., Burstein, J. C., Chodorow, M., Fowles, M. E., & Kukich, K. (2002a). Comparing the validity of automated and human scoring of essays. *Journal of Educational Computing Research, 26,* 407–425.

Powers, D. E., Burstein, J. C., Chodorow, M., Fowles, M. E., & Kukich, K. (2002b). Stumping e-rater: Challenging the validity of automated essay scoring. *Computers in Human Behavior, 18*(2), 103–134.

Ramineni, C., Trapani, C. S., Williamson, D. M., Davey, T., & Bridgeman, B. (2012a). *Evaluation of e-rater® for the GRE® issue and argument prompts (ETS RR-12–02).* Princeton, NJ: Educational Testing Service.

Ramineni, C., Trapani, C. S., Williamson, D. M., Davey, T., & Bridgeman, B. (2012b). *Evaluation of e-rater® for the TOEFL® independent and integrated prompts (ETS RR-12-06).* Princeton, NJ: Educational Testing Service.

Scott, J. (1999). Looking for the tidy mind, alas. *The New York Times,* January 31.

Sheehan, K. M., Kostin, I., Futagi, Y., & Flor, M. (2010). *Generating automated text complexity classifications that are aligned with targeted text complexity standards (ETS Research Report RR-10–28).* Princeton, NJ: Educational Testing Service.

Shermis, M. D., & Burstein, J. (2003). Introduction. In M. D. Shermis & J. Burstein (Eds.), *Automated essay scoring: A cross-disciplinary perspective.* Mahwah, NJ: Lawrence Erlbaum Associates, Inc.

Stenner, A. J., Horabin, I., Smith, D. R., & Smith, M. (1988). Most comprehension tests do measure reading comprehension: A response to McLean and Goldstein. *Phi Delta Kappan, 79,* 765–767.

Weigle, S. C. (1998). Using FACETS to model rater training effects. *Language Testing, 15,* 263–287.

Weigle, S. C. (1999). Investigating rater/prompt interactions in writing assessment: Quantitative and qualitative approaches. *Assessing Writing, 6,* 145–178.

Wolf-Quintero, K., Inagaki, S., & Kim, H. Y. (1998). *Second language development in writing: Measures of fluency, accuracy & complexity.* Honolulu, HI: University of Hawaii Press.

Yang, Y., Buckendahl, C., Juszkiewicz, P., & Bhola, D. (2002). A review of strategies for validating computer-automated scoring. *Applied Measurement in Education, 15,* 391–412.

12 Scaling and Norming for Automated Essay Scoring

Kristin L. K. Koskey and Mark D. Shermis

INTRODUCTION

In this chapter, we provide an overview of different methods used in scaling and norming essay scores starting with a general comparison of holistic and analytic rubrics. Next, scales applied for rating the quality of writing samples are reviewed with a focus on standardized writing development scales established for application in automated essay evaluation (AEE) providing for an examinee's writing ability to be meaningfully tracked over time and across essay prompts. Methods for formation of scores in AEE are then overviewed. Common standard-setting methods are summarized and, finally, differential item functioning methods are discussed. Throughout the chapter, we raise validity issues that continue to exist today, and make recommendations for future work in the effort of producing meaningful scores in the process of scaling and norming essay scores in general and in AES.

SCORING AND SCALING ESSAYS

There are three general approaches to scoring and scaling essays. The most common method is a criterion-referenced approach applying a rubric or set of standards defining lower to higher quality writing performance. The key feature of this approach is that the writing is compared to a set of criteria against which the essay is evaluated. This method is often used in combination with the second approach, normative scaling. In normative scaling, raters utilize a rubric, but the actual evaluation of writing performance is based on a set of norms established for making comparisons in examinees' relative writing performance. The higher the score an examinee is assigned, the higher the relative performance on the essay task. The last approach, which employs the Rasch model (1960, 1980), examines the relationship between examinees' ability and the probability of obtaining a particular score on an essay item of a given difficulty level. This approach has been combined with criterion and norm-referenced approaches. The Rasch model is a family of models consisting of the dichotomous, polytomous, partial credit, and many-facet Rasch models, to name a few. The many-facet Rasch model (MFRM; Linacre, 1994), also referred to as the multi-facet Rasch model, is becoming increasingly applied in scaling essays scores in general (see for a review Eckes, 2009) and in AEE in particular (e.g., Lee, Gentile, & Kantor, 2008). We elaborate on criterion-referenced approaches next, including the use of holistic and trait-scoring approaches, scales associated with such approaches, and efforts applying the Rasch model in attempt to scale essay ratings onto a common scale.

Holistic and Trait Scoring Approaches

Two classifications of rubrics are holistic rubrics and analytic or trait rubrics. Analytical scoring focuses on the component parts of writing (e.g., ideas, wording), whereas trait scoring evaluates the attributes of performance for a particular audience and writing purpose (Stiggins & Bridgeford, 1983). In applying a holistic rubric, the rater makes a judgment about the overall quality of an examinee's performance on an essay item. In this sense, the rater judges multiple criteria simultaneously when assigning a single rating. A single rating represents an examinee's performance on a conglomerate of characteristics such as word usage, writing conventions, voice, and organization. For example, the Florida Comprehensive Assessment Test® Writing Rubric in Table 12.1 applies a holistic approach. Only the description defining one rating from the 6-point scale is provided here for illustrative purposes. The description for rating 6 (the highest level) is characteristic of a holistic approach where multiple criteria are included in the single rating defining an examinee's performance on the focus of the topic, organizational pattern, use of supporting ideas, maturity of language usage, application of writing conventions, and so forth. In this sense, holistic rubrics assume that writing ability is a unidimensional construct defined by these criteria.

The holistic scoring approach has noted advantages over the trait scoring approach in terms of efficiency of the scoring process and degree of reliability of ratings assigned. Raters can efficiently assign scores applying a holistic rubric because they only need to make an overall judgment about an examinee's performance. Some researchers found that a holistic approach to scoring yields a higher degree of reliability compared to a trait approach (e.g., Page, Poggio, & Keith, 1997; Smith, 1993). For instance, Page, et al. (1997) concluded human ratings assigned to essays using a holistic approach are more consistent compared to when employing a trait scoring approach when nearly 500 essays for the National Assessment of Educational Progress (NAEP) were scored. Further, scores produced from holistic approaches are found to correlate moderately to highly with scores produced from analytic approaches (Graduate Management Admission Council®, 2006; Lee et al., 2008, Lee, Gentile, & Kantor, 2009). For example, the Graduate Management Admission Council (Graduate Management Admission Council®, 2006) found a high degree of agreement between average scores produced by the Vantage AEE system using a holistic scoring approach and human ratings using a trait scoring approach for two of the four domains rated, analysis and use of support. Some might conclude that because the two share a strong correlation, that the holistic rubric and analytic rubrics are measuring the same construct or are producing redundant information, thus supporting the adoption of the more efficient holistic scoring approach. This reasoning is consistent with Messick's (1980) framework for validity. However,

Table 12.1 Florida Comprehensive Assessment Test® Writing Rubric (Rating 6 Only)

Score	Description
6	The writing is focused on the topic, has a logical organizational pattern (including a beginning, middle, conclusion, and transitional devices), and has ample development of the supporting ideas. The paper demonstrates a sense of completeness or wholeness. The writing demonstrates a mature command of language including precision in word choice. Subject/verb agreement and verb and noun forms are generally correct. With few exceptions, the sentences are complete, except when fragments are used purposefully. Various sentence structures are used.

The Grade 4 Florida Comprehensive Assessment Test® (FCAT) Writing Rubric, Score 6 Description, appears by permission of the Florida Department of Education, Office of Assessment, Tallahassee, Florida 32399–0400.

just because two things are correlated does not mean that they are measuring the same construct, as Sechrest (2005) previously emphasized.

The major limitation noted for holistic rubrics is the lack of diagnostic insight on an examinee's performance. Because the criteria are grouped together, the end-user cannot determine the specific strengths and weaknesses of the writing product. In other words, the feedback is not specific, which can make it difficult for the end-user to understand what characteristics of the writing formed the basis for rater judgment. This phenomenon is similar to a student receiving a marking of "B" on a paper with a few general comments but no descriptive feedback. The lack of information on specific writing characteristics makes it difficult to adapt instruction to improve students' writing. Further, if educators want to weight different components of writing when making selection or categorization decisions, then an analytic scoring approach would be necessary (Graduate Management Admissions Council®, 2006). Indeed, in a study conducted by the GMAC (2006) to develop and pilot test an analytic rubric for use on the GMAT® Analytical Writing Assessment, it was found that the use of an analytic scoring approach provided greater discrimination among writers for two of four domains rated (analysis and language) compared to a holistic scoring model applied in the Vantage AES system.

Trait rubrics theoretically address these latter limitations by separating into the writing performance criteria more diagnostic information about the strengths and weaknesses of an examinee's writing ability (Bacha, 2001; Weigle, 2002). The "6+1 Traits®" Writing model is one of the more popular trait scoring models that was originally developed by a group of educators in the mid-1980s. The model was then adopted and tested in the early 1990s by the Northwest Regional Educational Laboratory (NWREL) in Portland, Oregon. This rubric is designed for teaching and assessing writing, and is made up of six qualities (traits) that define high quality writing (NWREL, 2012a). These traits include: (a) ideas, the content supporting the main message; (b) organization, the structure of the composition; (c) voice, the tone and flavor of the examinee's message; (d) word choice, the vocabulary used to convey meaning; (e) sentence fluency, the rhythm and flow of the language used; (f) conventions, the mechanical accurateness; and (g) presentation, the visual look of the composition on the page, which is not usually used in automated essay evaluation (NWREL, 2012a).

Four optional rating scales can be applied with this scoring model depending on whether the scoring model is being used for beginning or more experienced writers (NWREL, 2012b). NWREL suggests that two rating scales are appropriate when rating beginning writers ranging from kindergarten through second grade. The first rating scale is a 5-point rating scale ranging from "experimenting" to "experienced." The second is a 6-point rating scale ranging from "beginning" to "exceptional." For students in late second grade through twelfth grade, 5- and 6-point scales also exist. The 5-point scale is labeled numerically as 5, 3, and 1 (thus making it more of a 3-point ordinal scale). The 6-point scale ranges from "beginning" to "exceptional." This latter scale differs from the K–2 scale in that the six ratings are further divided into two proficiency levels: "not proficient" (beginning, emerging, or developing) and "proficient" (capable, experienced, or exceptional). NWREL has created professional development workshops, training materials, and other supporting measures to make the 6+1 Trait® Writing model and rating scales easy to adopt.

Research findings on the effectiveness of applying the 6+1 Trait® scoring model are mixed (e.g., Jarmer, Kozel, Nelson, & Salsberry, 2000; Kozlow & Bellamy, 2004). For instance, Jarmer et al. (2000) found that fifth-grade students taught writing using the scoring model as a guide had significantly better writing quality over time compared to students who were taught using traditional methods. Results from Kozlow and Bellamy's (2004) research showed no significant differences when testing the writing model with fourth through sixth graders. In comparing students receiving instruction using the writing model to a control group, no significant differences were found in writing achievement even when controlling for pre-existing differences in writing quality.

Two possibilities exist that might explain Kozlow and Bellamy's (2004) negative findings. The first is that the teachers were only exposed to a two-day workshop. The second involved the observation that some teachers in the experimental group reported not fully implementing the 6+1 Trait® Writing model, while some teachers in the control group were observed using characteristics of the writing model as part of their traditional instruction. Thus, experimental contamination may have confounded their results. Establishing a control group in future studies to test the effects of the writing model will likely continue to be a challenge because the characteristic of the scoring model are adopted as part of a number of school districts goals for developing students' writing ability (Kozlow & Bellamy, 2004).

One might think because the criteria are rated separately, that greater discrimination among writers would result. However, Shermis, Koch, Page, Keith, and Harrington (2002) did not find this to be the case. Instead, these researchers observed that a trait rubric did not discriminate writing performance any better than the use of a holistic evaluation scheme alone. Additionally, Page et al. (1997) argued that the value of a trait score over a holistic score is the ability to portray relative strengths of the writer in much the same way that a broad achievement test in reading can provide a similar diagnostics. It could be, however, that the use of a specific trait rubric is restricted to models based on single topics. If this were indeed the case, then a scoring model such as the 6+1 Trait® would have limited utility in AEE.

Future longitudinal research is needed to investigate the validity of the scoring model in scaffolding students' writing ability to determine if the 6+1 Trait® scoring model has a value-added component over more traditional instructional methods. Despite the wide adoption of this model, published research on its effectiveness is lacking. Moreover, research testing the reliability and validity of the rating scales applied with the writing model is required before it can be effectively applied to AEE.

Rating Scales

A variety of scaling options exist for rating an essay response. These scales tend to be either strictly numerical or a hybrid of numerical with associated qualitative labels for ease of interpretation. Essay scores fall onto one of four scales of measurement: nominal, ordinal, interval, or ratio. Nominal scales have no quantitative meaning and are typically not used in essay scoring. While arbitrary values may be assigned to represent an attribute (e.g., 1 = male, 2 = female), the numerical values assigned are not quantitatively meaningful. Ordinal scales, on the other hand, rank attributes from lowest to highest.

Many rubrics used to evaluate essay responses on high-stakes tests are rated on ordinal scales, ranking the quality of a writing sample from lower to higher quality. For example, the widely applied 6+1Traits™ rubric applies a scale labeled: 1 = beginning, 2 = emerging, 3 = developing, 4 = capable, 5 = experienced, 6 = exceptional. In this case, a writing sample rated as "exceptional" exhibits a higher writing quality than a writing sample rated as "experienced" on the rated trait. However, the distance between adjacent values is not necessarily equal. For instance, the jump from "beginning" to "emerging" is not necessarily equal to the distance between "experienced" and "exceptional." So, for example, it could be easier for a writing sample to move from being rated "beginning" to "emerging" than from being rated "experienced" to "exceptional." This potential limitation is similar to norm-referenced percentile rankings. It is easier for a student to move from the 85th to the 90th percentile than it is from the 95th to the 99th percentile.

The limitation of ordinal scales raises a question about a common method used in studies comparing the consistency between ratings assigned by human raters and AEE systems. Oftentimes, agreement is defined on exact *or* adjacent values. Ratings that are adjacent could indeed hold very different quantitative (and qualitative) meaning. Further, if the ratings of multiple traits along ordinal scales are summed to form an overall essay score, there is no meaning to the score since the distance between ratings are not equal. As a result, mathematical operations such as addition and subtraction cannot and should not be performed on scores measured on such ordinal scales (Linacre, 1994). Because a linear transformation is not applied, the quasi-equal intervals are not maintained (Bond & Fox, 2007; Embretson, 1996). Using scales in their ordinal form do not provide for meaningful comparisons to be made, which is problematic when assessing *how much* an examinee has progressed in their writing ability over time.

PROXES AND TRINS

A rubric is used to make valid judgments by identifying features of writing that have value in the assessment context. Inherent in the process is that some aspects of writing will be ignored or undervalued, generally those features that the developers of the rubric think are less essential. In formulating the rubric, the developers identify those characteristics that can be readily observed and use these characteristics as a placeholder for some intrinsic feature of the writing that is not so easily discernable. In the social science context, this would be analogous to the observed or latent distinction that is made in formulating models of systems or behaviors. Observed variables are ones that we measure whereas latent variables are the "real" underlying traits or characteristics that we are interested. Our measurement of a trait is hampered by the low degree of reliability or validity of the observed variables that we are constrained to use.

In the world of AEE, the same distinction is made between trins and proxes (Page & Petersen, 1995). Trins are intrinsic characteristics of interest whereas proxes are approximations of those characteristics (observed variables). At first glance, it may appear as if some of the proxes are rather superficial, but on closer inspection they may in fact reflect sophisticated thinking. For example, one of the automated evaluation systems counts the number of times "but" appears in a writing sample. From a grammatical standpoint, "but" is a simple conjunction and may not contribute all that much to our understanding of the writing. However, "but" is often used at the beginning of a dependent clause which occurs in the context of more complex writing. It could be that "but" is an appropriate proxy for writing sophistication or sentence complexity.

The point to keep in mind is that a proxy may act as a good or better indicator of quality than more authentic procedures for two basic reasons. First, one should be able to better train raters on observable features of the writing than on their intrinsic characteristics. Second, one has a better chance of obtaining expert consensus on the observable variables rather than arguing about the intrinsic features of the writing sample.

FORMATION OF SCORES

There are several ways to create scores for AEE. The most common method is to use a regression approach to make predictions about the quality of a particular essay. Usually, the AEE system parses the text and tags it according to an a priori variable set referred to as proxies. For example, the system might identify proxies or features proposed to be related to writing ability such as the number of sentences, use of verb/noun agreement, number of commas used, difficulty level of word usage, the use of conjunctions, and so forth. We discuss the types of classifications a parser might make in the following section. Once the parser has completed its work, the variables are summarized. To create a prediction equation, the variables are regressed against the scores provided by the raters for a set of essays randomly selected for model building. In this case, the evaluations from the raters serve as the criterion in the model.

The exception to this latter approach is embodied in the evaluation of content. The prediction weightings for content may be supplemented through techniques such as Latent Semantic Analysis (LSA; Landauer, Foltz, & Laham, 1998). For example, the Intelligent Essay Assessor (IEA; see Chapter 5 in this volume) evaluates content by analyzing the essay's propensity to contain keywords and synonyms or sets of keywords and synonyms, and comparing their Euclidean distance to words contained on a master list.

Most studies involve creating regression models using two data sets, one randomly selected for model building and the other randomly selected for validating the model. The number of variables used in a regression model varies from parser to parser. For example, the parser in Project Essay Grade (Page, 2003; see also Chapter 6) can classify over 200 variables, but only about 30 to 40 of them are typically identified as significant predictors in a multiple-regression equation. A randomly selected second set of data is then used to validate the multiple regression equation developed from the first data set (Page & Petersen, 1995; Shermis et al., 2002).

Most rubrics result in ratings ranging from 1 to 5 or 1 to 6. If a non-standardized linear multiple regression is used for model building, then scores that are returned from the computer model will (after truncation or rounding) be on the same scale. If a standardized regression equation is used, then the resulting mean of the distribution will be 0 with a standard deviation of 1. The non-standardized scores are what end-users (e.g., educator, parents, students) desire whereas the standardized scores are often used for research purposes. However, Page (1972) developed a "modified T-score," based on the standardized multiple regression, where the mean is transformed to 70 rather than 50 and the standard deviation remains at 10. The automated essay scorer has a range of 40 to 100, similar to the range of scores a teacher might assign to students completing an essay for classroom assessment.

Some variables may be weighted more than others in the linear regression equation such as in the *e-rater*® automated essay evaluation (AEE) system. In *e-rater*®, the linear regression model is built using the essay scores assigned by human raters as the criterion and any significant contributing essay features from the AEE system as the predictors in the regression model (Attali, Burstein, & Andreyev, 2003). Features might be differentially weighted in the equation. For instance, word count has been found to be a strong predictor of an examinee's essay score alone (Burstein, Chodorow, & Leacock, 2004). As a result, this might be assigned a lower weight in the regression equation compared to another feature so that the estimated essay scores are not artificially increased by the system (Burstein et al., 2004).

Although the regression approach is widely applied in model building in AEE, this approach not without validity concerns. Under such classical test theory, models may not replicate when applied to a different sample of essays. This loss of precision accuracy is referred to as "shrinkage" (Cohen & Swendlik, 2010). Haberman and Sinharay (2010) noted one limitation of linear regression model approaches being that such linear models assume that the criterion is on a continuous scale, when this might not be the case. The researchers argue that a more appropriate model is the cumulative logistic regression model where the ratings are treated as categorical (Haberman & Sinharay, 2010). The resultant estimated scores fall within the possible essay score range, thus making for more meaningful interpretation in the cumulative logistic regression model approach. Haberman and Sinharay's (2010) preliminary results show support for their argument but additional research is needed on other data sets.

Developmental Scales

Researchers such as Stenner, Burdick, Sanford, and Burdick (2007) and Attali and colleagues (Attali & Burstein, 2006; Attali & Powers, 2009) recognized the need to address the limitations of ordinal rating scales so that meaningful comparisons in writing performance could be made across different writing prompts, and over time. Stenner and colleagues (Stenner, Burdick, et al., 2007; Wright, & Stenner, 1999) addressed this issue by applying the Rasch model (1960, 1980) to develop a criterion-referenced scale referred to as the Lexile Scale for Reading, recently adapted to develop a parallel Writing Ability Developmental Scale (Burdick et al., under review; Stenner, Swartz, Burdick, Burdick, & Hanlon, 2007).

Briefly, the Rasch model is a family of measurement models that provides for scores to be converted onto an interval scale using a logarithmic transformation. The resultant scale units are called "logits." Rasch models are often mistakenly associated with Item Response Theory (IRT: Lee et al., 2008). Rasch models do not fall under IRT (see, for explanations, Bode & Wright, 1999; Bond & Fox, 2007; Linacre, 2005). The most simplistic form of the Rasch model is in its dichotomous form which can be extended for essay items scored on a polytomous scale with more than two ratings. The polytomous Rasch model is expressed in exponential form as (Andrich, 1978):

$$\pi_{nik} = \frac{e^{(\beta_n - \delta_i - \tau_k)}}{1 + e^{(\beta_n - \delta_i - \tau_k)}}$$

where π_{nik} is the probability that person n will be rated on rating k on item i, which is a function of the constant exponent equal to 2.71828 raised to the difference between a person's ability β_n, the item difficulty δ_i, and the difficulty of a given threshold τ_k divided by the same function plus 1. In this model, there are at least two thresholds on the latent continuum.

Translating this formula to essay scoring, β is an examinee's writing ability level and δ is the composition difficulty level where the probability of succeeding on prompt i is a function of an examinee's ability and the difficulty level of the essay prompt. The difference between the examinee and item parameter governs the probability of what will occur when a person with a specific ability encounters a prompt of a specific difficulty level (Wright & Masters, 1982). The prompt difficulty parameter is included in the mathematic function under the Rasch model where the examinee and item parameters are conjointly additive. An examinee's writing ability can then be plotted against the difficulty level of the writing prompt along common logit scale. The item mean is set at zero on the logit scale, whereas in IRT the origin of the scale is set at the average of the person ability in a given sample thus making IRT norm-referenced (Linacre, 2005).

The resultant interval-level Lexile scale provides for a common ruler to be used across examinees, essay prompts, grade levels, and contexts. The Lexile is advantageous compared to other norm-referenced scales because the scale intervals are fixed. Other scales can expand or contract depending on the item parameters. They are sometimes referred to as "rubber rulers." A Rasch analysis is performed to calibrate the scores onto the logit scale and then converted into Lexiles for ease of interpretation by applying the following equation (Stenner & Burdick, 1997, p. 13):

$$\text{Lexile} = (\text{logit} + \text{constant}) \times CF + 200$$

The constant and conversion factor (CF) are derived from the anchors (see for example, Stenner & Burdick, 1997). The Lexile scale ranges from 0 to above 2000 but typically anchors are set at 200 (considered mid-first-grade level) and 1200 Lexiles. Because the Lexile scale is an interval scale, the distance between points is equal. For example, the distance between 200 to 300 Lexiles is the same as the distance between 1100 and 1200 Lexiles (100 points). Each Lexile unit "is 1/1000th of the difference between the mean difficulty of the mid-first grade material and the mean difficulty of workplace passages" (Burdick et al., under review, p. 25).

To apply the Lexile Framework in AEE, writing samples are divided into smaller chunks referred to as slices of text consisting of about 125 words per slice or to the ending of a sentence within that slice. Each slice is treated as if it is an individual item and rated on two components. The first component is the syntactic complexity of the writing sample including the percentage of total words that were different parts of speech, and ratios of parts of speech to one another. The second component is the lexical complexity of the writing sample including lexical density (difficulty level of word usage), lexical diversity (total number of unique words used), and lexical sophistication (average word length and frequency) (Burdick et al., under review; Smith III, 2009).

The resultant Lexile scale provides for a common frame of reference to plot reading and writing ability along the same scale to make meaningful comparisons or to examine relationships among dimensions of writing and reading. For instance, it was found that students usually read 300 Lexiles higher than they write when plotting the two abilities on the Lexile scale (Smith III, 2009). It also provides for an equating mechanism because the scores are *calibrated onto a common interval scale*. Longitudinal trends in an examinee's performance can thus be examined rather than depending on a snapshot of his/her writing ability. These characteristics justify the Lexile scale as "developmental".

The Lexile Framework for reading has been applied to interpreting examinees' performances on a number of high-stakes tests such as the Metropolitan Achievement Tests, Standard Achievement Test Series, Iowa Tests, and TerraNova. Applications for converting scores onto the Lexile scale from scores produced from test such as the Tests of Adult Basic Education and Test of English as a Foreign Language (TOEFL) scores are also available. We expect that the Lexile Framework for writing has much to offer AEE given the promising preliminary results supporting the validity of the Writing Development Scale (Burdick et al., under review).

One study that supports our prediction is summarized in Burdick et al. (under review) examined the reliability and validity of essay scores produced from the Writing Development Scale by comparing the scores produced to human essay scores, a common method used in testing the validity of scores produced by AEE methods. A total of 19 human raters applied the NAEP scoring guide (U.S. Department of Education, Institute of Education Sciences 1998, 2002). A total of 589 students from one school district in the southern U.S. participated in the study from grades 4, 5, 8, 10, and 12. The sample was reported as being comparable to the state and national distribution of students by grade level, gender, ethnicity, free lunch, and socio-economic status. Supportive evidence for the validity of the essay scores produced from the Writing Development Scale was found, giving credence to the need for further testing and application in AEE (Burdick et al., under review). The Writing Development Scale and human essay scores progressed monotonically as expected with lower ratings indicating lower quality writing and higher ratings indicating higher quality writing. In addition, the students' essay scores on the Writing Development Scale and human essay scores increased with grade level as expected. Further, the Writing Development Scale was as discriminating among students' writing abilities over time as human essay scores. Specifically, the Writing Development Scale and human essay scores were reported to share 90% of the variance in discriminating among a student's writing ability level.

Finally, essay scores on the Writing Development Scale shared statistically significant and strong positive correlations ranging from .77 to .83 with the human essay scores across the different criteria rated. Reliability evidence of essay scores produced from the Writing Development Scale was also found with scores more consistent than those produced by the human raters. This latter finding is not surprising given a lower degree of subjectivity involved in AEE.

While these preliminary results are promising for the use of the Writing Development Scale in AEE, some differences between this scale and human ratings did exist. Lexile/human differences were found between some grade levels and by gender (Burdick et al., under review). Given these results coupled with the fact that limited research testing the reliability and validity of the Writing Development Scale exists, further research is needed to test if these findings replicate for other samples, grade levels, and different sets of essay items.

An earlier study conducted by Attali and Powers (2009) constructed developmental norms based on 20 writing prompts, 5 grade levels (4, 6, 8, 10, 12), and included 11,955 students. In this study each student wrote on approximately three of the essay prompts. The authors were able to collect enough data to develop a standardized scaling model across all essay prompts. Their results, shown in Table 12.2, suggest a progression in writing ability by grade level.

Table 12.2 Descriptive Statistics for Scaled Scores (Used by permission)

Grade	Students	M	SD	Weighted M	Weighted SD
4	3,346	−1.04	0.73	−1.06	0.73
6	6,837	−0.40	0.79	−0.39	0.80
8	9,967	0.13	0.80	0.15	0.79
10	8,169	0.54	0.79	0.51	0.82
12	6,312	0.75	0.78	0.75	0.76
All	34,631	0.12	0.95	0.00	1.00

Source: Yigal Attali and Donald Powers. Validity of Scores for a Developmental Writing Scale Based on Automated Scoring. Sage Publications, 2009. Reprinted with permission of Sage Publications. No further reproduction is permitted without written permission of Sage Publications.

Applications of the MFRM

The MFRM (Linacre, 1994) can be applied in scaling essays onto a common metric and also making meaningful comparisons on the common interval logit scale while taking into account multiple "facets." A "facet" refers to an aspect of the measurement process that could systematically affect the estimation of an examinee's ability (Bond & Fox, 2007; Linacre, 1994). Person and item parameters are the two facets calibrated in all Rasch models. In essay scoring, additional facets typically included in the model are rater severity, rating dimension, and item prompt.

Briefly, the MFRM is an extension of the Partial Credit Model (Masters, 1982) developed for analyzing responses and scales consisting of intermediate levels (e.g., open-ended items). In the Partial Credit Model, steps or thresholds for each item are created rather than for all items together. That is, each item can function on a unique scale. The MFRM is similar to the Partial Credit Model in that unconditional maximum likelihood (Fisher, 1922) is used to produce parameter estimates for multiple facets (Linacre & Wright, 2002). The MFRM is expressed as (Linacre, 1994):

$$\pi_{nikj} = \frac{e^{\left(\beta_n - \delta_i - F_k - C_j\right)}}{1 + e^{\left(\beta_n - \delta_i - F_k - C_j\right)}}$$

where C_j represents an additional difficulty estimate for an additional facet such as the severity C of rater j, which is part of the probability estimate for examinee n responding to essay item i for category (i.e., essay rating) threshold k for rater j.

In applying MFRM, one can choose to make additional facets "active" to test whether these additional facets influence, for instance, essay item difficulty measures or examinees' scores. When a facet systematically affects examinees' scores, this is referred to as differential facet functioning (Eckes, 2008). Additional facets such as demographic variables can also be included to adjust for any significant effect on an examinee's resultant ability measure.

The MFRM is used as an alternative to the common method of introducing a third rater to the scoring process if the first two raters disagree on an examinee's essay score. The use of a third rater might not resolve the disagreement and questions can be raised why the third rater's decision is weighted more. For instance, Rater 3 might agree with Rater 1 but this discounts Rater 2's expert opinion. The MFRM provides for examining if rater differences have a systematic effect on examinees' scores and then adjusts for these differences.

Consider the significance of including rater severity and writing prompt as two additional facets when scaling an examinee's writing performance in three different situations. Imagine that Examinee A and B have the same writing ability. In the first instance, Examinees A and B receive the same essay prompt but Examinee A is rated by rater who is consistently more severe. As a result, Examinee A receives a lower rating. MFRM can adjust for this main effect of rating severity. In the second instance, Examinees A and B are evaluated by the same rater. Examinee A completes the more difficult prompt and Examinee B completes the easier prompt. As a result, Examinee A is assigned a lower score. This situation is similar to a student receiving a final grade without the teacher first weighting the different assessments according to their difficulty level and comprehensiveness. MFRM can adjust for this main effect of this item difficulty level. Finally, in the third situation, Examinee A is not only evaluated by a more severe rater than Examinee

B, but also responds to the most difficult prompt. MFRM can also adjust for this interaction effect on Examinee's A score.

This model is widely applied in scaling essays scored by human raters and is also applied in AEE. For instance, Educational Testing Service applied MFRM to produce score profiles to analyze for the TOEFL® writing assessment using the *e-rater®* AEE system (Lee et al., 2008). Particular recommendations can be made for its further application in AEE. First, essay length has been proposed as an additional variable that might be controlled given that it has been found to be highly correlated with essay ratings (e.g., Lee et al., 2008). One suggestion is to classify essay length as an additional facet to be considered in the measurement process. One might also include scoring type (human vs. machine) as an additional facet. Including scoring type as an additional facet is an alternative to the method of comparing the correlation between average scores produced by human raters (the external criterion) and AES systems. MFRM permits examining several fit indices to determine whether the measures fit the specifications of the Rasch model and thus yield meaningful measures, but also whether scoring type has a systematic effect (i.e., differential facet functioning) on examinees' scores.

By including scoring type as an addition facet, human ratings can be directly plotted against machine ratings using the same metric. It is essential to provide for sufficient connectivity or linkage among the facets included in the model (Linacre, 1994). For example, sufficient connectivity by linking examinees by common raters or item prompts in the design. Figure 12.1 illustrates an example of five different facets plotted along a common interval scale ruler in logits. The higher on the ruler, the higher the degree on the underlying construct. The relative difficulty or severity level can be observed for each value on each facet across facets. In the figure, Raters 1 and 7 tend to be of the same severity level, within a standard error. However, these two raters tend to be much more severe than Rater 6, who is (empirically) the easiest rater. By including whether each rater was a human rater or machine rating, we can also make direct comparisons across the two types of scoring using a common frame of reference in studies examining reliability and validity question related to AEE.

STANDARD-SETTING METHODS

Standard-setting refers to systematic methods used to set performance standards classifying the level of an examinee's performance, e.g., writing quality (Cizek, 2012). *Performance* standards differ from *content* standards in that content standards refer to the "what" of learning, whereas performance standards focus on the "how well" or at "what level." As part of this process, cut-scores are established to determine what score is needed to achieve the lower bound of each performance standard. While systematic rules are followed and psychometrics can guide the process, all standard-setting methods involve a great degree of human judgment. Typically, panels made up of subject-matter experts ultimately set the cut-scores associated with the performance standards (Kane, 1994; Shepard, 1979).

The variety of standard-setting methods and modifications to each method continue to increase and be widely applied not only in high-stakes testing, but also placement decisions. Research will continue to grow in this area given the specifications under the No Child Left Behind Act ("No Child Left Behind Act of 2001," 2002) to establish performance standards as part of tracking students' achievement levels (U.S. Department of Education, 2009). Reviewing all of the methods applied in setting-standards for essays is beyond the scope of this chapter. We encourage the reader to see Cizek (2012) for

Measure in Logits	Examinees	Essay Prompt	Rating Dimension[1]	Rater	Scale

```
Measure                Examinees              Essay      Rating        Rater      Scale
in Logits                                     Prompt     Dimension¹

  2 + 1   27                              +        +         +      + 1    7 +   6
      |          Higher                   |  More   |  More   |        More    |
      |          Writing                  | difficult| difficult|     Severe   |
      |          Ability                  |         |         |        |       |
      |                                   |    4    |         |        |       |
      |                                   |         |         |        |       |
      | 4   18                            |         |    I    |        |       |
      |                                   |         |         |      |   3   |   5
  1 +                                     +        +    SF   +      |   4   +
      | 6                                 |         |         |        |       |
      | 14                                |         |    O    |        |       |
      | 10                                |         |         |        |       |
      | 6  1    18                        |         |         |        |       |
      | 19   22   23   19                 |    5    |         |        |       |
      | 4  14  20  16  22  11|            |         |         |        |       |
      | 10                                |         |         |        |     |   4
  0 * 16  24  21   3  24            *     *        *         *      | 2     *
      | 2   2   5  15  17  17       | 1   |         |         |        |
      | 5   8  21  23   7           | 2 3 |         |         |      | 5    |
      | 13  9  20                         |         |    WC   |        |
      | 15                                |         |         |        |
      | 8                                 |         |         |        |
      | 25  7  11                         |         |         |        |
      | 3  12  12                         |         |         |        |
 -1 + 25                                  +        +    C    +      + 8    9 +   3
      |                                   |    6    |         |        |
      | 13                                |         |         |        |
      |                                   |         |         |        |       |   2
      |                                   |         |         |        |
      | 26       Lower                    |         |         |      |   6   |
      |          Writing                  |         |         |        |       |
 -2 +            Ability                  +  Easier + Easier  +      | Less  +   1
      |                                   |         |         |      | Severe|
```

Figure 12.1 Example of multiple facets plotted against each other along a common metric in logits produced by the MFRM. The authors artificially created this figure for illustrative purposes. 1 I = Ideas; SF = Sentence Fluency; O = Organization; WC = Word Choice; C = Conventions.

a more comprehensive description of standard-setting. We also refer the reader to the *Standards for Educational and Psychological Testing* (American Educational Research Association, American Psychological Association, & National Council on Measurement in Education, 1999) for professional guidelines on implementing and testing the validity of standard-setting methods.

We focus next on the general major steps in standard-setting followed by a brief overview of the more commonly applied standard-setting methods for constructed-type responses. This is especially important with AEE since the standard-setting steps can be used in establishing the cut-points across a rubric scale (or highlighting the discrepancies between how human raters score a scale and what is specified in the rubric). In addition, setting alternative norms and equating methods are briefly discussed. Many frameworks are proposed for categorizing standard-setting methods (e.g., norm vs. criterion-referenced, examinee-centered vs. test-centered, compensatory vs. conjunctive). Consistent with Cizek (2012), we avoid categorizing each method here given that the distinction is not always 100% clear as many standard-setting methods cross the taxonomic boundaries.

General Steps in Standard-Setting

Select the Method

There are a variety of standard-setting methods that apply essays or assessments made up of both dichotomously and polytomously scored items. One factor to consider in selecting an appropriate method is the audience or client, e.g., a national organization, board, government, foundation, or school. Some clients such as national organizations may have strict policies regarding standard-setting methods. A second factor to consider is the purpose—to track growth in performance level over time, make funding decisions, simply classify proficiency level, or make placement decisions. A third factor to consider is whether item level or more holistic performance standards are required. Finally, consider the feasibility (e.g., time, cost) of implementing the different methods in the given context.

Define the Performance-Level Descriptors

Operationally define the Performance-Level Descriptors (PLDs) in such a way a panelist can understand. There should be clear distinction among the qualitative descriptors of the performance levels. This process is similar to generating qualitative descriptors for each category or value on a rubric applied when scoring examinees' essay responses. Defining the PLDs might not be complete until the end of the standard-setting process in some standard-setting methods such as the Bookmark Model (Lewis, Mitzel, Merado, & Schulz, 2012).

Select and Train the Panel

Panel refers to the group of individuals who will be the judges in making the standard or cut-scores. Three major factors should be considered when selecting a panel: quality, quantity, and feasibility. In terms of quality, the panel should consist of a number of individuals who are subject-matter experts in writing or English Language Arts. Additional panelists might include members of subgroups deemed to have an important stake in score outcomes. It is recommended that the subject-matter experts make up a majority of the panel and that at least two members from any subgroup are on the panel (Loomis, 2012; Morgan & Michaelides, 2005).

Recommendations differ in regards to quantity. Some have noted panel sizes as small as 8 (Loomis, 2012), 15–20 (Hambleton, Pitoniak, & Copella, 2012), or as high as 20–30 (Morgan & Michaelides, 2005). A larger number of panelists are typically included when setting actual standards in high-stakes situations, whereas fewer panelists are included when conducting empirical studies on standard-setting methods. Loomis (2012) recommended creating a split pool of panelists when working with a large number of essay items.

The third factor, feasibility, should be included in determining the composition of a panel. Geographical proximity can be a barrier to composing a quality panel and thus considering virtual methods as a means of conducting the standard-setting might be appropriate. Once formed, the panel must be trained on the standard-setting procedure and PLDs.

Facilitate Panel Judgments

The panelists then make individual judgments base on the criterion or criteria set. How panelists are instructed to make their judgments differs by standard-setting method. Typically, each panelist makes his or her individual cut-score judgment followed by a small group discussion based on empirical feedback in an effort to increase consistency among panelists' judgments. Two to three rounds of this process might occur.

Compute and Recommend Final Cut-Score(s)

One of the final steps in the process is computing the final cut-score associated with each performance level and perhaps the overall test, if applicable. The number of cut-scores varies depending on the number of proficiency levels. To achieve this, a measure of central tendency is typically computed such as the mean or median (in cases where the data are skewed). As others have recommended (Morgan & Michaelides, 2005), it is good practice to report plus or minus two standard errors associated with each cut-score for the overall population and any relevant subgroups.

Documentation

An essential step in the standard-setting process is to generate documentation to provide for defensible cut-scores. Document each step of the process, including the procedure of panel formulation to justification for the final cut-scores computed.

Modified Angoff

The Modified Angoff method (originally proposed by Angoff, 1971) is cited as one of the most widely applied standard-setting method for dichotomously scored items, but also can be applied for polytomously scored items (Plake & Cizek, 2012). When applying this method to essay items, panelists are asked to consider a hypothetical examinee whose work is borderline of achieving each performance level. Borderline examinees are also referred to as those who are "minimally competent." Plake and Cizek (2012) classify judgments as occurring in one of two ways. The first is by way of mean item estimation in which each panelist is asked what the mean score of an examinee performing at a minimally competent level (for each performance level) would score on a given item. Responses are aggregated across panelists and an average is computed for each item. Cut-scores can then also be summed to determine an estimated cut-score for the entire set of items making up the test. The second judgment method is the expected task score approach where each panelist judges the expected score of an examinee performing at a minimally competent level on a given item using the scale or categories provided. A related method asks each panelist to report what percentage of minimally competent students would fall into the different performance levels (Morgan & Michaelides, 2005). Typically two to three rounds of judgments are conducted with discussions occurring among panelists between each round.

One limitation cited for this method is that because the judgment process focuses on making item-level judgments, the degree of accuracy of representing the holistic performance level might be sacrificed (Morgan & Michaelides, 2005). Additionally, panelists are not provided with any information on the difficulty levels of the items to help inform their judgments or the stability of the construct (Stone, Koskey, & Sondergeld, 2011).

Bookmark Method and Methods Based on the Bookmark Method

The Bookmark method (Lewis, Green, Mitzel, Baum, & Patz, 1998; Mitzel, Lewis, Patz, & Green, 2001) is perhaps the most widely applied standard-setting method for polytomously scored items since the Angoff method (1971) was introduced. One of the key distinctions between this method and the Angoff method is the first step involves computing the item (or trait) difficulty level through the use of the IRT or Rasch model (1960, 1980). The items are then presented to panelists in ascending order in an ordered item booklet (OIB). The location where panelists place the bookmark indicates where a minimally competent examinee would master the items below but not above the bookmark.

After the OIB is created, panelists are to engage in three rounds of judgments. In round 1, the panelists review the OIB and discuss why each item is assigned a difficulty level relative to the other items and what skills are necessary to master that item (Karantonis & Sireci, 2006; Lewis et al., 2012). "Master" is defined in terms of probabilities of success, typically a probability of .67, although the values can differ (Lewis, et al., 2012). Panelists then individually mark their cut-scores and engage in round 2 where they are provided with feedback on their cut-scores and informed of the average or median cut-score across panelists. During round 2, panelists again discuss in small groups what an examinee must demonstrate to achieve a given performance level. Panelists are then provided the opportunity to mark new cut-scores or retain their cut-scores from round 1. Notice that this step also differs from the Angoff method in that the PLDs are not fully defined a priori. Finally, in round 3 the facilitator (typically a psychometrician) communicates the impact data such as what percentage of examinees ended up falling into each performance level and the average cut-score across panelists. Panelists are then given the opportunity to adjust their bookmarks from which the final cut-scores are computed.

Two advantages for the Bookmark method are that panelists can mark multiple cut-scores (Morgan & Michaelides, 2005) and the method is easy to understand (see, for a review, Karantonis & Sireci, 2006). One of the limitations is that panelists can have difficulty conceptualizing their judgments in terms of probabilities of, say, .67 (Skaggs & Tessema, 2001) and especially .50 (Karantonis & Sireci, 2006). Interestingly, a probability of .50 used for judgments has continuously been found to function better than other criteria employed (Karantonis & Sireci, 2006).

Variations of the Bookmark method have been proposed to overcome this latter limitation. One such variation is the Item Descriptor (ID) Matching method (Ferrara & Lewis, 2012) where panelists are not instructed to make judgments based on probability but rather to match each score level for an item and the required skills needed to master the item to the PLDs, which then serves as the guide for judging cut-scores. Another variation is Map-Marking (Schulz & Mitzel, 2009) where an item map is used as a replacement for an OIB. An item map illustrates the distribution of items in ascending order along a continuum with item difficulty increasing towards the upper-end of the continuum of the map. Panelists mark where on this map a minimally competent examinee would fall for a given performance level.

One final variation, though less widely applied, is Objective Standard Setting (Stone, 1995, 2004, 2008). The Rasch model is utilized for computing the item difficulty levels similar to in the Bookmark method; however, in this case panelists do not engage in rounds of discussion and judging cut-scores. Rather, judges engage in the standard-setting process while scoring examinees' essays. This results in a procedure that is more efficient and cost-effective. Preliminary results are promising in terms of how this method compares to more traditional methods of standard-setting (e.g., Stone, 2008). The cut-score judgment is then added as an additional facet to compute final cut-scores using the MFRM (Linacre, 1994).

Contrasting Groups

Contrasting Groups is yet another type of standard-setting method that can be used when a test consists of a combination of dichotomously and polytomously scored items. In this method, score distributions are plotted for students at the different levels or in contrasting groups (e.g., pass/fail). The cut-score is determined as the point where the score distributions intersect. As (Zieky, 2012) explains, "if judges believe that it is equally as harmful to pass a member of the unqualified group as it is to fail a member of the qualified group, the cut score is set at the score at which the probability of being qualified is .50" (p. 22).

A variation of this method is Body of Work. In this method, each examinee's essay responses are organized into booklets with a number of booklets ranging all possible score points (Kingston & Tiemann, 2012). After engaging in training on the PLDs and practice classifying examinee' responses, panelists engage in range-finding where they judge the cut-score points. The highest and lowest essays from each pinpointing booklet are extracted to create range-finding booklets that represented the range of possible performance levels (Kingston & Tiemann, 2012). Panelists judge the booklet holistically to classify each booklet into a performance level. The panelists' responses are organized into a table detailing the ascending ordering of responses within each range-finding folder and how many panelists classified each response in which performance level.

The cut-scores are determined by considering "the score above which all papers are placed in one category and below which all papers are placed in another category" (Kingston & Tiemann, 2012). If panelists agree on the performance-level classification of a given paper within a range-finding folder, no adjustments are needed. If they disagree on the classification, the responses' cut-score is defined as the probability of .50 that a panelist would assign the essay response to that performance level. Kingston and Tiemann (2012) explain that two criteria are considered to achieve this: 33% of the panelists judged at least one essay response in the range-finding folder as correctly classified at that performance level and 67% or more panelists did not agree that any essay response in the booklet should be classified at that performance level. While this process is easy for panelists to understand, it can be time-consuming.

Equating

Equating is a statistical technique that is used to ensure that different versions of the test, different essay prompts in this case, are equivalent. Equating is an essential step in the scaling process in order to make meaningful direct comparisons in examinee's performances over time and across tasks. Depending on the situation, item or person equating might be used. As is true with objective tests, it is quite likely that the difficulty level of prompts differ from one prompt to the next (Shermis, Rasmussen, Rajecki, Olson, & Marsiglio, 2001). Although some of the AEE systems may use a separate model for each prompt, it is likely that from one sample of examinees to the next, the prompts would be treated as being equal unless either the prompts or the models to score the prompts were equated.

Shermis, Rasmusses, et al. (2001) investigated the equivalency of prompts using both Project Essay Grade and Multiple Content Classification Analysis (MCCA), a content analysis package that was used to evaluate the content of advertisements for children (Rajecket, et al., 1993). Based on a Project Essay Grade model that involved 1,200 essays, each with four raters (Shermis, Mzumara, Olson, & Harrington, 2001), one thousand essays were randomly selected and analysed using MCCA. The essays included ratings across 20 different prompts. These researchers concluded that essays which were oriented more toward "analytical" responses were rated higher than prompts which elicited "emotional" responses. The authors concluded that prompts might be weighted in much the same way that dives in a swimming competition are assigned a variety of difficult levels.

DIFFERENTIAL ITEM FUNCTIONING

Differential item functioning (DIF) exists when the scores of examinees of similar writing ability but in different subgroups *systematically* differ on an item. DIF is often examined by gender, ethnic background, minority status, socio-economic status, and English language learning status (first or second language learner). While real differences in writing ability might indeed exist among some of these subgroups, DIF refers specifically to detecting differences that would not be expected on items for those across these subgroups who have comparable ability overall. Any systematic differences are thought to be associated with bias attributed when something other than the construct being measured manifests itself on the essay score. Performance on writing may be contingent on the mastery of several skills, making it multidimensional, and be influenced by rating biases. Thus, it is good practice to test for significant DIF even in AEE where the scoring process may have a higher degree of objectivity compared to using human raters.

Essay scores do not lend themselves to the commonly used dichotomous analysis of DIF because essay ratings are polytomous where there are more than two rating categories that increase as ability level increases. However, there are at least three problems limiting the use of polytomous DIF measures: (a) low reliability of polytomous scores, (b) the need to define an estimate of ability to match examinees from different demographic groups, and (c) the requirement of creating a measure of item performance for multiple categories of polytomous scores (Penfield & Lam, 2000).

To date, no single method will address all types of possible DIF under all possible situations (e.g., uniform and non-uniform DIF). Given this constraint, a variety of approaches continue to be tested adapting methods used for detecting DIF in dichotomously scored items for polytomous items with success (e.g., Penfield, 2007, 2008; Penfield & Lam, 2000; Wang & Shih, 2010). Penfield and Lam (2000) recommended using one of three approaches: Standardized Mean Difference, SIBTEST, and Logistic Regression. The first two approaches require a fairly sophisticated statistical and measurement expertise. Standardized Mean Difference is conceptually simple and produces reliable results with well-behaved items. SIBTEST, although computationally complex, is robust to departures from the equality of the mean abilities. Finally, Logistic Regression is an approach more familiar to consumers of tests than are some of the feasible alternatives.

An additional method more recently adapted for polytomous scales is the multiple indicators-multiple causes (MIMIC) confirmatory factor analytic approach. This approach was previously successfully used in detecting DIF on dichotomously scored items (Finch, 2005; Wang, Shih, & Yang, 2009), even in comparison to other commonly applied SIBTEST and Mantel-Haenszel methods (Finch, 2005). Preliminary testing of adaptations of the MIMIC approach for items scored on a polytomous scale are promising for detecting uniform DIF (Wang & Shih, 2010). Further investigations are needed to test whether adaptations to this method are successful in detecting non-uniform DIF (Wang & Shih, 2010).

Penfield (2008) has more recently argued for the need and outlined how to apply polytomous IRT models to examine what he refers to as Differential Step Functioning (DSF). DSF is operationally defined as "the between-group difference in measurement equivalence at the level of the step" (Penfield, 2008, p. 480). Examining systematic differences at the item level does not provide diagnostic insight into where the systematic differences are taking place on the polytomous scale with more than two ratings. Rather than examining the aggregated effects across an item, the notion is to detect more specifically where systematic group differences exist for which points on the rating scale rather than just for which items. That is, between which two ratings. This information can in turn be used to inform more specifically *where* revisions are needed for a given essay item (Penfield, 2008).

REFERENCES

American Educational Research Association, American Psychological Association, & National Council on Measurement in Education. (1999). *Standards for educational and psychological testing*. Washington, DC: AERA.

Andrich, D. (1978). Rating formulation for ordered response categories. *Psychometrica, 43*(4), 561–573.

Angoff, W. A. (1971). Scales, norms and equivalent scores. In R. L. Thorndike (Ed.), *Educational Measurement* (2nd ed., pp. 508–600). Washington, DC: American Council on Education.

Attali, Y., & Burstein, J. (2006). Automated essay scoring with e-rater V.2. *Journal of Technology, Learning, and Assessment, 4*(3). Retrieved from http://www.jtla.org

Attali, Y., Burstein, J., & Andreyev, S. (2003). *E-rater version 2.0: Combining writing analysis feedback with automated essay scoring*. Princeton, NJ: Educational Testing Service

Attali, Y., & Powers, D. (2009). Validity of scores for a developmental writing scale based on automated scoring. *Educational and Psychological Measurement, 69*, 978–993.

Bacha, N. (2001). Writing evaluation: What can analytic versus holistic essay scoring tell us? *Systems, 29*, 371–383.

Bode, R. K., & Wright, B. D. (1999). Rasch measurement in higher education. In J. C. Smart & W. G. Tierney (Eds.), *Higher education: Handbook of theory and research* (Vol. XIV, pp. 287–315). New York, NY: Agathon Press.

Bond, T. G., & Fox, C. M. (Eds.). (2007). *Applying the Rasch model: Fundamental measurement in the human sciences* (2nd ed.). Mahwah, NJ: Lawrence Erlbaum.

Burdick, H., Swartz, C. W., Stenner, A. J., Fitzgerald, J., Burdick, D., & Hanlon, S. T. (under review). *Measuring students' writing ability on a computer-analytic developmental scale: A validity study*.

Burstein, F., Chodorow, M., & Leacock, C. (2004). Automated essay evaluation: The Criterion Online writing service. *AI Magazine, 25*(3), 27–36.

Cizek, G. J. (Ed.). (2012). *Setting performance standards: Foundations, methods, and innovations* (2nd ed.). New York, NY: Routledge.

Cohen, R. J., & Swerdik, M. E. (2010). *Psychological testing and assessment* (47th ed.). Mountain View, CA: Mayfield Publishing Company.

Eckes, T. (2008). Rater types in writing performance assessments: A classification approach to rater variability. *Language Testing, 25,* 155–185.

Eckes, T. (2009). Many-facet Rasch measurement. In S. Takala (Ed.), *Reference supplement to the manual for relating examinations to the Common European Framework of Reference for Languages: Learning, teaching, assessment (Section H).* Strasbourg, France: Council of Europe/Language Policy Division.

Embretson, S. E. (1996). The new rules of measurement. *Psychological Assessment, 8,* 341–349.

Ferrara, S., & Lewis, D. M. (2012). The Item-Descriptor (ID) Matching method. In G. J. Cizek (Ed.), *Setting performance standards: Foundations, methods, and innovations* (2nd ed.). New York, NY: Routledge.

Finch, H. (2005). The MIMIC model as a method for detecting DIF: Comparison with Mantel-Haenszel, SIBTEST, and the IRT likelihood ratio. *Applied Psychological Measurement, 29,* 278–295.

Fisher, R. A. (1922). On the mathematical foundations of theoretical statistics. *Proceedings of the Royal Society, 222,* 309–368.

Graduate Management Admission Council. (2006). *GMAT® analytic rubric study report* (Vol. RR-06–04). Retrieved from http://www.gmac.com/~/media/Files/gmac/Research/research-report-series/RR0604_GMATAnalyticRubric.pdf

Haberman, S. J., & Sinharay, S. (2010). The application of the cumulative logistic regression model to automated essay scoring. *Journal of Educational and Behavioral Statistics, 35*(5), 586–602.

Hambleton, R. K., Pitoniak, M. J., & Copella, J. M. (2012). Essential steps in setting performance standards on educational tests and strategies for assessing the reliability of results. In G. J. Cizek (Ed.), *Setting performance standards: Foundations, methods, and innovations* (2nd ed.). New York, NY: Routledge.

Jarmer, D., Kozel, M., Nelson, S., & Salsberry, T. (2000). Six-trait writing model improves scores at Jennie Wilson Elementary. *Journal of School Improvement, 1*(2), 29–32.

Kane, M. (1994). Validating the performance standards associated with passing scores. *Review of Educational Research, 64*(3), 425–461.

Karantonis, A., & Sireci, S. G. (2006). The Bookmark standard-setting method: A literature review. *Educational Measurement: Issues and Practice, 25*(1), 4–11.

Kingston, N. M., & Tiemann, G. C. (2012). Setting performance standards on complex assessments: The Body of Work Method. In G. J. Cizek (Ed.), *Setting performance standards: Foundations, methods, and innovations* (2nd ed.). New York, NY: Routledge.

Kozlow, M., & Bellamy, P. (2004). *Experimental study on the impact of the 6+1 Trait® writing model on student achievement in writing.* Retrieved from http://educationnorthwest.org/webfm_send/13

Landauer, T. K., Foltz, P. W., & Laham, D. (1998). Introduction to latent semantic analysis. *Discourse Processes, 25*(2–3), 259–284.

Lee, Y.-W., Gentile, C., & Kantor, R. (2008). *Analytic scoring of TOEFL CBT essays: Scores from humans and e-rater®.* Retrieved from http://www.ets.org/Media/Research/pdf/RR-08-01.pdf

Lee, Y.-W., Gentile, C., & Kantor, R. (2009). Toward automated multi-trait scoring of essays: Investigating links among holistic, analytic, and text feature scores. *Applied Linguistics, 31*(3), 391–417. doi: 10.1093/applin/amp040

Lewis, D. M, Mitzel, H. C., Merado, R. L., & Schulz, E. M. (2012). The Bookmark standard setting procedure. In G. J. Cizek (Ed.), *Setting performance standards: Foundations, methods, and innovations* (2nd ed.). New York, NY: Routledge.

Lewis, D. M., Green, D. R., Mitzel, H. C., Baum, K., & Patz, R. J. (1998). *The Bookmark standard setting procedure: Methodology and recent implementations.* Paper presented at the National Council for Measurement in Education, San Diego, CA.

Linacre, J. M. (1994). *Many-facet Rasch measurement.* Chicago, IL: MESA Press.

Linacre, J. M., & Wright, B. D. (2002). Understanding Rasch measurement: Construction of measures from many-facet data. *Journal of Applied Measurement, 4,* 486–512.

Linacre, J. M. (2005). *A user's guide to Winsteps/Ministeps Rasch-model program.* Chicago, IL: MESA Press.

Loomis, S. C. (2012). Selecting and training standard setting participants: State of the art policies and procedures. In G. J. Cizek (Ed.), *Setting performance standards: Foundations, methods, and innovations* (2nd ed.). New York, NY: Routledge.

Masters, G. N. (1982). A Rasch model for partial credit scoring. *Psychometrika, 47,* 149–174.

Messick, S. (1980). Test validity and the measurement of ethics. *American Psychologist, 35,* 1012–1027.

Mitzel, H. C., Lewis, D. M., Patz, R. J., & Green, D. R. (2001). The Bookmark procedure: Cognitive perspectives on standard setting. In G. J. Cizek (Ed.), *Setting performance standards: Concepts, methods, and perspectives* (pp. 249–281). Mahwah, NJ: Lawrence Erlbaum Associates.

Morgan, D. L., & Michaelides, M. P. (2005). *Setting cut scores for college placement* (Research Report No. 2005–9). Retrieved from http://107.21.248.10/sites/default/files/publications/2012/7/researchreport-2005-9-setting-cut-scores-college-placement.pdf

No Child Left Behind Act of 2001, Public Law No. 107–110 115 Stat 1444–1446 C.F.R. (2002).

NWREL, Northwest Educational Research Laboratories. (2012a). *6+1 Trait® definitions.* Retrieved from http://educationnorthwest.org/resource/503

NWREL, Northwest Educational Research Laboratories. (2012b). *6+1 Trait® rubrics (aka scoring guides).* Retrieved from http://educationnorthwest.org/resource/464

Page, E. B. (1972). Seeking a measure of general educational advancement: The Bentee. *Journal of Educational Measurement, 9*(1), 33–43.

Page, E. B. (2003). Project Essay Grade: PEG. In M. D. Shermis & J. Burstein (Eds.), *Automated essay scoring: A cross-disciplinary perspective* (pp. 43–54). Mahwah, NJ: Lawrence Erlbaum Associates, Inc.

Page, E. B., & Petersen, N. S. (1995). The computer moves into essay grading: Updating the ancient test. *Phi Delta Kappan, 76,* 561–565.

Page, E. B., Poggio, J. P., & Keith, T. Z. (1997). *Computer analysis of student essays: Finding trait differences in the student profile.* Paper presented at the annual meeting of the American Educational Research Association, Chicago, IL, March.

Penfield, R. D. (2007). An approach for categorizing DIF in polytomous items. *Applied Measurement in Education, 20*(3), 335–355.

Penfield, R. D. (2008). Three classes of nonparametric differential step functioning effect estimators. *Applied Psychological Measurement, 32,* 480–591. doi: 10.1177/0146621607305399

Penfield, R. D., & Lam, T. C. M. (2000). Assessing differential item functioning in performance assessment: Review and recommendations. *Educational Measurement: Issues and Practice, 19*(3), 5–15.

Plake, B. S., & Cizek, G. J. (2012). Variations on a theme: The Modified Angoff, Extended Angoff, and yes/no standard setting methods. In G. J. Cizek (Ed.), *Setting performance standards: Foundations, methods, and innovations* (2nd ed.). New York, NY: Routledge.

Rajecki, D. W., Dame, J. A., Creek, K. J., Barrickman, P. J., Reid, C. A., & Appleby, D.C. (1993). Gender casting in television toy advertisements: Distributions, message content analysis, and evaluations. *Journal of Consumer Psychology, 2,* 307–327.

Rasch, G. (1960). *Probabilistic models for some intelligence and attainment tests.* Copenhagen: Danmarks Paedagogiske Institut.

Rasch, G. (1980). *Probabilistic models for some intelligence and attainment tests* (expanded ed.). Chicago, IL: University of Chicago Press.

Schulz, E. M., & Mitzel, H. C. (2009). A mapmark method of standard setting as implemented for the National Assessment Governing Board. In E. Smith & G. E. Stone (Eds.), *Criterion referenced testing: Practice analysis to score reporting using Rasch measurement* (pp. 194–235). Maple Grove, MN: JAM Press.

Sechrest, L. (2005). Validity of measures is no simple matter. *Health Research and Educational Trust, 40*, 1584–1604.

Shepard, L. (1979). Setting standards. In M. A. Bunda & J. R. Sanders (Eds.), *Practices and problems in competency-based education* (pp. 59–71). Washington, DC: National Council on Measurement in Education.

Shermis, M. D., Koch, C. M., Page, E. B., Keith, T. Z., & Harrington, S. (2002). Trait ratings for automated essay grading. *Educational and Psychological Measurement, 62*(1), 5–18.

Shermis, M. D., Mzumara, H. R., Olson, J., & Harrington, S. (2001). On-line grading of student essays: PEG goes on the web at IUPUI. *Assessment and Evaluation in Higher Education, 26*(3), 247–259.

Shermis, M. D., Rasmussen, J. L., Rajecki, D. W., Olson, J., & Marsiglio, C. (2001). All prompts are created equal, but some prompts are more equal than others. *Journal of Applied Measurement, 2*(2), 154–170.

Skaggs, G., & Tessema, A. (2001). *Item disordinality with the Bookmark Standard setting procedure.* Paper presented at the annual meeting of the National Council on Measurement in Education, Seattle, WA, April.

Smith III, M. (2009). *The reading-writing connection.* Retrieved from http://www.Lexile.com/m/uploads/positionpapers/ReadingWritingConnection.pdf

Smith, W. (1993). Assessing the reliability and adequacy of using holistic scoring of essays as a college composition placement technique. In M. M. Williamson & B. Huot (Eds.), *Validating holistic scoring for writing assessment: Theoretical and empirical foundations* (pp. 142–205). Cresskill, NJ: Hampton Press.

Stenner, A. J., & Burdick, D. S. (1997). *The objective measurement of reading comprehension: In response to technical questions raised by the California Department of Education's Technical Study Group.* Durham, NC: MetaMetrics, Inc.

Stenner, A. J., Burdick, H., Sanford, E. E., & Burdick, D. S. (2007). *The Lexile Framework for reading technical report.* Durham, NC: MetaMetrics, Inc.

Stenner, A. J., Swartz, C. W., Burdick, H., Burdick, D. S., & Hanlon, S. (2007). *The Lexile framework for writing.* Paper presented at the the annual meeting of the International Reading Association, Toronto, CA.

Stiggins, R. J., & Bridgeford, N. J. (1983). An analysis of published tests of writing proficiency. *Educational Measurement: Issues and Practice, 2*(1), 6.

Stone, G. E. (1995). *Objective Standard Setting.* Paper presented at the American Educational Research Association, San Francisco, CA.

Stone, G. E. (2004). Objective Standard Setting. In R. Smith & E. Smith (Eds.), *Introduction to Rasch measurement* (pp. 445–459). Minnesota: MN: JAM Press.

Stone, G. E. (2008). *Establishing criterion measures on graded essays using Objective Standard-Setting for judge-mediated examinations.* Paper presented at the 1st International Meeting on Evaluation for Mid-Higher Level Education and College Level, Veracruz, Mexico.

Stone, G. E., Koskey, K. L. K., & Sondergeld, T. A. (2011). Comparing construct definition in the Angoff and Objective Standard Setting models: Playing in a house of cards without a full deck. *Educational and Psychological Measurement, 71*(6), 942–962.

U.S. Department of Education, Institute of Education Sciences. (1998). *Sample questions: Writing 1998.* Retrieved from http://nces.ed/gov/nationsreportcard/

U.S. Department of Education, Institute of Education Sciences. (2002). *Sample questions: Writing 2002.* Retrieved from http://nces.ed/gov/nationsreportcard/

U.S. Department of Education (2009). *Race to the Top Program executive summary.* Retrieved from http://www2.ed.gov/programs/racetothetop/index.html

Wang, W.-C., & Shih, C.-L. (2010). MIMIC methods for assessing differential item functioning in polytomous items. *Applied Psychological Measurement, 43*(3), 166–180. doi: 10.1177/0146621609355279

Wang, W.-C., Shih, C.-L., & Yang, C.-C. (2009). The MIMIC method with scale purification for detection differential item functioning. *Educational and Psychological Measurement, 69*, 713–731. doi: 10.1177/0013164409332228

Weigle, S. C. (2002). *Assessing writing*. New York, NY: Cambridge University Press.

Wright, B. D., & Stenner, A. J. (1999). One fish, two fish: Rasch measures reading best. *Popular Measurement, 2*(1), 34–38.

Wright, B. D., & Masters, G. N. (1982). *Rating scale analysis*. Chicago, IL: MESA Press.

Zieky, M. J. (2012). So much has changed: An historical overview of setting cut scores. In G. J. Cizek (Ed.), *Setting performance standards: Foundations, methods, and innovations* (2nd ed., pp. 15–32). New York, NY: Routledge.

13 Human Ratings and Automated Essay Evaluation

Brent Bridgeman

INTRODUCTION

Because Automated Essay Evaluation (AEE) systems are typically built to predict human ratings (e.g., Attali & Burstein, 2006; Dikli, 2006; Shermis & Burstein, 2003; and Chapters 2 and 4 in this book), the quality of the human ratings can affect the quality of the scores generated by the automated system. If the human raters are inconsistent and unreliable and/or if they overuse one or two points on the score scale, the machine cannot be effectively trained.

The quality of human ratings is also an issue for testing programs in which the final score assigned to students is a combination of a human and a machine score. This type of combined scoring is used at Educational Testing Service (ETS) for large-scale assessments such as the Test of English as a Foreign Language Internet-based Test (TOEFL iBT) with over two million essays scored annually. Total scores are formed by summing or averaging the scores provided by the human rater and the machine. If the human and machine scores differ by a pre-specified threshold, an additional human score is obtained and the score that is most discrepant, whether it is the human or machine score, is then dropped from the average. The Graduate Record Examination (GRE) General Test also has used a combination of human and machine essay scores, though in a somewhat different manner. In the GRE model, the machine score is used as a check on the human score, and if the discrepancy is within the threshold, the single human score becomes the final score for that essay; if the discrepancy exceeds the threshold an additional human score is obtained. Thus, with this model the machine score never directly contributes to the final score. Nevertheless, the relationship of the human and machine scores is still important, as the value of the machine score in identifying discrepant essays is dependent on a close relationship of human and machine scores.

This chapter will summarize some of the procedures for monitoring and evaluating the quality of human essay ratings. Then some of the factors that may contribute to problematic human scores and ways to minimize the impact of these factors will be explored. Finally, the extent to which mimicking human scores should be the gold standard for the evaluation of machine scoring engines will be discussed.

ASSESSING RATER RELIABILITY

A traditional first step in evaluating the quality of human scoring is to get an estimate of how well two or more raters agree on the score that should be assigned to a given essay. At one time, the standard method was to compute the extent of exact agreement, and agreement within one score point (typically called adjacent agreement), between two raters. The primary reason for using this approach is that it is easy to understand without any statistical training. For well-trained raters using a 6-point scale, adjacent agreement rates close to 99% are not uncommon with exact agreement rates around 60% (Shermis & Burstein, 2003). Although apparently easily understood, percent agreement rates also can be deceptive. If raters are using only a few points on the rating scale a relatively high agreement rate can be reached by chance alone. In the worst case scenario, if all raters assigned a score of 3 to every essay, the exact agreement rate would be 100%, but the assessment would be worthless for evaluating individual differences. If it can be established that both raters are appropriately using a full score scale consisting of at least four points, then percent exact and adjacent agree rates make some sense although the method still makes no explicit adjustment for chance agreement. An alternative to percent agreement rate is Cohen's kappa coefficient or weighted kappa (Cohen, 1968). Ordinary kappa explicitly accounts for chance agreement, but treats all discrepancies the same. That is, ratings of 3 and 4 from two raters are considered the same as ratings of 1 and 6. A version of kappa that treats large discrepancies more severely than slight discrepancies is quadratic weighted kappa in which weights are proportional to the square of the deviation of individual ratings. Quadratic weighted kappa is virtually identical to Pearson r or the intra-class correlation for large-scale testing programs in which raters 1 and 2 for a particular essay are an essentially random draw from a large pool of raters. In such cases, the mean for "rater 1" is nearly identical to the mean for "rater 2," so a method that takes mean differences between raters into account (weighted kappa) will tend to produce very similar results to a method that does not consider such mean differences (e.g., Pearson r) as long as the number of score categories is fixed (Schuster, 2004). If the total rater pool is very small and the means for rater 1 and 2 differ, then quadratic weighted kappa can differ from the Pearson r. In analyses comparing scores from an automated essay evaluation system and scores from human raters, Pearson r may differ from quadratic weighted kappa when the automated system produces continuous scores while the human raters produce scores in just a few discrete categories. For example, with a 1 to 6 scale human raters could score an essay "4" or "5," but not 4.348; the decimal score would be possible with the machine rating. Pearson r can deal with the decimal scores, but if they are rounded to compute quadratic weighted kappa, results for the two methods will diverge. Quadratic weighted kappa is sensitive to the number of points in the scale and will generally increase as the number of points on the scale increases (Brenner & Kleissch, 1996). When comparing kappas across different studies, it is important to attend to which version of kappa is being reported as quadratic weighted kappa tends to produce a much larger number than unweighted kappa.

High rater reliability is sometimes confused with high score reliability, but an essay assessment could have high rater reliability but low score reliability. Multiple-choice tests have essentially perfect rater reliability because the optical scanners make very few errors, but such tests are not necessarily reliable if form to form variation is taken into account. The same is true for essay examinations in that high rater reliability does not assure high prompt to prompt reliability. Indeed, adding more essays per person to an essay assessment generally has a much greater impact on score reliability than does adding more raters per prompt. Breland, Bridgeman and Fowles (1999) reviewed a number of studies that varied the number of essays and the number of raters per essay. A typical finding in one of these studies indicated that a single essay read by four different readers produces a score reliability of .63 while four different essays with each read by only a single rater produced a score reliability of .73. In terms of rater costs, these two scenarios would be identical, although the latter scenario would require more testing time. A more realistic scenario that is frequently encountered in high stakes testing programs such as the GRE and TOEFL iBT has examinees write two essays with each essay read by two readers. The Breland et al. (1999) study demonstrates the advantages of using two readers in such cases; two essays each with a single reader produced a score reliability of .59 while two readers per essay showed a substantial improvement to a reliability of .70. This level of improvement also can be expected when the second reader of the essay is an automated system (Bridgeman, Trapani, & Attali, 2012).

Confusion between rater reliability and score reliability sometimes also can be observed when models based on Item Response Theory (IRT) are used. The generalized Partial Credit Model (Murakim, 1992) may be used to evaluate essay responses, and examinee proficiency is inferred directly from the rater scores. "A basic problem with this approach, however, is that it follows that more precise measurement of an examinee's proficiency can be obtained simply by using more raters instead of by giving the examinee more items!" (DeCarlo, Kim, & Johnson, 2011, p. 333). They note that following a traditional IRT approach, with enough raters, infinitely precise measurement of latent proficiency would be theoretically possible, though this is clearly not actually the case. They propose an alternative model that uses signal detection theory that appropriately accounts for various rater effects as part of a two-stage hierarchal model.

Generalizability theory (G theory) provides a mechanism for attending to the various factors that contribute to the differences among scores and avoids the overly-simplistic approaches that focus only on differences among raters. In G theory studies, it is possible to account for many different factors that may influence score variability in addition to rater effects; although many variations could be modeled such as testing location (classroom vs. test center), response mode (paper vs. computer) or time of day, for writing assessments attention is most frequently focused on effects of variation in test forms, which in a writing test often equates to different writing prompts. Although the basic concepts of G theory go back almost 50 years to Cronbach, Nageswari, and Gleser (1963), Robert Brennan's (2001) book on the topic renewed interest in the area and formalized computational procedures from an analysis of variance perspective. G studies allow researchers to evaluate how much of the variability in scores can be attributed to what they want to measures, i.e., differences among examinees, and how much should be attributed to different sources of error such as prompt, rater, and possible interactions of prompt and rater. Other interactions might also be of interest, such as the interaction of the rater with the native language of the examinee to identify whether some raters tend to give higher scores to examinees from particular language groups; this may be relevant whether the rater is a human or an automated system. Following a G study, a decision (D) study may be used to make decisions related to changing some aspects of the test administration. For example, a D study can be used to model the effects of increasing the number or raters or increasing the number of writing tasks. Lee and Kantor (2005) used results of a D study on pilot versions of the TOEFL to suggest, among other things, that it would be more efficient to increase the number of tasks rather than the number of raters and that larger gains in composite score reliability would be achieved by increasing the number of listening–writing tasks rather than reading–writing tasks. With a testing program that includes essay scores from an automated system, a D study might suggest the gains, in terms of score reliability, that might be achieved by adding one or more humans to the rating of an individual essay. Of course, the goal should always be to maximize validity, not reliability, and while improving reliability is generally a worthwhile goal, it is reasonable only if the reliability gains do not result in validity losses.

FACTORS AFFECTING RATER RELIABILITY

Writing scoring guides are frequently fairly complex and require evaluating several different dimensions simultaneously. For example, for GRE issue essays, a score of 5 on the 6-point scale is defined as follows:

> In addressing the specific task directions, a 5 response presents a generally thoughtful, well-developed analysis of the issue and conveys meaning clearly.
>   A typical response in this category:
>
> - presents a clear and well-considered position on the issue in accordance with the assigned task
> - develops the position with logically sound reasons and/or well-chosen examples
> - is focused and generally well organized, connecting ideas appropriately
> - conveys ideas clearly and well, using appropriate vocabulary and sentence variety
> - demonstrates facility with the conventions of standard written English, but may have minor errors
>
> (GRE analytical writing scoring guide, 2011)

One essay might have very "logically sound reasons and/or well-chosen examples" but have relatively poor sentence variety while another essay has the opposite pattern. Although raters are expected to balance all of these factors simultaneously, raters may differ in how they respond to these inconsistent patterns. Rigorous training may reduce some of these inconsistencies, but is unlikely to completely eliminate them. Greatly simplifying the scoring guide would likely improve rater reliability, but at the price of assessing only a portion of the intended construct. Suppose the scoring guide asked raters to focus only on "facility with the conventions of standard written English." Rater reliability would likely increase, but at a very high price. In an even more extreme case, raters could be asked to focus on verbal fluency as operationalized by a word count. Rater reliability estimates in the high .90s might be found, but would reveal very little about the potential value of the assessment.

In addition to non-systematic differences across raters in parts of the writing construct that they may differentially value, other more consistent rater characteristics must also be considered. Of the consistent effects, rater leniency/severity has received a considerable amount of attention (e.g., Engelhard, 1994; Myford & Wolfe, 2004; Wolfe, 2004). Some raters tend to assign scores that are systematically higher or lower than the scores assigned by other raters. When rater leniency/severity can be adequately documented, it is possible to statistically calibrate raters and adjust scores accordingly (Braun, 1988). Braun argued, "This statistical calibration appears to be a cost-effective approach to enhancing scoring reliability when compared to simply increasing the number of readings per paper" (p. 1). A complication with overly simplistic severity adjustments is that the severity of individual raters can change over an extended rating period or even just from one day to the next (Braun, 1988). Braun indicated that his findings suggested that, "we should explore the possibility of calibrating readers separately each day rather than once overall" (p. 9). Braun studied essays from the Advanced Placement (AP) program in which raters are seated at tables monitored by a table leader. He noted significant table effects that might also have to be accounted for if scores from raters seated at different tables are to be differentially adjusted. Congdon and McQueen (2000) studied essay scores given to 8,285 Australian elementary school children over a week-long rating period. They found significant fluctuations in day-to-day severity ratings such that the average severity rating over the entire week might not be appropriate on any given day. They concluded, "These findings cast doubt on the practice of using a single calibration of rater severity as the basis for adjustment of person measures" (p. 163). Significant instability in rater severity over time was also found in England's 2008 national curriculum English writing test for 14-year-olds (Leckie & Baird, 2011). Possible causes of some of these fluctuations are rater fatigue and rater learning. Raters can become fatigued at the end of an entire day of reading essays, especially if the day is at the end of a week-long (or longer) testing session. Fatigued raters may be more likely to look at external features of the essays, such as length or correctness of the grammar, rather than to truly evaluate the quality of reasoning in an argument. They may also tend to give scores near the middle of the scale, as identifying truly exemplary essays may require more effort. On the other hand, as raters gain more experience with grading essays on a particular topic and gain a fuller understanding of the range of writing abilities in a particular testing cohort, more valid and reliable scoring might be expected. In some individuals the fatigue affect may be dominant while others may differentially benefit from the learning opportunities, which could account for some of the inconsistencies noted in the studies mentioned above. Any attempts to provide statistical adjustments for rater severity or table effects must address potentially serious fairness concerns. Suppose a student happens to receive high scores (say a 6 on a 6-point scale) from each of two raters, both of whom are judged to be lenient raters. This student's 6 would then be adjusted downward. It is quite possible, but unknown, that this student would also have received a 6 from a more severe rater. The same would be true for table effects; a student whose essay happened to be read at a "lenient" table might have a score statistically adjusted downward even if that particular essay might have received the same score at a "strict" table. Over a very large number of essays these biases may average out, but a given student who writes only one or two essays would not benefit by the scoring being fair "on average."

Rather than attempting to adjust scores from individual raters, especially if these adjustments might vary from day to day, a potentially fairer procedure is to make an early identification of raters who are too lenient or too severe and retrain them to grade more appropriately. This requires real-time tracking of rater behavior. Such tracking also addresses a related problem—the tendency of raters to avoid the extremes of the score scale by overscoring low quality essays and underscoring high quality essays. Myford and Wolfe (2009) used a multifaceted Rasch approach to study changes in scale category use over time in ratings of Advanced Placement English Literature and Composition essays. In addition, they studied changes in level of accuracy over time. The raters used a 9-point holistic scale. The authors concluded some individual raters exhibited evidence of significant changes in accuracy and/or differential score category use over time, and they argued that these results underscore the importance of real-time rater monitoring, especially in high stakes testing programs.

RATER TRAINING AND MONITORING

Especially in high-stakes testing programs, such as the SAT, GRE, or TOEFL iBT, adequate rater training and monitoring is essential for producing fair and valid scores. Details may differ from program to program, but the essential features are as follows:

1. Rater training should include an opportunity to review and discuss scoring rubrics and scores assigned to sample essays. The discussion could either be in person or electronically via the Internet.

2. Before raters are certified as qualified, they should pass a certification test indicating that they can reasonably match scores assigned to essays by expert raters.

3. For raters who are scoring essays via the Internet, at the beginning of each testing day or when switching from one topic to another, a set of essays that has already had scores assigned by expert raters should be rated and a pre-specified level of agreement with the experts reached. As with all ratings, the raters would not be able to see the score from any other rating before they assigned a score to the essay. The rater should not be allowed to begin operational scoring on a test until they can satisfactorily pass this hurdle.

4. Throughout the scoring process, essays with predetermined expert scores should be blindly distributed to raters through the usual channel. That is, these essays should appear to the raters as just another essay and not as a special paper designed to monitor their performance.

5. Throughout the scoring process, statistics should be accumulated for each rater to indicate the level of agreement with the second rater of each essay and the number of scores at each score level that the rater has assigned. This can help to identify raters who are not using the full score scale. However, these data may be useful only after a substantial number of essays have been rated. This is especially true if the essays scored on any given day are not a random sample of the testing population. For example, in an international testing program the essays on a given day, or even in a given week, may come predominantly from one part of the world. If essay scores assigned to students from this part of the world are traditionally below average, raters on this day (or week) should not be expected to assign an average number of high scores when the average is determined over the entire testing population.

6. Identifying problematic raters or ratings is worthwhile only if meaningful steps are taken when the problems are identified. As suggested above, one step is to simply not allow a rater to provide operational scores before general competence and competence on a particular topic is demonstrated. At the extreme, a problematic rater might have to be let go, but less drastic action is usually feasible if proper mentoring and retraining is made available. Therefore, it should be the responsibility of scoring leaders to both monitor and mentor raters.

THE ROLE OF AEE IN RATER MONITORING

Automated essay scoring systems are potentially useful not only for scoring essays and providing diagnostic feedback to examinees but also for monitoring human raters. Indeed, this function is already a part of high-stakes essay assessments. Human raters and the machine are evaluating somewhat different aspects of the writing construct, so minor discrepancies between human and machine scores are to be expected. Large discrepancies, though sometimes legitimate, might also signal a fatigued human rater who overlooked some aspect of the essay that could be appropriately evaluated by the machine.

As noted previously, the GRE program has used a check score model in which the machine is used only as a check on the rating given by a human (Monaghan & Bridgeman, 2005). The research that supported the use of this model studied 5,950 examinees who had taken the standard operational GRE twice so that essay scores from two different occasions were available. The criterion was the total essay score from the second administration. This total was based on two different essays, one in response to an issue prompt and one in response to an argument prompt. The issue prompt asks examinees to make an argument supporting a particular position and the argument prompt asks the examinee to identify flaws in the argument presented in the prompt. Because each prompt was evaluated by two human raters, the final total score was based on at least four human ratings. ("At least," because an additional human rater would be used if the scores from the first two raters differed by more than one point.) The two essays from the first administration were also each rated by two humans and by e-rater. For the study, the first human score was compared with the e-rater score and if the human and e-rater scores differed by no more than one point, the single human score was taken as the final score. If they differed by more than a point, an additional human score was obtained so that the final reported score always reflected only human judgment. The need for a second human score was relatively rare as the human and e-rater agreed 85% of the time. For predicting the total score on the second administration, a single unchecked human score from time one agreed with the time two score (within .5 point) 73% of the time. The checked human score agreed 76% of the time, and the score from two humans at time one agreed 77% of the time. So, the checked score is noticeably better than a single unchecked human score and almost as good as the score from two humans, but with a substantial savings in the number of trained rates who must be in the rater pool. The strain on the rater pool could be relieved even further by simply averaging (or summing) the human and e-rater scores. The sum of the e-rater and human scores from time one provided the best prediction of the time two scores, agreeing within .5 point 78% of the time. Despite this apparent statistical superiority for the combined human/e-rater score, the check score model was initially adopted by the GRE program because of discomfort from test users or potential test users who did not believe that a machine should have any part in evaluating analytical writing ability.

For programs, such as the TOEFL iBT, that use a contributory score model (i.e., the sum of a human and e-rater score determines the reported score), the machine still serves a quality control function because large discrepancies between human and machine scores are still flagged and used as a trigger for an additional human reading. On one hand, this can be viewed as a quality control on the electronic score for cases in which the machine is not sensitive to problems that can be identified by humans (such as illogical reasoning), but it is also a quality control on humans who may have missed something that was identified by the machine. Indeed, experience with the TOEFL iBT program suggests that when flagged discrepant scores are sent to an additional human rater, that rater tends to agree with the machine more often than she or he agrees with the other human score.

FAIRNESS CONSIDERATIONS WHEN MACHINES ARE TRAINED TO MIMIC HUMAN SCORES

Automated essay scoring systems are typically developed to mimic scores produced by human raters. In general, they do this very well such that the correlation of human and machine scores is typically as high as the correlation between two humans. Means and standard deviations also can be set such that these statistics will match for the essays scored by machine and by human raters. However, just because a system works well on average, there is no guarantee that it will work equally well in all population subgroups. Bridgeman, Trapani, and Attali (2012) studied differences in the means from automated and human scoring on GRE essays for population subgroups defined by gender and race/

ethnicity within the United States. They also studied differences by language or native country groups for both the GRE and the TOEFL iBT.

For the GRE, they evaluated a random sample of approximately 3,000 essays for each of 133 issue prompts and 139 argument prompts that were drawn from operational test administrations from September 2006 to September 2007. For each prompt, e-rater models were built on 500 essays and the remaining 2,500 were used as a cross-validation set. Results from these sets were used in the analyses by averaging across the 133 issue prompts and separately averaging across the 139 argument prompts. The differences between human and machine mean scores by gender were very small—.10 or smaller in standard deviation units (d) for both issue and argument essays. Gender within race/ethnicity differences were also relatively small, with the largest difference ($d = -0.12$)[1] indicating that African American men tend to receive slightly higher scores from human raters than from e-rater on essays written in response to the issue prompt type. For the argument prompt type, African American men again showed the largest discrepancy ($d = -0.22$) with African American women showing the next largest discrepancy ($d = -0.18$).

Because the GRE is administered internationally, comparisons by native country are also of interest. For the issue prompt type, mean differences between human and machine scores were quite small (d less than .15) across the top 15 countries in terms of the number of examinees, with the notable exception of examinees from mainland China where the difference was .60 (indicating higher scores from e-rater than from human raters). (Note that there were over 9,000 examinees from mainland China in the sample, so the result could not be attributed to instability of mean differences in small samples.) It might be reasonable to suppose that an automated system trained primarily on students who are native speakers of English would have difficulty with Asian languages. But the difference noted in mainland China was much larger than differences noted in other East Asian countries. In Japan, for example, the standardized difference was a trivial .01 and in Korea the difference was .09. So, if it is not Asian languages generally, could it be something unique to Mandarin Chinese? This language is also spoken in Taiwan, and the difference in Taiwan was only .12. Although the reasons for the large discrepancy noted in mainland China are not fully understood, it might be related to essay length as essays from mainland China tend to be longer than essays from other regions. Although both human raters and e-rater tend to value longer essays, they are especially valued by e-rater. But as Bridgeman, et al. (2012) noted, "Although analyzing the feature weights assigned by e-rater is a straightforward process, determining which essay characteristics are most influential in determining human holistic scores is much more difficult, and more research in this area is clearly needed" (p. 36). Other factors could also be relevant, as the authors further note:

> Another possible explanation for the greater discrepancy between human and machine scores for essays from mainland China may be the dominance of coaching schools in mainland China that emphasize memorizing large chunks of text that can be recalled verbatim on the test. Human raters may assign a relatively low score if they recognize this memorized text as being somewhat off topic, though not so far off topic as to generate a score of 0. On the other hand, this grammatical and well-structured memorized text would receive a high score from e-rater. Although automated scoring engines can be trained to identify text that is not at all related to the assigned topic, they may not yet be sensitive enough to recognize this slightly off topic text.
>
> (Bridgeman et al., 2012, pp. 36–37)

For the argument prompt type, differences were again relatively trivial everywhere except in mainland China where the standardized difference between human and machine scores was .38. Nevertheless, this difference was considerably smaller than the difference for the issue prompt type. The authors speculated, "Because it may be more difficult to insert generic memorized text into argument essays, this finding supports the hypothesis that such text may contribute to the larger discrepancy between humans and machine noted for the issue prompts" (Bridgeman et al., 2012, p. 38).

The independent essay prompt type that is part of the TOEFL iBT is very similar to the GRE issue prompt type, but results differed somewhat from the results for the GRE. Although mainland China again showed the largest discrepancy between human and machine scores, the difference was only .25, compared to the .60 for the GRE. The difference in Taiwan was .18, and .10 and .01 in Korea and Japan, respectively. It is not clear why the difference in mainland China is smaller for the TOEFL iBT than for the GRE, but it might be related to the context of the rating experience for the human raters. Most GRE essays are written by native speakers of English, so the errors in a non-native essay may be more apparent; nearly all TOEFL iBT essays are written by non-native English speakers, so essays from China would not be seen as so different in this context. Two language groups, Arabic and Hindi, received somewhat higher scores from humans than from the machine (ds of –0.19 and –0.18 for Arabic and Hindi, respectively). The Hindi result is especially intriguing as there was essentially no difference ($d = .03$) for the other large Indian language group in the sample (Telugu). It is not clear whether this difference is related to linguistic or cultural features. What is clear is that more research is needed to better understand differences between human and machine scores, and particularly to better understand the features of writing that are most salient for human raters. It is easy to put precise weights on the features evaluated by automated essay scoring engines, but much more difficult to assign weights to the unknown features that influence human raters. Nevertheless, there have been a number of attempts to quantify, or at least to more fully describe, the factors that contribute to the scores that raters assign (e.g., Lumley, 2002; Suto, 2011). Think-aloud methods are one way in which attempts can be made to peer into the minds of essay raters (Wolfe, 2005).

THE GOLD STANDARD FOR DEVELOPING AND VALIDATING AEE REVISITED

The gold standard for developing and evaluating automated essay scoring engines has traditionally been agreement with a human rater when both humans and the machine are evaluating performance on the same prompt. Although this standard has the advantage of being relatively easy to compute, it is overly simplistic. As Bennett and Bejar (1997) argued, "a comprehensive discussion of validity and automated scoring includes the interplay among construct definition and test and task design, examinee interface, tutorial, test development tools, automated scoring, and reporting-for in the development process these components affect one another" (Abstract). Blindly selecting features that can be electronically evaluated just because they appear to predict human judgments may not lead to an assessment tool that can be said to represent the desired writing construct.

Bridgeman, Trapani, and Williamson (2011) evaluated the gold standard with respect to the integrated essay prompt on the TOEFL iBT. This prompt type is especially challenging for an automated scoring engine because it asks the examinee to listen to a lecture, read a relevant selection that may present a different point of view from that of the lecture, and then to write an essay integrating and reacting to these different points of view. By the traditional criteria, this prompt was not a good candidate for automated scoring. For the TOEFL iBT independent task, the correlation of automated and human scores exceeded the correlation of two humans (.72 vs. .68), but for the integrated task the human–human correlation was substantially higher (.83 vs. .62).[2]

Other evidence, not directly related to the gold standard (human ratings), but highly relevant to the overall validity argument were evaluated. Specifically, two additional criteria were considered. The first was designed to determine how well the automated score, compared to a human score, predicted other scores in the same general domain. The TOEFL iBT produces four scores, only one of which is a writing score based on essay responses; the other scores are reading, listening, and speaking. All four scores are designed to assess academic English language skills that are relevant for success at universities in which English is the primary language of instruction. Factor analyses suggest that these skills are highly related to the extent that it makes sense to add the four scores together to form a single total score (Sawaki, Stricker, & Oranje, 2009). This relationship among the tasks also suggests that the combination of the reading, listening, and speaking scores is a reasonable validity criterion for the writing score. The second criterion was the TOEFL writing score on a test taken at a later date. As the authors note:

> On a single task, humans may agree on aspects of a response that are unique to that task but that do not generalize to writing performance on a different occasion. Generalization beyond the task at hand is the goal of any test intended to be used in an admissions context . . .
>
> (Bridgeman et al., 2011, p. 12)

The criterion score was based on the sum of four different human ratings on this second test—two ratings on the independent task and two ratings on the integrated task.

In the sample of 141,203 TOEFL iBT examinees, the correlation of the e-rater score with the reading/listening/speaking total score was .66 and the human rater correlation with this criterion was only slightly higher (.71). As noted, this research focused on the generic e-rater score for practical implementation reasons, but for other testing programs it might be feasible to use a prompt-specific model. Thus, it is worth noting that a prompt specific model substantially outperformed a human rater for this criterion with a correlation of .78.

For the second criterion, total writing score from a different test administration (time 2), the human score and the generic e-rater score on the integrated task both correlated .62 with the criterion. For two human raters combined, the correlation was .65, and for one human rater combined with e-rater the correlation was .68. Because the total writing score, combining scores on the independent and integrated writing tasks, is what is reported to score users, it is the combination of these scores that should provide the most relevant data. If the time 1 score is based on two human scores on the independent task and two human scores on the integrated task, the correlation with the time 2 criterion is .72. If the time 1 score is based on a combination of one human score and one e-rater score on each task, the correlation with the time 2 criterion is .73. Eliminating the need for half of the human raters,[3] and substituting e-rater scores, can be accomplished with no loss in predictive power. When viewed in this broader context, an automated score that appeared to fail the usual gold standard test could be seen as providing valuable and valid information. In the future, the correlation of human and machine scores may become even less important as test users become more comfortable with the idea of letting machines do what they do best (e.g., counting objective grammatical and structural features) and letting people do what they do best (e.g., evaluating logic and persuasiveness of arguments), and not requiring that these separate functions be very highly correlated.

CONCLUSION

Even if agreement with human raters evaluating the same essay is not the only criterion for developing and evaluating automated essay scoring systems, the relationship of human and automated scores is likely to remain as a key consideration. This suggests that attention to the reliability and meaning of human ratings should remain as a focus for research for the foreseeable future.

NOTES

1 The negative sign denotes that the human score was higher than the e-rater score. Positive values indicate a higher e-rater score.
2 The 0.62 correlation was for a generic version of e-rater in which the same feature weights and intercept values (for the prediction of human scores) are used for every prompt. A prompt specific model which uses additional topical vocabulary features and different weights and intercepts for each prompt yielded a considerably higher correlation (0.77). However, because the prompt specific model requires a new model be built for each prompt, and because the TOEFL program must constantly add new prompts for test security reasons, only the generic model is a practical alternative.
3 In addition to the obvious cost savings in paying raters, reducing the stress on the size of the human rater pool allows greater ability to select and retain only the most skilled raters.

REFERENCES

Attali, Y., & Burstein, J. (2006). Automated essay scoring with e-rater V.2. *Journal of Technology, Learning, and Assessment, 4*(3). Available from http://www.jtla.org.

Bennett, R., & Bejar, I. (1997). *Validity and automated scoring: It's not only the scoring. (ETS RR-97–13)*. Princeton, NJ: Educational Testing Service.

Braun, H. I. (1988). Understanding score reliability: Experiments in calibrating essay readers. *Journal of Educational Statistics, 13*, 1–18.

Breland, H. M., Bridgeman, B., & Fowles, M. E. (1999). Writing assessment in admission to higher education: Review and framework. *College Board Report No. 99–3; GRE Board Research Report No. 96-12R; ETS RR 99–3*. New York, NY: College Entrance Examination Board.

Brennan, R. L. (2001). *Generalizability theory*. New York, NY: Springer-Verlag.

Brenner, H., & Kleissch, U. (1996). Dependence of weighted kappa coefficients on the number of categories. *Epidemiology, 7*, 199–202.

Bridgeman, B., Trapani, C., & Attali, Y. (2012). Comparison of human and machine scoring of essays: Differences by gender, ethnicity, and country. *Applied Measurement in Education, 25*, 27–40.

Bridgeman, B., Trapani, C., & Williamson, D. (2011). *The question of validity of automated essay scores and differentially valued evidence*. Paper presented at the National Council on Measurement in Education, New Orleans, LA.

Cohen, J. A. (1968). Weighted kappa: Nominal scale agreement with provision for scaled disagreement of partial credit. *Psychological Bulletin, 70*, 213–220.

Congdon, P. J., & McQueen, J. (2000). The stability of rater severity in large-scale assessment programs. *Journal of Educational Measurement, 37*, 163–178.

Cronbach, L. J., Nageswari, R., & Gleser, G. C. (1963). Theory of generalizability: A liberation of reliability theory. *The British Journal of Statistical Psychology, 16*(2), 137–163.

DeCarlo, J. T., Kim, Y. K., & Johnson, M. S. (2011). A hierarchical rater model for constructed responses, with a signal detection rater model. *Journal of Educational Measurement, 48,* 333–356.

Dikli, S. (2006). An overview of automated scoring of essays. *The Journal of Technology, Learning, and Assessment, 5*(1), http://ejournals.bc.edu/ojs/index.php/jtla/article/view/1640/1489

Engelhard, G., Jr. (1994). Examining rater errors in the assessment of written composition with a many-faceted Rasch model. *Journal of Educational Measurement, 31*(2), 93–112.

GRE analytical writing scoring guide (2011), from http://www.ets.org/gre/revised_general/prepare/analytical_writing/issue/scoring_guide

Leckie, G., & Baird, J. (2011). Rater effects on essay scoring: A multilevel analysis of severity drift, central tendency, and rater experience. *Journal of Educational Measurement, 48,* 399–418.

Lee, Y. W., & Kantor, R. (2005). Dependability of new ESL writing tests scores: Evaluating prototype tasks and alternative rating schemes *ETS-RR-05-14; TOEFL-MS-31*. Princeton, NJ: Educational Testing Service.

Lumley, T. (2002). Assessment criteria in a large-scale writing test: What do they really mean to the raters? *Language Testing, 19,* 246–276.

Monaghan, W., & Bridgeman, B. (2005). *E-rater as a quality control on human scores.* (R&D Connections RDC-02). Princeton, NJ: Educational Testing Service.

Murakim, E. (1992). A generalized Partial Credit Model: Applications of an EM algorithm. *Applied Psychological Measurement, 16,* 159–176.

Myford, C. M., & Wolfe, E. W. (2004). Detecting and measuring rater effects using many-facet Rasch measurement: Part II. *Journal of Applied Measurement, 5,* 189–227.

Myford, C. M., & Wolfe, E. W. (2009). Monitoring rater performance over time: A framework for detecting differential accuracy and differential scale category use. *Journal of Educational Measurement, 46,* 371–389.

Sawaki, Y., Stricker, L., & Oranje, A. (2009). Factor structure of the TOEFL Internet-based Test (TOEFL iBT). *Language Testing, 26,* 5–30.

Schuster, C. (2004). A note on the interpretation of weighted kappa and its relations to other rater agreement statistics for metric scales. *Educational and Psychological Measurement, 64,* 243–253.

Shermis, M. D., & Burstein, J. (2003). Introduction. In M. D. Shermis & J. Burstein (Eds.), *Automated essay scoring: A cross-disciplinary perspective.* Mahwah, NJ: Lawrence Erlbaum Associates, Inc.

Suto, I. (2011). *A critical review of some research used to explore rater cognition.* Paper presented at the annual conference of the American Educational Research Association New Orleans.

Wolfe, E. W. (2004). Identifying rater effects using latent trait models. *Psychological Science, 46,* 35–51.

Wolfe, E. W. (2005). Uncovering rater's cognitive processing and focus using think-aloud protocols. *Journal of Writing Assessment, 2,* 37–56.

14 Using Automated Scoring to Monitor Reader Performance and Detect Reader Drift in Essay Scoring

Susan M. Lottridge, E. Matthew Schulz, and Howard C. Mitzel

INTRODUCTION

With expediencies such as rapid turnaround time and economic benefits associated with reduced scoring costs, automated scoring is widely viewed as on a path to replace human labor, like so many prior innovative technologies. As a result, the focus of automated scoring development has tended to be on validity or measures of accuracy as compared to human efforts. This chapter is focused on a somewhat nearer-term process, the transition from human to machine scoring and how the two scoring methods can be used concurrently. Previously, the authors have referred to the use of both human and machine scoring for a single assessment program as a "blended" scoring model (Lottridge, Mitzel, & Chou, 2009). The central idea is to see if two imperfect scoring methods can be mutually leveraged in some optimal way to improve the overall accuracy of scoring. Although the authors have not yet achieved that goal, the studies presented here can be taken as a progress report toward that objective.

The general scenario under which these blended scoring models were investigated has some similarities to the next generation of computer-based K–12 assessments. Specifically, this assessment program is a No Child Left Behind (NCLB) high stakes end of course (EOC) program, where a writing prompt constitutes one session of a high school English test. The prompts are scored holistically on each of two dimensions, on a 0–4 scale. More detail is presented below. A key tenet of this program is that the "score of record," that is, the final score associated with a student response is always assigned by a human rater. This design, where final scores are assigned by humans, was adopted due to concerns around the public acceptance of machine-based scores. Automated scoring functions as a second read for all responses, under a fairly standard (hand) scoring design whereby non-adjacent scores, meeting some criterion (e.g., greater than a 1-point difference), are resolved by an expert human reader.

A second element of the assessment design is rapid turnaround of scores. Most students (99%) receive their standards-based scores, placing them in an NCLB achievement level within two working days. It is important to recognize that this rapid-turnaround design precludes post-equating studies, rescoring efforts should some scoring anomaly occur, along with the opportunity to review score distributions prior to the release of results for the entire administration. This means that test forms are pre-equated, including the writing prompts. In addition, the prompts are used in two or more administrations at differing time periods, so they must be scored comparably in each use. For this assessment program, then, it is an imperative that hand scoring be as accurate and unbiased as possible.

This chapter recounts a progression of studies designed to (1) identify (systematic) human rater bias or scoring drift occurring across an online administration window, (2) establish a criterion for identifying specific raters who are drifting, (3) examine more closely the role of expert readers and table leaders in preventing or contributing to rater drift, and (4) begin to consider what types of interventions can be applied within the live scoring window in the face of suspected reader drift. It is somewhat ironical that a new technology expected to eventually replace hand scoring is what is really required to effectively monitor hand-scoring accuracy. This is, in fact, to suggest that current monitoring methods, such as read-behinds, and re-scores of old sets of papers are well intentioned but manifestly inadequate for this purpose. Further evidence for this position is developed in the course of this chapter.

LITERATURE REVIEW

Stakeholders in K–12 assessment often appear to operate under the assumption that humans do not make errors or make very few errors in scoring. However, "Raters are human and therefore subject to all the errors to which humankind must plead guilty" (Guilford, 1936, as quoted in Engelhard, 1994, p. 108). Systematic reader errors, or bias, introduce construct-irrelevant variance into scores and therefore impacts validity of the scores (Messick, 1995).[1] Reader bias has also been referred to as reader effects (Braun, 1988) and reader drift (Wolfe, Myford, Engelhard, & Manalo, 2007). Reader bias affects the validity of student scores at the individual and group level, affects parameter estimation, especially if reader bias changes over time, and affects the quality of equating when hand-scored items are included in the anchor set. Ultimately, it is critical that reader bias is identified and managed in large-scale, high-stakes assessment programs because it has the potential to influence the overall reliability, validity and fairness of the test scores (American Educational Research Association, American Psychological Association, and National Council on Measurement in Education, 2004).

There has been little empirical research in the large-scale assessment literature that identifies reasons for reader bias; the reasons underlying bias are typically hypothesized but not scientifically explicated, for reasons cited above. The format of the scoring rubric is likely to impact bias (Guilford, 1954; Harik et al., 2009; Quellmalz, 1980; Saal, Downey, & Lahey, 1980). Operationally-defined scoring categories which include checklists or well-defined trait-level rubrics can serve to minimize bias because they reduce the need of readers to weigh and prioritize elements of a student response that may or may not properly contribute to the score. For instance, bias is less likely to be observed in the scoring of a constructed response math item with few correct answers. The distinction being drawn here is between the recognition of a correct response versus the evaluation of multiple elements of a student's response which are combined by some cognitive process into a score judgment. The evaluation of writing of course falls to the latter end of this continuum (Gere, 1980; Wiggins, 1994). Rubrics generally used in the scoring of writing in large-scale assessment often require the reader to simultaneously identify and weigh interrelated aspects of writing quality to produce either a holistic score or at most six trait-based scores. A typical example of a scoring rubric in writing is shown in Figure 14.1, which is a rubric assessing the "Ideas" trait in the 6+1® model produced by Education Northwest.

A reader using this rubric to score a student essay would need to consider multiple aspects of the essay and convert those into a performance level or holistic score. Note that there are multiple "opportunities" for the reader to make evaluations about the nature of the aspect, the quality of the aspects, and how each is cognitively weighed to contribute to the score. When confronted with the scoring of hundreds of essays, readers

6-POINT WRITER'S RUBRIC

IDEAS

| | Not proficient | | 3 Developing | 4 Capable | Proficient | |
	1 Beginning	2 Emerging			5 Experienced	6 Exceptional
	No main idea, purpose, or central theme exists; reader must infer this based on sketchy or missing details	Main idea is still missing, though possible topic/theme is emerging	Main idea is present; may be broad or simplistic	Topic or theme is identified as main idea; development remains basic or general	Main idea is well-marked by detail but could benefit from additional information	Main idea is clear, supported, and enriched by relevant anecdotes and details
A	No topic emerges	Several topics emerge; any might become central theme or main idea	Topic becomes clear, though still too broad, lacking focus; reader must infer message	Topic is fairly broad, yet author's direction is clear	Topic is focused yet still needs additional narrowing	Topic is narrow, manageable, and focused
B	Support for topic is not evident	Support for topic is limited, unclear; length is not adequate for development	Support for topic is incidental or confusing, not focused	Support for topic is starting to work; still does not quite flesh out key issues	Support for topic is clear and relevant except for a moment or two	Support is strong and credible, and uses resources that are relevant and accurate
C	There are no details	Few details are present; piece simply restates topic and main idea or merely answers a question	Additional details are present but lack specificity; main idea or topic emerges but remains weak	Some details begin to define main idea or topic, yet are limited in number or clarity	Accurate, precise details support one main idea	Details are relevant, telling; quality details go beyond obvious and are not predictable
D	Author is not writing from own knowledge/experience; ideas are not author's	Author generalizes about topic without personal knowledge/experience	Author "tells" based on others' experiences rather than "showing" by own experience	Author uses few examples to "show" own experience, yet still relies on generic experiences of others	Author presents new ways of thinking about topic based on personal knowledge/experience	Author writes from own knowledge/experience; ideas are fresh, original, and uniquely the author's
E	No reader's questions have been answered	Reader has many questions due to lack of specifics; it is hard to "fill in the blanks."	Reader begins to recognize focus with specifics, though questions remain	Reader generally understands content and has only a few questions	Reader's questions are usually anticipated and answered by author	Reader's questions are all answered
F	Author doesn't help reader make any connections	Author does not yet connect topic with reader in any way although attempts are made	Author provides glimmers into topic; casual connections are made by reader	Author stays on topic and begins to connect reader through self, text, world, or other resources	Author connects reader to topic with a few anecdotes, text, or other resources	Author helps reader make many connections by sharing significant insights into life

Key question: Does the writer stay focused and share original and fresh information or perspective on the topic?

Figure 14.1 Six-point scoring rubric for the Ideas trait. Source: Education Northwest, 2010.

are likely to develop an internal scoring model or policy, often leaning on mental heuristics to enable efficient scoring. Of course there may be as many policies as there are readers. At issue is whether the internal policy objectively reflects the scoring rubric and range finding history.

Biased scoring is thought to be due to various aspects of reader characteristics, reader psychology, and rating environment. Reader characteristics are factors such as teaching experience, rating experience, and content experience in areas for which the reader is scoring. Reader psychology is any factor that occurs internal to the reader such as fatigue, breaks from scoring that may result in forgetting the scoring procedures, attitude toward the essays or prompt, attitude toward response format, and inability to ignore factors irrelevant to score such as messy handwriting. The rating environment can also influence scoring: papers read, pressure to score many papers in short amount of time, pressure to achieve high agreement rates, impact of table leaders (Braun, 1988; Hoskins & Wilson, 2001; Quellmalz, 1980), and the social/psychological aspects such as the mood of the room or conversations between readers (Engelhard, 1994). In particular and important for this study, the pressure to achieve high agreement rates can encourage readers to adopt a "play it safe" strategy and restrict use of the full range of the scale (Wolfe et al., 2007).

Saal et al.'s (1980) review of the reader bias literature provided a categorization of four major outcomes of reader bias: severity/leniency, halo, central tendency, and restriction of range. Severity/leniency bias is the tendency of a reader to score responses easier (leniency) or harder (severity) than is called for by the response. Saal et al. define the halo effect as a "rater's failure to discriminate among conceptually distinct and potentially independent aspects of a ratee's behavior" (1980, p. 415). In writing, halo bias may be occurring when the inter-rater trait scores have higher correlations than what is expected, when pattern scores across traits are highly consistent, or when summed scores across the traits exhibit peaks (Engelhard, 1994). Central tendency bias occurs when the "ratings are clustered around the midpoint of the rating scale" (Saal et al., 1980). Restriction of range is similar to central tendency bias but the clustering can occur anywhere in the rating scale.

Central tendency/range restriction bias has been observed in a variety of rater effect studies (Braun, 1988; Engelhard, 1994; Guildford, 1954; Hoskins & Wilson, 2001; Leckie & Baird, 2011; Myford & Wolfe, 2009). This bias is often due to the pressure to achieve overly high agreement rates. In most large-scale assessment programs, score adjudication rules call for expert resolution when scores are non-adjacent. Readers who have "too many" non-adjacent scores may be identified to undergo retraining and/or possible removal from scoring. Thus, assigning middle scores can increase scoring adjacency and thereby allow a reader to stay under the radar or "play it safe."

Reader bias does not necessarily conform to expected behaviors. Numerous studies have found bias to be unstable over time (Braun, 1988; Cogdon & McQueen, 2000; Harik et al., 2009; Hoskins & Wilson, 2001; Leckie & Baird, 2011; Myford & Wolfe, 2009; Quellmalz, 1980). Also, experts can exhibit bias. Engelhard (1994) observed "some regression toward the mean . . . through the consensus process used by the validity committee" (p. 105) which served as the benchmark for detecting reader bias. Table leader bias has also been identified (Braun, 1988; Hoskins & Wilson, 2001; Leckie & Baird, 2011). Finally, entire groups of readers can exhibit bias. Quellmalz (1980) noted a type of context effect where readers scoring a set of low-performing essays exhibit leniency bias as a group because their reference point shifts. Rather than scoring to the rubric, readers use their previously scored papers as their referent, which shifts the score distribution higher.

As mentioned earlier, many assessment programs examine reader performance by monitoring reader agreement rates, with high agreement rates considered the primary benchmark of scoring validity. The assumption underlying the emphasis on reader agreement is that agreement between independent ratings suggests convergent validity. In addition, true score theory is generalized to suggest that only one score assignment is valid. However, "high agreement among the ratings assigned . . . by different readers does not necessarily imply predictable or valid ratings, and that disagreement among readers may be associated with predictability and possibly validity" (Buckner, 1959). This is because one can achieve high agreement rates at the expense of scoring accuracy. In this scenario, readers may "play it safe" to obtain high agreement rates by only assigning extreme scores in cases where they are certain the evaluation wouldn't be questioned. Alternatively, readers may adopt construct-narrowed heuristics that enable quick scoring. An example might be the use of factors such as a review of the essay for key words, number of paragraphs, existence of citations, and few misspellings or grammar errors rather than a careful reading of the essay against the scoring rubric.

One can reasonably conceive of essays as occurring on a continuum of writing ability. Range finding exercises often identify borderline papers (e.g., high–3 or low–2) suggesting that there is a range within rubric categories and papers can straddle adjacent score categories. Assuming that writing ability is distributed continuously and not categorically (like scoring rubrics), there will obviously be errors in classification. For instance, a borderline essay will veridically have a 50/50 chance of being classified into the below or above category. Note that the optimal agreement rate for a set of essays straddling a category border is only 0.50, which is well below most hand-scoring agreement criteria.

Given the above issues with reader bias, "constant monitoring of rater stability is desirable" (Cogden & McQueen, 2000). In operational large-scale assessment, readers are monitored using a variety of methods. These methods vary by vendor and program but include some combination of validity papers, read-behinds, second reads, and table leader back-reading of scored papers. In the case of validity papers (also called seed papers or check papers), a set of papers with expert vetted scores are seeded at regular intervals into each reader's scoring queue. Read-behinds are independent scores assigned by another human reader but these scores usually do not contribute to the final score and are used primarily for monitoring the first human reader. Second reads are independent scores assigned by another human reader and this score is usually included into the final score for the student depending on the specific scoring model. The scores from two readers are often resolved in the case of non-adjacency, and each reader is evaluated on the basis of the agreement rates with the set of second reads. The theory of unresolved adjacent reads is that scoring errors will "cancel out" one another, or, in the case of borderline papers, "average out" correctly. However, even adjacent scores can result in scoring bias, as is shown later.

Regardless of the use of validity papers, read-behinds, or second reads, readers are often evaluated using two metrics: (1) extent of agreement with the validity, second read, or read-behind score usually compared to a criterion; and, (2) comparison of the individual reader's score distribution to that of all readers, collectively. Read-behinds and validity papers usually don't occur with enough frequency to yield reliable detection of problems with readers. Additionally, problems with readers can't be detected with read-behinds or second reads if the second reader is displaying the same problem, such as central tendency, as the first reader. Two assumptions underlie the score distribution comparison: (1) papers are randomly administered to readers and as a result the score distributions should be similar within sampling error; and, (2) the group as a whole is scoring accurately. However, papers often arrive clustered by student ability, and readers will score at different speeds and at different intervals within the scoring window, possibly violating the first assumption. And, if the group of readers is exhibiting central tendency bias, then the score distribution comparison will not detect bias in an individual reader.

Finally, readers are usually organized into small teams led by team or table leaders. Table leaders will back-read a percentage of papers scored by each reader, monitoring for correctness of scores. As with other methods, this assumes that the team leader is accurately applying the scoring rubric and is reading sufficient numbers of papers to identify errant readers with some level of certainty.

Automated essay scoring presents a promising approach in monitoring human readers. Automated scores can serve as a benchmark on which to compare all readers and all essays scored by readers. This approach removes the sparse data problem outlined for the validity papers and read-behinds. In addition, because automated scoring engine scores are reproducible for any given essay, they are inherently consistent over time. This allows them to serve as a benchmark for measuring and hopefully mitigating group-level bias within a testing window or for the life of a writing prompt (i.e., across testing windows).

Automated essay scoring has also been shown to perform comparably to humans for a variety of prompt types and engines (Attali & Burstein, 2006; Landauer, Laham, & Foltz, 2003; Rudner, Garcia, & Welch, 2006; Shermis & Hamner, 2012). Interestingly, automated scoring to monitor reader performance has been reported in only isolated cases in large-scale assessment (Enright & Quinlan, 2010; Rudner et al., 2006; Williamson, Xi, & Breyer, 2012).

Once the engine has been trained, it can be configured to score all essays for a much lower cost than human scoring, meaning that large samples of scores can now be investigated where it was once cost prohibitive. In addition, one may choose the training sample for the engine that reflects program goals for monitoring human readers. For instance, the engine can be trained on expert scores to act as a high benchmark for human reader performance. Alternatively, the engine can be trained on typical reader scores to perform as an average human reader, to detect operational scoring readers who are significantly below average. This perspective, that different calibrations of the scoring engine may have different uses presents interesting possibilities for the future. Clearly, the choice of calibration impacts the interpretations applied to the monitoring data.

The CRASE Engine

Pacific Metrics automated scoring engine, CRASE™, scores responses to items typically appearing in large-scale assessments: (a) essay length writing prompts; (b) short answer constructed response items in mathematics, English Language Arts, and science; (c) math items eliciting formulae or numeric answers; and, (d) technology-enhanced items (e.g., Drag and Drop, Graphing). It has been used in both formative and high-stakes summative assessments, providing rapid turnaround and delivering cost savings over traditional hand-scoring methods. The system is customizable, both in terms of the configurations used to build machine scoring models and in terms of the how the system can blend human scoring and machine scoring (i.e., hybrid models). CRASE is a fully integrated Java-based application that runs as a web service. Integration refers to its ability to: (a) score any of several different item types as a single software application, (b) interface with web-based assessment delivery platforms for immediate turnaround of scores, and (c) integrate with vendor-based electronic hand-scoring systems for monitoring or dual scoring.

For the CRASE engine, categorization is critical to the scoring process. Using experience, along with training materials, scoring guides, etc., a human rater classifies a student's response into one of several defined categories or scores. CRASE analyzes a sample of already-scored student responses to produce a model of the raters' scoring behavior. In general, the system will score as reliably as the sample from which the scoring models are built. By emulating human scoring behavior, CRASE essentially predicts the score that a human rater would assign to a given student response. CRASE uses a sequential process to first analyze and then score students' responses. When a response is received from an online test administration system, it moves through three phases in the scoring process: (a) identifying non-attempts, (b) extracting features, and (c) predicting a score.

- Identifying non-attempts. The response is first reviewed to determine whether it is a valid attempt at the item. If it is not a valid attempt (e.g., it is blank or gibberish), the response is flagged and removed from the remaining feature extraction and scoring process.
- Extracting features. If it is a valid attempt, the response is submitted to one of the feature extraction engines. In this phase, a vector of values is generated that represents both the scoring rubric and the construct the item is intended to assess.
- Predicting a score. The vector of values is submitted to a scoring engine that uses a statistical model and/or a series of computational linguistic procedures to classify the response into a score category. It is at this stage that the model derived from the rater sample is applied to predict the score a rater would provide. The predicted score and any non-attempt flags are then returned to the test administration system.

For the scoring of writing prompts, the feature extraction step is organized around the 6+1 Trait® Model, a product of Education Northwest (http://educationnorthwest.org/traits) that is used in some form by most states for K–12 writing applications. The 6+1 Trait Model conceptualizes six traits of writing (ideas, sentence fluency, organization, voice, word choice, and conventions) along with the '+1' which is "written presentation." For writing prompts and essays, the feature extraction stage first pre-processes student responses by tokenizing elements in the response, counting and correcting misspellings, computing part-of-speech tags, and conducts stemming. One or more functions are associated with each of the six traits, and these functions are applied to the processed response to produce one or more variables that represent the trait. Examples of functions are: identifying usage and mechanics errors typically seen in student essays, measuring variation in sentence type, calculating extent of personal engagement, and idea development in phrasing. This step also produces text-based and numeric-based feedback that can be used to improve the essay (e.g., too-common words or sentence beginnings, spelling errors, grammatical errors). CRASE can be customized to score each of the six traits, or combinations of the traits. It can also be customized to score a number of points (e.g., 1 to 4, 1 to 6). The scoring step uses statistical modeling methods to produce a score using the variables produced in the feature extraction step. Bayesian methods can also be employed to incorporate priors into the scoring model.

STUDIES

As stated earlier, this chapter recounts a progression of studies designed to (1) identify (systematic) human rater bias or scoring drift occurring across an online administration window, (2) establish a criterion for identifying specific raters who are drifting, and

(3) examine more closely the role of expert readers and table leaders in preventing or contributing to rater drift. Each of these studies and their results are outlined in the following three sections. These studies focus on a single writing prompt although the program itself has multiple writing prompts. The prompts perform similarly to one another in terms of scoring and the CRASE system has been configured to score the prompts using similar training procedures.

Study 1: Identifying Rater Drift

Reader drift was suspected following a May 2009 administration, based on distributional changes within the administration window. As noted earlier, the assessment program is an online summative end of course program for high school English. The program has unusually tight scoring and reporting turnaround times, requiring test scores to be returned within 48 hours of the student completing the test and human reader scores to be returned within 24 hours. Following the administration, the CRASE system was trained on a random sample of 334 responses and reader-assigned scores from the May 2009 administration. Thus, the engine was configured to act as a typical human reader. The sample was taken from the first six days (time period 1) of the 15-day administration, when the central tendency bias appeared to be minimal. The engine results were used to demonstrate that central tendency bias was occurring later in the window during time periods 2 and 3.

Each writing prompt is scored against a general scoring rubric that assesses two traits: Ideas and Style. The two trait scores are very highly correlated for this prompt; the intra-trait correlations are around 0.93 across administrations. Given the similar scoring for both traits, the analyses presented in this study are focused on the first trait (Ideas) only.

Table 14.1 displays the performance of the engine and human readers across three time periods for the Ideas trait. In time period 1 (again, the source for the training sample) the

Table 14.1 Performance of Automated and Human Readers for the Ideas Trait Across Three Time Periods

Score	Time Period 1 (n=2,131)		Time Period 2 (n=1,808)		Time Period 3 (n=1,213)	
	HS	AS	HS	AS	HS	AS
Percent in Score Category						
1	4	4	2	4	4	6
2	28	28	24	28	24	30
3	53	53	62	53	61	50
4	15	15	12	15	10	15
Mean Score						
Mean	2.80	2.80	2.83	2.80	2.78	2.73
SD	0.74	0.74	0.66	0.73	0.68	0.78
Agreement with the Human Reader						
Exact	67%	68%	74%	70%	80%	67%
Adj	32%	31%	26%	30%	20%	33%
Relationship to Multiple Choice Score						
r_{MC}	0.43	0.44	0.49	0.55	0.47	0.48
Mean	22.44		22.85		21.75	
SD	9.28		8.70		9.02	

Note. HS—Human score. AS—Automated score. Engine trained on data from time period 1 and configured to match score distributions for this time period.

two sources performed similarly relative to one another and to the total multiple choice score. In time periods 2 and 3, the CRASE-assigned score distributions and agreement rates were similar to those in time period 1 and concordant with the multiple choice score means. However, for the second and third time periods, the human reader scores show about an 8% increase in scores of 3 and a decrease in scores assigned to all other categories. This appears to be a classic case of reader drift (i.e., bias), but note how difficult it can be to detect. The mean human rating is fairly stable across the time periods. Adjacent scores are not resolved, which permits the drift into score category 3. The human scores also showed higher than expected agreement rates in time periods 2 and 3. Note that the human–human agreement rates "improve" across the time periods. Figure 14.2 shows the daily agreement rate trends across the 16-day scoring window for the Ideas trait. As can be observed in Figure 14.2, the human–human agreement rates grew steadily as the window progressed, while the human–CRASE agreement rates remained stable. The steadily increasing curve reflects the human–human agreement for the Ideas trait across the window. The curve that hovers around 68% reflects the human–CRASE agreement for the Ideas trait across the window. The human–human agreement rates increase to unusual levels, exceeding 90% in the last few days of the window.

Study 2: Establishing a Criterion for Individual Rater Agreement Rates

Given the ability of the automated scoring engine to detect drift in the May 2009 administration, it was hoped that the introduction of automated scoring into the operational scoring process as a monitoring tool would help to reduce the central tendency drift. Starting with the May 2010 administration, CRASE was used as to provide 100% read-behind scores. The score of record on each of the two dimensions was assigned by the human reader. When a response was entered by a student, the response was first submitted to CRASE which returned either a numeric score (1 through 4) or a non-attempt score of 0. With the exception of blank responses and some refusal responses (e.g., "I don't know"), all other responses and scores were submitted to the hand-scoring vendor in

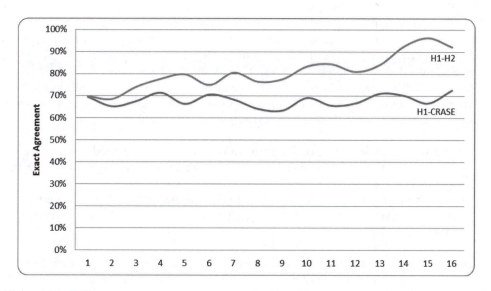

Figure 14.2 Daily exact agreement rates across the May 2009 testing window for two humans (H1–H2) and the automated scorer and one human (H1–AS). Dim1=Ideas.

batches multiple times per day. The hand-scoring vendor then distributed the responses to the human readers, who did not have knowledge of the CRASE-assigned scores. If the human reader and the CRASE-assigned scores differed by more than one point, then the response was submitted to an expert human reader for a final score. For all responses, only the human-assigned score (first human reader or expert reader) was instantiated as the score of record. Thus, the automated score was used only for monitoring purposes.

Exact agreement rates, but not score distributions, were monitored for individual readers. A reader's exact agreement rate with CRASE was compared to a criterion agreement rate. The criterion rate was prompt-specific, and was set at 5 points below the average human/CRASE agreement rate that was obtained when the engine was trained to score the prompt. This criterion was used under the assumption that raters will necessarily vary in their skill in applying the rubric, that the overall agreement rate across raters should be the observed human/CRASE agreement rate in the engine training sample, and that readers should be flagged only if they were "too far" below the observed human/CRASE agreement rate. While human/CRASE score distributions were not compared at the individual reader level, they were compared over all readers combined. That is, the score distribution for each reader was compared to the CRASE score distribution for all papers read. Additionally, the monitoring reports provided only cumulative results and did not explicitly connect individual reader agreement rates with score distributions relative to CRASE.

As a result of using automated scoring in this manner in three successive administrations (May 2010, December 2010, and May 2011), some limitations in the monitoring system became apparent. First, because reports were cumulative, the reliability of differences in exact agreement rates over time could not be evaluated. Differences in exact agreement rates were suspected to be not very reliable based on informal information by the hand-scoring vendor; however, state personnel wanted the hand-scoring vendor to intervene with readers whenever their exact agreement rates fell below criterion. If unreliable, then readers were potentially being flagged unnecessarily. Second, readers were able to maintain exact agreement rates above the criterion in part by displaying the central tendency bias that CRASE was introduced to help mitigate. For example, if CRASE assigned 55% of the papers a "3," readers could maintain an agreement rate above criterion despite assigning 65% or more of the same papers a "3."

In order to improve reader monitoring and provide information to state personnel concerning the reliability of the monitoring statistics, additional monitoring at the reader level was introduced in December 2011. This monitoring was both statistically-based and time-based. The new reports were produced daily and provided cumulative, past 72-hour, past 48-hour, and past 24-hour information. Reader exact agreement rates were compared to a criterion (63%). For each time period:

- A Z-score based on the binomial probability distribution was used to compute the statistical significance of the difference between a reader's exact agreement rate and the criterion.
- For each score point, the difference between the percent of papers assigned the score by the reader versus CRASE (reader percent minus CRASE percent), was computed.

Figure 14.3 presents an example of information that was available for one 24-hour period several days into the testing window. The report has been edited to show only three readers' performance statistics, plus a similar set of statistics for CRASE based on comparison to all other readers combined. Each reader has two sets of statistics—one

Reader ID	Item & Dimension	N	N Exact	% Exact	Z	prob	Reader/AS Difference by Score			
							1	2	3	4
1133	300450.1	64	37	57.81	−0.86	0.20	3.13	−10.94	−10.94	18.75
1133	300450.2	64	40	62.50	0.08	0.53	3.13	−10.94	−6.25	14.06
2262	300450.1	43	31	72.09	1.24	0.89	0.00	−9.30	9.30	0.00
2262	300450.2	43	30	69.77	1.05	0.85	0.00	−13.95	16.28	−2.33
3608	300450.1	115	75	65.22	0.49	0.69	0.00	−7.83	18.26	−10.43
3608	300450.2	115	74	64.35	0.52	0.70	0.00	−7.83	20.87	−13.04
AS	300450.1	684	467	68.27	2.86	1.00	−0.88	5.41	−10.53	5.99
AS	300450.2	684	461	67.40	2.91	1.00	−0.73	6.58	−14.04	8.19

Figure 14.3 Snapshot of Reader Monitoring Report

for each trait. The report shows that Reader 2262 scored 43 papers in the 24-hour period and assigned 31 of these papers (72.09%) scores that were in exact agreement with CRASE on the Ideas trait. However, the percentage of papers this reader assigned a "3" was 9.3 percentage points higher than the percent assigned a "3" by CRASE. The lines for AS in this figure shows that in comparison to all other readers in that 24-hour period, with a total of 684 papers scored, the percent of papers assigned a "3" by AS was 10.53 percentage points lower than the percent assigned a "3" by the readers, taken collectively.

The data for Readers 2262 and 3608 in Figure 14.3 illustrate the issue that readers are able to meet criterion agreement rates by over-assigning the 3 score relative to CRASE. The percentage of papers assigned a 3 by Reader 3608 was about 20 points higher than CRASE, yet the exact agreement rate with AS met the criteria for both dimensions. Reader 1133 demonstrates the opposite effect. By assigning fewer papers to the modal score, the exact agreement rate is more negatively impacted.

With data like that shown in Figure 14.3 for each time period, the following questions were addressed using the automated scoring engine as the benchmark: (1) How much do agreement rates vary among readers? (2) How reliable are differences in agreement rates among readers? (3) How much normal variance among readers' agreement rates should be allowed for when setting a criterion agreement rate for a prompt based on some minimally acceptable "average"? And, (4) How large and reliable are reader effects with regard to central tendency (i.e., over-assignment of 3s)? Underlying these questions is the broader question of whether and how automated scoring can be used to help guide interventions with readers by their supervisors with regard to scoring reliability (agreement rates) and drift. In order to determine how to use automated scoring in this way, it is necessary to understand the statistical behavior of indices of agreement and drift so that realistic, effective criteria can be set for flagging readers for closer monitoring and intervention.

To answer questions 1 through 3, the variability and correlation of agreement rates were studied within and across time periods. The variation in agreement rates across readers within a given time period provides a sense of how many readers will be flagged by setting the criterion a given distance below the average for all readers. For example, by setting the criterion one standard deviation below the average, one could expect to flag about 17% of the readers. The correlation of exact agreement rates across time periods provides an indication of the reliability of the agreement rates. For example, readers who have low agreement with CRASE on day k should have low agreement with CRASE on day $k+1$ and those with high agreement on day k should have high agreement on day $k+1$. Specifically, is reader 1133 in Figure 14.3 likely to have a low agreement rate in the next 24-hour period? If the relative performance of readers in 24-hour time periods is not correlated from one day to another, then it does not seem good policy to base reader interventions on a single day's worth of agreement rate information. But what about rates based on three consecutive days of data (72-hour rates)? Are three days' worth of data enough to measure reliable differences among readers? Are reader agreement rates based on days k, $k+1$, and $k+2$ correlated with agreement rates based on days $k+3$, $k+4$, and $k+5$? Underlying this question is another: How long should a reader be allowed to read poorly before removing the reader from scoring?

These questions were addressed in a second fashion in this study by simply computing the standard error of the agreement rates, based on sample size. This was done by assuming the true agreement rate for each reader was the average agreement rate for all readers and that the standard error of each reader's agreement rate was a function solely of the average agreement rate and the number of papers read. This seems to be a reasonable assumption given that a single benchmark (the CRASE score) was used for all readers. If there were no true variance among readers, then the observed standard deviation of the agreement rate among readers should be about equal to the root mean squared measurement error.

To answer question 4, the following analyses were performed. First, differences in percentages of assignment of 3s versus CRASE for each reader within each 24-hour and 72-hour time period were computed. Second, the differences in central tendency bias with the number of papers read were correlated. Moreover, these analyses were conducted at the table leader level. The results for question 4 were surprising, and appear in the subsequent section on the role of table leaders in drift.

Table 14.2 presents the mean and standard deviation of agreement rates across the readers by day (24-hour period) for the Ideas trait. Recall that the agreement rates are based upon the reader's agreement with CRASE on every paper scored by that reader. On day 1, 11 readers scored an average of 11 papers each. The mean and standard deviation of the readers' exact agreement rate with CRASE were, respectively, 69% and 15.3%, on day 1. The predicted standard deviation, based on binomial error variance, was 14.1%.

Table 14.2 Summary Statistics for Reader Agreement Rates With CRASE for Trait 1 (Ideas) by Day and 24-Hour Period

Day	Average N	Mean	Std Dev	Root Error Variance
1	11	69	15.3	14.1
2	12	74	11.8	12.9
3	92	74	3.3	4.6
4	68	69	8.2	5.6
5	96	69	4.5	4.7
6	93	68	6.2	4.8
7	48	69	6.1	6.7
8	59	73	5.6	5.8
9	84	72	8.2	4.9
10	51	78	3.5	5.8
11	57	70	8.2	6.1
Overall Average			6.2	5.6

Note. Average N is the average number of papers read per human reader. Mean is the average agreement rate across human readers.

Across the testing window, the average reader agreement rates ranged from 68% to 78%, with an average agreement rate of 71%. (This average is not shown in Table 14.2.) The average agreement rate was at least 5 points higher than the minimum threshold for flagging readers (63%), which was expected. As mentioned earlier, the minimum was set at 5 points below the May 2009 average. The weighted, average within-day standard deviation (6.2%) was slightly larger than the expected, weighted standard deviation based on binomial error variance alone (5.6%). Thus, the reader variation exceeds that expected by chance alone, suggesting some true error variance.

Table 14.3 shows similar statistics for successive 72-hour periods throughout the test window. The column labeled "Day" in this table shows the last day of the 72-hour (three-day) period. Day "3" represents the period including days 1 to 3. Day "4" represents the period including days 2 to 4. Because there are more papers scored in a 72-hour period, smaller variation in agreement rates across readers would be expected—perhaps a higher signal-to-noise ratio. Across the testing window, the average reader agreement rates ranged from 68% to 74%, with an average agreement rate of 71%, the same as for the one-day periods. (Again, this average is not shown in Table 14.3.) The weighted, average within-period standard deviation of agreement rates, 3.8%, was smaller as expected and again (as in Table 14.2) slightly larger than the corresponding expected value based solely on binomial error variance, 3.2%.

The next two tables present the correlation coefficients between agreement rates (paired within reader) from adjacent, non-overlapping periods of time, where the period is 24 hours (Table 14.4) or 72 hours (Table 14.5). Across all 11 days of the window,

Table 14.3 Summary Statistics for Reader Agreement Rates With CRASE for Trait 1 (Ideas) Each Day by 72-Hour Period

Day	Average N	Mean	Std Dev	Root Error Variance
3	114	74	3.3	4.1
4	172	72	3.7	3.4
5	257	70	2.7	2.8
6	257	68	4.8	2.9
7	237	69	3.8	3.0
8	194	70	3.3	3.3
9	176	71	3.8	3.4
10	194	74	3.7	3.2
11	192	73	4.8	3.2
			3.8	3.2

Table 14.4 Day-to-Day Correlation of Reader Agreement Rates Using 24-Hour Period

Days	Correlation
1,2	−0.51
2,3	−0.10
3,4	−0.08
4,5	0.19
5,6	0.52
6,7	−0.01
7,8	−0.22
8,9	−0.08
9,10	−0.07
10,11	0.11
Average:	−0.02

Table 14.5 Day-to-Day Correlation of Reader Agreement Rates Using 72-Hour Period

Last Day(s)	Correlation
3,6	−0.55
4,7	0.13
5,8	0.42
6,9	−0.23
7,10	−0.04
8,11	−0.06
Average:	−0.06

the average period-to-period correlation of agreement rates was −0.02 for the 24 hour periods (Table 14.4) and −0.06 for the 72-hour periods (Table 14.5). These correlations are somewhat worse than the results in Tables 14.2 and 14.3, which suggest at least some true variance in agreement rates. One possible explanation for the lower-than-expected correlations is that the correlations are more sensitive to interventions with weaker readers. An intervention with a weak reader (low agreement rate) would tend to produce a higher agreement rate for that reader in the next time period.

Overall, the results in Tables 14.2 through 14.5 show that reader agreement rates in the December 2011 administration were unreliable. This result supports the decision to flag readers based on practical and statistical significance. In other words, readers should be flagged on whether they fell below the minimum threshold and whether the difference is statistically significant. Due to this dual criterion for flagging, very few readers were flagged during this administration using the new reports.

Study 3: The Role of Table Leaders in Drift

An informal look at the data from previous administrations and scores assigned by table leaders themselves suggested that some table leaders were exhibiting central tendency bias and transmitting this tendency to the readers at their table through activities such as read-behinds and interventions. Table 14.6 presents the difference scores by scoring team (Tables 14.1 and 14.2) within period (72 hours). Positive values indicate that human readers assigned more 3 scores than the automated scoring engine. There are clear differences between tables with "table 1" showing small and varying differences each day and "table 2" exhibiting stronger over-assignment of 3s compared to team "table 1." Around

Table 14.6 Difference in 3-Assignment by Table and Day Using 72-Hour Period

	Table	
Day	1	2
3	3.8	12.9
4	5.9	13.2
5	1.4	11.4
6	−2.4	7.4
7	−5.4	4.2
8	−3.8	2.2
9	−1.9	2.7
10	−0.9	4.1
11	2.5	5.2

day 4, both team tables began to show a trend away from positive values and "table 1" eventually showed some negative values.

This trend of smaller positive or negative difference values was presumably due to an intervention. On or about day 4, the psychometricians who had developed the monitoring program discussed the over-assignment of 3s with the hand-scoring staff. The apparent table effects were also discussed. The team leader for "table 2" had been a team leader in the previous administration (May 2011), where there had been four tables and corresponding team leaders, and the same prompt had been scored. A similar analysis had been performed on the data for the May 2011 administration, the results of which are shown in Table 14.7. The CRASE scores in May 2011 were based upon the same model as those in December 2011. Thus, the scores served as both a within-window and across-window benchmark. The results for "table/team 2" presented in Table 14.7 correspond to the same team leader as those for "table 2" in Table 14.6. This team leader was apparently the strongest source of over-assignment of 3s in both administrations, and this was pointed out to the hand-scoring staff in the discussion on day 4 in the December administration.

Another interesting pattern to point out with regard to Tables 14.6 and 14.7 are the trends that developed across time periods. Readers didn't over-assign 3s early in the May administration. Rather, the over-assignment was a steady development for all four tables, with the last few time periods showing the strongest over-assignment. In December, the strong over-assignment seen for "table 2' at the outset of scoring appears to be a carry-over effect due to the fact that the team leader was the same one associated with table/team 2 in the prior May administration, where over-assignment of 3s was strongest. It is also interesting that, even after intervention on day 4 of the December administration, by day 8 over-assignment of 3s again began to creep upward and was approaching significance by the last day. No meeting similar to that held on day 4 to call out over-assignment of 3s was held subsequently during the administration.

Table 14.8 shows the correlation between the human-minus-CRASE difference in percent of 3s assigned and the number of papers read by table within period (72-hour periods). The correlations are substantially positive. That is, readers who read more papers in a 72-hour period were more likely to assign a score of 3. This tendency appears to be

Table 14.7 Difference in 3-Assignment by Table and Day Using 72-Hour Period in May, 2011 Administration

Day	Table			
	1	2	3	4
3	1.4	−0.2	−2.7	−4.1
4	3.9	1.5	−3.2	−2.2
5	4.9	3.4	−2.3	0.2
6	4.7	6.1	−2.9	2.6
7	4.6	7.3	−1.6	5.0
8	3.8	9.1	1.9	7.2
9	2.9	9.4	4.0	7.4
10	1.5	10.6	5.2	8.1
11	2.5	11.1	6.2	8.4
12	5.5	12.8	6.8	8.2
13	10.4	15.2	7.4	11.6
14	12.4	15.3	7.2	12.8
15	13.0	13.6	6.3	14.7
Average:	5.8	8.8	2.2	4.6

Table 14.8 Correlation Between Number of Papers Read and Difference in 3-Score Assignment, by Day and Team for 72-Hour Period

	Table	
Day	1	2
4	0.41	0.88
5	0.42	0.58
6	0.59	0.43
7	0.51	0.52
8	0.49	0.58
9	0.61	0.64
10	0.57	0.69
11	0.59	0.71

equally strong at both tables. This suggests that the scoring speed is associated with the central tendency bias exhibited by the readers.

CONCLUSION

Overall, the analyses suggest that automated scoring is a powerful method for monitoring reader performance and for detecting trends in overall and individual reader performance. Specifically, five elements of the study address the broader question of whether and how automated scoring can be used to help guide interventions with readers.

First, the results show the effect of the intervention after four days on reducing central tendency bias. The day following the intervention, the over-assignment of "3" scores began to decline. However, the over-assignment started to trend up as the window progressed, suggesting the need for continued monitoring and interventions.

Second, the results show that the period-to-period correlations of agreement rates averaged across the window were slightly negative and near zero. These correlations were lower than expected given that the observed standard deviation of agreement rates was higher than the expected standard deviation based on binomial error variance alone. In other words, there was some true variance in readers' agreement rates. One theory to explain this result is that the intervention with the weaker readers was working. In other words, intervention with a reader flagged for low agreement could cause that reader to have a higher agreement rate in the next time period, which could produce a zero or even negative correlation in agreement rates across time periods.

Third, the use of automated scoring in this context enabled the use of 100% read-behinds fairly inexpensively. This will lead to more powerful and better-understood monitoring indices. The study demonstrates that the need to consider both the magnitude of the agreement rate and its statistical significance using a well-researched criterion before readers are flagged for intervention. Otherwise, readers are flagged unnecessarily, wasting time and resources.

Fifth and finally, the study suggests that more scoring errors are due to bias than unreliability. It also suggests that automated scoring is a powerful tool for reducing scoring errors due to its unique ability to identify bias. This study shows that bias (here, in the form of central tendency) can exist for an entire table or even a group of raters, as shown with the May 2009 and May 2011 administrations. The study suggested that agreement rates can be inflated due to this type of bias, and that both need to be monitored. Also, the close monitoring now possible with the addition of automated scoring will lead to more effective intervention strategies with readers, although this is only the beginning of such investigations. Finally, the study found that bias is also positively associated with the number of papers read by a reader. Under these circumstances, it is not possible to identify one reader's bias since the readers providing the second read are equally biased. Only automated scoring can detect bias when an entire table or cohort of readers is drifting.

Two limitations of this study should be noted. First, the analyses were based on a single prompt in one state program and may not be generalizable in other situations. Second, the analyses were exploratory, in part because of the highly empirical nature of the work. One would expect that more formal hypothesis-driven approaches to monitoring human readers will occur as automated scoring becomes a more common part of the scoring process in large-scale assessment.

NOTE

1 Random errors, such as those caused by lapses of attention, are not the focus of this paper and should be considered an unavoidable part of the assessment process.

REFERENCES

American Educational Research Association, American Psychological Association, and National Council on Measurement in Education (2004). *Standards for educational and psychological testing.* Washington, DC: American Educational Research Association.

Attali, Y., & Burstein, J. (2006). Automated essay scoring with e-rater V.2. *Journal of Technology, Learning, and Assessment, 4*(3). Available from http://www.jtla.org

Braun, H. I. (1988). Understanding score reliability: Experiments in calibrating essay readers. *Journal of Educational Statistics, 13*, 1–18.

Buckner, D. N. (1959). The predictability of ratings as a function of inter rater agreement. *Journal of Applied Psychology, 43*, 60–64.

Cogdon, P. J., & McQueen, J. (2000). The stability of rater severity in large-scale assessment programs. *Journal of Educational Measurement, 37*(2), 163–178.

Education Northwest. (2010). http://educationnorthwest.org/webfm_send/773

Engelhard, G., Jr. (1994). Examining rater errors in the assessment of written composition with a many-faceted Rasch model. *Journal of Educational Measurement, 31*(2), 93–112.

Enright, M. K., & Quinlan, T. (2010). Complementing human judgment of essays written by English language learners with e-rater scoring. *Language Testing, 27*(3), 317–334.

Gere, A. R. (1980). Written composition: Toward a theory of evaluation. *College English, 42*(1), 44–48,53–58.

Guilford, J. P. (1954). *Psychometric methods.* New York: McGraw-Hill.

Harik, P., Clauser, B. E., Grabovsky, I., Nungester, R. J., Swanson, D., & Nandakumar, R. (2009). An examination of rater drift within a generalizability theory framework. *Journal of Educational Measurement, 46*(1), 43–58.

Hoskins, M., & Wilson, M. (2001). Real-time feedback on rater drift in constructed response items: An example from the Golden State Examination. *Journal of Educational Measurement, 38*, 121–146.

Landauer, T. K., Laham, D., & Foltz, P. W. (2003). Automated scoring and annotation of essays with the Intelligent Essay Assessor. In M. D. Shermis & J. Burstein (Eds.), *Automated essay scoring: A cross-disciplinary perspective* (pp. 87–112). Mahwah, NJ: Lawrence Erlbaum Associates, Inc.

Leckie, G., & Baird, J. (2011). Rater effects on essay scoring: A multilevel analysis of severity drift, central tendency, and rater experience. *Journal of Educational Measurement, 48*, 399–418.

Lottridge, S., Mitzel, H., & Chou, F. (2009). *Blending machine scoring and hand scoring for constructed responses*. Paper presented at the CCSSO National Conference on Student Assessment, June.

Messick, S. (1995). Validity of psychological assessment: Validation of inferences from persons' responses and performances as scientific inquiry into score meaning. *American Psychologist, 50*(9), 741–749.

Myford, C. M., & Wolfe, E. W. (2009). Monitoring rater performance over time: A framework for detecting differential accuracy and differential scale category use. *Journal of Educational Measurement, 46*, 371–389.

Quellmalz, E. (1980). *Problems in stabilizing the judgment process* (Vol. CSE Report No. 136). Los Angeles, CA: Center for the Study of Evaluation.

Rudner, L. M., Garcia, V., & Welch, C. (2006). An evaluation of the IntelliMetric Essay Scoring System. *Journal of Technology, Learning, and Assessment, 4*(4). Retrieved from http://www.jtla.org

Saal, F. E., Downey, R. G., & Lahey, M. A. (1980). Rating the ratings: Assessing the psychometric quality of rating data. *Psychological Bulletin, 88*, 413–428.

Shermis, M. D., & Hamner, B. (2012). *Contrasting state-of-the-art automated scoring of essays: Analysis*. Paper presented at the 2012 National Council of Measurement in Education Conference, Vancouver, BC, April.

Wiggins, G. (1994). The constant danger of sacrificing validity to reliability: Making writing assessment serve writers. *Assessing Writing, 1*(1), 129–139.

Williamson, D., Xi, X., & Breyer, J. (2012). A framework for evaluation and use of automated scoring. *Educational Measurement: Issues and Practice, 31*, 2–13.

Wolfe, E. W., Myford, C .M., Engelhard, G., & Manalo, J. R. (2007). *Monitoring rater performance and DRIFT in the AP® English Literature and Composition Examination using benchmark essay* (Vol. Research Report No. 2007–2). New York, NY: The College Board.

15 Grammatical Error Detection in Automatic Essay Scoring and Feedback

Michael Gamon, Martin Chodorow,
Claudia Leacock, and Joel Tetreault

MOTIVATION

In English-language essay scoring guides, such as the Test of English as a Foreign Language (TOEFL) or Graduate Record Examination (GRE), control of language is an important part of the rubric. Essay scoring rubrics include control of language as one of the criteria for a high-scoring essay and lack of control of language as a criterion for a low-scoring essay. For example, at the highest score point of 6, a TOEFL essay "displays consistent ability in the use of language." A mid-range essay, with a score of 3, may reveal one of the following weaknesses: "a noticeably improper choice of words or word forms" or "numerous errors in sentence structure and/or usage." A poor essay, with the lowest score of 1, "may contain severe and persistent writing errors."[1] This chapter is based on the assumption that the absence of grammatical errors in an essay, that is, correct usage and syntax, is a clear marker of a student's control of the English language. Thus, when a scoring engine can identify grammatical errors, these errors can be used as a feature to help determine an essay's score.

Leacock and Chodorow (2003) found independent evidence that grammatical errors influence TOEFL scores. They reported a negative correlation between TOEFL essay scores and the grammatical errors that they contained. Leacock and Chodorow found that it is the *variety* of errors that affects the score, rather than the total error count. They also found that not all errors are equal. The most useful predictors of lower scores were violations of a rule of syntax, such as subject–verb agreement (*my friend meet this guy*), ill-formed modal verbs (*People would said that . . .*), and determiner–noun agreement (*this things*). Somewhat less reliable predictors were commonly confused words (homophones or near homophones such as *their, there,* and *they're*) and confusion of a verb with its nominal form (*I will success*). Less costly errors involved pronoun use, missing commas, and apostrophes. Some errors appeared to have no effect on the score. For these, Leacock and Chodorow conjectured that the errors could likely be introduced when editing the essay (e.g., *a the book* or *straighten you desk*) and that the raters allow for sloppy proofreading.

Detecting errors in essays and using them as a feature for scoring is important in a summative assessment environment, but that is not the only application of scoring engines. They can also be used in a formative environment, where the engine not only provides a score but also provides students with feedback by flagging errors and suggesting one or more corrections.

What Do We Mean by Grammatical Error?

We find it useful to divide grammatical errors into two categories: syntactic errors and usage errors. However, we understand that, when evaluating student writing, it is not always clear which category to assign an error to. Syntactic errors involve violations of structural rules of syntax, such as agreement or pronoun case. Usage, or common use, errors can result from inaccurate memorization (as with collocations) or complex interactions between syntactic features, lexical features, discourse factors, and, in some cases, world knowledge.

Syntactic errors involve violations of structural syntactic rules that are clearly defined in any prescriptive grammar manual. These errors include ill-formed verb phrases, violations of subject–verb and determiner–noun agreement, and errors in pronoun case. Sentence fragments also involve syntactic rule violations, as do comma splices (where two sentences are joined with a comma instead of a conjunction). Syntactic errors often cause problems for automatic parsers, whereas usage errors tend not to. While it can be argued that the confusion of homophones is a usage error rather than a syntactic one, the result of such a confusion will often produce a syntactic error (*I want to see there house*).

With usage errors, there is usually no clear-cut syntactic rule that has been violated. For example, consider the use of the indefinite article (*a/an*) in English. An indefinite article is required to precede some nouns (a *car*) but not others (*an equipment)—which is determined by the noun's lexical property of countability. Yet the countability of a noun is not a binary property. Allan (1980) identified seven levels of noun countability ranging from fully countable, as with *car*, to uncountable, as with *equipment*. One of the remaining five levels is strongly countable nouns, for example, *maple* usually requires the indefinite article (*there is a maple in the yard*) except when the maple's wood is referenced (*the chest is made of maple*). Another level is that of weakly countable nouns, for example, while one says, "*I don't drink beer*" but, to a bartender, one says, "*I'd like a beer.*" Noun countability also depends on the sense of the noun being used. If referring to a newspaper, then *I read a paper*, but if referring to a sheet of paper, *I wrote on paper*. There are also syntactic agreement features as well as noun class features, discourse factors (use of the definite article, *the*, if there is a previous mention of the noun phrase). World knowledge is also a factor to contend with, for example, *the moon* for the Earth's moon but *a moon* for one of Jupiter's moons.

We make the distinction between syntactic and usage errors because, by and large, the best way to automatically identify errors depends upon whether the error involves syntax or usage. As will be discussed in "Error Detection Methods: Grammar-Based Versus Statistical," syntactic errors are best tackled through rule-based approaches while the more difficult to detect, and harder to correct, usage errors usually require machine-learned statistical methods.

Native and Non-Native Errors

When native speakers make errors, they tend to produce syntactic ones. English language learners (ELLs), of course, also make syntactic errors. On the other hand, ELLs tend to produce a great number of usage errors, which native speakers make fairly infrequently (Leacock, Chodorow, Gamon, & Tetreault, 2010). Most commercially available grammar checkers, such as Microsoft (MS) Word, are designed to be used by native speakers and thus focus on syntactic, not usage, errors. However, there is a large and growing need for coverage of usage errors for ELLs. Guo and Beckett (2007) estimate that "over a billion people speak English as their second or foreign language." To help second and foreign ELLs, many researchers have turned their attention to the types of usage errors that they produce. These errors are the focus of much of the work that is described in this chapter.

Figure 15.1 shows the relative frequencies of annotated English learner errors in the *Cambridge Learner Corpus*[2] (CLC). Note that CLC spelling error flags are not included in these error frequencies. Spelling flags comprise almost half of the total flags in the corpus, but spell-checking for language learners is an independent field of study. For an overview of research on spell-checking for language learners, see Heift and Schulze (2007).

By far, the most frequently occurring ELL grammatical error found in CLC is content word choice (choice of a noun, verb, adjective, or adverb). The next two most frequent errors involve the use of prepositions and determiners. The fourth most frequent error involves the omission or placement of a comma. Contrast this with a study of errors made by U.S. college students (Conners & Lunsford, 1988), where use of the comma was *the* most frequent error. They found that no comma after an introductory clause was the most frequent error, no comma in a compound sentence was the third most frequent error, no comma in a non-restrictive clause was the fifth most frequent error, and a comma splice was the eighth most frequent grammatical error produced by the students.

The error types that are italicized in Figure 15.1 are those errors that Conners and Lumsford found in the top 20 error categories that were made by U.S. college students. The only usage errors in these 20 categories are a wrong or missing preposition, which was the students' seventh most frequent error. Both groups produced the syntactic errors of pronoun and subject–verb agreement, run-on sentence, and confused words. While the students in the Conners and Lumsford study made quite a few tense errors, these involved tense shift in the discourse rather than the confusions of past, present, and future tenses that ELLs tended to produce.

Some of the errors are influenced by the writer's native language (L1). For example, speakers of East Asian languages (e.g., Chinese, Japanese, and Korean), have difficulty mastering the English article system (a large subset of the determiner errors), because their native language does not have articles. The German article system is quite similar to that of English, and native German speakers produce fewer article errors. Eighteen percent of the sentences written by Korean speakers contained at least one article error,

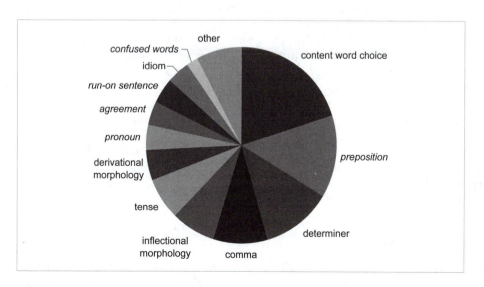

Figure 15.1 Learner errors from *Cambridge Learners Corpus*.

consisting of the inclusion and choice of an indefinite article (*a/an*) or definite article (*the*). In contrast, only one-half of a percent of the sentences produced by native German speakers had article errors.

Other errors are produced across the full range of L1s. For example, English prepositions are difficult for ELLs no matter what their L1 happens to be (Dalgish, 1985; Leacock, Chodorow, Gamon, & Tetreault, 2010). In this case, however, prepositions pose a very different kind of challenge: that of interference or negative transfer from the learner's L1, no matter what that language is. To compound the problem, prepositions perform many roles in English. The rules and lexical features governing preposition use and their interactions make preposition use difficult for *anyone* to learn (note that native speakers make them relatively frequently). In CLC, 13% of the sentences produced by Korean speakers include at least one preposition error, as do 10% of those produced by German speakers.

Due to the special problems that articles and prepositions pose for language learners, much of the remainder of this chapter focuses on their detection and correction.

ERROR DETECTION METHODS: GRAMMAR-BASED VERSUS STATISTICAL

In this section we give a high-level overview of the predominant techniques in grammatical error detection. This research area has received attention since at least the 1980s, with a strong resurgence in the past decade. For a more detailed overview and a comprehensive bibliography, the reader is advised to consult Leacock et al. (2010). Here, we focus mainly on relatively recent research, in some cases so recent that it was not available for inclusion in Leacock et al. (2010).

A useful high-level categorization of the basic approaches to grammatical error detection can be obtained by distinguishing rule-based from statistical systems. Amongst the rule-based systems, there are simple methods that use surface-based rules or pattern-matching, and there are the more prominent and powerful grammar-based systems that rely on a full grammatical analysis of a sentence provided by a manually crafted computational grammar. We will not deal with the pattern-based approaches here, instead we use the term "grammar-based" to comprise computational grammars that are manually crafted. In these grammar-based systems, either the grammar itself or a post-processing component then checks the structure for violations of grammatical rules such as subject–verb agreement. Grammar-based systems are best suited for grammatical errors, since they explicitly address deviations from a manually encoded grammar. The second approach to error detection is based on statistical methods, following a general trend in natural language processing (NLP) away from manually crafted analysis systems to "learned" systems that are trained on large amounts of language data. One of the strengths of a statistical system is that it can learn subtle regularities of "common use" that would be hard to express in simple rules. As a consequence, statistical systems are particularly well-suited for usage errors. We will illustrate examples of these two types of approaches in the following discussion.

Grammar-Based Techniques

Grammar-based systems for error detection have been, and are still, used widely. All of these systems have in common that they face a challenge in the design of their rules: a computational grammar that is supposed to process only grammatical, error-free sentences can be constructed by encoding the grammatical rules of a language. This in itself is by no means a trivial task; the construction of broad-coverage grammars takes time and linguistic expertise. By definition, such a grammar will fail to process sentences that do not conform to the rules of the grammar—but these are exactly the sentences that error correction is needed for. Without an analysis, however, it is impossible to provide diagnostics about the location and nature of the error, and about possible corrections. Hence, the computational grammar needs to be adapted to potentially erroneous input. While it is not feasible to analyze every kind of arbitrary error and/or combination of errors, it is possible to "build into" the grammar some knowledge about commonly occurring errors. For example, in the case of subject–verb agreement, a computational grammar could contain a rule that combines a subject noun phrase with a verb phrase into a declarative sentence even if the subject does not agree in number with the main verb. Such a rule—termed "mal-rule" in the literature—would also contain some sort of flag that indicates the presence of this specific error. Similarly, instead of adding a special new rule for an error, it is also possible to "relax" rules. In our example, the grammar could contain a subject-rule that encodes the constraint that the subject of a declarative sentence has to agree with the main verb, but this constraint can be less rigid than other constraints in the sense that it can be violated, at the cost of raising an error flag. A third method to allow for the analysis of erroneous input is to allow for the over-generation of analyses through the use of relatively permissive rules in combination with a ranking mechanism for analyses. If no completely well-formed analysis can be found, the highest-ranking "less ideal" analysis can be used to detect where an error might be present. Yet a fourth way to accommodate errors in a computational grammar is to allow partial parses that at least identify the main phrases in a sentence. Special post-processing rules can then examine the pieces of this analysis and try to find the sources for the failure to combine the pieces into a complete sentence analysis.

One example of a grammar-based error correction system is the grammar checker in MS Word. This grammar checker performs a complete analysis of all text, using the broad-coverage MS-NLP parsing engine and grammar. The MS-NLP grammar, as described in Jensen et al. (1993), permits parses that violate, for example, subject–verb agreement, but flags such agreement violations on nodes in the parse tree. A post-processing component examines the resulting top-ranked parse and suggests possible corrections for the detected error(s). This component also makes it possible to deal with interdependent multiple errors where the correction of one error depends on the correction of another error. Agreement errors are a perfect example of the types of errors that grammar-based systems are very well suited to detect and correct. The reason is that these errors are "non-local" in nature, or, in other words, they often involve words that are not near to each other. Consider the example. *Adults who went to colleges that this study ranked highly tends to achieve higher salaries in later employment.* The subject in this example is *adults* and it fails to agree with the main verb *tends*. These two words are separated by two nouns, two pronouns and two other verbs. Without a grammatical analysis that identifies *adults* as the subject of the verb *tends*, it is impossible to detect this long-distance relationship between the two words that are the culprits in the agreement error.

Statistically-Based Techniques

Turning now to the second major approach to grammatical error detection, statistical approaches have in general become more prominent in the NLP community over the last few decades. Some of the main reasons for this trend are:

1. Statistical approaches tend to be less brittle than manually created analysis systems since they are trained on large data sets.
2. There is no need for costly rule-engineering (although the creation of training corpora for statistical systems is not cost-free either).
3. Experimentation with new algorithms is straightforward, as it only requires retraining the new system on the same data that were used in training for the previous system, thus enabling rapid iterations on algorithm improvements.

This trend has also been reflected in grammatical error correction. Two statistical techniques that have been dominant are language modeling and classification. A statistical language model is a model that has been trained on a large set of language data. It has learned statistics about the probability of words (unigrams), word pairs (bigrams), and word sequences of greater length. Provided with a new, unseen sentence, the language model provides a score for the sentence based on the words and word sequences in that sentence and their probabilities as determined during training. For example, a simple sentence "It is raining" will most likely receive a high score since the words *it*, *is*, and *raining* are common words and are likely to have been seen many times during training of the language model. Similarly, the word pairs *it is* and *is raining* are also common. In contrast, a sentence such as "it be raining" is likely to receive a lower score. While the individual words in that sentence are common, the word pairs *it be* and *be raining* are much rarer. Using a language model to score sentences or phrases for error detection basically makes the generalization that *rare* word sequences are more likely to be erroneous than very common ones. This generalization cannot be applied naively, though; a simple counterexample is a sentence such as "I saw Aarthi yesterday" which contains a name that is rare in English, and may never have been encountered during training. The "unknown" word with its low probability will lead to a lower language model score for sequences containing this name, although there is no error in this sentence.

One example of a system that takes word sequence probabilities into account for error detection is Assessment of Lexical Knowledge (ALEK; Leacock & Chodorow, 2003). ALEK is based on bigram (word pair) statistics collected from a large part-of-speech tagged corpus of English news text. It is not a language model system in the sense that it assigns scores to word sequences of arbitrary length. Instead, it focuses on word pairs and their statistical association. Using two association metrics (pointwise mutual information and log likelihood ratio), it can identify highly unlikely word pairs. For example, the combination of two singular nouns "disk (sg. NOUN) drive (sg. NOUN)" will be a pair of very highly associated words, whereas the combination of a singular determiner and a plural noun "a (sg. DET) drives (pl. NOUN)" will have very little (if any) association. By detecting low-association bigrams in text from English Placement Tests, ALEK produces a candidate list of potential errors. Additional heuristics are then used to filter out candidates that are likely to be false positives. For example, "these (pl. DET) disk (sg. NOUN)" is a very low association word pair, but it does not indicate an error if followed by a plural noun as in "these disk drives." Using this approach of locating target bigrams with very low association and then applying heuristic filters to limit the number of false detections, ALEK can detect several types of error, including subject–verb agreement, determiner–noun agreement, and wrong verb form.

Classification approaches are statistical approaches that are more targeted towards a specific error rather than providing a score for any sequence of words. A statistical classifier is a model that makes a decision on new data, based on data seen at training time. For an example in non-native error correction, consider preposition choice errors. At training time, a classifier for this type of error will consider each observed preposition in a training corpus as a training case. Evidence will be presented to the classifier in the form of "features" of the individual training case. The most important feature is the choice of the preposition itself, which is often called the "target" feature, i.e., the target that we want the classifier to predict. Other features that the classifier needs to take into account in order to make its predictions can be measures such as "what is the word to the left/right of the preposition," "what is the governing verb of the preposition," "what are the part of speech tags of the words in the context around the preposition," etc. (see Tetreault and Chodorow (2008b) for a description of these and other features). Based on many such observations, the training algorithm will learn how much weight should be associated with each feature value with respect to a particular preposition choice. When presented with a new sentence such as "I rely to my friends," the classifier will extract the same features as at training time, i.e., it will detect that the word to the left of the preposition is *rely*, which also is the governing verb. Given that information and the weights assigned to these features at training time, the classifier will determine that the most likely preposition should be *on*, and that *to* is a much less likely choice. One great advantage of a classification approach is that it can use almost any kind of feature, including, for example, language model features (such as the language model score for a short window around the current preposition, or language model scores for all potential prepositions in that slot). While there are a number of highly efficient classification algorithms, system performance is often found to depend more on having a good set of features than on choosing a particular algorithm.

Combining language modeling and classification is, of course, also an option. Gamon (2010) combined language model scores and classification in a system that learns from a corpus of corrected errors how to best combine the two approaches to maximize accuracy on error detection. Recently, research has also begun to explore additional statistical models for error correction. Dahlmeier and Ng (2011) investigated Alternate Structure Optimization, a method of combining classifiers in a transfer learning manner, where error-free data are used for training and the model is then applied to data containing errors. Gamon (2011) experimented with sequence modeling, which is a technique that operates on the sequence of words in a sentence, modeling the probability of an error at a given position in the sentence by taking into account various features from the context, including a range of language model scores.

Rozovskaya and Roth (2011) showed another advantage of statistical models for non-native error correction, namely their capability of including information about typical errors that a learner with a particular L1 is likely to make. Incorporating that knowledge allows an error correction system to be targeted to specific groups of users based on regularities in their error patterns.

Recent research (Wagner, 2012) indicates that statistical grammars can be used for error detection. Statistical (or probabilistic) grammars are not based on hand-crafted rules, but instead learn rules and associated probabilities from a large corpus of syntactically annotated sentences, known as a "tree bank" such as the Penn Tree Bank (Marcus, Santorini, & Marcinkiewicz, 1993). No hand-tuned relaxation mechanisms or mal-rules are feasible for the probabilistic grammars. Nevertheless these grammars tend to be very permissible, i.e., they are usually able to analyze almost any erroneous sentence in some way, but with lower probability for the analysis than for a more "standard" and error-free sentence. Wagner (2012) showed that, along with other features, probability scores from such grammars can be utilized as a signal for error detection. Note that this direction of research blurs the line between grammar-based and statistical methods. Arguably it has more affinity to the statistical techniques, though, since the probabilistic grammars do not allow manual control of computational grammar rules.

Finally, there has been research on the use of a web search engine to compare preposition usage. In these experiments, web queries are issued with a small window of context around a preposition. The number of returned results is compared with the number of returned results for a query that contains the same words but with a different preposition (Bergsma, Lin, & Goebel, 2009; Gamon & Leacock, 2010). This is motivated by the fact that web search engines have billions of word sequences readily accessible. For example, consider the sentence *I am fond for beer*, where there is a preposition error. A possible window of context would be *fond <prep> beer*, and one would extract counts from a web search engine for *fond of beer*, *fond at beer*, *fond for beer*, etc. The string with the highest count would be considered the correction. This method can also be applied to determiners and other error types with a constrained set of alternatives. It should be noted that web search query results are not perfect, and that the size of the window as well as the presence of errors in the window can skew results (Tetreault & Chodorow, 2009).

Up to this point, we have mostly contrasted and compared different methods such as grammar-based and statistical algorithms. In practice, however, a good argument can be made for a combination of methods. Different error types exhibit different properties: some of them may be more amenable to a grammar-based system; others may lend themselves to a classification or language model method. As a rule of thumb, the more non-local errors are, the more likely they are to require a treatment involving a full grammatical analysis of a sentence. On the other hand, the more local an error is and the more its correction can involve cues from neighboring words, the better suited it is to a statistical method. The subject–verb disagreement error in the sentence *Adults who went to colleges that this study ranked highly tends to achieve higher salaries in later employment* that we discussed earlier in this section is an example of a non-local error—the subject noun phrase *Adults* is separated from the main verb *tends* by a number of words and much linearly intervening grammatical structure (including the relative clause *that this study ranked highly*). Without a clear notion of the grammatical structure of this sentence it is hard to imagine how this error could be detected. Another error category that we touched upon earlier consists of preposition errors. While the logic behind the appropriate choice of preposition is anything but trivial in English, proper preposition usage is often dictated by the governing verb, the governed noun (phrase) or both. Of course the governing verb can also be separated from the preposition, and so can the governed noun, but in the great majority of cases these dependencies are still relatively local. For error types like preposition choice, statistical methods such as classification and language modeling (or a combination of the two) tend to achieve sufficient accuracy to be deployed in operational systems.

Finally there also are non-negligible numbers of errors of a type that is both very local and only dependent on minimal (or even no) context. Consider the typical error made by children and non-native speakers of over-regularizing an irregular verb in English: *sleeped* instead of *slept*. This error will need neither full grammatical analysis nor sophisticated statistical models. A simple heuristic that detects regular past tense/past participle variants of irregular verbs will achieve high accuracy here, and the formulation of the heuristic will only need to take about 100 irregular verbs in English into account. Similarly, especially non-native speakers often have difficulty with the usage of English quantifiers with mass and count nouns. It is *much information*, and not *many informations*—an error that will require a minimum of context (taking both the quantifier and the noun into account), but again it is entirely reasonable to treat this error with a relatively straightforward rule that has access to the limited set of quantifiers and common mass nouns in English.

OVERVIEW OF EVALUATION ISSUES

In the previous section, we discussed different methods of creating grammatical error detection systems: some are grammar or rule based, while others are statistical. Regardless of the technique, there is one phase in developing an end-to-end grammatical error detector which is common to all methods—evaluation of system performance. How a system is evaluated can impact its development and tuning, and also whether it can be included as a component in an automated essay scoring engine. At a very high level, an evaluation consists of running the grammatical error detection system on a set of essays containing errors and then counting how many errors the system catches (the "hits"), how many it fails to catch (the "misses"), and how many non-errors it falsely flags (the "false positives"). However, in practice, evaluation can be quite complicated as there are a host of issues that a system designer must take into account to get an accurate assessment of performance. In the remainder of this section, we present a summary of these issues and discuss best practices for addressing them. For a more detailed treatment of these topics, see Leacock et al. (2010). While there are currently no agreed upon evaluation standards in the grammatical error detection community, progress is being made with a series of shared tasks on grammatical error detection (Dale & Kilgarriff, 2010) which provide a forum for researchers to discuss best practices.

Evaluation Metrics

To assess how well a system performs, researchers typically make use of the evaluation metrics of *precision* and *recall*. Precision, the number of hits divided by the sum of the hits and false positives, measures how often the system is correct when it reports that an error has been found. Recall, the number of hits divided by the sum of the hits and misses, measures the fraction of errors that are actually detected by the system. This can also be viewed as quantifying the coverage of the system.

The relationship between precision and recall can be thought of as a balancing act. Precision can be increased by allowing the system to flag only those cases where its confidence exceeds some threshold level, but this will reduce recall as the system will now miss errors where the confidence is lower. On the other hand, lowering the threshold too much will increase recall, but precision will suffer from an increase in false positives as the system flags even those cases where its confidence is low. Typically in grammatical error detection, systems are tuned for high precision, at the expense of low recall, so as to reduce the number of false positives since marking errors where none exist would misinform a student.

Another metric that is sometimes used to measure performance is *accuracy*. This metric is the ratio of correct judgments, which consists of hits plus true negatives (non-errors that are not flagged), divided by the total number of judgments. The advantage of using accuracy is that there is only one number to report, on a scale of 0.00 to 1.00. However, it is not as informative as the precision and recall metrics since accuracy does not directly show the relationships between the hits, false positives, and misses—all important measures of a system's performance that can inform improvements.

Evaluation Data

Another important aspect of system evaluation is the composition and size of the data set to be used in the evaluation. Ideally, the evaluation data should be as similar as possible to the data that the system will process in the operational setting. So if the grammatical error detection system will be used as a part of an automated scoring engine which assesses English as a Second Language (ESL) learner writing, the evaluation data should consist of ESL essays from a similar proficiency level and native language. It is also important to have a large enough data set during development to draw reliable conclusions about changes that are intended to improve system performance. For example, using only a few essays which may only contain ten examples of the error in question is too small a sample to inform system design. A data set consisting of hundreds or thousands of errors may be needed to determine if improvements are statistically significant.

Evaluation Methodologies

There are two main methodologies that system designers use to determine when the system correctly or incorrectly flags an error: the *verification* method and the *annotation* method. In the verification method, the system processes a set of data and flags any errors it finds. A trained human rater then checks all the cases where the system has flagged an error and decides if it is a hit or a false positive so that precision can be calculated. The primary drawback of this method is that it can be cumbersome for rapid system development because every time a system is changed, there must be a new round of manually checking (or verifying) the output, which can be time-consuming and costly. The annotation method is intended to avoid the need for multiple verification rounds by having a rater mark all the errors in a corpus before evaluation. This makes it possible to evaluate performance automatically and repeatedly.

Annotation

Manually checking errors, whether in verification or annotation mode, can require several important decisions as well. First, one must decide which errors to focus on. In some annotation efforts, such as the one found in the **CLC**, all errors are flagged by the raters. This has the advantage of being comprehensive but of course the process can be time-consuming and it may be unclear how to annotate a phrase that may have errors in the same context or multiple ways of correcting. In other schemes (Tetreault & Chodorow, 2008a) raters are asked to focus on only one error type so as to reduce the cognitive load created by having to simultaneously check for multiple types.

Another decision involves the number of annotators to use. Using only one rater can be problematic since fatigue and human error can cause inconsistencies which can then affect the evaluation of system performance. One alternative is to employ multiple raters to annotate an entire data set and then combine their judgments. The advantage of this approach is that each rater can serve as a check on the others, and differences can be discussed. However, the use of additional raters is more costly. Another consideration is the type of error being annotated. For some error types where there is usually high inter-rater agreement, such as subject–verb number agreement, one rater may be sufficient. For more contentious errors, such as usage errors involving prepositions and articles, multiple raters are often favored to provide a range of judgments.

Given the costliness of multiple raters, system designers and researchers tend to use just one rater. However, recently, the use of *crowdsourcing* has been shown to be an effective method of collecting multiple judgments at a fraction of the cost and time that trained raters would normally require. Web-based applications allow "requesters" to post jobs for untrained workers (or "turkers") on the web to complete for a nominal fee. Tetreault, Filatova and Chodorow (2010) and Madnani, Tetreault, Chodorow and

Rozovskaya (2011) showed that using this service can provide an efficient way of collecting multiple judgments on different types of usage errors with the same reliability as trained raters.

ERROR DETECTION IN PRACTICE

Error Detection and Essay Scoring in Practice

In this section, we discuss the grammatical error detection components of four different Automated Scoring Engines: Pacific Metrics' CRASE™, CTB/McGraw Hill's Automated Essay Evaluation (AEE), Measurement Incorporated's Project Essay Grade (PEG), and ETS's e-rater and Criterion systems. While detailed, in-depth information about commercial systems such as these is proprietary, representatives of each company were kind enough to provide high-level descriptions of their error detection components for this section. Although each system has a slightly different focus, such as type of assessment (high stakes or low), whether it is used as for assessment or feedback, and characteristics of its user population, there are some commonalities. Many of the systems target the same types of errors. For instance, most detect word choice errors, run-on sentences and sentence fragments, and punctuation errors. Three of the systems place special emphasis on minimizing false positives. The rationale is that in either an assessment or feedback condition, it is better to have high precision at the expense of recall to avoid giving a student false information which may slow the learning process.

Pacific Metrics' CRASE

CRASE™ uses a rule-based tool to identify grammatical errors in preprocessed, tokenized, part-of-speech tagged student essays. The rules were written to reflect the critical and common grammatical mistakes made by students which are considered important to teachers and are thought to influence the score on an essay. The grammar detection tool also provides possible corrections to the student. Grammar errors are categorized into mechanics errors and usage errors. Examples of error types identified by the system are those involving punctuation, subject–verb agreement, abbreviations, contractions, possessives, capitalization, fragments, run-ons, and homophones. The numbers of mechanics and usage errors are transformed so that they do not reflect essay length, and are then weighted by a statistical model into the holistic essay score and/or trait scores. If mechanics and usage are not a part of the construct assessed according to the rubric, then these variables can be removed from the prediction model.

CTB's Automated Essay Evaluation

The Automated Essay Evaluation (AEE) system has an NLP-based grammar and style error detection tool embedded within it. This software tool is used internationally and has been continuously updated and maintained since 2006. Its development was assisted by feedback from U.S. and Chinese users from grade 3 through adult. CTB's grammar and style tool detects the following eight major types of common writing errors: agreement (such as "school for boys *were* established"), missing words ("Beijing is (*the*) capital of China"), extra words ("you should *be* try this"), wrong words ("listen to *she*"), confused words (then vs. than), wrong word order ("how you *are*?"), and punctuation and white space errors.

Writing rubrics commonly require evaluation of word choice/grammar usage and mechanics as a means to identify grammatical and style errors. When automated error detection is employed in the classroom, customers require that the tool detect grammatical errors as teachers do. The performance of the automated grammatical and style error detection in the CTB AEE system is specifically evaluated based on the correlations between the engine and human scores for analytic traits of word choice/grammar usage and mechanics. For example, the engine–human score correlation on the two traits ranged from 0.64 to 0.87, and weighted kappa ranged from 0.68 to 0.91 across grades 3 through 11 from 2009 WESTEST2 operational testing (CTB/McGraw-Hill, 2010).

Measurement Incorporated's Project Essay Grade

Measurement Incorporated's (MI) grammar checker is built into Project Essay Grade (PEG™), its automated essay scoring system. The grammar checker employs a custom search language, modeled loosely on regular expressions, which allows linguists to write rules searching for complex grammatical constructions in the essays being evaluated. In formative applications, targeted feedback is provided when errors are flagged.

PEG's grammar checker detects and provides feedback for a wide variety of syntactic, semantic, and punctuation errors. These include, but are not limited to, run-on sentences, sentence fragments, comma splices, homophone errors and other errors of word choice, missing or misused commas, apostrophes, quotation marks, and end punctuation. In addition, the grammar checker locates and offers feedback on style choices inappropriate for formal writing. PEG currently uses a straightforward count of the number of grammatical errors and the number per type of grammatical errors per essay and per sentence in its model.

Because the program is used for writing improvement, the grammar checker is applied in a way that keeps false positives to a minimum. A consequence of this approach is that some grammatical errors may not be flagged if doing so would lead to an increase in the number of errors marked inappropriately. For example, in a recent research study of a set of 1,984 sentences, 1,389 were marked as having an error by human readers. On this set, the grammar rules achieved 99% precision and 52% recall.

Educational Testing Service (e-rater)

Educational Testing Service's (ETS's) automated essay scoring, *e-rater*, targets a wide variety of grammatical errors. E-*rater* is organized into 11 macro-features, three of which target grammatical errors: Grammar, Usage and Mechanics. Within each macro-feature there are several micro-features (represented by NLP error detection modules) which target specific errors. The micro-features can be rule-driven (that is, use ALEK to detect the error in question) or can be statistically-driven, as in the case of article and preposition usage errors. The Grammar macro-feature consists of micro-features which detect garbled sentences, run-on sentences, fragments, subject–verb agreement, ill-formed verbs, pronoun errors, possessive errors, and wrong or missing words. The Usage macro-feature detects incorrect articles, confused words, wrong word forms, faulty comparisons, incorrect prepositions, and incorrect negation. The Mechanics macro-feature detects errors in spelling, capitalization, punctuation, hyphen usage, fused words, compound words, and duplicate adjacent words. As in the other automated scoring systems, the micro-features are tuned so as to prioritize precision over recall.

The three grammatical error macro-features contribute to the overall *e-rater* holistic score. Each micro-feature produces a count of the number of errors it detects, and these counts are summed together for each macro-feature. The error counts for the three grammatical macro-features are combined with the values of the other macro-features in a regression model to produce a holistic score for the essay. The regression weights for the macro-features vary between assessments such as TOEFL and GRE, but generally they are strong contributors to the holistic score. For example, in one TOEFL model, Grammar, Usage, and Mechanics macro-features contribute up to 25% of the holistic score (see Table 15.1).

In addition to the macro-features described above, a new "Positive" macro-feature was recently added to *e-rater*. It is designed to represent the quality of the prepositions and collocations in the essay. In a sense, the positive feature "inverts" the information normally used in error detection. For example, in the case of preposition error detection, e-rater produces a score for the writer's preposition and then compares it to the scores of all other prepositions that could appear in the same location. When a competing preposition has a much higher score, the writer's preposition is marked as an error. In the case of the positive preposition feature, the real number value of the writer's preposition score is used as a measure of how *good* the preposition is, that is, how well it fits the context. By averaging all the preposition scores in an essay, it is possible to produce a measure of overall preposition quality. This feature has been found to correlate very strongly with holistic score, and it shows another way in which grammatical error detection methods can be used to assess student writing.

How Does Grammatical Feedback Affect Student Writing?

When used in formative assessment, an important goal of grammatical error detection is to improve the quality of the user's writing by highlighting errors, describing the types of mistakes the writer has made, and suggesting corrections. But does such feedback actually improve writing? There have been a number of studies documenting the effectiveness of high-quality, manually-generated error correction for language learners. But given their less-than-perfect performance, we might ask whether automated systems are beneficial overall or if they do more harm than good. To date, most research has focused on measuring the effectiveness of automated essay scoring systems by looking at users' essay scores or their overall performance on standardized writing tests (Elliot & Mikulas, 2004; Shermis, Burstein, & Bliss, 2004; Warschauer & Ware, 2006). In contrast to these holistic measures of writing, the four studies discussed below examine

Table 15.1 Relative Feature Weights in the E-Rater Generic Scoring Model Developed for the TOEFL Independent Essays

Feature	Relative Weight (%)
Organization	32
Development	29
Mechanics	10
Usage	8
Grammar	7
Lexical Complexity (Word Length)	7
Lexical Complexity (Use of Less Frequent Words)	4
Style	3

Source: Enright and Quinlan, 2010.

the specific effects of automated feedback on reducing the occurrence of grammatical errors.

Shermis et al. (2008) used Criterion to score and provide feedback on over 11,000 essays written by more than 2,000 students in grades 6 through 10. Statistical analyses showed significant increases in essay score across successive essays and significant decreases in the numbers of errors for grammar, usage, and mechanics. Unfortunately, this study did not have a control group for comparison, i.e., one that received writing instruction but without benefit of Criterion's scoring and feedback, so it is difficult to interpret the results in terms of a causal association between error feedback and error reduction. Chodorow et al. (2010) re-analyzed data that had originally been collected by Lipnevich and Smith (2009) from 463 university students who either received no feedback on the essays that they wrote or who were given feedback generated by Criterion. Lipnevich and Smith found significantly more improvement in essay score with feedback than without it. As a follow-up to this study, Chodorow et al. (2010) separated the data into native and non-native groups and studied changes in the number of article usage errors that the students made from the first draft of their essay to the final draft. Results showed a small but statistically significant decrease in article errors for nonnative speakers in the Criterion feedback condition. Choi (2010) looked at essay score and the number of grammar, usage, and mechanics errors in essays written by ESL and EFL students who received instruction under one of three conditions: with Criterion integrated into their writing course, with Criterion as an optional resource, and without use of Criterion. Results showed that, in two of the three writing assignments which the students were given, those in the Criterion integrated condition showed greater improvement in essay score and greater reduction in number of errors between drafting and revising their essays than the students in the other two conditions.

Clearly there is a need for more research on the effects of automated grammatical error feedback in improving the quality of writing. Ideally, large-scale longitudinal studies should be used to measure the effects for specific error types in native and non-native speakers at various levels of writing proficiency. Only then will we have a detailed picture of how writers use feedback when it is supplied by an automated system that misses many errors and, on occasion, falsely reports others.

NOTES

1 http://www.ets.org/toefl/pbt/scores/ writing_score_guide/
2 http://www.cambridge.org/elt/corpus/learner_corpus.htm

REFERENCES

Allan, J. (1980). Nouns and countability. *Language, 56*(3), 541–567.

Bergsma, S., Lin, D., & Goebel, R. (2009). *Web-scale n-gram models for lexical disambiguation*. Paper presented at the 21st International Joint Conference on Artificial Intelligence.

Chodorow, M., Gamon, M., & Tetreault, J. (2010). The utility of article and preposition error correction systems for English language learners: Feedback and assessment. *Language Testing, 27*(3), 419–436.

Choi, J. (2010). *The impact of automated essay scoring (AES) for improving English language learners' essay writing*. Unpublished Ph.D dissertation. University of Virginia.

Conners, R. J., & Lunsford, A. A. (1988). Frequency of formal errors in current college writing or Ma and Pa Kettle do research. *College Composition and Communication, 39*(4), 395–409.

CTB/McGraw-Hill. (2010). WVDE WESTEST 2 technical report. Monterey, CA.

Dahlmeier, D., & Ng, T. H. (2011). *Grammatical error correction with alternating structure optimization*. Paper presented at the Proceedings of the 49th Annual Meeting of the Association for Computational Linguistics: Human Language Technologies (ACL-HLT-2011).

Dale, R., & Kilgarriff, A. (2010). *Helping our own: Text massaging for computational linguistics as a new shared task*. Paper presented at the INLG.

Dalgish, G. (1985). Computer-assisted ESL research and courseware development. *Computers and Composition, 2*(4), 45–61.

Elliot, S., & Mikulas, C. (2004). *The impact of MY Access! use on student writing performance: A technology overview and four studies*. Paper presented at the the Annual Meeting of the American Educational Research Association, San Diego, CA, April.

Enright, M. K., & Quinlan, T. (2010). Complementing human judgment of essays written by English language learners with e-rater® scoring. *Language Testing, 27*(3), 317–334.

Gamon, M. (2010). *Using mostly native data to correct errors in learners' writing: A meta-classifier approach*. Paper presented at the NAACL 2010, Association for Computational Linguistics, June.

Gamon, M. (2011). *High-order sequence modeling for language learner error detection*. Paper presented at the Sixth Workshop on Innovative Use of NLP for Building Educational Applications, June.

Gamon, M., & Leacock, C. (2010). *Search right and thou shalt find . . . Using web queries for learner error detection*. Paper presented at the NAACL 2010, Association for Computational Linguistics, June.

Guo, Y., & Beckett, G. H. (2007). *The hegemony of English as a global language*. Paper presented at the International Symposium on Social Policy and Social Engineering.

Heift, T., & Schulze, M. (2007). *Errors and intelligence in computer-assisted language learning: Parsers and pedagogues*. New York, NY and London: Routledge.

Jensen, K., Heidorn, G. E. and Richardson, S. D. (1993). *Natural language processing: The PLNLP approach*. Dordrecht: Kluwer.

Leacock, C., & Chodorow, M. (2003). Automated grammatical error detection. In M. D. Shermis and J. C. Burstein (Eds.), *Automated essay scoring: A cross-disciplinary perspective* (pp. 195–207). Mahwah, NJ: Lawrence Erlbaum Associates.

Leacock, C., Chodorow, M., Gamon, M., & Tetreault, J. (2010). *Automated grammatical error detection for language learners*. Paper presented at the Synthesis Lectures on Human Language Technologies.

Lipnevich, A., and Smith, J. (2009). Effects of differential feedback on students' examination performance. *Journal of Experimental Psychology: Applied, 15*, 319–333.

Madnani, N., Tetreault, J., Chodorow, M., & Rozovskaya, A. (2011). *They can help: Using crowdsourcing to improve the evaluation of grammatical error detection systems*. Paper presented at the 49th Annual Meeting of the Association for Computational Linguistics: Human Language Technologies, Portland, OR, June 19–24.

Marcus, M. P., Santorini, B., & Marcinkiewicz, M. A. (1993). Building a large annotated corpus of English: The Penn Tree Bank. *Computational Linguistics, 19*, 313–330.

Rozovskaya, A., & Roth, D. (2011). *Algorithm selection and model adaptation for ESL correction tasks*. Paper presented at the 49th Annual Meeting of the Association for Computational Linguistics: Human Language Technologies (ACL-HLT-2011).

Shermis, M. D., Burstein, J., & Bliss, L. (2004). *The impact of automated essay scoring on high stakes writing assessments*. Paper presented at the annual meetings of the National Council on Measurement in Education, San Diego, CA, April.

Shermis, M. D., Wilson, C., Diao, G., & Diao, Y. (2008). *The impact of automated essay scoring on writing outcomes online submission*. Paper presented at the Annual Meetings of the National Council on Measurement in Education, New York, NY, March 25–27.

Tetreault, J., & Chodorow, M. (2008a). *Native judgments of non-native usage: Experiments in preposition error detection*. Paper presented at the COLING Workshop on Human Judgments in Computational Linguistics, Manchester, UK, August 23.

Tetreault, J., & Chodorow, M. (2008b). *The ups and downs of preposition error detection.* Paper presented at the COLING, Manchester, UK.

Tetreault, J., & Chodorow, M. (2009). *Examining the use of region web counts for ESL error detection.* Paper presented at the Web as Corpus Workshop (WAC-5), San Sebastian, Spain.

Tetreault, J., Filatova, E., & Chodorow, M. (2010). *Rethinking grammatical error annotation and evaluation with the amazon mechanical Turk.* Paper presented at the 5th Workshop on Innovative Use of NLP for Building Educational Applications, Los Angeles, CA, June 5.

Wagner, J. (2012). *Detecting grammatical errors with treebank-induced, probabilistic parsers.* Dublin City University, Dublin, Ireland.

Warschauer, M., & Ware, P. (2006). Automated writing evaluation: Defining the classroom research agenda. *Language Teaching Research, 10*(2), 1–24.

16 Automated Evaluation of Discourse Coherence Quality in Essay Writing

Jill Burstein, Joel Tetreault, Martin Chodorow, Daniel Blanchard, and Slava Andreyev

INTRODUCTION

Discourse coherence is an essential criterion for essay evaluation as illustrated in scoring rubric criteria for standardized writing assessments.[1] In this chapter we discuss different perspectives that aim to define text coherence; the tangible criteria that illustrate discourse coherence quality in scoring rubrics that motivate the need for including these analysis in automated essay scoring systems; linguistic properties in essay data that contribute to discourse coherence; and a description of how these features can be modeled to build a system that generates coherence quality scores for student and test-taker essay writing.

We begin by discussing a few differing perspectives on linguistic and cognitive factors contributing to the relative weak or strong coherence quality of a text. From Halliday and Hasan's (1976) perspective, a text is a semantic unit, as opposed to a large grammatical unit, or super-sentence. Further, there are a number of contributors to *textual continuity*—the ability of the reader to construct meaning from the text. These include a number of overt linguistic features, including relationships between words, well-formed sentences, and meaningful transitions. As well, interpretation of a text plays a role in a reader's perception of the text continuity, or quality of discourse coherence. Shriver (1989) asserted that the quality of a text can be judged to some extent by the *correct* (author-intended) inferences that readers draw from the text. In addition, from a cognitive psychology perspective, Graesser, McNamara, Louwerse, and Cai (2004) asserted that coherence is a psychological construct, and "*. . . coherence relations are constructed in the mind of the reader and depend on the skills and knowledge that the reader brings to the situation*" (p. 193) As is also pointed out in Graesser et al. (2004), readers' construction of meaning may differ based on individual inferences. A challenge, then, in the evaluation of discourse coherence quality is that a reader's perception of coherence is related to that reader's construction of meaning of a particular text. This can vary from reader to reader. We observed this in an annotation task in our research, and this is discussed later in the chapter in the context of an annotation task.

Given that readers' perceptions about the coherence quality of a text can vary, where might we look for criteria that could help us to understand the linguistic properties that contribute to human raters' decisions about discourse coherence quality? Further, how might assessment of discourse coherence play a role in the assignment of an overall essay score? At Educational Testing Service, holistic scoring is used by human raters to assign scores to essays. By design, holistic scoring guides developed for standardized writing assessments are meant to offer human raters guidelines in terms of how to assign an overall score that takes into account many aspects of writing (Coward, 1950; Godshalk, Swineford, & Coffman, 1966; Huddleston, 1952). These include linguistic characteristics such as word choice, syntactic variety, grammaticality, and organizational quality. With regard to discourse coherence, whereas scoring guides provide a general idea of linguistic features that might play a role in evaluating discourse coherence quality, they do not definitively prescribe, nor do they provide specific illustrations to the rater of the linguistic features that contribute specifically to higher and lower coherence quality. Example scoring rubric criteria are provided Figure 16.1.

In the context of automated essay scoring, there is a growing body of research that addresses the task of automated detection of discourse coherence quality. However, to our knowledge, no operational automated capabilities exist that evaluate coherence quality based on the broad set of linguistic properties expressed in holistic scoring rubric criteria discussed above. Large-scale standardized assessments clearly motivate continued research in automated essay scoring that more fully addresses aspects of the writing construct (see Chapters 4 and 20), and, specifically, discourse coherence. A more recent motivation for automated capabilities that handle different aspects of argumentation, including evaluation of discourse coherence quality of writing, is now also provided by increased requirements for state and national assessments and standardized classroom instruction. The need for a research agenda for text analysis is emphasized by the Common Core State Standards Initiative (CCSSI).[2] This initiative has now been adopted by most states for use in kindergarten through 12th grade (K–12) classrooms, and it is likely to have a strong influence on teaching standards in K–12 education. The CCSSI encodes what K–12 students should be learning with regard to reading, writing, speaking, listening, language, and media and technology. More specifically, it describes language structures that learners need to grasp as they progress to the higher grades in preparation for college and career readiness in reading and writing.[3] In terms of writing skill and discourse coherence, there is a strong focus on students' ability to develop argumentation in the context of a college readiness skill. In terms of its relationship to argumentation, discourse coherence essentially characterizes the landscape of the argumentation in a piece of writing. The quality of the overall discourse coherence of an essay can be said to be determined by the quality of the ordering, development, connectedness, and fluency of ideas. A breakdown in any of these characteristics might disturb the coherence landscape, making it a bit rough for the reader to navigate the writer's bumpy argumentation.

Given the continued emphasis on the need for feedback, and a specific interest in supporting students' ability to develop well-formed argumentation in student writing, the development of advanced automated capabilities that evaluate aspects of argumentation, such as discourse coherence quality, will be critical. Consistent with this, we have been developing a system for automated evaluation of discourse coherence quality (Burstein, Tetreault, & Andreyev, 2010). A major goal is to ensure that the system addresses scoring rubric criteria specifically related to discourse coherence in essay writing.

"displays unity, progression, and coherence, though it may contain occasional redundancy, digression, or unclear connections;[a] Is not clearly organized; some parts may be clear while others are disjointed or confused . . . errors in grammar interfere with reader understanding."[b]

Figure 16.1 Excerpts from Scoring Rubric Criteria for Essay Writing Assessments.

Notes:
a Excerpt from: http://www.ets.org/Media/Tests/TOEFL/pdf/Writing_Rubrics.pdf
b Excerpt from: http://www.ets.org/Media/Products/Criterion/topics/hs12_dress.htm

RELATED WORK

As discussed in the previous section, *discourse coherence* might be described as the landscape of the argumentation in an essay. Whether or not an essay is coherent to an individual reader may depend on the ordering, development, connections, and the fluency with which the ideas in the essay are expressed. Coherence breakdowns may occur for an individual reader due to a number of factors, including, but not limited to, grammatical and word usage errors, lack of transitions resulting in unexpected topic shifts, and single ideas that seem to be mini-idea islands, not necessarily tied to other ideas in the text. By contrast, the notion of *text cohesion* has typically been discussed in the context of vocabulary (topic) use and distribution in a text. The literature that discusses text cohesion has also typically been focused on well-formed texts (e.g., textbooks).

There is quite an extensive literature that describes the characteristics contributing to text cohesion, specifically, how vocabulary usage in text contributes to text cohesion (Deane, Sheehan, Sabatini, Futagi, & Kostin, 2006; Kintsch, 1988; McNamara, 2001; McNamara & Kintsch, 1996; Van Dijk & Kintsch, 1983). There is also a growing body of work in natural language processing (NLP)[4] that addresses text cohesion, but again, mostly on well-formed texts. Some of this work is related to the identification of linguistic variability in text for the purpose of assigning a grade (readability) level to a text (Graesser, McNamara, & Kulikowich, 2011; Sheehan, Kostin, Futagi, & Flor, 2010). NLP research that addresses readability (i.e., assignment of grade levels to texts) typically handles well-formed texts. We are not aware of studies in the readability research domain that handles *noisy* essay data. This makes sense because the traditional goal of readability measures has been to identify grade levels of text, not specifically to determine the quality of the text within the grade level.

In this chapter, we specifically investigate how to characterize and automatically evaluate the quality of discourse coherence in *noisy* essay texts—specifically, essays written by test-takers or students.

Data Modeling Approaches

In NLP work, there are two main approaches to data modeling: *unsupervised* and *supervised* approaches. We use supervised modeling to build our discourse coherence detection systems. We will discuss each of these to provide the reader with background about both approaches.

Unsupervised Modeling

Unsupervised modeling approaches do not require annotated data sets. Such approaches for analyzing the discourse coherence of texts have, in general, been *limited* to lexical cohesion, specifically, repetition of vocabulary in a text (Foltz, Kintsch, & Landauer, 1998; Hearst, 1997). TextTiling, for instance, identifies lexical chains (essentially, repetition of vocabulary) across adjacent sentences following the notion of identifying subtopic structure in text (Hearst, 1997). Similarly, Foltz et al. (1998) described systems that measure lexical relatedness between text segments by using vector-based similarity between adjacent sentences.

Moving beyond vocabulary, Graesser et al. (2004) developed Coh-Metrix, a text analysis system designed to analyze *text cohesion*—the text features that render a text easier or more difficult to read. The system incorporates approximately 200 features related to vocabulary and syntax that are aligned with theoretical frameworks of comprehension (Graesser et al., 2011). However, Coh-Metrix was designed to evaluate text cohesion (as discussed above), specifically for assessing readability in well-formed text, in contrast to *noisy* essay data. Evaluations of Coh-Metrix (and cohesion features) have typically been performed on well-formed texts to determine grade level and genre (Graesser et al., 2011). Therefore, the system does not include features related to grammatical or spelling errors that are characteristic of noisy data, such as essays or social media texts (e.g., blogs). SourceRater[5] is a more recent system that uses similar kinds of features to identify the grade level of a text (Sheehan et al., 2010). Like Coh-Metrix, SourceRater does not address errors in grammar and spelling to address coherence quality in text, which makes sense when dealing with well-formed, academic texts. Systems like Coh-Metrix and SourceRater look for characteristics present in well-formed text that render them more or less comprehensible.

Supervised Modeling

Supervised modeling approaches require annotated data. Miltsakaki and Kukich (2000) were the first to complete an annotation study focusing on discourse coherence in essay data. They implemented a annotation task that was independent of writing mode that requires significant expertise related to Centering Theory (Grosz et al., 1995). The goal of this work was to use Centering Theory to identify topic shift in essays. In Miltsakaki and Kukich, 100 essays were manually annotated to label specific features that identified where Centering information occurred in text. The data were used to show that essays with a higher proportion of *topic shifts* (i.e., *Rough Shifts* in Centering Theory) tended to have lower scores (based on a standard 6-point holistic scoring scale, where 6 indicates the best writing and lower scores indicate degraded writing skill). Higgins, Burstein, Marcu, and Gentile (2004) implemented an annotation method that was dependent on writing mode and system to predict discourse coherence quality in essays. The annotation scheme required expertise about essay-based discourse structure, specifically, the ability to rate the coherence between specific essay-based discourse elements, such as an essay's *thesis statement* and each of its *main points*. This method showed some success, but it was reliant on organizational structures that are most consistent with responses to expository and persuasive writing.

Barzilay and Lapata (2005, 2008) implemented a method to predict discourse coherence quality in well-formed texts. In their approach, an entity grid (matrix) is built by extracting the entities (nouns and pronouns) in a text, and keeping track of their syntactic roles in each sentence. The information about entities and their associated syntactic roles in the grid is then used to compute the distributional and syntactic properties of text entities (nouns and pronouns) in a text. Theoretically, their method is aligned with a linguistic theory called Centering Theory (Grosz, Joshi, & Weinstein, 1995). Centering Theory asserts that the discourse in a text contains a set of textual segments, each containing discourse entities. Entities are then ranked by their importance. The theory can be used to track entities as well as topic clusters and shifts. Barzilay and Lapata's algorithm keeps track of the distribution of entity transitions between adjacent sentences and computes a value for all transition types based on the proportion of occurrence in a text. Barzilay and Lapata (2008) evaluated the algorithm with three tasks using well-formed newspaper corpora: text ordering, summary coherence evaluation, and readability assessment. For *summary evaluations*, their approach successfully predicted coherence quality of summaries written by humans versus machine-generated summaries. System predictions were compared to human judgments of discourse coherence quality where annotators assigned a holistic quality rating on a 7-point scale, with 1 indicating the lowest quality and 7 the highest quality. Similar to the Coh-Metrix and SourceRater evaluations, for the *readability assessment evaluation*, Barzilay and Lapata (2008) used their algorithm to determine if a well-formed text was from an elementary-level text versus an adult-level text. Texts included pairs of articles taken from *Encyclopaedia Britannica* for each of these levels. They found increased performance for a system that predicted readability (higher or lower grade level) when standard readability syntactic measures were added to the model. This is consistent with Graesser et al. (2004, 2011). Barzilay and Lapata's (2008) measures used syntactic parse tree information (Charniak, 2000) and included sentence length, average parse tree height, average number of noun phrases, average number of verb phrases, and average number of subordinate clauses (Schwarm & Ostendorf, 2005). Like other evaluations of readability assessment, features addressing technical quality were not included because this work involved well-formed texts.

Other discourse coherence schemes for well-formed text, such as Wolf and Gibson's (2005), have required annotators to label text segments with particular discourse coherence relations, for instance, *cause-effect, example*, and *elaboration*. This work is similar to Miltsakaki and Kukich (2000), and to Higgins et al.'s (2004), feature-specific annotation task, both of which require significant expertise.

Using well-formed texts, Pitler and Nenkova (2008) showed that a text coherence detection system yields the best performance when it includes features using the Barzilay and Lapata (2008) algorithm, syntactic features, discourse relations from the Penn Discourse Treebank (Prasad et al., 2008), and vocabulary and length features. Evaluations were based on 30 *Wall Street Journal* articles that were annotated for coherence by at least three college students. The coherence annotation scheme, similar to our holistic scheme (see "Developing an Intuitive, Flexible Annotation Scheme," below), required annotators to provide a rating on a scale of 1 to 5 in response to each of these four questions related to the article's coherence: (1) *How well-written is this article?* (2) *How well does the text fit together?* (3) *How easy was it to understand?* and (4) *How interesting is this article?*

Crossley and McNamara (2011) also developed an annotation scheme for discourse coherence in essays. This is the only other work to our knowledge that includes a technical quality measure (i.e., an annotation measure that assesses standard English conventions) for evaluating a system for automated detection of coherence quality. In this study, raters assigned a holistic score (from 1 to 6) to multiple traits of an essay which were believed to contribute to essay coherence. These addressed the following categories: (a) quality of the introductory paragraph, including connections between thesis and essay discourse; (b) connections between topic across paragraphs in the essay; and (c), grammar, syntax, and mechanics. As Crossley and McNamara discuss, their annotators were experts, and so this was a higher cost annotation task with regard to *expertise*. Their findings differ from Burstein et al.'s (2010) findings and those reported later in this paper in the following way. In contrast to Crossley and McNamara's results, our work indicates that technical quality (e.g., grammatical errors) is a strong predictor of coherence quality in the context of test-taker essay writing. The fact that a relationship between coherence and grammatical errors was not found in Crossley and McNamara's work may be related to the nature of their essay data, which consisted only of essays written by native speakers, during an undergraduate composition course. This is possibly a population of more proficient writers who are less likely to make grammatical and spelling errors in their writing.

Pitler and Nenkova's (2008) annotation scheme most closely reflects the annotation approach that we use in our work (Burstein et al., 2010), which is described in "Developing an Intuitive, Flexible Annotation Scheme," below. Like Pitler and Nenkova, our annotators use a holistic annotation scheme to rate the overall coherence of a text. The task is completed at the document level and requires no specific linguistic or essay-scoring expertise. The major difference between our work and Pitler and Nenkova's is the data itself. They annotate well-formed text, and we annotate noisy essay data. Given that, it is not surprising that our feature set for predicting coherence includes a technical quality feature, and theirs does not.

Burstein et al. (2010) also showed that the use of data sets from three different test-taker populations also demonstrated coherence model differences across populations. These modeling differences could be attributed to how coherence is represented in texts, which could be influenced by essay mode, and the language use in the particular population. For instance, grammatical errors might be more likely to influence coherence in non-native speaking younger writers. Findings in Burstein et al. (2010) suggest that this is true, since grammatical errors seemed to play a strong role in accurate prediction of high- and low-coherence quality.

Lin, Ng, and Kan (2011) performed a study that demonstrates how outputs from a discourse parser can be used to model coherence, using the Penn Discourse Treebank-style discourse parser developed by Lin et al. (2011). This parser automatically identifies the discourse relations, labels the argument spans, and classifies the relation types including rhetorical relations, such as *Antithesis*, *Cause*, *Contrast*, and *Elaboration*. Lin et al. process text through the parser and evaluate the small sequences of two or three adjacent relations (or, n-gram sequences). The authors introduce the idea of a discourse transition matrix similar in nature to Barzilay and Lapata's (2008) entity grid. In Lin et al.'s (2011) system, the matrix contains the associated relations present in each sentence in the text for each text entity. By contrast, Barzilay and Lapata created a grid that represents the syntactic roles of entities in each sentence in the text. Lin et al. created a grid that specifies *discourse transitions* across adjacent sentences, and Barzilay and Lapata create a grid that specifies *syntactic roles* across adjacent sentences. Lin et al. model the transition probabilities from the discourse transition matrix to perform a text ranking task that predicts the relative ranking of a text pair (see Lin et al., 2011 for details about the modeling approach). Using 50 texts from the *Wall Street Journal*, Lin et al. report that their method using a discourse transition matrix outperformed Barzilay and Lapata on a coherence ranking task.

DEVELOPING AN INTUITIVE, FLEXIBLE ANNOTATION SCHEME

Human readers who score essays in response to standardized writing exams are instructed to take coherence into account. By design, the holistic scoring guides developed for these writing assessments do not pinpoint the linguistic features that contribute specifically to coherence breakdown, nor do they provide specific examples that indicate where such breakdowns take place in essays. See Figure 16.1 for example rubric criteria.

While no clear definition exists that we can use to target specific linguistic structures, we have a strong interest in developing a measure of discourse coherence quality that we can use to enhance e-rater®, an operational automated essay scoring system (Attali & Burstein, 2006). In order to build a system, we developed an annotation scheme that was broadly aligned with the high-level descriptions provided in rubric criteria that might bring into play the linguistic information that could contribute to coherence quality in test-taker writing. Specifically, these include clarity of relationships of main ideas in an essay, and sufficient technical quality—both of which are likely to contribute to the discourse coherence quality (or, the relative smoothness of the flow of ideas) in a test-taker essay. Our annotation scheme does not require annotators to annotate specific structures in essays (Higgins et al., 2004; Miltsakaki & Kukich, 2000). It is authentic in that it is designed to emulate (but, not imitate) the holistic scoring process, in which readers assign a score based on a general impression, given fuzzy criteria (above). In this case, our annotators assign a (impressionistic) score specifically for discourse coherence quality based on a few features that may contribute to an essay's coherence (flow of ideas). The annotation scheme was developed and refined over a period of about one month, and training two annotators to achieve moderate agreement (kappa = 0.67) took approximately one week. The annotations were then successfully used to build a discourse coherence system across a number of test domains, including writing samples from native and non-native writers, spanning from sixth to twelfth grade, and across undergraduate and graduate-level assessments. Writing task types were also varied, including expository and persuasive writing, subject-based writing, and summary writing. In previous research, Miltsakaki and Kukich (2000) used a Centering Theory (Grosz et al., 1995) approach to indicate topic shift in essays. This approach, while successful, is quite time-consuming. In Higgins et al. (2004), an annotation scheme for discourse coherence was developed to capture topical relationships between specific essay-based discourse elements, for example an essay's *thesis statement* and each of its *main points*. This method had some success; however, it is reliant on organizational structures that are consistent with responses to expository and persuasive writing. The newer annotation scheme described in this chapter is more intuitive and flexible. It does not require specific linguistic expertise, and it can be applied across writing modes (e.g., expository and persuasive essay writing). In our work, we have collected annotations for approximately 1550 essays from across these different grade levels, writing modes, and task types. The same annotation protocol that was originally developed for only expository and persuasive writing (Burstein et al., 2010) has been successful in examining linguistic properties of discourse coherence, and subsequently developing features based on these properties to model discourse coherence *across* different populations, writing modes, and domains.

Annotation Scheme

The annotation scheme used in the study described here was first described in Burstein et al. (2010). Essentially, the scheme asks annotators to consider the following question: "*When reading an essay, how often did I become confused?*" The annotation scheme uses a 3-point scale, where 1 = incoherent (low, or total confusion); 2 = somewhat coherent (medium, or a little confusing); and, 3 = no problems with coherence (high, or not at all confusing). For instance, Score Point 1 represents an essay which is *largely incoherent*, so that the annotator cannot even identify specific points in the text where coherence degrades. By contrast, Score Point 3 represents an essay where the annotator had *no problem* understanding the essay. Score Point 2 represents an essay with *one or two easily identifiable points* where coherence breakdowns occurred. (Specifically, the reader could not construct a meaningful connection between the breakdown points in the text, and other parts of the text.) For Score Point 2, annotators had to do an additional task. Score Point 2 essays represent those essays in which most of the meaning of the text can easily understood, but there are one or two *identifiable points* where coherence breakdown has occurred. For these essays, annotators had to label the "awkward sentence(s)" where the coherence breakdown occurred. Annotators could also add comments to describe the confusion points in the essays where it may have taken a few tries to construct meaning at those points, or where meaning construction might have been unsuccessful.

The annotation protocol includes specific examples of essays at each of the three score points. For Score Point 2, the protocol also contains example awkward sentences that illustrate where sources of coherence breakdown appear in an essay, as in the essay excerpt in (1) below. While there may be different interpretations of this text, we have indicated in *italicized bold* font our judgments about which sentences might be inter-preted as awkward. In the short essay excerpt in (1) below, the sentence [1] reference to "these companies" does not have a natural antecedent and is confusing. In sentence [2], we are not clear who or what "posers" are. In sentence [3], there is a similar issue, and "products" does not have a natural antecedent. These points of confusion can be resolved using some inference, so that we can essentially construct meaning for this text. It is therefore assigned to Score Point 2.

In the protocol, annotators were instructed not to consider grammatical or spelling errors as lowering coherence scores, unless these errors interfered with the annotators' ability to construct meaning. This is aligned with Shriver's (1989) assertion that such error types are not notable, and we tend to ignore them while reading unless they slow down our reading and make us re-read. That said, the interference of grammatical and spelling errors should appear in essays that annotators assign a Score 1 or Score 2. In the case of Score 2 writing, these would be cases where such errors caused the annota-tor (reader) to have to re-read a part of the text because grammatical or spelling errors interfered with understanding of a particular section of the text.

(1)

Media in all physical or visual forms from magazines, to movies, to billboards, and television display images of beauty from both male and female. Not a day goes by when a person is not exposed to these campaigns. **These companies are trying to promote their product or service in the most elegant way, but the qualities seen on the images are compared with themselves who may not match up by far.** [1] **When look at these images, it's easy to forget that the posers depend on their careers to look the way they do, but the observers do not.** [2] *Thus, a desire to have the same look continuously builds and results in taking action. It is the state of mind that they are dissatisfied with their appearance and they will take any steps to gain that appearance. Psychological problems may occur and lead to serious disorders such as anorexia.* **Furthermore, the products or others related to that kind, are sold leading to obsessive and unnecessary spending.** [3]

Data and Annotator Training

Data

Essay data included writing samples from native and non-native English speakers, rang-ing from sixth to twelfth grade, and across undergraduate and graduate-level writing assessments. Writing task types were varied and included expository and persuasive writ-ing, subject-based writing, and summary writing. The total number of essays was 1555 across five data sets, described in the evaluation section in Tables 16.1 and 16.2. Data sample sizes ranged from approximately 250 to 400 essays.

Annotator training

During the initial training and annotation scheme development (Burstein et al., 2010), two annotators worked with two of the authors. Both annotators were research assist-ants and had experience doing varied kinds of linguistic annotation. However, neither annotator had previous experience with annotating discourse coherence.

The annotation scheme was developed and refined over a period of about one month in discussion with two of the authors and the two annotators. Training began at the point at which the authors and the annotators agreed on the annotation protocol instructions, and the examples of essays that illustrated coherence at each of the three score points. Fifty essays were annotated using a training set that contained essays from different task types, grade levels, and domains. Annotations took approximately one week. Annotators had below acceptable agreement for Score Point 2. Therefore, we collapsed the essays assigned to Score Point 2 and Score Point 3 into a single category (*high*). Moderate agreement (kappa = 0.67) for a 2-point scale was achieved: *low* (all essays at Score Point 1) and *high* (all essays at Score Points 2 and 3). The annotations were then successfully used to build a discourse coherence system that assigned low and high coherence scores to essays across a number of test domains.

A possible explanation for low agreement for Score Point 2 may be related to individual readers' inferencing decisions. More research is underway to better understand the kinds of structures that contributed to Score 2 assignments. Initial observations based on rater comments indicate that raters described awkward sentences or clauses indicating *topic shifts*, *lacking transitions*, *requiring a new paragraph*, and simply *not understanding the content* in a sentence or clause (which typically seemed to be related to a serious grammatical error).

SYSTEM DESCRIPTION

In the following section, we describe the system features and their relationship to scoring rubric criteria, and system evaluations.

Feature Set Descriptions

The set of features used in each model is intended to capture holistic rubric criteria from scoring guides that correspond to discourse coherence from Figure 16.1. The specific aspects that our features address are underlined: "*displays unity, progression, and coherence, though it may contain occasional redundancy, digression, or unclear connections;*" *Is not clearly organized; some parts may be clear while others are disjointed or confused . . . errors in grammar interfere with reader understanding.*" These features include the following: proportion of grammatical errors using error features from e-rater (Attali & Burstein, 2006), entity-grid transition probabilities (Barzilay & Lapata, 2005, 2008), rhetorical structure theory (RST) features (Mann & Thompson, 1988) derived from an RST parser (Marcu, 2000), and a type-token feature that computes the entity type/token ratios from specific words and terms recovered from the entity grid. Below, we describe each feature type and its corresponding scoring rubric criterion. (For more detailed descriptions of the entity-grid approach, refer to Barzilay and Lapata, 2008; for more detail about the rhetorical structure tree parser, see Marcu, 2000.)

E-rater Grammatical Error Features

These features address *errors in grammar* that could interfere with reader understanding. E-rater identifies more than 30 kinds of errors in grammar, such as subject-verb agreement errors, word usage, missing article errors, and spelling (Attali & Burstein, 2006). Aggregate counts of these individual errors are used as features in e-rater, and these same features were used in our model.

Entity-Grid Transition Probabilities

Entity-grid transition probabilities (Barzilay & Lapata, 2005, 2008) are intended to address *unity, progression* and *coherence* by tracking nouns and pronouns in text. The entity grids characterize occurrences of words across a text in syntactic roles. An entity grid is constructed in which all entities (nouns and pronouns) are represented by their roles in a sentence (i.e., Subject, Object, Other). *Entity-grid transitions* track how the same word appears in a syntactic role across adjacent sentences. Examples of transition types are Subject–Object, Object–Object, and Object–Other. *Entity transition probabilities* represent the proportions of different entity transition types in a text. These probability values are used as features to build coherence models.

Type/Token Ratios for Entities

Type/token ratios can be used to track redundancy in essay writing. The entity-grid transition probabilities are used as features in the coherence models, but they measure only local transition patterns in adjacent sentences rather than more global reuse of words. For instance, if there is a high probability for the "Subject–Subject" transition to occur in an essay, this indicates that the writer is repeating an entity in Subject position in adjacent sentences, but we do not know if same word is being repeated throughout the text or if a variety of words are. The type/token feature can distinguish between these two cases. For instance, if there are ten Subject–Subject transitions, and five different word types appear in these transitions, the type/token ratio would be 5/10 (0.50); if, on the other hand there is only one word type (e.g., "*I*"), the type/token ratio would be 1/10 (0.10). Thus, higher ratios indicate that more concepts are being introduced in a given syntactic role, and lower ratios indicate fewer concepts.

RST-Derived Features

Rhetorical relations tell us how clauses and sentences in a text are rhetorically linked. RST relations include, for example, *Antithesis, Cause, Comparison, Elaboration* and *Example*. Essays are submitted to a rhetorical structure tree parser (Marcu, 2000). We derived features from the rhetorical structure trees to evaluate if and how certain rhetorical relations, combinations of rhetorical relations, or rhetorical relation tree structures might contribute to discourse coherence quality. These included the following: (a) relative frequencies of n-gram rhetorical relations in the context of the tree structure (<u>unigram</u>, or occurrences of a single relation; <u>bigrams</u>, or occurrences of two adjacent relations, for example, "*Contrast->Example*"; and <u>trigrams</u>, or occurrences of three adjacent relations, for example, "*CohesionElaboration->Example->Contrast*"; (b) relative proportions of leaf–parent relation types in rhetorical structure trees; and, (c) counts of root node relation types in rhetorical structure trees.

System Evaluation

Using the features described above, discourse coherence systems were evaluated on each of the five data sets. Our more comprehensive analyses indicated that building coherence models by data set (task and population) produced more accurate systems. Using C5.0,[6] a decision-tree machine learning approach, n-fold cross-validation was used to evaluate system performance for each data set.

System performance on high and low coherence essays is measured in terms of *precision, recall*, and *F-score*. A system's precision on high coherence essays, for example, is

the number of essays that both the system and the human annotator agreed are "high," divided by the number of essays that the *system* labeled "high." Recall is the number of essays that both the system and the human annotator agreed are "high," divided by the number of essays that the *human* labeled "high." The F-score is the harmonic mean of precision and recall. Precision, recall, and F-score can be calculated for "low" coherence essays in a similar manner.

Three baseline systems were used to compare with our novel system: (a) majority class assignment, where all essays were assigned a score of 1 (High); (b) e-rater, where e-rater features were used; and (c) e-rater grammar, usage, and mechanics features. The baselines of performance were all relatively high, with overall F-scores for low- and high-coherence assignments in the range of 0.80 to 0.90. This is undoubtedly driven by the larger proportion of essays with high coherence. Overall precision, recall, and F-scores for the best systems (as compared to baselines) for the five data sets ranged from 0.83–0.91. Tables 16.2 and 16.3 show separate performance measures for high and low predictions, respectively. These are more informative about system performance than the overall values where low and high predictions are collapsed.

The "Best System" was our novel system which outperformed the baselines for all data sets, with the exception of a professional licensure proficiency exam. It should be noted that the data for this exam had about 50% fewer Score Point 1 essays than the other data sets. The system had a difficult time predicting the low coherence essays. Note that in Tables 16.1 and 16.2, the "Best System" (boldface) for each data set was built using a combination of the features described above in "Feature Set Descriptions." Table 16.3 illustrates the features that contributed to the best system for each data set.

Table 16.1 Precision (P), Recall (R), and F-scores (F) (x 100) for "**High**" Discourse Coherence

System	EP/ NNC n=196	Summary/NNC n=304	EP/GL n=210	PPE n=355	EP/ 6–12 n =220
	P/R/F	**P/R/F**	**P/R/F**	**P/R/F**	**P/R/F**
Majority Class	77/100/87	76/100/76	82/100/90	91/100/95	87/99/92
E-rater	87/86/86	81/90/86	87/97/92	91/97/94	89/91/90
ERGramError	90/85/88	78/93/86	86/97/91	91/100/95	90/94/92
Best System	**91/93/92**	**84/95/89**	**90/100/95**	**93/98/95**	**93/97/95**

EP/NNC is expository and persuasive, non-native, college level assessment writing; Summary/NNC is summary, non-native, college level assessment writing; EP/GL is expository and persuasive, graduate level assessment writing; PPE is the Professional Proficiency Exam; and EP/6–12 is elementary, middle, and high school writing. E-rater—E-rater system features. ERGramError—E-rater Grammatical Error features.

Table 16.2 Precision (P), Recall (R), and F-scores (F) (x 100) for "**Low**" Discourse Coherence

System	EP/ NNC n=58	Summary/NNC n=94	EP/GL n=47	PPE n=37	EP/ 6–12 n =33
	P/R/F	**P/R/F**	**P/R/F**	**P/R/F**	**P/R/F**
Majority Class	0/0/0	0/0/0	0/0/0	0/0/0	0/0/0
E-rater	54/57/55	56/33/40	73/34/46	14/5/8	32/27/30
ERGramError	58/69/63	39/14/20	68/32/43	0/0/0	41/37/33
Best System	**75/69/72**	**72/44/55**	**100/49/66**	**56/27/36**	**71/52/60**

EP/NNC is expository and persuasive, non-native, college level assessment writing; Summary/NNC is summary, non-native, college level assessment writing; EP/GL is expository and persuasive, graduate level assessment writing; PPE is the Professional Proficiency Exam; and EP/6–12 is elementary, middle, and high school writing. E-rater—E-rater system features. ERGramError—E-rater Grammatical Error features.

Table 16.3 Feature Sets Used in the Best System for Each Data Set

Data Set	Best System Feature Set
EP/ NNC	EntityGrids + ERGramError + Type/Token + RST
Summary/NNC	EntityGrids + ERGramError + Type/Token
EP/GL	EntityGrids + ERGramError + Type/Token
PPE	EntityGrids + ERGramError + Type/Token + RST
EP/ 6–12	EntityGrids + ERGramError + Type/Token + RST

EP/NNC is expository and persuasive, non-native, college level assessment writing; Summary/NNC is summary, non-native, college level assessment writing; EP/GL is expository and persuasive, graduate level assessment writing; PPE is the Professional Proficiency Exam; and EP/6–12 is elementary, middle, and high school writing. ERGramError—E-rater Grammatical Error features.

DISCUSSION AND CONCLUSIONS

As is discussed in the introduction of this chapter, coherence quality is a critical, yet ill-defined characteristic in the essay evaluation domain. Specifically, coherence is expressed in scoring rubric criteria in the context of organization as it pertains to the unity and progression of ideas, and also with regard to the technical quality of a student or test-taker essay.

Based on an intuitive annotation scheme, we collected annotations for high and low discourse coherence for a set of about 1500 annotated essays. These annotations were used to build and evaluate systems that could generate high- and low- coherence quality scores for essays across domains and populations. Note that this differs from work related to text cohesion which typically handles only vocabulary repetition in text. By contrast, the research reported in this chapter suggests that the coherence of a text depends not only on the words used, but how these words are distributed in a text. In addition to vocabulary, the research also indicates that rhetorical relations and the technical quality of writing contribute to overall coherence in the context of student or test-taker essay writing (or, *noisy data*).

The current state of the art in automated essay evaluation addresses mostly the higher-level features in essays that relate to technical quality: grammatical error detection, presence and absence of essay-based organization elements (e.g., *thesis statement, main points*), and general vocabulary usage. As we continue to develop analysis capabilities in automated essay scoring systems, new capabilities should reflect scoring rubric criteria that are not currently handled, and, in addition, capabilities should be developed with feedback in mind. Feedback should be aligned with the interests of educators and should promote the development of student and test-taker writing skills, such that the more difficult aspects of writing, such as *argumentation*, can be evaluated. Discourse coherence quality does relate to an aspect of argumentation; specifically, it tells us how clearly the ideas in the text structure are expressed. The influential Common Core State Standards for Writing prioritize students' ability to develop clear and logical argumentation in writing, and across modes. As the volume of standardized testing increases, automated essay scoring capabilities will need to accommodate this appropriately, by making sure to incorporate rubric-relevant scoring features. As the volume of standardized assessments grows, especially in anticipation of large-scale state assessments related to the Common Core Standards, the need for relevant feedback for instructional and practice assessments is likely to grow along with it. The more relevant the feedback is to the scoring rubric criteria, the more meaningful and helpful the feedback is likely to be for students and test-takers using online essay evaluation systems for instruction and practice.

The current state of the art in automated evaluation of discourse coherence is presented in this chapter. Note that this research stream is ongoing, and like many NLP-based technologies, is likely to change and improve very quickly. The goal is to be able to include discourse coherence quality ratings as new features in e-rater for use with essay scoring in the near future. In the longer term, we hope to gain greater understanding of how to offer explicit feedback about discourse coherence quality in essay evaluation systems, such as Criterion^SM.

NOTES

1 Example scoring guides for different writing tests may be found at these links: http://www.ets.org/gre/revised_general/scores/how/http://www.ets.org/gre/revised_general/scores/how/ http://www.ets.org/Media/Tests/TOEFL/pdf/Writing_Rubrics.pdf
2 See http://www.corestandards.org/
3 See http://www.corestandards.org/assets/Publishers_Criteria_for_3-12.pdf
4 For a basic discussion of NLP, the reader should refer to Chapter 4.
5 SourceRater has been renamed as Text Evaluator™.
6 http://wwww.rulequest.com/

REFERENCES

Attali, Y., & Burstein, J. (2006). Automated essay scoring with e-rater V.2. *Journal of Technology, Learning, and Assessment, 4*(3). Available from http://www.jtla.org

Barzilay, R., & Lapata, M. (2005). *Modeling local coherence: An entity-based approach.* Paper presented at the ACL, Ann Arbor, MI.

Barzilay, R., & Lapata, M. (2008). Modeling local coherence: An entity-based approach. *Computational Linguistics, 34,* 1–34.

Burstein, J., Tetreault, J., & Andreyev, S. (2010). *Using entity-based features to model coherence in student essays.* Paper presented at the Proceedings of the HLT/NAACL Annual Meeting, Los Angeles, CA, June.

Charniak, E. (2000). *A maximum-entropy-inspired parser.* Paper presented at the North American Chapter of the Association for Computational Linguistics, San Francisco, CA.

Coward, A. F. (1950). *The method of reading the Foreign Service Examination in English composition.* Princeton, NJ: Educational Testing Service.

Crossley, S. A., & McNamara, D. S. (2011). Understanding expert ratings of essay quality: Coh-Metrix analyses of first and second language writing. *International Journal of Continuing Engineering Education and Life-Long Learning, 21,* 170–191.

Deane, P., Sheehan, K. M., Sabatini, J., Futagi, Y., & Kostin, I. (2006). Differences in text structure and its implications for assessment of struggling readers. *Scientific Studies of Reading, 10,* 257–275.

Foltz, P. W., Kintsch, W., & Landauer, T. K. (1998). The measurement of textual coherence with Latent Semantic Analysis. *Organizational Process, 25*(2–3), 285–307.

Godshalk, F. I., Swineford, F., & Coffman, W. E. (1966). *The measurement of writing ability.* New York, NY: College Entrance Examination Board.

Graesser, A. C., McNamara, D. S., Louwerse, M. M., & Cai, Z. (2004). Coh-Metrix: Analysis of text on cohesion and language. *Behavioral Research Methods, Instruments, and Computers, 36,* 193–202.

Graesser, A. C., McNamara, D. S., & Kulikowich, J. (2011). Coh-Metrix: Providing multilevel analyses of text characteristics. *Educational Researcher, 40,* 223–234.

Grosz, B., Joshi, A., & Weinstein, S. (1995). Centering: A framework for modeling the local coherence of discourse. *Computational Linguistics, 21*(2), 203–226.

Halliday, M. A. K., & Hasan, R. (1976). *Cohesion in English.* London: Longman.

Hearst, M. (1997). TextTiling: Segmenting text into multi-paragraph subtopic passages. *Computational Linguistics, 23*(1), 33–64.

Higgins, D., Burstein, J., Marcu, D., & Gentile, C. (2004). Evaluating multiple aspects of coherence in study essays. *Proceedings of the Annual Meeting of HLT/NAACL.*

Huddleston, E. M. (1952). *Measurement of writing ability at the college-entrance level: Objective vs. subjective testing techniques.* Princeton, NJ: Educational Testing Service.

Kintsch, W. (1988). The use of knowledge in discourse processing: A construction-integration model. *Psychological Review, 95,* 163–182.

Lin, Z., Ng, H. T., & Kan, M.-Y. (2011). *Automatically evaluating text coherence using discourse relations.* Paper presented at the 49th Annual Meeting of the Association for Computational Linguistics Portland, OR.

Mann, W. C., & Thompson, S. A. (1988). Rhetorical structure theory: Toward a functional theory of text organization. *Text, 8,* 243–281.

Marcu, D. (2000). *The theory and practice of discourse parsing and summarization.* Cambridge, MA: The MIT Press.

McNamara, D. S. (2001). Reading both high and low coherence texts: Effects of text sequence and prior knowledge. *Canadian Journal of Experimental Psychology, 55,* 51–62.

McNamara, D. S., & Kintsch, W. (1996). Learning from text: Effects of prior knowledge and text coherence. *Discourse Processes, 22,* 247–287.

Miltsakaki, E., & Kukich, K. (2000). *Automated evaluation of coherence in student essays.* Paper presented at the LREC 2000, Athens, Greece.

Pitler, E., & Nenkova, A. (2008). *Revisiting readability: A unified framework for predicting text quality.* Paper presented at the EMNLP, Honolulu, HI.

Prasad, R., Dinesh, N., Lee, A., Miltsakaki, E., Robaldo, L., Joshi, A., & Webber, B. (2008). *The Penn Discourse Treebank 2.0.* Paper presented at the LREC'08.

Schwarm, S. E., & Ostendorf, M. (2005). *Reading level assessment using support vector machines and statistical language models.* Paper presented at the 43rd Annual Meeting of the Association for Computational Linguistics, Ann Arbor, MI.

Sheehan, K. M., Kostin, I., Futagi, Y., & Flor, M. (2010). *Generating automated text complexity classifications that are aligned with targeted text complexity standards (ETS Research Report RR-10-28).* Princeton, NJ: Educational Testing Service.

Shriver, K. A. (1989). Evaluating text quality: The continuum from text-focused to reader-focused methods. *IEEE Transactions on Professional Communication, 32*(4), 238–255.

Van Dijk, T. A., & Kintsch, W. (1983). *Strategies of discourse comprehension.* New York: Academic Press.

Wolf, F., & Gibson, E. (2005). Representing discourse coherence: A corpus-based study. *Computational Linguistics, 31*(2), 249–288.

17 Automated Sentiment Analysis for Essay Evaluation

Jill Burstein, Beata Beigman-Klebanov,
Nitin Madnani, and Adam Faulkner

INTRODUCTION

Sentiment analysis systems have typically been designed for use with specific domains, such as product and movie reviews, and political and newspaper domains. To our knowledge, the research discussed in this chapter is the first attempt to build a sentiment analysis system for the purpose of identifying sentiment and polarity (positivity, negativity, and neutrality) in student and test-taker essay writing (Beigman-Klebanov, Burstein, Madnani, Faulkner, & Tetreault, 2012).

As is discussed in Chapter 4, feature development for e-rater, Educational Testing Services' automated essays scoring system, is aligned with scoring rubric criteria to ensure that relevant aspects of the writing construct (writing characteristics we want to evaluate)[1] are addressed in the context of automated essay evaluation. As is also discussed in Chapters 4 and 16, the Common Core State Standards Initiative (CCSSI) specifications stress the teaching and evaluation of argumentation in student writing. Sentiment analysis research is relevant to the evaluation of argumentation in writing. It incorporates the detection of *personal opinion* ("*I agree with the statement that . . .*"); *attributed opinion* ("*The author believes that . . .*"); and, *statements about positive and negative events* ("*There was a decrease in unemployment this month*"). In the identification of personal or attributed opinion, sentiment analysis systems can also be used to determine the polarity of the opinion (positivity, negativity, and neutrality), and the relative strength or intensity of the polarity ("*I loved that movie!*" versus "*It was a pretty good movie*").

In essay writing, the presence of personal opinion, attributed opinion, and positive and negative statements related to events or circumstances that support the writer's opinion, can all be relevant factors in argument construction. How the expression of sentiment might contribute to essay quality will, most likely, play out differently for varying essay modes (e.g., expository, persuasive, or summary writing). For instance, in an expository essay writing task, the writer might be asked to form an opinion about an issue (e.g., *Sports figures should earn higher salaries than medical doctors.*). A simple illustration of how a sentiment analysis system might be used to evaluate essay quality would be the following. The writer forms a specific opinion in response to an issue. In the context of evaluating the essay, to ensure that the writer is on-task, a system that could identify the presence or absence of a personal opinion would be relevant to this task. Further, it would be useful to determine if the writer expresses a *personal opinion* (e.g., *I disagree with the statement that . . .*), or only makes reference to and discusses the issue in the prompt text, but never actually expresses a personal opinion (e.g., "*Some people believe that sports figures should earn higher salaries than medical doctors. People with this opinion argue that . . .*"). If a writer incorporates only an *attributed opinion* and never forms his or her own opinion, this might indicate that the essay response is off-task (i.e., has not responded to the specific writing task). In this case, the absence of personal opinion could affect the quality of the writing relative to the specific task.

In this chapter, we discuss the development and evaluation of a sentiment (subjectivity) analysis prototype system for the essay writing domain. This research effort will ultimately play a significant role in the analysis and evaluation of the quality of argumentation in student and test-taker essay writing.

RELATED WORK

Natural language processing (NLP)[2] research in sentiment analysis typically addresses three primary research streams, related to identification of: (a) words and terms that are linked to sentiment, used to build subjectivity lexicons; (b) subjectivity in sentences, clauses, phrases, and words in a context—that is, classifications of subjective and objective statements, and of positive, negative, and neutral polarity; and (c) subjectivity for specific applications, such as determining the sentiment orientation of reviews (Pang & Lee, 2004; Popescu & Etzioni, 2005; Turney, 2002), news headlines (Strapparava & Mihalcea, 2007), new articles (Wiebe, Wilson, & Cardie, 2005; Wilson, Wiebe, & Hoffmann, 2005), and blogs (Godbole, Srinivasaiah, & Skiena, 2007).

The research presented in this chapter focuses on the creation and evaluation of subjectivity lexicons which are critical in the development of automated sentiment analysis systems. We use vocabulary from essay data for this task. We discuss an innovation into the lexicon building process by using a paraphrase generation system to do automated expansion of a small seed lexicon. Further, this work investigates how the role of *intensity estimations* for sentiment words in our lexicon may obtain greater accuracy of a sentiment analysis system, i.e., improved accuracy for the assignment of sentiment and related polarity to sentences. Intensity estimations will be discussed in more detail later in the chapter. However, the general concept challenges the traditional notion that a word is associated with a single polarity (positive, negative, or neutral) (Wilson, Wiebe, & Hwa, 2004). Rather, we assume that a word is associated with varying degrees of positivity, negativity, and neutrality. For instance, "*happy*" has a strong positive intensity, and "*sad*" has a strong negative intensity. By contrast, our research has indicated that for some words, such as "*ambiguous*," the polarity is not as clear-cut. We will show later how the use of intensity profiles that express a word's relationship to positivity, negativity, and neutrality contribute to improved system performance. Improved performance allows us to make better predictions about the sentiment and polarity of sentences in our essay data. This is critical in the larger picture of accurate detection of argument construction in essay writing (e.g., where the writer's opinions or claims occur). The concept of intensity of a word is discussed further in this section in the context of other research. Later in the chapter, our method for estimating a word's intensity profile is described.

The first step in our work was to compile a comprehensive list of words with clear *prior polarity*. *Prior polarity* is a term used to refer to the mostly likely polarity for a word when that word is in isolation. For example, "*happy*" is likely to have positive prior polarity, and "*sad*" is likely to have negative prior polarity. Of course, the prior polarity of a word can change given a context (e.g., *not happy*; *not sad*). Probably the largest research initiative in this area is the work of Wiebe and colleagues. A concrete outcome of various annotation studies is the Multi-Perspective Question Answering (MPQA) subjectivity lexicon, freely available for research[3] (Riloff & Wiebe, 2003; Wiebe et al., 2005; Wilson et al., 2005). This lexicon contains a list of words labeled with information about polarity, and the *intensity* of the polarity (strong or weak). In more recent work, lexicons that include word sense information are also freely available and are extensions of this work (Gyamfi, Wiebe, Mihalcea, & Akkaya, 2009; Wiebe & Mihalcea, 2006). Additional lexicons include the classic General Inquirer (GI; Stone, Dunphy, Smith, & Ogilvie, 1966), and SentiWordNet (Esuli & Sabastiani, 2006). Custom-built lexicons with wide coverage exist as well (Taboada, Brooke, Tofiloski, Voll, & Stede, 2011). In our work, the lexicons we develop are compared to both MPQA and GI to provide comparative performance and coverage evaluations. These are the standard evaluation resources in the NLP literature about lexicon creation and evaluation for automated sentiment analysis.

A central part of the work described in this chapter discusses our work on lexicon building (Andreevskaia & Bergler, 2006; Esuli & Sabastiani, 2006; Hu & Liu, 2004; Kamps, Marx, Mokken, & de Rijke, 2004; Kanayama & Nasukawa, 2006; Kim & Hovy, 2004; Strapparava & Valitutti, 2004; Takamura, Inui, & Okumura, 2005). In the context of lexicon building, we describe and show evaluations for three methods for automated lexicon expansion. The first two mentioned are common in the literature. The most popular source for expansion is WordNet (Miller, 1995). In other research, distributional similarity methods are used to expand a lexicon, given a small "starter" seed set of positive and negative words (Turney, 2002; Turney & Littman, 2003; Yu & Hatzivassiloglou, 2003). Similarly, we use Lin's (1998) distributional thesaurus for lexicon expansion. In a nutshell, this thesaurus offers a list of words that are related based on the likelihood that they will appear in the same context in a text. For each word in the thesaurus, there is an associated word list, and each word has a value that suggests the likelihood (a value between 0 and 1) that the word will appear in the same context as the source word. For example, in the Lin thesaurus, the adjective, "*astonished*," is shown to be strongly related to "*bemused*," "*shocked*," and "*awestruck*," while other words, such as "*amazed*," "*surprised*," and "*perplexed*," are also shown to be related—these words have weaker relationships based on their lower likelihood values. In a third method, we use a paraphrase generation system for lexicon expansion. Over the last decade, data-driven paraphrase generation has become an extremely active area in NLP. In particular, it has been used to improve several tasks such as query expansion in information retrieval (Metzler, Dumais, & Meek, 2007; Riezler, Vasserman, Tsochantaridis, Mittal, & Liu, 2007), evaluation of NLP systems (Kauchak & Barzilay, 2006; Owczarzak, Groves, van Genabith, & Way, 2006; Zhou, Lin, Muntenau, & Hovy, 2006), and statistical machine translation (Callison-Burch, Koehn, & Osborne, 2006; Madnani & Dorr, 2010; Madnani, Resnik, Dorr, & Schwartz, 2008). To our knowledge, ours is the first attempt to use a paraphrase generation system for expanding a subjectivity lexicon.

As discussed above, the MPQA lexicon contains *intensity* labels that indicate the strength of a particular sentiment word. This is the outcome of early research by Wilson, Wiebe, and Hwa (2004) who used intensity values to evaluate a system for detecting not only subjective versus objective sentences in text, but the intensity (or strength) of a subjective statement. An example of *low* and *high* intensity words is "*support*," and "*accused*," respectively. Wilson et al. (2004) use various machine learning approaches to evaluate systems that identify opinion statements at the clause level, whereby in nested clause structures, the clause with the highest strength determines the sentiment strength of the whole sentence. For example, due to their strong negative sentiment, the words <u>accused</u> and <u>warmongering</u> would drive the negative sentiment of this sentence: "*President Mohammad Khatami of Iran, whose attempt at reforms have gotten American support, <u>accused</u> the United States of <u>warmongering</u>.*" In this research, Wilson et al. collected annotations on vocabulary polarity, and the strength (*high*, *medium*, and *low*) of the polarity for a given word. In addition to the relative intensity of a word, they also introduce a number of syntactic features that contribute to intensity assignment; their system combines both lexical and syntactic clues. Evaluations indicated that lexical intensity labels in combination with syntactic clues (i.e., grammatical structures) yielded the best performance.

Previously, Andreevskaia and Bergler (2006) challenged the conventional notion that all sentiment words are equal in the context of a sentiment class: *positive*, *negative*, and *neutral*. Rather, they asserted that there was some fuzziness among words represented in the three sentiment classes. So, while some members of a sentiment class, such as *good* (positive) and *bad* (negative) have clear membership in a polarity class, membership for other words may be less well-defined (fuzzier). Our work, as described in this chapter, is consistent with this approach. However, it takes this notion a step further in the context of system building. In terms of how to obtain information about "fuzziness," Andreevskaia and Bergler point out, for instance, that in annotation studies, lower inter-annotator agreement about a word's sentiment can be an indicator that a word might not be clearly defined in a particular sentiment class. Andreevskaia and Bergler use WordNet lexical relations and glosses to automatically annotate lists of sentiment words. Their method starts with creating 58 non-intersecting seed word sets from a set of manu-ally-annotated adjectives from Hatzivassiloglou and McKeown (HM; 1997). The system expands on these seed words using WordNet synonyms and antonyms. Then entries that contain the definitions for the set of sentiment-bearing words from the extended seed list are added to further expand the list. Clean-up is performed by removing "expan-sion" words that do not match the part-of-speech of the source words. The seed sets plus the unique expansions are used to build a final sentiment word lexicon. For their experiments, the GI (Stone, Dunphy, Smith, & Ogilvie, 1966) list of adjectives is used as the gold-standard for comparison to evaluate the accuracy of polarity assignments in the final set. To determine the *centrality* (strength) of a particular word, Andreevskaia and Bergler (2006) subtracted the number of times a word retrieved from WordNet was assigned negative polarity (based on its source word) from the number of times it was assigned positive polarity (based on its source word) to compute a score that describes, for each word, its strength with regard to a particular polarity. For instance, if a word was retrieved five times from source words with negative polarity, and five times from source words with positive polarity, it was more likely to have *less* strong, ambiguous (or neutral) polarity, than be assigned to any particular polarity. They also point out that for words with neutral polarity based on this formula in the HM data (which had been manually annotated for polarity), that inter-annotator agreement tended to be lower at about 20%. There is, therefore, a positive relationship between inter-annotator agree-ment on the polarity of a word and the strength of its polarity. In part, Andreevskaia and Bergler's work motivated our *crowdsourcing* annotation effort with CrowdFlower (CF).[4] Briefly, crowdsourcing is an efficient and less costly process of collecting intel-ligence from the broader population. For linguistic annotation, for instance, researchers can post annotation tasks through online businesses (such as CF), and collect thousands of annotations in a number of hours or days for a relatively low cost (depending on the complexity of the task). In our CF annotation effort, we collected manual annotations for sentiment words in our lexicons, and generated *intensity estimations*. Our notion was that a word is *not* necessarily associated with a strict polarity. Rather, words can have a relative intensity, with respect to a particular polarity. Our specific crowdsourcing task and results are discussed later in this chapter.

Taboada et al. (2011) describe a sentiment detection system that uses polarity and inten-sity to classify polarity (i.e., whether a statement is positive or negative). Taboada et al., similarly to Wilson et al. (2004) and Andreyevskaya and Bergler (2006) use the working assumption that words cannot be assumed to have equal polarity, even if they tend to be used more often with one polarity than another. Taboada et al. (2011) collect manual annotations for intensity on a 5-point scale for entries in a subjectivity lexicon. Annotators labeled positive words on a +1 through +5 scale, and negative words on a −1 through −5 scale. Higher absolute numbers indicated stronger intensity, so +5 (*masterpiece*) would indicate the strongest level of positivity, and −5 (*monstrosity*) would indicated the strongest level of negativity. Using their lexicon with + and − values associated with each word, they identified sentiment words in a sentence, and used the total sum of the values to determine if a sentence was positive, negative, or neutral. Morphological analyses were used to assign values to words in texts that were not in the lexicon, using stemming to assign the same values to words with the same stem. More complex assignments were performed to handle cases where modifiers, such as negation, for instance, might shift a word's polarity. Essentially, Taboada et al.'s (2011) work uses a scale instead of uniform values for assigning polarity to words which ultimately determine the polarity of a sentence. The scale was validated using an Amazon Mechanical Turk (AMT)[5] crowdsourcing annotation task.

In our work described in the following sections, we describe the creation and evaluation of a family of lexicons, starting with a standard seed lexicon, and using various expansion methods to automatically build a set of lexicons. An annotation study is conducted to collect annotations for the purpose of deriving intensity estimate values for words in the lexicons. These values were derived from inter-annotator agreement values from a large set of crowdsourced annotations from CF. The intensity profile estimates tell us if the strength of a particular word as a positive, negative, or neutral entity. This is consistent with Wiebe et al.'s (2005) research that asserts that the higher the inter-annotator agreement with regard to subjective expressions, the stronger the intensity of the expression. It is also consistent with Andreevskaia and Bergler's (2006) findings that lower inter-annotator agreement about word polarity suggests that the word is more likely to be neutral.

We develop and evaluate systems that challenge the conventional notion that a word is a member of a single polarity class, specifically, *positive, negative, or neutral.* In this scenario, some words have a more strict membership to a polarity, while others have a softer membership. The development of a set of subjectivity lexicons is described, and an evaluation of these lexicons is conducted to determine the quality of the expansion methods in the assignment of sentiment and polarity labels at the sentence level. An annotation study is conducted to derive estimation values used to build the intensity profiles. Another evaluation is conducted to show the affect of enhancing lexicons with intensity profiles that represent the degrees positivity, negativity, and neutrality for a word.

THE PROCESS OF BUILDING SUBJECTIVITY LEXICONS

Seed Lexicon

First, we randomly sampled 5,000 essays from a corpus of about 100,000 essays containing writing samples across many topics. Essays were responses to several different writing assignments, including graduate school entrance exams, non-native English speaker proficiency exams, and a professional licensure exam. We manually selected sentiment words with more clear positive and negative sentiment (e.g., *happy* and *sad*) from the full list of word types in these data; these constitute our Lexicon 0 which contained 407 words.

We sampled 878 sentences containing at least one word from the Lexicon 0 to increase the number of sentiment-bearing, positive (POS) and negative (NEG) sentences, and to decrease the proportion of neutral sentences (NEU). Using these sentences, the following annotation task was performed. Two research assistants annotated the set of 878 sentences as positive, negative, or neutral; 248 of these sentences were also annotated to indicate the specific words in a sentence that contributed to the sentiment of the sentence, and additional sentiment bearing words that may have opposite polarity (as in the example below). The following sentence, (1), was labeled as positive. Words contributing to the positive sentiment are bold-faced, and words and phrases with secondary (negative) polarity are underlined.

(1)

> Some may even be **impressed** that we are **confident** enough to <u>risk</u> showing a <u>lower net income</u>.

We refer to the 248 sentence set as S-1, and to the 630 sentence set as S-2.

In addition, positive and negative sentences from the TRAIN-1 data set (see "Training and Testing Data Sets" below) were annotated using the crowdsourcing resource AMT. In this task, five AMT annotators identified words that contributed to the overall sentiment of the sentence; all words marked by at least three AMT annotators were retained for inclusion in the lexicon.

Finally, the Seed Lexicon was created by adding to Lexicon 0 all words[6] marked in S-1 annotations and all words retained from the AMT annotations; the authors then performed a manual clean-up. The resulting Seed Lexicon contained 750 words: 406 positive and 344 negative. (S-2 was not used in lexicon creation. However, S-2 labeled sentences in that set were used in the evaluation experiments described in "Training and Testing Data Sets.")

Automatically Expanding the Seed Lexicon

We used three sources to automatically expand the Seed Lexicon: WordNet (Miller, 1995), Lin's distributional thesaurus (Lin, 1998), and a broad coverage pivot-based paraphrase generation tool (Madnani & Dorr, forthcoming). The resulting lexicons will be called Lexicon-WN, Lexicon-Lin, and Lexicon-Para, respectively; they were created as follows (also see Beigman-Klebanov et al., 2012).

Lexicon-WN

We used WordNet to extract the first three synonyms of the first sense of each word in the Seed Lexicon, restricting returned words to those with the same part-of-speech as the original word. The selection process was based on previous research (Burstein & Pedersen, 2010), that showed that these constraints are likely to produce strong synonym candidates without a large number of false positives.

Lexicon-Lin

Lin's proximity-based thesaurus trained on our in-house essay data as well as on well-formed newswire texts provided an additional resource for lexicon expansion (Leacock & Chodorow, 2003). All words with the proximity score greater than 1.80 to any of the Seed Lexicon words were included in the expansion. This threshold was empirically determined through a manual evaluation of outputs (see Burstein & Pedersen, 2010 for details), and also happens to be close to the mean score, 0.172. Values lower than 0.180 tended to produce a large number of contextually-similar antonyms, thus undermining the separation between POS and NEG parts of the lexicon.

Lexicon-Para

We used a pivot-based lexical and phrasal paraphrase generation system. This system operates by extracting bilingual correspondences from a bilingual corpus, identifying phrases and words in language A that all correspond to the same phrase or word in language B and, finally, pivoting on the common phrase or word in order to extract all the language A words and phrases as paraphrases of each other. More details about the system can be found in Bannard and Callison-Burch (2005). We use the French–English parallel corpus (approx. 1.2 million sentences) from the corpus of European parliamentary proceedings (Koehn, 2005) as the data on which pivoting is performed to extract the paraphrases. However, the base paraphrase system is susceptible to large amounts of noise due to the imperfect bilingual word alignments. Therefore, we implement additional heuristics in order to minimize the number of noisy paraphrase pairs (Madnani & Dorr, forthcoming). For example, one such heuristic filters out any pairs where a function word may have been inferred as a paraphrase of a content word. For lexicon expansion experiments, we use the top 15 single-word paraphrases for every word from the Seed Lexicon, excluding morphological variants of the seed word.

We note that *only* the distributional thesaurus is based on in-domain data, while the other expansions use either a general-purpose dictionary (WordNet), or out-of-domain training materials (parliamentary proceedings). It therefore remains to be seen whether the generated expansions are sufficiently general to apply to our domain.

Manual Clean-up of Expanded Lexicons

The expanded lexicons did require some clean-up. For example, antonyms of positive words ended up in the positive lexicon. This could happen, especially when using the distributional thesaurus, since antonyms and their synonyms tend to appear in the same distributions (for example, a *good* paper; a *bad* paper). In order to narrow down the expansions to words that carry positive or negative sentiment, we employed AMT again. All words generated by at least one expansion mechanism were included in this new task. This time, AMT annotators were asked to label single words as positive, negative, or neutral. Each word received three annotations. Two filtering criteria were used to generate the Cleaned versions based on the original Lexicon- expanded lexicon: (a) each word had be tagged as POS or NEG polarity by the majority of the three annotators, and (b) the majority polarity had to match the expected polarity of the word, that is, the polarity of the word from the Seed Lexicon for which the current word had been generated as an expansion. The clean-up procedures resulted in a 35% to 45% reduction in the Lexicon-lexicon sizes (see Table 17.2 for the sizes of the Lexicon- and Cleaned lexicons), although the cleaned lexicons are still at least twice the size of the Seed Lexicon.

Automatic Clean-up of Expanded Lexicons Through Lexicon Combination

We experimented with an alternative, automated strategy for noise reduction in the expanded lexicons. This strategy is based on the assumption that the three sources and mechanisms of expansion are sufficiently different to provide independent evidence of a word's relatedness to the seed word it was expanded from. Therefore, in the generation of new lexicons, where automated clean-up was applied, we introduced into the new lexicon *only* words that were produced by both of the two expansion methods of choice. Thus, we created the Lexicon-WN + Lexicon-Lin lexicon that contains the Seed Lexicon expanded with words with the same polarity that were in both Lexicon-WN and Lexicon-Lin. Lexicon-WN + Lexicon-Para and Lexicon-Lin + Lexicon-Para were generated in a similar fashion. This procedure resulted in the elimination of up to 67% of the larger of the two Lexicon- lexicons; for the lexicon sizes, see Table 17.2. Still, these new lexicons are 21–58% larger than the Seed Lexicon, providing significant expansion without human intervention.

EVALUATING THE QUALITY OF THE LEXICONS

Evaluation Methodology

We used C5.0 (Quinlan, 1993), a decision-tree classifier, to evaluate the effectiveness of the different lexicons for *classifying sentiment polarity of sentences*. Two features were created using our lexicons: (1) the number of positive words from the lexicon in the sentence, and (2) the number of negative words from the lexicon in the sentence. A number of experiments were conducted with additional features, but using only these two features produced the highest accuracies. For instance, an additional feature that was tried was the difference between the number of positive and negative words in a sentence. This is relevant since a sentence with a positive polarity, for instance, can contain negative words as shown in the example sentence (1), above. We hypothesized that a large difference in counts might help to predict the dominant polarity. However, adding this difference feature did not improve performance.

Training and Testing Data Sets

To generate the data for training and testing, the following strategies were employed. We used our pool of 100,000 essays to sample a second, non-overlapping set of 5,000 essays. From these essays, we randomly sampled 550 sentences, and these were annotated for sentiment polarity by the two research assistants. Fifty of the sentences were annotated by both annotators. Kappa was 0.8 for inter-annotator agreement on these sentences. Sentences labeled as incomprehensible or those where the annotators disagreed on positive or negative polarity were removed. The remaining sentences were randomly split between TRAIN-1 and TEST sets, except for the 43 sentences out of the 50 double-annotated ones for which the annotators were in agreement. These 43 sentences were added to the TEST set. TRAIN-1 contained 247 sentences. TEST contained 281 sentences, and was the set used for the blind testing reported in Table 17.3.

As a second step, in order to augment the training set, we utilized the data initially used for lexicon development. Recall that S-1 and S-2 had been created with a bias towards positive and negative polarity sentences (see "Seed Lexicon," above); this resulted in a significantly smaller proportion of neutral sentences in S-1 and S-2 (11%) than in the TRAIN-1 set (39%). In order to create a larger training set that matched, we sampled data from S-1 and S-2 for the purpose of matching the category distributions in TRAIN-1. Adding the new items to TRAIN-1, we now have TRAIN-2 (482 sentences), doubling the amount of training data and retaining the TRAIN-1 distribution of categories.

In order to further expand the training data without changing its category distribution, we used the remaining positive and negative annotated sentences in S-1 and S-2 and undertook the following procedure to collect more neutral sentences. Using a different essay pool with the same sub-modes of essays, we randomly sampled 1000 sentences with a condition that was complementary to the one used to produce S-1 and S-2, that is, *none* of the sampled sentences match any word in Lexicon 0 (see "Seed Lexicon," above).

Table 17.1 Sizes of the Training and Test Sets for C5.0 Experiments

Data set	# Sentences
TRAIN-1	247
TRAIN-2	482
TRAIN-3	1631
TEST	281

This way, we obtained a higher percentage of neutral sentences in the sample. This new 1000 sentence set was submitted to AMT, and all sentences with a majority vote of neutral out of three AMT annotator labels were considered to be acceptable neutral sentences. We then added these neutral sentences, along with the appropriate number of positive and negative sentences from S-1 and S-2[7] to maintain the category distribution of TRAIN-1 and TRAIN-2, and produced the final, largest training set, TRAIN-3. Table 17.1 summarizes the sizes of all three training sets and of the test set. The distribution of categories is the same in all training sets: 39% NEU, 35% POS, 26% NEG.

Effective Coverage

Before moving to a system evaluation that examines the performance of lexicons in a sentence-level sentiment polarity classification task, we checked whether or not the expansion strategies actually succeeded in expanding the *effective coverage* of our training data. Specifically, we examined whether the words added during expansion appear in our three training sets. This question is especially pertinent to our expansion strategies that used corpus-independent material (such as WordNet) or out-of-domain material, like the paraphrase generation tool. Table 17.2 shows the sizes of the lexicons as well as the number of different words from the lexicon that were in fact observed in the TRAIN-1, TRAIN-2, and TRAIN-3 data sets. Note that there is no guarantee that an observed word is a sentiment-bearing word; performance of each lexicon in the evaluation through sentiment classification as reported in the next section addresses this aspect of the expansion process.

Table 17.2 shows that even the most conservative expansion (Lexicon-WN + Lexicon-Lin) is 20% bigger than the Seed Lexicon and has 17% more coverage than the Seed Lexicon for the largest training set. We also note that both the manually- and the auto-

Table 17.2 Sizes and Effective Sizes of the Various Subjectivity Lexicons

Lexicon	# Words#	Words in TRAIN-1	#Words in TRAIN-2	#Words in TRAIN-3
Seed Lexicon	750	202	398	688
Lexicon- WN	2929	546	957	1527
Lexicon- Lin	2106	348	652	1119
Lexicon- Para	3437	771	1287	2022
Cleaned WN	1599	292	553	947
Cleaned Lin	1611	265	508	896
Cleaned Para	1951	430	758	1266
Lexicon-WN + Lexicon-Lin	981	241	471	804
Lexicon-WN + Lexicon-Para	1182	350	627	999
Lexicon-Lin + Lexicon-Para	1162	267	515	876
MPQA	7629	261	518	1022
GI	4204	263	514	940

Table 17.3 Accuracy of C5.0 Classification of Sentiment Polarity

Lexicon	TRAIN-1	TRAIN-2	TRAIN-3
Majority Baseline	0.390	0.390	0.390
Seed Lexicon	0.520	0.513	0.513
Lexicon- WN	0.451	0.469	0.448
Lexicon- Lin	0.455	0.448	0.469
Lexicon- Para	0.422	0.505	0.469
Cleaned WN	0.495	0.523	0.523
Cleaned Lin	0.538	0.505	0.491
Cleaned Para	0.473	0.484	0.498
Lexicon- WN + Lexicon- Lin	0.545	0.505	0.491
Lexicon- WN + Lexicon- Para	0.498	0.484	**0.556**
Lexicon- Lin + Lexicon- Para	0.509	0.516	0.487
MPQA	0.520	0.538	0.542
GI	0.462	0.527	0.487

matically-cleaned lexicons are on par with MPQA and GI, the state-of-the-art lexicons, in terms of effective coverage, even though they are at least 50% smaller in overall size.

Prediction of Sentiment Polarity

Table 17.3 summarizes the accuracy of C5.0 classifier on TEST using counts of POS and NEG words as features, across various lexicons and the three cumulatively larger training sets. For the best system (0.556) the following are the Precision (P), Recall (R), and F-measures (F) for the POS, NEG, and NEU categories: POS: P = 0.58, R = 0.46, F = 0.51; NEG: P = 0.49, R = 0.34, F = 0.40; NEU: P = 0.56, R = 0.73, F = 0.63. A system's Precision on a specific sentence polarity (e.g., POS) is the number of positive assignments that both the system and the human annotator agreed are "positive," divided by the number of sentences that the system labeled "positive." Recall is the number of positive sentences that both the system and the human annotator agreed are "positive," divided by the number of sentences that the human labeled "positive." The F-score is the harmonic mean of precision and recall.

Summary

The top system outperformed systems that used the state-of-the-art MPQA lexicon (0.542) and GI lexicon (0.527). Recall that the current nature of the MPQA and GI licensing agreements does not allow us to use these lexicons in our commercial systems, so we had to develop our own lexicon using our essay data. Therefore, we have shown that it is feasible to build a competitive subjectivity lexicon from scratch using the steps described in this paper. In the next section, we discuss the more innovative phase of our lexicon development research using crowdsourcing to derive *intensity profile estimations* of words. Enhancement of lexicons with intensity profiles continues to be a building block of in this research effort.

INTENSITY PROFILE ESTIMATION FOR SYSTEM BUILDING

As discussed in "Related Work" above, other research that uses intensity for prediction of sentiment and polarity in sentiment analysis systems assigns intensity estimation values to words based on the strength of their membership to a particular polarity class—specifically, *positive*, *negative*, or *neutral*. Consistent with Andreeskaya and Bergler (2006), our research challenges this standard notion and assumes that words are not necessarily associated with a particular polarity. Rather, words belong to all three polarities, but with varying degrees (or likelihood).

Intensity Annotation With CF

The intensity estimation values that were derived from a CF annotation task yield a likelihood value about a word's relative intensity across *all* three polarity classes. Details about the annotation task, intensity profile estimations, and use of the estimated profile values for system evaluations are described in the following sections.

CF Annotation Task

The CF[8] crowdsourcing site was used for this annotation task. All words from our Seed Lexicon, Lexicon-WN, Lexicon-Lin, and Lexicon-Para lexicons (see "The Process of Building Subjectivity Lexicons" above) were annotated by at least 20 annotators. Recall that the Seed Lexicon was created manually, and the Lexicon-WN, Lin, and Para lexicons were each created based on a different automated expansion method. This final, combined word list was composed of over 4900 words. In this task, annotators were instructed to assign a word a positive, negative, or neutral label. The word was shown in isolation. Strong, unambiguous examples of positive, negative, and neutral words were provided in the following instructions.

> In this task, you will be shown a word. Your job is to label the word as positive, negative or neutral. Positive words are used to describe something good, negative words are used to describe something bad and neutral words are neither positive nor negative. For example, the words "politeness", "lovely" and "fairness" are positive. The words "attacked", "misgivings" and "insufficiently" are negative. The words "say", "there", and "desk" are neutral. This task will help us design a system to detect the sentiment of a sentence in a piece of text.

For the CF task, a set of gold-standard answers (i.e., words that we are fairly certain had clear positive or negative a priori polarity) are distributed among the larger set of words for the annotators to label. In crowdsourcing tasks, annotators may just randomly click on responses to earn money quickly, and don't necessarily take the task seriously. To reduce the number of non-serious annotators, annotators must respond correctly to a high proportion of the gold answers, or they are not allowed to complete the full task. Therefore, we have reasonable confidence that our annotations are reasonable. Annotators were shown words in sets of ten, and responded to as many sets of ten as they wanted to. Annotations were collected until we had at least 20 annotations per word. Data collection took less than eight hours.

Each of the words in the final word list was labeled as positive, negative, or neutral by at least 20 annotators. From these annotations, we created a final COMBINED Lexicon. For each of the approximately 4900 words, a proportion was derived representing the proportion of positive and negative judgments based on the 20 annotations. Each word now had a value indicating its likelihood of being positive, negative, or neutral. An excerpt of the list is in Table 17.4. The total POS + NEG + NEU intensity will add up to 1.0. *Intensity profile estimations* were computed by dividing the total number of

Table 17.4 Example Intensity Profile Estimations for Lexicon Words

Word	POS	NEG	NEU
familiarize	0.70	0.00	0.30
fancy	1.0	0.00	0.00
logically	0.70	0.00	0.30
lone	0.00	1.00	0.00
ludicrous	0.03	0.93	0.03
mad	0.00	1.00	0.00
made	0.13	0.00	0.87
magic	0.80	0.00	0.20
magical	0.95	0.00	0.05
unequaled	0.45	0.10	0.45

judgments for a specific polarity by the total 20 judgments. For instance, for the first example "*familiarize*," the intensity profile estimates are as follows: POS = 0.70 (14/20); NEG = 0.0 (0/20); NEU = 0.3 (6/20).

Evaluation

In state-of-the-art sentiment analysis systems, words have intensity profiles specific to a single polarity class. In this section, we present results that illustrate that the use of intensity estimations in which a word that has an intensity value for positive, negative, and neutral classes outperforms a system that uses the conventional notion in which words are assigned strict positive, negative, and neutral polarity.

Data Sets

For this evaluation, the larger, TRAIN-3, set containing 1631 sentences labeled for polarity was used for training. The TEST data set containing 281 sentences labeled for polarity was used for the blind test set. The number of sentences for each polarity is shown in Table 17.1.

System Building Methods

In this section, we describe the lexicon-based features developed for system evaluation, and we report system results using a baseline system that *does not* make use of the intensity profiles, and two systems that *do*. The methods for each system used in the comparison are described in this section. Feature descriptions are illustrated in Table 17.5.

Features

As illustrated in Table 17.5, three feature sets were used, each using different information about polarity and intensity. The Baseline system simply used counts of words associated with a single polarity. The SUMS system summed each word's positive and negative intensity estimation values. The 10-BINS method took advantage of the fine-grained intensity profile estimation values associated with polarity membership for a word. The confidence intervals of 0.2 (bin sizes) were computed following Goodman (1965) and Quesenberry and Hurst (1964).

Table 17.5 System Features and Descriptions

System	# of Features	Feature Descriptions
Baseline	2	• Feature 1 : <u>Lexicon- counts</u> of words labeled as *positive* in lexicons (no intensity estimations) • Feature 2 : <u>Lexicon- counts</u> of words labeled as *negative* in lexicons (no intensity estimations)
SUMS	2	• Feature 1 : the <u>sum</u> of *positive* intensity estimation values for sentiment words • Feature 2 : the <u>sum</u> of *negative* intensity estimation values for sentiment words.
10 BINS	10	• Feature 1 : <u>Lexicon- counts</u> of words with intensity estimations: $0.0 < = x <= 0.2$ for *positivity* • Feature 2 : <u>Lexicon- counts</u> of words with intensity estimations: $0.2 < x < = 0.4$ for *positivity* • Feature 3 : <u>Lexicon- counts</u> of words with intensity estimations: $0.4 < x < = 0.6$ for *positivity* • Feature 4 : <u>Lexicon- counts</u> of words with intensity estimations: $0.6 < x < = 0.8$ for *positivity* • Feature 5 : <u>Lexicon- counts</u> of words with intensity estimations: $0.8 < x <= 1.0$ for *positivity* • Feature 6 : <u>Lexicon- counts</u> of words with intensity estimations: $0.0 <= x <= 0.2$ for *negativity* • Feature 7: <u>Lexicon- counts</u> of words with intensity estimations: $0.2 < x < = 0.4$ for *negativity* • Feature 8 : <u>Lexicon- counts</u> of words with intensity estimations: $0.4 < x < = 0. 6$ for *negativity* • Feature 9 : <u>Lexicon- counts</u> of words with intensity estimations: $0.6 < x < = 0.8$ for *negativity* • Feature 10 : <u>Lexicon- counts</u> of words with intensity estimations: $0.8 < x < = 1.0$ for *negativity*

Referring to Table 17.5 note that there are 10 "bins," each representing an interval of 0.2. Here is an example of how the bins are used to make feature assignments for sentiment-bearing words in a sentence. Using the intensity estimation values for "*familiarize*," from Table 17.4 (0.7, 0.0, 0.3), the positivity value is 0.7, so "1" (presence of this feature) would be assigned to Feature 4, and "0s" would be assigned to all other features (absence of these features).

Evaluation

For these evaluations, results for sentence-level assignment of <u>sentiment</u> (sentiment or non-sentiment bearing) are shown in Table 17.6; results for sentence-level assignment of <u>polarity</u> (positive, negative, and neutral) are presented in Table 17.7. Three machine learners are used in the evaluation: C5.0, Support Vector Machine (SVM), and Logistic Regression (LR). We wanted to see if different learners affected performance, and if the performance trends were consistent across learner. The three learners have fairly competitive results, and trends are identical. In Tables 17.6 and 17.7, best performance (boldface values) is competitive across machine learners using the Lexicon-Para Lexicon with the binning method. Lexicon-Para had generated the largest number of expansions with the greatest range of intensity estimations and so this was selected for this evaluation to compare using traditional single polarity assignments for words versus intensity estimations for words to classify sentences as sentiment or non-sentiment-bearing, and with specific polarity, positive, negative, or neutral. Results in Tables 17.6 and 17.7 illustrate that systems using binning methods that incorporate the intensity estimations outperform the baseline systems. Baseline systems use the version of the lexicon in which words are labeled only as positive or negative, and do not include the intensity estimations values in the feature set, but only counts of positive and negative word tokens (see Figure 17.2). Table 17.6 indicates performance for sentiment assignment only; specifically, the system's ability to classify a sentence as sentiment-bearing, or non-sentiment-bearing. Table 17.7 shows performance for the assignment of a specific polarity—positive, negative, and neutral.

CONCLUSIONS

Argumentation in essays is a critical measure of writing quality, as seen in scoring rubrics for standardized essay writing, as well as in the Common Core State Standards Initiative specifications for the teaching and evaluation of student writing. In this chapter, we have discussed automated sentiment analysis research that supports the advancement of capabilities for the analysis of argumentation in essay writing. While this is a highly relevant area for essay evaluation, given its potential to identify and evaluate argumentation, it has not yet been addressed in automated essay scoring. The work presented in this chapter shows promise toward building a sentiment analysis systems that can be used for essay scoring.

The longer-term aim of this research is build a system that can identify relevant aspects of essays related to sentiment that contribute to essay quality. We acknowledge the relevance of sentiment with regard to essay quality is also likely to vary by essay mode. For instance, the presence or absence of personal opinion (as discussed earlier), may contribute to the quality of expository writing. By contrast, in a summarization task that requires the writer to summarize to contrasting perspectives offered in the prompt text, the proportion of sentiment polarity in relation to the sentiment in the prompt text might be relevant to essay quality.

Table 17.6 System Performance—*Accuracy* of Sentiment Assignment

Machine Learner	Lexicon	Baseline	SUMS	10-BINS
C5.0	Seed	61.6	63.7	66.2
	Lexicon- Para	61.2	65.1	**68.7**
SVM	Seed	61.5	62.2	64.8
	Lexicon- Para	58.7	65.1	**67.9**
Logistic Regression	Seed	61.5	62.6	64.7
	Lexicon- Para	60.1	65.8	**70.4**

Table 17.7 System Performance—Accuracy of Polarity Assignment

Machine Learner	Lexicon	Baseline	SUMS	10-BINS
C5.0	Seed	51.2	56.6	58.7
	Lexicon- Para	45.9	61.6	**64.1**
SVM	Seed	52.6	54.8	57.3
	Lexicon- Para	46.2	60.1	**64.4**
Logistic Regression	Seed	54.4	55.5	58.3
	Lexicon- Para	51.2	58.3	**61.5**

As part of our effort to develop an operational system for identifying sentiment and polarity, we are, in parallel, exploring how sentiment analysis might apply to different essay modes. It is our longer-term goal to clearly identify relevant aspects of sentiment in essays that contribute to more construct- and mode-relevant scoring, but also as a way to provide explicit feedback related to sentiment and argumentation in essays.

ACKNOWLEDGMENTS

We would like to thank Joel Tetreault for his support in the annotation tasks associated with the first experiments for lexicon creation. We are very grateful to Daniel Blanchard and Diane Napolitano for software engineering support throughout this project.

NOTES

1 See Chapters 4 and 20 for more detailed discussions of the writing construct.
2 See Chapter 4 for a general discussion of NLP.
3 The lexicon is here: http://people.cs.pitt.edu/~wiebe/. Due to the nature of the licensing agreement, we cannot use this lexicon for commercial systems.
4 http://www.crowdflower.com
5 https://www.mturk.com/mturk/welcome
6 When annotators could not attribute sentiment to single words, they marked phrases. Our current lexicons make no use of multi-word annotations.
7 We added 160 positive sentences from the newly annotated 1000 to TRAIN-3, in order to retain the distribution of categories the same as in TRAIN-1.
8 http://crowdflower.com/

REFERENCES

Andreevskaia, A., & Bergler, S. (2006). *Mining WordNet for a fuzzy sentiment: Sentiment tag extraction from wordnet glosses.* Paper presented at the EACL.

Bannard, C., & Callison-Burch, C. (2005). *Paraphrasing with bilingual parallel corpora.* Paper presented at the ACL, Ann Arbor, MI.

Beigman-Klebanov, B., Burstein, J., Madnani, N., Faulkner, A., & Tetreault, J. (2012). Building subjectivity lexicon(s) from scratch for essay data. In A. Gelbulkh (Ed.), *Springer lecture notes in computer science.* Berlin: Springer-Verlag.

Burstein, J., & Pedersen, T. (2010). *Towards improving synonym options in a text modification application* (Vol. UMSI 2010/165), University of Minnesota Supercomputing Institute Research Report Series, November.

Callison-Burch, C., Koehn, P., & Osborne, M. (2006). *Improved statistical machine translation using paraphrases.* Paper presented at the NAACL, New York.

Esuli, A., & Sabastiani, F. (2006). *Determining term subjectivity and term orientation for opinion mining.* Paper presented at the EACL.

Godbole, N., Srinivasaiah, M., & Skiena, S. (2007). *Large scale sentiment analysis for news and blogs.* Paper presented at the ICWSM.

Goodman, L. (1965). On simultaneous confidence intervals for multinomial proportions. *Technometrics, 7*(2), 247–254.

Gyamfi, Y., Wiebe, J., Mihalcea, R., & Akkaya, C. (2009). *Integrating knowledge for subjectivity sense labeling.* Paper presented at the NAACL.

Hatzivassiloglou, V., & McKeown, K. (1997). *Predicting the semantic orientation of adjectives.* Paper presented at the ACL.

Hu, M., & Liu, B. (2004). *Mining and summarizing customer reviews*. Paper presented at the ACM SIGKDD International Conference on Knowledge Discovery and Data Mining, Seattle, WA.

Kamps, J., Marx, M., Mokken, R., & de Rijke, M. (2004). *Using WordNet to measure semantic orientation of adjectives*. Paper presented at the LREC.

Kanayama, H., & Nasukawa, T. (2006). *Fully automatic lexicon expansion for domain-oriented sentiment analysis*. Paper presented at the EMNLP.

Kauchak, D. and Barzilay, R. (2006). Paraphrasing for automatic evaluation. In *Proceedings of HLT-NAACL* (pp. 455–462), New York.

Kim, S., & Hovy, E. (2004). *Determining the sentiment of opinions*. Paper presented at the COLING.

Koehn, P. (2005). *EUROPARL: A parallel corpus for statistical machine translation*. Paper presented at the Machine Translation Summit.

Leacock, C., & Chodorow, M. (2003). C-rater: Scoring of short-answer questions. *Computers and the Humanities, 37*(4), 389–405.

Lin, D. (1998). *Automatic retrieval and clustering of similar words*. Paper presented at the 38th Annual Meeting of the Association for Computational Linguistics, Hong Kong.

Madnani, N., & Dorr, B. (2010). Generating phrasal & sentential paraphrases: A survey of data-driven methods. *Computational Linguistics, 36*(3), 341–387.

Madnani, N., & Dorr, B. (forthcoming). Generating targeted paraphrases for improved translation. *ACM Transactions on Intelligent Systems and Technology (Special Issue on Paraphrasing)*.

Madnani, N., Resnik, P., Dorr, B., & Schwartz, R. (2008). *Are multiple reference translations necessary? Investigating the value of paraphrased reference translations in parameter optimization*. Paper presented at the Eighth Conference of the Association for Machine Translation in the Americas (AMTA), Waikiki, HI.

Metzler, D., Dumais, S., & Meek, C. (2007). *Similarity measures for short segments of text*. Paper presented at the European Conference on Information Retrieval (ECIR), Rome

Miller, G. (1995). WordNet: A lexical database. *Communications of the ACM 38, 11*, 39–41.

Owczarzak, K., Groves, D., van Genabith, J., & Way, A. (2006). *Contextual bitext-derived paraphrases in automatic MT evaluation*. Paper presented at the Workshop on Statistical Machine Translation, New York.

Pang, B., & Lee, L. (2004). *A sentimental education: Sentiment analysis using subjectivity summarization based on minimum cuts*. Paper presented at the ACL.

Popescu, A., & Etzioni, O. (2005). *Extracting product features and opinions from reviews*. Paper presented at the HLT/EMNLP.

Quesenberry, C., & Hurst, D. (1964). Large sample simultaneous confidence intervals for multinomial proportions. *Technometrics, 6*, 191–195.

Quinlan, J. R. (1993). *C4.5: Programs for machine learning*. Burlington, MA: Morgan Kaufmann Publishers.

Riezler, S., Vasserman, A., Tsochantaridis, I., Mittal, V., & Liu, Y. (2007). *Statistical machine translation for query expansion in answer retreival*. Paper presented at the 45th Annual Meeting of the Association of Computational Linguistics, Prague, Czech Republic, June.

Riloff, E., & Wiebe, J. (2003). *Learning extraction patterns for subjective expressions*. Paper presented at the EMNLP.

Stone, P., Dunphy, D., Smith, M., & Ogilvie, D. (1966). *The General Inquirer: A computer approach to content analysis*. Cambridge, MA: MIT Press.

Strapparava, C., & Mihalcea, R. (2007). *SemEval-2007 task 14: Affective text*. Paper presented at the SemEval, Prague, Czech Republic.

Strapparava, C., & Valitutti, A. (2004). *WordNet-affect: And affective extension of Word-Net*. Paper presented at the LREC, Lisbon, Portugal.

Taboada, M., Brooke, J., Tofiloski, M., Voll, K., & Stede, M. (2011). Lexicon-based method for sentiment analysis. *Computational Linguistics, 37*(2), 267–307.

Takamura, H., Inui, T., & Okumura, M. (2005). *Extracting semantic orientation of words using spin model*. Paper presented at the ACL.

Turney, P. (2002). *Thumbs up or thumbs down? Semantic orientation applied to unsupervised classification of reviews*. Paper presented at the ACL, Philadelphia.

Turney, P., & Littman, M. (2003). Measuring praise and criticism: Inference of semantic orientation from association. *ACM Transactions on Information Systems 21*(4), 315–346.

Wiebe, J., & Mihalcea, R. (2006). *Word sense and subjectivity*. Paper presented at the ACL.

Wiebe, J., Wilson, T., & Cardie, C. (2005). Annotating expressions of opinions and emotions in language. *Language Resources and Evaluation, 39*(2–3), 165–210.

Wilson, T., Wiebe, J., & Hoffmann, P. (2005). *Recognizing contextual polarity in phrase level sentiment analysis*. Paper presented at the HLT-EMNLP.

Wilson, T., Wiebe, J., & Hwa, R. (2004). *Just how mad are you? Finding strong and weak opinion clauses*. Paper presented at the AAAI-2004.

Yu, H., & Hatzivassiloglou, V. (2003). *Towards answering opinion questions: Separating facts from opinions and identifying the polarity of opinion sentences*. Paper presented at the EMNLP, Morristown, New Jersey

Zhou, L., Lin, C., Muntenau, D., & Hovy, E. (2006). *ParaEval: Using paraphrases to evaluate summaries automatically*. Paper presented at the HLT-NAACL, New York.

18 Covering the Construct

An Approach to Automated Essay Scoring Motivated by a Socio-Cognitive Framework for Defining Literacy Skills

Paul Deane

1. INTRODUCTION

Much of the literature on automated essay scoring (AES) frames it as an attempt to model human essay scoring, with its assignment of scores or grades based upon a rubric. This is certainly the way that Project Essay Grade was originally conceptualized (Page, 1966, 1967), and it continues to be the default approach in most AES systems, including e-rater (Burstein & Chodorow, 2010; Burstein, Chodorow, & Leacock, 2003; Chodorow & Burstein, 2004; Powers, Burstein, Chodorow, Fowles, & Kukich, 2000, 2001), and the Intelligent Essay Assessor (Landauer, Laham, & Foltz, 2003), among others (Larkey & Croft, 2003). Some of the other chapters in this volume explore the strengths and limitations of this approach and possible ways to move beyond it (e.g., the chapters by Attali, Bridgman, Burstein and Williams). In this chapter, however, a slightly different approach will be explored. Rather than starting with human rubrics and human scores, and examining how much of the same information can be captured in an AES system, analysis will begin by considering a general cognitive framework, a construct model for writing, and then work forward to consider what aspects of the construct can and should be modeled in current and future approaches to automated writing assessment.

Since 2006, Educational Testing Service (ETS) has been developing an innovative approach to K–12 assessment that incorporates a developmental framework that links assessment goals with best instructional practices and the results of cognitive and learning sciences research. Several major themes emerge when this approach, "Cognitively Based Assessment of, for, and as Learning," or CBAL (Bennett, 2011; Bennett & Gitomer, 2009) is applied to literacy skills—to reading, writing, and their use to support thinking and learning (cf. Deane, 2011; Deane, Fowles, Baldwin, & Persky, 2011; Deane, Quinlan, & Kostin, 2011; Deane, Quinlan, Odendahl, Welsh, & Bivens-Tatum, 2008). In particular, the CBAL model emphasizes the critical roles of reading and writing, the importance of coordinating them, and the strong connection between reading, writing, and critical thinking skills. Similar themes emerge directly from the literature on the best practices in reading and writing instruction (Graham & Perin, 2007; Hillocks, 1986; Perin, 2009). In the present context, the CBAL initiative provides a detailed delineation of the skills and abilities that contribute to writing proficiency. These construct considerations have implications not only for the selection of features to include in AES applications, but also for the ways in which multiple sources of information—not just human scores—may be combined to provide stable criterion measures. This paper will examine the implications of the CBAL framework for AES, with an emphasis not just on assessing current systems, but on exploring potentially fruitful new research directions that would build on and extend current methods for automated writing assessment.

In particular, the following questions will be explored:

- What should be measured?
- How should AES interact with instruction?
- How do we define use cases for AES?

Note that these issues arise whether or not one explicitly makes use of a formal construct framework. The contribution of the framework is to systematize our thinking about various key elements—the construct definition, use cases, best practices in instruction, and measurement issues—and thus enables a more consistent approach to the entire range of issues.

The CBAL approach is a *socio-cognitive* approach, since it pays attention not only to the cognitive elements (skills, knowledge, and strategies) that enter into writing, but also to the social contexts and purposes for which it is deployed. This approach has important implications for construct definition. In particular, we may note the following points.

- **Product vs. Process.** Current AES engines focus on the final written product, and on writing quality as measured by human raters. A socio-cognitive perspective suggests that over the long term, it is also important to gather information about the writing process and the strategies employed by novice versus skilled writers.
- **Text Quality vs. Writing Skill.** Similarly, since current AES engines emphasize features extracted from the final written product, they provide direct evidence about text quality, not about writing skill as a teacher would understand it. When evaluated from a socio-cognitive perspective, text quality is a secondary and indeed, unstable, construct since writers may produce high quality text in one context and purpose (where they are familiar with the content, context, and social purpose of a writing task), and low quality text in another; and indeed, one and the same text may be considered high quality for some contexts and purposes, and low quality for others. A replicable definition of text quality, such as may be found in the Six Traits model or in holistic scoring rubrics and procedures, by definition makes assumptions about purpose, audience, and genre: i.e., that the text is written to inform or convince through rational argument; that the audience has no specialized knowledge of the subject nor any specific relationship with the author; and that it is to be read as an independent work, without presuppositions about what other texts the audience may have read. It is thus important to consider why particular features are positively associated with judgments of increased text quality, since the relationship between measurable features and writing skill is even more indirect than the relationship between measurable features and text quality.
- **Use Cases for AES.** AES is a perfect example of how specific use cases drive technological design, by creating assumptions that the software designers have no reason to question, even if (as may often be the case), other, different assumptions might create a different, and better, user experience. The technology and interface design of most current-generation AES systems are intended to provide a partial substitute for human holistic (or more recently, trait) scoring in which individual scorers apply a rubric to the final student text. Holistic scoring, in turn, was intended as a systematization of, and partial replacement for, the traditional school model in which a teacher sits in a room with a stack of student themes and a red pen. In both cases, the prototypical use case involves a student text, a score, and text mark-up intended to provide feedback to the writer. Formative applications of AES replicate this exact

use case, and are accepted, or attacked, on that basis. When evaluated from a socio-cognitive perspective, this is just one use case among many. It is easy to imagine how other kinds of interactions could be supported by AES systems. For instance, the features underlying an automated writing evaluation system could be used to provide different kinds of feedback during different stages of the writing process, or to provide differentiated feedback that was sensitive to differences in the genre of the text or the skill level of the writer. Automated methods could be used to support peer review, collaboration on joint projects, or a variety of other writing situations that do not fit the traditional school model. Since changing the use case may change the decisions one makes in building a model, this is not a trivial matter. Over the long term, AES systems may need to be re-imagined and reworked to support a broader range of use cases that will align well with modern best practices in writing instruction.

2. OVERVIEW OF THE CBAL LITERACY FRAMEWORK

More specific implications can be identified by considering the details of the CBAL literacy framework, or "competency model," which identifies relevant dimensions on which student writing skill may vary and which places these dimensions within a larger model of how novice writers gain in expertise. These dimensions are shared among a set of related constructs—reading, writing, critical thinking—which differ in how they mobilize these common resources to achieve different kinds of literate performance. For instance, effective writing demands skills that might more strictly be thought of as reading skills (such as re-reading to support revision and planning), while effective reading depends upon skills that critically incorporate writing, such as note-taking and summarization.

2.1 Key Analytical Elements

Several elements enter into the CBAL competency model. At the highest level of analysis, we must consider two fundamental dimensions:

- Basic types of cognitive process (interpretive processes such as reading and listening; expressive processes such as writing and speaking; deliberative processes requiring executive control, strategic planning, and reflection).
- Different modes of cognitive representation, e.g., print and auditory representations; verbal (linguistic) representations of form and meaning; textual/discourse (macrostructural) representations; conceptual representations; social representations involving communicative purpose, beliefs, affect, and social roles.

These elements combine to define the basic space of skills that support reading, writing, and critical thinking, as shown in Figure 18.1 (slightly modified from Deane, 2011, p. 8). At this level of abstraction, core writing processes involve expressive, or text production skills, in which the author engages with audience and purpose, conceptualizes what to say, structures those ideas into a coherent rhetorical plan, finds the right way to phrase those ideas, and transcribes them through handwriting or keyboarding processes to produce a text. But actual skilled writing processes may presuppose reading of source texts (and re-reading of one's own drafts), and may draw heavily on deliberative skills to support a nonlinear, iterative writing process in which a text may go through many

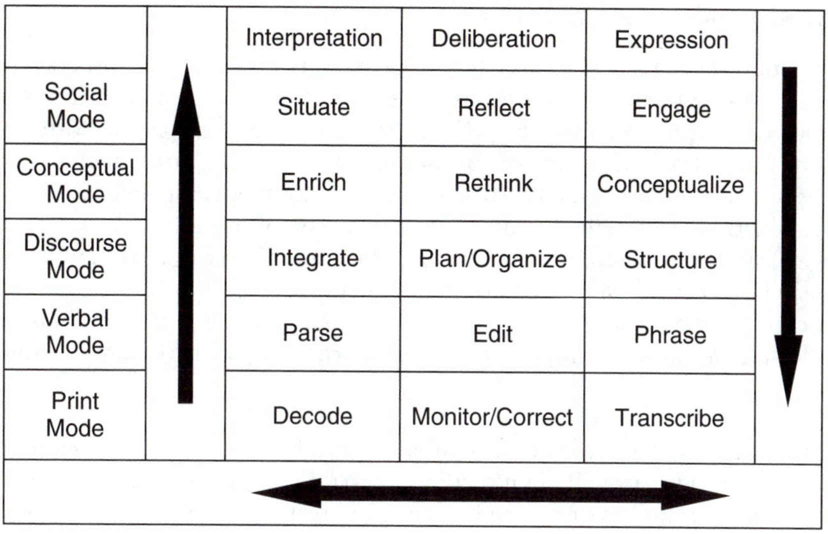

		Interpretation	Deliberation	Expression	
Social Mode		Situate	Reflect	Engage	
Conceptual Mode		Enrich	Rethink	Conceptualize	
Discourse Mode		Integrate	Plan/Organize	Structure	
Verbal Mode		Parse	Edit	Phrase	
Print Mode		Decode	Monitor/Correct	Transcribe	

Figure 18.1 Basic cognitive dimensions of literacy.

drafts as the writer works and reworks it at every level (Bereiter & Scardamalia, 1988; Hayes & Flower, 1980).

Obviously, the demands made by writing tasks will vary, both in the emphasis they place on particular cells in Figure 18.1, and in the specific skills on which they draw. Writing a persuasive text may require the writer to make use of rhetorical appeals (a social skill) and argument (a conceptual skill). By contrast, writing a narrative may require the writer to capture character traits, motivation and purpose (which will draw upon a different set of social and conceptual skills). In other words, no single skill will be equally useful in every genre and equally active at every stage of the writing process. It is useful to think of writing skill as involving the internalization of a set of activity systems (Hung & Chen, 2002; Jonassen & Rohrer-Murphy, 1999) that draw upon a general pool of literacy and reasoning skills.

Within this conceptualization, the development of writing skill involves the following elements:

1. Increased fluency and automatization of component skills, enabling the writer to address more challenging conceptual and rhetorical problems (Bereiter & Scardamalia, 1988).
2. Acquisition of new strategies for solving an ever-wider range of writing problems (Graham & Perin, 2007).
3. Internalization of previously-learned strategies, thus freeing up cognitive resources for more complex writing and thinking tasks (McCutchen, 1996, 2000).

It also emphasizes connections and co-dependencies among reading, writing, and thinking skills. Writing draws upon a common base of literacy skills, but expert writers can deploy those skills effectively and efficiently across a range of writing tasks that may impose very different specific requirements.

2.2. Defining the Writing Construct

The conception sketched in the preceding pages implies an expansive, process-oriented view of the writing construct. The resulting approach is consistent with the National Conference of Teachers of English (NCTE) Framework for Success in Postsecondary Education (Council of Writing Program Administrators, 2011), rather than with a view that focuses strictly on text quality, such as the Six Trait model (Spandel, 2005). A specific piece of writing may reflect a complex combination of specific skills and the impact of a range of strategies for coordinating them, which means, in turn, that a wide range of factors may influence the rubrics deployed in human scoring.

These considerations have important implications for how we reason about writing skill, and therefore how we approach AES. In particular, we may note the following points:

- **The Complexity of a Single Performance.** No writing task can be reduced to a single criterion. Rubric traits will often correspond to different levels of cognitive representation. Since the final written product is an indirect measure of key skills, no single writing sample is likely to provide strong and unambiguous evidence about any single skill. Much of a writer's skill lies in how they manage multiple, and competing, demands to produce an effective piece of writing.
- **The Ecology of Multiple Performances.** There are many different genres of writing, many different kinds of writing practices, and many different social roles that people may play within the ecology of written communication. We must concern ourselves not only with the written genre of the *essay*, but with other genres too. We must think about how we might measure not only the core text production process of *drafting a document*, but with other writing practices, such as planning, revision, and editing. We must worry not only about whether people can function well as authors, but whether they understand how to operate in such roles as reviewer, editor, and copyeditor. Somewhere in this space of possibilities we must draw the difference between different, but related, constructs. What skills make someone a good researcher, or a good editor, instead of a good writer?

A construct like "writing" is thus a compound, complex thing. It clearly includes everything that helps build expressive fluency, and all five modes of cognitive representation. But if we want to encourage skills realistically linked to the practices we want people to learn, we must consider other roles and skills where students must develop appropriate practices and strategies, and include those practices that also help to make people into effective writers.

3. IMPLICATIONS FOR AES

3.1. Limitations

One of the implications of the CBAL competency model is that we cannot expect all features of writing skill to be represented in the final written product. For example, if we examine the features used in e-rater, it is evident that these features provide direct evidence almost exclusively about three cells in Figure 18.1:

- **Structure** (e.g., paragraphs and transitions, thesis and topic sentences, transitional discourse markers, and cohesion across sentences).

- **Phrase** (e.g., vocabulary; sentence length and complexity, and stylistic choices).
- **Transcribe** (e.g., adherence to written conventions, such as those that govern grammar, usage, spelling, and mechanics).

Moreover, they do not provide equally strong information about all aspects of text quality, even if we focus attention on these three cells. The features included represent some kind of compromise between what is desirable (from a construct perspective), what is measurable (from a computational linguistics perspective), and what is feasible (in terms of the computing power and complexity of programming required to get reliable results).

The strong agreement observed between human scores and AES-derived scores may thus be partly due to reliance on similar rubrics, and partly due to a trade-off between text production and problem solving, as outlined in McCutchen (1996, 2000). Students who get low scores on writing tasks are likely to be challenged both by the requirements of text production and by the demands of social and conceptual reasoning. Conversely, students who score well on writing tasks are likely to display both fluent reading and fluent text production. To the extent that this situation holds, current AES systems may do well. But it is important to highlight the fact that they reflect a specific aspect of writing skill, and that analysis of writing from a broad construct perspective may reveal criteria that do not fall within the scope of the current AES construct.

Perhaps the simplest way to illustrate the point is to consider actual rubrics used to score CBAL tests. In recent pilots, two writing forms were administered: a persuasive essay topic ('Ban Ads') and a literary essay topic (an analysis of selections from *The House on Mango Street*). In 2011 pilot administrations (which sampled 8th-grade students from more than 20 middle schools across the U.S., cf. Cline, 2012) each essay was scored twice: once with a general writing rubric designed to cover the same construct that AES systems are intended to cover, and once with a genre-specific rubric focusing on the rhetorical and critical-thinking requirements of the task. Table 18.1 shows the correlations among the three rubrics for the 644 students who took both Ban Ads and *Mango Street*.

While there was a strong correlation between the general writing quality rubric and the argumentation rubric for Ban Ads (.79), there was a much lower correlation between the general writing quality rubric and the literary analysis rubric for *Mango Street* (.62). Despite the same rubric being used, the correlation between the general writing quality rubric for Ban Ads and *Mango Street* was only .53, presumably reflecting differences in performance contingent on genre and topic. Examination of the rubrics (Figures 18.2 through 18.4) demonstrates how very differently they are focused, despite the moderate to strong correlations between them.

Table 18.1 Correlations Among Human Essay Scores on Different Rubrics

	Ban Ads I (General Writing Quality)	**Ban Ads II** (Quality of Argumentation)	**Mango Street I** (General Writing Quality)
Ban Ads II (Quality of Argumentation)	.79		
Mango Street I (General Writing Quality)	.53	.49	
Mango Street II (Quality of Literary Analysis)	.42	.46	.62

**CBAL GENERIC SCORING GUIDE: DISCOURSE-LEVEL FEATURES
IN A MULTI-PARAGRAPH TEXT**

EXEMPLARY (5)

An EXEMPLARY response meets <u>all</u> of the requirements for a score of 4 but *distinguishes itself by skillful use of language, precise expression of ideas, effective sentence structure, and/or effective organization*, which work together to control the flow of ideas and enhance the reader's ease of comprehension.

CLEARLY COMPETENT (4)
A CLEARLY COMPETENT response typically displays the following characteristics:

<u>It is adequately structured.</u>
o   *Overall, the response is clearly and appropriately organized for the task.*
o   *Clusters of related ideas are grouped appropriately and divided into sections and paragraphs as needed.*
o   *Transitions between groups of ideas are signaled appropriately.*
<u>It is coherent.</u>
o   *Most new ideas are introduced appropriately.*
o   *The sequence of sentences leads the reader from one idea to the next with few disorienting gaps or shifts in focus.*
o   *Connections within and across sentences are made clear where needed by the use of pronouns, conjunctions, subordination, etc.*
<u>It is adequately phrased.</u>
o   *Ideas are expressed clearly and concisely.*
o   *Word choice demonstrates command of an adequate range of vocabulary.*
o   *Sentences are varied appropriately in length and structure to control focus and emphasis.*
<u>It displays adequate control of Standard Written English</u>
o   *Grammar and usage follow SWE conventions, but there may be minor errors.*
o   *Spelling, punctuation, and capitalization follow SWE conventions, but there may be minor errors.*

DEVELOPING HIGH (3)

A response in this category displays some competence but <u>differs from</u> Clearly Competent responses in at least one important way, including *limited development; inconsistencies in organization; failure to break paragraphs appropriately; occasional tangents; abrupt transitions, wordiness; occasionally unclear phrasing; little sentence variety; frequent and distracting errors in Standard Written English; or relies noticeably on language from the source material.*

DEVELOPING LOW (2)

A response in this category <u>differs from</u> Developing High responses because it displays serious problems such as *marked underdevelopment; disjointed, list-like organization; paragraphs that proceed in an additive way without a clear overall focus; frequent lapses in cross-sentence coherence; unclear phrasing; excessively simple and repetitive sentence patterns; inaccurate word choices; errors in Standard Written English that often interfere with meaning; or relies substantially on language from the source material.*

MINIMAL (1)

A response in this category <u>differs from</u> Developing Low responses because of serious failures such as *extreme brevity; a fundamental lack of organization; confusing and often incoherent phrasing; little control of Standard Written English; or can barely develop or express ideas without relying on the source material.*

NO CREDIT (0): *Not enough of the student's own writing for surface-level features to be judged, not written in English; completely off topic, blank, or random keystrokes.*

Figure 18.2 Generic rubric focusing on print, verbal and discourse features.

CBAL SCORING GUIDE:
CONSTRUCTING AN ARGUMENT

EXEMPLARY (5)

An EXEMPLARY response meets <u>all</u> of the requirements for a score of 4 <u>and distinguishes</u> <u>itself</u> with such qualities as *insightful analysis (recognizing the limits of an argument, identifying possible assumptions and implications of a particular position); intelligent use of claims and evidence to develop a strong argument (including particularly well-chosen examples or a careful rebuttal of opposing points of view); or skillful use of rhetorical devices, phrasing, voice and tone to engage the reader and thus make the argument more persuasive or compelling.*

CLEARLY COMPETENT (4)

The response demonstrates a competent grasp of argument construction and the rhetorical demands of the task, by displaying all or most of the following characteristics:

<u>Command of Argument Structure</u>
♦ *States a clear position on the issue*
♦ *Uses claims and evidence to build a case in support of that position*
♦ *May also consider and address obvious counterarguments*

<u>Quality and Development of Argument</u>
♦ *Makes reasonable claims about the issue*
♦ *Supports claims by citing and explaining relevant reasons and/or examples*
♦ *Is generally accurate in its use of evidence*

<u>Awareness of audience</u>
♦ *Focuses primarily on content that is appropriate for the target audience*
♦ *Expresses ideas in a tone that is appropriate for the audience and purpose for writing*

DEVELOPING HIGH (3)

While a response in this category displays considerable competence, it <u>differs from</u> Clearly Competent responses in at least one important way, such as a *vague claim; somewhat unclear, limited, or inaccurate use of evidence; simplistic reasoning; or occasionally inappropriate content or tone for the audience.*

DEVELOPING LOW (2)

A response in this category <u>differs from</u> Developing High responses because it displays problems that seriously undermine the writer's argument, such as *a confusing claim, a seriously underdeveloped or unfocused argument, irrelevant or seriously misused evidence, an emphasis on opinions or unsupported generalizations rather than reasons and examples, or inappropriate content or tone throughout much of the response.*

MINIMAL (1)

A response in this category <u>differs from</u> Developing Low responses in that it displays little or no ability to construct an argument. For example, there may be *no claim, no relevant reasons and examples, no development of an argument, or little logical coherence throughout the response.*

NO CREDIT (0)

Completely off task, consists almost entirely of copied source material, random key strokes, blank, etc.

Figure 18.3 Rubric for "Ban Ads" test form focusing on rhetorical effectiveness and quality of reasoning

CBAL SCORING GUIDE:
LITERARY ANALYSIS

EXEMPLARY (5)

An EXEMPLARY response meets all of the requirements for a score of 4 and distinguishes itself with
such qualities as *insightful analysis; thoughtful evaluation of alternative interpretations; particularly well-chosen quotations, details, or other supporting evidence; skillful use of literary terms in discussing the texts; or perceptive comments about the author's use of language, perspective, setting, mood, or other literary techniques.*

CLEARLY COMPETENT (4)

A typical essay in this category *presents an understanding of the story that includes not only s* elements (such as sequence of events) but also appropriate inferences about characters, their motivations, perspectives, interactions and/or development.* More specifically, it:

Analyzes and interprets the texts with reasonable clarity and accuracy

♦ *Goes beyond summarization by advocating a specific interpretation (or alternative interpretations) of the story as a whole)*

♦ *Justifies the interpretation(s) by using relevant quotations, details, or other evidence from all three texts*

♦ *Makes clear connections between the interpretation and supporting evidence from the texts*

Shows an awareness of audience

♦ *Presents ideas in a way that makes it easy for the reader to see that the interpretation is valid*

♦ *Expresses ideas in a tone that is appropriate for the intended reader*

DEVELOPING HIGH (3)

While a response in this category displays considerable competence, it differs from Clearly Competent responses in at least one important way, such as a *simplistic or limited interpretation of the story (e.g., mentioning the writing but ignoring its importance); an interpretation based on fewer than three texts but which deals with the significance of Esperanza's writing; limited or occasionally inaccurate use of evidence; somewhat unclear or undeveloped explanations; mostly a summary; content not well-suited to the audience; or an occasionally inappropriate tone.*

DEVELOPING LOW (2)

A response in this category differs from Developing High responses in at least one of the following ways: *a somewhat confusing or seriously limited interpretation (e.g., based on two texts but which ignores the writing); an interpretation based only on the third text; some inaccurate or irrelevant evidence from the story; an emphasis on opinions or unsupported statements; a confusing explanation of how the evidence supports the interpretation; merely a summary; or an inappropriate tone throughout much of the response.*

MINIMAL (1)

A response in this category differs from Developing Low responses in that it displays little or no ability to justify an interpretation of literary texts. For example, there may be *an unreasonable or inaccurate interpretation of the story's characters, their motivations, perspectives, interactions and/or development; use of only the first or second text; a serious lack of relevant or accurate references to the text; a poor summary; or little coherence throughout the response.*

NO CREDIT (0)

A response receives "No Credit" for any one of the following reasons: Does not comment on Esperanza or Mango Street; Not long enough for critical-thinking skills to be judged; Not written in English; Off topic; Blank; Only random key strokes

Figure 18.4 Rubric for *Mango Street* test form focusing on quality of literary interpretation

The strength of the correlation between the two Ban Ads rubrics may illustrate one reason why AES systems may perform well despite focusing on a relatively limited sub-construct: because the same people who perform well on the sub-construct also perform well overall. On the other hand, the rather lower correlation between the two *Mango Street* rubrics highlights the fact that the constructs are different, while the variability of individual performance across tasks and rhetorical situations is illustrated by the moderate correlations that obtain between *Mango Street* and Ban Ads essay scores. Modeling human scores, in other words, is not the same thing as modeling the writing construct. The rubric selects those aspects of the text that will matter to humans, and the choice of AES features selects those aspects of the text that will matter to the computer. This is not to say that the selection is unjustified, but, rather, to point out that it is a selection, and that it embodies decisions about what matters and what can be measured, which entail specific limitations on how the scores produced by the current generation of AES systems can be interpreted and applied.

3.2. Potential Extensions to the AES Feature Set

While the features used in current-generation AES systems measure a specific range of skills (essentially, a subset of the criteria specified in the general writing rubric in Figure 18.2), there is nothing that requires technology to stand still. There are a wide range of ways that AES models could be improved, both by improving the modeling of traits that are already (partially) measured by existing features, and by expanding the evidence measured to include new aspects of the writing construct. One advantage of having a comprehensive model like the CBAL literacy framework is that it provides an independent taxonomy of skills and abilities that matter in the writing process, and thus can support the development of a systematic research program for extending the construct coverage of an AES system.

Such extensions logically exemplify some combination of the following categories:

1. adding new sub-constructs to the model;
2. adding new sources of evidence to the model;
3. developing new methods of measurement and making improvements to existing methods

Adding New Sub-Constructs

Figures 18.2 and 18.4 illustrate a common way in which AES systems are likely to measure less than the full construct. Both rubrics require the author to demonstrate control of a particular type of reasoning and a particular use of evidence. In other words, in terms of the CBAL literacy framework, they require particular kinds of reasoning at the conceptual level, and particular uses of source texts at the discourse level.[1] None of these elements are modeled in existing AES systems. In principal one might develop automated features to assess elements of argumentation (see Feng & Hirst, 2011, for a first step in this direction) or of literary analysis, though such features are likely to be significantly more challenging to implement, if feasible at all, in the current state of natural language processing technology. In all probability, automated analysis of conceptual or social elements of writing are likely to require much more advanced natural language processing and artificial intelligence techniques than current AES systems require, but might help to address some of the concerns that have been expressed about their limitations (Ericsson & Haswell, 2006).

Note, however, that many such potential additions to an AES model will be genre-specific. Quality of argumentation (or of literary analysis) only matters if that element is critical to the writing task. One reason for the selection of features present in current-generation AES systems is precisely their generality, and hence relevance, across a wide range of writing tasks. As most AES systems stand now, they provide general measurement, but less specific measurement at the level of genres, though AES models can and are often differentiated by assigning different feature weights depending on the prompt or genre. But any effort to extend AES to cover a broader writing construct will need to take into account the fact that different kinds of writing tasks require different combinations of skills, which may require different features to be selected in the process of building a scoring model.

Adding New Sources of Evidence

As noted earlier in this paper, existing AES systems use only the final submitted text as a source of evidence. This source of evidence, by its very nature, can provide very little information about the interpretive and deliberative skills that support writing, nor about the ways in which writing quality is affected by the way that a writer organizes the writing process. For instance, writers may pause longer within words or other text production units if they are encountering processing difficulties (Breitvelt, Van den Bergh, & Rijlaarsdam, 1994; Will, Nottbusch, & Weingarten, 2006). There is an extensive literature on the use of keystroke logs to support analysis of writing processes (Sullivan & Lindgren, 2006) although as yet there has been no operational use of process data to supplement or support AES. Within the CBAL project at ETS, these possibilities are being explored in depth (Deane & Quinlan, 2010; Deane, Quinlan & Kostin, 2011). More generally, electronic, online delivery systems can support collection of a variety of ancillary data that can supplement direct analysis of final, submitted texts; but such additional sources of evidence remain largely unexploited in the current state of the art in AES.

Developing New Methods of Measurement; Improving Old Ones

Finally, there are a variety of ways in which measurement of writing constructs can be improved by advances in natural language processing methods. Such advances are often fed by identification of phenomena for which an automated analysis method is feasible. The role that a literacy framework such as CBAL can play in this process is by identifying specific skills and processes, ranging from paraphrase and vocabulary usage through argument analysis and analysis of stance and tone, which may be relevant to identifying and developing new measurement techniques. As these kinds of advances are being developed on a regular basis as part of ongoing research, relatively little needs to be said in this context.

3.3. New Ways to Support Writing Assessment and Instruction

Finally, as noted earlier in this paper, typical uses of AES in education can best be conceptualized as automated versions of the traditional school model in which essays are graded, and feedback takes the form of mark-up on the student text. The kinds of socio-cognitive analyses that are being built into the CBAL literacy framework (e.g., genres and writing occasions, natural learning trajectories, and best practices in writing instruction) can help to identify other models of interaction to which automated scoring can contribute. At this point, relatively few such applications exist, though there are some prototypes and suggestive studies. The following examples should therefore be considered illustrative rather than definitive.

- **Tutorial Feedback During the Writing Process.** Instead of following the model used in ETS' Criterion product and similar products from other vendors, AES could be applied to support a tutorial approach in which feedback was selected dynamically based upon where the student was in the writing process (McNamara et al., in press). Such a model would have the advantage of putting off feedback (for instance) about grammatical errors until a final editing/proofreading stage.
- **Peer Review Quality Assurance.** Peer review is one of the best practices recommended for effective writing instruction (Graham & Perin, 2007), but is potentially problematic, as students must be trained to give appropriate peer review. One approach to this problem is to have students review and score a fixed set of training essays before they review one another's work (Carlson & Berry, 2003), but this approach suffers from the need to restrict the prompts used to those for which a pre-scored set of sample prompts have been developed. Within a formative system that incorporated an AES system and a large library of prompts, it would be possible to use the AES model to assess the quality of student peer reviews, as long as those reviews included qualitative judgments such as holistic or trait scores, and not just textual responses. Yigal Attali (personal communication) has suggested that AES could also be used to order essays by their predicted score before presentation to human raters, and thus increase the reliability of human evaluation by reducing it to a reordering task, in which raters only had to decide whether an essay should be rated above or below its neighbors. Such an application would be natural in the context of peer review, where it would be straightforward to provide students with a set of reference essays and ask students to rank an essay they were peer-reviewing relative to the reference set.
- **New Forms of Curriculum-Based Measurement.** Curriculum-Based Measurement (CBM) has a long history before the advent of computerized instruction, but has been implemented in online and computerized versions as well (Deno, 1985, 2003; Stecker, Fuchs, & Fuchs, 2005). Since AES provides a way to measure features of student writing automatically, without need for instructor evaluation, it is clearly applicable in a CBM context. Moreover, the emphasis on text production that it would provide (particularly if supplemented by data from keystroke logs) is far more strongly justified in a CBM context, where it would serve to monitor progress in fluency and accuracy of text production, than in many pure writing class settings, where the emphasis is on teaching students strategies that draw heavily upon rhetorical (social) and conceptual elements.

These are not the only ways that AES could be applied in settings very different than typical contexts for the current generation of AES products, but they illustrate the kinds of thinking and applications that might be possible if a systematic effort were made to find the most useful contexts within which AES could be applied.

CONCLUSIONS

This chapter is, more than anything else, an exploration of possibilities. AES is a contingent, historical product that has grown up from specific contexts of use, but the technologies it exploits have a wide range of applications that go well beyond those contexts. It would be a mistake to focus AES research entirely within the space circumscribed by the holistic scoring rubric, or by traditional school essay grading. Future research may make it possible to cover a much larger portion of the writing construct, and to construct use cases that exploit the capabilities of automated writing analysis, that create new possibilities for analyzing text quality and writing performance, and that provide new ways to support assessment and instruction, under different conditions of use than the current generation of AES engines. These are possibilities that should be exploited in order to bring the technology to its full potential, and to support a rich and nuanced account of writing skill that will fit well with best practices and what is known about the way novice writers develop greater expertise.

NOTE

1 Figure 18.1 only presents the highest level of the CBAL literacy framework. A more detailed picture, including both specific sub-skills and developmental hypotheses, can be accessed at https://session.wikispaces.net/29156/auth/auth?authToken=016a2acdca18bce4c83a9bc06a5a424cb

REFERENCES

Bennett, R. (2011). CBAL: Results from piloting innovative K-12 assessments. *ETS Research Report* (Vol. RR-11–23). Princeton, NJ: Educational Testing Service.

Bennett, R. E., & Gitomer, D. H. (2009). Transforming K-12 assessment: Integrating accountability testing, formative assessment and professional support. In C. Wyatt-Smith & J. J. Cumming (Eds.), *Educational assessment in the 21st century* (pp. 43–62). Dordrecht, Heidelberg, London and New York: Springer.

Bereiter, C., & Scardamalia, M. (1988). *The psychology of written composition*. Hillsdale, NJ: Lawrence Earlbaum.

Breitvelt, I., Van den Bergh, H., & Rijlaarsdam, G. (1994). Relationships between writing processes and text quality: When and how. *Cognition and Instruction, 12*(2), 103–123.

Burstein, J., & Chodorow, M. (2010). Progress and new directions in technology for automated essay evaluation. In R. Kaplan (Ed.), *The Oxford handbook of applied linguistics* (2 ed., pp. 487–497). Oxford: Oxford University Press.

Burstein, J., Chodorow, M., & Leacock, C. (2003). *Criterion: Online essay evaluation: An application for automated evaluation of test-taker essays*. Paper presented at the Fifteenth Annual Conference on Innovative Applications of Artificial Intelligence, Acapulco, Mexico, August 12–14.

Carlson, P. A., & Berry, F. C. (2003). *Calibrated peer review and assessing learning outcomes*. Paper presented at the 33rd ASEE/IEEE Frontiers in Education Conference, Boulder, Colorado, USA.

Chodorow, M., & Burstein, J. (2004). Beyond essay length: Evaluating e-rater's performance on TOEFL essays. *ETS Research Report* (Vol. RR-04–04). Princeton, NJ: Educational Testing Service.

Cline, F. (2012). *2011 CBAL Multi-state reading and writing study*. Internal ETS Project Report.

Council of Writing Program Administrators, National Council of Teachers of English & National Writing Project (2011). Framework for success in postsecondary writing, from http://wpacouncil.org/files/framework-for-success-postsecondary-writing.pdf

Deane, P. (2011). Writing assessment and cognition. *ETS Research Report* (Vol. RR-11–14). Princeton, NJ: Educational Testing Service.

Deane, P., Fowles, M., Baldwin, D., & Persky, H. (2011). The CBAL summative writing assessment: A draft eighth-grade design. In *ETS Research Memorandum* (Vol. RM-11–01). Princeton, NJ: Educational Testing Service.

Deane, P., & Quinlan, T. (2010). What automated analyses of corpora can tell us about students' writing skills. *Journal of Writing Research 2*(2), 151–177.

Deane, P., Quinlan, T., & Kostin, I. (2011). Automated scoring within a developmental, cognitive model of writing proficiency. *ETS Research Report* (Vol. RR-11–16). Princeton, NJ: Educational Testing Service.

Deane, P., Quinlan, T., Odendahl, N., Welsh, C., & Bivens-Tatum, J. (2008). Cognitive models of writing: Writing proficiency as a complex integrated skill. In *CBAL literature review—writing* (Vol. RR-08–55). Princeton, NJ: Educational Testing Service

Deno, S. L. (1985). Curriculum-Based Measurement: The emerging alternative. *Except Child, 52*(3), 219–232.

Deno, S. L. (2003). Developments in Curriculum-Based Measurement. *Journal of Special Education, 37*(3), 184–192.

Ericsson, P. F., & Haswell, R. H. (Eds.). (2006). *Machine scoring of student essays: Truth and consequences.* Logan, UT: Utah State University Press.

Feng, V. W., & Hirst, G. (2011). *Classifying arguments by scheme.* Paper presented at the 49th Annual Meeting of the Association for Computational Linguistics.

Graham, S., & Perin, S. (2007). A meta-analysis of writing instruction for adolescent students. *Journal of Educational Psychology, 99,* 445–476.

Hayes, J. R., & Flower, L. (1980). Identifying the organization of writing processes. In L. Gregg & E. R. Steinberg (Eds.), *Cognitive processes in writing* (pp. 3–30). Hillsdale, NJ: Lawrence Erlbaum Associates.

Hillocks, G. (1986). *Research on written composition: New directions for teaching.* Urbana, IL: National Council of Teachers of English.

Hung, D., & Chen, V. (2002). Learning within the context of communities of practices: A reconceptualization of the tools, rules and roles of the activity system. *Education Media International, 39*(3–4), 248–255.

Jonassen, D. H., & Rohrer-Murphy, L. (1999). Activity theory as a framework for designing constructivist learning environments. *Educational Technology, Research and Development, 47*(1), 61–79.

Landauer, T. K., Laham, R. D., & Foltz, P. W. (2003). Automated scoring and annotation of essays with the Intelligent Essay Assessor. In M. D. Shermis & J. Bernstein (Eds.), *Automated essay scoring: A cross-disciplinary perspective.* Mahwah, NJ: Lawrence Erlbaum Associates, Inc.

Larkey, L., & Croft, W. B. (2003). A text categorization approach to automated essay grading. In M. D. Shermis & J. Burstein (Eds.), *Automated essay scoring: A cross-disciplinary perspective* (pp. 55–70). Mahwah, NJ: Lawrence Erlbuam Associates, Inc.

McCutchen, D. (1996). A capacity theory of writing: Working memory in composition. *Educational Testing Review, 8*(3), 299–325.

McCutchen, D. (2000). Knowledge, processing, and working memory: Implications for a theory of writing. *Educational Psychologist, 35*(1), 13–23.

McNamara, D. S., Raine, R., Roscoe, R., Crossley, S., Jackson, G. T., Dai, J., Graesser, A. C. (in press). The Writing-Pal: Natural language algorithms to support intelligent tutoring on writing strategies. In P. M. McCarthy & C. Boonthum (Eds.), *Applied natural language processing and content analysis: Identification, investigation, and resolution.* Hershey, PA: IGI Global.

Page, E. B. (1966). The imminence of grading essays by computer. *Phi Delta Kappan, 48,* 238–243.

Page, E. B. (1967). *Statistical and linguistic strategies in the computer grading of essays.* Paper presented at the International Conference on Computational Linguistics Morristown, NJ, August 23–25.

Perin, D. (2009). Best practices in teaching writing to adolescents. In C. MacArthur & J. Fitzgerald S. Graham (Eds.), *Best practices in writing instruction.* New York: Guilford Press.

Powers, D. E., Burstein, J., Chodorow, M., Fowles, M. E., & Kukich, K. (2000). Comparing the validity of automated and human essay scoring. GRE Board Research Report No. 98–08a, *ETS Research Report* (Vol. RR-00–10). Princeton, NJ Educational Testing Service.

Powers, D., Burstein, J. C., Chodrow, M., Fowles, M. E., & Kukich, K. (2001). *Stumping E-Rater: Challenging the validity of automated essay scoring GRE Board Professional (Rep. No. 98–08bP).* Princeton, NJ: Educational Testing Service.

Spandel, V. (Ed.). (2005). *Creating writers through 6-trait writing assessment and instruction* (4 ed.). Boston, MA: Pearson, Allyn & Bacon.

Stecker, P. M., Fuchs, L. S., & Fuchs, D. (2005). Using Curriculum-Based Measurement to improve student achievement: Review of research. *Psychology in the Schools, 48*(8), 795–819.

Sullivan, K. P. H., & Lindgren, E. (Eds.). (2006). *Computer keystroke logging and writing.* Oxford and Amsterdam: Elsevier.

Will, U., Nottbusch, G., & Weingarten, R. (2006). Linguistic units in word typing: Effects of word presentation modes and typing delay. *Written Language and Literacy, 9*(1), 153–176.

19 Contrasting State-of-the-Art Automated Scoring of Essays

Mark D. Shermis and Ben Hamner[1]

INTRODUCTION

With the press for developing innovative assessments that can accommodate higher-order thinking and performances associated with the Common Core Standards, there is a need to systematically evaluate the benefits and features of automated essay evaluation (AEE). While the developers of AEE engines have published an impressive body of literature to suggest that the measurement technology can produce reliable and valid essay scores (when compared with trained human raters; Attali & Burstein, 2006; Shermis, Burstein, Higgins, & Zechner, 2010), comparisons across the multiple platforms have been informal, involved less-than-ideal sample essays, and were often associated with an incomplete criterion set.

The purpose of this chapter is to present the results of a comparison of nine AEE engines on responses to a range of prompts, with some targeting content and others relatively content-free, from multiple grades. The AEE engines were compared on the basis of scores from independent raters using state-developed writing assessment rubrics. This study was shaped by the two major consortia associated with implementing the Common Core Standards, the Partnership for Assessment of Readiness for College and Careers (PARCC) and SMARTER Balanced Assessment Consortium (SMARTER Balanced), as part of their investigation into the viability of using AES for their new generation of assessments.

Comprehensive independent studies of AEE platforms have been rare. Rudner, Garcia, and Welch (2006) conducted a two-part independent evaluation of an automated essays scoring engine from one vendor, IntelliMetric by Vantage Learning. After reviewing data drawn from the Graduate Management Admission Test™ (GMAT), the investigators concluded, "the IntelliMetric system is a consistent, reliable system for scoring AWA (Analytic Writing Assessment) essays." While such individual endorsements are heartening, there has yet to be a comprehensive look at machine scoring technology. This is particularly important as the assessments for the Common Core Standards are under development. In part, this vendor demonstration was designed to evaluate the degree to which current high-stakes writing assessments, and those envisioned under the Common Core Standards, might be scored through automated methods.

This study was the first phase of a three-part evaluation. Phase I examines the machine scoring capabilities for extended-response essays, and consists of two parts. The first part reports on the capabilities of already existing commercial machine scoring systems. Running concurrently with the vendor demonstration was a public competition in which the study sponsor (The William and Flora Hewlett Foundation) provided cash prizes for newly-developed scoring engines created by individuals or teams. Phase II will do the same thing for short answer constructed responses, followed with an evaluation of math items (i.e., proofs, graphs, formulas) for Phase III.

PARTICIPANTS

Student essays (N = 22,029) were collected for eight different prompts representing six PARCC and SMARTER Balanced states (three PARCC states and three SMARTER Balanced states). To the extent possible, an attempt was made to make the identity of the participating states anonymous. Three of the states were located in the Northeastern part of the U.S., two from the Midwest, and one from the West Coast. Because no demographic information was provided by the states, student characteristics were estimated from a number of different sources, as displayed in Table 19.1. Student writers were drawn from three different grade levels (7, 8, 10) and the grade-level selection was generally a function of the testing policies of the participating states (i.e., a writing component as part of a 10th grade exit exam), were ethnically diverse, and evenly distributed between males and females.

Samples ranging in size from 1527 to 3006 were randomly selected from the data sets provided by the states, and then randomly divided into three sets: a training set, a test set, and a validation set. The training set was used by the vendors to create their scoring models, and consisted of scores assigned by at least two human raters, a final or adjudicated score, and the text of the essay. The test set consisted of essay text only and was used as part of a blind test for the score model predictions. The purpose of the second test set was to calculate scoring engine performance for a public competition that was launched at approximately the same time as the vendor demonstration. It was also to be used as a test set for any of the commercial vendors who might have subsequently elected to participate in the public competition. The second test set consisted of essay text only. The distribution of the samples was split in the following proportions: 60% training sample, 20% test sample, 20% validation test sample. The actual proportions vary slightly due to the elimination of cases containing either data errors or text anomalies. The distribution of the samples is displayed in Table 19.1.

Instruments

Four of the essays were drawn from traditional writing genre (persuasive, expository, narrative) and four essays were "source-based," that is, the questions asked in the prompt referred to a source document that students read as part of the assessment. In the training set, average essay lengths varied from M = 94.39 (SD = 51.68) to M = 622.24 (SD = 197.08), Traditional essays were significantly longer (M = 354.18, SD 197.63) than source-based essays (M = 119.97, SD = 58.88; $t_{(13334)}$ = 95.18, p < .05).

Five of the prompts employed a holistic scoring rubric, one prompt was scored with a two-trait rubric, and two prompts were scored with a multi-trait rubric, but reported as a composite score. The type of rubric, scale ranges, scale means and standard deviations, are reported in Tables 19.2 and 19.3. Table 19.2 shows the characteristics of the training set and Table 19.3 shows the characteristics of the test set. Human rater agreement information is reported in Tables 19.2 and 19.3 with associated data for exact agreement, exact + adjacent agreement, kappa, Pearson r, and quadratic-weighted kappa. Quadratic weighted kappas ranged from 0.62 to 0.85, a typical range for human rater performance in statewide high-stakes testing programs.

PROCEDURE

Six of the essays sets were transcribed from their original paper-form administration in order to prepare them for processing by AEE engines. At a minimum, the scoring engines

Table 19.1 Sample Characteristics Estimated From Reported Demographics of the State*

	Data Set #							
	1	2	3	4	5	6	7	8
State	#1	#2	#3	#3	#4	#4	#5	#6
Grade	8	10	10	10	8	10	7	10
Grade Level N	42,992	80,905	68,025	68,025	71,588	73,101	115,626	44,289
n	2,968	3,000	2,858	2,948	3,006	3,000	2,722	1,527
Training n	1,785	1,800	1,726	1,772	1,805	1,800	1,730	918
Test n	589	600	568	586	601	600	495	304
Validation n†	594	600	564	590	600	600	497	305
Gender M%｜F%	51.2 48.8	51.4 48.6	51.0 49.0	51.0 49.0	49.6 50.4	49.2 50.8	51.2 48.8	48.7 51.3
Race W%｜N%	63.8 36.2	77.8 22.2	42.9 57.1	42.9 57.1	70.2 29.9	69.5 30.5	70.2 29.8	66.3 33.7
Free/Reduced Lunch %	32.9	40.0	32.24	32.2	34.2	34.2	46.6	41.3

* Taken primarily from: National Center for Education Statistics, Common Core of Data (CCD), (2010). State Non-fiscal Survey of Public Elementary/Secondary Education, 2009–10, Version 1a. Washington, DC: U.S. Department of Education. This information was supplemented with state department of education website information or annual reports for each participating state.

† The validation set was not used in this study.

M—Male
F—Female
W—White
N—Non-White

Table 19.2 Training Set Characteristics

	Data Set #							
	1	2	3	4	5	6	7	8
N	1,785	1,800	1,726	1,772	1,805	1,800	1,730	918
Grade	8	10	10	10	8	10	7	10
Type of Essay	persuasive	persuasive	source-based	source-based	source-based	source-based	expository	narrative
M # of Words	366.40	381.19	108.69	94.39	122.29	153.64	171.28	622.13
SD # of Words	120.40	156.44	53.30	51.68	57.37	55.92	85.20	197.08
Type of Rubric	holistic	trait (2)	holistic	holistic	holistic	holistic	composite*	composite+
	2a	2b						
Range of Rubric	1–6	1–6 1–4	0–3	0–3	0–4	0–4	0–12	0–30
Range of RS	2–12	1–6 1–4	0–3	0–3	0–4	0–4	0–24	0–60
M RS	8.53	3.42 3.33	1.85	1.43	2.41	2.72	19.98	37.23
SD RS	1.54	0.77 0.73	0.82	0.94	0.97	0.97	6.02	5.713
Exact Agree	0.65	0.78 0.80	0.75	0.77	0.58	0.62	0.28	0.28
Exact + Adj Agree	0.99	0.93 1.00	1.00	1.00	0.98	0.99	0.54	0.49
κ	0.45	0.65 0.66	0.61	0.67	0.42	0.46	0.17	0.15
Pearson r	0.72	0.81 0.80	0.77	0.85	0.75	0.78	0.73	0.63
Quadratic Weighted κ	0.72	0.81 0.80	0.77	0.85	0.75	0.78	0.73	0.62

RS—Resolved Score
Agree—agreement
Adj—adjacent
* composite score based on four of six traits
+ composite score based on six of six traits

Table 19.3 Test Set Characteristics

	Data Set #							
	1	2	3	4	5	6	7	8
N	589	600	568	586	601	600	495	304
Grade	8	10	10	10	8	10	7	10
Type of Essay	persuasive	persuasive	source-based	source-based	source-based	source-based	expository	narrative
M # of Words	368.96	378.40	113.24	98.70	127.17	152.28	173.48	639.05
SD # of Words	117.99	156.82	56.00	53.84	57.59	52.81	84.52	190.13
Type of Rubric	holistic	trait (2)	holistic	holistic	holistic	holistic	composite*	composite+
Range of Rubric	1–6	1–6 1–4	0–3	0–3	0–4	0–4	0–12	0–30
Range of RS	2–12	1–6 1–4	0–3	0–3	0–4	0–4	0–24	0–60
M RS	8.62	3.41 3.32	1.90	1.51	2.51	2.75	20.13	36.67
SD RS	1.54	0.77 0.75	0.85	0.95	0.95	0.87	5.89	5.19
Exact Agree	0.64	0.76 0.73	0.72	0.78	0.59	0.63	0.28	0.29
Exact + Adj Agree	0.99	1.00 1.00	1.00	1.00	0.98	0.99	0.55	0.49
κ	0.45	0.62 0.56	0.57	0.65	0.44	0.45	0.18	0.16
Pearson r	0.73	0.80 0.76	0.77	0.85	0.74	0.74	0.72	0.61
Quadratic Weighted κ	0.73	0.80 0.76	0.77	0.85	0.75	0.74	0.72	0.62

RS—Resolved Score
Agree—agreement
Adj—adjacent
* composite score based on four of six traits
+ composite score based on six of six traits

require the essays to be in American Standard Code for Information Interchange (ASCII) format. This process involved retrieving the scanned copies of essays from the state or a vendor serving the state, randomly selecting a sample of essays for inclusion in the study, and then sending the selected documents out for transcription.

Both the scanning and transcription steps had the potential to introduce errors into the data that would have been minimized had the essays been directly typed into the computer by the student, the normal procedure for AEE. Essays were scanned on high quality digital scanners, but occasionally student writing was illegible because the original paper document was written with an instrument that was too light to reproduce well, was smudged, or included handwriting that was undecipherable. In such cases, or if the essay could not be scored by human raters (i.e., essay was off-topic or inappropriate), the essay was eliminated from the analyses. Transcribers were instructed to be as faithful to the written document as possible keeping in mind the extended computer capabilities had they been employed. For example, more than a few students hand-wrote their essays using a print style in which all letters were capitalized. To address this challenge, we instructed the transcribers to capitalize beginning of sentences, proper names, etc. This modification may have corrected errors that would have otherwise been made, but limited the over-identification of capitalization errors that might have otherwise been made by the AEE engines.

The first transcription company serviced four prompts from three states and included 11,496 essays. In order to assess the potential impact of transcription errors, a random sample of 588 essays was re-transcribed and compared on the basis of punctuation, capitalization, misspellings, and skipped data. Accuracy was calculated on the basis of the number of characters and the number of words with an average rate of 98.12%. The second transcription company was evaluated using similar metrics. From a pool of 6006 essays, a random sample of 300 essays was selected for re-transcription. Accuracy for this set of essays was calculated to be 99.82%.

Two of the essays were provided in ASCII format by their respective states. The 10th grade students in those states had typed their responses directly into the computer using web-based software that emulated a basic word processor. Except that the test had been administered by a computer, the conditions for testing were similar to those in states where the essays had been transcribed.

One of the key challenges to both sets of data, those that were transcribed and those that were directly typed, was that carriage returns and paragraph formatting meta-tags were missing from the ASCII text. For some of the scoring engines, this omission could have introduced a significant impediment in the engine's ability to accurately evaluate the underlying structure of the writing, one component in their statistical prediction models. Other than asking each student to retype their original answers into the data sets, there was no way to ameliorate this.

Vendors were provided a training set for each of the eight essay prompts. Up to four weeks were allowed to statistically model the data during the "training" phase of the demonstration. In addition, vendors were provided with cut-score information along with any scoring guides that were used in the training of human raters. This supplemental information was employed by some of the vendors to better model score differences for the score points along the state rubric continuum. Two of the essay prompts used trait rubrics to formulate a composite score by summing some or all of the trait scores. For these two essays, both the composite and trait scores were provided to the vendors.

During the training period, a series of conference calls, with detailed questions and answers, were conducted to clarify the nature of the data sets or to address data problems that arose while modeling the data. For example, the guidelines from one state indicated that the final or resolved score was to be the higher of the two rater scores, but in several cases this was not the case. Rather than modify the resolved score, the vendors were instructed to use it in their prediction models even though it was apparently inconsistent with the state's guidelines.

This operational decision had the potential to negatively impact the scoring engines' reported capacity to adequately model what the state was trying to accomplish in assigning scores to essays. However, it is acceptable, adding to the robustness of whatever results were obtained, since the study was designed to test how vendors would perform when applying their scoring engines to state-generated data under pragmatic conditions. Stated somewhat differently, the consideration of these inconsistencies provided a representation of the typical contextual conditions within which the scoring engines were actually employed.

In the "test" phase of the evaluation, vendors were provided data sets that had only the text of essays associated with them, and were asked to make integer score predictions for each essay. They were given a 59-hour period in which to make their predictions and were permitted to eliminate up to 2% of the essay score predications in each data set in case their scoring engine classified the essay as "unscorable." Even though human raters had successfully rated all the essays in the test set, there were a variety of reasons why any one essay might prove problematic for machine scoring. For example, an essay might have addressed the prompt in a unique enough way to receive a low human score, but be deemed as "off-topic" for machine scoring. In real-life situations provisions would be made for these to be scored by human raters.

Procedure-Scoring Engines

Eight of the nine AEE engines that were evaluated in the demonstration represented commercial entities and captured over 97% of the current automated scoring market in the United States. The lone non-commercial scoring engine was invited into the demonstration because it was an already existing open-source package that was publicly available on their web site. Below are short descriptions of each engine.

AutoScore, American Institutes for Research

Autoscore is an essay scoring engine developed by the American Institutes for Research (AIR). The engine is designed to create a statistical proxy for prompt-specific rubrics. The rubrics may be single or multiple trait rubrics. A training set, including known, valid scores, is required to train the engine.

The system takes a series of measures on each essay in the remaining training set. These measures include:

- semantic measures based on the concepts that discriminate between high- and low-scoring papers,
- other semantic measures that indicate the coherence of concepts within and across paragraphs, and
- a range of word-use and syntactic measures.

In addition, where clear, proposition-based, prompt-specific rubrics are available, the system can integrate measures based on AIR's *Proposition Scoring Engine*, which recognizes pre-specified "propositions," allowing a wide variation in the expression of those propositions.

For each trait in the rubric, the system estimates an appropriate statistical model relating the measures described above to the score assigned by humans. This model, along with its final parameter estimates, is used to generate a predicted or "proxy" score.

LightSIDE, Carnegie Mellon University, TELEDIA Lab

LightSIDE is a free and open-source software package developed at Carnegie Mellon University. This program is designed as a tool for non-experts to quickly utilize text mining technology for a variety of purposes, including essay assessment. LightSIDE incorporates numerous options for extending its data representation, machine learning, or visualization through plugins. However, to train the models used in the Automated Student Assessment Prize (ASAP) competition, no additional programming was required. Models were trained and tuned using standard options available through the user interface. With instruction, a beginner user with no programming experience could reproduce the results we report for this competition in less than one hour of work.

Bookette, CTB/McGraw-Hill

CTB's Bookette automated writing evaluation analytics ("scoring engines") are able to model trait level and/or holistic level scores for essays with a similar degree of reliability to an expert human rater. The engines use a natural language processing system with a neural network to model expert human scores. The engines are trained using essays that have been scored by expert raters and validated against a separate set of papers also scored by expert raters during the model building phase. The engines are then monitored by using human-to-engine comparisons during the implementation phase for uses in which students are scored "live'" for accountability purposes.

CTB has been using automated writing evaluation in large-scale accountability testing contexts since 2009 and in classroom settings since 2005. CTB has expertise in building prompt-specific and generic engines. Prompt-specific engines have demonstrated high fidelity to human scoring on a prompt-by-prompt basis, but they may only be reliably used with the particular prompt for which they have been trained. Generic engines, on the other hand, are not quite as reliable as prompt-specific engines, but they generalize to a variety of prompts, thereby allowing them to be more flexibly used in the classroom. Their technology when applied in the classroom for formative purposes provides both holistically and trait level performance feedback through the use of the information found in the scoring rubric and through feedback on grammar, spelling, and conventions at the sentence level.

CTB's *Bookette* engines operate on approximately 90 text features classified as structural-, syntactic-, semantic-, and mechanics-based. Most commonly, the features are used to model trait level scores which may be reported separately and/or combined to produce a total writing score. The analytic scoring guide underlies the CTB system produces integer scores (ranging from 1 to 6 points) based on well-recognized traits of effective writing: Organization, Development, Sentence Structure, Word Choice/Grammar Usage, Mechanics.

E-rater®, Educational Testing Service

The e-rater® scoring engine is an automated scoring system designed to evaluate essay quality. The system scores essays based on dozens of features, each of which is designed to measure specific aspects of essay quality. These features are derived using a variety of techniques from a subfield of artificial intelligence called natural language processing. Some of these techniques are based on linguistic analysis, some are from empirical modeling using statistical techniques from several fields of study, while others are developed on the basis of hybrid approaches. These features form the basis for performance feedback to students in learning environments through products such as Criterion, a learning tool for writing in a classroom setting (www.ets.org/criterion). These features are grouped together into conceptually similar sets to comprise blocks of features covering major areas of writing, including grammar, usage, mechanics, style, organization and development, lexical complexity, and content relevance. These feature sets are the basis for the production of essay scores and are typically calibrated on a provided set of human scores to produce statistically optimal weights for score production.

The scores from e-rater are not only used in learning environments, but also for scoring practice tests, placement tests, and in high-stakes assessment. In 1999 the scores from e-rater were the first to be deployed operationally in high-stakes assessment as one of two scores for the GMAT and have since been used in the Graduate Record Examination (GRE) and the Test of English as a Foreign Language (TOEFL) assessments following similar models of providing one of the two scores on each essay.

Lexile® Writing Analyzer, MetaMetrics

Lexile® Writing Analyzer is a grade-, genre-, prompt-, and punctuation-independent automatic essay scoring engine for establishing Lexile writer measures. A vertical scale is employed to measure the writing construct and, as such, training is not necessary to evaluate an essay.

A Lexile writer measure refers to an underlying individual trait, which is defined as the power to compose written text, with writing ability embedded in a complex web of cognitive and sociocultural processes. Individuals with higher-level writing ability are more facile with at least some of the aspects of a writer-composition-reader transaction than are individuals with lower-level writing ability. Facets of a writer-composition-reader transaction may be related to, reflected in, or reflective of, an individual's writing ability, but they are not, in themselves, "writing ability." Rather, writing ability is an individual trait that is brought to bear to a greater or lesser extent within each transaction occasion.

Through a research study to examine the relationship between text complexity, text features, and writing ability, a parsimonious set of significant predictors emerged—predictors consistent with the hypothesis that selected kinds of composition surface text features may be proxies for a degree of executive functioning and working memory capacity and efficiency. The resulting combination consisted of lexical representations alone—without syntax signifiers. Specifically, a combination of a small number of variables—degree of diverse use of vocabulary and greater vocabulary density, controlling for production fluency—predicted 90% of the true variance in rater judgments of essays.

The "training" phase of the study involved the categorization of Lexile essay scores into distinct groups corresponding to teacher ratings (similar to changing actual temperature measurements into categories of "very hot," "hot," "cool," and "cold").

Project Essay Grade (PEG), Measurement, Inc.

Measurement, Inc.'s (MI's) AEE engine, Project Essay Grade (PEG), has undergone 40 years of study and enhancement. Replication studies for a number of state departments of education have indicated that PEG demonstrates accuracy that is very similar to that of trained human scorers. It has been used to score millions of essays in formative and summative assessments, including statewide formative assessments, online writing improvement systems for a network of international schools, and the Utah Direct Writing Assessment, the state's census assessment in grades 5 and 8. PEG utilizes training sets of human-scored student constructed responses to build models with which to assess the quality of unscored responses. The training responses are analyzed across multiple dimensions and, from this analysis, features are calculated, including various measures of structure, mechanics, organization, semantics, and syntax. Once the features have been calculated, PEG uses them to build statistical models for the accurate prediction of scores, holistically or by trait. In order to create these features, MI has developed a number of tools that respond well to student error. One such tool is a custom search language that allows our linguists to locate complex structures within a text quickly and accurately. More recently, MI created a set of tools that evaluate text on a deeper semantic level, generating high-dimensional data. To handle this data adequately, we have drawn on recent advances in statistical machine learning, including prediction algorithms specifically designed to deal with noisy, high-dimensional data.

Intelligent Essay Assessor, Pearson Knowledge Technologies

The Intelligent Essay Assessor (IEA) evaluates the structure, style, and content of writing using a range of artificial intelligence- (AI-) based technologies. It derives some of its measures through using semantic models of English (or any other language) from an analysis of large volumes of text equivalent to all the reading a student may have done through high school (about 12 million words). The IEA combines background knowledge about English in general and the subject area of the assessment in particular, along with prompt-specific algorithms to learn how to match student responses to human scores. Using a representative sample of responses that are double-scored by humans, the computer compares the content and relevant qualities of the writing of each student response, along with the scores given to the responses by the human scorers. From these comparisons, a prompt-specific algorithm is derived to predict the scores that the same scorers would assign to new responses. IEA can be trained and ready to score in a matter of days.

IEA provides an immediate overall evaluation of a response as well as feedback on specific traits, spelling, grammar errors, and on content categories. IEA can be tuned to understand and evaluate text in any language (Spanish, Arabic, Hindi, etc.) or in any subject area. It includes built-in detectors for off-topic responses, highly unusual essays and other special situations that may need to be referred to human readers. In addition, products based on the technology provide feedback that is easy to understand. IEA has been used in situations including scoring English Language Arts (ELA) and science responses for grade schools, assessing and giving feedback on reading comprehension and summarization skills, assessing scenario-based learning for college students and for assessing military leadership skills. It has been used for scoring millions of essays in high-stakes testing as a second score or in formative evaluations.

CRASE™, Pacific Metrics

Pacific Metrics automated scoring engine, CRASE™, scores responses to items typically appearing in large-scale assessments: (a) essay length writing prompts; (b) short answer constructed response items in mathematics, ELA, and science; (c) math items eliciting formulae or numeric answers; and, (d) technology-enhanced items (e.g., Drag and Drop, Graphing). It has been used in both formative and high-stakes summative assessments, providing rapid turnaround and delivering cost savings over traditional hand scoring methods. The system is highly customizable, both in terms of the configurations used to build machine scoring models and in terms of the how the system can blend human scoring and machine scoring (i.e., hybrid models). CRASE is a fully integrated Java-based application that runs as a web service. By integrated, this refers to its ability to: (a) score any of several different item types as a single software application, (b) interface with web-based assessment delivery platforms for immediate turnaround of scores, and (c) integrate with vendor-based electronic hand scoring systems for monitoring or dual scoring.

At its most basic level, categorization is critical to the scoring process. Using experience, along with training materials, scoring guides, etc., a human rater classifies a student's response into one of several defined categories or scores. CRASE analyzes a sample of already-scored student responses to produce a model of the raters' scoring behavior. In general, the system will score as reliably as the sample from which the scoring models are built. By emulating human scoring behavior, CRASE essentially predicts the score that a human rater would assign to a given student response. CRASE uses a sequential process to first analyze and then score students' responses. When a response is received from an online test administration system, it moves through three phases in the scoring process: (a) identifying non-attempts, (b) feature extraction, and (c) scoring.

- Identifying non-attempts. The response is first reviewed to determine whether it is a valid attempt at the item. If it is not a valid attempt (e.g., it is blank or gibberish), the response is flagged and removed from the remaining feature extraction and scoring process.
- Extraction of features. If it is a valid attempt, the response is submitted to one of the feature extraction engines. In this phase, a vector of values is generated that represents both the scoring rubric and the construct the item is intended to assess.
- Predicting a score. The vector of values is submitted to a scoring engine that uses a statistical model and/or a series of computational linguistic procedures to classify the response into a score category. It is at this stage that the model derived from the rater sample is applied to predict the score a rater would provide. The predicted score and any non-attempt flags are then returned to the test administration system.

For the scoring of writing prompts, the feature extraction step is organized around the 6+1 Trait® Model, a product of Education Northwest (http://educationnorthwest.org/traits) that is used in some form by most states for K–12 writing applications. The 6+1 Trait Model conceptualizes six traits of writing (ideas, sentence fluency, organization, voice, word choice, and conventions) along with the "+1" which is "written presentation." For writing prompts and essays, the feature extraction stage first preprocesses student responses by tokenizing elements in the response, counting and correcting misspellings, computing part-of-speech tags, and conducting stemming. One or more functions are associated with each of the six traits, and these functions are applied to the processed response to produce one or more variables that represent the trait. Examples of functions are: identifying usage and mechanics errors typically seen in student essays, measuring variation in sentence type, calculating extent of personal engagement, and idea development in phrasing. This step also produces text-based and numeric-based feedback that can be used to improve the essay (e.g., too-common words or sentence beginnings, spelling errors, grammar errors). CRASE can be customized to score each of the six traits, or combinations of the traits. It can also be customized to score a number of points (e.g., 1 to 4, 1 to 6). The scoring step uses statistical modeling methods to produce a score using the variables produced in the feature extraction step. Bayesian methods can also be employed to incorporate priors into the scoring model.

IntelliMetric, *Vantage Learning*

IntelliMetric is an intelligent machine scoring system that emulates the processes carried out by human scorers. IntelliMetric draws its theoretical underpinnings from a variety of areas, including cognitive processing, AI, natural language understanding, and computational linguistics in the process of evaluating the quality of written text. IntelliMetric learns to score essays in much the same manner as human raters are trained. In the typical human scoring scenario, expert raters develop anchor papers for each score point thereby becoming the basis for training human scorers on the proposed protocol. Human scorers use these anchor papers as reference points, and learn to distinguish the features embedded in the anchor papers that translate to their respective scores. Similarly, IntelliMetric is trained to score test-taker essays. Each prompt (essay) is first scored by expert human scorers, who develop anchor papers for each score point. A number of papers for each score point are loaded into IntelliMetric, which runs multiple algorithms to determine the specific writing features that translate to various score points.

EVALUATION CRITERIA

In the field of performance assessment there are few "gold standards" and occasionally there is disagreement about the objectivity of the standards that are in place. So for instance, in a shooting competition one can obtain an "objective" score based on how well one hits the areas of a stationary target, but the debate among enthusiasts centers on how realistic the conditions for shooting on a target range actually are (i.e., the lack of variables such as target motion, weather, wind that might impact shooting accuracy) compared to, say, hunting in the wild.

Essay assessment, which has no gold standard, often employs rubrics (quantifiable declarations of what human raters are instructed to score as being important, typically on a scale ranging from "poor" to "excellent") to guide the assignment of a score that reflects writing standards. Trained human raters, as with subject-matter or writing experts, can read the same paper and assign the same or different scores for different reasons. To compensate for possible differences, most states use the scores from two trained human raters as the criterion measure. Human raters are generally hired with some writing background, given extensive training, provided scoring guides to help standardize their score assignments, and periodically compare their assessments with essays that have been previously scored by writing experts (i.e., "training sets"). The higher the agreement among human raters, the more reliable the assessment is thought to be. However, the metrics used to assess agreement are sometimes impacted or modified by the rubric scales that have been adopted or by the way in which a final score is resolved. So for example, some states simply add the equally weighted scores from human raters to determine a final score assignment rather than employ a third rater or supervisor to resolve a score discrepancy between them, and thereby preserve the original rating score values.

Scoring

Rather than try to evaluate machine scoring on the basis of one metric, this study will evaluate scoring performance on the basis of a set of measures that are standard in the field, including:

- Distributional differences. Correspondence in mean and variance of the distributions of human scores to that of automated scores.
- Agreement. Measured by correlation, weighted kappa, and percent agreement (exact and exact + adjacent).
- Agreement delta > Degree of difference between human-human agreement and automated-human agreement by the same agreement metrics as above.

Results

Eight of the nine vendors provided predictions for 100% of the test set. The one vendor who did not resulted in the elimination of ten essays from their predictions. The proportion is so small (10/4343 = .002) that for comparison purposes, the results will be treated as if they had reported at the 100% rate.

Table 19.4 shows the mean distributions across all nine vendors for the eight data sets. For comparison purposes, three additional calculations are provided. H1 refers to the mean calculations based on the scores assigned by the first human rater and H2 shows the same calculations based on the score assignments for the second human rater. In the three data sets (1, 7, and 8) where the final or resolved score was the equally weighted sum of the two human raters, the scores for H1 and H2 were doubled to be on the same scale.

The results for data set #2 were a bit of an anomaly. In addition to being scored on two traits, this data set differed from the others in how scores were assigned. While two raters evaluated the essays, only the rating from the first rater determined the score assignment. The second rater was used as a "read behind" to monitor rating quality. However, the second rater had no influence on the actual score assignment. Because of this unique situation, only the means for the second human rater are listed in Table 19.4.

RS refers to the final or resolved score. This was the score that was provided by the state. As mentioned previously, determining the resolved score was accomplished differently by the different states, but is a function of human ratings. So where one state might have used the equally weighted sum of the raters to determine the resolved score, another state might have issued the guideline to use the higher of the two human rater scores. The H1 and H2 metrics (H1H2) are provided throughout the results section for comparison purposes.

By and large, the scoring engines did a good job of replicating the mean scores for all of the data sets. Figure 19.1 illustrates these in graphic form. Table 19.5 shows the deviation scores (deltas) from the means of each data set. Accuracy was most likely influenced by the size of the scale. For example, all vendor engines generated predicted means within 0.10 of the human mean for data set #3 which had a rubric range of 0–3. However, even when the range was much larger as in data set #8 (0–60), mean estimates were generally within 1 point, and usually smaller.

Table 19.6 shows analogous information for the standard deviations for each of the data sets with Table 19.7 illustrating the deltas. With the exception of data sets 1, 7, and 8, where the two rater scores were summed to get a resolved score, most of the predicted scores had standard deviations within 0.10 of the resolved scores. Figure 19.2 graphically depicts this and shows some scatter for data sets 7 and 8 where the scale ranges were much wider than with some of the earlier data sets.

Table 19.8 begins the sequence of agreement statistics for the data sets. The human exact agreements ranged from 0.28 on data set #8 to .76 for data set #2. Machine scoring exact agreements ran from 0.07 on data set #2 to 0.72 on data sets 3 and 4. An inspection of the deltas on Table 19.9 shows that machines performed particularly well on data sets

Table 19.4 Test Set Means

Essay Set	N	M # of Words	H1	H2	RS	AIR	CMU	CTB	ETS	MI	MM	PKT	PM	VL
1*	589	366.40	8.61	8.62	8.62	8.54	8.51	8.56	8.57	8.53	8.56	8.57	8.49	8.80
2aᵗ	600	381.19	—	3.39	3.41	3.41	3.36	3.39	3.39	3.37	3.33	3.41	3.36	3.40
2bᵗ	600	381.19	—	3.34	3.32	3.37	3.18	3.35	3.32	3.21	3.26	3.29	3.32	3.34
3	568	108.69	1.79	1.73	1.90	1.90	1.90	1.92	1.88	1.95	1.91	1.84	1.89	1.92
4	586	94.39	1.38	1.40	1.51	1.50	1.47	1.50	1.34	1.48	1.46	1.39	1.47	1.57
5	601	122.29	2.31	2.35	2.51	2.49	2.51	2.49	2.47	2.51	2.44	2.49	2.50	2.54
6	600	153.64	2.57	2.58	2.75	2.79	2.71	2.83	2.54	2.76	2.74	2.76	2.74	2.83
7*	495	171.28	20.02	20.24	20.13	20.05	19.63	19.46	19.61	19.80	19.63	19.58	19.52	19.91
8*	304	622.13	36.45	36.70	36.67	37.32	37.43	37.18	37.24	37.23	37.54	37.51	37.04	37.79

H1—Human Rater 1
H2—Human Rater 2
RS—Resolved Score (based on human ratings)
AIR—American Institutes for Research
CMU—TELEDIA, Carnegie Mellon University
CTB—CTB McGraw-Hill
ETS—Educational Testing Service

PKT—Pearson Knowledge Technologies
PM—Pacific Metrics
VL—Vantage Learning
MI—Measurement, Inc.
MM—MetaMetrics

* RS score was obtained by summing the equally weighted ratings from H1 and H2. To be on the same scale as the RS, the original ratings for H1 and H2 were doubled.
t For data set #2, the first rater determined the score assignment. The second rater was employed as a "read behind," but did not influence the score assignment.

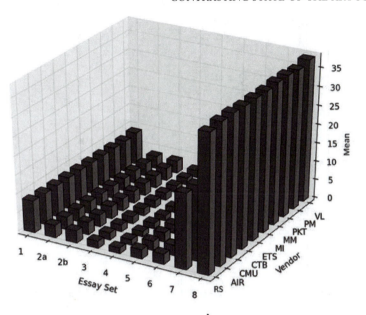

Figure 19.1 Bar chart for vendor performance on mean estimation across the eight essay data
sets

#5 and 6, two of the source-based essays. Figure 19.3 illustrates the exact agreement sta-
tistics in bar graph form. With one exception most of the bars hover around the resolved
score exact agreements.

   Adjacent agreements refer to the combined exact and adjacent score agreements. This
calculation is based on the generally accepted convention of considering rater score
assignments within one score point as being a "match." If the scores differ by more than
one point, many states will ask a third rater to evaluate the essay or they may have some
other rule about how to handle the score difference. For data sets 1, 7, and 8, the calculation for adjacent agreement was slightly different than for the other data sets. These
data sets came from states where the resolved score was the unweighted sum of the two
human raters. While the calculation of adjacent agreement could be based on the original
scale for the two human raters, the machine score predictions were on the unweighted
summed (i.e., doubled) scale. In order to compensate for this scaling difference, the calculation of adjacent agreement for the machine scores were predicated on an adjacent
score difference of two points, not one. Adjacent agreements are shown on Table 19.10,
and for data sets 1–6, they range in the mid–high 90s. Data sets 7 and 8 are lower, but
are in line with human rater performance. Table 19.11 shows that the differences are
generally minor. Figure 19.4 displays these differences.

   Kappa is a measure of agreement that takes into consideration agreement by chance
alone. For the resolved score, based on human ratings, the ranges ran from 0.16 on
data set #8 to 0.65 on data set #4. Overall machine performance ran from 0.04 on
data set #8 to 0.59 on several data sets. These are given in Table 19.12 and graphically
represented in Figure 19.5. Table 19.13 shows the deltas for the kappa statistics. In
general, performance on kappa was slightly less with the exception of essay prompts
#5 and #6. On these data sets, the AES engines, as a group, matched or exceeded
human performance.

Table 19.5 Test Set Mean Deltas (M – M$_{(RS)}$)

Essay Set	N	M # of Words	H1	H2	RS	AIR	CMU	CTB	ETS	MI	MM	PKT	PM	VL
1*	589	366.40	-0.01	0.00	—	-0.08	-0.11	-0.06	-0.05	-0.09	-0.06	-0.05	-0.13	0.18
2a†	600	381.19	—	-0.02	—	0.00	-0.05	-0.02	-0.02	-0.04	-0.08	0.00	-0.05	-0.01
2b†	600	381.19	—	0.02	—	0.05	-0.14	0.03	0.00	-0.11	-0.06	-0.03	0.00	0.02
3	568	108.69	-0.11	-0.17	—	0.00	0.00	0.02	-0.02	0.05	0.01	-0.06	-0.01	0.00
4	586	94.39	-0.13	-0.09	—	-0.01	-0.04	-0.01	-0.17	-0.03	-0.05	-0.12	-0.04	0.06
5	601	122.29	-0.20	-0.16	—	-0.02	0.00	-0.02	-0.04	0.00	-0.07	-0.02	-0.01	0.03
6	600	153.64	-0.18	-0.17	—	0.04	-0.04	0.08	-0.21	0.01	-0.01	0.01	-0.01	0.08
7*	495	171.28	-0.11	0.11	—	-0.08	-0.50	-0.67	-0.52	-0.33	-0.50	-0.55	-0.61	-0.22
8*	304	622.13	-0.22	0.03	—	0.65	0.76	0.51	0.57	0.56	0.87	0.84	0.37	1.12

H1—Human Rater 1
H2—Human Rater 2
RS—Resolved Score (based on human ratings)
AIR—American Institutes for Research
CMU—TELEDIA, Carnegie Mellon University
CTB—CTB/McGraw-Hill
ETS—Educational Testing Service

PKT—Pearson Knowledge Technologies
PM—Pacific Metrics
VL—Vantage Learning
MI—Measurement, Inc.
MM—MetaMetrics

* RS score was obtained by summing the equally weighted ratings from H1 and H2. To be on the same scale as the RS, the original ratings for H1 and H2 were doubled.
† For data set #2, the first rater determined the score assignment. The second rater was employed as a "read behind," but did not influence the score assignment.

Table 19.6 Test Set Standard Deviations

Essay Set	N	M # of Words	H1	H2	RS	AIR	CMU	CTB	ETS	MI	MM	PKT	PM	VL
1*	589	366.40	1.64	1.68	1.54	1.23	1.45	1.26	1.54	1.51	1.57	1.34	1.44	1.29
2a^t	600	381.19	—	0.78	0.77	0.67	0.84	0.65	0.79	0.69	0.83	0.83	0.78	0.64
2b^t	600	381.19	—	0.73	0.75	0.68	0.83	0.67	0.69	0.84	0.80	0.68	0.72	0.65
3	568	108.69	0.79	0.78	0.85	0.76	0.91	0.75	0.79	0.89	0.81	0.72	0.83	0.77
4	586	94.39	0.89	0.90	0.95	0.83	0.97	0.88	1.00	0.86	1.12	0.88	0.95	0.82
5	601	122.29	0.96	0.97	0.95	0.89	1.00	0.89	1.02	1.08	1.08	0.88	0.94	0.93
6	600	153.64	0.90	0.86	0.87	0.82	1.01	0.73	0.95	0.95	1.06	0.85	0.88	0.78
7*	495	171.28	6.40	6.31	5.89	4.17	6.37	5.30	6.27	6.43	6.51	5.17	5.71	4.99
8*	304	622.13	5.93	5.68	5.19	4.11	4.44	3.83	4.52	5.38	5.91	4.63	5.16	4.21

H1—Human Rater 1
H2—Human Rater 2
RS—Resolved Score (based on human ratings)
AIR—American Institutes for Research
CMU—TELEDIA, Carnegie Mellon University
CTB—CTB McGraw-Hill
ETS—Educational Testing Service

PKT—Pearson Knowledge Technologies
PM—Pacific Metrics
VL—Vantage Learning
MI—Measurement, Inc.
MM—MetaMetrics

* RS score was obtained by summing the equally weighted ratings from H1 and H2. To be on the same scale as the RS, the original ratings for H1 and H2 were doubled.
t For data set #2, the first rater determined the score assignment. The second rater was employed as a "read behind," but did not influence the score assignment.

Table 19.7 Test Set Standard Deviation Deltas $(SD - SD_{(RS)})$

Essay Set	N	M # of Words	H1	H2	RS	AIR	CMU	CTB	ETS	MI	MM	PKT	PM	VL
1*	589	366.40	0.10	0.14	—	-0.31	-0.09	-0.28	0.00	-0.03	0.03	-0.20	-0.10	-0.25
2aᵗ	600	381.19	—	0.01	—	-0.10	0.07	-0.12	0.02	-0.08	0.06	0.06	0.01	-0.14
2bᵗ	600	381.19	-0.02	—	—	-0.07	0.08	-0.08	-0.06	0.09	0.05	-0.07	-0.03	-0.10
3	568	108.69	-0.06	-0.07	—	-0.09	0.06	-0.10	-0.06	0.04	-0.04	-0.13	-0.02	-0.08
4	586	94.39	-0.06	-0.05	—	-0.12	0.02	-0.07	0.05	-0.09	0.17	-0.07	0.00	-0.13
5	601	122.29	0.01	0.02	—	-0.06	0.05	-0.06	0.07	0.13	0.13	-0.07	-0.01	-0.02
6	600	153.64	0.03	-0.01	—	-0.05	0.14	-0.14	0.08	0.08	0.19	-0.02	0.01	-0.09
7*	495	171.28	0.51	0.42	—	-1.72	0.48	-0.59	0.38	0.84	0.62	-0.72	-0.18	-0.90
8*	304	622.13	0.74	0.49	—	-1.08	-0.75	-1.36	-0.67	0.19	0.00	-0.56	-0.03	-0.98

H1—Human Rater 1
H2—Human Rater 2
RS—Resolved Score (based on human ratings)
AIR—American Institutes for Research
CMU—TELEDIA, Carnegie Mellon University
CTB—CTB McGraw-Hill
ETS—Educational Testing Service

PKT—Pearson Knowledge Technologies
PM—Pacific Metrics

VL—Vantage Learning
MI—Measurement, Inc.
MM—MetaMetrics

* RS score was obtained by summing the equally weighted ratings from H1 and H2. To be on the same scale as the RS, the original ratings for H1 and H2 were doubled.

t For data set #2, the first rater determined the score assignment. The second rater was employed as a "read behind," but did not influence the score assignment.

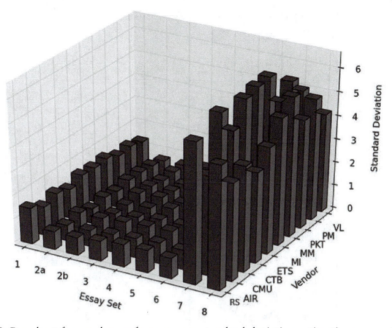

Figure 19.2 Bar chart for vendor performance on standard deviation estimation across the eight essay data sets.

Kappa is typically applied as an agreement measure when the scoring categories have no ordinality associated with them. Quadratic-weighted kappa is appropriate when the categories have some underlying ordinal trait that establishes an ordering for the categories (e.g. when scoring essays, scores may be ordered from 0 to 3). These assumptions are met for the scoring rubrics applied to the data for this demonstration. Human quadratic-weighted kappas ranged from 0.61 to 0.85 and were closely followed by the machine ranges which went from 0.60 to 0.84 (see Table 19.14 where these data are organized). Table 19.15 displays the delta values for quadratic-weighted kappa. Of particular interest are the delta values for data sets #5 and #6 which are generally positive. These two data sets were drawn from source-based essays and were shorter than the other data sets. Figure 19.6 illustrates the quadratic-weighted kappas in graphic form.

Finally the values for the correlation coefficients are given in Table 19.16. The values for the correlation coefficients generally mirror that of quadratic-weighted kappa. These values might have been higher except that the vendors were asked to predict integer values only. Had they been given leeway to predict values containing decimal places, the correlation might have been higher. The correlation values are graphically represented in Figure 19.7. The deltas are provided in Table 19.17.

DISCUSSION

The findings clearly show that in replicating the distributions of the eight essays, the scores of the AEE engines performed quite well. Most of the mean predictions were within 0.10 of the means of the resolved score. Not unexpectedly, the mean estimates deviated where the scales of the essays were large. So for example, in data set #8, the range of scores ran from 0–60 whereas in data set #3, the range only ran from 0–3. The

Table 19.8 Test Set Exact Agreements

Essay Set	N	M # of Words	H1	H2	H1H2	AIR	CMU	CTB	ETS	MI	MM	PKT	PM	VL
1*	589	366.40	0.64	0.64	0.64	0.44	0.44	0.44	0.42	0.46	0.31	0.43	0.43	0.47
2a^t	600	381.19	—	0.76	0.76	0.68	0.64	0.70	0.69	0.70	0.55	0.64	0.68	0.70
2b^t	600	381.19	—	0.73	0.73	0.68	0.59	0.66	0.69	0.66	0.55	0.66	0.67	0.69
3	568	108.69	0.89	0.83	0.72	0.68	0.70	0.66	0.69	0.72	0.63	0.61	0.69	0.69
4	586	94.39	0.87	0.89	0.76	0.65	0.68	0.64	0.66	0.72	0.47	0.60	0.64	0.70
5	601	122.29	0.77	0.79	0.59	0.71	0.67	0.68	0.65	0.68	0.47	0.68	0.65	0.71
6	600	153.64	0.80	0.81	0.63	0.67	0.61	0.63	0.62	0.69	0.51	0.64	0.68	0.69
7*	495	171.28	0.28	0.28	0.28	0.10	0.15	0.12	0.12	0.17	0.07	0.09	0.12	0.12
8*	304	622.13	0.35	0.35	0.29	0.12	0.26	0.23	0.17	0.16	0.08	0.14	0.20	0.10

H1—Human Rater 1
H2—Human Rater 2
H1H2—Human Rater1, Human Rater 2
AIR—American Institutes for Research
CMU—TELEDIA, Carnegie Mellon University
CTB—CTB McGraw-Hill
ETS—Educational Testing Service

PKT—Pearson Knowledge Technologies
PM—Pacific Metrics
VL—Vantage Learning
MI—Measurement, Inc.
MM—MetaMetrics

* RS score was obtained by summing the equally weighted ratings from H1 and H2. To be on the same scale as the RS, the original ratings for H1 and H2 were doubled.
t For data set #2, the first rater determined the score assignment. The second rater was employed as a "read behind," but did not influence the score assignment.

Table 19.9 Test Set Exact Agreement Deltas ($Exact - Exact_{(RS)}$)

Essay Set	N	M # of Words	H1	H2	H1H2	AIR	CMU	CTB	ETS	MI	MM	PKT	PM	VL
1*	589	366.40	0.00	0.00	—	-0.20	-0.20	-0.20	-0.22	-0.18	-0.33	-0.21	-0.21	-0.17
2a^t	600	381.19	—	0.00	—	-0.08	-0.12	-0.06	-0.07	-0.06	-0.21	-0.12	-0.08	-0.06
2b^t	600	381.19	—	0.00	—	-0.05	-0.14	-0.07	-0.04	-0.07	-0.18	-0.07	-0.06	-0.04
3	568	108.69	0.17	0.11	—	-0.04	-0.02	-0.06	-0.03	0.00	-0.09	-0.11	-0.03	-0.03
4	586	94.39	0.11	0.13	—	-0.11	-0.08	-0.12	-0.10	-0.04	-0.28	-0.16	-0.12	-0.05
5	601	122.29	0.18	0.20	—	0.12	0.08	0.09	0.06	0.09	-0.12	0.09	0.06	0.12
6	600	153.64	0.17	0.18	—	0.04	-0.02	0.00	-0.01	0.06	-0.12	0.01	0.05	0.06
7*	495	171.28	0.00	0.00	—	-0.18	-0.13	-0.16	-0.16	-0.11	-0.21	-0.19	-0.16	-0.16
8*	304	622.13	0.06	0.06	—	-0.17	-0.03	-0.06	-0.11	-0.12	-0.20	-0.14	-0.09	-0.19

H1—Human Rater 1
H2—Human Rater 2
H1H2—Human Rater1, Human Rater 2
AIR—American Institutes for Research
CMU—TELEDIA, Carnegie Mellon University
CTB—CTB McGraw-Hill
ETS—Educational Testing Service

PKT—Pearson Knowledge Technologies
PM—Pacific Metrics
VL—Vantage Learning
MI—Measurement, Inc.
MM—MetaMetrics

* RS score was obtained by summing the equally weighted ratings from H1 and H2. To be on the same scale as the RS, the original ratings for H1 and H2 were doubled.
t For data set #2, the first rater determined the score assignment. The second rater was employed as a "read behind," but did not influence the score assignment.

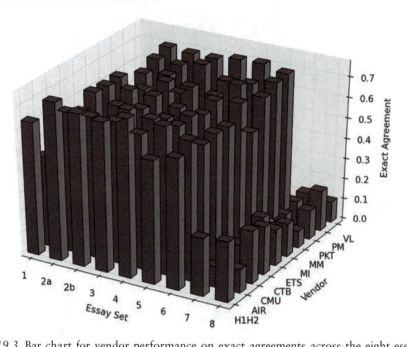

Figure 19.3 Bar chart for vendor performance on exact agreements across the eight essay data sets.

range in data set #8 was an artifact of the way the state scored the essay by summing the two equally weighted rater scores (based on a trait rubric). Had they employed some other approach which utilized a more restricted range, it is quite likely that the performance of the machines would have been improved further. Figure 19.1, however, suggests that with regard to the mean estimates, the machines scores were very close to the resolved score. The same is true for the estimates of the standard deviations (see Figure 19.2).

With the exception of data sets #5 and #6, the pattern of exact agreements was slightly lower with the predicted machine scores than with the actual scores assigned by human raters. On data sets #1, #7, and #8 where the scores reflected the equally weighted sums of the two human raters, most of the deviation scores averaged less than 0.10 from the human raters. Even with the scaling issues associated with these three data sets, the average performance of most of the vendors closely mirrors that of the human raters. The same pattern was observed for the calculations of the kappas which corrected for chance agreement. On data sets #5 and #6, most of the vendors obtained exact agreements that matched or exceeded that of the human raters. This was a bit surprising because the conventional wisdom was that the machine scoring engines would likely do better with essays drawn from the traditional writing genre where the scoring of content was less important. With regard to the adjacent agreements, vendor performance was very close to that of human raters.

Overall vendor performance on quadratic-weighted kappa was particularly impressive. This measure of agreement takes into account the ordinality of the scales developed for each prompt. It is numerically equivalent to the intra-class correlation coefficient. Even on data sets #1, #7, and #8 where the exact agreements and kappas had been lower, the pattern included quadratic-weighted kappas that were higher than with human raters. Data sets #5 and #6 also showed similar patterns. Because the values of the correla-

Table 19.10 Test Set Exact and Adjacent Agreements

Essay Set	N	M # of Words	H1	H2	H1H2	AIR	CMU	CTB	ETS	MI	MM	PKT	PM	VL
1*	589	366.40	0.99	0.99	0.99	0.99	0.99	0.98	0.99	0.99	0.95	0.99	0.99	0.99
2a†	600	381.19	—	1.00	1.00	1.00	0.99	1.00	1.00	1.00	0.99	0.99	1.00	1.00
2b†	600	381.19	—	1.00	1.00	0.99	0.98	0.99	1.00	0.99	0.97	0.99	1.00	1.00
3	568	108.69	1.00	1.00	1.00	0.98	0.97	0.98	0.98	0.97	0.97	0.98	0.97	0.99
4	586	94.39	1.00	1.00	1.00	0.99	0.99	0.98	0.99	0.99	0.96	0.99	0.98	0.99
5	601	122.29	1.00	1.00	0.98	0.99	0.99	0.99	0.99	0.99	0.93	0.99	0.99	1.00
6	600	153.64	1.00	1.00	0.99	0.99	0.99	0.97	0.99	1.00	0.95	1.00	1.00	1.00
7*	495	171.28	0.55	0.55	0.55	0.47	0.52	0.50	0.52	0.56	0.38	0.50	0.52	0.56
8*	304	622.13	0.53	0.52	0.49	0.52	0.51	0.51	0.52	0.52	0.41	0.52	0.48	0.53

H1—Human Rater 1
H2—Human Rater 2
H1H2—Human Rater1, Human Rater 2
AIR—American Institutes for Research
CMU—TELEDIA, Carnegie Mellon University
CTB—CTB McGraw-Hill
ETS—Educational Testing Service

PKT—Pearson Knowledge Technologies
PM—Pacific Metrics
VL—Vantage Learning
MI—Measurement, Inc.
MM—MetaMetrics

* RS score was obtained by summing the equally weighted ratings from H1 and H2. To be on the same scale as the RS, the original ratings for H1 and H2 were doubled.
† For data set #2, the first rater determined the score assignment. The second rater was employed as a "read behind," but did not influence the score assignment.

Table 19.11 Test Set Exact and Adjacent Agreement Deltas $(Exact+Adjacent - Exact+Adjacent_{(RS)})$

Essay Set	N	M # of Words	H1	H2	H1H2	AIR	CMU	CTB	ETS	MI	MM	PKT	PM	VL
1*	589	366.40	0.00	0.00	—	0.00	0.00	-0.02	0.00	0.00	-0.05	0.00	-0.01	0.00
2aᵗ	600	381.19	—	0.00	—	0.00	-0.01	0.00	0.00	0.00	-0.01	-0.01	0.00	0.00
2bᵗ	600	381.19	—	0.00	—	-0.01	-0.02	-0.01	0.00	-0.01	-0.03	-0.01	0.00	0.00
3	568	108.69	0.00	0.00	—	-0.02	-0.03	-0.02	-0.02	-0.03	-0.03	-0.02	-0.03	-0.01
4	586	94.39	0.00	0.00	—	-0.01	-0.01	-0.02	-0.01	-0.01	-0.04	-0.01	-0.02	-0.01
5	601	122.29	0.02	0.02	—	0.01	0.01	0.01	0.01	0.01	-0.05	0.01	0.01	0.02
6	600	153.64	0.01	0.01	—	0.00	0.00	-0.02	0.00	0.01	-0.04	0.01	0.01	0.01
7*	495	171.28	0.00	0.00	—	-0.08	-0.03	-0.05	-0.03	0.01	-0.17	-0.05	-0.03	0.01
8*	304	622.13	0.04	0.03	—	0.03	0.01	0.02	0.03	0.02	-0.08	0.02	-0.02	0.04

H1-Human Rater 1
H2-Human Rater 2
H1H2-Human Rater1, Human Rater 2
AIR—American Institutes for Research
CMU—TELEDIA, Carnegie Mellon University
CTB—CTB McGraw-Hill
ETS—Educational Testing Service

PKT—Pearson Knowledge Technologies
PM—Pacific Metrics
VL—Vantage Learning
MI—Measurement, Inc.
MM—MetaMetrics

* RS score was obtained by summing the equally weighted ratings from H1 and H2. To be on the same scale as the RS, the original ratings for H1 and H2 were doubled.
t For data set #2, the first rater determined the score assignment. The second rater was employed as a "read behind," but did not influence the score assignment.

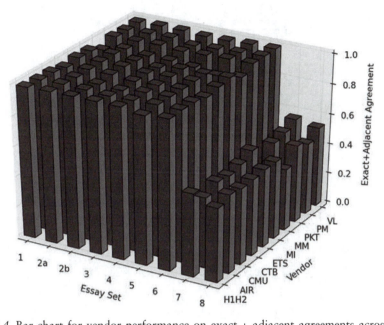

Figure 19.4 Bar chart for vendor performance on exact + adjacent agreements across the eight essay data sets.

tion coefficient were similar to that of quadratic-weighted kappa, the same pattern was observed on this measure as with quadratic weighted kappa.

The premise of this demonstration was to illustrate the general capacity of machine scoring to evaluate extended response essays, and not to single out any one vendor. However, as with human scorers there is some vendor variability in performance. A few vendors scored impressively well across all of the essay metrics while others performed better with certain types of essays (i.e., source-based essays). We view this variability as a strength rather than as a limitation. Exploring the reasons as to why there might be better performance on certain types of essays may lead to programming that better optimizes the scoring for any new assessments developed by the two major Race-to-the-Top consortia. If one were to simply focus on the performance of the majority of vendors across all the measures described in this demonstration, the results meet or exceed that of the human raters.

In the procedures section of this paper, there were several limitations of this study which likely restricted the performance of the automated scoring engines. For example, six of the essays sets had to be transcribed into machine form in order to be processed by AEE. This step had the possibility of introducing transcription and formatting errors. In addition, the rubrics and scoring rules applied by the different states likely resulted in scaling artifacts which impacted on the optimal scoring for both human raters and machine scoring engines. With all of these challenges, the performance of the AEE engines should be viewed as a "floor" rather than a ceiling for what the AEE engines can do under operational conditions. Moreover, we acknowledge some of the limitations from the current study:

• Agreement with human ratings is not necessarily the best or only measure of students' writing proficiency (or the evidence of proficiency in an essay). We can look at

Table 19.12 Test Set Kappas

Essay Set	N	M # of Words	H1	H2	H1H2	AIR	CMU	CTB	ETS	MI	MM	PKT	PM	VL
1*	589	366.40	0.53	0.53	0.45	0.29	0.29	0.25	0.28	0.33	0.16	0.29	0.27	0.32
2a†	600	381.19	—	0.62	0.62	0.46	0.44	0.49	0.51	0.51	0.30	0.43	0.48	0.50
2b†	600	381.19	—	0.56	0.56	0.46	0.35	0.42	0.49	0.46	0.27	0.43	0.45	0.48
3	568	108.69	0.83	0.77	0.57	0.52	0.56	0.50	0.54	0.59	0.45	0.43	0.55	0.53
4	586	94.39	0.82	0.84	0.65	0.49	0.56	0.50	0.53	0.60	0.30	0.44	0.50	0.58
5	601	122.29	0.69	0.71	0.44	0.59	0.55	0.55	0.51	0.56	0.28	0.54	0.51	0.59
6	600	153.64	0.70	0.71	0.45	0.49	0.44	0.40	0.44	0.55	0.31	0.46	0.51	0.51
7*	495	171.28	0.23	0.23	0.18	0.05	0.09	0.07	0.08	0.12	0.03	0.05	0.07	0.07
8*	304	622.13	0.26	0.26	0.16	0.06	0.13	0.11	0.08	0.10	0.04	0.09	0.11	0.04

H1—Human Rater 1
H2—Human Rater 2
H1H2—Human Rater1, Human Rater 2
AIR—American Institutes for Research
CMU—TELEDIA, Carnegie Mellon University
CTB—CTB McGraw-Hill
ETS—Educational Testing Service

PKT—Pearson Knowledge Technologies
PM—Pacific Metrics
VL—Vantage Learning
MI—Measurement, Inc.
MM—MetaMetrics

* RS score was obtained by summing the equally weighted ratings from H1 and H2. To be on the same scale as the RS, the original ratings for Hx1 and H2 were doubled.
† For data set #2, the first rater determined the score assignment. The second rater was employed as a "read behind," but did not influence the score assignment.

Table 19.13 Test Set Kappa Deltas ($\kappa - \kappa_{RS}$)

Essay Set	N	M # of Words	H1	H2	H1H2	AIR	CMU	CTB	ETS	MI	MM	PKT	PM	VL
1*	589	366.40	0.08	0.08	—	-0.16	-0.16	-0.20	-0.17	-0.12	-0.29	-0.16	-0.18	-0.13
2a^t	600	381.19	—	0.00	—	-0.16	-0.18	-0.13	-0.11	-0.11	-0.32	-0.19	-0.14	-0.12
2b^t	600	381.19	—	0.00	—	-0.10	-0.21	-0.14	-0.07	-0.10	-0.29	-0.13	-0.11	-0.08
3	568	108.69	0.26	0.20	—	-0.05	-0.01	-0.07	-0.03	0.02	-0.12	-0.14	-0.02	-0.04
4	586	94.39	0.17	0.19	—	-0.16	-0.09	-0.15	-0.12	-0.05	-0.35	-0.21	-0.15	-0.07
5	601	122.29	0.25	0.27	—	0.15	0.11	0.11	0.07	0.12	-0.16	0.10	0.07	0.15
6	600	153.64	0.25	0.26	—	0.04	-0.01	-0.05	-0.01	0.10	-0.14	0.02	0.06	0.06
7*	495	171.28	0.05	0.05	—	-0.13	-0.09	-0.11	-0.10	-0.06	-0.15	-0.13	-0.11	-0.11
8*	304	622.13	0.10	0.10	—	-0.10	-0.03	-0.05	-0.08	-0.06	-0.12	-0.07	-0.05	-0.12

H1—Human Rater 1
H2—Human Rater 2
H1H2—Human Rater1, Human Rater 2
AIR—American Institutes for Research
CMU—TELEDIA, Carnegie Mellon University
CTB—CTB McGraw-Hill
ETS—Educational Testing Service

PKT—Pearson Knowledge Technologies
PM—Pacific Metrics
VL—Vantage Learning
MI—Measurement, Inc.
MM—MetaMetrics

* RS score was obtained by summing the equally weighted ratings from H1 and H2. To be on the same scale as the RS, the original ratings for Hx1 and H2 were doubled.

t For data set #2, the first rater determined the score assignment. The second rater was employed as a "read behind," but did not influence the score assignment.

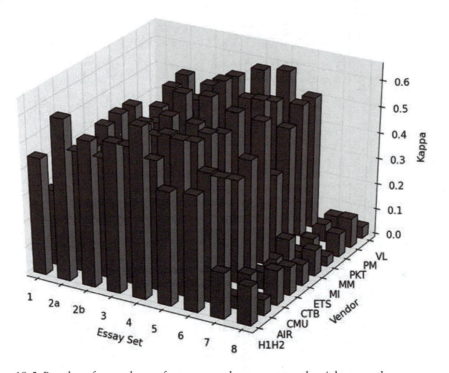

Figure 19.5 Bar chart for vendor performance on kappas across the eight essay data sets.

other measures as well, including alternate-form reliabilities, and correlations with external measures such as state assessment scores or course grades (and some of our studies have done so). The limitation of human scoring as a yardstick for automated scoring is underscored by the human ratings used for some of the tasks in this study, which displayed strange statistical properties and in some cases were in conflict with documented adjudication procedures (Williamson et al., 2012).

- Another issue not addressed by this study is the question of construct validity. A predictive model may do a good job of matching human scoring behavior, but do this by means of features and methods which do not bear any plausible relationship to the competencies and construct that the item aims to assess. To the extent that such models are used, this will limit the validity argument for the assessment as a whole.
- A related issue is that of potential washback on test-taking behavior and instruction. Before using a system operationally, some consideration will need to be given to the question of how the measures used in scoring might be subject to manipulation by test-takers and coaches with an interest in maximizing scores. This study does not conduct any evaluations relevant to this question.
- An important aspect of system performance to evaluate before operational use is fairness—whether subgroups of interest are treated differentially by the scoring methodology. This study does not conduct any evaluations relevant to this question.

CONCLUSION

As a general scoring approach, AEE appears to have developed to the point where it can be reliably applied in both low-stakes assessment (e.g., instructional evaluation of essays)

Table 19.14 Test Set Quadratic Weighted Kappas

Essay Set	N	M # of Words	H1	H2	H1H2	AIR	CMU	CTB	ETS	MI	MM	PKT	PM	VL
1	589	366.40	0.77	0.78	0.73	0.78	0.79	0.70	0.82	0.82	0.66	0.79	0.76	0.78
2a	600	381.19	—	0.80	0.80	0.68	0.70	0.68	0.74	0.72	0.62	0.70	0.72	0.70
2b	600	381.19		0.76	0.76	0.66	0.63	0.63	0.69	0.70	0.55	0.65	0.69	0.68
3	568	108.69	0.92	0.89	0.77	0.72	0.74	0.69	0.72	0.75	0.65	0.65	0.73	0.73
4	586	94.39	0.93	0.94	0.85	0.75	0.81	0.76	0.80	0.82	0.67	0.74	0.76	0.79
5	601	122.29	0.89	0.90	0.74	0.82	0.81	0.80	0.81	0.83	0.64	0.80	0.78	0.83
6	600	153.64	0.89	0.89	0.74	0.76	0.76	0.64	0.75	0.81	0.65	0.75	0.78	0.76
7	495	171.28	0.78	0.77	0.72	0.67	0.77	0.74	0.81	0.84	0.58	0.77	0.80	0.76
8	304	622.13	0.75	0.74	0.61	0.69	0.65	0.60	0.70	0.73	0.63	0.69	0.68	0.68

H1—Human Rater 1
H2—Human Rater 2
H1H2—Human Rater1, Human Rater 2
AIR—American Institutes for Research
CMU—TELEDIA, Carnegie Mellon University
CTB—CTB McGraw-Hill
ETS—Educational Testing Service

PKT—Pearson Knowledge Technologies
PM—Pacific Metrics
VL—Vantage Learning
MI—Measurement, Inc.
MM—MetaMetrics

* RS score was obtained by summing the equally weighted ratings from H1 and H2. To be on the same scale as the RS, the original ratings for Hx1 and H2 were doubled.
t For data set #2, the first rater determined the score assignment. The second rater was employed as a "read behind," but did not influence the score assignment.

Table 19.15 Test Set Quadratic Weighted Kappa Deltas ($\kappa_w - \kappa_{w(RS)}$)

Essay Set	N	M # of Words	H1	H2	H1H2	AIR	CMU	CTB	ETS	MI	MM	PKT	PM	VL
1	589	366.40	0.04	0.05	—	0.05	0.06	-0.03	0.09	0.09	-0.07	0.07	0.03	0.06
2a	600	381.19	—	0.00	—	-0.12	-0.10	-0.11	-0.06	-0.08	-0.18	-0.10	-0.08	-0.10
2b	600	381.19	—	0.00	—	-0.09	-0.13	-0.12	-0.06	-0.06	-0.21	-0.11	-0.07	-0.08
3	568	108.69	0.15	0.12	—	-0.05	-0.03	-0.08	-0.05	-0.02	-0.12	-0.12	-0.04	-0.04
4	586	94.39	0.08	0.09	—	-0.10	-0.04	-0.09	-0.04	-0.03	-0.18	-0.10	-0.08	-0.05
5	601	122.29	0.15	0.16	—	0.07	0.07	0.05	0.06	0.09	-0.10	0.05	0.03	0.08
6	600	153.64	0.15	0.15	—	0.02	0.03	-0.10	0.01	0.07	-0.09	0.01	0.04	0.02
7	495	171.28	0.06	0.05	—	-0.05	0.06	0.03	0.09	0.12	-0.14	0.05	0.08	0.09
8	304	622.13	0.14	0.13	—	0.07	0.03	-0.01	0.09	0.12	0.00	0.08	0.07	0.07

H1—Human Rater 1
H2—Human Rater 2
H1H2—Human Rater1, Human Rater 2
AIR—American Institutes for Research
CMU—TELEDIA, Carnegie Mellon University
CTB—CTB McGraw-Hill
ETS—Educational Testing Service

PKT—Pearson Knowledge Technologies
PM—Pacific Metrics
VL—Vantage Learning
MI—Measurement, Inc.
MM—MetaMetrics

* RS score was obtained by summing the equally weighted ratings from H1 and H2. To be on the same scale as the RS, the original ratings for Hx1 and H2 were doubled.
t For data set #2, the first rater determined the score assignment. The second rater was employed as a "read behind," but did not influence the score assignment.

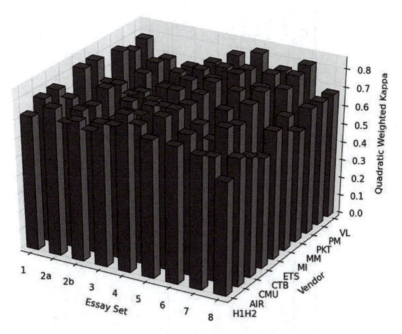

Figure 19.6 Bar chart for vendor performance on quadratic weighted kappas across the eight essay data set.

and perhaps as a second scorer for high-stakes testing. Many of the vendors have software that integrates AEE as part of an instructional package (e.g., MyAccess!, Criterion). Moreover, they have developed generic models that can be used to score essay prompts developed by teachers. AEE is also used as second reader for high stakes assessment in several general tests (e.g., TOEFL, GMAT) and in a similar fashion for some licensing exams (e.g., the American Institute of Certified Public Accountants (AICPA)). And AES is used in large-scale K–12 summative assessment programs either as the only score with human read-behind for monitoring (e.g., Utah) or as a 100% read-behind for reader monitoring (e.g., Louisiana).

Finally, the results of this demonstration apply to commercial vendors who cover most of the extended response machine scoring market. As of this writing, there is a pubic competition underway that will demonstrate the programming skill of individuals or teams with regard to the established capacities of the commercial vendors. So far, the best aggregate (though unverified) performance of a public competitor suggests that these systems may be comparable to the performance of commercial systems with respect to agreement between human and automated scores. The hope is to link the public competitors with the commercial vendors to get the best possible product available for use in scoring the new assessments.

AUTHORS' NOTE

1 Mark D. Shermis, Department of Educational Foundations and Leadership and the Department of psychology, The University of Akron; Ben Hamner, Kaggle, Inc.
   This work was supported through funding from the William and Flora Hewlett Foundation. The opinions expressed in this paper are those of the authors and do not necessarily represent the

Table 19.16 Test Set Pearson Moment Product Correlation Coefficient, *r*

Essay Set	N	M # of Words	H1	H2	H1H2	AIR	CMU	CTB	ETS	MI	MM	PKT	PM	VL
1*	589	366.40	0.93	0.93	0.73	0.80	0.79	0.71	0.82	0.82	0.66	0.80	0.76	0.80
2a†	600	381.19	—	0.80	0.80	0.68	0.71	0.69	0.74	0.72	0.62	0.70	0.72	0.71
2b†	600	381.19	—	0.76	0.76	0.67	0.64	0.64	0.70	0.71	0.55	0.65	0.69	0.69
3	568	108.69	0.92	0.89	0.77	0.72	0.74	0.69	0.72	0.75	0.65	0.66	0.73	0.73
4	586	94.39	0.94	0.94	0.85	0.76	0.81	0.76	0.82	0.82	0.68	0.75	0.76	0.80
5	601	122.29	0.89	0.90	0.75	0.82	0.81	0.80	0.81	0.84	0.65	0.80	0.78	0.83
6	600	153.64	0.89	0.89	0.74	0.76	0.77	0.65	0.77	0.81	0.66	0.75	0.78	0.77
7*	495	171.28	0.93	0.93	0.72	0.71	0.78	0.75	0.81	0.84	0.58	0.78	0.80	0.82
8*	304	622.13	0.87	0.88	0.61	0.71	0.66	0.63	0.71	0.73	0.62	0.70	0.68	0.72

H1—Human Rater 1
H2—Human Rater 2
H1H2—Human Rater1, Human Rater 2
AIR—American Institutes for Research
CMU—TELEDIA, Carnegie Mellon University
CTB—CTB McGraw-Hill
ETS—Educational Testing Service

PKT—Pearson Knowledge Technologies
PM—Pacific Metrics
VL—Vantage Learning
MI—Measurement, Inc.
MM—MetaMetrics

* RS score was obtained by summing the equally weighted ratings from H1 and H2. To be on the same scale as the RS, the original ratings for Hx1 and H2 were doubled.
† For data set #2, the first rater determined the score assignment. The second rater was employed as a "read behind," but did not influence the score assignment.

Table 19.17 Test Set Pearson Moment Product Correlation Coefficient Deltas $(r - r_{(RS)})$

Essay Set	N	M # of Words	H1	H2	H1H2	AIR	CMU	CTB	ETS	MI	MM	PKT	PM	VL
1*	589	366.40	0.20	0.20	—	0.07	0.06	-0.02	0.09	0.09	-0.07	0.07	0.03	0.07
2a†	600	381.19	—	0.00	—	-0.12	-0.09	-0.11	-0.06	-0.08	-0.18	-0.10	-0.08	-0.09
2b†	600	381.19	—	0.00	—	-0.09	-0.12	-0.12	-0.06	-0.05	-0.21	-0.11	-0.07	-0.07
3	568	108.69	0.15	0.12	—	-0.05	-0.03	-0.08	-0.05	-0.02	-0.12	-0.11	-0.04	-0.04
4	586	94.39	0.09	0.09	—	-0.09	-0.04	-0.09	-0.03	-0.03	-0.17	-0.10	-0.09	-0.05
5	601	122.29	0.14	0.15	—	0.07	0.06	0.05	0.06	0.09	-0.10	0.05	0.03	0.08
6	600	153.64	0.15	0.15	—	0.02	0.03	-0.09	0.03	0.06	-0.12	0.01	0.04	0.03
7*	495	171.28	0.21	0.21	—	-0.01	0.06	0.03	0.09	0.12	-0.14	0.06	0.08	0.10
8*	304	622.13	0.26	0.27	—	0.10	0.05	0.02	0.10	0.12	0.01	0.09	0.07	0.11

H1—Human Rater 1
H2—Human Rater 2
H1H2—Human Rater1, Human Rater 2
AIR—American Institutes for Research
CMU—TELEDIA, Carnegie Mellon University
CTB—CTB McGraw-Hill
ETS—Educational Testing Service

PKT—Pearson Knowledge Technologies
PM—Pacific Metrics
VL—Vantage Learning
MI—Measurement, Inc.
MM—MetaMetrics

* RS score was obtained by summing the equally weighted ratings from H1 and H2. To be on the same scale as the RS, the original ratings for Hx1 and H2 were doubled.
† For data set #2, the first rater determined the score assignment. The second rater was employed as a "read behind," but did not influence the score assignment.

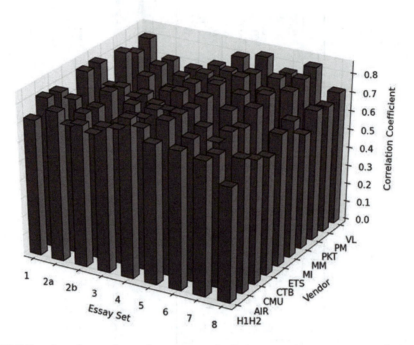

Figure 19.7 Bar chart for vendor performance on the Pearson product moment correlation across the eight essay data sets.

policy or views of the William and Flora Hewlett Foundation or their Board of Directors. This chapter was originally presented as a paper with a similar title at the 2012 annual conference of the National Council on Measurement in Education in Vancouver, British Columbia. The authors would like to thank Jaison Morgan (The Common Pool), Tom Vander Ark and Lynn Van Deventer (OpenEd Solutions), Tony Albert (SBAC), and Jeff Nellhouse (PARCC) for their tireless efforts in executing this study. Correspondence concerning this article should be addressed to Mark D. Shermis, 213 Crouse Hall, The University of Akron, Akron, OH 44325. Electronic mail may be sent via Internet to mshermis@uakron.edu.

REFERENCES

Attali, Y., & Burstein, J. (2006). Automated essay scoring with e-rater V.2. *Journal of Technology, Learning, and Assessment, 4*(3), available from http://www.jtla.org

Rudner, L. M., Garcia, V., & Welch, C. (2006). An evaluation of the IntelliMetric essay scoring system. *Journal of Technology, Learning, and Assessment, 4*(4), retrieved from http://www.jtla.org

Shermis, M. D., Burstein, J., Higgins, D., & Zechner, K. (2010). Automated essay scoring: Writing assessment and instruction. In E. Baker, B. McGaw & N. S. Petersen (Eds.), *International encyclopedia of education* (Vol. 4, pp. 20–26). Oxford, UK: Elsevier.

Williamson, D. M., Xi, X., & Breyer, F. J. (2012). A framework for the evaluation and use of automated essay scoring. *Educational Measurement: Issues and Practice, 31*(1), 2–13.

20 The Policy Turn in Current Education Reform

The Common Core State Standards and Its Linguistic Challenges and Opportunities

Kenji Hakuta

INTRODUCTION

The Common Core State Standards Initiative (CCSSI) has been referred to in the Introduction to this volume, as well as in several chapters in this volume. This influential initiative is tied to a number of related initiatives in the area of national-level efforts at shifting education standards. The new standards will change the United States' educational landscape in significant ways for the next decade, and will thus affect the demand for the sorts of tools and technologies created from natural language processing (NLP) technologies. While the focus of this volume is on automated essay evaluation, much of the NLP research and development that has come to fruition for use in that context might be used for additional innovation in education. The aim of this chapter is to provide an overview of this new policy landscape, its implications for educational practice, and for the need for NLP-supported tools. Readers should refer to the book Introduction and to Chapter 4 (*The E-rater® Automated Essay Scoring System*) for discussions of NLP and related technologies.

THE COMMON CORE AND RELATED INITIATIVES

The Common Core State Standards Initiative is a state-led effort (in collaboration with the National Governors' Association and the Council of Chief State School Officers) to develop a common set of education standards in Language Arts/Literacy and Mathematics that consists of college- and career-readiness standards and K–12 standards which address expectations at each grade level. The development of the standards began in 2009, and after a series of input from experts and the public, was released in June 2010. They have been adopted, as of this writing, by 45 states, two territories, and the District of Columbia. The Standards have already been hugely influential in shifting the education reform discussion of the nation. The shift is attributable not only to its widespread adoption, but also to major corollary activities that it has spawned and which are discussed below.

The *American Recovery and Reinvestment Act of 2009* (ARRA), better known as the stimulus bill, provided significant funding (US$350 million) to two consortia of states to develop assessment systems aligned to the new standards, adding teeth to the standards (Center for K-12 Assessment and Performance Management at ETS, 2012). As a result, the two consortia known as the Smarter Balanced Assessment Consortia (SBAC) and the Partnership for Assessment of Readiness of College and Careers (PARCC) are actively working with their member states, developing frameworks and specifications based on the standards to develop assessment systems, and many local school districts are gearing up their capacity, through professional development and curriculum and instructional supports, to "prepare for the Common Core."

A corollary effort has been the development of the *Next Generation Science Standards* (NGSS). While the effort is technically not associated with the Common Core, it is another effort riding on the wake created by the Common Core. NGSS began with the release of a "Framework for K-12 Science" that was developed through a National Research Council committee process (Council, 2011). This framework has now been drafted into a set of Next Generation Science Standards (2012) through a process facilitated by Achieve, Inc. Once the standards are finalized, states will eventually go through a process of common adoption much like the CCSSI. Widespread adoption is anticipated.

A third corollary comes from the cascading effect of CCSSI on state *English Language Proficiency* (ELP) *Standards*. The ELP Standards are mandated under Title III of No Child Left Behind (NCLB),[1] for each state to adopt standards for ELP for their English language learners (ELLs) and develop assessments that align to these standards. Although there is no requirement for common ELP Standards, NCLB requires assessment in the four domains of listening, speaking, reading and writing, and for the assessments to align to their respective state content standards. Now that the CCSSI has been adopted, the next logical move is for each state to modify the ELP Standards to align to the CCSSI, which would create greater similarity across the state ELP Standards.

This alignment of ELP with CCSS was set in motion by the Obama Administration through its Elementary and Secondary Education Act (ESEA) Flexibility memorandum (issued on September 23, 2011) providing guidance to states seeking regulatory relief from the accountability provisions of NCLB, particularly the Adequate Yearly Progress (AYP) requirements that put states and districts under increasing thresholds for meeting adequacy. In order to qualify:

> An SEA must also support English Learners in reaching such standards (CCSSI) by committing to adopt ELP Standards that correspond to its college- and career-ready standards and that reflect the academic language skills necessary to access and meet the new college- and career-ready standards, and committing to develop and administer aligned ELP assessments.
>
> (U.S. Department of Education, 2011)[2]

As a result of this requirement that states commit to adopt ELP Standards that "correspond"[3] to the CCSSI, the Council of Chief State Schools Officers (CCSSO)[4] developed a document to help states determine whether their ELP Standards correspond to CCSS. This document, still in development as of the writing of this chapter, will serve as another common base for standards adopted across states in the domain of English language proficiency, and may also serve as the basis from which a common set of ELP Standards may eventually be delivered.

The policy landscape on the level of standards has thus changed. How will these policy developments impact the ways in which the concept of "language" is represented in the increasingly common standards across states? What implications and opportunities does this have for NLP applications in supporting instructional materials and supports, teacher capacity, and assessment systems that include a linguistic focus?

THE COMMON CORE STATE STANDARDS: A LANGUAGE-PROMINENT STATEMENT

Standards are policy instruments intended to align various components of a system. In a highly-decentralized system such as the United States where there is little room for top-down leadership, commonly agreed-upon standards by entities distributed around the system is one of the few policy mechanisms available for systemic reform (Smith & O'Day, 1991). What gets put into the standards provides guidance to state education agencies, local school districts, school leaders (including principals), teachers, publishers, professional development providers, test publishers, and teacher credentialing institutions, among others.

Understanding Language

For a linguist, what stands out about the Common Core is its privileging of the uses of language. The Understanding Language Initiative at Stanford University (http://ell.stanford.edu), a national group of academics and professionals based in universities, non-profits and school districts, has paid special attention to this characteristic of the Common Core as well as the Next Generation Science Standards because of its interest in the challenges and opportunities that the new standards pose for ELLs. At the same time, the language demands inherent in the new standards are by no means limited to ELLs—indeed it is a challenge for *all* students.

The Understanding Language Initiative has paid particular attention to the macro-level shifts inherent in the CCSSI, and they are summarized in Table 20.1. In English Language Arts (ELA), for example, the emphasis on text-based evidence for argumentation poses a significant shift worthy of attention. Writing Standard 9, for example, requires the integration of reading for evidence with writing that displays analysis and reflection of the evidence. In mathematics, there is considerable emphasis on the language of reasoning and the encouragement of discourse as well as writing around understanding mathematical practices. Students are encouraged to write explanations, critique the writings of others, and to revise their explanations. It is in these sorts of writing tasks where we can see application for NLP. NLP approaches can be used to flag words and features that signal logical argumentation, sentiment, and other features of the text related to argumentation. Readers should refer to Chapters 16 and 17 for discussions related to NLP applications about the automated evaluation of discourse coherence quality, and sentiment analysis, respectively.

Table 20.1 Macro-Level Analysis of Major Shifts Found in the New Standards

Major Shifts in New Standards		
ELA	*Math*	*Science*
• Regular practice with complex text and its vocabulary	• Provide opportunities for student access to the different mathematical (discourse) practices described in the CCSS	• Developing and using models
• Building knowledge through content-rich informational texts	• Support mathematical discussions and use a variety of participation structures	• Constructing explanations (for science) and developing solutions (for engineering)
• Emphasis on reading, writing, and speaking that is grounded in evidence from the text	• Focus on students' mathematical reasoning, NOT on students' flawed or developing language	• Engaging in argument from evidence
		• Obtaining, evaluating, and communication information

Source: http://ell.stanford.edu

In the ELA standards, it is also noteworthy that the standards single out Literacy in History/Social Studies, Science, and Technical Subjects, signaling the importance of content-area teachers working together to address the needs of students grappling with complex subject-matter texts and writing about the content, but with a strong emphasis on aspects of argumentation. Consider the writing standard for Literacy in History/Social Studies, Science, and Technical Subjects 6–12 for Text Type and Purposes on writing arguments focused on discipline-specific content. These aspects of the writing construct open the door for NLP for the development and refinement of NLP approaches that capture content knowledge, and argumentation.

a. Introduce precise, knowledgeable claim(s), establish the significance of the claim(s), distinguish the claim(s) from alternate or opposing claims, and create an organization that logically sequences the claim(s), counterclaims, reasons, and evidence.
b. Develop claim(s) and counterclaims fairly and thoroughly, supplying the most relevant data and evidence for each while pointing out the strengths and limitations of both claim(s) and counterclaims in a discipline-appropriate form that anticipates the audience's knowledge level, concerns, values, and possible biases.
c. Use words, phrases, and clauses as well as varied syntax to link the major sections of the text, create cohesion, and clarify the relationships between claim(s) and reasons, between reasons and evidence, and between claim(s) and counterclaims.
d. Establish and maintain a formal style and objective tone while attending to the norms and conventions of the discipline in which they are writing.
e. Provide a concluding statement or section that follows from or supports the argument presented.

What is remarkable about this standard is that this would strike the English teacher as familiar, but it might seem quite alien to most teachers of other content areas, such as the science or history teacher. Teachers across subject areas would need to collaborate, and I would claim that NLP-based tools that help them collaborate in working on text features that help with the teaching of such standards would prove invaluable.

Innovative tools for flagging words and relating them to databases, such as WordNet (Miller, 1990) to find word relations (such as synonyms and antonyms); identifying sentences and larger portions of text that contain key ideas; as well as, identifying text segments that potentially mark key claims and evidence is now automatically feasible, and can help teachers identify and prepare for students as they productively struggle to read complex text which they may need to understand fully to complete a writing assignment. Linguistic feedback applications such as *Language Muse*[SM] (Burstein, Sabatini, & Shore, in press), and *Wordsift* (Roman, Wientjes, Thompson, & Hakuta, 2009; http://www.wordsift.com) have already been placed in the hands of teachers, and are seen by teachers as valuable resources to support their instruction. As NLP continues to expand its ability to flag relevant text, and text structures, and to deal with the imperfections that are expected in student writing through work such as those represented in this volume, and especially if teachers begin seeing how NLP tools can support their implementation of the Common Core, we can expect a large demand for the implementation of NLP tools for classroom use to support the writing process.

From the viewpoint of the education of ELLs, there is further elaboration necessary about the implications of the new standards for what is generally called "English as a Second Language" (ESL), which stands in somewhat of a limbo status because language itself is the content. Policy requires that both the academic content and access to the development of the English language be provided to ELLs. All states have adopted ELP

Standards that guide the content of ESL instruction, and these can be typically characterized as oriented to the forms and functions of language. More recently, they have focused on what has come to be referred to as generic "academic English," often focused on Tier 2[5] vocabulary (Beck, McKeown, & Kucan, 2002, 2008) that typically occurs in academic instruction and textbooks not specifically tied to content-specific vocabulary. The aspect of language, however, that is highlighted in the new standards is distinctly tied to the expected instructional expectations of the disciplinary area. Thus, the Council of Chief State School Officers' ELP framework (referred to earlier) honors this and proposes separate specifications of language functions by subject area.

Student *productive* language, for example, should include the following.

Language Arts

- Describing discernible points of comparison (e.g., point of view or focus, style, amount and quality of evidence, differences in emphasis, significant omissions and/or inclusions of ideas, etc.).
- Providing explanation of an argument through the logical presentation of its steps.
- Presenting a synthesis of ideas in two or more texts to show a coherent understanding on similar topics or events.
- Describing how a linguistic structure (e.g., an appositive) is used for particular rhetorical effect.
- Describing how certain word choice impacts meaning.

Math

- Explain (or draw diagrams that show) relationships between quantities and representations (such as objects, drawings, words, math symbols, graphs, equations, tables).
- Explain reasoning as it relates to situation, problem, and quantities.
- Describe and define how a model relates to a phenomenon or system.

Science

- Elicit clarification of a statement just made by another or further details of models or explanations of others.
- Propose investigations to be carried out through further observations or measurements.
- Describe how a model relates to a phenomenon or system.
- Produce a written plan for an investigation.
- Make predictions.
- Describe observations.
- Describe conditions and record measurements.
- Discuss the quality of scientific information obtained from text sources based on investigating the scientific reputation of the source, and comparing information from multiple sources.

What impact will this framework have on how states set up expectations for ELP Standards? My belief is that the impact will be profound because the way in which language used in disciplinary instruction receives focus in this framework will require a major shift from conceptualizations of language currently in place. At present, language is typically defined with respect to forms, vocabulary, and functions, separated by modality (and assessed through listening, speaking, reading and writing items as required by NCLB). The shift to a more function-embedded language that is furthermore context-sensitive to the discipline poses a challenge not just for assessments, but for teachers and school administrators.

The shift required will be from thinking of ELP development as primarily the domain of the ESL teacher to that of the content teacher (science, math, language arts) as the teacher of the language uses within the discipline. Literacy, also, is interwoven in the Common Core across subject areas in grades 6–12, with the standards singling out literacy in the social studies/history, science and technical subjects. The bottom line is that there will be an intense need for all content teachers to develop their instructional repertoire to be deliberate and adept at engaging students in language and literacy activities of their discipline. School and district instructional leaders, in turn, will need to become better able to support this instructional shift across all teaching staff in their buildings or districts. NLP tools that enable all teachers to readily analyze and identify specific characteristics of language and texts that can help support their instruction of ELLs, such as through the identification of sentiment words and structures, argumentation, coherence, as well as the identification of key vocabulary, such as collocations, would be extremely valuable for teachers.

Another area in great need of attention will be in formative assessment practices, defined as instructional practices that give teachers information for effective instruction, students' feedback on their performance, and additionally provides students with opportunities for self-assessment (Heritage, 2010, based on Black & William, 1998). The Common Core implementation will benefit greatly by identifying formative assessment practices that help teachers and students prepare for and engage with challenging, complex texts. If the formative assessment practice involves students writing into digitized formats, this would even be better! This again is an opportunity for added value from NLP tools that identify and support student engagement with complex language functions.

CONCLUSIONS: THE NEED FOR A FIELD OF EPISTEMOLOGICAL LINGUISTICS

While there are important niches for NLP that will be created by the shift in the policy environment to the Common Core, it is also important to push the limits of basic theory and knowledge that can help inform the work in computational modeling. I have used the term "epistemological linguistics" to label such a field, which might be seen as the analysis of the relationship between knowledge domains, linguistic representations, as applied to cognitive representations and the social interactions involved in the educational curriculum and instruction.

A central question that such a field might address is: What are features of a linguistic representation of texts, monologues, and discourse that vary with epistemological domains of the subject area (causation in historical analyses vs. causation in the natural sciences), or between subtopics within a subject area where the representational form of the topics are different (as in algebraic reasoning vs. geometric reasoning)?

A deep and thoughtful analysis of this question would bring to bear fundamental questions about the relationship of language and cognition. Its methods would draw in interdisciplinary ways from linguistics, psychology, and the cognitive neurosciences, addressing developmental processes, the sociolinguistic conditioning of language forms and functions, and illuminating educational and computational applications. Basic foundations in these areas are absolutely critical to the establishment of a healthy field of epistemological linguistics which in turn would fuel the NLP tools and supports for instruction and assessment.

The Common Core and its related initiatives have opened up a huge opportunity for language scientists and educators to explore overlapping interests that can have enormous positive consequences for all students. The developments documented in this volume indicate the many promising avenues by which this can happen.

NOTES

1 A description of Title III of NCLB can be found here: http://www.cde.ca.gov/fg/aa/ca/nclbtitleIII.asp
2 SEA is the acronym for State Education Agency.
3 This terminology "correspond" was used in this context to contrast with "alignment" which has a more specific and technical term of linking two similar constructs. See discussion in the CCSSO ELP Framework (U.S. Department of Education, 2011).
4 Information about the Council of Chief State School Officers can be found here: http://www.ccsso.org/
5 Readers may also refer to a discussion of the Three Tiers of Vocabulary here: http://www.corestandards.org/assets/Appendix_A.pdf

REFERENCES

Beck, I. L., McKeown, M. G., & Kucan, L. (2002). *Bringing words to life: Robust vocabulary instruction*. New York: Guilford.

Beck, I. L., McKeown, M. G., & Kucan, L. (2008). *Creating robust vocabulary: Frequently asked questions and extended examples*. New York: Guilford.

Black, P., & William, D. (1998). Assessment and classroom learning. *Assessment in Education principles, policy and practice, 5*, 7–73.

Burstein, J., Sabatini, J., & Shore, J. (in press). Developing NLP applications for educational problem spaces. In R. Mitkov (Ed.), *Oxford handbook of computational linguistics*. New York: Oxford University Press.

Center for K-12 Assessment & Performance Management at ETS (2012). Coming together to raise achievement: New assessments for the common core state standards, from http://www.k12center.org/rsc/pdf/Coming_Together_April_2012_Final.PDF

Council, National Research. (2011). *A framework for K-12 science education: Practices, crosscutting themes, and core ideas*. Washington, DC: National Academy Press.

Heritage, M. (2010). *Formative assessment and next-generation assessment systems: Are we losing an opportunity?* Washington, DC: Council of Chief State School Officers.

Miller, G. A. (1990). An on-line lexical database.' *International Journal of Lexicography, 3*(4), 235–312.

Roman, D., Wientjes, G., Thompson, K., & Hakuta, K. (2009). WordSift: An interactive web-based vocabulary tool. *AccELLerate (National Clearinghouse for English Language Acquisition), 1*(4).

Smith, M. S., & O'Day, J. (1991). Systemic school reform. In S. Fuhrman & B. Malen (Eds.), *The Politics of Curriculum and Testing*. London: Falmer Press.

Standards, Next Generation Science. (2012), from http://www.nextgenscience.org/

U.S. Department of Education, National Assessment Governing Board (2011). Writing framework for the 2011 National Assessment of Educational Progress, from http://www.nagb.org/publications/frameworks/writing-2011.pdf

Index